D0204270

Tikal Report No. 25B

THE CERAMIC SEQUENCE OF TIKAL

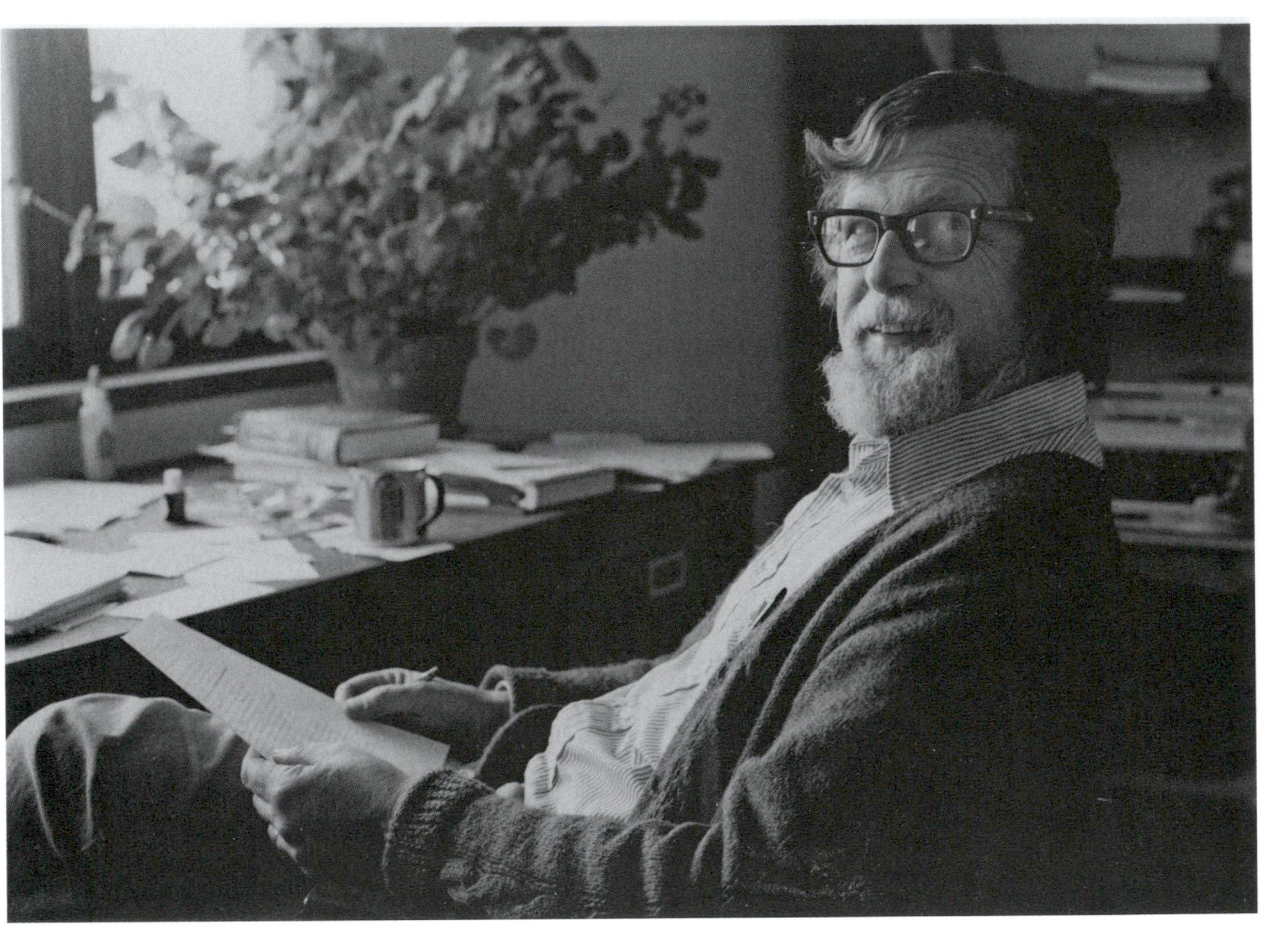

Frontispiece. Pat Culbert in Santa Fe, NM 1982.
(Photograph courtesy of Bobbi Culbert.)

University Museum Monograph 152

Tikal Report No. 25B

THE CERAMIC SEQUENCE OF TIKAL

By T. Patrick Culbert

and

Laura J. Kosakowsky

Content editor: Hattula Moholy-Nagy

Series Editors

William A. Haviland

Simon Martin

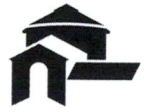

Published by

UNIVERSITY OF PENNSYLVANIA MUSEUM
of Archaeology and Anthropology
Philadelphia
2019

Library of Congress Cataloging-in-Publication Data

Names: Culbert, T. Patrick, author. | Kosakowsky, Laura J., author. |
  Moholy-Nagy, Hattula, editor.
Title: The ceramic sequence of Tikal / by T. Patrick Culbert and Laura J.
  Kosakowsky ; content editor, Hattula Moholy-Nagy.
Description: Philadelphia : University of Pennsylvania Museum of Archaeology
  and Anthropology, 2019. | Series: University museum monograph ; 152 |
  Series: Tikal report ; No. 25B | Includes bibliographical references.
Identifiers: LCCN 2019014200| ISBN 9781949057034 (hardcover : alk. paper) |
  ISBN 1949057038 (hardcover : alk. paper)
Subjects: LCSH: Tikal Site (Guatemala) | Maya pottery. |
  Pottery--Guatemala--Tikal Site--Classification. |
  Pottery--Guatemala--Tikal Site--Themes, motives. | Mayas--Antiquities. |
  Excavations (Archaeology)--Guatemala.
Classification: LCC F1465.1.T5 C85 2019 | DDC 972.81/01--dc23
LC record available at https://lccn.loc.gov/2019014200

Distributed for the University of Pennsylvania Museum of Archaeology and Anthropology
by the University of Pennsylvania Press.

Printed in the United States of America on acid-free paper.

Table of Contents

Tables

Illustrations

Ceramic Types and Varieties

(in alphabetical order)

Foreword

I came to the University of Arizona in 1976 to begin work on my doctorate, after completing an undergraduate degree in anthropology at Stanford University. I chose Arizona not only because of its overall superb reputation and four-field approach, but also because I knew I wanted to specialize in Maya archaeology and there were two renowned Mayanists on the faculty: the late T. Patrick Culbert and the late William L. Rathje. Both Pat and Bill, along with the other members of my dissertation committee, Raymond H. Thompson and the late William Longacre, provided excellent advice and support throughout my graduate career.

I was fortunate indeed that my first introduction to Maya ceramics was under the tutelage of Pat Culbert with the Tikal collections. I cannot imagine a better teacher and patient mentor, nor a more impressive set of pottery with which to study and learn. It formed the foundation for my own decades of ceramic research in Belize and Guatemala. I was afforded the opportunity to conduct my dissertation research in Belize, at the site of Cuello by Norman Hammond, and I owe him a debt of gratitude for taking a chance on me, and then including me in numerous other interesting field projects over the years. My first year in the field in Belize, I was able to learn from the grand-master of Maya ceramic studies, Joseph W. Ball, and from Duncan Pring. Both generously shared their immense knowledge of and expertise with Maya ceramics, and taught me how to analyze ceramics utilizing a rigorous methodological approach, applying type: variety-mode classifications.

Throughout my career, I have benefited from the help and support of many colleagues and friends. I would like to thank especially Carol Gifford, whose experience producing the monograph on the Barton Ramie ceramics, after James Gifford passed away, provided an excellent model to follow, and who always has freely shared invaluable advice and superb editing assistance. Since we were graduate students together, Laura J. Levi, one of the few archaeologists who took the time to also learn Maya ceramics, has provided years of friendship and intellectual discussions. My fellow ceramicists, Robin Robertson and Kerry L. Sagebiel, have from beginning to end, alternately discussed, argued, reasoned, compared, and shared their insights, and the result is better for their support.

They say "it takes a village," and it couldn't be truer than when producing a monograph on the Tikal Project. When I asked Hattula Moholy-Nagy to look over some of the initial rewrites, little did she realize that by saying "yes" she would end up serving as a content editor for the entire volume. Her knowledge of Tikal and her meticulous attention to detail is incomparable; I could not have completed this without her. Other Tikal Project members who unfailingly stepped up to help me with every request, no matter how small or large, include Virginia Greene, the late Peter Harrison, and William Haviland. As someone who didn't participate in the Tikal excavations, I relied heavily on their expertise and shared history. I would like to thank Prudence M. Rice who reviewed this monograph, and whose detailed comments have made for a much better end product. I would especially like to thank Michael G. Callaghan, the second reviewer, who also provided superb, helpful suggestions, and who is one of the most talented next-generation ceramicists carrying Pat Culbert's legacy forward, which makes me very hopeful for the future of Maya ceramic studies. I would also like to thank Page Selinsky, editor of

Penn Museum publications, who did a remarkable job of copy editing this monograph.

Pat always said that if anything ever happened to him, I would have to complete the Tikal ceramic monograph and for many years I responded that he was simply not allowed to die. I worried that I wouldn't be up to the task, or meet the impossibly high standard that Pat's research always upheld. When Pat's widow, Bobbi Culbert, contacted me after he passed away in 2013, I knew immediately why, and without hesitation agreed to take on Pat's life's work. Pat started writing up the Tikal ceramic sequence in the 1970s and his reevaluations and rewrites spanned the next four decades, with the last version written in 2009. The Early Classic, Late Classic, and Terminal Classic complexes didn't require major typological revisions, although for all complexes I have attempted to update the descriptions with recent research from other sites in the Maya Lowlands, as the original type descriptions did not include any comparative site information. I also have simplified the shape classification for all complexes, and changed some of Pat's terminology so that it is now in line with other published material. The Preclassic complexes, however, required major revisions; there has been so much recent research particularly on the Early Middle and Late Middle Preclassic, which Pat had not included even in his last rewrite. The Eb and Tzec Complexes have been largely redone based on my own reevaluations of the Tikal ceramics. The three Late Preclassic Complexes, Chuen, Cauac, and Cimi, have also been rewritten to reflect the addition of some types that Pat did not recognize in his original analysis. In all cases I have listed both the original typological designations, as well as the changes I have made in this work. Since this volume was designed as a companion to TR. 25A *The Ceramics of Tikal: Vessels from the Burials, Caches, and Problematical Deposits* (Culbert 1993), I reference the illustrations in this prior publication and also describe the new typological designations for the whole vessels in that monograph, when appropriate. Unfortunately, while working through all of Pat's files it became clear that some data were missing, because they have simply been lost or were never collected, and, where there are gaps, I have made note in the text. I have tried whenever possible to honor Pat's original intent for the Tikal ceramics, but could not in good conscience publish an out of date manuscript.

Finally, I would like to thank my late husband, Henry Truebe, and my children, Sarah and Brian Truebe. While growing up, my children coped with long absences when I was conducting research in Belize and Guatemala and also were coerced often into washing, counting, and sorting many, many sherds (although they did get paid pennies for the honor). My most heartfelt thanks go to Bobbi Culbert, and Pat's four children, Chris, Martin, Michael, and Tricia. Over the years, they unfailingly welcomed me into Pat's life and their home, and shared him with me and all the other graduate students, friends, and colleagues who showed up on their doorstep. When I chose to follow closely in Pat's footsteps by studying ancient Maya ceramics, it brought us ever closer and we used to joke about which of us would publish their ceramics volume first. My Cuello volume, a far less ambitious endeavor than the Tikal ceramics was published in 1987, and I gleefully lorded that over Pat's 1993 publication date for the Tikal whole vessels whenever I had the opportunity. He was always gracious in defeat; always the epitome of the gentleman scholar. I was also very aware that Pat was able to be Pat because of Bobbi, and I would like to dedicate this volume to her. I hope that the end result measures up to Pat's standards and would have made him happy and proud.

Laura J. Kosakowsky
Tucson, AZ
November 12, 2017

Preface

The two volumes of the central Tikal ceramic reports (Tikal Reports 25A and 25B) present the information gathered from the analysis of all ceramics recovered by the Penn Museum research project at Tikal between 1956 and 1970. Tikal Report 25A (Culbert 1993) contains illustrations and brief descriptive captions for all whole vessels recovered from burials, caches, and problematical deposits. Because Tikal Report 25A illustrates the often spectacular decorated vessels from major burials, it is of the most general interest for comparative purposes. This volume, Tikal Report 25B, presents the Tikal sequence of nine ceramic complexes (the analysis of the small sample of Postclassic Caban ceramics was not completed), describes the ceramics from each complex, presents the data for all counted lots, and illustrates the material from sherd collections. It is a specialist volume, primarily of interest to those actively involved in research with Maya ceramics. The material is complemented by data in the Tikal Reports devoted to excavations and by the analysis of non-ceramic artifactual material in Tikal Reports 27A and 27B.

I joined the Tikal Project in the spring of 1961. My initial assignment was to finish analysis of the ceramics from Groups 4F-1 and -2 (Tikal Report 19). Until the fall of 1962, I lived in Guatemala City and worked on ceramics that were shipped out to me (visiting the site occasionally). From 1963 through the end of the project in 1970, I spent summers at Tikal continuing ceramic analysis, and directing some test excavations to expand collections from some complexes.

A number of individuals had worked on Tikal ceramics before I joined the project, though little from their results was passed on to me. These included: (1) A 1958 report from Richard E. W. Adams on the ceramics from Op. 12A, the section of the North Acropolis trench that cut through the frontal stairway, and (2) A number of papers from James C. Gifford, who was in charge of ceramics in 1960, but most of them deal with laboratory organization and the handling of collections. The only data from Gifford dealing directly with ceramics are a 30-page consideration of the ceramics and stratigraphy of Str. 5D-34 and a very detailed description of each of the vessels in Bu. 22. Mary Ricketson also worked with ceramics from Str. 5D-34; Keith Dixon worked with ceramics from Groups 4F-1 and -2 in 1959 and 1960; and Vivian Broman worked peripherally with ceramics in the laboratory. I have no written information on the work of these individuals.

Previous workers on the Tikal Project ceramics based dating and type names on the Uaxactun sequence (Smith 1955; Smith and Gifford 1966), as was inevitable in the early stages of analysis. Although they surely recognized that Tikal needed an independent sequence, they did not have time to develop one. At the beginning of my work, I decided that given the importance of Tikal and the enormous collections being amassed, I would not rely on the Uaxactun sequence, so I in effect slammed the Uaxactun report shut. I obviously had general knowledge about Uaxactun and other Maya ceramics before starting my work, but in the beginning it was very important to work on the Tikal sequence without further reference to Uaxactun. It prevented any temptation to be biased in classification or on decisions about chronology. It turned out the Uaxactun sequence is superb and identical to the Tikal sequence in everything except minor details, and, in fact, the Tikal collections made possible a greatly expanded treatment of the Preclassic. The closeness of the two sequences provided evidence not only of the excellence of the original Uaxactun analysis, but also of the validity of the sequence derived at Tikal.

The first objective of my research with Tikal ceramics was to establish a full ceramic sequence for the site. The enormous quantity of ceramics available, the presence of stratigraphic sequences, and the variety of contexts sampled in Tikal excavations made it obvious that to depend on already established sequences would be unacceptable. A second objective was to be a service person for other members of the project. At Tikal, as is true at most other sites, excavators depended upon the analysis of ceramics for temporal evaluations. Thirdly, the variety of contexts represented meant that ceramic research could not be confined to chronology. The analysis also had to deal with cultural questions of production distribution and use of ceramics. Finally, the necessity of publishing the results of the ceramic studies was an enormous responsibility and, as it turned out, a lifetime one.

T. Patrick Culbert
Santa Fe, NM
2011

Abbreviations

Bu.: Burial
Ca.: Cache
Ch.: Chultun
Gp.: Group
LG.: Lot Group
Op.: Operation
PD.: Problematical Deposit
Plat.: Platform
Rm.: Room
Str.: Structure
U.: Unit

I

Introduction

The ceramics from Tikal are presented in two separate but complementary volumes. Tikal Report (TR.) 25A described the whole vessels from special deposits including burials, caches, and problematical deposits. This volume is focused on the massive sherd collections and constructing a ceramic chronology for the site utilizing multiple approaches including type: variety classification and crosscutting modal analyses of ceramic pastes and vessel shapes. From the very beginning of the Tikal Project, it was obvious that the sheer quantity of ceramic material provided both a wonderful opportunity and an enormous challenge. What follows is a discussion of the sampling methodology used, the kinds of deposits from which the sherd collections were excavated, an overview of how the ceramic types are presented, and a description of the modal paste and shape analyses. Finally, we summarize the entire ceramic sequence of Tikal beginning with the Early Middle Preclassic and ending in the Postclassic.

Sampling Methodology

The first ceramic analysis conducted at Tikal by the senior author was the analysis of sherds from the small structure groups 4F-1 and 4F-2. The excavations of these eighteen structures, reported in TR. 19, most of which were done in detail during 1959 and 1960, produced three tons of sherds. Given this and in view of the huge volume of material recovered from other operations throughout the site,

it was clear that full classification and total counts could never be made of all the sherds in each lot.

Consequently decisions had to be made very early about which lots should be fully analyzed. Several criteria were used for selecting lots for analysis. First, the quantity of sherds in a lot had to be large enough to be significant. In almost all cases this meant at least 100 rim sherds (although exceptions were made if necessary). Secondly, the lot should be relatively temporally "pure"; i.e., it should represent material from only a single ceramic complex. The criterion of temporal "purity" was modified in ways to be described later for large lots of fill from major structures. Finally, with lots where more than one-quarter of the sherds were too badly weathered to show surface characteristics, no type counts were made, although counts of shapes could be done.

These restrictions on classifying and counting sherds did not mean that any lots were left uninspected. The excavators had the right to at least a quick chronological evaluation of material from each lot. Consequently, each bag of material was dumped on a table, chronologically indicative material noted, and brief summaries such as "a lot of Imix and Ik; some Manik; no Preclassic" were recorded and given to the excavators. Before evaluation of lots was undertaken, excavators were responsible for supplying information about the location of each lot, including potential stratigraphy in relation to other lots, and an evaluation of probable source; e.g., "probably slumped fill from Str. 4F-7." Excavators were also responsible for suggesting potential Lot Groups, groups of lots that probably were similar, e.g. "all lots from surface levels outside of Str. 4F-15." The lots in a lot group could be combined to provide a sample of sufficient size if the material warranted quantification. Finally, excavators indicated lots that were particularly significant, for example: "This lot of sealed fill is critical in supplying a date for Str. 4F-19-2nd." Such lots were more carefully analyzed so that critical information would not be missed in a rapid inspection.

Kinds of Deposits

Meaningful archaeological analysis is impossible without a careful consideration of a set of factors that provide or limit possibilities for various types of analyses. Such considerations are especially true for a lengthy project at a very large site, where a huge variety of different situations will be encountered. Far too often, archaeologists have a tendency to consider only certain deposits useful for analysis. This is particularly true for claims that only "primary" deposits are useful, a claim that frequently ignores the formation processes to which deposits have been subjected.

Several factors are important in determining the utility of deposits for providing specific kinds of information. These include (1) The nature (e.g., size, preservation, quantity) of the artifactual material; (2) The amount of time represented by the deposit; (3) The stratigraphic situation involved; and (4) The formation processes, both cultural and natural, that have affected the material. Taking these factors into account, the Tikal deposits are classified into several categories.

"Mixed grab bag"

This is a term for the typical deposit encountered at Tikal, especially in association with small structures. A "mixed grab bag" includes a mixture of artifacts from all periods during which people engaged in activity at a location. There is no stratigraphic order to the deposits. Why such randomness should be typical becomes clear if one considers the cultural and natural processes to which refuse deposits were subjected after discard. The Maya were accustomed to use refuse as fill for new structures. In the process, they moved material from one location to another,

and disturbed things that might have been left in place. For centuries after abandonment, the deposits were subjected to such natural processes as erosion, animal burrowing, root action, and especially, tree falls. When a dead tree is blown over in the typically shallow soil of the forest, its roots remove soil and artifacts and strip an area clear down to bedrock. Eventually, the roots decay, the soil and artifacts are released and are slowly washed back into the hole in random order. The effect is like a giant mixing machine. Information contained in such mixed deposits is mostly chronological. The excavator may be able to make sense of the relative amounts of material from different periods of occupation. Most of the demographic history of Tikal (Culbert et al. 1990), in fact, was derived from such deposits.

Middens

If one defines a midden as an archaeological deposit left untouched by cultural or natural processes after being discarded by the ancient inhabitants of a site, such deposits are rare at Tikal. Stratified middens—deposits in which middens accumulate stratigraphically over long intervals of time—are almost unknown. The closest thing to true middens at Tikal were the often large accumulations of material left within rooms by the Terminal Classic inhabitants of range structures. In addition, some deposits found in chultuns seem to represent rapid dumping episodes that approach true midden status. Some deposits found outside of small structures also represent relatively short periods of deposition, although they may be presumed to have been somewhat mixed by the processes noted above.

Fill deposits

Often disdained by archaeologists, fill deposits were among the most useful in the Tikal ceramic analysis. Deposits from structure fill are critical for excavators to date construction. When fill is sealed, it is obvious that the structure can have been built no earlier than the latest sherd it contains (*terminus post quem*). Large fill samples provide some security that the construction date is actually represented by the latest sherd; small samples may be problematic. For information in addition to date of construction, other data become important factors to consider.

These data include the size of the structure involved, the group to which it pertains, and the number of reconstructions at the location.

Fill from small structure groups (TR. 19, 20A, 22) provides an excellent source of information. Sherd fits between structure fill and refuse materials from outside of other structures in the same group make it clear that the Maya moved accumulated refuse into platforms that were being constructed or remodeled. Such fill often represents a relatively unmixed sample from a short time interval, probably because contemporary refuse deposits within the group were readily available and provided enough material for filling operations.

Fill from large structures is another matter. Large construction usually involved dismantling of earlier structures at the same location, resulting in a constant "upwelling" of early material into later constructions that makes unmixed samples rare. Sealed fill from large structures, however, can provide important opportunities. Preservation of sherd surfaces is usually much better than in small structures, allowing description and analysis of decorated types and varieties. In addition, sequences of construction involving large quantities of sealed fill related to architectural stratigraphy can provide exceedingly precise information about the points at which ceramic features were introduced. The Preclassic levels in the North Acropolis (TR. 14) are an outstanding example of this phenomenon. Level upon level of construction provided huge samples of ceramics in an excellent state of preservation. The exact point in the sequence when a new ceramic element made its appearance can be documented. After being introduced, most elements showed a trend of increase followed by a decline in typical battleship curve fashion. The curves, however, are not as well defined as in less mixed deposits.

Special Deposits

The utility of burial and cache artifacts (including ceramics) for providing information about chronology, social status, and ritual practices is well known. These data, including a significant amount of published Tikal data, have been used by Krejci and Culbert (1995) for a consideration of social status and change over time during the Preclassic and Early Classic periods in the Maya Lowlands. In addition,

the Early Classic burials 10, 22, and 48 provide an excellent source of information about the impact of Teotihuacan on the Maya elite of Tikal and Kaminaljuyu (Reents-Budet et al. 2003). Recent advances in Maya epigraphy (Harrison 1999; Martin and Grube 2000), providing historic information, have also enhanced our ceramic interpretations. Problematical Deposits (PD.) at Tikal, however, represent such a mixed group of situations and contents (as they were appropriately designed to do) that they cannot be considered a single category for analysis. Some types of PD. are rich and varied in their ceramic contents and provide very important collections for ceramic analysis (TR. 27A:67–68).

Type: variety Classification

We will not rehash in detail the various theoretical arguments critiquing the type: variety system of classification for Maya pottery; there have been numerous publications (cf. Aimers 2013; Culbert and Rands 2007; Forsyth 1983; Rice 2013), especially concerning the focus on prioritizing surface finish of ceramics over other attributes. However, despite these critiques it remains the most useful system of classification for Maya pottery and, in conjunction with other modal analyses, allows ease of comparison between sites. Therefore, a combined type: variety-mode analysis was used in this volume. The identification of ceramic types, varieties, and modes has the advantage of informing on the temporal placement of the occupation and construction history of a site, as well as allowing one to place it in a regional and interregional context. In the absence of well-preserved surfaces, modal characteristics such as rim and lip shape, vessel form (Sabloff 1975; Thompson 1939), and visual paste and temper characteristics are also extremely useful in pottery identification.

Sherds were classified utilizing the type: variety-mode system (see Gifford 1976), with classification primarily confined to surface treatment, which has always been the major characteristic used in establishing types and varieties. As the system has proliferated, however, using such characteristics as vessel shape or paste as the basis for varieties has led many to ask whether there are rules in naming types and varieties. As a matter of fact, some shape-based varieties were originally used in TR. 25A and have been eliminated in this volume, as they are inconsistent with the rules of nomenclature. Instead varieties of a type are identified on the basis of secondary decorative elements.

Another complaint about traditional type-variety analysis is that the concept of "ware" was found to be altogether less useful, unless it is used in the old-fashioned traditional sense of paste difference such as Fine Orange Ware or Mars Orange Ware. In this traditional sense the term had meaning because it referred to quite unique combinations of paste with surface color. When, however, ware is incorporated as a hierarchical level above the ceramic group in the type: variety system, it has lost most meaning. As an example, the term "Petén Gloss Ware" has been applied for the entire Classic period in the Petén; it includes what must be dozens of types, a number of which are not, in fact, particularly glossy. The only surface characteristic the types have in common is that all are slipped and/or painted, a feature that is abundantly clear from type names. However, in the interests of producing type descriptions for Tikal that are easily comparable to types described in other ceramic monographs the decision was made to use standardized type: variety formats that include ware. This does not mean that the technical features in pottery production that produce glossiness in contradistinction to the frequently waxy surface of Preclassic ceramics are meaningless. But they should be considered as a general description and not applied like a mantra to all types of the applicable periods.

As indicated above, ceramic type: variety descriptions have been written using a standardized format (Gifford 1976; Willey, Culbert, and Adams 1967) (Table 1.1). In some instances, missing data from the original analyses has resulted in only partially complete type descriptions, although every effort was made to provide as much information as possible. There are also a number of types for which there were no illustrations in the Tikal files, though some are illustrated in TR. 25A, and others are cross-referenced in the intersite comparisons so they can be found elsewhere in the literature. The one area in which the Tikal type descriptions differ from a completely standardized format is the category of vessel shape. While the most common shapes are listed for each type, within the type description, a separate, detailed modal vessel shape classification is also presented for each complex.

Multiple Classifications

The procedures used in the analysis of Tikal ceramics differ, as mentioned above, from those common in many ceramic reports. At Tikal, a system of multiple classifications advocated by Culbert and Rands (2007) is followed, rather than collapsing all information under the type-variety system, although the typological classification takes precedence. From the beginning of the analysis, completely different sortings were done for types, pastes, and shapes.

Type: variety-mode

As mentioned above, ceramics are described using traditional type: variety nomenclature (Gifford 1976; Willey, Culbert, and Adams 1967), however, a detailed modal vessel shape analysis is also employed and found to be extremely useful in identifying chronological change in the Tikal ceramics. The original type descriptions produced by the senior author did not include any information on intrasite locations at Tikal, and it is not known whether this information was never collected or has been lost in the intervening years. Intersite and regional comparisons were also not done in the original classification but have been added in this volume by the junior author. Additionally complete type frequency counts were apparently never collected consistently for minor types and varieties, for all sample locations, or for all ceramic complexes by the senior author. A decision was made to include type frequencies in this volume when available, despite the inconsistencies, as being better than none at all. Therefore, the tables in each chapter that highlight type frequencies are inconsistent. In some instances percentages include both types and varieties, and in others they are differentiated only to the level of the ceramic group. Often there were no counts for minor types or groups included in the original data.

Paste Classification

Rather than relying only on the designations of wares to identify technological differences on the Tikal ceramic assemblage, technological information on the ceramics is provided in greater detail using an analysis of changes in pastes throughout

TABLE 1.1
Format for Type: Variety Descriptions

Type: Variety	Name
Established	Reference for first use of type and variety name according to priority of publication.
Ceramic Group	Connects types to all others with similar surface treatment.
Ware	General and standardized name based on broad technological similarity.
Ceramic Complex	Site specific ceramic complex name.
Ceramic Sphere	Regional connection for Tikal Complexes.
Illustrations	Includes a cross-reference for illustrations in TR. 25A (Culbert 1993) as well as illustrations in this volume for both types and vessel shapes.
Principal Identifying Attributes	Includes the most common attributes utilized to identify the type and variety.
Identifying characteristics and sorting problems	If there are any sorting problems between types they are noted.
Paste	Describes the most common pastes on which the type is manufactured, as well as any inclusions.
Firing	Describes firing conditions.
Slip	Describes slip texture and condition.
Polish	Describes degree of polish if present.
Color	Utilizes standard Munsell Soil Color designations.
Surface finish and decoration	Describes any decoration or other surficial defining characteristics.
Shapes	The most common shapes are listed within the type description and then described in detail in the vessel shape classification.
Temporal Distribution	Listed by ceramic complex.
Comments	Includes any additional information.
Intersite comparisons	Cites the most relevant literature where the type is found at other sites.

the sequence. The Tikal ceramic analysis was based on the assumption that paste composition is an independent variable, the correlation of which, with surface finish, should be tested rather than assumed. It became clear that certain pastes are in fact tied to specific ceramic types and varieties.

However, this separate classification done for pastes was conducted by the senior author in the 1960s and was restricted in scope and entirely non-technical. Analysis and sorting were done by a simple visual description of paste that includes color, texture, amount and general appearance of inclusions, but sadly no detailed mineralogical or compositional analyses were ever conducted. Dilute hydrochloric acid was used to test for carbonate compounds, but no other chemical tests were made and more sophisticated mineralogical identifications were not attempted. Counts of paste types were done only for small samples from type collections and the results are less secure and representative than the quantitative treatment of types and shapes. Nevertheless, even these techniques provided useful information and showed changes in paste composition through time in the Tikal ceramic sequence.

Vessel Shape Classification

In the classification of vessel shapes, a two-level system is used. At one level are shape classes, major groups defined by basic proportions and size (see Table 1.2). Shape classes are closely related to vessel function. As an example, vessels of the shape class wide-mouth jars are characterized by wide mouth and large body size. Narrow-mouth jars have narrow mouths and are of much smaller size. Because wide-mouth jars are too heavy to carry any distance when filled, they have little potential for transporting water but could be used to store water and the wide mouth allows water to be dipped from them for use. Narrow-mouth jars are transportable and the narrow mouth prevents spilling. These two shape classes persist among Maya ceramic producers today (Thompson 1958; Culbert 1965). Similarly, cylindrical vessels would be appropriate for drinking, but not easily usable for serving solid food. Plates, on the other hand, would be awkward to drink from but good for serving or eating solid or liquid food. Most shape classes persist through time and would have counterparts in almost all societies that use ceramic vessels. Variations in frequencies of shape classes have little temporal meaning but may indicate differences in social meaning (e.g., between social classes).

Shapes are subdivisions of shape classes (e.g., wide-mouth jar with tall neck or wide-mouth jar with short neck, tripod cylinder or cylinder) based on more detailed features. Shapes change through time and are among the most useful diagnostics for defining ceramic complexes. Modal differences within shapes, such as flanges, supports, or lip shapes, provide even more detail and are often temporally specific.

A final kind of quantification used four "categories." Three of these categories are the shape classes wide-mouth jars, narrow-mouth jars, and large capacity bowls. The fourth category combined all the shapes classes commonly considered "serving vessels." The first three categories are usually considered "utilitarian"; i.e., vessels that would be used within households. The serving vessel category includes vessels that could indeed, be used for serving food, but might also have ritual uses. Serving vessels is the category that includes the great majority of vessels that appear in burials and caches.

At Tikal, from the beginning to the end of the sequence, there is close to a 100% correspondence

TABLE 1.2
Tikal Shape Classes and Dimensions

Shape Class	Rim Diameter Range
1. Wide-mouth Jars	20.0–30.0 cm
2. Narrow-mouth Jars	<20.0 cm
3. Very Wide-mouth Jars	>40.0 cm
4. Large Capacity Bowls	>30.0 cm
5. Medium Diameter Bowls and Dishes	20.0–30.0 cm
6. Small Diameter Bowls and Dishes	10.0–20.0 cm
7. Cylindrical Vessels	—
8. Medium Plates	20.0–30.0 cm
9. Large Plates	>30.0 cm
10. Specialized Cache and Burial Vessels and Covers	—
11. Miniature Vessels	<10 cm
12. Covers	—
13. Effigy Vessels	—

of unslipped/striated types, with a coarse paste with heavy carbonate tempering, and wide-mouth jars. In the Early Classic, vessels in the serving vessel category are sometimes monochrome and sometimes decorated, but, in the Late Classic, serving vessels are almost always made in types from one of the polychrome groups and have pastes different from other types. In the Terminal Classic, as polychromes decline drastically, serving vessels are again usually of monochrome types. While it is clear that the Tikal sequence exhibits quantifiable changes through time, the relationship of type, paste, and vessel shape is a matter to be investigated rather than assumed.

It is also important to note that unfortunately there are gaps in the data presented in the descriptions of the ceramic complexes. When producing a monograph decades after the excavations, it is perhaps not surprising that some of the information has been lost. When these gaps occur, they are indicated in the chapters on the ceramic complexes. What follows first is a summary of the Tikal ceramic sequence that highlights the temporal changes and presents a general ceramic chronology (Table 1.3).

Social Dimensions of Tikal Types

An additional aspect of the Tikal ceramic analysis, beyond chronological, is an attempt to examine intrasite variation across different contexts at Tikal. In order to quantify this, structure groups, structures, and associated contexts (such as chultuns for example) were loosely grouped into broad categories that do not necessarily match their architectural designations by the excavator. A good example of this is Group 7F-1 which Haviland (TR. 22) would consider an elite residential group, comparable to the Central Acropolis residences, but because of its location outside of the Great Plaza is grouped with other intermediate size residential groups. This was done to facilitate comparisons and produce groupings that were more or less similar in terms of location within the site, group and structure size, and hypothesized functions. The civic-ceremonial category is used to describe non-residential large temples and pyramids within the site center of Tikal, while elite residential groups can serve both residential and administrative functions within the site center. Intermediate structure groups are the most broad, and problematical, in that they cover a large range of sizes and functions (elite residential as well as administrative) but were separated to distinguish from small structure groups that are clearly household structures.

The Ceramic Sequence: The Preclassic

The ceramic sequence at Uaxactun (Smith 1955; Smith and Gifford 1966), the previous standard for central Petén ceramics, managed to achieve only the two-part division of Mamom and Chicanel for the Preclassic, and Matzanel for the Terminal Preclassic. The much more voluminous collections and superb stratigraphy at Tikal, especially in the North Acropolis, made possible the separation of five sequential complexes: Eb, Tzec, Chuen, Cauac, and Cimi based on changes in predominant ceramic types and vessel shapes (see Table 1.3). Ceramic complexes are assemblages "with specific temporal, spatial, and cultural integrity and boundaries" (Ball 1977:3).

The construction of an independent ceramic sequence is dependent on the kinds, quantity, preservation, and stratigraphy of the collections available. These factors differed considerably between the contexts of the various complexes at Tikal, so that different methods had to be used in the construction of different segments of the sequence.

TABLE 1.3
Tikal Chronology

PERIOD	LONG COUNT	DATE	CERAMIC COMPLEX	CERAMIC SPHERE
Early Postclassic		c. A.D. 950	Caban	
Terminal Classic	10.2.0.0.0	A.D. 869	Eznab	Tepeu 3
Late Late Classic	9.13.0.0.0	A.D. 692	Imix	Tepeu 2
Early Late Classic	9.6.0.0.0	A.D. 554	Ik	Tepeu 1
Early Classic	8.11.0.0.0	c. A.D. 250	Manik	Tzakol
Terminal Preclassic		c A.D. 150	Cimi	Chicanel
Late Late Preclassic		c. 1 B.C.	Cauac	Chicanel
Early Late Preclassic		c. 350 B.C.	Chuen	Chicanel
Late Middle Preclassic		c. 600 B.C.	Tzec	Mamom
Early Middle Preclassic		c. 800 B.C.	Eb	Pre-Mamom

The Eb Complex

Two temporal facets were originally defined for the Eb Complex. Early Eb was the first pre-Mamom horizon material recognized in the central Petén, although similar to material found in the Yaxha-Sacnab region (Rice 1979a). Since the definition of Early Eb at Tikal, pre-Mamom ceramics have been identified at many sites throughout the Maya Lowlands and more samples have been uncovered in significant quantities in the Mundo Perdido Complex (Hermes 1993; Laporte and Fialko 1995). In the Penn Museum collections, Early Eb ceramics occurred in quantity only in two locations, a pit in bedrock underlying the North Acropolis and in Chultun 5G-15, 1.5 km east of the site center. The deposit underneath the North Acropolis establishes the temporal priority of Early Eb.

Early Eb ceramics include types and shapes that distinguish them from later Mamom horizon material, particularly the types. Although there are contemporary ceramic complexes known both from sites in the Río Pasión area (Adams 1971; Sabloff 1975; Inomata et al. 2013) and from Belize (Gifford 1976; Kosakowsky 1987; Kosakowsky and Pring 1998; Sagebiel and Haines 2015) (as well as from neighboring areas outside the Maya lowlands), these other complexes show relatively little relationship to Eb or to each other. The great heterogeneity of the earliest ceramics from different regions of the Maya lowlands has long been recognized (Culbert 1977) as suggesting that the initial populations moved into the lowlands from several different directions, but no collections from surrounding areas seem similar enough to Early Eb to suggest a specific area of origin. Elsewhere the junior author and others (Kosakowsky, Sagebiel, and Pring 2018; Castellanos and Foias 2017) have suggested naming the pre-Mamom as the Eb Sphere, centered on Tikal in the central Petén; a ceramic sphere "exists when two or more complexes share a majority of their most common types" (Willey, Culbert, and Adams 1967:306).

Late Eb ceramics came mostly from the tunnel excavated by the Tikal Project into Str. 5C-54, the great pyramid in the Mundo Perdido Complex. Late Eb is now defined as part of the Mamom Tzec Complex. Because the sample on which Late Eb was originally based was fill from a large structure, it included a mixture of pre-Mamom Eb and Mamom Tzec ceramics.

The Tzec Complex

The Tzec Complex is the first one that shows links to many other lowland Maya sites and is part of the Mamom ceramic horizon. The complex was sparsely represented in the Tikal collections. Only one location (a quarry pit underlying structures 5F-17 and -18 about 1 km east of site center) provided a Tzec sample that could be analyzed quantitatively. The collections from this location, however, were very large and the deposits deep enough to demonstrate ceramic change within the Tzec Complex and a gradual transition to the succeeding Chuen Complex that overlies it. Like the Mamom Complex at Uaxactun (Smith 1955), a principal defining characteristic of Tzec was a huge abundance of plates. This characteristic, also shared with the Mamom-equivalent San Felix Complex at Altar de Sacrificios (Adams 1971), is difficult to explain in a functional sense. Whatever activity was represented by the use of plates, it was shared across the southern Maya lowlands.

The Chuen Complex

The Chuen Complex represents the beginning of the Late Preclassic (Chicanel Horizon) complexes at Tikal. The archaeological evidence for the complex is more complete than that for the Eb and Tzec Complexes. The Chuen samples represent increased contextual variety, a greater number of locations, more samples per location, and an increased total quantity of sherds. It also is the point at which the North Acropolis floor sequence, which seals large quantities of ceramics, begins.

Typologically, Tzec and Chuen ceramics are relatively easy to distinguish, but with the beginning of the Chuen Complex, Tikal ceramics entered a long period of typological stability during which the types that comprised the bulk of the collections changed very little for a period of 600 years. The time of the Chicanel Horizon is also the time at which there were very strong similarities in ceramics across the Maya lowlands and even outside to such areas as the Central Depression of Chiapas (Willey, Culbert, and Adams 1967).

The Cauac Complex

The Cauac Complex is the best defined of the Late Preclassic complexes at Tikal, both because more diagnostic shapes mark the complex and because the ceramic collections are more abundant. Typologically, there was little change in either types represented or the frequency thereof between the Chuen and Cauac Complexes. The only change in types that is worthy of mention is the appearance of the first types with Usulutan decoration. That such decoration had its home to the south of the Maya lowlands in El Salvador (Demarest and Sharer 1982) seems fairly clear. In this sense, its introduction represents cultural contact. It is important, however, to make a distinction between the term "Usulutan Style" and "Usulutan Ware" (Brady et al.1998; Pring 2000). Usulutan Style consists of multiple parallel wavy line decoration, presumably made with a multipronged instrument of unknown manufacture. Usulutan Ware was made by a resist technique in which sections of the first slip are covered with something like wax before a second slip was added. Although resist techniques were used at Tikal, in other types in the Tzec and Chuen Complexes, resist pieces in Usulutan style were rare at the site, and most of them were probably trade items. Usulutan Style vessels in the entire Petén and Belize were usually decorated using a "wipe-off" technique. This involves adding a second slip over the first and then removing it, while still wet, with a multipronged instrument to reveal sections of the underlying first slip. There are also some pieces in which a second slip is positively painted with a multipronged instrument. In effect then, the Maya of Tikal copied the stylistic approach of Usulutan, but produced it with their own techniques.

Despite the small amount of typological change between Chuen and Cauac, the separation between the two complexes is made relatively easy by the fact that there are quite distinctive changes in shapes that occur in vessels that are common in the collections. Of these, the appearance of medial-flange bowls and dishes is the most obvious.

The Cimi Complex

The last of the Preclassic ceramic complexes of the Tikal sequence is the Cimi Complex. The Cimi Complex is both controversial and the most difficult to recognize of the Tikal complexes. Therefore, it is necessary to consider in some detail the basis on which it was defined, its content, and its position in relation to the Tikal sequence and to other sequences in the Maya area.

The Cimi Complex was based primarily on the North Acropolis stratigraphy and associated ceramics that showed minor but significant additions to the preceding Cauac Complex. Collections included all lots sealed by the seventh, eighth, and ninth floors from the top of the Acropolis (TR. 14). This was an important interval of time in the Acropolis. A massive construction, raising the overall North Acropolis platform took place at some time that was probably close to the beginning of the Cimi time span. The rebuilding associated with the new platform set a basic pattern of structures that would persist for centuries. The only chamber burial (Bu. 125) that occurred in this interval involved a very large chamber that was empty except for the remains of multiple individuals. At the end of Cimi, but clearly before the start of the Manik Complex, the entire approach to the Acropolis from the Great Plaza was changed by completion of a single frontal stairway that replaced what had previously been two separate stairways. Probably more than a century later and well into Manik times, a pit was dug through the fifth floor of the Acropolis sequence and filled with PD. 87, a collection of Cimi ceramics, including a large quantity of utilitarian pottery, and human bones that Coe (TR. 14:831) suggests may have been a redeposited Cimi burial, but may also have included redeposited material from elsewhere. If so (the ceramics seem appropriate for a burial), it would indicate that major chamber burials were still being made in the North Acropolis in Cimi times.

The Cimi ceramic samples were large and included 10,178 sherds counted for types and 2,849 rims counted for shapes. The differentiation between Cauac and Cimi is minimal, and consists mostly of the addition of new Usulutan varieties produced using a very liquid black slip that is easily given to jagged patterns, and tetrapodal vessels with mammiform feet. The Cimi markers never occur in frequencies greater than 5%; consequently, their absence in small collections is not significant.

The Usulutan varieties that identify Cimi also appear at sites in Belize (Willey et al. 1965;

Gifford 1976) and on the Pasion River (Adams 1971; Sabloff 1975) in ceramic complexes that have traditionally been termed "Protoclassic" (Brady et al. 1998; Pring 2000). In this work, we do not use the term Protoclassic and call the time of the Cimi Complex "Terminal Preclassic." The term Protoclassic has been used in such a variety of ways that almost every recent use results in generating endless verbiage about the ways in which "Protoclassic" has been used previously, usually followed by a new definition (Brady et al. 1998; Pring 2000), and the continued use of the term seems to result in nothing more than compounding the confusion.

It is also important to stress that the Cimi Complex is clearly Preclassic. However, it is marked by the presence of a few sharp z-angle bowls and annular bases, shapes that are more characteristic of the Early Classic Manik 1 and 2. In decoration, however, not a single true polychrome sherd occurred in the huge sealed lots of pure Cimi Complex date. Instead, the decorative message was carried by Usulutan types and a few dichrome decorations with simple designs. In addition, there was not a single example of either a basal flange bowl or a scutate lid (also called a scutate cover), shapes that were strongly associated with polychromes in Manik.

It is no surprise that a transition between complexes might occur gradually, with different elements appearing at different times. A ceramic complex is a heuristic device that summarizes the major characteristics of ceramics during a given time interval. It is not a closed box that overnight replaces the box of a previous complex. Very often, however, our collections are not adequate to demonstrate the details of changes, as will be apparent when we discuss the transition between the Early and Late Classic as reflected in the Tikal Project data.

The Ceramic Sequence: The Early Classic

The Manik Complex

Although the Penn Museum collections for the Early Classic Manik Complex at Tikal were abundant, they did not give sufficient information for subdividing the complex. A major problem was that the very large collections of ceramics from sequent architectural levels that were so critical in defining the Preclassic sequence did not occur in the Classic architectural levels. However, Coggins (1975), focusing on decorated vessels, achieved a three-part sequence (Manik 1, 2, and 3a, 3b) that was successful.

The situation has been greatly clarified by the very detailed analysis of Manik materials made possible by the excavations of the Proyecto Nacional Tikal, especially in the Mundo Perdido Complex (Laporte and Fialko 1987, 1990, 1995). In the Proyecto Nacional material, an excellent sequence of Manik 1, 2, 3a, and 3b has been defined. Combining that material with the North Acropolis data, there is now a superb understanding of the ceramic transition between the Late Preclassic and the Early Classic. The changes are profound and represent a replacement of all types and shapes, both utilitarian and decorated, albeit a gradual one.

The elaborate burials discovered in the Mundo Perdido Group by the Proyecto Nacional Tikal (Laporte and Fialko 1987) give a very rich picture of Manik 2. In those burials, polychromes were abundant, mostly on sharp-z-angle bowls, although a few basal flange bowls occurred. Scutate lids were added to the repertoire, often with elaborate polychrome decoration and modeled handles. None of the Usulutan types occurred. Large mammiform feet, which characterized Cimi, continued to appear in the Manik 1–2 burials.

A sharp transition in serving vessels took place at the beginning of Manik 3 (Coggins 1975: Krejci and Culbert 1995). Sharp z-angle bowls and scutate lids disappeared, the polychrome tradition continued, but became less important in burial offerings, and the tripod cylinder, often of decorated incised and gouged-incised types became a key feature, especially in chamber burials. The influences from Teotihuacan, which mark Burials 10, 22, and 48, typify the transition. Krejci and Culbert (1995) note that in addition to ceramics, other very significant changes occur in burials and caches related to the dynastic change from Chak Tok Ich'aak I (Jaguar Paw) to Nuun Yax Ayiin I (Curl Nose). In the Tikal sherd collections, the tripod cylinder is not confined to ceremonial-elite contexts at the site center but occurs as a significant component of refuse in small mound groups.

The Ceramic Sequence: The early Late Classic and the late Late Classic

The appearance of Late Classic ceramics represents another drastic change in which all types and shapes were replaced with the single exception of unslipped and striated large-mouth jars. How abrupt was this change? Unlike the Preclassic/Early Classic transition, where the North Acropolis sequence showed the early introduction of some Early Classic markers, there was no key to the pace of change at this boundary in the Tikal Project data. In the research of the Proyecto Nacional Tikal (Laporte et al. 1992), however, several special deposits indicate a transitional period between AD 550 and 600 in which the majority of the ceramics were still Early Classic, but Late Classic types and shapes had begun to appear corresponding to Coggins's Manik 3b (1975). It would seem, then, that the Early Classic/Late Classic transition was also a gradual one.

For the Late Classic, the derivation of the ceramic sequence was based primarily on a seriation of lots, most of which came from the abundant collections provided by excavation of small structure groups. Because these collections were very poorly preserved, most of the information available concerned vessel shapes. A description of decorated types was possible, however, because of a few large and well-preserved collections from the fills of large structures (such as Str. 5D-33-1st). Burials, of course, provided critical information on changes in decorated vessels (Coggins 1975).

Within the Late Classic, there was great continuity in all categories except serving vessels. Unslipped and monochrome types are undifferentiated between Late Classic complexes. So are basic shapes of jars and large bowls, although quantitative changes in such minor modes as lip shapes provide clues to differentiate complexes. But the shapes of serving vessels, which were almost entirely polychrome until the Terminal Classic Eznab Complex, changed sharply and serve as an unmistakable key to the separation of the Ik, Imix and Eznab Complexes.

The Ik Complex

The Ik Complex marked the appearance of almost all the types and shapes that distinguish the early Late Classic from the Early Classic. Unslipped types and the wide-mouth jars produced from them changed very little from the Early Classic, but Tinaja Red became the dominant monochrome type and the shapes of small-mouth jars and large capacity bowls were quite different from those of the Early Classic. Decorated material was almost entirely of the Saxche Polychrome Group, with plates with medial ridges, barrels, and outflaring to slightly outcurving-side bowls and dishes the most characteristic shapes.

The Imix Complex

Only minor changes in such modes as lip shape and the decoration (e.g., incised lines, fingernail punctations, etc.) of large capacity bowls separate the late Late Classic Imix Complex utilitarian vessels from those of the preceding Ik Complex. The Palmar Polychrome Group replaced the Saxche Group as the primary decorated ceramic. At Tikal, the two groups are easy to distinguish because types of the Palmar Group were produced using an initial white underslip that underlay all further painting. In addition, there are differences in shades of color and in pastes between the two ceramic groups, although at other sites they are often difficult to differentiate and are lumped together (Sabloff 1975). To make the differences between Ik and Imix decorated serving vessels even more distinctive, outflaring to slightly outcurving-side plates replaced the plates with medial ridges of Ik and barrels became much less common while cylinders increased in frequency. The changes in serving vessel shapes are so striking and the shapes are so common even in small structures that the two complexes can hardly be confused.

The Ceramic Sequence: The Terminal Classic

The Eznab Complex

Definition of the Eznab Complex was made easy by the abundant surface debris found in range structure groups, especially in the Central Acropolis. As the last phase of occupation, these deposits remained largely undisturbed thereafter. With the beginning of the Terminal Classic Eznab Complex, a set of changes even more obvious than those that separated the Ik and Imix Complexes took place. An Eznab sample of even modest size can hardly fail to be identified. Typologically, unslipped and monochrome types remained the same as earlier, except that the use of black slip became considerably more common for some types of serving vessels. Polychromes diminished greatly in frequency. Polychromes represented 10–30% of vessels in Imix, and rarely more than 2–6% in most Eznab contexts. In addition, many of the polychromes that continued to be produced were off-color and poorly painted in comparison with those of Imix. A few Fine Orange vessels and local imitations of Fine Orange were added to the typological inventory. Among vessel shapes, such characteristic Imix shapes as outflaring to slightly outcurving-side plates and cylinders continued to be common, but were now almost invariably red-slipped, which they would never have been in Imix times. In addition, new serving vessel shapes were added to the inventory including large tripod plates and pyriform vases with pedestal bases. It must be stressed, however, that the tradition of ceramic production was continuous from earlier complexes. There is absolutely no indication from the ceramics that the Eznab inhabitants of the site were anything other than descendants of earlier occupants of Tikal.

The Ceramic Sequence: The Early Postclassic

The Caban Complex

A final Early Postclassic occupation, in a few locations at Tikal, is represented by the Caban Complex. Collections are very sparse, similar to the site of Seibal (Sabloff 1975:218–228), and the complex cannot be completely described, although the majority of sherds are monochrome red or unslipped. One Caban unnumbered PD., previously designated as Bu. 5, includes a Paxcaman Red tripod plate and an Ixpop Polychrome tripod plate (see TR. 25A: fig. 98g1–2; TR. 14:603). The slips and pastes are markedly different from the preceding complex, however they appear similar to ceramics of the Early Facet Postclassic New Town Complex at Barton Ramie (Gifford 1976). Given this lack of continuity, it seems quite sure that the complex represents reoccupation by a few settlers with totally new ceramics closely related to the Early Postclassic complexes encountered along the lakes of the central zone of the Petén (Chase 1984; Rice 1979b) or perhaps elsewhere as well.

II

Eb Ceramic Complex

Eb Complex Collections

Introduction

The Eb Ceramic Complex was sparsely represented at Tikal. Only three locations produced Eb samples of significant size and although the samples permitted a good description of the complex, they provided little information about intrasite variation. Although the Eb locations were originally thought to be temporally unmixed, the reanalysis has made it clear that in fact the ceramics are mixed with later Tzec Complex sherds of the Mamom Ceramic Sphere and, in some cases, early Chuen as well. Other occurrences of Eb pottery were scanty and consisted of no more than a few sherds mixed into later lots, however subsequent excavations at the Mundo Perdido have produced deposits with Eb Complex ceramics (Laporte and Valdes 1993). The Eb population of Tikal must have been small and scattered.

Originally, a combination of new type names and Mamom type names were used to describe the Eb Complex pottery (TR. 25A), in part because at the time there was little evidence from other sites and regions of comparative early ceramics (Culbert 1977). This decision to use known Mamom type names was also the result of a lack of recognition that the three sample locations with Eb pottery at Tikal were temporally mixed. However, since that time numerous southern Maya Lowland sites have produced pre-Mamom ceramics and the decision was made to reserve Mamom type names for the succeeding Tzec Complex. In utilizing the term "pre-Mamom," we do not mean to imply that there is sufficient concordance between the Eb Complex at Tikal and early complexes at other lowland Maya sites to define a ceramic sphere, but rather we use the term to identify the time period. Elsewhere the junior author has proposed a pre-Mamom Ceramic Sphere centered on the central Petén at Tikal (Kosakowsky, Sagebiel, and Pring 2018) that has been corroborated by others (Castellanos and Foias 2017).

Eb samples were not stratigraphically related to the succeeding Tzec Complex, or to each other, but the position of the Eb Complex at the beginning of the Tikal ceramic sequence is secure on typological grounds and through comparison with pre-Mamom ceramic sequences at other sites. Though the Eb Complex unfortunately lacks temporally unmixed stratigraphic deposits in the three sample locations, it is described in this work as a pre-Mamom Early Middle Preclassic complex.

The social contexts of Eb samples are difficult to define. Neither Eb Location 1 nor Eb Location 2 could be associated with architectural remains and although Eb Location 3 was sealed within a structure buried beneath a temple pyramid, the buried structure was not thoroughly explored and its nature is unclear. Neither burials nor caches were discovered in association with Eb ceramics.

Information on the three locations that provide Eb Complex samples is presented in Table 2.1. The three locations produced a total of 5,811 sherds, of which 625 are rims.

TABLE 2.1
Locations of Eb Complex Samples

Sample #	Op.Sub-Op./Lot	Structure Group and Structure Number	Structure Group Type	Total Sherds-Types	Total Sherds-Shapes	Comments	TR.
1	27B/1–9	Gp. 5G-1 Chultun 5G-15	Uncertain in Eb, Intermediate Structure Group (residential) later	2724	198	Combined sample that includes PD 1.	21
2	12P/151	Gp. 5D-2 Lowest levels underlying North Acropolis	Uncertain in Eb; Civic-ceremonial later	1489	143	One lot	14
3	90C/6–14	Gp. 5C-11 Sealed fill below Str. 5C-54	Uncertain in Eb; Civic-ceremonial later	1598	284	Combined sample of 9 lots	23C
GRAND TOTAL				5811	625		

EB LOCATION 1

This location is Ch. 5G-15, a chultun located in the southeastern quadrant of Tikal about 1.5 km E of the civic-ceremonial center. Nearby Str. 5G-4 through 9 are of Classic date and there is no evidence of Eb or other Preclassic construction in the area (see TR. 21). The chultun was filled with a large and well-preserved sample of Eb material mixed with later ceramics (Tzec and early Chuen Complex vessels), including PD. 1. Although the material was separated into lots on the basis of depth, the ceramics are homogeneous and were combined into a single sample for analytical purposes. A possible Manik vessel and some Imix Complex sherds were mixed into the upper levels of the chultun but were easily separated on a typological basis. Above-ground deposits near the chultun do not contain Eb ceramics and there is no information about the nature of the occupation that produced the Eb sample. It is likely that ceramics from an outlying area of the site with no architectural remains are domestic refuse. For this location, 2,724 sherds were counted for types and 198 rims for shapes.

EB LOCATION 2

This location consisted of the lowest level of cultural material in the trench that sectioned the North Acropolis (TR. 14). The material occurred in a depression in bedrock underlying all construction, and was excavated as a single lot. This sample was covered by Chuen Complex deposits associated with the earliest known construction in the North Acropolis. Although the Eb deposit was not sealed, there is no indication of serious mixture with later material. No evidence of Eb architecture was encountered, so no inferences can be made about the nature of the activities that produced the ceramic sample. Although the North Acropolis was clearly a ceremonial center by Chuen times, there is no good reason to assume that the location had developed ceremonial connotations as early as the time of the Eb Complex. For this location, 1,489 sherds were counted for types, and 143 rims for shapes.

EB LOCATION 3

Eb Location 3 consisted of fill sealed by an early wall buried by the large Cauac pyramid Str. 5C-54. In the excavation of 5C-54, an axial tunnel was cut into the structure at base level. The tunnel encountered the early wall and then penetrated it to produce the Eb sample of concern here. The lack of any later sherds suggests an Eb date for construction. It was not possible to explore the nature of the structure of which this wall had been a part, but the extent of fill suggests that it was of large size. By the end of the Preclassic, when Str. 5C-54 was built, the area was certainly ceremonial in character. It is tempting to guess that ceremonialism had begun in this location by Eb times, but in the absence of more extensive excavation this remains speculative. Nine lots were separated in the excavation of the Eb deposit, but the contents do not differ meaningfully and the entire collection is treated here as a single sample. For this location, 1,598 sherds were counted for types, and 284 rims for shapes.

Pastes of the Eb Complex

Introduction

This section provides a classification of the paste types that occur in the Eb Complex without regard to surface finishes. Entries under both paste and type descriptions indicate the degree of correspondence between the two categories. Three kinds of variables were used in classifying Eb Complex pastes: the amount and particle size of inclusions; presence, or absence, of carbonate inclusions; and presence or absence of secondary clay inclusions. Here and throughout this report, the term "inclusion" is used for materials other than the clay fabric to avoid any connotation of whether or not particular substances are present or were added intentionally by the potter.

There are three classes of pastes based on the quantity and size of particles: coarse, medium, and fine. The coarse pastes correlate strongly with the unslipped ceramic groups of the Eb Complex, while pastes with medium and fine inclusions generally occur in slipped types. Carbonate and secondary clay particles are added to the paste recipes resulting in seven different paste compositions for Eb types.

Throughout the Tikal ceramic analysis the assumption was made that paste composition is an independent variable, the correlation of which with surface finish is an independent variable that should be tested rather than assumed. However, it is clear that certain paste compositions are strongly correlated with specific types, so although the Eb pastes are described separately in the following section, the paste compositions are listed in the type descriptions as well.

Eb Complex Paste Descriptions

CANHEL PASTE

Identifying Characteristics: Abundant amounts of non-carbonate inclusions that give a spotty, granular appearance.

Color: Brown to light brown (7.5YR 5/8 to 10YR 6/3); rarely, light red (2.5YR 6/6).

Texture: Fine to medium.

Inclusions: Medium to high amounts of fine and medium particles of diverse nature. Frequent inclusions are (1) a black shiny material that often takes the form of rectangular crystals; (2) clay, orange to brown in color; (3) white, amorphous particles that contain tiny black specks. Crystalline carbonate occurs in about two-thirds of the sherds in quantities ranging from medium to sparse; the other one-third have no carbonate.

Types: This paste is the defining characteristic of the Canhel Ceramic Group. Because of its complete correspondence with the group, the group name rather than a descriptive name is used for the paste. [Note: This was a somewhat confusing decision on the part of Culbert (TR. 25A) to use the same name for the paste as well as the ceramic group. Rather than renaming already published material, the decision was made to keep the names as is in this volume since this paste only occurs within the Canhel Group.]

MEDIUM-CARBONATE AND CLAY PASTE

Identifying Characteristics: Includes both medium-size carbonate particles and particles of a second clay.

Color: Usually very pale brown to reddish yellow (10YR 7/4 to 7.5YR 6/6).

Texture: Medium.

Inclusions: Medium amounts of gray amorphous and crystalline carbonate particles. Occasional fine to quite large particles of orange clay different from the basic clay of the paste are common.

Types: This is one of the dominant pastes of Calam Buff; otherwise, it is rare in other Eb Complex sherds.

MEDIUM-CARBONATE PASTE

Identifying Characteristics: Medium-size carbonate inclusions.

Color: Usually very pale brown to reddish yellow (10YR 7/4 to 7.5YR 6/6).

Texture: Medium.

Inclusions: Medium amounts of carbonate particles that range in size from very fine to quite large. Both amorphous gray and crystalline carbonate are represented. Occasional white amorphous particles and rare lumps of hematite are also present.

Types: This is one of the dominant pastes in Calam Buff. It is rare in other Eb Complex types.

FINE-CARBONATE PASTE

Identifying Characteristics: Finely divided carbonate inclusions.

Color: Covers a wide range from pale or yellowish browns (10YR 6/3 to 6/8) through red-yellows (7.5YR 6/6 to 5YR 5/6) to reds (2.5YR 4/8 to 6/8).

Texture: Fine.

Inclusions: Medium amounts of fine carbonate particles; occasional fine white amorphous particles.

Types: This paste is the most common paste for Cob Red-impressed and occurs as a minor paste in all the slipped types of the Eb Complex.

FINE-INCLUSIONS PASTE

Identifying Characteristics: Inclusions are finely divided; lacks carbonate.

Color: Light gray (2.5Y 6/2, 7/2) and pale or yellowish brown (10YR 5/4, 6/3) are common.

Texture: Fine.

Inclusions: Low to medium amounts of finely divided material. White amorphous particles are most common; occasional black, plate like particles; and occasional golden mica.

Types: Fine-inclusions Paste is by far the most common paste in the Unnamed Monochrome Black, Ainil Orange, and Boolay Brown Groups.

Comments: There is no outstanding criterion that identifies Fine-inclusions Paste. Rather, the lack of carbonate, clay, and coarse inclusions combine to define it.

YELLOW PASTE

Identifying Characteristics: The distinctive yellow (10YR 7/6) color of the paste is the principal identifying characteristic.

Types: Occurs only in the Unnamed Monochrome Red Group.

Comments: Aside from the paste color, this paste is like Fine-inclusions Paste. This paste is confined to the Eb Complex.

As mentioned previously, Eb ceramics demonstrate a number of interesting paste-type correlations. Throughout the complex there is a good correlation between coarse pastes and unslipped ceramic groups and the distinction in pastes between the Eb Complex Canhel Group and the Achiotes Group in the subsequent Tzec Complex is well defined. The set of inclusions that characterizes the Canhel Group is very distinctive and is unique among coarse pastes in the Tikal sequence. The Coarse-carbonate Paste of the Achiotes Group, on the other hand, marks the appearance of a standard paste for unslipped pottery that continues with no noticeable change for the remainder of the Tikal ceramic sequence.

Among slipped types, the Unnamed Monochrome Red, Unnamed Monochrome Black, Ainil Orange, and Boolay Brown groups are made primarily from Fine-inclusions Paste, accounting for 75–90% of the sherds. In the succeeding Tzec Complex, the frequencies of Fine-inclusions Paste declines and Fine- and Medium-carbonate Pastes become more important. The patterns of paste composition and distribution among ceramic types of the Eb Complex suggest both considerable variety in the choice of materials and a fair degree of specificity in making choices for particular types. The low population density indicated by the sparseness of Eb remains at Tikal makes it seem unlikely that variation can be attributed to the presence of a series of specialized centers of pottery manufacture. The variability, then, may lie in choice of materials and combinations made by individual local potters, or was brought to Tikal by various exchange mechanisms.

Eb Ceramic Complex Types

Introduction

The Eb Ceramic Complex consists of 11 ceramic groups and 20 types (composed of 24 varieties) listed in Table 2.2. Incising is the only decorative technique that appears with any frequency during the complex and the designs usually consist of no more than one or more lines encircling the vessels. The frequencies of types in the samples of Eb ceramics appear in Table 2.3. Typological frequencies are based on a count of all sherds, including body sherds, given the relatively small sample size, and include the subsequent Tzec Complex types because the samples are chronologically mixed.

Two facets of the Eb Complex, an Early and Late, originally were defined based on the quantitative differences in type frequencies between Sample Location 3 compared with both Sample Locations 1 and 2 (TR. 25A). The reanalysis demonstrates that these frequency differences are the result of temporal mixing and greater quantities of Mamom Tzec Complex types in the Sample Location 3 lots. There were no illustrations for Unnamed Monochrome Red Fluted, Unnamed Monochrome Black Fluted, Xtoyil Fluted (Ainil Ceramic Group), Xkili Fluted (Boolay Ceramic Group), Bil White, and Baadz Tan located in the Tikal files.

Eb Complex Type Descriptions

CANHEL CERAMIC GROUP

Canhel Unslipped: Canhel Variety

Established: TR. 25A (Culbert 1993)

Group: Canhel

Ware: Unspecified

Ceramic Complex: Eb

Ceramic Sphere: Eb

Illustrations: Fig. 2.10, 2.56, 2.62; 3.1–7; 5.2, 5.3, 5.5, 5.7–10, 5.35, 5.36. See TR. 25A: fig. 119*d–e*.

Principal Identifying Attributes: Light brown to orange, well smoothed, and unslipped surfaces mostly on jar forms.

Identifying characteristics and sorting problems: Because Canhel Paste is distinctive, the type is relatively easy to sort by inspection of the paste.

Paste: Characterized by Canhel Paste.

Firing: Dark cores rare. About two-thirds of the sherds are smudged on one or both surfaces.

Color: Strong (7.5YR 5/8) to pale (10YR 6/3) brown; rare examples are light red (2.5YR 6/6).

Surface finish: Usually smoothed.

Shapes: Wide-mouth jars with medium-tall and short-necks, wide-mouth jars, and rare examples of bowls. Most vessels are between 6 and 9 mm in thickness.

Temporal distribution: Confined to the Eb Complex.

Intersite comparisons: Canhel Unslipped is identified at Buenavista-Nuevo San José (Castellanos and Foias 2017) and Holmul (Callaghan 2008). The smoothed surfaces and color range are similar to

TABLE 2.2 (part 1)
Ceramic Groups and Types of the Eb Complex

Culbert and Kosakowsky	Culbert (1993*)
Tzec Complex Group	ACHIOTES CERAMIC GROUP
Tzec Complex Type	Achiotes Unslipped: Achiotes Variety
Tzec Complex Type	Achiotes Unslipped: Ahtzums Variety
CANHEL CERAMIC GROUP	**CANHEL CERAMIC GROUP**
Canhel Unslipped: Canhel Variety	Canhel Unslipped: Canhel Variety
CABCOH CERAMIC GROUP	**CABCOH CERAMIC GROUP**
Cabcoh Striated: Cabcoh Variety	Cabcoh Striated: Cabcoh Variety
CALAM CERAMIC GROUP	**CALAM CERAMIC GROUP**
Calam Buff: Calam Variety	Calam Buff: Calam Variety
Aac Red-on-buff : Aac Variety	Aac Red-on-buff : Aac Variety
UNNAMED MONOCHROME RED CERAMIC GROUP	**JOVENTUD CERAMIC GROUP**
Unnamed Monochrome Red: Fine Inclusions Variety	Eb Complex Type
Unnamed Monochrome Red Incised: Fine Inclusions Variety	Eb Complex Type
Unnamed Monochrome Red Fluted: Unspecified Variety	Xexcay Fluted: Xexcay Variety
Unnamed Monochrome Red: Yellow-paste Variety	Joventud Red: Yellow-paste Variety
Unnamed Monochrome Red Incised: Yellow-paste Variety	Eb Complex Type
Tzec Complex Type	Guitara Incised: Simple- and Design-incised Varieties
Tzec Complex Type	Joventud Red: Joventud Variety
Tzec Complex Type	Desvario Chamfered: Desvario Variety
COB CERAMIC GROUP	**COB CERAMIC GROUP**
Cob Red-impressed: Cob Variety	Cob Red-impressed: Cob Variety
UNNAMED MONOCHROME BLACK CERAMIC GROUP	**CHUNHINTA CERAMIC GROUP**
Unnamed Monochrome Black: Fine Inclusions Variety	Chunhinta Black: Fine Inclusions Variety
Unnamed Monochrome Black Incised: Fine Inclusions Variety	Deprecio Incised: Simple-incised Variety
Unnamed Monochrome Fluted: Unspecified Variety	Centenario Fluted: Centenario Variety
Tzec Complex Type	Deprecio Incised: Design Incised Variety
Tzec Complex Type	Chunhinta Black: Chunhinta Variety

TABLE 2.2 (part 2)
Ceramic Groups and Types of the Eb Complex

Culbert and Kosakowsky	Culbert (1993*)
AINIL CERAMIC GROUP	**AINIL CERAMIC GROUP**
Ainil Orange: Ainil Variety	Ainil Orange: Ainil Variety & Fine Inclusions Variety
Xpokol Incised: Simple-incised Variety	Xpokol Incised: Simple-incised Variety
Xpokol Incised: Design-incised Variety	Xpokol Incised: Design-incised Variety
Xtoyil Fluted: Xtoyil Variety	Xtoyil Fluted: Xtoyil Variety
BOOLAY CERAMIC GROUP	**BOOLAY CERAMIC GROUP**
Boolay Brown: Boolay Variety	Boolay Brown: Boolay Variety & Fine Inclusions Variety
Bechh Incised: Simple-incised Variety	Bechh Incised: Simple-incised Variety
Bechh Incised: Design-incised Variety	Bechh Incised: Design-incised Variety
Xkili Fluted: Xkili Variety	Xkili Fluted: Xkili Variety.
BIL CERAMIC GROUP	**BIL CERAMIC GROUP**
Bil White: Bil Variety	Bil White: Bil Variety
BAADZ CERAMIC GROUP	**BAADZ CERAMIC GROUP**
Baadz Tan: Baadz Variety	Baadz Tan: Baadz Variety
HALEB CERAMIC GROUP	**HALEB CERAMIC GROUP**
Haleb Composite: Haleb Variety	Haleb Red-on-cream Fluted-grooved: Haleb Variety
Tzec Complex Group	**SAVANA CERAMIC GROUP**
Tzec Complex Type	Savana Orange: Savana Variety
Tzec Complex Type	Reforma Incised: Reforma Variety

*The Achiotes, Joventud, Chunhinta, and Savana Ceramic Groups are Tzec Complex groups. The use of Mamom type names by Culbert (1993) has been changed to use pre-Mamom type names for the Eb Complex.

Jocote Orange-Brown in the Jenney Creek Complex at Barton Ramie (Gifford 1976).

CABCOH CERAMIC GROUP

Cabcoh Striated: Cabcoh Variety

Established: TR. 25A (Culbert 1993)

Group: Cabcoh

Ware: Unspecified

Ceramic Complex: Eb

Ceramic Sphere: Eb

Illustrations: Fig. 2.22, 2.63; 3.8–10; 5.1, 5.4, 5.6. See TR. 25A: fig. 119*a–c*; 120*a–f.*

Paste: Characterized by Canhel Paste.

Principal Identifying Attributes: Light brown to orange, well smoothed, and unslipped surfaces same as Canhel Unslipped, with secondary decoration of striations on the exterior of vessels on the body of jars and up the neck to the lip.

TABLE 2.3
Ceramic Type Frequencies of the Eb Complex

Ceramic Groups/Types	Sample Loc 1 %	Sample Loc. 2 %	Sample Loc. 3 %
Eb Complex			
Canhel Group	8.0	7.5	3.3
Cabcoh Group	43.3	9.0	2.9
Calam Buff: Calam Variety	6.7	11.5	9.7
Aac Red-on-buff : Aac Variety	0.2	0.3	0.3
Unnamed Monochrome Red Group	8.4	11.9	5.3
Cob Group	2.6	0.0	0.1
Unnamed Monochrome Black Group	5.3	3.5	6.5
Ainil Orange: Ainil Variety	3.2	2.0	5.2
Xpocol Incised: Simple and Design-Incised Variety	<0.1	0.0	0.6
Xtoyil Fluted: Xtoyil Variety	0.0	0.0	0.1
Boolay Brown: Boolay Variety	3.2	2.2	6.8
Bechh Incised: Simple and Design-Incised Variety	<0.1	0.1	1.0
Ikili Fluted: Ikili Variety	0.0	0.0	0.3
Bil Group	0.0	0.0	0.8
Baadz Group	0.0	0.0	0.6
Haleb Group	<0.1	0.0	0.5
Tzec Complex			
Achiotes Group	4.1	7.5	13.0
Joventud Red: Ahcax Variety	6.3	9.9	8.1
Guitara Incised: Simple and Design-Incised Variety	0.5	1.8	1.2
Amil Chamfered: Amil Variety	0.1	0.0	0.0
Chunhinta Black: Maach Variety	2.0	3.5	7.0
Deprecio Incised: Simple and Design-Incised Variety	0.1	0.1	1.6
Ahmax Chamfered: Ahmax Variety	0.0	0.0	0.1
Savana Orange: Savana Variety	0.1	0.1	3.3
Reforma Incised: Reforma Variety	0.1	0.1	2.1
Unknown Complex			
Unnamed odd type	0.2	0.4	2.0
Weathered	5.5	28.5	16.9
Weathered Incised	0.1	0.1	0.7
TOTAL SHERDS	2724	1489	1598

Identifying characteristics and sorting problems: Cabcoh Striated: Cabcoh Variety is identical to Canhel Unslipped except for the characteristics noted below. The combination of the distinctiveness of Canhel Paste, which makes even body sherds easy to sort, and the continuation of striation to the lip of the vessels makes Cabcoh Striated an easily identifiable type.

Surface Finish: Dominant striations are broad but shallow; fine striations frequently appear on raised areas between the broad striations. The striations seem to have been made while the clay was still moist. Striation patterns are parallel and meet at angles on only a few sherds. An important diagnostic of the type is that striations continue all the way up to the lip of the vessel on the outside and occasionally occur on the inside of the neck.

Shapes: Wide-mouth jars with medium-tall and short-necks.

Temporal Distribution: Striated ceramics in pre-Mamom and Mamom contexts are less common than in the Late Preclassic.

Intersite comparisons: Identified at Buenavista-Nuevo San José (Castellanos and Foias 2017) and Holmul (Callaghan 2008).

CALAM CERAMIC GROUP

Calam Buff: Calam Variety

Established: Type named by Coe (1963); Variety named by Culbert (1993 [TR. 25A]).

Group: Calam

Ware: Unspecified

Ceramic Complex: Eb

Ceramic Sphere: Eb

Illustrations: Fig. 2.3, 2.4, 2.11, 2.17–21, 2.23, 2.55; 4.2, 4.19, 4.24. See TR. 25A: fig. 117*a–d*.

Principal Identifying Attributes: Thin buff slip or self-slip through burnishing of vessel surfaces which results in lightly polished vessel exteriors.

Identifying characteristics and sorting problems: The better-smoothed examples are distinctive because of color and present no problems; some of the less-smoothed examples could be confused with unslipped types. The distinctive vessel shapes that occur in Calam Buff aid in the identification of rim sherds. This type, with its heavy carbonate temper, is easily separated from Canhel Unslipped.

Paste: Medium-carbonate Paste and Medium-carbonate and Clay Paste occur with about equal frequency and are by far the most common pastes in Calam Buff. Fine-carbonate Paste occurs occasionally. In general, Calam Buff shows more and larger inclusions than most other slipped types of the Eb Complex.

Firing: Dark cores are rare. About one-quarter of the sherds show fireclouding on either interior or exterior.

Slip: Whether Calam Buff is primarily slipped or unslipped is uncertain, although it is classified as a monochrome type. Some sherds clearly show a surface coat of fine buff-colored clay, while others look as though the surface finish was produced when polishing of the vessel brought finer particles to the surface.

Polish: There is a wide range from well smoothed to poorly smoothed.

Color: Pale brown (10YR 6/3, 7/4, 8/3) to reddish yellow (7.5YR 8/6). Surface color of the sherds is generally lighter than the paste color.

Shapes: More than half the examples of Calam Buff are medium size slightly incurving to round-side bowls with bolstered lips. Tecomates, medium plates, and slightly incurving to round-side bowls are represented with frequencies of 10–15% and several other bowl forms occur with low frequencies. Most sherds are between 6 and 8 mm in thickness.

Temporal distribution: Calam Buff is one of the most easily identified markers for the Eb Complex. It does not seem to have occurred in the subsequent Tzec Complex at Tikal or in the Mamon collections at Uaxactun (Smith 1955; Smith and Gifford 1966).

Intersite comparisons: Buenavista-Nuevo San José (Castellanos and Foias 2017); Holmul (Callaghan 2008); and Yaxha-Sacnab (Rice 1979a).

Aac Red-on-buff: Aac Variety

Established: Type named by Coe (1963).

Group: Calam

Ware: Unspecified

Ceramic Complex: Eb

Ceramic Sphere: Eb

Illustrations: Fig. 5.34, 5.40–42. See TR. 25A: fig. 116*a–b,e*.

Principal Identifying Attributes: Burnished buff surfaces, same as Calam Buff, with the addition of a thin red matte slip applied in bands or stripes.

Identifying characteristics and sorting problems: This type consists of sherds that have a matte red slip applied over the surface of pottery that is otherwise identical to Calam Buff. All entries are the same as those for Calam Buff except the following:

Slip: The red is a wash of thin to medium thickness; the buff is the same as in Calam Buff.

Polish: The red is unpolished; the buff shows the same range of polish as Calam Buff.

Color: The red ranges from yellowish red (5YR 5/8) to red (10R 4/6).

Design Patterns: The red is applied in bands, in broad, curving stripes, or in simple patterns. Some sherds are completely red, but they are not large enough to determine whether they are indicative of entirely red-slipped vessels.

Shapes: A variety of bowl forms are represented with no form predominating. The medium size slightly incurving to round-side bowl with bolstered lip that is so important in Calam Buff is not represented.

Temporal Distribution: The type is a rare type that occurs only in the Eb Complex.

Intersite comparisons: Holmul (Callaghan 2008) and Yaxha-Sacnab (Rice 1979a). There is some similarity to the northern Belize type Tower Hill Red-on-cream at Blue Creek (Kosakowsky and Lohse 2003); Colha (Valdez 1987); Cuello (Kosakowsky 1987); and Ka'kabish (Sagebiel and Haines 2015), as well as an Unnamed Buff-on-red at Cahal Pech (Sullivan and Awe 2013).

UNNAMED MONOCHROME RED CERAMIC GROUP

Unnamed Monochrome Red: Fine Inclusions Variety

Established: Type named in this work; Variety named by Culbert (1993 [TR. 25A]).

Group: Unnamed Monochrome Red

Ware: Unspecified

Ceramic Complex: Eb

Ceramic Sphere: Eb

Illustrations: Fig. 2.6, 2.7, 2.14–16, 2.29, 2.61; 3.19, 3.20, 3.34–35. See TR. 25A: fig. 116*f–j*, 117*e–i*.

Principal Identifying Attributes: Smoothed surfaces with a thin lightly polished monochrome red slip over a distinctive fine paste.

Identifying characteristics and sorting problems: The slip color and fine paste are defining characteristics of the type. Originally misidentified and included in Joventud Red (TR. 25A).

Paste: The identifying characteristic of the type is the use of Fine-inclusions Paste.

Firing: A small percentage of the sherds show dark cores.

Slip: The clay surfaces are usually well smoothed before the application of a thin slip.

Polish: Usually low.

Color: The surface color is red (10R 5/8 to 2.5YR 5/8).

Shapes: Small diameter bowls and dishes, and medium diameter bowls, dishes, and plates. There do not appear to be any examples of jars.

Temporal Distribution: This type is confined to the Eb Complex and the Fine-inclusions Paste does not continue into Joventud Red in the Tzec Complex.

Intersite comparisons: None noted, however, the surface finish of the type overlaps with examples of Ramgoat Red (Pring 1977; Sagebiel and Haines 2015) and Consejo Red (Kosakowsky 1987) in Northern Belize and Abelino Red at Altar de Sacrificios (Adams 1971) and Seibal (Sabloff 1975), as well as Uck Red in the Belize Valley (Sullivan and Awe 2013).

Comments: While naming a variety on the basis of paste is in violation of basic nomenclature rules for type: variety (Gifford 1976) the decision was made in this case to keep the Fine-inclusions Paste examples separate from the Yellow Paste examples as it is unclear if these are simply paste variants of the same type or if the variants have more significant chronological or contextual differences.

Unnamed Monochrome Red Incised: Fine Inclusions Variety

Established: Type named in this work; Variety named by Culbert (1993 [TR. 25A]).

Group: Unnamed Monochrome Red

Ware: Unspecified

Ceramic Complex: Eb

Ceramic Sphere: Eb

Illustrations: Fig. 2.13, 2.42, 2.50; 3.28; 4.27. See TR. 25A: fig. 116*c,d,l.*

Principal Identifying Attributes: Thin lightly polished monochrome red slip on fine paste. Secondary decoration is by means of simple fine line incisions on the exterior of vessels.

Comments: In all other respects the same as the Unnamed Monochrome Red: Fine Inclusions Variety described above. Originally misidentified and included in Guitara Incised (TR. 25A).

Intersite comparisons: Similar in decoration to Pico de Oro Incised at Altar de Sacrificios (Adams 1971) and Seibal (Sabloff 1975) and to Backlanding Incised in northern Belize (Kosakowsky 1987).

Unnamed Monochrome Red Fluted: Unspecified Variety

Established: Type named this work. Originally called Xexcay Fluted by Culbert (1993 [TR. 25A]).

Group: Unnamed Monochrome Red

Ware: Unspecified

Ceramic Complex: Eb

Ceramic Sphere: Eb

Principal Identifying Attributes: Same as the Unnamed Monochrome Red: Fine Inclusions Variety with the addition of shallow, widely spaced fluting. Smoothed surfaces with a thin lightly polished monochrome red slip over a distinctive fine paste.

Identifying characteristics and sorting problems: The slip color, fine paste, and fluted decorations are defining characteristics of the type. Originally misidentified and included in Joventud Red (TR. 25A).

Paste: The identifying characteristic of the type is the use of Fine-inclusions Paste.

Firing: A small percentage of the sherds show dark cores.

Slip: The clay surfaces are usually well smoothed before the application of a thin slip.

Polish: Usually low.

Color: The surface color is red (10R 5/8 to 2.5YR 5/8).

Shapes: Small diameter bowls and dishes and medium diameter bowls, dishes, and plates. There do not appear to be any examples of jars.

Temporal Distribution: This type is confined to the Eb Complex and the Fine-inclusions Paste does not continue into Joventud Red in the Tzec Complex.

Intersite comparisons: None noted, however the surface finish of the type overlaps with examples of Ramgoat Red (Pring 1977; Sagebiel and Haines 2015) and Consejo Red (Kosakowsky 1987) in Northern Belize and Abelino Red at Altar de Sacrificios (Adams 1971) and Seibal (Sabloff 1975), as well as Uck Red in the Belize Valley (Sullivan and Awe 2013).

Unnamed Monochrome Red: Yellow-paste Variety

Established: Type named in this work; Variety named by Culbert (1993 [TR. 25A]).

Group: Unnamed Monochrome Red

Ware: Unspecified

Ceramic Complex: Eb

Ceramic Sphere: Eb

Illustrations: Fig. 3.23; 4.20–23.

Principal Identifying Attributes: Smoothed surfaces with a flaky non-waxy monochrome red slip over a distinctive yellow paste.

Identifying characteristics and sorting problems: The combination of paste color and flaking of the slip makes the variety easy to identify. Originally named a Yellow-paste Variety of Joventud Red (TR. 25A). However, the surfaces of the yellow paste examples are glossier than typical examples of Joventud Red and are restricted to the pre-Mamom Eb Complex. Therefore, these examples were separated out, but because of the small sample size, left unnamed.

Paste: Characterized by Yellow Paste.

Firing: Dark cores rare.

Slip: The clay surface was well smoothed before application of the slip. The slip tends to flake off in patches.

Polish: Low to medium.

Color: The underlying yellow clay gives a reddish-orange cast (2.5YR 6/8) to the surface color.

Shapes: The sample of rim sherds was too small to give much idea of shape distribution, although most likely bowl and dish forms.

Temporal distribution: Occurs only in one sample of Eb.

Comments: The paste is a good marker for the Eb Complex, and shows through the red slip. While naming a variety on the basis of paste is in violation of basic nomenclature rules for type: variety (Gifford 1976) the decision was made in this case to keep the Yellow Paste examples separate from the Fine-inclusions Paste examples as it is unclear if these are simply paste variants of the same type or if the variants have more significant chronological or contextual differences.

Intersite comparisons: None noted, however the surface finish of the type overlaps with examples of Ramgoat Red in Northern Belize (Pring 1977) and Abelino Red at Altar de Sacrificios (Adams 1971) and Seibal (Sabloff 1975), as well as Uck Red in the Belize Valley (Sullivan and Awe 2013).

Unnamed Monochrome Red Incised: Yellow-paste Variety

Established: Type named in this work; Variety named by Culbert (1993 [TR. 25A]).

Group: Unnamed Monochrome Red

Ware: Unspecified

Ceramic Complex: Eb

Ceramic Sphere: Eb

Illustrations: Fig. 3.18.

Principal Identifying Attributes: Smoothed surfaces with a flakey non-waxy monochrome red slip over a distinctive yellow paste. Secondary decoration by means of simple fine line incisions on the exterior of vessels. Originally misidentified as a variety of Guitara Incised (TR. 25A).

Comments: In all other respects the same as the Unnamed Monochrome Red: Yellow-paste Variety described above.

Intersite comparisons: Similar in decoration to Pico de Oro Incised at Altar de Sacrificios (Adams 1971) and Seibal (Sabloff 1975) and to Backlanding Incised in northern Belize (Kosakowsky 1987).

COB CERAMIC GROUP

Cob Red-impressed: Cob Variety

Established: TR. 25A (Culbert 1993)

Group: Cob

Ware: Unspecified

Ceramic Complex: Eb

Ceramic Sphere: Eb

Illustrations: Fig. 2.57–60; 5.11.

Principal Identifying Attributes: Thin red slip applied to the exterior surfaces of possible jars (few rim sherds found in the sample) and incurving bowls or tecomates. Pre-slip crescent-shaped impressions alternate with unimpressed zones, separated by shallow grooves.

Identifying characteristics and sorting problems: The decoration is unique to this type in the Eb Complex. None.

Paste: Fine-carbonate Paste predominates with some examples of Fine-inclusions Paste and rare examples of other pastes.

Firing: Dark cores rare; fireclouding occurs on better than half of the sherds in a small sample.

Slip: A thin slip that adheres well was applied after the impressions had been made.

Polish: Matte finish.

Color: Weak red (10R 5/4) through red (2.5YR 4/6) to reddish yellow (5YR 6/6).

Surface Finish and Decoration: Many small impressions, usually crescent-shaped; some sherds show alternation between zones with and without impressions, sometimes with a shallow groove delimiting the zones. There are no examples of neck or rim sherds with impressions.

Shapes: The impressions that characterize the type occur only on body sherds of jars, which are mostly 4 to 6 mm thick.

Temporal Distribution: Cob Red-impressed is a rare type found only in Eb Complex collections.

Intersite comparisons: None noted. However, the decoration may be antecedent to the fingernail crescent-shaped impressions on Hongo Composite (Adams 1971) in the Joventud Red Group in the succeeding Tzec Complex.

UNNAMED MONOCHROME BLACK CERAMIC GROUP

Unnamed Monochrome Black: Fine Inclusions Variety

Established: Type named in this work; Variety named by Culbert (1993 [TR. 25A]).

Group: Unnamed Monochrome Black

Ware: Unspecified

Ceramic Complex: Eb

Ceramic Sphere: Eb

Illustrations: Fig. 2.8; 3.24, 3.25, 3.31.

Principal Identifying Attributes: Thin lightly polished monochrome black slip on fine paste.

Identifying characteristics and sorting problems: Fine-inclusions Paste is more uniform and distinct from other pastes, greatly reducing the number of sorting problems. Originally misidentified as Chunhinta Black (TR. 25A).

Firing: Many sherds are darkened at the surface of the paste or throughout their sections. Dark cores distinguishable from surface darkening are rare. Deep blackening beneath the slip indicates reducing conditions in firing.

Slip: Thin slip that adheres well.

Polish: Usually medium, sometimes low.

Color: The black occasionally shades into patches of orange or brown.

Paste: The identifying characteristic of the type is the use of Fine-inclusions Paste.

Shapes: Medium outflaring to slightly outcurving-side plates as well as small bowl forms.

Temporal distribution: Occurs only in the Eb Complex.

Comments: While paste characteristics should not be used as the basis for defining a type or variety, the combination of the Fine-inclusions Paste and lightly polished surfaces are distinct.

Intersite comparisons: The lightly polished surfaces are similar to Machaca Black in northern Belize (Kosakowsky 1987) and Chi Black in the Belize Valley (Sullivan and Awe 2013).

Unnamed Monochrome Black Incised: Fine Inclusions Variety

Established: Type named in this work; Variety named by Culbert (1993 [TR. 25A]).

Group: Unnamed Monochrome Black

Ware: Unspecified

Ceramic Complex: Eb

Ceramic Sphere: Eb

Illustrations: Fig. 2.30.

Principal Identifying Attributes: Thin, lightly polished, monochrome black slip on fine paste. Secondary decoration is by means of simple fine line incisions on the exterior of vessels. Originally misidentified as Deprecio Incised (TR. 25A).

Comments: In all other respects the same as the Unnamed Monochrome Black: Fine Inclusions Variety described above.

Intersite comparisons: Decoration similar to Chompipi Incised at Altar de Sacrificios (Adams 1971) and Seibal (Sabloff 1975), and to Chacalte Incised in northern Belize (Kosakowsky 1987).

Unnamed Monochrome Black Fluted: Unspecified Variety

Established: This work. Originally called Centenario Fluted by Culbert (1993 [TR. 25A]).

Group: Unnamed Monochrome Black

Ware: Unspecified

Ceramic Complex: Eb

Ceramic Sphere: Eb

Principal Identifying Attributes: Same as the Unnamed Monochrome Black: Fine Inclusions Variety with the addition of shallow, widely spaced fluting. Thin, lightly polished, monochrome black slip on fine paste.

Identifying characteristics and sorting problems: Fine-inclusions Paste is more uniform and distinct from other pastes, greatly reducing the number of sorting problems. Originally placed in the Chunhinta Group (TR. 25A).

Firing: Many sherds are darkened at the surface of the paste or throughout their sections. Dark cores distinguishable from surface darkening are rare. Deep blackening beneath the slip indicates reducing conditions in firing.

Slip: Thin slip that adheres well.

Polish: Usually medium, sometimes low.

Color: The black occasionally shades into patches of orange or brown.

Paste: The identifying characteristic of the type is the use of Fine-inclusions Paste.

Shapes: Medium outflaring to slightly outcurving-side plates as well as small bowl forms.

Temporal distribution: Occurs only in the Eb Complex.

Comments: While paste characteristics should not be used as the basis for defining a type or variety, the combination of the Fine-inclusions Paste and lightly polished surfaces are distinct.

Intersite comparisons: The lightly polished surfaces are similar to Machaca Black in northern Belize (Kosakowsky 1987) and Chi Black in the Belize Valley (Sullivan and Awe 2013).

AINIL CERAMIC GROUP

Ainil Orange: Ainil Variety

Established: TR. 25A (Culbert 1993)

Group: Ainil

Ware: Unspecified

Ceramic Complex: Eb

Ceramic Sphere: Eb

Illustrations: Fig. 2.24–26, 2.36, 2.37; 3.21, 3.38; 4.28, 4.41. See TR. 25A: fig. 118*j*.

Principal Identifying Attributes: Monochrome orange to brown thin, lightly polished slip on narrow-mouth jars.

Identifying characteristics and Sorting Problems: Sorting problems for the type involve color separations. The orange color of Ainil Orange is relatively distinct from other types, but fireclouded surfaces overlap considerably with Boolay Brown. There is little problem in distinguishing Ainil Orange from later red monochrome sherds of the Tzec Complex. Culbert (TR. 25A) originally identified two separate varieties of Ainil Orange dependent on paste differences and slight surface color differences, however, it is felt that the overlap is too great to keep this varietal distinction and both varieties have been combined into the Ainil Variety.

Paste: There are two different pastes that comprise this type. The use of Fine-inclusions Paste may be more common earlier, and then is replaced with Medium-carbonate Paste later, however, the lack of good stratigraphy and mixed deposits for the Eb Complex makes this observation difficult to quantify.

Firing: About one-fifth of the sherds have dark cores. Fireclouding is very common, occurring on about one-quarter of the bowl sherds and better than one-half of the jar sherds.

Slip: The surface of the vessel was well smoothed before the application of a thin slip that adheres well.

Polish: Low to medium.

Color: The Fine-inclusions Paste examples are usually reddish yellow (7.5YR 6/6) fireclouded to strong brown (7.5YR 5/6) and yellowish brown (10YR 5/4). The Medium-carbonate Paste examples are commonly reddish yellow (5YR 6/6, 6/8) and yellowish red (5YR 5/6, 5/8), though the color differences overlap. Fireclouding occurs on most sherds. In fact, erosion of slip and fireclouding are so extreme that it is difficult to find examples on which color can be measured consistently.

Shapes: Narrow-mouth jars, outflaring to slightly outcurving-side plates, and small bowl forms. Most sherds are between 5 and 7 mm in thickness.

Temporal distribution: Ainil Orange is confined to the Eb Complex.

Intersite comparisons: Found at Buenavista-Nuevo San José (Castellanos and Foias 2017); Nixtun-Ch'ich (Rice 2009); and Trinidad de Nosotros (Moriarty 2012).

Xpokol Incised: Simple-incised Variety

Established: TR. 25A (Culbert 1993)

Group: Ainil

Ware: Unspecified

Ceramic Complex: Eb

Ceramic Sphere: Eb

Illustrations: Fig. 2.2; 3.22, 3.26, 3.27, 3.30; 5.16, 5.21.

Principal Identifying Attributes: Monochrome orange to brown, thin, lightly polished slip on mostly narrow-mouth jars. Secondary decoration is by means of single or multiple incised lines, which are almost always located on the exterior of the vessel near the rim.

Comments: Xpokol Incised: Simple-incised Variety is identical to Ainil Orange in all other aspects.

Xpokol Incised: Design-incised Variety

Established: TR. 25A (Culbert 1993)

Group: Ainil

Ware: Unspecified

Ceramic Complex: Eb

Ceramic Sphere: Eb

Illustrations: Fig. 2.28.

Principal Identifying Attributes: Monochrome orange to brown thin, lightly polished slip on most-

ly narrow-mouth jars. Secondary decoration is by means of incised lines, which create simple patterns.

Shapes: Most commonly medium size composite silhouette dishes.

Comments: Xpokol Incised: Design-incised Variety is identical to Ainil Orange in all other aspects.

Xtoyil Fluted: Xtoyil Variety

Established: TR. 25A (Culbert 1993)

Group: Ainil

Ware: Unspecified

Ceramic Complex: Eb

Ceramic Sphere: Eb

Principal Identifying Attributes: Monochrome orange to brown thin, lightly polished slip on narrow-mouth jars. Secondary decoration is by means of shallow fluting.

Comments: The sample of Xtoyil Fluted was too small to permit a reliable description. It would appear that the type, except for the fluted decoration, is identical to Ainil Orange in all other aspects.

BOOLAY CERAMIC GROUP

Boolay Brown: Boolay Variety

Established: TR. 25A (Culbert 1993)

Group: Boolay

Ware: Unspecified

Ceramic Complex: Eb

Ceramic Sphere: Eb

Illustrations: Fig. 2.9; 3.32, 3.33; 4.40; 5.43.

Principal Identifying Attributes: Thin, lightly polished, monochrome brown slip that overlaps with fireclouded examples of Ainil Orange.

Identifying characteristics and sorting problems: There are strong color overlaps between Boolay Brown and fireclouded surfaces of Ainil Orange. Only those sherds where the brown color covered most or all of the sherd were sorted into Boolay Brown.

Paste: A wide variety of paste types were used in the production of Boolay Brown, including the use of Fine-inclusions Paste. Originally Culbert (TR. 25A) used this paste distinction to define separate varieties, however, since the surfaces are indistinguishable, both varieties have been subsumed into this single variety.

Firing: Dark cores occur in about one-tenth of the sherds. Fireclouding is common, occurring on better than half of the examples.

Slip: The slip is thin to medium and adheres well.

Polish: Low to medium.

Color: Brown to pale brown (10YR 6/3 to 5/3), ranging to strong brown (7.5YR 5/6) and yellow (10YR 6/5).

Shapes: Narrow-mouth jars with short necks, tecomates, medium plates, and small bowls. Most sherds are of medium thickness, between 5 to 8 mm.

Temporal Distribution: Boolay Brown is confined to the Eb Complex.

Comments: The brown sherds could have been subsumed into other types without the definition of a separate brown type, however, because enough sherds show a steady brown color it was felt that the production of the color was intentional.

Intersite comparisons: Buenavista-Nuevo San José (Castellanos and Foias 2017) and Nixtun-Ch'ich (Rice 2009).

Bechh Incised: Simple-incised Variety

Established: TR. 25A (Culbert 1993)

Group: Boolay

Ware: Unspecified

Ceramic Complex: Eb

Ceramic Sphere: Eb

Illustrations: Fig. 3.29; 4.12, 4.13; 5.17, 5.19, 5.20.

Principal Identifying Attributes: Thin, lightly polished, monochrome brown slip that overlaps with fireclouded examples of Ainil Orange. Secondary decoration is by means of single or multiple incised lines that are almost always located on the exterior of vessels near the rim.

Comments: Bechh Incised: Simple-incised Variety is identical to Boolay Brown in all other aspects.

Bechh Incised: Design-incised Variety

Established: TR. 25A (Culbert 1993)

Group: Boolay

Ware: Unspecified

Ceramic Complex: Eb

Ceramic Sphere: Eb

Illustrations: Fig. 2.12.

Principal Identifying Attributes: Thin, lightly polished, monochrome brown slip that overlaps with fireclouded examples of Ainil Orange. Secondary decoration is by means of fine line incisions that create simple patterns.

Comments: Bechh Incised: Design-incised Variety is identical to Boolay Brown in all other aspects.

Xkili Fluted: Xkili Variety

Established: TR. 25A (Culbert 1993)

Group: Boolay

Ware: Unspecified

Ceramic Complex: Eb

Ceramic Sphere: Eb

Principal Identifying Attributes: Thin, lightly polished, monochrome brown slip that overlaps with fireclouded examples of Ainil Orange. Secondary decoration is by means of shallow fluted decoration.

Shapes: Medium composite silhouette dishes.

Comments: The sample of Xkili Fluted was too small to permit a reliable description. It would appear that the type, except for the fluted decoration, falls within the range of Boolay Brown.

BIL CERAMIC GROUP

Bil White: Bil Variety

Established: TR. 25A (Culbert 1993)

Group: Bil

Ware: Unspecified

Ceramic Complex: Eb

Ceramic Sphere: Eb

Principal Identifying Attributes: Thin, medium polished, white slip on bowls.

Identifying characteristics and sorting problems: Surface colors are a true white which does not overlap with any other Eb types so it is easy to sort this type.

Paste: Most examples in the small sample are Medium-carbonate and clay Paste with textures that range from fine to medium. Some examples fall within the range of Fine-inclusions Paste.

Firing: Better than one-half the examples have dark cores; fireclouding occurs on about one-quarter of the sherds.

Slip: Thin to medium slip; adheres well.

Polish: Low to medium.

Color: White (10YR 8/2 to 2.5Y 8/2).

Shapes: Most of the body sherds are from small bowls; the only rim sherd is a small indeterminate shape that might be either a bowl or jar. Vessel wall thickness ranges from 6 to 9 mm.

Temporal distribution: Bil White is confined to the Eb Complex.

Intersite comparisons: The surface finish of Bil White is similar to Huetche White at Altar de Sacrificios (Adams 1971) and Seibal (Sabloff 1975). There is also some overlap with Cocoyol Cream at Cahal Pech (Sullivan and Awe 2013) and Quamina Cream at Cuello (Kosakowsky 1987), although the latter two examples are not a true white in color.

BAADZ CERAMIC GROUP

Baadz Tan: Baadz Variety

Established: TR. 25A (Culbert 1993)

Group: Baadz

Ware: Unspecified

Ceramic Complex: Eb

Ceramic Sphere: Eb

Principal Identifying Attributes: Burnished and polished slipped surfaces that are a light or pale brown. Thin walled vessels, including bowls and jars, with an unusual brownish-yellow paste.

Identifying characteristics and sorting problems: The color overlaps with the range of variation of Boolay Brown, but thinness and paste characteristics suggest the possibility that this may be a separate, possibly trade, type.

Paste: Most sherds have a brownish-yellow paste that contains reddish secondary clay particles, black mineral particles, and small amounts of carbonate; it is likely that this is a foreign paste. A few examples have paste that falls within the range of local Fine-inclusions Paste.

Firing: Dark cores occur on 3 of 10 examples; fire-clouding occurs on 3 of 10 examples.

Slip: Medium slip that adheres well.

Polish: Medium to high; some examples show a burnished effect.

Color: Ranges from light or very pale brown (7.5YR 6/4 to 10YR 7/3) to reddish yellow (7.5YR 7/6); considerable color variation occurs on individual sherds.

Shapes: Both small bowls and narrow-mouth jars are represented among body sherds; rim sherds are small and not distinctive. Sherds are fairly thin, ranging from 4 to 7 mm.

Temporal distribution: Known only from a small sample in the Eb Complex.

Intersite comparisons: None noted.

HALEB CERAMIC GROUP

Haleb Composite: Haleb Variety

Established: Type named in this work; variety named by Culbert (1993 [TR. 25A]).

Group: Haleb

Ware: Unspecified

Ceramic Complex: Eb

Ceramic Sphere: Eb

Illustrations: Fig. 5.31–33.

Principal Identifying Attributes: Polished red-on-cream slip on composite silhouette vessels. Secondary decoration is by means of deep broad grooving and fluting.

Identifying characteristics and sorting problems: Some small sherds could be sorted to red, tan, or red-on-cream types when they lack both slip colors.

Paste: A brownish-yellow to red-colored paste that includes red secondary clay particles, black mineral particles, and usually a small amount of finely divided carbonate. This paste is outside of the usual range of variation of Eb pastes and could probably be defined as a separate paste type except that the sample is too small to be certain of its total characteristics. The same paste is common in Baadz Tan and may represent a trade type.

Firing: Dark cores very common and fireclouding is uncommon.

Slip: Both slips are of medium thickness; the cream slip was applied first, but the two slips overlap only in a narrow band where they meet.

Polish: Highly polished on all surfaces.

Color: The red slip is centered on a true red (10R 4/6, 5/6). The cream ranges from a very pale brown (10YR 7/3, 8/4) to light brownish gray (10YR 6/2).

Surface Finish and Decoration: Deep, broad grooves were made before the application of the slips as well as fluting that is carefully executed. Cream is the predominant color on most vessels, with red applied as a broad band on the upper section of the exterior. Flutes and grooves run horizontally, encircling the exterior of the vessel. One vessel shows a simple line and dot design painted in red on the cream interior.

Shapes: All examples are from composite-silhouette vessels except for one small round-side bowl.

Temporal distribution: Occurs only in the Eb Complex.

Intersite comparisons: There is some similarity to the northern Belize type Tower Hill Red-on-cream at Blue Creek (Kosakowsky and Lohse 2003); Colha (Valdez 1987); Cuello (Kosakowsky 1987); and Ka'kabish (Sagebiel and Haines 2015), as well as an Unnamed Buff-on-red at Cahal Pech (Sullivan and Valdez 2013).

UNTYPED UNUSUAL SHERDS

After types were sorted and named, all of the Tikal complexes yield a residue of odd sherds that did not fit established typological categories. Since it is unjustified to establish types when samples are too small to permit an understanding of the range of variation, these sherds are left outside of the typological system. Because some of the typological features within this group are interesting and might prove meaningful in other contexts, the following descriptions of scantily represented categories are appended here.

Unslipped-impressed Pottery

Several sherds in the Eb samples show fingernail impressions on unslipped pottery. The examples range from coarse unslipped jars with impressions at the juncture of neck and body to a small round-side bowl with restricted orifice that is encircled by a fillet of clay with deep impressions. These may be similar to Baldizon Impressed in the Xe Complex at Seibal (Sabloff 1975).

Slipped-impressed Pottery

Two sherds show a quite similar pattern in which a row of fingernail impressions outlined the border between slipped and unslipped areas on the exterior of round-side bowls with everted rims. The slip color of one of these sherds would fall into Ainil Orange and that of the second is within the range of Boolay Brown. Another sherd shows an unslipped and impressed exterior and an orange interior.

Matte Red Pottery

There are a few examples of very poorly finished matte red sherds in Eb Complex collections. These sherds, which are mostly characterized by coarse pastes as well, were originally separated as a tentative matte-red type. They do not seem to have enough coherence for typological status, since they form the end of a continuum with other red sherds.

Non-coarse Paste Unslipped Pottery

The vast majority of unslipped sherds are of one of the coarse textured pastes discussed in earlier sections. There are a few unslipped sherds, however, that are made from pastes of considerably finer texture. Since these sherds also associate with unusual vessel shapes, they would seem to be outside the

range of variation of named unslipped types and may represent trade pieces.

Eb Complex Decorated Pottery

Decoration of pottery during the Eb Complex consisted largely of surface manipulation that falls under the generic heading "incising." The frequency of incising in the total sherd sample that included body sherds ranged from 1% to 7% in the Eb samples. Total sherd counts, however, are not very indicative of the frequency with which vessels were decorated because the counts are dominated by quantities of body sherds from large jars. Counts that include only rim sherds are a better measure of the number of whole vessels that were decorated. Among rim sherds, incising occurs with frequencies of 10% to 25%.

The term "incised" covers a continuum between extremes that might be called "fine-incised" and "grooved." Width of the lines varies considerably between the extremes and there is a strong tendency in the Eb Complex for fine-incised examples to show post-slip scoring while grooved examples were almost always scored before the application of slip. No attempt was made to separate fine-incised and grooved sherds for quantitative analysis, but a brief inspection of the collections suggested that the two techniques occur with about equal frequency. As the width of lines increases, grooving merges gradually into examples that are classified as fluted. In sorting, only those sherds in which the depressions are considerably wider than the raised areas between them were counted as fluted. Chamfering is a special kind of fluting in which the depressions, rather than being symmetrical, are deeper at one edge than at the other. The distinction between fluting and chamfering is difficult to apply for most examples, and few sherds were clear enough examples of chamfering to be so classified.

In the analysis of incised types, each type is divided into a simple-incised variety, in which decoration consists of single or parallel straight lines, and a design-incised variety in which the incised lines cross or make patterns. Simple incising is considerably more common than design incising, making up 70–80% of the sample for most incised types. Simple-incised sherds are about equally divided between examples that show only a single incised line and those that show multiple lines. On multiple-line examples, the lines occur in sets of between two and six parallel lines. The design-incised sherds show very simple patterns. Better than half of the design-incised examples consist of nothing more than straight lines meeting at an angle. Incised decoration is distributed among a series of shapes. Incising occurs on most shapes in about the same frequency as in the total rim sherd sample, suggesting that shape and incised decoration are independent variables. Decoration is almost invariably on the exterior of vessels, usually near the lip.

Bichrome decoration is very rare in the Eb Complex. The only two bichrome types, Aac Red-on-buff and Haleb Composite, both use large contrasting color areas as the principal decorative feature and only a few examples of simple patterns using finer lines exist in the collections. Cob Red-impressed uses zones of impressions in the same fashion as the contrasting color zones of the painted types.

Eb Types: Chronological Change

Given the nature of the Eb sample locations it is difficult to determine if there is chronological change among types in the Eb Ceramic Complex. Although the three sample locations were treated as homogeneous for typological assessments, both Sample Locations 1 and 3 showed some minor quantitative variation between the lower and upper lots. Among unslipped ceramics, Canhel Unslipped and Cabcoh Striated are restricted to the Eb Complex, and are replaced by Achiotes Unslipped in the succeeding Tzec Complex. With the decline of Cabcoh Striated, there appears to be an absence of striated vessels in the succeeding Tzec Complex. There are also features of unslipped pottery distribution among the Eb samples that do not seem to have a chronological explanation, most notably the extremely high frequency of Cabcoh Striated in Eb Location 1, which as a chultun deposit may distinguish it from other domestic refuse (Op. 27B).

Among slipped pottery types, there may be a decrease of Fine-inclusions Paste varieties of monochrome types through time based on the stratigraphy of lots at Sample Locations 1 and 3, as well as an abrupt rise of incised types. The total frequency of all incised types is 7.2% in the upper levels, as compared to 0.8 and 2.2% in the lower lots.

When the Eb Complex is compared with later Preclassic complexes at Tikal, some types of Eb ceramics are unique, i.e., they are largely confined to Eb and do not seem to give rise to descendant types in succeeding complexes. Other Eb types mark the beginning of traditions that continue in a gradual progression through later periods.

There are several features in which unslipped pottery of the Eb Complex stands apart from later unslipped types. Canhel Paste, with its abundance of non-calcareous inclusions, is quite unlike the paste that characterizes later types. The striation of Cabcoh Striated that covers both the necks and bodies of jars is another unique feature since in all later types striation stops below the necks of vessels. The separateness of Cabcoh Striated is further emphasized by the disappearance of striated pottery in the Tzec Complex, before the beginning of the standard kind of striation in the Chuen Complex.

Calam Buff is another type in Eb that stands apart from later Preclassic tradition. Both the technique of finishing and the surface color separate Calam Buff from later buff or cream types. The uniqueness of Calam Buff is accentuated by the fact that the principal shapes for which the type was used have no successors in later complexes.

Eb Types: Social Variation

Although there is little solid information on which to judge the social contexts of the three Eb locations, an examination of variation that does not seem to arise from temporal change must be attempted. The chief frequency differences among the Eb samples are the high frequency of Cabcoh Striated in the sample from Location 1 and higher frequencies of monochrome types in the other two locations. A part of these differences in unslipped type frequencies may be simply the result of differential preservation. Paste studies demonstrate that the sherds classified as "weathered" in these and other samples from Tikal do not represent a random cross section of ceramic types, but instead are heavily weighted toward unslipped types. If a majority of the weathered sherds in the three Eb samples were, in fact, of unslipped types, the difference between Location 1 and the other locations (especially Location 2 with its high frequency of weathered sherds) would be much less than it seems. Whatever adjustments were made, Location 1 would still be highest in unslipped types and lowest in slipped types. Another point of difference is that Location 1 has the lowest frequency of incised types among all Eb locations.

The net result is that Locations 2 and 3, the two locations that have ceremonial connotations in later times, produced samples higher in slipped and decorated types than the single sample from a presumably domestic location.

Eb Complex Shape Descriptions

There are 6 shape classes and 11 shapes listed in Table 2.4 that comprise the Eb Complex. The median sizes or range of sizes within each shape are presented in Table 2.5.

TABLE 2.4
Shape Classes and Shapes of the Eb Complex

1. Wide-mouth Jars
    Wide-mouth Jar (with Medium-tall Neck)
    Wide-mouth Jar (with Short Neck)
2. Narrow-mouth Jars
    Narrow-mouth Jar (with Medium Neck)
    Narrow-mouth Jar (with Short Neck)
4. Large Capacity Bowls
    Tecomate
5. Medium Diameter Bowls and Dishes
    Slightly Incurving to Round-side Bowl
    Composite Silhouette Bowl or Dish
6. Small Diameter Bowls and Dishes
    Slightly Incurving to Round-side Bowl
    Composite Silhouette Bowl or Dish with Restricted Orifice
8. Medium Plates
    Outflaring to Slightly Outcurving-side Plate
    Widely-everted Rim Plate

SHAPE CLASS 1: WIDE-MOUTH JARS

Wide-mouth Jar (with Medium-tall Neck)

Illustrations: Fig. 2.10, 2.22, 2.23; 5.1–4, 5.6, 5.35, 5.36. See TR. 25A: fig. 119*b–c*; 120*a–f.*

Identifying characteristics and sorting problems: Identified by lack of slip, mouth size and neck height; few sorting problems. Originally called Eb Wide-mouth jar (TR. 25A).

Base and Body: No complete examples in the collections. On the basis of large sherds, the body seems to have been globular. Since there are no unslipped or striated flat bases, the base must have been rounded.

Neck-body juncture: Usually vague; fairly well marked on rare examples.

Orientation of neck: Wide outflare.

Neck: Wide outcurve.

Rim: Direct, but not infrequently accentuates outcurve of neck.

Lip: Rounded; sometimes thickened.

Appendages: Loop handles on the body of the jars are quite common.

Surface: Unslipped, either smoothed or striated; striations continue to the lip on the exterior and sometimes also occur on the interior of the neck.

Types: Cabcoh Striated and Canhel Unslipped.

Diameter of lip: Range 14–34 cm; median 22 cm.

Neck height: median 4.9 cm.

Diameter/Height Ratio: median 4.8.

Shape class: 1, Wide-mouth jars

Temporal distribution: Eb Complex.

Comments: The medium to tall necked wide-mouth jar shape is quite distinctive among the wide-

TABLE 2.5
Shape Dimensions of the Eb Complex

Shape Class and Shape	Median Diameter or Range (cm)	Median Height or Range (cm) (Neck Height for Jars)	Median Diameter/ Height Ratio or Range (cm)
1. Wide-mouth Jar (with Medium-tall Neck)	22.0	4.9	4.8
1. Wide-mouth Jar (with Short Neck)	20.0	2.8	7.4
2. Narrow-mouth Jar (with Medium Neck)	12.0	4.0	2.6
2. Narrow-mouth Jar (with Short Neck)	14.0	2.4	5.8
4. Tecomate	18.0 (restricted orifice)	—	—
5. Slightly Incurving to Round-side Bowl	24.0	9.4–14.8	1.8–1.9
5. Composite Silhouette Bowl or Dish	26.0–34.0	—	—
6. Slightly Incurving to Round-side Bowl	20.0	8.0	2.0
6. Composite Silhouette Bowl or Dish with restricted orifice	16.0–18.0	—	—
8. Outflaring to Slightly Outcurving-side Dish or Plate	31.0	6.0	4.4–5.0
8. Widely Everted-rim Plate	32.0	5.6–6.2	4.2–5.0

mouth jars of the Preclassic complexes. Although the diameter is almost identical to other wide-mouth jars in both range and median, the neck height is much greater. The vague neck-body juncture is also unusual. Because of these features, the shape is a good marker for the Eb Complex.

Wide-mouth Jar (with Short Neck)

Illustrations: Fig. 2.55, 2.62, 2.63; 3.1–8; 5.5, 5.7–8. See TR. 25A: fig. 119*a,d*.

Identifying characteristics and sorting problems: Easy to distinguish on the basis of short neck, large lip diameter, and unslipped surface.

Base and body: No whole examples, but body seems to have been globular.

Neck-body juncture: Usually rounded but well defined.

Orientation of neck: Medium to wide outflare.

Neck: Outcurves in varying degrees.

Rim: Direct.

Lip: Usually rounded to pointed; a few examples are beveled or flattened.

Surface: Striated below neck-body juncture; variable care in finishing.

Types: A few examples of Canhel Unslipped and Cabcoh Striated.

Lip diameter: Range 10–24 cm; median 20 cm.

Neck height: Range 1.4–4.6 cm; median 2.8 cm.

Lip diameter/neck height ratio: Range 4.8–12.8; median 7.4.

Shape class: 1, wide-mouth jars.

Temporal Distribution: Occurs rarely in the Eb Complex.

Comments: This shape is not so common in the Eb Complex as it is in later Preclassic complexes. The only feature in which the Eb Complex examples of the shape differ from later examples is that loop handles occasionally occur on the body of the vessel.

SHAPE CLASS 2: NARROW-MOUTH JARS

Narrow-mouth Jar (with Medium Neck)

Illustration: Fig. 2.8; 3.31. See TR. 25A: fig. 119*e–g*.

Base and body: There were no whole examples, but large sherds suggest that the body was globular. Since there are few flat jar bases in the collections, the base was probably rounded.

Neck-body juncture: A well-marked, angular juncture is characteristic.

Orientation of neck: Slight outflare to nearly vertical.

Neck: Slight to medium outcurve. Some examples are nearly straight near the juncture with the body and become outcurving toward the lip.

Rim: Direct; rounded everted; some examples of marked, but short eversion.

Lip: Rounded.

Surface: Carefully finished on exterior and the interior of the neck. Incised decoration occurs as single lines on the neck or at the juncture of neck and body. More complex decoration is absent.

Types: Ainil Orange and Baadz Tan.

Diameter of lip: Range 8–24 cm; median 12 cm.

Height of neck: Range 3.0–5.0 cm; median 4.0 cm.

Diameter of lip/neck height ratio: Range 2.0–5.0; median 2.6.

Shape class: 2, narrow-mouth jars.

Identifying characteristics and sorting problems: Since neck height is the only characteristic that separates this shape from the narrow-mouth jar with short-neck, small sherds cannot be attributed to specific shape.

Temporal distribution: About equally common in the Eb and Tzec Complexes, although rare later.

Comments: The separation of the medium-neck jar shape from the short-neck jar shape is artificial to the extent that it involves an arbitrary distinction within a continuous range of neck heights. The form is distinct, however, in the sense that if all jar necks were lumped into a single shape there would be a bimodal peak for height. The medium-height jar is also discrete in that jars with necks of this height were very rare in later Preclassic complexes.

Narrow-mouth Jar (with Short Neck)

Illustrations: Fig. 2.9; 3.32–35.

Identifying characteristics and sorting problems: The short neck makes it fairly easy to distinguish this jar from earlier and later shapes.

Base and body: The few complete examples have globular bodies of small size, but these examples—all from special deposits—may not be representative.

Neck-body juncture: Usually well marked; most frequently angular but sometimes rounded.

Orientation of neck: Medium outflare.

Neck: Ranges from medium outcurve to nearly straight.

Rim: Usually direct; a subclass has sharp to rounded eversion of the rim.

Lip: Rounded or pointed; some examples of the everted rim subclass have flattened lips.

Surface: Slipped on exterior and on interior of neck; remainder of interior unslipped. Care in finishing varies.

Types: Ainil Orange, Boolay Brown, and Baadz Tan.

Diameter: Range 10–30 cm; median 14 cm.

Neck Height: Range 1.2–4.0 cm; median 2.4 cm.

Lip diameter/neck height ratio: Range 3.6–11.7; median 5.8. The ratio shows a wide distribution with little central tendency; it seems unlikely that the ratio was of much significance to the users.

Shape class: 2, narrow-mouth jars.

Temporal distribution: Present in both the Eb and Tzec Complexes, but more common in the Chuen, Cauac, and Cimi Complexes.

Comments: This shape occurs in all Preclassic complexes, but is somewhat less common in the Eb Complex than in later complexes.

SHAPE CLASS 4: LARGE CAPACITY BOWLS

Tecomate

Illustrations: Fig. 2.3, 2.4, 2.6–7, 2.28–30, 2.36–37; 4.12–13, 4.19–24; 5.11. See TR. 25A: fig. 116*a–b*.

Base: Unknown.

Orientation of side: Slightly to highly restricted orifice.

Side: Rounded, the degree of curvature varies from low to medium.

Rim: Direct; a few examples show a slight, rounded eversion.

Lip: Rounded or Bolstered. Includes tecomates originally identified as tecomates with bump lip.

Surface: The exterior is slipped, with wide variation in the care of finishing. The interior may be slipped just inside the lip, but otherwise interiors are unslipped, although smoothed. Incised decoration, when present, occurs just below the lip on the exterior of the vessel.

Type: All slipped types are about equally represented in a small sample though most common in Boolay Brown and Calam Buff. Incised types are quite common.

Diameter: Range 10–22 cm; median 18 cm. Other dimensions are unknown since there are no complete examples in the collections. The curvature of the side suggests that tecomates were usually of large size, although the highly restricted orifice results in a small measurement for the rim diameter.

Shape class: 4, large capacity bowl.

Identifying characteristics and sorting problems: The restricted orifice, low curvature of wall and unslipped interior were used as diagnostics for sorting. There are some problems of overlap with small round-side bowls with restricted orifice.

Temporal distribution: The tecomate shape was at peak frequencies in the Eb Complex, and occurrences in later complexes are rare and sporadic.

SHAPE CLASS 5: MEDIUM DIAMETER BOWLS AND DISHES

Slightly Incurving to Round-side Bowl

Illustrations: Fig. 2.18–21, 2.24–26, 2.29–30; 3.18; 5.33, 5.40. See TR. 25A: fig. 117*a–d*.

Base: Flat or concave.

Orientation of side: Most examples have nearly vertical sides with only a slight incurve. The exteriorly bolstered lip is characteristic and easy to identify.

Side: Straight to slightly rounded.

Rim: Direct.

Lip: Thickened by a bolster on the exterior.

Surface: Varies from well to carelessly finished.

Types: About 90% of the examples are Calam Buff.

Diameter: Range 16–40 cm; median 24 cm. The sample scatters evenly between 16 and 30 cm with a few larger examples.

Height: (3 examples) range 9.4–14.8 cm.

Diameter/height ratio: (3 examples) range 1.8–1.9. In size this shape overlaps both the medium and large size, but the majority, as well as the median diameter is more securely on the medium size of vessels.

Shape class: 5, medium diameter bowls and dishes.

Identifying characteristics and sorting problems: The angle and thickness of the wall, bolstered lip, and frequent use of Calam Buff combine to make the shape very easy to identify, even from small rim sherds.

Temporal distribution: It may be slightly more common in the earlier lots of the Eb Complex.

Comments: This shape with the exteriorly bolstered lip is one of the best markers for the Eb Complex. While succeeding examples in later complexes of slightly incurving to round-side bowls occur, they lack the characteristic exteriorly bolstered lip.

Composite Silhouette Bowl or Dish

Illustrations: Fig. 2.2; 5.31–32.

Base: Unknown

Orientation of side: Slight outflared to vertical.

Side: Upper section, straight to slight outcurve; lower section, seems to be straight.

Break between sections: Angular.

Rim: Direct or slightly everted.

Lip: Rounded, pointed, or flattened.

Surface: Exterior of upper section is encircled by a series of flutes or deep grooves; vessels are very carefully finished and well polished.

Types: Haleb Red-on-cream and Xkili Fluted are important; fluted or incised types in black and orange also occur.

Diameter: (5 examples) range 26–34 cm. In size this shape overlaps both the medium and large size, but the majority, as well as the median diameter is more securely on the medium size of vessels.

Shape class: 5, medium-diameter bowls and dishes.

Identifying characteristics and sorting problems: The fluting or grooving is very characteristic and makes the shape easy to identify, although small sherds could be confused with those from cuspidors.

Temporal distribution: Securely identified only in a few examples in the Eb Complex, although some small sherds from the Tzec Complex may also have been of this shape.

Comments: Although examples are numerically insignificant, the overall shape is quite distinctive. The shape relates to cuspidors and other composite silhouette shapes. It was originally called Fluted Dish with Composite Silhouette (TR. 25A). However, the name has been changed in this work to reflect the shape rather than the fluted decoration.

SHAPE CLASS 6: SMALL DIAMETER BOWLS AND DISHES

Slightly Incurving to Round-side Bowl

Illustrations: Fig. 2.11, 2.13–16, 2.24–26, 2.56, 2.61; 4.28; 5.17. See TR. 25A: fig. 116*c–k*.

Identifying characteristics and sorting problems: This shape includes examples with restricted orifices, which were originally separated (TR. 25A) on the basis of higher curvature of the side and slightly thinner walls. There was, however, considerable overlap between the shapes and they are combined in this work.

Base: Flat in the few examples that show complete sections.

Side: Rounded; usually high curvature.

Rim: There are two rims that characterize this shape. The first is direct. The second includes examples with an everted rim that is usually marked by incising or grooving on the exterior. The rim eversion might be described as a recurving-side bowl, however the sample size is small and the decision was made to include both rim forms in the same basic shape.

Lip: Usually rounded.

Surface: Well-finished both inside and out. This was a favorite form for incised decoration, which invariably occurs on the exterior, usually as a line or lines on the upper part of the vessel.

Types: Occurs in low frequencies for all monochrome slipped types.

Diameter: 20 cm.

Height: 8 cm.

Diameter/Height Ratio: 2 cm.

Shape class: 6, small-diameter bowls and dishes.

Temporal distribution: This shape was common during the Eb Complex.

Composite Silhouette Bowl or Dish with Restricted Orifice

Illustrations: Fig. 4.25–26.

Base: Unknown.

Orientation of side: Slight to medium restriction of orifice.

Side: Straight to slightly rounded above shoulder; rounded below shoulder.

Break between sections: The juncture of the upper and lower sections is usually rounded and does not make a clear line.

Rim: Direct.

Lip: Rounded.

Surface: Slipped on both interior and exterior.

Types: Unnamed Monochrome Red and Boolay Brown as well as incised types.

Diameter: Range 16–18 cm. Sample too small to have confidence in a median; no whole sections available, so other dimensions unknown.

Shape class: 6, small-diameter bowls and dishes.

Identifying characteristics and sorting problems: Examples large enough to show the break between upper and lower sections are easy to identify; small rim sherds would not be recognized.

Temporal distribution: The shape was never common throughout the Eb Complex.

Comments: This is little more than a variant of the slightly incurving to round-side bowl with restricted orifice but possesses a composite silhouette vessel wall.

SHAPE CLASS 8: MEDIUM DISHES AND PLATES

Outflaring to Slightly Outcurving-side Plate

Identifying characteristics and sorting problems: The flat lip when present is a good marker for this shape. Originally called a Flat-lip dish (TR. 25A), however, shapes are not defined by their lip form and those with flattened lips overlap with other outflaring to slightly outcurving-side plates in all other aspects.

Illustrations: Fig. 2.17; 3.38; 4.2, 4.6–7, 4.10, 4.25–26, 4.29, 4.39, 4.40, 4.41; 5.16.

Base: Flat.

Orientation of side: Medium outflare or outcurve.

Side: Outflaring to outcurving.

Rim: Direct; occasionally the rim accentuates the outcurve of the side.

Lip: Rounded, pointed, or most commonly flattened; sometimes takes beveled or semi-beveled inward form. The lip is usually thicker than the rest of the wall.

Surface: Slipped on both interior and exterior; care of finish varies; incising occurs occasionally on the exterior wall.

Types: Unnamed Monochrome Black, Unnamed Monochrome Red, Ainil Orange, Boolay Brown, and Calam Buff.

Diameter: Range 16–58 cm; median 31 cm. While there is a wide range of diameters, some of which would be considered large plates, the majority is of medium size.

Height: Range 3.8–11.1 cm; median 6.0 cm. Height measurements show a wide scatter without much tendency to cluster.

Diameter/height ratio: Range 3.2–6.9; median 4.4–5.0. In both height measurements and in D/H ratio there is wide scatter with little central tendency.

Shape class: 8, medium dishes and plates.

Temporal distribution: Begins in the Eb Complex and continues into the Tzec Complex.

Widely-everted Rim Plate

Illustrations: Fig. 2.42, 2.55; 4.12–13.

Base: Flat.

Orientation of side: Medium to wide outflare.

Side: Straight.

Rim: Widely everted, usually to horizontal; the rim section is broad.

Lip: Usually rounded.

Surface: Slipped on interior; carelessly finished, sometimes unslipped on exterior. The upper surface of the everted rim is almost invariably marked by one or two grooves; pattern incising on the rim also occurs.

Types: About equally divided between Calam Buff, Unnamed Monochrome Red, and incised types.

Diameter: Range 20–38 cm, median 32 cm.

Height: (2 examples) 5.6 and 6.2 cm.

Diameter/height ratio: (2 examples) 4.2 and 5.0.

Shape class: 8, medium dishes and plates.

Identifying characteristics and sorting problems: No other shape in the Tikal sequence duplicates this particular rim treatment.

Temporal distribution: Begins in the Eb Complex and continues into the Tzec Complex.

Comments: Since this shape is so distinctive and is completely confined to Eb and Tzec, it makes an excellent temporal marker for these two complexes.

UNIDENTIFIABLE SMALL RIMS

In each ceramic lot there is an inevitable residue of rim sherds too small to be identified by shape. The size of this category depends on the state of preservation, i.e., the size of sherds in a given lot and also upon the degree of complexity or simplicity of the shapes. Since one of the characteristics of the Eb Complex is relative simplicity of shape, with many shapes that depend upon nearly whole sections for identification, unidentifiable rim counts ran relatively high in Eb samples.

Eb Complex Shape Classes

The six shape classes represented in the Eb Complex cover a wide range of sizes and proportions that must relate to the uses of the vessels. Correlations between shape classes, surface finish, and care of production lend support to the idea of functional variability, as do parallels with vessels produced by modern Maya potters.

Shape class 1 consists of wide-mouth jars made from unslipped pottery. The lip diameter distribution is identical for the two subclasses and demonstrates a tight normal curve. Although there are no complete examples in the collections, the curvature of body sherds suggests that capacities were large. Data on modern Maya pottery (Reina and Hill 1978) indicate that vessels in shape class 1 are very similar to those still used for water storage. These modern vessels not only show dimensions similar to those of shape class 1, but are, like vessels of that shape class, unslipped.

Shape class 1 is divided into two subclasses on the basis of differences in neck height and, consequently, lip diameter/neck height ratios. Although neck height distributions for the two subclasses are clearly distinct, it is unlikely that the difference was functionally meaningful. Height measurements for both subclasses gave scattered distributions without much central tendency. This suggests that potters did not carefully control neck-heights and probably means that this dimension was not critical to the intended use. Furthermore, throughout the Tikal sequence there is great stability in the neck diameters of unslipped, wide-mouth jars, but considerable variation in neck heights. If different neck heights related to different uses, this apparently stable form would have changed drastically in use through time, a situation that seems unlikely.

Shape class 2, narrow-mouth jars, presents a situation similar to that just discussed for shape class 1. Lip diameter is uniform and was apparently carefully controlled, while neck height, although it can be used as a criterion for subdivision, shows a variability that does not seem consistent with functional necessity. Although there are not enough large sherds to give satisfactory measurements of average capacity, the vessels were certainly much smaller than those in shape class 1. In comparison with modern Maya pottery, shape class 2 is a direct counterpart of jars still used for transporting water.

A surprising gap in the shape repertoire of the Eb Complex is the scarcity of large capacity bowls. Vessels of this class are common in most Tikal complexes and probably served for bulk storage. The tecomate, tentatively classed as a large-capacity bowl (shape class 4), may have filled this function, but the average capacity and proportions of the shape are uncertain because of the lack of complete examples and the frequency of the shape was never high.

Medium-diameter bowls and dishes (shape class 5) are less common in the Eb collections than in most other Tikal complexes, but small bowls and dishes (shape class 6) are strongly represented both in frequency and variety. The distinction between these two shape classes, however, may not be very meaningful. Measurements of the individual shapes that comprise the shape classes do not show tight clustering around a mode, and the overall distribution of all shapes within each shape class does not show the bi-modality or multi-modality that one would expect if there had been production of classes of carefully controlled size. The use of vessels in shape classes 5 and 6 is difficult to determine. Such vessels would have been appropriate for serving food, as suggested by any number of archaeologists, but the shapes are also adaptable for a variety of other uses such as small volume storage, religious offerings, or even manufacture for aesthetic reasons. Care in finish and decoration is more obvious in these shape classes than in most others, but this fact does not lead to any single interpretation about use.

Shape class 8 is represented by medium dishes and plates. Their larger size suggests they probably were used for serving or for storage-display. Offerings and other religious uses are also possible functions.

Eb Shapes: Temporal Change

Relative frequencies of Eb shapes by sample location are presented in Table 2.6, but as with Eb Complex types, the small sample size and mixed chronological stratigraphy make it difficult to identify chronological differences in Eb shapes.

Because there are only three samples that are stratigraphically unrelated, it also is difficult to demonstrate which differences arise from temporal rather than other sources of variation such as social or functional differences.

The shape class of wide-mouth unslipped jars varies considerably among the three Eb samples. The sum of all vessels in the shape class varies from 45.4% of total rim sherds in Sample Location 1 to only 19.9% in Sample Location 2, and 15.3% in Sample Location 3 in Eb, less common in the Tzec Complex, and absent in later complexes. This is clearly an early shape that has a relatively short history in the Tikal sequence. The wide-mouth jar with short neck, a very long-lived shape that is common throughout the Tikal Preclassic, shows frequencies that diminish between Eb Location 1 and Eb Location 3. This may not be a temporally significant variation, however, because in the context of the whole Preclassic, frequencies of the shape vary in a manner that does not relate to the temporal position of samples.

The tecomate, (shape class 4: Large Capacity Bowls), is a common form in the Eb Complex and may decline through time as they become considerably less common by the succeeding Tzec Complex. Among medium- and small-diameter bowls and dishes (shape classes 5 and 6), some minor shapes differ in frequency throughout the Eb Complex. In particular, the composite silhouette dish may become more common in later levels and is a likely precursor to the cuspidor of the Tzec Complex. Similarly, shape class 8: Medium Dishes and Plates may

TABLE 2.6
Shape Frequencies of the Eb Complex

Shape Class and Shape	Sample Location 1	Sample Location 2	Sample Location 3
	%	%	%
1. Wide-mouth Jar (with Medium-tall Neck)	20.9	4.3	2.6
1. Wide-mouth Jar (with Short Neck)	24.5	15.6	12.7
2. Narrow-mouth Jar (with Medium Neck)	3.5	3.4	2.1
2. Narrow-mouth Jar (with Short Neck)	4.2	4.3	7.4
4. Tecomate	13.7	14.7	6.9
4. Slightly Incurving to Round-side Bowl	10.1	15.6	6.3
5. Composite Silhouette Bowl or Dish	—	—	3.2
6. Slightly Incurving to Round-side Bowl	7.5	19.8	15.9
6. Composite Silhouette Bowl or Dish with Restricted Orifice	4.8	7.7	1.6
8. Outflaring to Slightly Outcurving-side Plate	8.9	3.4	38.6
8. Widely Everted-rim Dish or Plate	1.9	11.2	2.7
TOTAL RIM SHERDS	**198**	**143**	**284**

appear in greater quantities in later Eb levels, a trend that continues into the Tzec Complex where even larger plates are a more common shape class than in the Eb Complex.

Comparisons of Eb shapes with those of later Preclassic complexes indicate two shapes that are unique to the complex. These shapes are: the composite silhouette dish and the composite silhouette bowl or dish with restricted orifice. Five Eb shapes make up a cluster common to the Eb and Tzec Complexes but are rare or absent in later complexes. These shapes are: (1) the flat-lip dish or plate; (2) the outflaring to slightly outcurving-side plate (usually with a flattened lip); (3) the widely everted-rim dish or plate; (4) the Eb wide-mouth jar; and (5) the Eb-Tzec narrow-mouth jar. The remaining shapes in the Eb Complex are long-lived shapes shared with other Preclassic complexes.

Eb Shapes: Social Dimension

It is difficult to interpret the activities indicated by Eb ceramics because of the lack of information about the archaeological context of the samples. Eb Location 1 is likely to have been a residential site because it is located well away from the center of Tikal in an area that shows no evidence of large Preclassic structures. Eb Location 3, fill from the heart of Str. 5C-54, is the most likely to represent ceremonial/elite activity. The sample was sealed within what seems to have been a contemporaneous large structure that was covered by a later Preclassic structure of undeniably ceremonial nature. Location 2 (underlying the North Acropolis) is even more difficult to fix in an activity context. Although the North Acropolis was an important ceremonial site within a few centuries after the sample in Location 2 was produced, there is no indication of the use of the area in Eb times.

The vessel shapes themselves provide another basis for inferring ceramic use. Wide-mouth jars and large bowls are associated with residential areas throughout the Tikal sequence while small bowls, dishes, and plate shape classes have frequent ceremonial-elite associations.

The distribution of shapes across the three sample locations is a surprisingly good match for the best guesses about what the contexts represent. Location 1 fits perfectly with the expected pattern of domestic debris, while Location 3, except for the low frequency of large plates, fits the ceremonial-elite pattern. Location 2 provides mixed results, perhaps indicating the mixing of material from more than one set of activities.

Special Deposits of the Eb Complex

There are no special deposits classified as burials or caches in the Eb Complex at Tikal, and the later excavations in the Mundo Perdido (Laporte and Valdes 1993) did not uncover Eb burials or caches, but did describe some additional problematical deposits.

Problematical Deposits of the Eb Complex

There is one special deposit defined as problematical that includes Eb Complex pottery. This deposit, PD. 1, was located in Chultun 5G-15 (Gp. 5G-15), an intermediate structure group in later times, but of uncertain size during Eb. Originally defined as Early Facet Eb (TR. 25A), PD. 1 includes Eb Complex and Tzec Complex vessels and, in the uppermost levels in the chultun, Chuen, Manik, and Imix Complex pottery. A reevaluation of the 48 whole vessels in PD. 1 is presented in Table 2.7.

TABLE 2.7 (part 1)
Problematical Deposits of the Eb Complex

PD. No.	Op.SubOp./Lot	Location	Structure Group Type	TR. 25A Illustration	TR.	Estimated No. of Vessels	Culbert (1993) TR. 25A	Culbert and Kosakowsky Revised Types	Ceramic Complex
1	27B/4, 7–9	Gp. 5G-1 Chultun 5G-15	Uncertain in Eb, Intermediate Structure Group (residential) later	116*a*	21	48	Joventud Red	Aac Red-on-buff	Eb
				116*b*			Joventud Red	Aac Red-on-buff	Eb
				116*c*			Guitara Incised	Unnamed Monochrome Red Incised: Fine Inclusions Variety	Eb
				116*d*			Guitara Incised	Unnamed Monochrome Red Incised: Fine Inclusions Variety	Eb
				116*e*			Unnamed red-on-natural	Aac Red-on-buff	Eb

TABLE 2.7 (part 2)
Problematical Deposits of the Eb Complex

PD. No.	Op.SubOp./Lot	Location	Structure Group Type	TR. 25A Illustration	TR.	Estimated No. of Vessels	Culbert (1993) TR. 25A	Culbert and Kosakowsky Revised Types	Ceramic Complex
				116f			Joventud Red	Unnamed Monochrome Red: Fine Inclusions Variety	Eb
				116g			Joventud Red	Unnamed Monochrome Red: Fine Inclusions Variety	Eb
				116h			Joventud Red	Unnamed Monochrome Red: Fine Inclusions Variety	Eb
				116i			Joventud Red	Unnamed Monochrome Red: Fine Inclusions Variety	Eb
				116j			Joventud Red	Unnamed Monochrome Red: Fine Inclusions Variety	Eb
				116k			Joventud Red	Unnamed Monochrome Red: Fine Inclusions Variety	Eb
				116l			Guitara Incised	Unnamed Monochrome Red Incised: Fine Inclusions Variety	Eb
				117a			Calam Buff	Calam Buff	Eb
				117b			Calam Buff	Calam Buff	Eb
				117c			Calam Buff	Calam Buff	Eb
				117d			Calam Buff	Calam Buff	Eb
				117e			Joventud Red	Unnamed Monochrome Red: Fine Inclusions Variety	Eb
				117f			Joventud Red	Unnamed Monochrome Red: Fine Inclusions Variety	Eb
				117g			Joventud Red	Unnamed Monochrome Red: Fine Inclusions Variety	Eb
				117h			Joventud Red	Unnamed Monochrome Red: Fine Inclusions Variety	Eb
				117i			Joventud Red	Unnamed Monochrome Red: Fine Inclusions Variety	Eb

TABLE 2.7 (part 3)
Problematical Deposits of the Eb Complex

PD. No.	Op.SubOp./Lot	Location	Structure Group Type	TR. 25A Illustration	TR.	Estimated No. of Vessels	Culbert (1993) TR. 25A	Culbert and Kosakowsky Revised Types	Ceramic Complex
				118a			Joventud Red	Joventud Red	Tzec
				118b			Joventud Red	Joventud Red	Tzec
				118c			Joventud Red	Joventud Red	Tzec
				118d			Joventud Red	Joventud Red	Tzec
				118e			Joventud Red	Joventud Red	Tzec
				118f			Joventud Red	Joventud Red	Tzec
				118g			Joventud Red	Joventud Red	Tzec
				118h			Joventud Red	Joventud Red	Tzec
				118i			Chunhinta Black	Chunhinta Black	Tzec
				118j			Ainil Orange	Ainil Orange	Eb
				118k			Joventud Red	Joventud Red	Tzec
				118l			Guitara Incised	Guitara Incised	Tzec
				119a			Cabcoh Striated	Cabcoh Striated	Eb
				119b			Cabcoh Striated	Cabcoh Striated	Eb
				119c			Cabcoh Striated	Cabcoh Striated	Eb
				119d			Canhel Unslipped	Canhel Unslipped	Eb
				119e			Canhel Unslipped	Canhel Unslipped	Eb
				119f			Ahchab Red-on-buff	Ahchab Red-on-buff	Early Chuen
				119g			Joventud Red	Joventud Red	Tzec
				119h			Joventud Red	Joventud Red	Tzec
				120a			Cabcoh Striated	Cabcoh Striated	Eb
				120b			Cabcoh Striated	Cabcoh Striated	Eb
				120c			Cabcoh Striated	Cabcoh Striated	Eb
				120d			Cabcoh Striated	Cabcoh Striated	Eb
				120e			Cabcoh Striated	Cabcoh Striated	Eb
				120f			Cabcoh Striated	Cabcoh Striated	Eb
				121a			Joventud Red	Sierra Red	Chuen
				121b			Chunhinta Black	Unknown monochrome red and black	Unknown
				121c			Aguila Orange	Aguila Orange	Manik
				121d			Achiotes Unslipped	Achiotes Unslipped	Tzec
				121e			Aguila Orange	Aguila Orange	Manik

III

Tzec Ceramic Complex

Tzec Complex Collections

Introduction

The Tzec Ceramic Complex was sparsely represented in the Tikal collections. Only one location provided Tzec samples that could be analyzed quantitatively, but the collection from this location was very large and the deposits deep enough to demonstrate some ceramic change within the Tzec Complex and a gradual transition to the succeeding Chuen Complex. Despite the lack of other pure samples, Tzec sherds were more abundant throughout the site than those of the Eb Complex. Preclassic levels in major structural precincts frequently contained some Tzec sherds mixed in later deposits even in outlying areas of the site. The Tzec occupation density, although still quite low, had increased from that of the Eb Complex (Culbert et al. 1990).

Information on the location that provides Tzec Complex samples is presented in Table 3.1. The sample locations are described as "Tzec-Chuen" as the deep stratigraphy at this location provided lots with ceramics from both complexes. There is also the small sample of Tzec ceramics mixed in with earlier Eb pottery as described in Chapter 2.

TZEC-CHUEN LOCATION 1

This location about 1 km E and slightly N of the Great Plaza is the platform that supports Str. 5F-17 and 18 (TR. 20A). It consists of a 30m² platform surmounted by structures. The only ones visible from

surface indications are typical Late Classic house mounds, but excavations revealed a long sequence of construction and occupation extending back to the Tzec-Chuen deposits that are of concern here.

Excavation at Tzec-Chuen Location 1 revealed two low platforms that were not visible from surface contours, a hearth, and probable remains of a perishable kitchen structure. There were also a hearth and a small pit in bedrock entered by two stone-cut steps, and a deep quarry hole excavated into bedrock. The small platforms and possible kitchen were used during subsequent Chuen and Cauac times as well, but there is no construction that can definitely be assigned a Tzec date. Filling of the quarry pit with midden debris began during the Tzec Complex and continued into the Late Preclassic, suggesting considerable quarrying activity at a very early date.

The best ceramic samples came from the quarry pit, which was large enough to permit excavation of five adjacent stratigraphic columns. Since there were no easily definable natural strata, arbitrary 20 cm levels were used in the excavation. Continuous occupation during the time of the Tzec and Chuen Complexes resulted in gradual accumulation of a deep midden deposit. The Tzec samples include a total of 3,321 sherds indentified for types and 695 rim sherds identified for type and shape. (It should be noted that there were no Tzec samples 1-1, 1-2, and 1-3. These top three levels of the quarry pit are dated to the Chuen Complex.)

Tzec Sample 1-4: This sample came from the uppermost Tzec level in the quarry pit and included all

TABLE 3.1
Locations of Tzec Complex Samples

Sample #	Op.Sub-Op./Lot	Structure Group and Structure Number	Structure Group Type	Total Sherds-Types	Total Sherds-Shapes	Comments	TR.
Location 1 [Samples 1-1 to 1-3 are Chuen]		Gp. 5F-1 In quarry pit near Str. 5F-17, -18	Small Structure Group				20A
Sample 1-4	71F/6,13,23,42			1057	151	100–120 cm level	
Sample 1-5	71F/7,14,24,43			1068	195	120–140 cm level	
Sample 1-6	71F/15,25,44,48			637	148	140–160 cm level	
Sample 1-7	71F/16,26,45,56,57			559	201	160–180 cm level (Includes PD. 108)	
GRAND TOTAL				3321	695		

sherds from the 100–120 cm level of five contiguous stratigraphic columns. The sample included 1057 sherds counted for types and 151 rims counted for shapes

Tzec Sample 1-5: This sample included sherds from the 120–140 cm level of the five columns. It included 1,068 sherds counted for types and 195 rims counted for shapes.

Tzec Sample 1-6: This sample included sherds from the 140–160 cm level of the five columns. It included 637 sherds counted for types and 148 rims counted for shapes.

Tzec Sample 1-7: This sample included sherds from the 160–180 cm level of the five columns. It included 559 sherds counted for types and 201 rims counted for shapes.

By Chuen times, the construction complex at Tzec-Chuen Location 1 was clearly residential, based on the small size of the platforms, the presence of a hearth, and an abundance of ash and snail shells in the midden, all of which point toward domestic activities. Even in the absence of definable Tzec structures, it seems safe to assume a domestic context for the Tzec material as well.

Pastes of the Tzec Complex

Introduction

Three paste types were common in the Tzec Complex collections, and there may be some small quantities of Tzec ceramics that are still manufactured using the Eb Complex Fine-inclusions Paste. Tzec pastes are transitional between those of the Eb Complex, which stand somewhat apart from previously known Petén Preclassic ceramics, and later traditions that are well known from a variety of sites. After the Tzec Complex, pastes entered a period of stability that persisted until the end of the Preclassic.

Red-particles Paste, the most common paste in Tzec Complex slipped types, was a distinctive, short-lived phenomenon that was almost completely confined to the time of the Tzec Complex, while Coarse-carbonate and Preclassic Monochrome Pastes were ones that were to become standard in all later Preclassic complexes. In addition to the kind and amount of inclusions that served as the principal basis for defining pastes, paste color proved a significant characteristic and was one of the bases for making varietal distinctions in unslipped types made from Coarse-carbonate Paste and slipped types produced from Preclassic Monochrome Paste.

Tzec Paste Descriptions

COARSE-CARBONATE PASTE

Identifying characteristics: Abundant carbonate inclusions.

Color, Regular Variety: Strong to yellowish brown (7.5YR 5/6 to 10YR 5/4), pale to grayish brown (10YR 5/2 to 6/3).

Color, Red Variety: Red to reddish yellow (10YR 5/8, 7.5YR 7/6 to 7.5YR 5/6).

Texture: Medium to coarse.

Inclusions: High to medium amounts of medium to large particles most of which are gray to white crystalline carbonate; also some finely divided sparkly particles, hematite, reddish clay, and black mineral particles.

Types: Achiotes Unslipped.

RED-PARTICLES PASTE

Identifying characteristics: The presence of red and black particles in a light-colored paste.

Color: Usually yellow (10YR 6/6); ranges to strong brown (7.5YR 5/6) and reddish yellow (5YR 6/8).

Texture: Medium.

Inclusions: Medium amounts of fine to medium particles that include several different kinds of materials: (1) reddish particles that seem to be a second clay; (2) black shiny particles; (3) translucent crystalline carbonate particles; and (4) white amorphous particles. The multicolored effect of the different inclusions is quite striking in sherds with large quantities of inclusions.

Types: Common in the Joventud and Chunhinta ceramic groups, and continues into early Chuen on the Ahuacan Variety of Sierra Red.

Temporal distribution: Red-particles Paste is most common in Tzec, but continues to appear in early Chuen types.

Comments: Red-particles Paste is very distinctive in appearance and is quite different from Preclassic pastes of both earlier and later complexes, although it does continue into the start of the Chuen Complex.

PRECLASSIC MONOCHROME PASTE

Identifying characteristics: The best identifying characteristic is a "fruitcake" appearance caused by the occurrence of inclusions of several different colors seen against a background paste color that varies from one part of a sherd to another.

Color: Tzec samples differ from those of later complexes in that almost all examples are of reddish colors (usually red to light red, 2.5YR 6/8 to 5/8; some examples reddish yellow 5YR 6/8), while color ranges are broader in later samples.

Texture: Medium.

Inclusions: This paste incorporates unusually large amounts of inclusions for a paste used with slipped ceramic types. Translucent or gray carbonate particles are invariably present, as are shiny black particles. Reddish-orange particles of secondary clay are visible in many sherds, but cannot be distinguished where the paste itself is red. White amorphous particles occur sporadically.

Types: Preclassic Monochrome Paste is used for monochrome and dichrome types, often with crazed slips, although it is less common than Red-particles Paste in the Tzec Complex.

Comments: Sherds classified within Preclassic Monochrome Paste show a considerable amount of variation in all characteristics, but potential subgroups failed to show chronological or other significance. This paste becomes the predominant paste in monochrome types during the subsequent Chuen through Cimi ceramic complexes, after its first appearance in the Tzec Complex.

Discussion

Correlations between pastes and surface finish helped in the separation of types. Coarse-carbonate Paste relates directly and almost exclusively to unslipped types, and was established as a major paste type during Tzec. Red-particles Paste proved to be an excellent marker for the Tzec Complex; it was easily recognizable, common in Tzec samples, and rare or absent in other complexes. Preclassic Monochrome Paste made its first appearance in Tzec Complex samples, but did not become common until later Preclassic complexes.

In comparison to the Eb Complex, Tzec pastes demonstrate a reduction in variety, both in the number of common paste types and in the variability within types. Although this might suggest increased standardization in production, such a conclusion must be considered tentative because only a single location with Tzec ceramics at Tikal was analyzed.

Ceramic Types of the Tzec Complex

Introduction

The Tzec Ceramic Complex includes the 8 ceramic groups and 14 types (composed of 16 varieties) listed in Table 3.2. Originally, Culbert (TR. 25A) chose Late Preclassic Chicanel names to describe the monochrome red, black, and cream types. In part, this decision was made because at the time of the analysis there were few pre-Mamom and Mamom complexes at other sites with which to compare the Tikal chronology [see for example: Altar de Sacrificios (Adams 1971); Seibal (Sabloff 1975); and Yaxha-Sacnab

TABLE 3.2 (part 1)
Ceramic Groups and Types of the Tzec Complex

Culbert and Kosakowsky	Culbert (1993)*
Eb Complex Group	**CANHEL CERAMIC GROUP**
Eb Complex Type	Canhel Unslipped: Canhel Variety
Eb Complex Type	**CABCOH CERAMIC GROUP**
Eb Complex Type	Cabcoh Striated: Cabcoh Variety
ACHIOTES CERAMIC GROUP	**ACHIOTES CERAMIC GROUP**
Achiotes Unslipped: Achiotes Variety	Achiotes Unslipped: Achiotes Variety
Included in Achiotes Variety	Achiotes Unslipped: Ahtzum Variety
JOCOTE CERAMIC GROUP	**JOCOTE CERAMIC GROUP**
Palma Daub: Palma Variety	Palma Daub: Palma Variety
Chuen Complex Group	**SAPOTE CERAMIC GROUP**
Chuen Complex Type	Sapote Striated: Sapote Variety
JOVENTUD CERAMIC GROUP	**SIERRA CERAMIC GROUP**
Joventud Red: Ahcax Variety	Sierra Red: Ahcax Variety
Early Chuen Complex Type	Sierra Red: Ahuacan Variety
Guitara Incised: Simple-incised Variety	Laguna Verde: Simple-incised Variety
Guitara Incised: Design-incised Variety	Laguna Verde Incised: Design-incised Variety
Amil Chamfered: Amil Variety	Amil Chamfered: Amil Variety

TABLE 3.2 (part 2)
Ceramic Groups and Types of the Tzec Complex

Culbert and Kosakowsky	Culbert (1993)*
Early Chuen Complex Type	Ahchab Red-on-buff: Ahchab Variety
Early Chuen Complex Type	Ahchab Red-on-buff: Ahlapp Variety
Placed in Boolim Ceramic Group	Boo Incised-dichrome: Simple Incised Variety
CHUNHINTA CERAMIC GROUP	**POLVERO CERAMIC GROUP**
Chunhinta Black: Maach Variety	Polvero Black: Maach Variety
Deprecio Incised: Simple-incised Variety	Lechugal Incised: Simple-incised Variety
Deprecio Incised: Design-incised Variety	Lechugal Incised: Design-incised Variety
Ahmax Chamfered: Ahmax Variety	Ahmax Chamfered: Ahmax Variety
Eb Complex Group	**AINIL CERAMIC GROUP**
Eb Complex Type	Ainil Orange: Ainil Variety
BACLAM CERAMIC GROUP	**BACLAM CERAMIC GROUP**
Baclam Red-orange: Ahtau Variety	Baclam Orange: Ahtau Variety
Eb Complex Group	**BOOLAY CERAMIC GROUP**
Eb Complex Type	Boolay Brown: Fine Inclusions Variety
Chuen Complex Group	**BOXCAY CERAMIC GROUP**
Chuen Complex Type	Boxcay Brown: Boxcay Variety
PITAL CERAMIC GROUP	**FLOR CERAMIC GROUP**
Pital Cream: Unspecified Variety	Flor Cream: Flor Variety
BOOLIM CERAMIC GROUP	**NEW TZEC CERAMIC GROUP**
Boolim Red-on-cream: Boolim Variety	Boolim Red-on-cream: Boolim Variety
Boo Composite: Boo Variety	Boo Incised-dichrome: Simple Incised Variety
SAVANA CERAMIC GROUP	**SAVANA CERAMIC GROUP**
Savana Orange: Savana Variety	Savana Orange: Savana Variety
Reforma Incised: Reforma Variety	Reforma Incised: Reforma Variety

*The Canhel, Cabcoh, Ainil, and Boolay Ceramic Groups originally identifed in the Tzec Complex by Culbert (1993) are Eb Complex groups. The Sapote and Boxcay Ceramic Groups are Chuen Complex. The use of Chicanel type names by Culbert (1993) has been changed to use Mamom type names for the Tzec Complex.

(Rice 1979a)]. However, in the decades since the original analysis, many sites have identified pre-Mamom and Mamom sequences [see for example: Cahal Pech (Awe 1992; Sullivan and Awe 2013); Cuello (Kosakowsky 1987; Kosakowsky and Pring 1998); Colha (Valdez 1987); Holmul (Callaghan 2008); K'axob and Pulltrouser Swamp (Fry 1989; Lopez Varela 1996); and Ka'kabish (Sagebiel and Haines 2015)].

In light of more recent research, this volume now identifies the types in the Tzec Complex using Mamom names, and the monochrome red, black, and cream ceramic groups and types are renamed Joventud in place of Sierra, Chunhinta in place of Polvero, and Pital in place of Flor. Chicanel type names are reserved for the succeeding Chuen, Cauac, and Cimi Complexes. The original types as outlined by Culbert (TR. 25A) are listed along with their new names in Table 3.2. A number of transitional Mamom/Chicanel types such as Sierra Red: Ahuacan Variety and Ahchab Red-on-buff (originally placed in the Joventud Group by Culbert), as well as transitional forms, are included in the early part of the Chuen Complex.

Unslipped sherds, mostly Achiotes Unslipped, make up between one-quarter and one-half of the sherds in Tzec samples. Joventud Red is the most common monochrome type, occurring in frequencies ranging from 16% to 28%. Incised decoration is common. Most incised sherds show simple patterns of parallel lines on vessel exteriors, but there is an increasing amount of other types of incised patterns, as well as incising on the interior of rims of outcurving or outflaring dishes and plates (Guitara Incised). Dichrome decoration becomes important with the appearance in Tzec of the Boolim Ceramic Group. There are no illustrations available for sherds of the Jocote Ceramic Group (Palma Daub: Palma Variety) and the Savana Group (Savana Orange: Savana Variety and Reforma Incised: Reforma Variety), however, similar examples are illustrated for Barton Ramie (Gifford 1976).

The only Tzec Complex lots available for quantitative analysis were those obtained from the lower levels of the deep pit in Tzec-Chuen Location 1, and all lots were temporally mixed. Because the quantity of material obtained was large, full typological counts were not made for all of the stratigraphic columns sunk into this deposit. For the columns analyzed, all sherds were counted. Frequencies of Tzec types in the four stratigraphic levels in Tzec-Chuen Location 1 are given in Table 3.3.

Tzec Type Descriptions

ACHIOTES CERAMIC GROUP

Achiotes Unslipped: Achiotes Variety

Established: Smith and Gifford (1966)

Group: Achiotes

Ware: Uaxactun Unslipped

Ceramic Complex: Tzec

Ceramic Sphere: Mamom

Illustrations: Fig. 3.11–17; 5.22–23; 6.1–11, 6.17–22, 6.24–25, 6.28–29, 6.34–35. TR. 25A: fig. 121*d*.

Principal Identifying Attributes: Unsmoothed, unslipped surfaces confined to wide-mouth jars.

Identifying characteristics and sorting problems: Both surface and paste are quite characteristic and overlap little with other types. Originally there were two varieties of Achiotes Unslipped identified (TR. 25A), however, this involves segmenting a continuum in which there are many intermediate examples. Later Tikal excavations did not separate these two varieties and placed all unslipped examples in the Achiotes Variety (Laporte and Valdes 1993). Therefore, the decision was made to combine both into the Achiotes Variety in this work, rather than distinguishing varieties based on paste variants.

Paste: There are two paste variants of Achiotes Unslipped that were originally described as two varieties of the type, the Achiotes Variety and the Ahtzum Variety (TR. 25A). The first paste variant (originally the Achiotes Variety) is characterized by Coarse-carbonate Paste. Most examples are of the brown to gray regular variety of Coarse-carbonate Paste, but some are of the red variety. The second paste variant (originally called the Ahtzum Variety) is characterized by the red variety of Coarse-carbonate Paste.

Firing: Many examples are darkened completely, but less than one-quarter show separable dark cores. Cores showing two or more shades of paste color are common. About half of the sherds show fireclouding of the surface.

Color: Highly variable, even on individual sherds. Light brown (7.5YR 6/4), strong brown (7.5YR 5/6), very pale brown (10YR 8/3), yellowish brown (10YR 5/4), and dark yellowish brown (10YR 4/4) all occur. Red (10YR 4/8 to 2.5YR 4/6) to light red (2.5YR 6/6) and reddish brown (10R 4/5, 5YR 4/3, 2.5YR 5/4) also occur; these latter reddish colored sherds formed the continuum that was originally identified as the Ahtzum Variety (TR. 25A).

Surface finish and decoration: Examples are both

TABLE 3.3
Ceramic Type Frequencies of the Tzec Complex

Ceramic Groups/Types	Tzec-Chuen Location 1			
	100–120 cm level	120–140 cm level	140–160 cm level	160–180 cm level
	%	%	%	%
Eb Complex				
Cabcoh Group	—	1.0	1.3	2.7
Ainil Group	5.7	3.8	2.5	3.6
Boolay Group	1.0	0.2	0.9	0.5
Tzec Complex				
Achiotes Group	24.0	17.7	44.3	42.2
Jocote Group	0.4	1.1	0.6	1.1
Joventud Red: Ahcax Variety	5.0	1.7	3.3	5.6
Guitara Incised: Simple and Design-Incised Variety	0.9	1.9	1.3	0.7
Amil Chamfered: Amil Variety	0.2	1.1	0.9	0.4
Chunhinta Black: Maach Variety	4.9	3.7	3.9	6.4
Deprecio Incised: Simple and Design-Incised Variety	0.2	0.4	0.3	0.5
Ahmax Chamfered: Ahmax Variety	0.5	0.3	—	—
Baclam Group	1.7	4.5	1.5	2.5
Pital Group	1.0	1.1	0.8	1.1
Boolim Red-on-cream: Boolim Variety	—	0.2	—	0.4
Boo Composite: Boo Variety	3.6	2.1	0.2	1.1
Savana Group	0.7	1.5	1.3	1.2
Early Chuen Complex				
Sapote Group	2.4	24.2	—	—
Sierra Red: Ahuacan Variety	8.6	14.6	7.5	6.3
Ahchab Red-on-buff: Ahchab Variety	4.6	4.3	6.4	5.0
Polvero Group	2.3	2.3	1.9	3.9
Boxcay Group	3.2	2.4	1.9	1.4
Unclassified	3.2	1.7	7.0	5.0
Weathered	25.9	8.2	12.2	8.4
Number of Sherds	1057	1068	637	559

smoothed as well as more carelessly finished and many sherds show smoothing marks and poor obliteration of coils. A few examples are medium smooth and have a surface coat of matte-red clay applied over the paste, which may be related to the Palma Daub type.

Shapes: Confined to the various wide-mouth jar shapes.

Temporal distribution: Begins in the Tzec Complex. After the Tzec Complex, the type becomes rare and although there is still a fairly abundant sherd-sorting category for Achiotes Unslipped, it contains mostly jar necks that are almost certainly from vessels that were actually striated.

Comments: Following the lead established by Adams (1971) with Altar de Sacrificios pottery, Achiotes Unslipped is a generalized unslipped category that begins in Mamom and continues until the end of the Preclassic complexes.

Intersite comparisons: Achiotes Unslipped is used as the predominant unslipped type at Acanmul (Ball and Taschek 2015); Altar de Sacrificios (Adams 1971); Becan (Ball 1977); El Mirador (Forsyth 1989); El Perú/Waka' (Eppich 2011); Holmul (Callaghan 2008; 2016a); Nakbe (Forsyth 1993); the Petexbatun (Foias and Bishop 2013); and Seibal (Sabloff 1975).

JOCOTE CERAMIC GROUP

Palma Daub: Palma Variety

Established: Smith and Gifford (1966)

Group: Jocote

Ware: Uaxactun Unslipped

Ceramic Complex: Tzec

Ceramic Sphere: Mamom

Principal Identifying Attributes: Well-smoothed, unslipped brown to orange surfaces decorated with "daubs" or zones of a monochrome red slip that is lightly applied.

Identifying characteristics and sorting problems: The presence of an unpolished red slip on a sherd with coarse paste is quite distinctive, but in many examples the slip is applied so lightly it is difficult to determine if it is present.

Paste: The paste falls within the range of variation of Coarse-carbonate Paste and includes examples of both color varieties. In texture, the examples are toward the finer end of the range of Coarse-carbonate Paste.

Firing: Dark cores occur in more than half of the examples.

Surface: Color ranges from brown (5YR 4/1, 5/1, 5/2, 5/3; 7.5YR 5/2) to yellowish brown (7.5YR 5/6 to 10YR 5/4); red to reddish yellow (10YR 5/8, 7.5YR 7/6 to 7.5YR 5/6) and a dull orange (2.5YR6/6, 6/8). The monochrome red zones are (2.5YR 5/6).

Surface finish and decoration: Unpolished red slip over all or part of the vessel.

Shapes: Sherds all seem to be from jars.

Temporal distribution: Tzec Complex.

Comments: Although some examples may not have been identified because of the difficulty of distinguishing the slip, it is evident that the type is far less common at Tikal than at Uaxactun.

Intersite comparisons: Barton Ramie (Gifford 1976); Chan (Kosakowsky 2012); Colha (Valdez 1987); Nakbe (Forsyth 1993); Punta de Chimino (Bachand 2007); Ceibal (Inomata et al. 2013); and Uaxactun (Smith 1955; Smith and Gifford 1966).

JOVENTUD CERAMIC GROUP

Note: Originally categorized as the Sierra Ceramic Group by Culbert (1993 [TR. 25A]).

Joventud Red: Ahcax Variety

Established: Type named by Smith and Gifford (1966); variety named by Culbert (1993 [TR. 25A]).

Group: Joventud

Ware: Flores Waxy

Ceramic Complex: Tzec

Ceramic Sphere: Mamom

Illustrations: Fig. 2.31–34, 2.39, 2.46–49, 2.51–54; 3.36–37, 3.42–45; 5.12–15, 5.24, 5.27–30, 5.37; 6.12–13, 6.15–16, 6.26–27; 7.11–12, 7.22, 7.24, 7.35–36, 7.42–46 See TR. 25A: fig. 118*a–h*; 118*k*; 119*g–h*; 121*a*.

Principal Identifying Attributes: Monochrome red slip that is heavily crazed on a characteristic red paste.

Identifying characteristics and sorting problems: The red color of the paste makes the Ahcax Variety easy to identify as does the crazed monochrome red slip.

Paste: Characterized by Preclassic Monochrome Paste.

Firing: About 20% have dark cores and fireclouding rare.

Slip: The surface of the vessels was smoothed before application of a slip of medium thickness. The slip is somewhat waxy, although the waxiness is less pronounced than in the monochrome reds of the Late Preclassic. The slip crazes badly and tends to flake off.

Polish: Usually medium, sometimes low.

Color: The most common examples tend to fall in the fully red range (10R 5/8) rather than shading toward orange.

Surface finish and decoration: Smoothed surfaces and a slightly waxy red slip. There are some examples where only one surface of the vessel is slipped red, and the other surface is left unslipped, though well smoothed. The sample was not large enough to identify a separate type, although they may be similar to Chito Red-and-unslipped at Holmul (Callaghan 2016a).

Shapes: Slightly outflaring to outcurving-side bowls, dishes, and plates; small slightly incurving to round-side bowls; narrow-mouth jars; and cuspidors.

Temporal distribution: The Ahcax Variety appears at the start of the Tzec Complex.

Intersite comparisons: The Ahcax Variety is similar to the Joventud Variety identified at other sites during the Middle Preclassic such as Uaxactun (Smith 1955; Smith and Gifford 1966) and Holmul (Callaghan 2016a); the Unspecified Variety at Barton Ramie (Gifford 1976), El Pozito (Eppich 2000) and Seibal (Sabloff 1975); the Jolote Variety at Altar de Sacrificios (Adams 1971) and Becan (Ball 1977); and the Sampopero Variety in the Belize Valley (Ball and Taschek 2003).

Guitara Incised: Simple-incised and Design-incised Varieties

Established: Type named by Smith and Gifford (1966); varieties named by Culbert (1993 [TR. 25A]).

Group: Joventud

Ware: Flores Waxy

Ceramic Complex: Tzec

Ceramic Sphere: Mamom

Illustrations: Fig. 2.1, 2.35, 2.40–41, 2.43–45; 3.50, 3.53; 4.14; 5.18, 5.26; 7.25, 7.29. See TR. 25A: fig. 118*l*.

Principal Identifying Attributes: Monochrome red slip similar to the Ahcax Variety of Joventud Red with the addition of a band with simple groove incising on the interior or exterior of rims, or geometric groove incising on the exterior of vessels.

Identifying characteristics and sorting problems: Identical to Joventud Red: Ahcax Variety except for the characteristics noted below. The slip characteristics and decoration make it easy to identify.

Paste: Characterized by Preclassic Monochrome Paste.

Firing: About 20% have dark cores and fireclouding rare.

Slip: The surface of the vessels was smoothed before application of a slip of medium thickness. The slip is somewhat waxy, although the waxiness is less pronounced than in later varieties. The slip crazes badly and tends to flake off.

Polish: Usually medium, sometimes low.

Color: The most common examples tend to fall in the fully red range (10R 5/8) rather than shading toward orange.

Surface finish and decoration: The Simple-incised Variety is decorated with single or multiple lines encircling the vessels almost always on the exterior or interior near the rim. Patterns of the Design-incised Variety are usually no more than curving lines or straight lines that cross. Very few sherds were large enough to demonstrate overall vessel patterns.

Shapes: Widely everted-rim plates (medium and large) and small-diameter bowls and dishes are the most common shape represented in all incised types.

Temporal distribution: Decoration, such as these examples, on monochrome red vessels begins and is most common during the Tzec Complex. Becomes less common in the succeeding Preclassic complexes.

Intersite comparisons: Guitara Incised has been identified at Altar de Sacrificios (Adams 1971); Barton Ramie (Gifford 1976); Becan (Ball 1977); Cuello (Kosakowsky 1987; Kosakowsky and Pring 1998); Colha (Valdez 1987); Holmul (Callaghan 2016a); El Mirador (Forsyth 1989); Ka'kabish (Sagebiel and Haines 2015); Seibal (Sabloff 1975); Uaxactun (Smith 1955; Smith and Gifford 1966); and Yaxha-Sacnab (Rice 1979a).

Amil Chamfered: Amil Variety

Established: TR. 25A (Culbert 1993)

Group: Joventud

Ware: Flores Waxy

Ceramic Complex: Tzec

Ceramic Sphere: Mamom

Illustrations: Fig. 2.5, 2.27, 2.38; 4.4–5, 4.30, 4.37; 7.2–3, 7.19, 7.49,–50. See TR. 25A: fig. 142*d5*; 155*e*.

Principal Identifying Attributes: Monochrome red slip similar to the Ahcax Variety of Joventud Red with the addition of chamfering on the exterior of cuspidors.

Identifying characteristics and sorting problems: There is a major problem in drawing a line between grooved-incised and chamfered decoration in the Tikal samples. The cuspidor shape is frequent-ly decorated with a raised section that is delimited from the remainder of the vessel by deep groove incising that often approaches chamfering. Sorted were only those chamfered examples that showed several parallel bands of very typical chamfering. In all other aspects the same as Joventud Red: Ahcax Variety.

Paste: Most examples have Red-particles Paste, but there are a few examples of Preclassic Monochrome Paste.

Surface finish and decoration: Chamfering occurs in bands encircling the exterior of vessels.

Shapes: Mostly cuspidors.

Temporal distribution: Most chamfering occurs in the Tzec Complex with a few Chuen examples.

Intersite comparisons: Similar to Desvario Chamfered at Altar de Sacrificios (Adams 1971); Becan (Ball 1977); Cuello (Kosakowsky 1987); Colha (Valdez 1987); Holmul (Callaghan 2016a); Ka'kabish (Sagebiel and Haines 2015); K'axob (Lopez Varela 1996); Nakbe (Forsyth 1993); the Petexbatun (Foias and Bishop 2013); Seibal (Sabloff 1975); and Uaxactun (Smith 1955; Smith and Gifford 1966).

CHUNHINTA CERAMIC GROUP

Chunhinta Black: Maach Variety

Established: Type named by Smith and Gifford (1966); Variety named by Culbert (1993 [TR. 25A]).

Group: Chunhinta

Ware: Flores Waxy

Ceramic Complex: Tzec

Ceramic Sphere: Mamom

Illustrations: Fig. 3.39–40, 3.46, 3.48, 3.55; 4.1, 4.8–9; 6.14, 6.23, 6.30–33; 7.48, 7.51. See TR. 25A: fig. 2*a3*; 118*i*; 142*d6*; 143*a7*.

Principal Identifying Attributes: Thick black, sometimes waxy slip, which tends to flake and craze.

Identifying characteristics and sorting problems: The type is quite distinct from the Unnamed Monochrome Black: Fine Inclusions Variety in the preceding Eb Complex on the basis of paste differences, thickness and waxiness of slip, and control of color.

Paste: Mostly Red-particles Paste and Preclassic Monochrome Paste.

Firing: Quite a few examples have completely darkened cores, but cores darkened only in the center are rare.

Slip: A slip of medium thickness was applied over a clay surface that was already smoothed. There is a tendency to a waxy slip and crazing is common. A number of sherds show no darkening of the surface under the black slip, so it is possible that a pigment that fires black under oxidizing conditions was used.

Polish: Medium.

Color: Good control of firing for the black color with only a few sherds with reddish patches. Surface color is black (5YR 2.5/1, 7.5YR N 2/, 10YR 2/1, 2.5Y N 2/).

Shapes: Evenly distributed among a variety of shapes.

Temporal distribution: The type occurs in the Tzec Complex and grades into Polvero Black: Polvero Variety during the succeeding Chuen Complex.

Intersite comparisons: Chunhinta Black occurs at Altar de Sacrificios (Adams 1971); Barton Ramie (Gifford 1976); Becan (Ball 1977), Cuello (Kosakowsky 1987); Colha (Valdez 1987); El Mirador (Forsyth 1989); El Pozito (Eppich 2000); Holmul (Callaghan 2016a); Seibal (Sabloff 1975); Tayasal (Chase 1984); and Uaxactun (Smith 1955; Smith and Gifford 1966).

Deprecio Incised: Simple-incised Variety and Design-incised Variety

Established: Type named by Smith and Gifford (1966); varieties named by Culbert (1993 [TR. 25A]).

Group: Chunhinta

Ware: Flores Waxy

Ceramic Complex: Tzec

Ceramic Sphere: Mamom

Illustrations: Fig. 3.41, 3.47, 3.49, 3.51, 3.54; 4.31–32, 4.34, 4.36, 4.42; 7.28, 7.54, 7.55. See TR. 25A: fig. 143*a*1,*a*8.

Principal Identifying Attributes: Monochrome black slip same as Chunhinta Black decorated with incising. In all other respects same as Chunhinta Black.

Identifying characteristics and sorting problems: The Simple-incised Variety which consists of groove incising of single or double lines encircling the exterior of vessels and the interior of rims is less common than the Design-incised Variety. Small sherds of the Design-incised Variety may overlap with the Simple-incised Variety of Deprecio Incised, so only those with obvious designs are separated out. In all other respects except for paste, the varieties are the same as Chunhinta Black.

Paste: Some examples have Preclassic Monochrome Paste. More common, however, is a reddish paste that includes very finely divided carbonate particles, with occasional amorphous white particles, and secondary clay particles. This paste may simply be a finer variant of Red-particles Paste.

Surface finish and decoration: Includes both pre-slip groove incising as well as post-slip, fine line incising of simple lines, parallel lines, and patterns of crosshatching.

Shapes: Small-diameter bowls and dishes and narrow mouth jars.

Temporal distribution: Appears in the Tzec Complex, and may lead into Lechugal Incised in the Late Preclassic.

Comments: This type, the incised counterpart of Chunhinta Black, was not common during the Tzec Complex because black slip was rarely used for plates or cuspidors, the two shapes on which incised decoration most commonly appeared. Deprecio Incised: Simple-incised Variety includes only a few examples of jars and small bowls with incised lines. The small sample provided little idea of the total range of variation.

Intersite comparisons: Nakbe (Forsyth 1993) highlights the transitional nature of these Tzec types between Mamom and Chicanel.

Ahmax Chamfered: Ahmax Variety

Established: TR. 25A (Culbert 1993)

Group: Chunhinta

Ware: Flores Waxy

Ceramic Complex: Tzec

Ceramic Sphere: Mamom

Illustrations: Fig. 4.33, 4.38; 7.1.

Principal Identifying Attributes: Monochrome black slip same as Chunhinta Black decorated with chamfering on the exterior of vessels.

Comments: Identical to Chunhinta Black except as noted below.

Decoration: Chamfered bands encircle the vessel exterior.

Shapes: Cuspidors.

Temporal distribution: Tzec Complex.

Comments: The type begins in the Tzec Complex. Chamfered decoration is most common in Mamom complexes elsewhere.

Intersite comparisons: There is an unnamed and incised chamfered example illustrated in the Chunhinta Group at Nakbe (Forsyth 1993).

BACLAM CERAMIC GROUP

Baclam Red-orange: Ahthau Variety

Established: Type renamed in this work from Baclam Orange to Baclam Red-orange; variety named by Culbert (1993 [TR. 25A]).

Group: Baclam

Ware: Flores Waxy

Ceramic Complex: Tzec

Ceramic Sphere: Mamom

Illustrations: Fig. 4.3,4.6; 7.10, 7.13–14, 7.29.

Principal Identifying Attributes: Slightly waxy monochrome orange slip that overlaps with monochrome red types.

Identifying characteristics and sorting problems: Surface color is the sole identifying characteristic of the type. The range of color grades continuously into that of Joventud and Sierra Red, so there are many borderline examples. Only the most clearly orange examples were classified in sorting as Baclam Red-orange.

Paste: Preclassic Monochrome Paste.

Slip: Usually medium thickness. On some examples, the clay surface was well polished before application of the slip. In these examples, the slip tends to flake off, revealing sections of light clay.

Polish: Low to medium. Waxiness variable.

Color: The most typical examples are reddish yellow (2.5YR 6/8), but the color ranges to red (2.5YR 5/8) as well.

Shapes: Narrow-mouth jars with short-necks and outflaring to slightly outcurving-side bowls, dishes, and plates are the most common shapes.

Temporal Distribution: A low frequency of Baclam Red-orange sherds begins with the Ahthau Variety in the Tzec Complex, and other varieties continue into the Late Preclassic.

Comments: This type derives from arbitrarily separating the orange end of a color continuum between red and orange. In sorting Tzec samples, sherds were separated that were the strongest orange color and counted as Baclam Red-orange. It is probable that some red-orange examples are sorted with more abundant monochrome reds at other sites.

Intersite comparisons: El Perú/Waka' (Eppich 2011).

PITAL CERAMIC GROUP

Pital Cream: Unspecified Variety

Established: Type established Smith and Gifford (1966); variety established Kosakowsky (1987).

Group: Pital

Ware: Flores Waxy

Ceramic Complex: Tzec

Ceramic Sphere: Mamom

Illustrations: Fig. 4.15–18; 7.7–8, 7.26, 7.38–41.

Principal Identifying Attributes: Lustrous, slightly waxy cream slip that is variable in color.

Identifying characteristics and sorting problems: Pital Cream presents few sorting problems.

Paste: Preclassic Fine Paste predominates, but Preclassic Monochrome Paste is also represented.

Firing: Dark cores and fireclouding are rare.

Slip: Slightly waxy, thick slip that adheres better and shows less tendency to flake or craze than other Preclassic monochrome slips.

Polish: High.

Surface color and decoration: Slip color of Pital Cream is extremely variable. Very pale brown (10YR 8/3), pale brown (10YR 6/3), brown (10YR 5/3), and light yellowish brown (10YR 6/4) are most common, but white (10YR 8/1, 8/2; 2.5Y 8/2) and gray (10YR 6/1; 5Y 5/1) also occur. It is common for sherds to show patches of two different colors and mottling, as well as fireclouding.

Shapes: Sherd sample and sherd size are too small to determine common shapes.

Temporal distribution: Restricted to the Tzec Complex.

Comments: The total sample is too small to say more than that it is quite variable in paste and surface color.

Intersite comparisons: Acanmul (Ball and Taschek 2105); Altar de Sacrificios (Adams 1971); Barton Ramie (Gifford 1976); Becan (Ball 1977); Blue Creek (Kosakowsky and Lohse 2003); Cahal Pech (Awe 1992); Chan (Kosakowsky 2012); Colha (Valdez 1987); Cuello (Kosakowsky 1987); El Mirador (Forsyth 1989); K'axob (Lopez Varela 1996); Holmul (Callaghan 2016a); the Petexbatun (Foias and Bishop 2013); Piedras Negras (Muñoz 2006); Punta de Chimino (Bachand 2007); Seibal (Sabloff 1975); Uaxactun (Smith 1955; Smith and Gifford 1966).

BOOLIM CERAMIC GROUP

Boolim Red-on-cream: Boolim Variety

Established: TR. 25A (Culbert 1993)

Group: Boolim (established this work). Originally placed in the Flor Ceramic Group (Culbert 1993 [TR. 25A]).

Ware: Flores Waxy

Ceramic Complex: Tzec

Ceramic Sphere: Mamom

Illustrations: Fig. 5.25, 5.38–39, 5.44.

Principal Identifying Attributes: Lustrous, slightly waxy, cream slip that is variable in color usually on the interior of vessels, and a monochrome red slip on the exterior of vessels.

Identifying characteristics and sorting problems: Colors red and cream on opposite faces of the vessel. No sorting problems if both sides preserved.

Paste: Usually Red-particles Paste; some examples of Preclassic Monochrome Paste.

Slip: The two colors are used on opposite sides of the vessel, with red usually on the interior and cream on the exterior.

Surface color and decoration: The red includes the same range of colors found in Joventud Red; the cream is pinkish white (7.5YR 8/2) to pink (7.5YR 8/4).

Shape: Usually outflaring to slightly outcurving-side bowls and dishes; some slightly incurving to round-side bowls.

Temporal distribution: Tzec Complex.

Comments: In basic characteristics, Boolim Red-on-cream is identical to Muxanal Red-on-cream from Uaxactun without the more elaborate geometric decorations that occur on some examples of Muxanal. While this type was originally classified in the cream group at Tikal (TR. 25A), it has been placed in a separate ceramic group in this work to parallel the identification of a separate Muxanal Group at other sites.

Intersite comparisons: See Muxanal Red-on-cream in Mamom Complexes at other sites. Acanmul (Ball and Taschek 2015); Altar de Sacrificios (Adams 1971); Becan (1977); Calakmul (Dominguez Carrasco 1994); Chan (Kosakowsky 2012); Cuello (Kosakowsky 1987; Kosakowsky and Pring 1998); Colha (Valdez 1987); El Mirador (Forsyth 1989); Holmul (Callaghan 2016a); Ka'kabish (Sagebiel and Haines 2015); K'axob (Lopez Varela 1996); Nakbe (Forsyth 1993); the Petexbatun (Foias and Bishop 2013); Uaxactun (Smith 1955; Smith and Gifford 1966); and Yaxha-Sacnab (Rice 1979a).

Boo Composite: Boo Variety

Established: Originally called Boo Incised-dichrome: Simple-incised Variety Culbert (1993 [TR. 25A]); renamed in this work in keeping with type: variety nomenclature rules.

Group: Boolim (established this work). Originally included in the Sierra Group by Culbert (1993 [TR. 25A]).

Ware: Flores Waxy

Ceramic Complex: Tzec

Ceramic Sphere: Mamom

Illustrations: Fig. 4.11; 6.36–57. See TR. 25A: fig. 143*a*2–5.

Principal Identifying Attributes: A red monochrome slip is applied along with a resist agent over a monochrome cream to buff underslip, leaving design patterns that include triangles, dots, crossed lines, and a series of formless blobs and patches. Additional decoration is by means of pre-slip groove incising on the lips of vessels.

Identifying characteristics and sorting problems: There are no sorting problems as the decoration on Boo Composite is distinctive. In all other aspects it is the same as Boolim Red-on-cream.

Shapes: Mostly medium and large plates.

Comments: Boo Composite is Boolim Red-on-cream with more elaborate resist and incised decoration. The overwhelming majority of examples are incised-lip plates. No incised decoration more complex than parallel lines occurs; hence, there is no design-incised variety.

Intersite comparisons: See Muxanal Red-on-cream in Mamom Complexes at other sites. Acanmul (Ball and Taschek 2015); Altar de Sacrificios (Adams 1971); Becan (1977); Calakmul (Dominguez Carrasco 1994); Chan (Kosakowsky 2012); Cuello (Kosakowsky 1987; Kosakowsky and Pring 1998); Colha (Valdez 1987); El Mirador (Forsyth 1989); Holmul (Callaghan 2016a); Ka'kabish (Sagebiel and Haines 2015); K'axob (Lopez Varela 1996); Nakbe (Forsyth 1993); the Petexbatun (Foias and Bishop 2013); Uaxactun (Smith 1955; Smith and Gifford 1966); and Yaxha-Sacnab (Rice 1979a).

SAVANA CERAMIC GROUP

Savana Orange: Savana Variety

Established: Smith and Gifford (1966)

Group: Savana

Ware: Mars Orange

Ceramic Complex: Tzec

Ceramic Sphere: Mamom

Illustrations: None

Principal Identifying Attributes: Thin red slip applied over an easily identifiable bright orange soft paste.

Identifying characteristics and sorting problems: The paste is so characteristic that even the smallest sherds can be easily recognized.

Paste: A silty paste with very consistent red (2.5YR 5/8, 6/8) color. Most examples show only a few tiny white inclusions, but some sherds have larger quantities.

Firing: Dark cores do not occur; fireclouding is rare.

Thickness: Medium-thin, mostly 5–6 mm.

Slip: Although a few sherds, mostly bases, are unslipped, most show a thin slip that is frequently rootlet-marked.

Polish: Low to medium.

Surface color and decoration: Red (10R 5/8) to light red (2.5YR 6/8).

Shapes: There are few sherds large enough to give an indication of vessel shape. Small jars, small slightly incurving to round-side bowls, and small outflaring to slightly outcurving-side bowls and dishes.

Temporal distribution: Tzec Complex.

Intersite comparisons: Acanmul (Ball and Taschek 2015); Altar de Sacrificios (Adams 1971); Barton Ramie (Gifford 1976); Cahal Pech (Awe 1992;); Chan (Kosakowsky 2012); Holmul (Callaghan 2016a); Seibal (Sabloff 1975); Uaxactun (Smith 1955; Smith and Gifford 1966).

Reforma Incised: Reforma Variety

Established: Smith and Gifford (1966)

Group: Savana

Ware: Mars Orange

Ceramic Complex: Tzec

Ceramic Sphere: Mamom

Illustrations: None

Principal Identifying Attributes: Thin red slip applied over an easily identifiable bright orange soft paste, with pre-slip groove incised decoration.

Comments: Identical to Savana Orange except for the presence of incising or grooving. Designs consist of single or multiple parallel lines.

Temporal distribution: Tzec Complex.

Intersite comparisons: Altar de Sacrificios (Adams 1971); Barton Ramie (Gifford 1976); Cahal Pech (Awe 1992;); Chan (Kosakowsky 2012); Holmul (Callaghan 2016a); Seibal (Sabloff 1975); Uaxactun (Smith 1955; Smith and Gifford 1966).

Tzec Complex Decorated Pottery

Decoration of vessels is very common in the Tzec Ceramic Complex, but the decorative patterns are simple and repetitive. Two kinds of decoration occur, incising and resist painting. Incised decoration involves a series of variables such as the stage in the manufacture of the vessel at which incising was done, the width and depth of incisions, and the kinds of patterns produced. In the Tzec sample, differences in techniques of production correlate strongly with the differences in the design pattern used to establish simple-incised and design-incised varieties.

Simple-incised decoration in the Tzec Complex consists of lines (occasionally single, but usually multiple) that encircle vessels parallel to the lip on the interior or exterior of the rim. The incisions were almost always made before the vessels were slipped and typically consist of relatively broad and shallow depressions.

Simple-incised decoration is strongly shape-correlated and a high percentage occurs on the interior lips of plates and on the exterior of small bowls and cuspidors. Simple incising in the Tzec Complex seems more controlled in both technique and field of decoration than it was in the Eb Complex. Lines in the Tzec samples have little variation in width and depth of incision, and the design fields used for decoration on both plates and cuspidors are carefully delimited. Vessels on which incised lines occur in unexpected locations were common in the Eb Complex but relatively rare in Tzec.

Design-incised patterns, defined as examples in which incisions did anything other than running parallel to the vessel lip were less common than simple-incising in the Tzec Complex. However, in comparison with Eb samples, design incising seems to be both more common and slightly more complex in Tzec, but in both complexes it is rare in comparison to simple incising.

The resist-painted decoration used in Boo Composite provides both a very different technique and a separate set of design problems. The resist technique seems to have been difficult to control and designs are vague, splotchy, and poorly defined. Triangles pendant from the lips of vessels, dots, and crossing lines can occasionally be identified as motifs but "blobs" and "patches" of color are far more common. It is regrettable that there are not more whole vessels of resist-painted types because far more design composition was likely present than is apparent from the small (and seemingly meaningless) areas of color that appear on sherds. Boo Composite uses a resist technique similar to Tierra Mojada Resist (Rice 1979a), which occurs elsewhere in Mamom Complexes, and these techniques may lead directly into Repasto Black-on-red in the subsequent Chuen Complex.

Tzec Types: Chronological Change

As mentioned previously, Culbert (TR. 25A) considered Tzec as a transitional complex that overlapped the boundary between the Mamom and Chicanel ceramic horizons in part because he did not recognize that the Eb Complex samples were temporally mixed. At other Petén sites for this time period, red types were represented by a Joventud Red-Sierra Red series, with the point of separation corresponding to the boundary between Joventud Red in Mamom and Sierra Red in the succeeding Chicanel ceramic horizons (Willey, Culbert, and Adams 1967). Since the Eb Complex now has been described more appropriately as pre-Mamom, that leaves Tzec as a fully Mamom Horizon Complex. Red pottery in the Tikal Late Preclassic complexes that followed the Tzec Complex are certainly Sierra Red, and Tzec red pottery, then, is best classified as a variety of Joventud Red on the basis of surface characteristics (note the inclusion of the Tzec Complex in the Mamom horizon in Willey, Culbert, and Adams [1967:295]).

The original decision to utilize Mamom type names for the Eb Complex (TR. 25A), and Chicanel type names for the Tzec Complex, masked important chronological comparisons with other sites. Although the original set of type names are utilized in TR. 25A, the companion volume to this one, it was decided to make changes in this volume and use Mamom type names for Tzec in order to facilitate comparisons with other site chronologies. As discussed previously, Table 3.2 lists the original types from Culbert (TR. 25A) alongside the new type names outlined in this volume.

This lengthy discourse on classificatory problems has not been intended solely as a demonstration of typological befuddlement. Instead, it is important to establish the point that behind the seeming solidity of a list of type names lies a series of decisions about archaeological material. In the analysis of any collection, some of the decisions will be clear-cut and easy to make while others will rest on subtle choices between nearly equal alternatives. If cultural change is a gradual process, as is usually the case, such problems are only to be expected. In the present case, the Tzec Complex provides the Tikal equivalent of Mamom Complexes at other sites that transition into Chicanel ceramic horizons.

The most distinctive Tzec innovations in slipped types are in paste, where relatively heavy inclusions of clay and carbonate are characteristic, and in the techniques of slipping that produce a waxy feel and heavy crazing of the slip surface. The occurrence of Red-particles Paste is a useful diagnostic of the Tzec Complex. Except for persistence into early Chuen samples from Location 1, this highly distinctive paste is confined entirely to Tzec. One of the most striking features of the Tzec Complex is an almost complete absence of striated types of pottery. The few sherds of Cabcoh Striated that appear in the collections are probably a minor persistence from the Eb Complex, and the later Sapote Striated appears in only small quantities in the uppermost levels of the Tzec deposits as a result of temporal mixing. In the absence of striated pottery, Achiotes Unslipped is very common and, in fact, reaches the highest frequencies ever attained by an unslipped and unstriated type at Tikal.

A new tradition in decoration appears in the Tzec Complex with the introduction of the resist technique used in Boo Composite, which continues into early Chuen with Ahchab Red-on-buff. These types also provide useful time markers because they are easily recognized, common, and rarely occur outside of Tzec and early Chuen samples at Tikal, and at other sites they are clearly linked to the Mamom horizon. Incised decoration continues to be strong in Tzec, as it was in the Eb Complex, with simple patterns still in overwhelming predominance, but with a slight increase in more complex designs in the Tzec samples.

Two types that are markers for the Mamom Complex at Uaxactun (Smith and Gifford 1966), Savana Orange and Palma Daub, are also present in Tzec samples at Tikal. Even in Tzec, however, these types are relatively rare and their temporal specificity is not as good as some of the other types mentioned above. The four Tzec Complex levels in the deep midden encountered in Tzec-Chuen Location 1 show frequency changes in several types (see Table 3.3 above). In sum, these changes fit the anticipated pattern of decrease in frequency through time of the elements that give Tzec continuity with Eb and an increase in the types in which Tzec presages later ceramics.

Tzec Types: Social Dimension

Since only a single excavation context is represented in the Tzec Complex samples, comparative analysis that might demonstrate social variation in the use of types within the complex is impossible. Some insights prove possible through comparison of the Tzec sample with samples from other complexes close to Tzec in time. The Tzec Complex samples probably represent debris from domestic activities. If this is so, one would expect functional similarity

between the Tzec samples and those from Eb Location 1 and the Chuen levels from Tzec-Chuen Location 1, both of which are samples of likely domestic origin. These samples should differ from those obtained from Eb Location 2 and 3, presumed non-domestic locations.

There are, however, few clues to function inherent in the characteristics of Preclassic types. Unslipped types, on the basis of their strong correlation with wide-mouth jars, presumably had largely domestic uses, although they have been used in feasting events elsewhere (Rice and Pugh 2017). All other types included a wide range of vessel shapes among which a variety of functions must have been represented. In essence, then, the only typological prediction one would be tempted to make about functional variation is that the total of striated and unslipped sherds should be high in domestic contexts. Such seems to be the case. The total percentage of these types in Tzec samples is 26% to 45%, while frequencies run from 33% to 35% in the Chuen samples in Tzec-Chuen location 1 and to 56% in Eb Location 1. On the other hand, the two presumed non-residential contexts from the Eb Complex show only 19% and 25% unslipped sherds. Slipped types conversely occur in lower frequencies in residential than in non-residential contexts. Since all slipped types are about equally affected, the lower frequencies in domestic contexts are probably no more than a result of higher unslipped frequencies.

Vessel Shapes of the Tzec Complex

Introduction

There are 7 shape classes and 13 vessel shapes listed in Table 3.4 that occur in Tzec Complex samples. Although the list of shapes is respectably long, the shape frequencies given in Table 3.5 show that Tzec samples were dominated by a very few shapes, chief among which were large and medium plates. Another measure of the lack of variety of Tzec Complex shapes is the fact that many of the shapes that occur are common in other ceramic complexes as well. The Tzec Complex is not differentiated from other complexes by a large repertoire of its own characteristic shapes but is strongly differentiated by frequency distributions.

TABLE 3.4
Shape Classes and Shapes of the Tzec Complex

1. **Wide-mouth Jars**
   Wide-mouth Jar (with Short Neck)
   Wide-mouth Jar (with Thin-lip)
2. **Narrow-mouth Jars**
   Narrow-mouth Jar (with Medium Neck)
   Narrow-mouth Jar (with Short Neck)
4. **Large Capacity Bowls**
   Tecomate
5. **Medium Diameter Bowls and Dishes**
   Slightly Incurving to Round-side Bowl
   Outflaring to Outcurving-side Bowl or Dish
6. **Small Diameter Bowls and Dishes**
   Slightly Incurving to Round-side Bowl
   Cuspidor
8. **Medium Plates**
   Outflaring to Slightly Outcurving-side Plate
   Widely Everted-rim Plate
9. **Large Plates**
   Outflaring to Slightly Outcurving-side Plate
   Widely Everted-rim Plate

Tzec Shape Descriptions

SHAPE CLASS 1: WIDE-MOUTH JARS

Wide-mouth Jar (with Short Neck)

Illustrations: Fig. 5.22–23; 6.1, 6.3–11, 6.17–22, 6.24–25, 6.28–29, 6.34–35.

Identifying characteristics and sorting problems: Easy to distinguish on the basis of short neck, large lip diameter, and unslipped surface.

Base and body: No whole examples, but body seems to have been globular.

Neck-body juncture: Usually rounded but well defined.

Orientation of neck: Medium to wide outflare.

Neck: Outcurves in varying degrees.

Rim: Direct.

Lip: Usually rounded to pointed; a few examples are beveled or flattened.

Surface: Variable care in finishing.

Types: Achiotes Unslipped.

Lip diameter: Range 10–24 cm; median 20 cm.

Neck height: Range 1.4–4.6 cm; median 2.8 cm.

Lip diameter/neck height ratio: Range 4.8–12.8; median 7.4.

Shape class: 1, wide-mouth jars.

Temporal Distribution: Occurs rarely in the Tzec Complex, however, common in the Late Preclassic Chuen, Cauac, and Cimi Complexes.

Comments: Considerable variability occurs in the shape, but it is not distinctive enough to allow meaningful subdivision.

Wide-mouth Jar (with Thin Lip)

Illustrations: Fig. 3.11–17; 6.2. See TR. 25A: fig. 121d.

Identifying characteristics and sorting problems: The thinning of the lip on characteristic examples is easily identified, though there is some overlap with the range of variation of the wide-mouth jar with short neck.

Base and body: No whole examples, but body seems to have been globular.

Neck-body juncture: Usually vague.

Orientation of neck: Wide outflare.

Neck: Wide outcurve.

Rim: Increases curvature of neck; sometimes direct or everted.

Lip: Round, slightly flattened, or small bolster on exterior. The lip is thinner than the rest of the neck.

Surface: Variable; well finished for an unslipped type.

Types: Achiotes Unslipped.

Lip diameter: Range 16–26 cm; median 20–22 cm.

Neck height: Range 1.9–3.4 cm; median 2.8 cm.

Lip diameter/neck height ratio: 4.8–10.0; median 7.2–7.4.

Shape class: 1, wide-mouth jars.

Temporal distribution: Tzec Complex. Wide-mouth jars that are thinned from the rim to the lip are characteristic of the Tzec Complex.

SHAPE CLASS 2: NARROW-MOUTH JARS

Narrow-mouth Jar (with Medium Neck)

Illustration: Fig. 2.39; 6.12–16,23; 7.3, 7.11–12, 7.15, 7.50. See TR. 25A: fig. 143*a*7.

Identifying characteristics and sorting problems: Since neck height is the only characteristic that separates this shape from the narrow-mouth jar with short-neck, small sherds cannot be attributed to specific shape.

Base and body: There were no whole examples, but large sherds suggest that the body was globular. Since there are few flat jar bases in the collections, the base was probably rounded.

Neck-body juncture: A well-marked, angular juncture is characteristic.

Orientation of neck: Slight outflare to nearly vertical.

Neck: Slight to medium outcurve. Some examples are nearly straight near the juncture with the body and become outcurving toward the lip.

Rim: Direct; rounded everted; some examples of marked, but short eversion.

Lip: Rounded.

Appendages: One example had a spout that left the body about halfway between shoulder and base. Other broken off spouts in the collections were probably associated with this shape. All spouts were unbridged and probably extended upward vertically.

Surface: Carefully finished on exterior and the interior of the neck. Incised decoration occurs as single lines on the neck or at the juncture of neck and body. More complex decoration is absent.

Types: Joventud Red, Baclam Red-orange, Chunhinta Black. There is a small Joventud Red jar (missing its rim) that is 9.6 cm in height. It is described as a miniature jar (TR. 25A:fig. 119*h*) but it is simply an unusually small jar. It is not included in the measurement range for this shape as it is lacking its neck and rim.

Diameter of lip: Range 8–24 cm; median 12 cm.

Height of neck: Range 3.0–5.0 cm; median 4.0 cm.

Diameter of lip/neck height ratio: Range 2.0–5.0; median 2.6.

Shape class: 2, narrow-mouth jar with medium neck.

Temporal distribution: About equally common in the Eb and Tzec Complexes, although rare later.

Comments: The separation of the medium-neck jar shape from the short-neck jar shape is artificial to the extent that it involves an arbitrary distinction within a continuous range of neck heights. The form is distinct, however, in the sense that if all jar necks were lumped into a single shape there would be a bimodal peak for height. The medium-height jar is also discrete in that jars with necks of this height were very rare in later Preclassic complexes.

Comments: This shape occurs in all Tzec samples in low frequencies.

Narrow-mouth Jar (with Short Neck)

Illustrations: Fig. 2.47; 7.13. See TR. 25A: fig. 143*a*8.

Identifying characteristics and sorting problems: The short neck makes it fairly easy to distinguish this jar from earlier and later shapes.

Base and body: The few complete examples have globular bodies of small size, but these examples, all from special deposits, may not be representative.

Neck-body juncture: Usually well marked; most frequently angular but sometimes rounded.

Orientation of neck: Medium outflare.

Neck: Ranges from medium outcurve to nearly straight.

Rim: Usually direct; a subclass has sharp to rounded eversion of the rim.

Lip: Rounded or pointed; some examples of the everted rim subclass have flattened lips.

Surface: Slipped on exterior and on interior of neck; remainder of interior unslipped. Care in finishing varies.

Types: Guitara Incised, Deprecio Incised.

Diameter: Range 10–30 cm; median 14 cm.

Neck Height: Range 1.2–4.0 cm; median 2.4 cm.

Lip diameter/neck height ratio: Range 3.6–11.7; median 5.8. The ratio shows a wide distribution with little central tendency; it seems unlikely that the ratio was of much significance to the users.

Shape class: 2, narrow-mouth jars.

Temporal distribution: Present in both the Eb and Tzec Complexes, but more common in the Chuen, Cauac, and Cimi Complexes.

Comments: This shape occurs in all Preclassic complexes.

SHAPE CLASS 4: LARGE CAPACITY BOWLS

Tecomate

Illustrations: Fig. 5.12, 5.25–26, 5.40; 7.7, 7.47.

Base: Unknown.

Orientation of side: Slightly to highly restricted orifice.

Side: Rounded, the degree of curvature varies from low to medium.

Rim: Direct; a few examples show a slight, rounded eversion.

Lip: Rounded.

Types: Joventud Red.

Diameter: Range 10–22 cm; median 18 cm. Other dimensions are unknown since there are no complete examples in the collections. The curvature of the side suggests that tecomates were usually of large size.

Shape class: 4, large-capacity bowl.

Identifying characteristics and sorting problems: The restricted orifice, low curvature of wall and unslipped interior were used as diagnostics for sorting. There are some problems of overlap with small round-side bowls with restricted orifice.

Temporal distribution: This shape occurs rarely in the Tzec Complex and may be a hold over from the preceding Eb Complex.

SHAPE CLASS 5: MEDIUM DIAMETER BOWLS AND DISHES

Slightly Incurving to Round-side Bowl

Illustrations: Fig. 2.31–32, 3.45, 3.48; 4.31, 4.33; 5.13, 5.15, 5.32–33; 7.8, 7.51. See TR. 25A: fig. 117*g–i*.

Identifying Characteristics and Sorting Problems: This shape is distinguished by its incurved side and most examples can be sorted without difficulty. There is an overlap in size range between some examples of the small slightly incurving to round-side bowl with the two shapes differentiated by size and wall thickness.

Base: Usually flat.

Side: Rounded, low to medium curvature.

Rim: Direct.

Lip: Rounded, pointed.

Surface: Well-finished interior and exterior.

Types: Joventud Red and Chunhinta Black.

Diameter: Range 28.0–30.0 cm.

Height: Range 6.0–8.5 cm.

Diameter/height ratio: Range 3.3–4.2.

Shape class: 5, medium-diameter dishes.

Temporal distribution: Round-side dishes occur in all ceramic complexes, but are most frequent in the subsequent Chuen Complex.

Comments: This basic Preclassic shape is not as common in the Tzec Complex samples, as in the later Chuen Complex.

Outflaring to Outcurving-sided Bowl or Dish

Illustrations: Fig. 2.33–34, 2.38, 2.46, 2.49; 3.36, 3.40–44, 3.46–48, 3.50–55; 4.1, 4.4–9, 4.11, 4.16–17, 4.25–26, 4.29, 4.34–36, 4.42; 5.27–29, 5.31, 5.34; 6.26–27, 6.30–33; 7.26, 7.28–29.

Identifying characteristics and sorting problems: Small sherds that show straight, outflaring sides could have belonged to any of a number of different shapes. Consequently, counted in this category are only examples that show a complete section to the base or that are long enough in preserved section to make it unlikely that they could have deviated from a simple shape.

Base: Flat; occasional examples that are slightly concave.

Orientation of side: Outflaring or outcurving

Side: Straight.

Rim: Direct or everted.

Lip: Rounded; occasionally thickened or bolstered on the exterior.

Surface: Slipped both inside and out.

Types: Almost entirely Joventud Red, but other monochrome types such as Chunhinta Black and Baclam Red-orange also represented in small numbers.

Diameter: Range 18–33 cm; median 22 cm. The size range places this shape between small and medium diameter bowls and dishes, however the majority are of medium size.

Height: range 4.0–6.4 cm.

Diameter/height ratio: range 3.2–5.4.

Shape class: 5, medium diameter bowls and dishes.

Temporal distribution: Occurs throughout the Tzec Complex.

SHAPE CLASS 6: SMALL DIAMETER BOWLS AND DISHES

Slightly Incurving to Round-side Bowl

Illustrations: Fig. 2.27, 2.51–54; 4.37–38; 5.18, 5.24, 5.37, 5.42, 5.44; 7.19, 7.38–46, 7.49, 7.54–55.

Identifying characteristics and sorting problems: In sorting, this shape was separated from the medium size bowls based on rim diameter and vessel thickness.

Base: Flat in the few examples that show complete sections.

Side: Rounded; usually high curvature.

Rim: Direct.

Lip: Usually rounded.

Surface: Well-finished both inside and out. This was a favorite form for incised decoration, which invariably occurs on the exterior, usually as a line or lines on the upper part of the vessel.

Types: Occurs in low frequencies for all monochrome slipped types.

Diameter: 20 cm.

Height: 8 cm.

Diameter/Height Ratio: 2.0.

Shape class: 6, small-diameter bowls and dishes.

Temporal distribution: Small round-side bowls occur in all Tzec samples, in variable, but generally low, frequencies.

Cuspidor

Illustrations: Fig. 4.15, 4.30, 4.32, 4.39; 5.39; 7.1–2. See TR. 25A: fig. 142*d*5.

Identifying characteristics and sorting problems: When present, the break between upper and lower sections of the vessel is a clear diagnostic. On sherds that do not include the break, the position and kind of decoration on the exterior are useful diagnostics. Originally Culbert (TR. 25A) described two additional vessel shapes, the interior-slipped jar and semi-cuspidor, both of which fall within the range and description of cuspidors and have been included in this shape in the current work. Culbert (TR. 25A) also identified what he thought was a vertical-side vessel, with incising or chamfering, however, none of the examples were complete rim to base profiles, and they all appear to be the upper wall sections of cuspidors.

Base: Small flat or concave section at base.

Orientation of side: Upper section, medium-to-wide outflare; lower section, restricted.

Side: Upper section, nearly straight to medium outcurve; lower section, rounded.

Break between sections: The break between sections is usually marked by a line on the interior where the upper section overhangs the lower. On the exterior, the break ranges from a rounded recurve to angular.

Rim: Direct.

Lip: Rounded or pointed.

Surface: Well finished both inside and out.

Decoration: The area above the break in curvature on the exterior of the vessel is used as a design field. On many examples, this field is bordered chamfering or incising to make it stand out. Undecorated examples are rare.

Types: Guitara Incised, Amil Chamfered, Ahmax Chamfered.

Diameter: Range 12–32 cm; median 20 cm. The size range places this shape between small and medium diameter bowls and dishes, however the majority are of small size.

Height: Range 8.6–13.5 cm; median 11.0 cm.

Diameter/height ratio: Range 1.6–2.3.

Shape class: 6, small-diameter bowls and dishes.

Temporal distribution: Tzec and Chuen Complexes.

SHAPE CLASS 8: MEDIUM DISHES AND PLATES

Outflaring to Slightly Outcurving-side Plate

Illustrations: Fig. 2.33; 3.39, 3.45, 3.49; 4.10; 5.14; 6.37–57; 7.53.

Identifying characteristics and sorting problems: The flat lip is the sole criterion that separates this shape from similar shapes without flat lips. Usually, the lips are clearly flat and present no problems in sorting. The flat lip was used as a criterion to separate this shape from others that are very similar in general conformation because it is easy to distinguish. In dimensions, this shape seems to be identical to the outcurving-side dish or plate, and shares with that form the lack of a central size-shape tendency.

There are problems in distinguishing some examples from others in the flat-lip dish category and other examples from straight-side dishes.

Base: Flat.

Side: Outflaring to medium outcurve.

Rim: Direct; occasionally the rim accentuates the outcurve of the side.

Lip: Rounded, pointed, or flattened; sometimes takes beveled or semi-beveled form. The lip is usually thicker than the rest of the wall.

Surface: Slipped on both interior and exterior; care of finish varies; incising occurs occasionally on the exterior wall.

Types: Joventud Red, Chunhinta Black, Baclam Red-orange.

Diameter: Range 16–58 cm; median 30 cm.

Height: Range 3.8–11.1 cm; height measurements show a wide scatter without much tendency to cluster.

Diameter/height ratio: Range 3.2–6.9. In both height measurements and in D/H ratio there is wide scatter with little central tendency. It is possible that earlier examples tend to fall within the lower end of the scatter, while later examples, tend to have higher ratios.

Shape class: 8, medium dishes and plates.

Temporal distribution: Begins in the Eb Complex and continues into the Tzec Complex.

Comments: The measurements suggest that this shape is not a well-defined unit in terms of size or basic dimensions. It is likely that the vessels included in this class may have served several different functions.

Widely-everted Rim Plate

Illustrations: Fig. 2.35; 4.14,18.

Identifying characteristics and sorting problems: No other shape in the Tikal sequence duplicates this particular rim treatment.

Base: Flat.

Orientation of side: Medium to wide outflare.

Side: Straight.

Rim: Widely everted, usually to horizontal; the rim section is broad.

Lip: Usually rounded.

Surface: Slipped on interior; carelessly finished, sometimes unslipped on exterior. The upper surface of the everted rim is almost invariably marked by one or two grooves; pattern incising on the rim also occurs.

Types: Common on all monochrome incised types as well as Boolim Red-on-cream and Boo Composite.

Diameter: Range 20–38 cm.; median 28cm. There is a wide variation in size of this shape and it overlaps both medium size and large size plates in diameter, however, most examples fall within the medium shape class.

Height: 5.6–6.2 cm.

Diameter/height ratio: 4.2–5.0.

Shape class: 8, medium dishes and plates.

Temporal distribution: Begins in the Eb Complex and continues into the Tzec Complex.

Comments: Since this shape is so distinctive and is completely confined to Eb and Tzec, it makes an excellent temporal marker for these two complexes.

SHAPE CLASS 9: LARGE PLATES

Outflaring to Slightly Outcurving-side Plate

Illustrations: Fig. 5.38; 6.36; 7.26, 7.35.

Identifying characteristics and sorting problems: This shape is distinguished from the medium sized example only on the basis of size and proportion, and in the smaller examples overlaps in size.

Base: Flat or slightly concave.

Orientation of side: Medium outflare to outcurve.

Side: Outcurved.

Rim: Direct.

Lip: Usually rounded and rather thick; sometimes rounded bevel.

Surface: Well finished on all surfaces except exterior base.

Types: Joventud Red predominates; and Chunhinta Black are fairly common. There are two unusual examples of a Deprecio Incised and Boo Composite (See TR. 25A: fig. 143a1–2) from PD. 108 that are rounded to a slightly concave base, although the upper wall orientation is outcurving.

Diameter: Range 28–42 cm; median 34 cm.

Height: Range 4.6–6.8 cm.

Diameter/height ratio: Range 5.4–6.2.

Shape class: 9, large plates.

Temporal distribution: Begins in the Eb Complex and continues into the Tzec Complex.

Widely Everted-rim Plate

Illustrations: Fig. 2.1, 2.40–41, 2.43–44; 5.30; 7.22, 7.24–25.

Identifying characteristics and sorting problems: This is the only shape that is incised on the interior lip; consequently, identification is easy even from small sherds. No other shape in the Tikal sequence duplicates this particular rim treatment. It is differentiated from the medium size plate solely on the basis of size and proportions although there is some overlap.

Base: Flat or slightly concave.

Orientation of side: Medium outflare to outcurve.

Side: Usually medium outcurve.

Rim: Mostly sharply everted; some examples are a more rounded eversion.

Lip: Usually thickened and beveled to give flat surface; some rounded.

Surface: Well finished on all surfaces except exterior base.

Decoration: Incised lines on interior lip surface.

Types: Mostly Boo Composite and Guitara Incised; rare examples of Deprecio Incised.

Diameter: Range 24–50 cm; median 38 cm.

Height: Range 3.8–7.2 cm; median 5.2 cm.

Diameter/Height ratio: Range 6.0–10.0; median 7.2.

Shape class: 9, large plates.

Temporal distribution: Very common in the Tzec Complex.

Tzec Shapes: Chronological Change

Almost all Eb shapes continue into Tzec, and only two new shapes of minor importance (cuspidors and large plates) are introduced in the Tzec Complex. When the frequency distributions of shape classes and shapes are taken into account, the two complexes are very different. In terms of shape classes, the very high frequency of plates and the low frequencies of both large- and medium-size bowls make the Tzec Complex unique among Tikal complexes (see Table 3.5). In addition, many specific shapes show large frequency changes between the Eb and Tzec Complexes (Table 3.6).

Shape class 1 (wide-mouth jars) is dominated in the Tzec Complex by the thin-lip jar, a characteristic and short-lived shape that rarely occurs in other complexes. Thin-lip jars occur in Tzec samples in frequencies ranging from 11% to 20% of rim sherds. The wide-mouth jar with short neck, a general Preclassic shape, has lower frequencies (1% to 9%) in Tzec samples than in any other Preclassic complex.

The two narrow-mouth jar shapes (shape class 2) occur with low but steady frequencies in all Tzec samples and show no trend of change from the Eb Complex. Tecomates (shape class 4) occur in all Tzec samples, but their scarcity continues a trend of decline that continues into the Late Preclassic. Medium-diameter dishes (shape class 5) continue in the same low frequencies as in Eb before beginning an abrupt increase in the Chuen Complex.

The overall total for shape class 6 (small-diameter bowls and dishes) declines markedly between the Eb and Tzec Complexes, however, it is marked by the appearance of the cuspidor shape in Tzec. The cuspidor, a diagnostic shape for the Tzec Complex that continues in the Chuen Complex, occurs in frequencies ranging from 8% to 13% except in the uppermost Tzec level where its frequency declines to 3%.

Medium and large plates (shape classes 8 and 9) show very distinctive changes in frequency between the Eb and Tzec Complexes. The widely everted-rim plate, undoubtedly the single most characteristic Tzec shape, occurs in frequencies between 24% and 26%, higher than in the preceding Eb Complex as well as in the succeeding Chuen Complex samples. In summary, three shapes are highly diagnostic of the Tzec Complex: the thin-lip jar, the cuspidor, and the widely everted rim plate (especially in larger sizes than in the Eb Complex). All three are common in Tzec samples and rare or absent in later complexes.

Although four levels of Tzec ceramics were metrically separated in Tzec-Chuen Location 1, they demonstrate little internal change and most variations between levels seem random. The best conclusion is that the Tzec levels in Tzec-Chuen Location 1 are a homogeneous sample that probably represents deposition within a short period of time.

TABLE 3.5
Shape Dimensions of the Tzec Complex

Shape Class and Shape	Median Diameter or Range (cm)	Median Height or Range (cm) (Neck Height for Jars)	Median Diameter/ Height Ratio or Range (cm)
1. Wide-mouth Jar (with Short Neck)	20.0	2.8	7.4
1. Wide-mouth Jar (with Thin Lip)	21.0	2.8	7.3
2. Narrow-mouth Jar (with Medium Neck)	12.0	4.0	2.6
2. Narrow-mouth Jar (with Short Neck)	14.0	2.4	5.8
4. Tecomate	18.0	—	—
5. Slightly Incurving to Round-side Bowl	28.0–30.0	6.0–8.5	3.3–4.2
5. Outflaring to Outcurving-side Bowl or Dish	22.0	4.0–6.4	3.2–5.4
6. Slightly Incurving to Round-side Bowl	20.0	8.0	2.0
6. Cuspidor	20.0	11.0	1.6–2.3
8. Outflaring to Slightly Outcurving-side Plate	30.0	3.8–11.1	3.2–6.9
8. Widely Everted-rim Dish or Plate	28.0	5.6–6.2	4.2–5.0
9. Outflaring to Slightly Outcurving-side Plate	34.0	4.6–6.8	5.4–6.2
9. Widely Everted-rim Plate	38.0	5.2	7.2

TABLE 3.6
Shape Frequencies of the Tzec Complex

Shape Class and Shape	100–120cm %	120–140cm %	140–160cm %	160–180cm %
1. Wide-mouth Jar (with Short Neck)	9.3	3.6	2.2	0.5
1. Wide-mouth Jar (with Thin Lip)	12.6	12.3	20.1	10.9
2. Narrow-mouth Jar (with Medium Neck)	1.3	4.1	3.4	2.0
2. Narrow-mouth Jar (with Short Neck)	4.0	2.1	1.4	5.5
4. Tecomate	0.7	0.5	1.4	2.0
5. Medium Bowls and Dishes (Includes both Slightly Incurving to Round-side Bowls and Outflaring to Slightly Outcurving-side Bowls and Dishes)	2.6	—	0.7	1.5
6. Slightly Incurving to Round-side Bowl	6.0	1.5	0.7	2.5
6. Cuspidor	5.9	11.8	12.8	17.9
8. Medium Plates (Includes both Outflaring to Slightly Outcurving-side Plates and Widely Everted-rim Plates)	13.2	19.0	8.3	18.4
9. Large Plates (Includes both Outflaring to Slightly Outcurving-side Plates and Widely Everted-Rim Plates)	25.8	23.6	24.3	26.4
Eb Complex Types/Shapes	3.3	2.0	0.7	2.0
Unidentified Rims	15.3	19.5	24.0	10.4
TOTAL RIM SHERDS	151	195	148	201

Tzec Shapes: Social Dimension

In the absence of multiple samples from a variety of archaeological contexts, inferences about the use of vessels during the Tzec Complex must be drawn from the nature of functional classes in the one location represented and comparison with samples from the Eb Complex. The assignment of a residential use of Tzec-Chuen Location 1 seems sound, but the ceramic assemblage is a poor fit for the vessel mix that one might expect from domestic activities. The scarcity of large storage vessels, the relatively low frequency of wide-mouth jars, and the abundance of dishes and plates (which are uncommon in most residential contexts at Tikal) deviate from other domestic contexts.

These results raise the question of whether the collections from Tzec-Chuen Location 1 may represent some special activity rather than those associated with residence. Comparative evidence from other sites, however, suggests that a predominance of dishes and plates at the expense of deeper bowl shapes is characteristic of other complexes in the Maya Lowlands in this time range. At Uaxactun, dishes and plates comprise 57% of the vessels in the Mamom phase sample (calculations based on Smith's [1955] classification and data). Although quantitative data for vessel shapes are not given in the Altar de Sacrificios ceramic report, Adams (1971) indicates that dishes and plates are very common in the Xe and San Felix complexes and give way to bowls and dishes in the Plancha Complex. As at Tikal, definition of the complexes at these sites is based on samples from only a few locations and one might entertain the thought that the same specialized activities happened to be sampled at all three sites. Such a conclusion seems to stretch the laws of probability and it is more likely that the shape-class distributions, peculiar though they may be, reflect general ceramic usage in the Maya Lowlands during the Mamom Horizon. The results are a useful reminder that pottery vessels are only a part of container assemblages. Gourds, baskets, and wooden containers are all functional equivalents of ceramics and the balance between the various materials chosen for vessels can vary in response to changing economic, aesthetic, or stylistic preferences. It is safe to conclude that during the early ceramic horizons in the Maya Lowlands extensive use was made of perishable materials for the manufacture of containers, especially large-capacity containers for the storage of dry materials.

Special Deposits of the Tzec Complex

Burials of the Tzec Complex

A single special deposit, classified as a burial (Bu. 158) was dated originally to the Tzec Complex (TR. 20A, 25A), however based on the ceramics it is better described as transitional between Tzec and Chuen, at the Mamom/Chicanel divide (Table 3.7). The burial contained three vessels and was encountered in the excavation of the platform that supports Str. 5F-17 and 5F-18, a small structure group that is residential. Two are partial vessels typed as Ahchab Red-on-buff (TR. 25A), which is an Early Chuen type. The first is a cuspidor, and the second is a plate, however, they overlap as well with examples of Boo Composite. The third vessel is a Chunhinta Black: Maach Variety outcurving-side dish from the Tzec Complex.

Problematical Deposits of the Tzec Complex

Only three special deposits classified as problematical were originally defined as containing Tzec Complex ceramics (Table 3.8). One (PD. 108) was encountered in the excavation of the platform that

TABLE 3.7
Burials of the Tzec Complex

Burial No.	Op.SubOp./Lot	Location Gp. Str.	Structure Group Type	TR. 25A Illustration	TR.	Culbert and Kosakowsky Types	Culbert (1993) Types	Ceramic Complex
158	71F/50	Gp. 5F-1 Platform Str. 5F-17, -18	Small Structure Group	2a1	20A	Ahchab Red-on-buff	Ahchab Red-on-buff	Early Chuen
				2a2		Ahchab Red-on-buff	Ahchab Red-on-buff	Early Chuen
				2a3		Chunhinta Black	Polvero Black	Tzec

TABLE 3.8
Problematical Deposits of the Tzec Complex

PD. No.	Op.SubOp./Lot	Location	Structure Group Type	TR. 25A Illustration	TR.	Estimated No. of Vessels	Culbert (1993) Types	Culbert and Kosakowsky Types	Ceramic Complex
1	27B/4, 7–9	Gp. 5G-1 Chultun 5G-15	Uncertain in Eb, Intermediate Structure Group (residential) later	116–121	21	48	See Table 2.8	See Table 2.8	Eb/ Tzec
108	71F/56,57	Gp. 5F-1 In quarry pit near Str. 5F-17, -18	Small Structure Group	142d1	20A	9–14	Laguna Verde Incised: Design Incised Variety	Laguna Verde Incised: Design Incised Variety	Chuen
				142d2			Laguna Verde Incised: Design Incised Variety	Laguna Verde Incised: Design Incised Variety	Chuen
				142d3			Laguna Verde Incised: Simple Incised Variety	Laguna Verde Incised: Simple Incised Variety	Chuen
				142d4			Ahchab Red-on-Buff	Ahchab Red-on-Buff	Early Chuen
				142d5			Amil Chamfered	Amil Chamfered	Tzec
				142d6			Polvero Black	Chunhinta Black	Tzec
				143a1			Polvero Black	Deprecio Incised	Tzec
				143a2			Boo Incised Dichrome	Boo Composite	Tzec
				143a3			Boo Incised Dichrome	Boo Composite	Tzec
				143a4			Boo Incised Dichrome	Boo Composite	Tzec
				143a5			Boo Incised Dichrome	Boo Composite	Tzec
				143a6			Ahchab Red-on-Buff	Ahchab Red-on-Buff	Early Chuen
				143a7			Chunhinta Black	Chunhinta Black	Tzec
				143a8			Lechugal Incised	Deprecio Incised	Tzec
266	12P/144	Gp. 5D-2 Platform 5D4-10	Civic-ceremonial later	155e	14	1	Amil Chamfered	Amil Chamfered	Tzec
267	12P/145	Gp. 5D-2 Platform 5D4-10	Civic-ceremonial later	155f	14	1	Laguna Verde Incised: Simple Incised Variety	Laguna Verde Incised: Simple Incised Variety	Chuen

supports Str. 5F-17 and 5F-18 about 1 km E and slightly N of the Great Plaza. The other two problematical deposits (PD. 266 and 267) were located in the trench through the North Acropolis. Additionally, PD. 1, originally classified as pure Eb Complex (TR. 25A) is in fact a mix of Eb and Tzec ceramics and should be considered a Tzec problematical deposit (see Chapter 2).

PD. 108 included 14 vessels according to Culbert, illustrated in TR. 25A figures 142*d* and 143*a*. However, Haviland (TR. 20A:409) reports a discrepancy with the excavation notes, which recorded only 9 vessels and suggests that some of the vessels may come from the midden in which PD. 108 is found. Four were Boo Composite; three were Chunhinta Black (and Deprecio Incised); and one was Amil Chamfered, all pertaining to the Tzec Complex. Two are Ahchab Red-on-buff, which are Early Chuen, and four are Laguna Verde Incised from the Chuen Complex. There was a strong emphasis in PD. 108 on decorated types and vessels in the serving-vessel category, especially cuspidors and plates. These were the kinds of vessels favored for burials throughout the history of Tikal, but the exact nature of the problematical deposit cannot be determined. PD. 108 is dated to the late Tzec/early Chuen divide, based on the ceramic types and shapes, and should be considered an early Chuen deposit.

The other two problematical deposits originally described as pertaining to the Tzec Complex consisted of a single vessel each. PD. 266 contained a fragmentary Amil Chamfered cuspidor that dates to the Tzec Complex. PD. 267 included an eroded vessel that may be a Laguna Verde Incised: Simple-incised Variety bucket from the Chuen Complex and should be dated to the Chuen Complex based on typological comparisons. Both pots are decorated types and their likely function was serving vessels.

Chuen Ceramic Complex

Chuen Complex Collections

Introduction

The archaeological evidence for the Chuen Ceramic Complex is more complete than that for the Eb and Tzec Complexes. The Chuen samples represent increased contextual variety, a greater number of locations, more samples per location, and an increased total quantity of sherds. The Chuen samples also begin a series of stratigraphically related samples with excellent architectural control that continues to the end of the Preclassic. Across the site, the frequency of minor occurrences of Chuen ceramics either as pure lots is either too small for quantitative analysis or occurs as admixture with later material, but the frequency increases considerably over such Tzec Complex occurrences. A substantial population increase must be postulated for Chuen (Culbert et al. 1990), but nothing in the ceramics indicates the arrival of new populations from elsewhere.

Seven separate locations provided quantifiable samples of Chuen Complex ceramics (Table 4.1). The transition from the Tzec Complex to the Chuen Complex was demonstrated by midden stratigraphy at Tzec-Chuen Location 1, while a series of sequential levels within the North Acropolis (Chuen-Cimi Location 2) showed change within the complex and a transition to the succeeding Cauac Complex. Three of the Chuen locations are from civic-ceremonial contexts in the site center, as well as one from the area of a later Classic Period range structure

group, and the other three are in small groups at some distance from the site center. Four special deposits classified as burials and three classified as caches included ceramics that date to the Chuen Complex. Burials and caches came from the main civic-ceremonial center of Tikal, while six problematical deposits came from civic-ceremonial groups at the site center and one (with questionable dating) from a small structure group.

TZEC-CHUEN LOCATION 1

This location about 1 km east and slightly south of the Great Plaza, Gp. 5F-1 (see TR. 20A), is the platform that supports Str. 5F-17 and 18. It consists of a 30m^2 platform surmounted by structures. The only visible structures from surface indications are typical Late Classic housemounds, but excavation revealed a long sequence of construction and occupation extending back to the Tzec Complex. The most abundant ceramics at the location pertain to the Tzec and Chuen Complexes.

Excavation at Tzec-Chuen Location 1 revealed two low platforms that were not visible from surface contours, a hearth and the probable remains of a perishable kitchen structure. There were also a hearth and a small pit in bedrock entered by two stone-cut steps and a deep quarry hole excavated into bedrock. The small platforms and possible kitchen were used during Chuen and Cauac times, but there is no construction that can definitely be assigned an earlier Tzec date. Filling of the quarry pit with midden debris began during the Tzec Complex, suggesting considerable quarrying activity at a very early date.

TABLE 4.1 (part 1)
Locations of Chuen Complex Samples

Sample #	Op.Sub-Op./Lot	Structure Group and Structure Number	Structure Group Type	Total Sherds-Types	Total Sherds-Shapes	Comments	TR.
Location 1	71F	Group 5F-1 Platform supporting Str. 5F-17, -18	Small Structure Group				20A
Sample 1-1	71F/27, 47, 72, 83, 99, 101, 110, 152, 126, 150, 160			95	*	Quarry pit levels 40–60 cm.	
Sample 1-2	71F/104, 114, 124, 136			195	53*	*Combined sample from Sample 1-1 and 1-2 for shape analysis. Quarry pit levels 60–80 cm.	
Sample 1-3	71F/105, 115, 137			352	43	Lowest levels of quarry pit 80–100 cm.	
Sample 1-4	Unknown lots			—	77	Small pit cut into bedrock	
Sample 1-5	Unknown lots			—	106	Combined sample	
Sample 1-6	Unknown lots			—	84	From above floor of earliest construction phase; probable fill from second phase of construction	
Location 2 (Samples 2-1 through 2-3 are Cimi; Samples 2-4 through 2-6 are Cauac)	12P	Group 5D-2 North Acropolis Platform 5D-4-8th, -9th, -10th	Civic-Ceremonial				14
Sample 2-7	12P/101, 102, 104, 105, 107, 108, 117, 122, 126, 130, 133, 157, 158, 163, 164, 165, 166, 167, 168, 169, 171, 172, 173, 175			104	—	Sample sealed by the 14th acropolis floor	
Sample 2-8				454	55	Sample from between the 16th and 17th acropolis floors	

TABLE 4.1 (part 2)
Locations of Chuen Complex Samples

Sample #	Op.Sub-Op./Lot	Structure Group and Structure Number	Structure Group Type	Total Sherds-Types	Total Sherds-Shapes	Comments	TR.
Sample 2-9				962	101	Sample from between the 17th and 18th acropolis floors	
Sample 2-10				1044	329	Combined sample from between the 18th and the 19th acropolis floors	
Sample 2-11				1309	387	Sample sealed by the 20th acropolis floor	
Location 3		Group 5D-9 Seven Temples Platform between Str. 5D-87 and -96	Civic-Ceremonial				23C, 23D
Sample 3-1	64A/3, 64B/5, 6, 64C/6,7, 64D/5–7, 64E/6,7, 64F/6–8, 64G/7,8, 64H/6, 64I/5, 64N/4, 64P/6,7, 64S/4,6, 64T/1, 64U/5,7			547	103	Combined sample from 5 test pits 80–140 cm. below the surface	
Sample 3-2	64B/7,8, 64C/8,9, 64D/8, 64E/8,10, 64F/9–11, 64G/9,10, 64H/8, 64I/8, 64K/10, 64L/8,10			739	152	Combined sample from 5 test pits 140–200 cm. below the surface	
Sample 3-3	64D/10,11,13, 64E/11–13, 64F/12,13, 64R/9,11, 64S/12,13			368	149	Combined sample from 5 test pits 200–260 cm. below the surface	
Sample 3-4	64D/14–17, 64E/14,15, 64R/12–14, 64S/14.			452	136	Combined sample from 4 test pits 260–320 cm. below the surface	
Sample 3-5	64E/17–19, 64R/14, 15, 64S/18			532	158	Combined sample from 4 test pits 320–380 cm. below the surface	
Sample 3-6	64S/20–22			495	72	Combined sample from 2 test pits 380–440 cm. below the surface	

TABLE 4.1 (part 3)
Locations of Chuen Complex Samples

Sample #	Op.Sub-Op./Lot	Structure Group and Structure Number	Structure Group Type	Total Sherds-Types	Total Sherds-Shapes	Comments	TR.
Location 4		Group 6E-1	Small Structure Group				20A
Sample 4-1	68I/46,47	Platform 6E-1 supporting Str. 6E-25, -26		—	67	Sample sealed by the 8th floor from the top of the platform	
Location 5		Group 5D-10	Range Structure Group				17
Sample 5-1	66T/1–14	Chultun 5D-2 at southern edge of West Plaza		329	92	Combined sample from entire chultun	
Location 6		Group 5D-2	Civic-Ceremonial				15[†]
Sample 6-1	79C/42–46	Platform 5D-1- 4th		64	187	Combined sample from beneath floors of Great Plaza at the base of Str. 5D-119	
Location 7		Group 2F-1	Small Structure Group				
Sample 7-1	118E/2,4,5,6,7,10,11,12,13, 20,22, 23,24,25	Str. 2F-32 and –33		—	77	Combined sample from all lots	20A
TOTAL SHERDS				8041	2375		

[†] Forthcoming

The best ceramic samples came from the quarry pit, which was large enough to permit excavation of five adjacent stratigraphic columns. Since there were no easily definable natural strata, arbitrary 20 cm levels were used in the excavation. Continuous occupation during the time of the Tzec and Chuen Complexes resulted in gradual accumulation of a deep midden deposit. The bottom four levels (from 1.0 to 1.8 m below the present ground surface) were Tzec, while the three levels immediately above them were of Chuen date. The top two levels contained mixed material that was not analyzed quantitatively.

Chuen ceramics were more widely distributed at the location than Tzec ceramics. Three levels in the filled quarry pit document the transition between the two complexes. In addition, three Chuen samples were recovered from small structures at the location. The small size of the structures and the presence of a hearth and possible remains of a pole-and-thatch kitchen structure in the center of the group suggest that the group was a Preclassic counterpart of later small structure groups.

Chuen Sample 1-1: This sample included all sherds from the 40 to 60 cm level of five contiguous stratigraphic columns in the quarry pit. Overlying levels in the quarry pit were mixed and were not included in the analysis. Counts included 95 sherds counted for types.

Chuen Sample 1-2: This sample was the summation of sherds from the 60 to 80 cm levels of the stratigraphic columns in the quarry pit. Counts included 195 sherds counted for types. Because Chuen Samples 1-1 and 1-2 did not individually provide sufficient rim sherds for a shape analysis, a combined sample of 53 rim sherds from the two samples was used in the vessel shape analysis instead.

Chuen Sample 1-3: This sample came from the 80 to 100 cm level, the lowest of the Chuen Complex levels in the quarry pit midden. Counts included 352 sherds counted for types and 43 rims counted for shapes.

Chuen Sample 1-4: This sample was obtained from the fill of a small round pit that had been cut into bedrock just outside of the structures. The function of the pit is uncertain, but because it had two rock-cut steps at the entrance it must have been entered and used regularly. Counts included 77 rims counted for shapes.

Chuen Sample 1-5: This sample combined 10 small lots recovered from excavations within and to the north of the structures. Some of the lots were probably fill from the structures, while others were debris from the area near the hypothesized kitchen structure. Soil was shallow throughout the area and artifacts were not abundant. Counts included 106 rims counted for shapes.

Chuen Sample 1-6: Sherds in this sample were obtained from the excavation of a small platform at the western edge of the group about 10 m from the area of the samples previously described. Most of the material lay above the floor of the earliest construction stage and represented fill of the second stage of construction. The platform was small and seems likely to have been the base for residences. Counts included 84 rims counted for shapes.

CHUEN-CIMI LOCATION 2

Chuen-Cimi Location 2 included all Preclassic floors and architecture encountered in the trench that sectioned the North Acropolis, Gp. 5D-2, Platform 5D-4 (see TR. 14). Control of architectural stratigraphy was superb and construction levels were sealed so that no material later than the date of sealing could have been intruded into the deposits. Consequently, there was a splendid sequence of "points of introduction" in which the first appearances of ceramic features could be fitted into the sequence of Acropolis floors. Most of the material recovered was structural fill, which included both ceramics contemporaneous with construction and material derived from the destruction of earlier units. The "upwelling" of early sherds blurred quantitative patterns of change.

The numbering sequence for acropolis floors starts with the latest (uppermost) and gets larger as they get earlier (TR. 14). The eight earliest floors of the North Acropolis series were of Chuen date, with samples sealed by five of the floors large enough for quantitative analysis. The quantity of material for a number of lots in Chuen-Cimi Location 2 was very large. These lots were sampled rather than counted completely; the samples were chosen by picking bags of sherds at random, although not by a statistically random procedure.

The earliest structures encountered in the North Acropolis trench were civic-ceremonial, as were all later buildings at the location. The most readily available source of fill material would almost certainly have been refuse from the ceremonial precinct and any elite residences that may have been associated with it. Samples 2-1 through 2-6 did not contain Chuen ceramics and dated to later Cauac and Cimi times.

Chuen Sample 2-7: This sample, the uppermost Chuen Complex sample from the North Acropolis, was sealed by the 14th Acropolis floor. It was a small sample that contained 104 sherds that could be analyzed for type, but too few rims for quantitative analysis.

Chuen Sample 2-8: This sample came from between the 16th and 17th floors of the North Acropolis (there were too few sherds between the 15th and 16th floors for analysis). Counts included 454 sherds for types and 55 rims for shapes.

Chuen Sample 2-9: This sample, from between the 17th and 18th floors, was somewhat larger than those just described. Counts included 962 sherds counted for types and 101 rims counted for shapes.

Chuen Sample 2-10: Material between the 18th and 19th acropolis floors provided too few sherds for analysis, so this sample was obtained from deposits below the 19th and above the 20th floors. A total of 329 rim sherds for shape counts were obtained by combining sherds from eleven lots, two of which were large enough for individual quantification. Type counts were made on 1,044 sherds from the two largest lots.

Chuen Sample 2-11: This sample, the earliest quantifiable one from Chuen-Cimi Location 2, was sealed by the 20th floor from the top of the North Acropolis. Twenty lots were included in the sample; four lots were large enough for separate shape quantification and six were large enough for type quantification. Consequently, there was a good check on consistency in content within the total sample. In all, 1,309 sherds were counted for types and 387 rims counted for shapes.

CHUEN LOCATION 3

Chuen Location 3 was a very deep deposit of Preclassic fill beneath the floors of Gp. 5D-9, the Seven Temples Platform. Located by a test pit during the spring of 1963, the deposit was sampled later that year by a series of test pits that began on the east side of the plaza in front of Str. 5D-96 and extended nearly to Str. 5D-87 on the opposite side of the plaza. The lowest of a series of plaza floors occurred at 80 cm below the ground surface, just above the Preclassic deposit, and the filling operation that the deposit represents may have been done to establish the level for the floor. The uppermost sample of the six into which the material from Chuen Location 3 was divided began just below the floor, while the deepest samples reach a depth of 440 cm below the present ground surface.

Hopes that the deep and abundant Preclassic refuse would prove to have been a gradual accumulation were disappointed, for the samples were homogeneous throughout and, although predominately Chuen, a few sherds of the Cauac Complex occurred even in the lowest level. It seems likely that a major filling operation, comparable to the largest of such enterprises evident in the North Acropolis trench, took place in the Seven Temples Plaza at some time during the Cauac Complex, using a fill source that provided an almost pure deposit of Chuen Complex material.

The general area of Chuen Location 3 seems to have been an important focal point for Preclassic ceremonialism at Tikal, because it contains both large Preclassic deposits and several important standing structures of Preclassic and Early Classic date. Operating on the same assumption used in connection with North Acropolis fill samples, the most likely source of Chuen Location 3 deposits would have been refuse from civic-ceremonial activities.

Chuen Sample 3-1: This is a combined sample of sherds from five test pits, from 80 to 140 cm levels below the present ground surface. Because the floors of the plaza were almost exactly parallel to the ground surface, measurements continued to be made from ground surface rather than from the plaza floor that sealed the Preclassic deposits. Counts included 547 sherds counted for types and 103 rims counted for shapes.

Chuen Sample 3-2: This sample came from the 140 to 200 cm level in all test pits in the Seven Temples Plaza. Counts included 739 sherds counted for types and 152 rims counted for shapes.

Chuen Sample 3-3: Sherds in this sample were from the 200 to 260 cm level in the test pits. Counts included 368 sherds counted for types and 149 rims counted for shapes.

Chuen Sample 3-4: At this stratigraphic depth, the test pit closest to Str. 5D-96 had encountered bedrock. Chuen Sample 3-4 consisted of all sherds from the 260 to 320 cm level in the remaining four test pits. Counts included 452 sherds counted for types and 136 rims counted for shapes.

Chuen Sample 3-5: This sample combined sherds from the 320 to 380 cm level in the four Seven Temples Plaza test pits that were still open. Counts included 532 sherds counted for type and 158 rims counted for shape.

Chuen Sample 3-6: The second and third test pits from Str. 5D-96 reached bedrock at the depths included in the previous sample. Consequently, this sample includes sherds from 380 to 440 cm level in the two test pits that were still producing cultural material. Counts included 495 sherds counted for types and 72 rims counted for shapes.

CHUEN LOCATION 4

Chuen Location 4 was the platform for Gp. 6E-1, a small structure group with a relatively high platform supporting Str. 6E-25 and 26 (see TR. 20A). The platform is located about 600 m southwest of the Great Plaza. Excavation in the platform revealed a complex series of construction and rebuilding operations that began in Chuen times and continued into the Late Classic. Although Chuen ceramics were widely distributed in the early levels of platform construction, only one pure sample of Chuen material large enough for quantitative analysis was obtained.

Chuen Sample 4-1: This sample from Gp. 6E-1 was sealed by the eighth floor from the top of the platform and was a construction of unknown function. Counts included 67 rims counted for shape. Type sherds were not counted.

CHUEN LOCATION 5

Chuen Location 5 was Ch. 5D-2 in Gp. 5D-10, about 35 m from the back of Temple II (see TR. 17). No Preclassic structures were encountered in the immediate vicinity of Ch. 5D-2.

Chuen Sample 5-1: Although a series of stratigraphic lots was separated during excavation, sherd quantities were too small for lots to be analyzed separately and contents of the entire chultun were combined into a single sample. Counts included 329 sherds counted for types and 92 rims counted for shapes.

CHUEN LOCATION 6

Chuen Location 6 was an excavation in Gp. 5D-2, beneath the floors of the Great Plaza, in Plat. 5D-1-4th, at the base of Str. 5D-119 (see TR. 15). A Preclassic deposit more than 1 m deep underlay the lowest plaza floor. Because sherds from a nearby location beneath the lowest Great Plaza floor pertained to the Cauac Complex, the floor seems to have been laid no earlier than Cauac times and it is uncertain whether the material in Chuen Sample 6-1 was debris that was redeposited when the floor was laid or an in situ Chuen deposit. The most likely source of the sample, based simply on its location so near the center of Tikal, was from civic-ceremonial activity.

Chuen Sample 6-1: The material from Chuen Location 6 was separated into six stratigraphically superimposed lots, but there was no significant difference between the small samples, which were combined into a single sample for analysis. Counts included 64 sherds counted for types and 187 rims counted for shapes.

CHUEN LOCATION 7

The excavation at this location, in the northeastern quadrant of Tikal 1.8 km from the Great Plaza, began as a test of seemingly vacant terrain near Ch. 2F-2 in Gp. 2F-1, a small structure group (see TR. 20A). Excavation revealed Str. 2F-32 and -33, low mounds not visible from the surface. Collections from the operation included a series of lots too small for individual analysis in which ceramics of the Chuen Complex predominated.

Chuen Sample 7-1: This sample was the summation of sherd counts from 14 small lots excavated in and around Str. 2F-32 and -33. Counts included 77 rims counted for shapes. Type sherds were not counted.

Pastes of the Chuen Complex

Chuen Paste Descriptions

COARSE-CARBONATE PASTE

Identifying characteristics: The large amounts of carbonate particles in Coarse-carbonate Paste are so unique that there is little danger of confusion with any other pastes. There is considerable variety in the paste color within and between complexes and examples of Coarse-carbonate Paste from all other complexes are indistinguishable.

Color: A broad range of colors often within single sherds marks the paste. The most common colors include various shades of brown and yellow (10YR 6/6 to 6/3; 5/8 to 5/3; 7.5YR 7/6, 6/6, 6/4; 5/6, 5/4, 4/4). A red variety includes shades of red to reddish yellow (10YR 5/8, 7.5YR 7/6 to 7.5YR 5/6).

Texture: Coarse.

Inclusions: Large amounts of carbonate particles of all size. The particles range from white to translucent and from powdery to soft crystalline.

Types: Striated types of all complexes, as well as most unstriated unslipped types. Vessels represented are almost entirely wide-mouth jars.

Temporal distribution: common in all complexes from Tzec through Eznab.

PRECLASSIC MONOCHROME PASTE

Identifying characteristics: The best identifying characteristic is a "fruitcake" appearance caused by the occurrence of inclusions of several different colors seen against a background paste color that varies from one part of a sherd to another.

Color: Most examples show reddish tones that range from light red (2.5YR 6/8) and red (2.5YR 5/8

to 4/6) to reddish yellow (5YR 6/8). Tan to brown tones are not uncommon, ranging from reddish yellow (7.5YR 6/6) to strong brown (7.5YR 5/6). Characteristic of the paste is color variation between the surface and core or between different sections of the same sherd.

Texture: Medium.

Inclusions: Inclusions are heavy for a paste used with slipped ceramic types. Translucent or gray carbonate particles are invariably present, as are shiny black particles. Reddish-orange particles of secondary clay are visible in many sherds but cannot be distinguished where the paste itself is red. White amorphous particles occur sporadically.

Types: Preclassic Monochrome Paste is the most common paste in both monochrome and dichrome types in the Chuen, Cauac, and Cimi Complexes.

Comments: Sherds classified within Preclassic Monochrome paste show a considerable amount of variation in all characteristics, but potential subgroups failed to show chronological or other significance.

RED-PARTICLES PASTE

Identifying characteristics: The presence of red and black particles in a light-colored paste.

Color: Usually yellow (10YR 6/6); ranges to strong brown (7.5YR 5/6) and reddish yellow (5YR 6/8).

Texture: Medium.

Inclusions: Medium amounts of fine to medium particles that include several different kinds of materials: (1) reddish particles that seem to be a second clay; (2) black shiny particles; (3) translucent crystalline carbonate particles; and (4) white amorphous particles. The multicolored effect of the different inclusions is quite striking in sherds with large quantities of inclusions.

Types: Common in the Joventud and Chunhinta ceramic groups in the Tzec Complex but continues on the Ahuacan Variety of Sierra Red and Ahchab Red-on-buff in the Chuen Complex.

Temporal distribution: Red-particles Paste is most common in Tzec but continues to appear in early Chuen samples.

Comments: Red-particles Paste is very distinctive in appearance and is quite different from Preclassic pastes of both earlier and later complexes.

Discussion

The degree of variability in Chuen pastes is not as low as might be inferred from the presence of only two common pastes (and the continuation of Red-particles Paste into early Chuen), because both Chuen pastes are broadly defined and show considerably more internal variation than the pastes of earlier complexes. Chuen Complex pastes mark a distinct break with traditions of earlier complexes. With the exception of the ubiquitous Coarse-carbonate Paste, most pastes that had characterized the Eb Complex had disappeared by Chuen, and the characteristic Red-particles Paste of the Tzec Complex appeared in only a few of the early Chuen samples. With Chuen, the almost universal use of carbonate inclusions and the relatively heavy amount of inclusions in all sherds were traditions that held until the end of the Tikal Preclassic.

Ceramic Types of the Chuen Complex

Introduction

The Chuen Ceramic Complex consists of the eight ceramic groups and eighteen types (composed of 23 varieties) listed in Table 4.2. Because the preceding Tzec Complex is characteristic of the Mamom Ceramic Sphere, Chuen is the first of the Tikal ceramic complexes that pertains unequivocally to the Chicanel Ceramic Sphere. With the Chuen Complex, Tikal ceramics entered a period of typological stability and the major types and their relative frequencies changed little through the remaining Preclassic complexes.

Monochrome types predominated during the time of the Chuen Complex. Sierra Red was the most frequent type in almost all collections, averaging about one-third of total sherds. Polvero Black

consistently accounted for 10 to 15% of the collections, and there were smaller amounts of Flor Cream, Baclam Red-orange, and Boxcay Brown. Unslipped types declined somewhat in importance from earlier complexes, although 10 to 20% of Sapote Striated and a low frequency of Achiotes Unslipped occurred in all samples. Decorated types also declined in frequency. Incised types were relatively rare during the Chuen Complex and Repasto Black-on-red—although a good horizon marker for the complex—occurred only in low frequencies. Mixed chronological fills included small frequencies of some Tzec types in later deposits (Table 4.3). Frequencies of Chuen ceramic types were calculated for only two locations, Gp. 5F-1 (small structure group) comprised of three sample locations (Loc 1-1, 1-2, and 1-3), and Gp. 5D-2 (civic-ceremonial), which includes five sample locations (Loc. 2-7, 2-8, 2-9, 2-10, and 2-11).

Chuen Type Descriptions

ACHIOTES CERAMIC GROUP

Achiotes Unslipped: Achiotes Variety

Established: Smith and Gifford (1966)

Group: Achiotes

Ware: Uaxactun Unslipped

Ceramic Complex: Chuen (continues into Cauac and Cimi)

Ceramic Sphere: Chicanel

Illustrations: Fig. 7.47, 7.69; 9.1–63; 13.20–22; 14.14.

Principal identifying attributes: Unslipped, only partially smoothed, surfaces that reflect highly variable paste colors on wide-mouth jars.

Identifying characteristics and sorting problems: Both surface and paste are quite characteristic and overlap little with other types.

Paste: Characterized by Coarse-carbonate Paste. Most examples are of the brown to gray regular va-

TABLE 4.2
Ceramic Groups and Types of the Chuen Complex

Culbert and Kosakowsky	Culbert (1993)
ACHIOTES CERAMIC GROUP	**ACHIOTES CERAMIC GROUP**
Achiotes Unslipped: Achiotes Variety	Achiotes Unslipped: Achiotes Variety
SAPOTE CERAMIC GROUP	**SAPOTE CERAMIC GROUP**
Sapote Striated: Sapote Variety	Sapote Striated: Sapote Variety
SIERRA CERAMIC GROUP	**SIERRA CERAMIC GROUP**
Sierra Red: Ahuacan Variety	*Tzec Complex Type*
Ahchab Red-on-buff: Ahchab Variety	*Tzec Complex Type*
Sierra Red: Sierra Variety	Sierra Red: Sierra Variety
Society Hall Red: Society Hall Variety	Society Hall Red: Society Hall Variety
Laguna Verde Incised: Simple-incised Variety	Laguna Verde Incised: Simple-incised Variety
Laguna Verde Incised: Design-incised Variety	Laguna Verde Incised: Design-incised Variety
Lagartos Punctated: Lagartos Variety	Lagartos Punctated: Lagartos Variety
Tzec Complex Type	Amil Chamfered: Amil Variety
Repasto Black-on-red: Repasto Variety	Repasto Black-on-red: Repasto Variety
Xcuican Incised-dichrome: Xcuican Variety	Xcuican Incised-dichrome: Xcuican Variety
POLVERO CERAMIC GROUP	**POLVERO CERAMIC GROUP**
Polvero Black: Polvero Variety	Polvero Black: Polvero Variety
Lechugal Incised: Simple-incised Variety	Lechugal Incised: Simple-incised Variety
Lechugal Incised: Design-incised Variety	Lechugal Incised: Design-incised Variety
Tzec Complex Type	Ahmax Chamfered: Ahmax Variety
BACLAM CERAMIC GROUP	**BACLAM CERAMIC GROUP**
Baclam Red-orange: Baclam Variety	Baclam Orange: Baclam Variety
Cay Incised: Simple-incised Variety	Cay Incised: Simple-incised Variety
Cay Incised: Design-incised Variety	Cay Incised: Design-incised Variety
BOXCAY CERAMIC GROUP	**BOXCAY CERAMIC GROUP**
Boxcay Brown: Boxcay Variety	Boxcay Brown: Boxcay Variety
Xtabcab Incised: Simple-incised Variety	Xtabcab Incised: Simple-incised Variety
Xtabcab Incised: Design-incised variety	Xtabcab Incised: Design-incised variety
FLOR CERAMIC GROUP	**FLOR CERAMIC GROUP**
Flor Cream: Flor Variety	Flor Cream: Flor Variety
Deleted	Flor Cream: Cozom Variety
Accordian Incised: Simple-Incised Variety	Accordian Incised: Simple-Incised Variety
XIK CERAMIC GROUP	**XIK CERAMIC GROUP**
Xik Double-slipped Orange: Xik Variety	Xik Double-slipped Orange: Xik Variety

TABLE 4.3
Ceramic Type Frequencies of the Chuen Complex

Ceramic Groups/Types	Location 1 Gp. 5F-1 Small Structure Group			Location 2 Gp. 5D-2 Civic-Ceremonial				
	Sample Loc. 1-1	Sample Loc. 1-2	Sample Loc. 1-3	Sample Loc. 2-11	Sample Loc. 2-10	Sample Loc. 2-9	Sample Loc. 2-8	Sample Loc. 2-7
	%	%	%	%	%	%	%	%
Achiotes Group	11.7	13.8	21.1	4.5	3.1	3.9	3.3	3.8
Sapote Group	21.3	20.0	11.4	10.1	18.0	18.9	13.2	12.5
Sierra Group	20.2	24.1	22.0	22.3	31.1	31.1	28.2	46.2
Society Hall Red: Society Hall Variety	0.0	0.0	0.0	0.6	1.8	0.3	1.0	0.0
Repasto Black-on-red: Repasto Variety	0.0	1.0	0.0	0.5	1.7	1.4	0.8	0.0
Polvero Group	0.0	0.5	1.5	13.9	14.3	15.3	10.0	15.4
Flor Group	1.1	1.0	1.8	1.4	0.1	1.3	2.4	0.9
Baclam Group	0.0	0.5	1.0	6.3	4.5	3.4	2.4	0.0
Boxcay Group	3.2	6.7	3.0	0.4	0.5	2.7	2.4	12.6
Unclassified and Rare Types	0.0	5.6	6.8	4.3	0.5	2.7	2.4	12.6
Tzec Types	8.5	7.5	11.2	0.0	0.0	0.0	0.0	0.0
Weathered	34.0	24.1	19.5	32.9	17.4	19.5	32.6	5.3
Number of Sherds	95	195	395	1309	1044	1063	509	104

riety of Coarse-carbonate Paste, but some are of the red variety.

Firing: Many examples are darkened completely, but less than one-quarter show separable dark cores. Cores showing two or more shades of paste color are common. About half of the sherds show fireclouding of surfaces.

Color: Highly variable, even on individual sherds. Light brown (7.5YR 6/4), strong brown (7.5YR 5/6), very pale brown (10YR 8/3), yellowish brown (10YR 5/4), and dark yellowish brown (10YR 4/4) all occur.

Surface finish and decoration: Most examples were carelessly finished and many sherds show smoothing marks and poor obliteration of coils; some examples are medium smooth.

Shapes: Almost entirely confined to the various

wide-mouth jar shapes: wide-mouth jar with short neck and very large-diameter jar.

Temporal distribution: Begins in the Tzec Complex. After the Tzec Complex, the type becomes rare and although there is still a fairly abundant sherd-sorting category for Achiotes Unslipped, it contains mostly jar necks that may be from vessels that were actually striated.

Comments: Following the lead established by Adams (1971) at Altar de Sacrificios, Achiotes Unslipped is used as a generalized unslipped category until the end of the Preclassic complexes. The characteristics of the type are identical to those of Sapote Striated except for the lack of striation. It seems unlikely that vessels of completely unstriated unslipped pottery were made in Chuen times, for almost all sherds sorted into this category are jar neck fragments that probably would have been Sapote Striated jars had larger sections been available. It should also be noted that the designation Paila Unslipped, used for Chicanel phase unslipped pottery at Uaxactun (Smith and Gifford 1966), has not been used at Tikal because there are no discernible differences between the preceding Mamom Tzec Complex, and Late Preclassic unslipped vessels.

Intersite comparisons: Achiotes Unslipped is used as the predominant unslipped type at Acanmul (Ball and Taschek 2015); Altar de Sacrificios (Adams 1971); Becan (Ball 1977); El Mirador (Forsyth 1989); El Perú/Waka' (Eppich 2011); Holmul (Callaghan 2008, 2016b); Nakbe (Forsyth 1993); the Petexbatun (Foias and Bishop 2013); and Seibal (Sabloff 1975). In Belize there is some variation noted from the Achiotes Ceramic Group and Paila Unslipped is used in its place at Barton Ramie; (Gifford 1976); Blue Creek (Kosakowsky and Lohse 2003); Chan (Kosakowsky 2012); and La Milpa (Sagebiel 2005). Paila Unslipped is also used at Uaxactun (Smith and Gifford 1966) for the Late Preclassic. Richardson Peak Unslipped is used at Cerros (Robertson 2016); Cuello (Kosakowsky 1987; Pring 1977); and Colha (Valdez 1987).

SAPOTE CERAMIC GROUP

Sapote Striated: Sapote Variety

Established: Smith and Gifford (1966)

Group: Sapote [It is included in the Achiotes Group elsewhere]

Ware: Uaxactun Unslipped

Ceramic Complex: Chuen (continues into Cauac and Cimi)

Ceramic Sphere: Chicanel

Illustrations: Fig. 7.9–10; 9.1–63; 13.1–19; 15.13. See TR. 25A: fig. 144*a*1.

Principal identifying attributes: Unslipped surfaces with closely spaced striations only on the bodies of wide-mouth jars, with the neck left unstriated.

Identifying characteristics and sorting problems: The type is quite characteristic. Sapote Stri-

ated may be separated from Cabcoh Striated on the basis of paste characteristics and the fact that striation in Cabcoh Striated continues onto the necks of the jars.

Paste: Coarse-carbonate Paste.

Firing: One-quarter to one-half of the sherds in individual lots have dark cores. Many sherds without dark cores have different paste color near the core than at the surface. Nearly half the sherds exhibit fireclouding of the surface.

Color: Highly variable in color, ranging from reddish tones (red, 10R 5/6, 2.5YR 5/6 to 4/8; light red, 2.5YR 6/6; reddish brown, 5YR 4/8) to brown (10YR 4/3, 5/3).

Surface finish and decoration: Striations are closely spaced, ranging from shallow to quite deep and from narrow to broad lines. Striations occur only on the bodies of jars.

Shapes: Almost entirely wide-mouth jars: widemouth jar with short neck and very large-diameter jar.

Temporal distribution: Becomes common in the earliest Chuen Complex samples and continues unchanged until the end of the Preclassic.

Comments: In initial sorting, a tentative separation was made between "thin-walled" and "regular" examples of Sapote Striated. Thin-walled examples are relatively thin (median 4 mm) and have fewer inclusions than the regular examples. Because there is a continuum between the ranges of the two potential varieties, the differences are not worth formalizing at even the varietal level. Thin-walled examples are most common in the Chuen Complex and decrease in frequency in later Preclassic complexes.

Intersite comparisons: Acanmul (Ball and Taschek 2015); Altar de Sacrificios (Adams 1971); Barton Ramie (Gifford 1976); Becan (Ball 1977); Blue Creek (Kosakowsky and Lohse 2003); Calakmul (Dominguez Carrasco 1994); Chan Chich (Valdez 1998, Valdez and Houk 2000); Cerros (Robertson-Freidel 1980); Colha (Valdez 1987); Cuello (Kosakowsky

1987); Holmul (Callaghan 2008; 2016b); El Pozito (Eppich 2000); El Mirador (Forsyth 1989); K'axob (Lopez Varela 1996); La Milpa (Sagebiel 2005); Naachtun (Walker and Reese-Taylor 2012); Nakbe (Forsyth 1993); Nohmul (Kosakowsky and Pring 2001); "Zapote" in the Petexbatun (Foias and Bishop 2013); Rio Azul (Adams 1999); Seibal (Sabloff 1975); Uaxactun (Smith and Gifford 1966); Yaxchilan (Lopez Varela 1989).

SIERRA CERAMIC GROUP

Sierra Red: Ahuacan Variety

Established: Type named by Smith and Gifford (1966). Originally named by Culbert (1993 [TR. 25A]) as a variety of Joventud Red. Type changed to Sierra Red by Kosakowsky (1983; 1987).

Group: Sierra

Ware: Paso Caballo Waxy

Ceramic Complex: Early Chuen

Ceramic Sphere: Chicanel

Illustrations: Fig. 8.3–4,6–8,11–13.

Identifying Attributes: Monochrome red-orange slip that is heavily crazed on a characteristic yellowish paste with red inclusions (Red-particles Paste).

Identifying characteristics and sorting problems: Paste, color, and the distinctive appearance, produced by heavy crazing make a characteristic combination. Originally identified as a variety of late Joventud Red in the Tzec Complex (TR. 25A), but it overlaps more with Sierra Red than Joventud Red, and is more appropriately a variety of Sierra Red.

Paste: Almost entirely Red-particles Paste. This yellowish paste with red particles is more commonly used in earlier complexes and marks this type as early Chuen.

Firing: Dark cores rare; fireclouding in one-fifth of the examples.

Slip: The surface was smoothed before the application of a slip of medium thickness. The slip tends to have a waxy feel, although waxiness is not so pronounced as in later varieties. The slip crazes badly and tends to erode easily.

Polish: Medium; the slip takes a polish well, but the effect is diminished by crazing and flaking.

Color: Slip color ranges farther toward red-orange than in most varieties of Sierra Red but does overlap with Sierra Variety. Standard color is red (2.5YR 5/8), with some examples at 10R 5/8 or even 7.5R 4/8. Lighter patches are reddish yellow (5YR 6/8). Streakiness of color is common.

Shapes: Composite silhouette vessels and outcurving-side bowls are most common. A number of other shapes occur with lower frequencies.

Temporal distribution: Begins and is most frequent in Early Chuen. This type and variety are transitional between Joventud Red and Sierra Red and, in fact, the surface color overlaps with both Joventud Red and Sierra Red at Tikal.

Intersite comparisons: At Cuello (Kosakowsky 1987), it is a variety of Sierra Red. It is likely that some transitional Mamom/Chicanel Reds are not sorted at other sites but would fit well within this variety.

Ahchab Red-on-buff: Ahchab Variety

Established: Culbert (1993 [TR. 25A]), originally as a Joventud Group type. Placed in the Sierra Group by Kosakowsky (1983; 1987).

Group: Sierra

Ware: Paso Caballo Waxy

Ceramic Complex: Early Chuen

Ceramic Sphere: Chicanel

Illustrations: Fig. 7.53; 8.5, 8.10, 8.14, 8.32, 8.35.

Identifying Attributes: A red monochrome slip is applied along with a resist agent over a monochrome buff underslip, leaving irregular blotchy design patterns on a characteristic yellowish paste with red particles (Red-particles Paste).

Identifying characteristics and sorting problems: Many sherds that actually belonged to vessels of Ahchab Red-on-buff must have been classified as Sierra Red because they lacked areas that showed the two-color decoration. When both colors are present, there are no major sorting problems.

Paste: Almost entirely Red-particles Paste. Originally an Ahlapp Variety was defined (TR. 25A) for sherds manufactured from Preclassic Monochrome Paste, however, varieties should not be differentiated based on paste in strict type: variety nomenclature (Gifford 1976). The Ahlapp Variety has been subsumed as a paste variant in the originally defined Ahchab Red-on-buff: Ahchab Variety in this work. Red-particles Paste is more commonly used in earlier complexes, marking this type as early Chuen.

Firing: Dark cores and fireclouding are rare.

Slip: The buff slip was applied first, followed by a resist agent and the red slip. Boundaries between the two colors are usually poorly defined, although they are sharp on a few examples. Slips have a waxy feel. Heavy crazing of both slips is characteristic.

Polish: Usually medium.

Color: The buff covers a wide range of color that includes reddish yellow (7.5YR 7/6, 5YR 7/6), brown (7.5YR 5/4), light brown (7.5YR 6/4), and pink (7.5YR 7/4). The red includes the same range of colors found in Sierra Red: Ahuacan Variety: red (2.5YR 5/8, 10R 5/8) and reddish yellow (5YR 5/8). Considerable color variation on a single sherd is common.

Decoration: Design patterns are generally areas that are red interspersed with yellow/brown/pink that appear as formless blobs and patches. Decoration occurs on both the interior and exterior of vessels.

Shapes: Cuspidors as well as outflaring to slightly outcurving-side bowls occur, as do rare examples of other shapes.

Temporal distribution: Occurs in the early part of the Chuen Complex.

Comments: The techniques used to produce Ahchab Red-on-buff are similar to Repasto Black-on-red. It is also related to the Tzec Complex Boo Composite, and may also be related to both Muxanal Red-on-cream and Tierra Mojada Resist identified in Mamom complexes at other sites: Acanmul (Ball and Taschek 2015); Altar de Sacrificios (Adams 1971); Becan (Ball 1977); Blue Creek (Kosakowsky and Lohse 2003); Calakmul (Dominguez Carrasco 1994); Colha (Valdez 1987); Cuello (Kosakowsky 1987); Holmul (Callaghan 2008, 2016b); K'axob (Lopez Varela 1996); Nakbe (Forsyth 1993); the Petexbatun (Foias and Bishop 2013); Piedras Negras (Muñoz 2006); Seibal (Sabloff 1975); and Uaxactun (Smith and Gifford 1966).

Intersite comparisons: Identified at Blue Creek (Kosakowsky and Lohse 2003) and Cuello (Kosakowsky 1987).

Sierra Red: Sierra Variety

Established: Smith and Gifford (1966)

Group: Sierra

Ware: Paso Caballo Waxy

Ceramic Complex: Chuen (continues into Cauac and Cimi)

Ceramic Sphere: Chicanel

Illustrations: Fig. 7.4–5, 7.20, 7.23, 7.27, 7.30–7.34, 7.37, 7.56, 7.59, 7.61–64, 7.66–68; 8.1, 8.9, 8.15, 8.26, 8.34, 8.38, 8.44, 8.49; 10.24–27, 10.32–37, 10.39, 10.41–46, 10.49, 10.51, 10.53–62; 11.1–8, 11.28–31, 11.39–40; 12.11, 12.21, 12.22, 12.28–31, 12.33, 12.39–45, 12.47–53, 12.55–58, 12.63–64, 12.67–73, 12.75–77; 13.26–28, 13.32–38, 13.43–46, 13.48–50, 13.55–57, 13.60; 14.8–10, 14.36, 14.39–40, 14.43–46. See TR. 25A: fig. 2*b*1–2,*c*,*d*2; 3*b*2–4; 99*a*,*b*; 139*a*; 141*a*,*b*1; 142*a*; 144*a*2.

Principal identifying attributes: Monochrome red, thick, waxy slip that fireclouds to brown and black on numerous bowl and dish shapes.

Identifying characteristics and sorting problems: Because almost all whole vessels of Sierra Red include areas in which the color variegates to black or light brown, sherds from variegated areas may be difficult to attribute to a specific type. In non-variegated areas, the color range of Sierra Red is small and quite distinct from that of other monochrome types. The Sierra Variety is easy to distinguish from the Ahuacan Variety of the Tzec Complex because the two have different pastes.

Paste: Preclassic Monochrome Paste.

Firing: Dark cores occur in about one-third of the sherds, usually in thicker sections. Fireclouding occurs on 30% to 45% of the sherds in individual lots, more frequently on jars than on bowls.

Slip: The slip is thick and tends to flake. In most cases, the surface was not well polished before application of the slip.

Polish: Usually low to medium. Waxiness is common but by no means universal.

Color: Good control of color. Most sherds are red (10R 4/8 to 2.5YR 5/6); a few examples range to reddish yellow (7.5YR 6/6).

Shapes: Sierra Red occurs in a great variety of shapes. Outflaring to slightly outcurving-side bowls and dishes are most common (30%), followed by short neck narrow-mouth jars (20%), and slightly incurving to round-side bowls and dishes (14%). Bowls and dishes often have everted rims. Also occurs on large buckets and widely outcurving-side bowls, as well as medium and large plates, and the occasional recurving-side bowl.

Temporal distribution: Chuen Complex to the end of the Preclassic.

Intersite comparisons: Extremely widespread throughout lowland Maya sites in the Late Preclassic. Acanmul (Ball and Taschek 2015); Altar de Sacrificios (Adams 1971); Barton Ramie (Gifford 1976); Becan (Ball 1977); Blue Creek (Kosakowsky and Lohse 2003); Calakmul (Dominguez Carrasco 1994); Chan (Kosakowsky 2012); Chan Chich (Valdez 1998, Valdez and Houk 2000); Cerros (Robertson-Freidel 1980); Colha (Valdez 1987); Cuello (Kosakowsky 1987); Holmul (Callaghan 2008, 2016b); El Mirador (Forsyth 1989); El Perú/Waka' (Eppich 2011); El Pozito (Eppich 2000); Kichpanha (McDow 1997); La Milpa (Sagebiel 2005); Nakbe (Forsyth 1993); Nohmul (Kosakowsky and Pring 2001); the Petexbatun (Foias and Bishop 2013); Rio Azul (Adams 1999); Seibal (Sabloff 1975:77–81); Uaxactun (Smith and Gifford 1966, Smith 1955).

Society Hall Red: Society Hall Variety

Established: Named as a variety by Smith and Gifford (1966). Elevated to the status of a type by Kosakowsky (1983; 1987).

Group: Sierra

Ware: Paso Caballo Waxy

Ceramic Complex: Chuen

Ceramic Sphere: Chicanel

Illustrations: Fig. 10.17–23; 11.25–26.

Principal identifying attributes: Monochrome red slip similar to Sierra Red but applied in a wipe-off technique that results in the streakiness of the surface ranging in color from red to orange.

Identifying characteristics and sorting problems: The streaky effect described below is the sole identifying characteristic of the variety. Because the Sierra Variety is rarely streaky, sorting problems are not severe.

Slip: The identifying characteristic of the Society Hall Variety is a streaky effect in which the red slip shades off into very fine streaks of orange. The effect appears to be the result of a polishing or burnishing process that wipes off some of the slip, because the streaks are too delicate and irregular to be due to a painting procedure. It is possible that multiple coats of slip or a single thick coat partially wiped off may be the source of the effect, because such techniques were used in later complexes to produce local Usulutan-style types.

Color: The red areas are the standard red color (10R 4/8 to 2.5YR 5/6) of Sierra Red. The orange is a clear bright reddish yellow exceeding 5YR 6/8 on the chroma scale.

Shapes: There were too few examples of rim sherds of the Society Hall Variety to provide reliable statistics, but the small sample suggests a strong representation of large buckets and widely outcurving-side bowls, as well as various vessels with bolstered lips.

Temporal distribution: Society Hall Red may be entirely confined to the Chuen Complex. No examples are known from earlier complexes and the rare examples in Cauac samples may be due to mixing.

Intersite comparisons: Barton Ramie (Gifford 1976); Blue Creek (Kosakowsky and Lohse 2003); Cerros (Robertson-Freidel 1980); Chan (Kosakowsky 2012); Chan Chich (Valdez 1998); Colha (Valdez 1987); Cuello (Kosakowsky 1987); El Pozito (Eppich 2000); El Perú/Waka' (Eppich 2011); Holmul (Callaghan 2008, 2016b); K'axob (Lopez Varela 1996); Kichpanha (McDow 1997); La Milpa (Sagebiel 2005); Nohmul (Kosakowsky and Pring 2001); Uaxactun (Smith and Gifford 1966).

Laguna Verde Incised: Simple-incised Variety and Design-incised Variety

Established: Type named by Smith and Gifford (1966). Varieties named by Culbert (1993 [TR. 25A]).

Group: Sierra

Ware: Paso Caballo Waxy

Ceramic Complex: Chuen (continues into Cauac and Cimi)

Ceramic Sphere: Chicanel

Illustrations: Fig. 7.16–17, 7.57; 8.16–19, 8.21–25, 8.30–31, 8.33, 8.36, 8.39–41, 8.43, 8.45–48; 10.1–12, 10.28–31, 10.40, 10.47. See TR. 25A: fig. 142*d*1–3; 155*f.*

Principal identifying attributes: Sierra Red slip decorated secondarily with pre-slip groove incising around vessel exteriors.

Surface finish and decoration: The Simple-incised Variety is decorated with single or multiple lines encircling the vessels almost always on the exterior near the rim. Patterns of the Design-incised Variety are usually no more than curving lines or straight lines that cross. Very few sherds were large enough to demonstrate overall vessel patterns.

Shapes: Small-diameter bowls and dishes are the most common shape represented in all incised types including cuspidors. Narrow-mouth jars occur with somewhat lesser frequencies.

Temporal distribution: Begins and is most common during the Chuen Complex. Incising and grooving are considerably less common in the Sierra Group in the succeeding Preclassic complexes.

Intersite comparisons: Varieties of Laguna Verde Incised are found at Acanmul (Ball and Taschek 2015); Altar de Sacrificios (Adams 1971); Becan (Ball 1977); Barton Ramie (Gifford 1976); Blue Creek (Kosakowsky and Lohse 2003); Calakmul (Dominguez Carrasco 1994); Cerros (Robertson-Freidel 1980); Chan (Kosakowsky 2012); Chan Chich (Valdez 1998, Valdez and Houk 2000); Colha (Valdez 1987); Cuello (Kosakowsky 1987); El Mirador (Forsyth 1989); El Perú/Waka' (Eppich 2011); El Pozito (Eppich 2000); Holmul (Callaghan 2008, 2016b); La Milpa (Sagebiel 2005); Nakbe (Forsyth 1993); Nohmul (Kosakowsky and Pring 2001); the Petexbatun (Foias and Bishop 2013); Rio Azul (Adams 1999); Seibal (Sabloff 1975); Uaxactun (Smith 1955; Smith and Gifford 1966).

Lagartos Punctated: Lagartos Variety

Established: Smith and Gifford (1966)

Group: Sierra

Ware: Paso Caballo Waxy

Ceramic Complex: Chuen (continues into Cauac and Cimi)

Ceramic Sphere: Chicanel

Illustrations: Fig. 7.21.

Principal identifying attributes: Monochrome red slip same as Sierra Red with the addition of secondary decoration of punctations on the exterior.

Identifying characteristics and sorting problems: There are only a few examples of punctated sherds in Chuen Complex collections. In typological characteristics, the sherds are identical to Sierra Red and are too small to permit comments about the patterns of punctation.

Temporal distribution: Begins in Chuen and continues through Cauac and Cimi.

Intersite comparisons: Lagartos Punctated is named as a type or unnamed within the Sierra Red Group at Altar de Sacrificios (Adams 1971); Blue Creek (Kosakowsky and Lohse 2003); Cuello (Kosakowsky 1987); El Mirador (Forsyth 1989); El Pozito (Eppich 2000); Holmul (Callaghan 2008, 2016b); Seibal (Sabloff 1975); Uaxactun (Smith and Gifford 1966).

Repasto Black-on-red: Repasto Variety

Established: Smith and Gifford (1966)

Group: Sierra

Ware: Paso Caballo Waxy

Ceramic Complex: Chuen (continues into Cauac)

Ceramic Sphere: Chicanel

Illustrations: Fig. 15.1–2. See TR. 25A: fig. 2*d*1; 3*d*; 141*b*2.

Principal identifying attributes: Identical to Sierra Red with the addition of secondary decoration by means of black resist. This decoration is dots, patches, and irregular lines of black on red.

Identifying characteristics and sorting problems: The irregular boundaries between red and black areas are quite characteristic. Sherds of the type that do not include areas of black would be classified as Sierra Red, though fireclouding on Sierra Red can be mistaken for Repasto Black-on-red.

Slip: A standard Sierra Red slip is applied first. After the intended design areas have been covered with a protective coating, one or both sides of the vessel are coated with a black pigment.

Color: Red identical to that of Sierra Red. Black ranges from a good clear black to dark red (2.5YR 4/6) in areas where the black pigment is inadequate.

Surface finish and decoration: Irregular lines, dots, and patches of the base red color appear on sherds. Whole vessels show overall designs that usually divide the vessel into sections. Because control of the areas of application was poor, only broad-line patterns were attempted.

Shapes: Slightly incurving to round-side bowls and dishes are by far the dominant shape followed by large outflaring to slightly outcurving-side plates. Various other shapes occur in low frequencies including cuspidors and other medium-diameter bowls and dishes.

Temporal distribution: Repasto Black-on-red does not occur before the Chuen Complex and is rare in the succeeding Cauac Complex. The type is one of the best "type fossils" for the Chuen Complex.

Comments: The resist technique on Repasto Black-on-red is identical to those used in Ahchab Red-on-buff.

Intersite comparisons: Altar de Sacrificios (Adams 1971); Barton Ramie (Gifford 1976); Becan (Ball 1977); Blue Creek (Kosakowsky and Lohse 2003); Cerros (Robertson 2016); Edzna (Forsyth 1983); El Mirador (Forsyth 1989); Holmul (Callaghan 2016b); La Milpa (Sagebiel 2005); Nohmul (Kosakowsky and Pring 2001); Uaxactun (Smith and Gifford 1966, Smith 1955).

Xcuican Incised-dichrome: Xcuican Variety

Established: TR. 25A (Culbert 1993)

Group: Sierra

Ware: Paso Caballo Waxy

Ceramic Complex: Chuen

Ceramic Sphere: Chicanel

Principal identifying attributes: Similar to Repasto Black-on-red with the addition of incising.

Identifying characteristics and sorting problems: A few sherds that were otherwise identical to Repasto Black-on-red have incised lines. Although in a strict type-variety nomenclature this makes a separate type, the sherds probably represent no more than occasional impulses to combine two decorative techniques.

Intersite comparisons: None noted but see Repasto Black-on-red above for intersite distribution of the type without incising.

POLVERO CERAMIC GROUP
Polvero Black: Polvero Variety

Established: Smith and Gifford (1966)

Group: Polvero

Ware: Paso Caballo Waxy

Ceramic Complex: Chuen (continues into Cauac and Cimi)

Ceramic Sphere: Chicanel

Illustrations: Fig. 7.6, 7.60, 7.65; 8.2, 8.20, 8.37, 8.42; 10.50; 12.6, 12.65–66, 12.74; 13.29–31, 13.41, 13.51–54, 13.58–59, 13.61–63; 17.3. See TR. 25A: fig. 3*b*1.

Principal identifying attributes: Thick black, sometimes waxy slip, which tends to flake and craze, and fireclouds to red and brown.

Identifying characteristics and sorting problems: Polvero Black is easily separated from the earlier Chunhinta Black by paste characteristics. The separation of small sherds of various monochrome types frequently presents sorting problems because of the poor control of color and firing in all types.

Paste: Preclassic Monochrome Paste.

Firing: Darkening of the paste beneath the surface indicates firing in a reducing atmosphere. Completely darkened paste bodies or separate dark cores are common.

Slip: Medium to relatively thick slip that tends to craze and flake. Polish: Low to medium. Most, but not all, sherds have a waxy feel.

Color: Color ranges from black (5YR 2.5/1, 7.5YR 2.5/1, 10YR 2/1, 2.5Y 2.5/1) to dark reddish brown (5YR 2.5/2). Control of the reduction process was not good, and few vessels are completely black. Blemishes are reddish and gray to tan.

Shapes: Short-neck, narrow-mouth jars make up nearly half of the sample. Slightly incurving to round-side bowls and dishes are common, and a variety of other shapes including outflaring to outcurving-side bowls and dishes, composite silhouette bowls and dishes, recurving bowls, and large plates occur with low frequencies.

Temporal distribution: Polvero Black is fully established by Chuen and continues until the end of the Preclassic with little change.

Intersite comparisons: Altar de Sacrificios (Adams 1971); Barton Ramie (Gifford 1976); Becan (Ball 1977); Blue Creek (Kosakowsky and Lohse 2003); Calakmul (Dominguez Carrasco 1994); Chan (Kosakowsky 2012); Chan Chich (Valdez 1998, Valdez and Houk 2000); Colha (Valdez 1987); Cuello (Kosakowsky 1987); Edzna (Forsyth 1983); El Perú/ Waka' (Eppich 2011); El Pozito (Eppich 2000); Holmul (Callaghan 2008, 2016b); El Mirador (Forsyth 1989); La Milpa (Sagebiel 2005); Naachtun (Walker and Reese-Taylor 2012); Nakbe (Forsyth 1983); Nohmul (Kosakowsky and Pring 2001); the Petexbatun (Foias and Bishop 2013); Piedras Negras (Muñoz 2006); Seibal (Sabloff 1975); Uaxactun (Smith and Gifford 1966, Smith 1955); Yaxchilan (Lopez Varela 1989).

Lechugal Incised: Simple-incised Variety and Design-incised Variety

Established: Type named by Smith and Gifford (1966); varieties named by Culbert (1993 [TR. 25A]).

Group: Polvero

Ware: Paso Caballo Waxy

Ceramic Complex: Chuen (continues into Cauac and Cimi)

Ceramic Sphere: Chicanel

Illustrations: Fig. 8.30, 8.33.

Principal identifying attributes: Monochrome black slip same as Polvero Black decorated with fine line incising in geometric designs.

Identifying characteristics and sorting problems: See Polvero Black above. In typological characteristics, Lechugal is indistinguishable from Polvero Black. The same comments on decoration and shape made for Laguna Verde Incised apply to Lechugal Incised.

Temporal distribution: Begins in Chuen and continues through Cauac and Cimi.

Intersite comparisons: Lechugal Variety used at Calakmul (Dominguez Carrasco 1994); Holmul (Callaghan 2008, 2016b); La Milpa (Sagebiel 2005); and Uaxactun (Smith and Gifford 1966; Smith 1955). Unspecified Variety used at Altar de Sacrificios (Adams 1971); Blue Creek (Kosakowsky and Lohse 2003); Chan (Kosakowsky 2012); El Mirador (Forsyth 1989); Seibal (Sabloff 1975). Macaw Bank Variety is used at Barton Ramie (Gifford 1976); Chan Chich (Valdez 1998; Valdez and Houk 2000), Colha (Valdez 1987). Grooved-incised Variety used at Cuello (Kosakowsky 1987); Nohmul (Kosakowsky and Pring 2001) and Gouged-incised Variety used at Edzna (Forsyth 1983).

BACLAM CERAMIC GROUP

Baclam Red-orange: Baclam Variety

Established: Named Baclam Orange by Culbert (1993 [TR. 25A]). Renamed Baclam Red-orange in this work.

Group: Baclam

Ware: Unspecified

Ceramic Complex: Chuen (continues into Cauac and Cimi)

Ceramic Sphere: Chicanel

Illustrations: Fig. 11.34, 11.39–40; 13.23–25, 13.42, 13.64–65.

Principal identifying attributes: Slightly waxy, monochrome, red-orange slip that overlaps with Sierra Red on the extreme and is difficult to sort from Sierra Red.

Identifying characteristics and sorting problems: Surface color is the sole identifying characteristic of the type. The range of color grades continuously into that of Sierra Red, so there are many borderline examples. Only the most clearly red-orange examples were classified in sorting as Baclam Red-orange.

Paste: Preclassic Monochrome Paste.

Slip: Usually medium thickness. On some examples, the clay surface was well polished before application of the slip. In these examples, the slip tends to flake off, revealing sections of light clay.

Polish: Low to medium. Waxiness variable.

Color: The most typical examples are reddish yellow (2.5YR 6/8); however, the color ranges to red (2.5YR 5/8) and overlaps the range of color of Sierra Red.

Shapes: Narrow-mouth jars with short neck, out-flaring to outcurving-side bowls and dishes, and slightly incurving to round-side bowls dishes are the most common shapes, as well as some examples of medium plates.

Temporal Distribution: A low frequency of Baclam Red-orange sherds occurs in all the Preclassic complexes beginning with Chuen, and continues in use through the Late Preclassic, relatively unchanged.

Comments: Because Baclam Red-orange is the end of a continuum in color shared with Sierra Red, it is impossible to say whether prehistoric potters deliberately produced red-orange pottery or whether the examples so classified represent color variants due to firing or other chance circumstances.

Intersite comparisons: El Perú/Waka' (Eppich 2011). It is probable that some red-orange examples are sorted with Sierra Red at other sites.

Cay Incised: Simple-incised Variety and Design-incised Variety

Established: TR. 25A (Culbert 1993)

Group: Baclam

Ware: Unspecified

Ceramic Complex: Chuen (continues into Cauac and Cimi)

Ceramic Sphere: Chicanel

Principal identifying attributes: Slightly waxy, monochrome, red-orange slip that overlaps with Sierra Red on the extreme and is difficult to sort from Sierra Red. Decorated secondarily with both pre-slip and post-slip incising.

Comments: A few red-orange slipped sherds show uncomplicated incised decoration. The sample was too small to permit a full typological characterization, but in all observable features the sherds are identical to Baclam Red-orange.

Intersite comparisons: None noted; however, at other sites red-orange incised examples are likely included in the Sierra Red Group, Laguna Verde Incised type.

BOXCAY CERAMIC GROUP

Boxcay Brown: Boxcay Variety

Established: TR. 25A (Culbert 1993)

Group: Boxcay

Ware: Unspecified

Ceramic Complex: Chuen (continues into Cauac and Cimi)

Ceramic Sphere: Chicanel

Illustrations: Fig. 11.44, 11.46; 13.39–40.

Principal identifying attributes: Slightly lustrous rather than waxy, monochrome, brown slip that exhibits crazing,

Identifying characteristics and sorting problems: Because the color of Boxcay Brown ranges into the colors of Polvero Black and Flor Cream, separation is not always clear. Boxcay Brown can be easily separated from the earlier Boolay Brown that has a fine paste with few inclusions.

Paste: Preclassic Monochrome Paste.

Firing: Dark cores occur in half of the sample. Better than half of the sherds show fireclouding.

Slip: Medium thickness.

Polish: Low to medium; waxiness not common.

Color: Ranges from dark yellowish brown (10YR 4/4) to olive brown (2.5Y 4/4).

Shapes: Short-neck jars are the most common shape, followed by slightly incurving to round-side dishes and outflaring to outcurving-side bowls and dishes.

Temporal distribution: The type begins in the Chuen Complex and continues until the end of the Preclassic period relatively unchanged.

Comments: The separation of this type on the basis of surface color from among the highly variegated monochromes of the Chuen Complex may be simply an artifact of sorting. Because a few large sherds show only brown color, there is a possibility that the production of brown pottery was intentional.

Intersite comparisons: El Perú/Waka' (Eppich 2011); Holmul (Callaghan 2008, 2016b); Piedras Negras (Muñoz 2006).

Xtabcab Incised: Simple-incised Variety and Design-incised Variety

Established: TR. 25A (Culbert 1993)

Group: Boxcay

Ware: Unspecified

Ceramic Complex: Chuen (continues into Cauac and Cimi)

Ceramic Sphere: Chicanel

Principal identifying attributes: Same as Boxcay Brown with the addition of simple incised decoration.

Comments: A few sherds of brown pottery in Chuen Complex collections are incised. Compared to most Chuen incised types, the sample of Xtabcab Incised pottery is heavily weighted to incised rather than grooved examples and has an unusually high frequency of design, rather than simple incision.

Intersite comparisons: None noted with incising but see Boxcay Brown above.

FLOR CERAMIC GROUP

Flor Cream: Flor Variety

Established: Smith and Gifford (1966)

Group: Flor

Ware: Paso Caballo Waxy

Ceramic Complex: Chuen (continues into Cauac and Cimi)

Ceramic Sphere: Chicanel

Illustrations: Fig. 7.58; 8.27–29; 10.13–16, 10.48; 12.19–20, 12.23–27, 12.32, 12.54, 12.59.

Principal identifying attributes: Lustrous, slightly waxy cream slip that is variable in color.

Identifying characteristics and sorting problems: Except for slight overlap with the color range of Boxcay Brown on fireclouded sherds, Flor Cream presents few sorting problems. Originally a Cozom Variety (TR. 25A) was separated out based upon a slightly whiter color and pinkish paste, however, these characteristics overlap with the descriptions of the Flor Variety at other lowland Maya sites and therefore both the Flor Variety and the Cozom Variety have been combined and are included in the Flor Variety in this work.

Paste: Preclassic Monochrome Paste.

Firing: Dark cores and fireclouding occur.

Slip: Thick slip that adheres better and shows less tendency to flake or craze than other Preclassic monochrome slips.

Polish: Examples are lightly to highly polished.

Color: Slip color of Flor Cream is extremely variable. Very pale brown (10YR 8/3), pale brown (10YR 6/3), brown (10YR 5/3), and light yellowish brown (10YR 6/4) are most common, but white (10YR 8/1, 8/2; 2.5Y 8/2) and gray (10YR 6/1; 5Y 5/1) also occur. The most common surface colors for the subsumed Cozom variety, very pale brown (10YR 7/3) to pale yellow (2.5Y 8/4), occur largely on flanged dishes and dish-lip plates and tend to exhibit less fireclouding, though it is common for most Flor Cream sherds to show patches of two different colors.

Shapes: Most common shape is outflaring to slightly outcurving-side bowl or dish with a labial flange, followed by other outflaring to slightly outcurving-side bowls or dishes, and large plates. Occasional examples of slightly incurving to round-side bowls and dishes.

Temporal distribution: Flor Cream begins in the Chuen Complex but the peak frequency occurs in Cimi lots. Pink paste examples are more common in the Chuen Complex than the succeeding Cauac and Cimi Complexes.

Intersite comparisons: Altar de Sacrificios (Adams 1971); Barton Ramie (Gifford 1976); Becan (Ball 1977); Blue Creek (Kosakowsky and Lohse 2003); Chan Chich (Valdez 1998; Valdez and Houk 2000); Colha (Valdez 1987); Cuello (Kosakowsky 1987); El Perú/Waka' (Eppich 2011); El Mirador (Forsyth 1989); Holmul (Callaghan 2016b); La Milpa (Sagebiel 2005); Nakbe (Forsyth 1993); Piedras Negras (Muñoz 2006); Nohmul (Kosakowsky and Pring 2001); Seibal (Sabloff 1975); and Uaxactun (Smith 1955; Smith and Gifford 1966). It is an Unspecified Variety at Chan (Kosakowsky 2012); Edzna (Forsyth 1983); K'axob (Lopez Varela 1996); the Petexbatun (Foias and Bishop 2013); and Yaxchilan (Lopez Varela 1989).

Accordian Incised: Simple-incised Variety

Established: Type named Smith and Gifford (1966); variety named Culbert (1993 [misspelled as Accordion in TR. 25A])

Group: Flor

Ware: Paso Caballo Waxy

Ceramic Complex: Chuen (continues into Cauac and Cimi)

Ceramic Sphere: Chicanel

Illustrations: Fig. 12.46.

Principal identifying attributes: Monochrome cream slip similar to Flor Cream: Flor Variety with the addition of incised decoration on the exterior of vessels.

Comments: Typologically, sherds of Accordian Incised are identical to sherds of Flor Cream with the addition of incising. Seven of the nine examples are grooved, while two are incised. No sherds were recovered that would fit into a design-incised category.

Intersite comparisons: Identified as the Accordian Variety at Holmul (Callaghan 2008, 2016b) and Uaxactun (Smith and Gifford 1966). It is an Unspecified Variety at Barton Ramie (Gifford 1976); Becan (Ball 1997); and Edzna (Forsyth 1983); and

called Acordeon Incised in the Petexbatun (Foias and Bishop 2013). There are unnamed examples at Seibal (Sabloff 1975).

XIK CERAMIC GROUP

Xik Double-slipped Orange: Xik Variety

Established: TR. 25A (Culbert 1993)

Group: Xik

Ware: Unspecified

Ceramic Complex: Chuen

Ceramic Sphere: Chicanel

Principal identifying attributes: Highly polished surfaces with a double orange slip.

Identifying characteristics and sorting problems: Typical examples are distinctive and can be identified with ease, but less highly polished examples in which the final slip completely covers the surface would probably be classified with orange or even red-orange types.

Paste: Preclassic Monochrome Paste.

Slip: The examples of the type show a highly polished bright orange surface interspersed with patches of darker color. In most cases, it is difficult to determine how the effect was produced but some examples reveal that a darker base slip was covered with a second thin slip that received the final high polish. The areas in which the base slip shows seem to be the result of inadequate coverage rather than an intentional decorative effect.

Polish: Very high except in areas were the base slip shows through. Hard, polished surface is not characteristic of most other Chuen Complex types but is similar to Chunux Hard Ware at Cerros (Robertson-Freidel 1980).

Color: The darker base slip is reddish yellow (5YR 6/6). The final coat is also reddish yellow (5YR 7/6, 7/8) but actually exceeds /8 on the chroma scale.

Shapes: The sample was too small to permit quantitative measures of vessel shape frequencies, but narrow-mouth jars are common, and a variety of bowl and dish forms also occur.

Temporal distribution: Most of the examples occur in the Chuen Complex, although the type probably persisted into the Cauac Complex.

Intersite comparisons: None noted for monochrome orange, however, similar double slips are used in the Late Preclassic on Cabro Red at Cerros (Robertson-Freidel 1980); Blue Creek (Kosakowsky and Lohse 2003); Cuello (originally called Big Pond Variety of Sierra Red) (Kosakowsky 1987); El Pozito (Eppich 2000); and Naachtun (Walker and Reese-Taylor 2012).

Chuen Complex Decorated Pottery

There was a drastic decline in frequency of decorated pottery in the Chuen Complex samples compared to those of the Tzec Complex. Decorated types made up about 1% of total sherds in Chuen samples as compared to 10% in the Tzec Complex. Incising was the most common decorative technique in the Chuen Complex, followed by resist painting, and rare examples of positive painting.

In the sample of Chuen incised sherds, grooved examples were about twice as common as fine-incised examples, a division about the same as in Tzec Complex samples. In Chuen, the fine-incised sherds were divided about equally between simple incision and design incision, a slight increase in relative frequency of design incision as compared to the Tzec Complex. Patterns in the design-incised varieties were still very simple. Groove-incising and fine line incising was used on all of the monochrome slip colors. Incising in the Chuen Complex was associated strongly with a limited number of vessel shapes. Small slightly incurving to round-side bowls were the vessels most commonly incised, followed by outflaring to slightly outcurving bowls, dishes and plates with everted rims, cuspidors, and narrow-mouth with short necks jars. The great preponderance of incised decoration occurred on vessel exteriors, usually in bands near the lip. Only occasional bowls and plates showed incised decoration on interiors, almost always on vessel lips. Repasto Black-on-red used large, whole-vessel designs that are difficult to comprehend from sherds.

The three whole vessels of the type are illustrated in TR. 25A (Fig. 2*d*1, 3*a*, 141*b*2) and are indicative of the kinds of patterns used.

As is true for all Tikal complexes for which there are large samples, a great variety of decorative techniques including punctation, appliqué, impression, and fluting occurred (largely in the Sierra Group) and, in a few examples, on the same sherd creating an occasional composite type. These stray examples have not been dignified with a separate type name, as this would have generated an almost interminable list of types based on single examples for which range of variation is essentially unknown.

Chuen Types: Chronological Change

There were pronounced typological changes between the Mamom and Chicanel Complex ceramics at Tikal. The Chuen levels may be characterized as follows when compared with earlier complexes:

1. Incised types showed a sharp decrease between Tzec and Chuen levels.

2. The use of Red-particles Paste decreased in the Chuen levels.

3. Achiotes Unslipped, the predominant unslipped type in Tzec samples, declined in frequency in the Chuen Complex. This may be the result of an increase in the frequency of Sapote Striated.

4. Sierra Red and Sapote Striated increase in frequency.

5. Chuen marker types include Repasto Black-on-red and Society Hall Red.

In later samples, despite the long sequence of deposits from the North Acropolis (Chuen-Cimi Location 2) there was little further change in ceramic types or frequencies. In fact, the typological changes throughout the rest of the Preclassic at Tikal were not great and did not involve the addition of major types. After the establishment of the pattern represented in the earliest Chuen samples in the North Acropolis (Location 2), there were no changes in types or type frequencies throughout the remainder of the Chuen Complex, despite five separate Chuen levels in the North Acropolis.

Chuen Types: Social Dimension

Chuen Complex types provided little information about social variation in ceramic use. Only one location for which type counts are available, Location 1, represents a likely residential area from a small structure group; all other locations are areas near the center of the site where a civic-ceremonial origin of ceramics is likely. A further factor complicating social inferences about Chuen (and other Late Preclassic ceramic complex) types is the fact that few types are closely tied to any particular inferred use. Unslipped types are from large jars likely representing domestic use, but the monochromes that comprise the bulk of the collections include both large vessels that may have had utilitarian functions such as storage, and smaller vessels of the serving or ceremonial category. The few decorated types are too rare in all samples to supply much information.

Given these factors, it is not surprising that there was little significant variation in type frequencies between Chuen locations (see Table 4.3). The sample from Location 1, small structure Gp. 5F-1, with the clearest residential context but also the earliest of the samples, stood slightly apart in producing more Achiotes Unslipped—giving it a higher total of unslipped pottery—and less Sierra Red and Polvero Black than other samples. These results could be interpreted as showing greater emphasis on the unslipped utilitarian wares in this domestic location. They might also be temporal, for Achiotes Unslipped was an early type, while Sierra Red showed a gradual increase over time for which its low frequencies in Location 1 are quite appropriate. The other locations, alike in their inferred civic-ceremonial contexts, showed strikingly similar type frequencies.

Vessel Shapes of the Chuen Complex

Introduction

There are 8 shape classes and 15 vessel shapes listed in Table 4.4 that appear in Chuen Complex samples. The relatively small number of shapes in the Chuen Complex masks the great variety in both rim and lip treatments that became common in the

TABLE 4.4
Shape Classes and Shapes of the Chuen Complex

1. Wide-mouth Jars
Wide-mouth Jar (with Short Neck)

2. Narrow-mouth Jars
Narrow-mouth Jar (with Short Neck)
Narrow-mouth Jar (with Tall Neck)

3. Very Wide-mouth Jars
Very Large-diameter Jar

4. Large Capacity Bowls
Widely Outcurving-side Bowl
Bucket

5. Medium Diameter Bowls and Dishes
Slightly Incurving to Round-side Bowl or Dish
Outflaring to Slightly Outcurving-side Bowl or Dish
Labial-flange Bowl or Dish
Recurving-side Bowl
Composite Silhouette Bowl or Dish

6. Small Diameter Bowls and Dishes
Slightly Incurving to Round-side Bowl or Dish
Cuspidor

8. Medium Plates
Outflaring-side Plate

9. Large Plates
Outflaring to Slightly Outcurving-side Plate

Late Preclassic. Profound changes, in both the shapes represented by these more elaborated rims and lips and in shape frequencies, occur between the preceding Mamom Tzec Complex and the Chicanel Chuen Complex. With the Chuen samples, the basic Late Preclassic shape patterns become established.

Chuen Shape Descriptions

SHAPE CLASS 1: WIDE-MOUTH JARS

Wide-mouth Jar with Short Neck

Illustrations: Fig. 7.9, 7.10, 7.69; 9.1–18, 9.21–23; 13.1–20, 19.22.

Identifying characteristics and sorting problems: Easy to distinguish on the basis of short neck, large lip diameter, and unslipped surface.

Base and body: No whole examples, but body seems to have been globular.

Neck-body juncture: Usually rounded but well defined.

Orientation of neck: Medium to wide outflare.

Neck: Outcurves in varying degrees.

Rim: Direct.

Lip: Usually rounded to pointed; a few examples are beveled or flattened.

Surface: Striated below neck-body juncture; variable care in finishing.

Types: Usually Sapote Striated; rarely, Achiotes Unslipped.

Lip diameter: Range 10–24 cm; median 20 cm.

Neck height: Range 1.4–4.6 cm; median 2.8 cm.

Lip diameter/neck height ratio: Range 4.8–12.8; median 7.4.

Shape class: 1, wide-mouth jars.

Temporal Distribution: Occurs rarely in the preceding Eb and Tzec Complexes, however, common in the Late Preclassic Chuen, Cauac, and Cimi Complexes.

Comments: Considerable variability occurs in the shape, but it is not distinctive enough to allow meaningful subdivision. Examples with thinner walls seem slightly more common in the Chuen Complex than in later complexes.

SHAPE CLASS 2: NARROW-MOUTH JARS

Narrow-mouth Jar (with Short Neck)

Illustrations: Fig. 7.47, 7.62, 7.65; 8.20, 8.33–34;

13.23–65. See TR. 25A: fig. *3b*3–4; *144a*1.

Identifying characteristics and sorting problems: For sherds that do not show the neck-body juncture, it is often difficult to distinguish narrow-mouth jars from interior-slipped jars. The short neck makes it fairly easy to distinguish this jar from earlier and later shapes.

Base and body: The few complete examples have globular bodies of small size, but these examples, all from special deposits, may not be representative.

Neck-body juncture: Usually well marked; most frequently angular but sometimes rounded.

Orientation of neck: Medium outflare.

Neck: Ranges from medium outcurve to nearly straight.

Rim: Usually direct; a subclass has sharp to rounded eversion of the rim.

Lip: Rounded or pointed; some examples of the everted rim subclass have flattened lips.

Surface: Slipped on exterior and on interior of neck; remainder of interior unslipped. Care in finishing varies.

Types: Sierra Red makes up about one-half the sample, Polvero Black one-quarter, and Baclam Red-orange one-twelfth; most other slipped such as Boxcay Brown, Xik Double-slipped Orange, and decorated types occur in low frequencies.

Diameter: Range 10–30 cm; median 14 cm. There is some indication of a secondary peak of diameters in the 20–26 cm range.

Height: Range 1.2–4.0 cm; median 2.4 cm.

Lip diameter/neck height ratio: Range 3.6–11.7; median 5.8. The ratio shows a wide distribution with little central tendency; it seems unlikely that the ratio was of much significance to the users.

Shape class: 2, narrow-mouth jars.

Temporal distribution: Present in both the Eb and Tzec Complexes, but more common in the Chuen, Cauac, and Cimi Complexes. The frequency of the shape is quite stable, both through time and between lots at the same time range.

Narrow Mouth Jar (with Tall Neck)

Illustrations: Fig. 7.68; 8.37,38; 10.53.

Identifying characteristics and sorting problems: Identified by spout. A few random spouts have been found in Chuen deposits, but no whole vessels. The few examples are similar to tall necked "chocolate pots" in the Late Preclassic at other sites.

Spout: Spout cross section is round.

Types: Sierra Red.

Shape class: 2, narrow-mouth jars.

Comments: This shape was most common during the Cauac Complex, but a few separate spouts that probably came from the shape occurred in Chuen Complex samples.

SHAPE CLASS 3: VERY WIDE-MOUTH JARS

Very Large-Diameter Jar

Illustrations: Fig. 9.19–20; 13.20.

Identifying characteristics and sorting problems: The diameter is so large that the shape stands far apart from other jars. It is unclear whether some of the taller fragments without neck-body juncture might be bowls.

Base and body: No information available.

Neck-body juncture: Vague in the few instances where present.

Orientation of neck: Outflaring.

Neck: Slight Outcurve.

Rim: Direct.

Lip: Rounded, very thick.

Surface: Unslipped.

Type: Either Achiotes Unslipped or Sapote Striated, though more commonly Sapote Striated.

Lip diameter: Range 40–50 cm; median 44 cm.

Neck height: Range 1.7–3.2 cm; median 2.7 cm.

Lip diameter/neck height ratio: Range 15.3–26.7; median 18.2.

Shape class: 3, very wide-mouth jars.

Temporal distribution: Occurs in low frequencies in all Preclassic complexes.

SHAPE CLASS 4: LARGE CAPACITY BOWLS

Widely Outcurving-side Bowl

Illustrations: Fig. 10.1–10; 11.28, 11.37–38; 12.19, 12.31–33.

Identifying characteristics and sorting problems: The identifying features are the broad lip grooves combined with the widely outcurving side on a deep bowl. Originally a shape called widely outcurving-side bowl with thin walls was sorted separately (TR. 25A), however, the two overlap and have been combined.

Base: Flat.

Orientation of side: Medium to wide outflare at lip.

Side: Outcurving to nearly straight.

Rim: Variant 1: Rounded outward eversion that may be pronounced. The entire rim section is often thickened. Variant 2: Incurved rim (though this rim variant is more common in Cauac and Cimi.

Lip: Pointed or rounded, usually thickened. One to three broad grooves on interior of lip.

Surface: Interior carefully finished; exterior less carefully done.

Types: Sierra Red, Society Hall Red.

Diameter: Range 24–58 cm; median 38 cm.

Height: Range 14–39 cm.

Diameter/height ratio: 2.6–3.8.

Shape class: class 4, large-capacity bowls.

Temporal distribution: The shape first appears in a few examples in the Chuen Complex. Frequency increases in the Chuen Complex, and peaks in samples from the Cauac and early Cimi Complexes. Thin walled examples may be slightly more frequent in the Chuen Complex.

Bucket

Illustrations: Fig. 8.42–48; 10.45; 11.30. See TR. 25A: fig. 99*e*; 141*b*1.

Identifying characteristics and sorting problems: Originally the shape described as a widely outcurving-side bowl (TR. 25A) included buckets as well as deep bowls.

Base: Flat.

Orientation of side: Medium to wide outflare at lip.

Side: Outcurving to nearly straight.

Rim: Rounded eversion that may be pronounced. The entire rim section is often thickened.

Lip: Rounded, usually thickened.

Surface: Slipped both interiorly as well as exteriorly.

Types: Sierra Red, Society Hall Red.

Diameter: Range 24.0–58.0 cm; (median 38 cm). The median has little meaning because of a split distribution between a group of smaller vessels with diameters between 24.0 and 42.0 cm and a group of larger vessels with diameters between 44.0 and 58.0 cm. Some examples could be considered shape class 5, medium-diameter.

Height: Range 21.0–39.0 cm.

Diameter/height ratio: 1.4 to 1.8

Shape class: 4, large-capacity bowls.

Temporal distribution: The shape first appears in the Chuen Complex. Frequency increases throughout the Late Preclassic, and peaks in samples from the Cauac and early Cimi Complexes.

SHAPE CLASS 5: MEDIUM DIAMETER BOWLS AND DISHES

Slightly Incurving to Round-side Bowl or Dish

Illustrations: Fig. 7.21, 7.31, 7.33–34, 7.64, 7.66; 11.39–40; 12.39–45, 12.54, 12.59, 12.65–66, 12.67–77; 15.1–2. See TR. 25A: fig. 3*a,b*1; 141*b*2.

Identifying Characteristics and Sorting Problems: There is some overlap with smaller examples of slightly incurving to round-side bowls and dishes, with the two shapes differentiated by size and wall thickness.

Base: Flat or slightly concave.

Side: Rounded, low to medium curvature.

Rim: Variant 1: Direct. Variant 2: Incurved just below the lip; the side curves inward either in a rounded curve accentuating curvature of the side or with a more abrupt break, sometimes marked by a slight groove on the interior. Variant 3: Everted

Lip: Rounded; pointed; beveled; flattened bolster; flat (rare).

Surface: Well-finished interior and exterior; exterior sometimes less carefully done. Occasional examples of Sierra Red are slipped on the exterior but not on the interior, especially those with everted rims, however, this is very rare.

Types: Samples of this shape were large enough to trace variation in type frequencies between complexes. In the Chuen Complex, most of the examples are Sierra Red, followed by Polvero Black, Repasto Black-on-red, Baclam Red-orange, Flor Cream,

Boxcay Brown, and various incised types occur in low frequencies.

Diameter: Range 14–58 cm (most examples 20–40 cm); median 30 cm. While the range of diameters includes both smaller and larger examples, the median clusters within the medium size shape class.

Height: Range 4.8–10.0 cm; median 6.0 cm.

Diameter/height ratio: Range 3.2–6.4; median 4.2.

Shape class: 5, medium-diameter dishes.

Temporal distribution: Slightly incurving to round-side bowls and dishes occur in all ceramic complexes.

Comments: Chuen examples of the shape differ from later examples only in the frequency of types represented.

Outflaring to Slightly Outcurving-side Bowl or Dish

Illustrations: Fig. 7.32, 7.37, 7.56–59; 8.30, 8.32; 10.16–30, 10.36–44; 11.31; 12.47–53. See TR. 25A: fig. 3*b*2; 139*a*.

Identifying characteristics and sorting problems: The gradual eversion, with a broad everted rim, identifies this shape. It differs from the outflaring-side bowl or dish with sharply everted rim only in the nature of the eversion.

Base: Probably flat.

Orientation of Side: Medium to wide outflare or outcurve.

Side: Outcurving to nearly straight in upper section. Some large sherds and whole vessels suggest that some examples have sides rounding to the base in lower sections of the vessel.

Rim: Variant 1: Direct; Variant 2: sharply everted or everted with a rounded eversion that does not make a sharp break with the side of the vessel. The everted section is broad. Variant 3: Slightly incurving-side rim.

Lip: Rounded, pointed, flattened, or beveled; frequently thickened or bolstered on the exterior. Many examples have a labial flange. The bolstered lip is an excellent temporal marker for the Chuen Complex, particularly when made from the rare Society Hall Red type, as are vessels with labial flanges.

Surface: Slipped on both interior and exterior.

Types: Most of the examples are Sierra Red, followed by Flor Cream, Polvero Black, Society Hall Red, Baclam Red-orange, Boxcay Brown, and incised varieties of all monochrome types.

Diameter: Range 18–32.0 cm; median 30.0 cm. There is a wide range of diameters in this vessel shape that runs from small to quite large, but the vast majority of examples are of medium size.

Height: 8.0–16.0 cm.

Diameter/Height ratio: 1.4–4.2

Shape Class: 5, medium-diameter bowls and dishes.

Temporal distribution: The basic shape is present in all Preclassic complexes.

Labial-flange Bowl or Dish

Illustrations: Fig. 10.14–15, 10.62; 12.6, 12.11, 12.20–30.

Identifying characteristics and sorting problems: The position of the flange is quite distinctive, especially if the shape is cream-slipped, a rare slip color for other flanged dishes.

Base: Probably flat.

Orientation of side: Medium outflare.

Side: Straight to slightly rounded. There is no break in curvature at the flange.

Rim: Direct.

Lip: Pointed. The lip is only a tiny section above the flange.

Flange: The flange is located just below the lip of the vessel. It is most frequently pointed in cross section, occasionally rounded. Usually, the flange is quite narrow, but there are a few examples of broad lip flanges. Originally described as a lip-flange dish by Culbert (TR. 25A).

Surface: Slipped on both interior and exterior.

Types: Chuen samples show a preponderance of Flor Cream (60%) and only about 25% Sierra Red.

Diameter: Range 20–42 cm; median 28 cm.

Shape class: shape class 5, medium-diameter dishes.

Temporal distribution: In contrast to medial-flange dishes, which never appear before the Cauac Complex, the labial-flange bowl or dish first appears in early Chuen samples and is most common in the Late Chuen Complex. There may be some examples in Cauac and Cimi but this may be the result of temporal mixing rather than the continued use of this shape, which is a good marker for the Chuen Complex.

Recurving-side Bowl

Illustrations: Fig. 7.4–5, 7.23, 7.60–61, 7.67; 8.23, 8.27–28, 8.35; 10.32; 11.1–8.

Identifying characteristics and sorting problems: Some overlap in sorting with the cuspidor shape, though recurving-side bowls tend to be larger. Culbert (TR. 25A) originally identified two shapes called an interior-slipped jar and an interior-slipped jar with lateral ridge. Most of the interior-slipped jar shapes are cuspidors and the interior-slipped jars with lateral ridge are recurving-side bowls.

Base: Unknown. Probably flat.

Orientation of side: Medium outflare.

Side: Outcurving at rim; recurves below to rounded side.

Rim: Direct or accentuates outcurve with rounded eversion.

Lip: Frequently thickened wall slightly below lip; lip is rounded, pointed, or rounded bevel.

Surface: Slipped on both interior and exterior; on some examples there is a slight ridge below the lip on the exterior.

Types: Mostly Sierra Red; some Polvero Black.

Diameter: Range 16–32 cm; median 23.0 cm.

Shape class: 5, medium-diameter bowls and dishes.

Temporal distribution: Most common in Chuen, but rare even then.

Composite Silhouette Bowl or Dish

Illustrations: Fig. 11.45–46.

Identifying characteristics and sorting problems: The composite silhouette is the identifying feature.

Base: Unknown.

Orientation of side: Slight to medium outflare.

Side: Composite silhouette; upper section outcurving; lower section straight to rounded.

Rim: Direct or everted.

Lip: Rounded with direct rim; beveled or semi-beveled with everted rim.

Break between sections: Usually angular shelf; sometimes rounded.

Surface: Slipped on both interior and exterior.

Types: Most commonly Polvero Black, followed closely by the Ahuacan Variety of Sierra Red. Other types represented infrequently.

Diameter: There is a wide range 14–44 cm.; median 28.0 cm. Examples are scattered evenly throughout range, but the median falls within the medium-diameter shape class.

Shape class: 5, medium-diameter bowls and dishes.

Temporal distribution: This shape is most common in the Chuen Complex, but examples occur occasionally in all Preclassic complexes.

SHAPE CLASS 6: SMALL DIAMETER BOWLS AND DISHES

Slightly Incurving to Round-side Bowl or Dish

Illustrations: Fig. 7.16–20, 7.27, 7.30, 7.33, 7.63; 8.26, 8.49.

Identifying characteristics and sorting problems: There is some overlap with examples that have a more restricted orifice, which necessitated frequent difficult decisions. Some examples have an exterior groove below the lip that was originally identified as a separate shape as were examples with a thickened lip (TR. 25A), but these two variants are now included in this shape.

Base: Rounded or flat.

Side: Rounded; medium to high curvature.

Rim: Variant 1: Direct. Variant 2: slightly everted.

Lip: Usually rounded, and sometimes thickened.

Surface: Well-finished both inside and out. This was a favorite form for incised decoration, which invariably occurs on the exterior, usually as a line or lines on the upper part of the vessel.

Types: Occurs in low frequencies on slipped types. Most common are Sierra Red, Polvero Black, and Repasto Black-on-red.

Diameter: 13.0–30.0 cm.; median 20.0 cm. Most examples are of the smaller size range, though some overlap with shape class 5, medium-diameter bowls and dishes.

Height: median 8.0 cm.

Diameter/Height ratio: median 2.0

Shape class: 6, small-diameter bowls and dishes.

Temporal distribution: The shape occurs in low frequencies in the Chuen, Cauac, and Cimi Complexes. It is somewhat more common in the Chuen Complex.

Cuspidor

Illustrations: Fig. 7.6; 8.17–19, 8.21–22, 8.24–25, 8.31, 8.36, 8.39–40; 10.46. See TR. 25A: fig. 2*d*1; 99*a–b*.

Identifying characteristics and sorting problems: The shape can be identified by the small diameter, outcurving side, slight degree of outflare, and vessel wall that recurves to base. However, in the absence of a complete rim to base profile, small sherds are difficult to distinguish from narrow-mouth jar sherds. Culbert (TR. 25A) originally used a sorting category of vertical-side vessels that are most likely the upper portion of cuspidors or outflaring to slightly outcurving-side bowls or dishes.

Base: Flat in the few examples where present.

Body: Three complete examples have a composite silhouette with an angular shoulder very low on the body. Other examples from large sherds suggest that some of the vessels had rounded bodies without composite silhouette.

Orientation of side: Slight outflare to nearly vertical.

Side: Outcurving in upper section, rounded toward base.

Rim: Direct or rounded eversion.

Lip: Usually rounded.

Surface: Slipped on both exterior and interior. In most examples careful finishing of the surface extends to the interior base.

Types: Better than three-fourths of the samples are Sierra Red, especially Laguna Verde Incised; Ahchab Red-on-buff, and Repasto Black-on-red occur occasionally.

Diameter: Range 12–28 cm, median 16 cm.

Height: (3 examples) Range 10–13 cm.

Diameter/Height ratio: (3 examples) Range 1.2–1.4.

Shape class: 5, small-diameter bowls and dishes.

Temporal distribution: The shape occurs in the Chuen, Cauac, and Cimi Complexes in about equal frequencies.

SHAPE CLASS 8: MEDIUM PLATES

Outflaring-side Plate

Illustrations: Fig. 7.53; 8.1–16; 10.11, 10.33–35, 10.48–51, 10.54, 10.56–61.

Identifying characteristics and sorting problems: Originally called a ridged dish or plate with thickened-beveled lip (TR. 25A). However, the basic shape is a medium-diameter outflaring-side plate. The combination of exterior ridge or ridges and thickened beveled lips characterizes the shape.

Base: Flat.

Orientation of side: Slight to medium outflare.

Side: Straight to slightly rounded.

Rim: Direct.

Lip: Thickened on exterior; reverse bevel.

Surface: The ridge or ridges on the vessel exterior create a surface that resembles horizontal fluting.

Types: Mostly Sierra Red; some Baclam Red-orange.

Diameter: (4 examples) Range 16–38 cm.

Height: (3 examples) Range 4.4–6.0 cm.

Diameter/height ratio: (3 examples) 3.3–6.3.

Shape class: 8, medium plates.

Temporal distribution: Similar shapes occur in all Preclassic complexes, but the shape is never common.

SHAPE CLASS 9: LARGE PLATES

Outflaring to Slightly Outcurving-side Plate

Illustrations: Fig. 8.29; 10.12–13, 10.31, 10.47, 10.55; 11.29. See TR. 25A: fig. 2b1–2,c,d2; 141a; 142a.

Identifying characteristics and sorting problems: Originally called the dish-lip plate (TR. 25A). The very characteristic lip shape is easily recognized and there are only a few examples in which the shape overlaps that of the outflaring-side bowl or dish with sharply everted rim.

Base: Flat.

Orientation of side: Medium to wide outflare.

Side: Slight to pronounced outcurve.

Rim: Sharply everted to horizontal.

Lip: The interior wall of the vessel comes up to make a point that delimits the top of the vessel. The everted section is added at right angles on the exterior to make what approaches a lip flange. The section of this appendage closest to the vessel wall is pinched in from both sides and then goes outward to form a bump-like lip.

Surface: Slipped on both interior and exterior.

Types: About 80% of the examples are Sierra Red. Flor Cream, Polvero Black, and Repasto Black-on-red follow in order of frequency.

Diameter: Range 22–48 cm; median 38 cm.

Height: Range 4–17 cm; median 6 cm.

Diameter/Height ratio: Range 1.9 to 7.0; median 6.2–6.6.

Shape class: 9, large plates.

Temporal distribution: The shape begins in the Tzec Complex and continues in Chuen.

In each sample some rim sherds are too small to indicate overall vessel shape and lack any diagnostic rim or lip features. These sherds are assigned to the indeterminate category. The median vessels dimensions for all Chuen vessel shapes are presented in Table 4.5.

Chuen Shapes: Chronological Change

A relatively even distribution among a number of vessel shapes is characteristic of the Chuen Complex. Because typological changes between the Chuen, Cauac, and Cimi Complexes were relatively small, changes in vessel shapes and shape frequencies are used along with typological changes for chronological distinctions of these complexes. The transition from the Tzec Complex to the Chuen Complex is marked by dramatic changes in rim and lip elaboration on vessel shapes. Additionally, a number of earlier vessel shapes disappear and new ones appear while the frequencies of both shapes and shape classes change drastically (see Table 4.6).

The total frequency of wide-mouth jars does not vary significantly between the two complexes, but the shapes represented do. The wide mouth jar with thin-lip, which is the predominant wide-mouth jar during the Tzec Complex, disappears in the Chuen Complex, and there is a sharp increase in the frequency of the wide-mouth jar with short neck. The narrow-mouth jar with medium to tall neck no longer appears in Chuen, and there is a substantial increase in the narrow-mouth jar with short neck.

Medium-diameter bowls and dishes increase between Tzec and Chuen from 3% to often more than 30–40% of rim sherds, although there is some variability among sample locations. Small-diameter bowls and dishes also increase between the two complexes, from frequencies of less than 6% in Tzec samples to

TABLE 4.5
Shape Dimensions of the Chuen Complex

Shape Class and Shape	Median Diameter or Range (cm)	Median Height or Range (cm) (Neck Height for Jars)	Median Diameter/ Height Ratio or Range (cm)
1. Wide-mouth Jar (with Short Neck)	20.0	2.8	7.4
2. Narrow-mouth Jar (with Short Neck)	14.0	2.4	5.8
2. Narrow-mouth Jar (with Tall Neck) (No whole vessels)	—	—	—
3. Very Large-diameter Jar	44.0	2.7	18.2
4. Widely Outcurving-side Bowl	38.0	14.0–39.0	—
4. Bucket	28.0–58.0	21.0–39.0	1.4–1.8
5. Slightly Incurving to Round-side Bowl or Dish	30.0	6.0	4.2
5. Outflaring to Slightly Outcurving-side Bowl or Dish	30.0	8.0–16.0	1.4–4.2
5. Labial-flange Bowl or Dish	28.0	—	—
5. Recurving-side Bowl	23.0	—	—
5. Composite-silhouette Bowl or Dish	28.0	—	—
6. Slightly Incurving to Round-side Bowl or Dish	20.0	8.0	2.0
6. Cuspidor	16.0	12.0	1.3
8. Outflaring-side Plate	16.0–38.0	4.4–6.0	3.3–6.3
9. Outflaring to Slightly Outcurving-side Plate	38.0	6.0	6.4

TABLE 4.6 (part 1)
Shape Frequencies of the Chuen Complex

	Group 5F-1				
	Small Structure Group				
Shape Class and Shape	Sample Loc. 1-1&2 40–80cm	Sample Loc. 1-3 80–100cm	Sample Loc. 1-4 Trench 4	Sample Loc. 1-5 Trench 2	Sample Loc. 1-6 Str. 17
	%	%	%	%	%
1. Wide-mouth Jar (with Short Neck)	13.0	18.6	9.1	25.4	17.8
2. Narrow-mouth Jar (with Short Neck)	1.9	4.7	11.7	8.5	4.8
3. Very Large-diameter Jar	—	—	—	—	—
4. Widely Outcurving-side Bowl	5.6	—	6.5	2.8	2.4
4. Bucket	1.9	—	2.6	1.9	—
Total Shape Class 4: Large Capacity Bowls	**7.5**	—	**9.1**	**4.7**	**2.4**
5. Slightly Incurving to Round-side Bowl or Dish	7.4	4.7	10.4	6.6	8.3
5. Outflaring to Slightly Outcurving-side Bowl or Dish	5.6	4.6	29.9	28.3	20.2
5. Labial-flange Bowl or Dish	—	—	—	—	—
5. Recurving-side Bowl	—	—	1.3	—	—
5. Composite-silhouette Bowl or Dish	—	—	1.3	—	—
Total Shape Class 5: Medium Diameter Bowls and Dishes	**13.0**	**9.3**	**42.9**	**34.9**	**28.5**
6. Slightly Incurving to Round-side Bowl or Dish	3.7	7.0	9.1	2.8	14.3
6. Cuspidor	1.9	4.7	—	1.9	—
Total Shape Class 6: Small Diameter Bowls and Dishes	**5.6**	**11.7**	**9.1**	**4.7**	**14.3**
8. Outflaring-side Plate	—	—	—	—	—
9. Outflaring to Slightly Outcurving-side Plate	1.9	—	—	—	2.4
Total Shape Classes 8 & 9: Medium and Large Plates	**1.9**	—	—	—	**2.4**
Unidentified Small Rims	11.2	20.8	10.3	12.3	11.9
Odd shapes	20.0	7.0	—	0.9	—
Tzec Rims	25.9	27.9	7.8	8.6	17.9
TOTAL RIM SHERDS	**53**	**43**	**77**	**106**	**84**

frequencies that range between 6% through more than 20% in Chuen samples, again with a high degree of variability among sample locations.

The most striking difference between the Tzec and Chuen Complexes is the drastic decline in the frequency of plates. From frequencies that range from 33 to 45% in the Tzec Complex, plates are reduced to totals from 1 to 12% in Chuen samples. As a group, the frequency of medium and larger size bowls and dishes increases in the Chuen Complex when compared with the Tzec Complex, which may replace the plates in the Tzec Complex,

TABLE 4.6 (part 2)
Shape Frequencies of the Chuen Complex

Shape Class and Shape	Group 5D-2 Civic-Ceremonial			
	Sample Loc. 2-11	Sample Loc. 2-10	Sample Loc. 2-9	Sample Loc. 2-8
	%	%	%	%
1. Wide-mouth Jar (with Short Neck)	17.8	13.7	16.8	21.8
2. Narrow-mouth Jar (with Short Neck)	16.0	14.3	11.9	18.2
3. Very Large-diameter Jar	—	0.6	—	—
4. Widely Outcurving-side Bowl	0.8	2.4	—	—
4. Bucket	0.5	0.9	2.0	—
Total Shape Class 4: Large Capacity Bowls	**1.3**	**3.3**	**2.0**	**—**
5. Slightly Incurving to Round-side Bowl or Dish	4.7	6.1	9.9	5.5
5. Outflaring to Slightly Outcurving-side Bowl or Dish	18.3	16.6	18.0	23.6
5. Labial-flange Bowl or Dish	2.1	0.3	2.0	5.5
5. Recurving-side Bowl	0.5	0.6	3.0	1.8
5. Composite-silhouette Bowl or Dish	1.5	0.9	2.0	1.8
Total Shape Class 5: Medium Diameter Bowls and Dishes	**27.1**	**24.5**	**34.9**	**38.2**
6. Slightly Incurving to Round-side Bowl or Dish	10.3	16.1	17.0	5.5
6. Cuspidor	3.6	3.0	5.0	1.8
Total Shape Class 6: Small Diameter Bowls and Dishes	**13.9**	**19.1**	**22.0**	**7.3**
8. Outflaring-side Plate	1.8	0.6	1.0	—
9. Outflaring to Slightly Outcurving-side Plate	1.5	7.3	4.0	3.5
Total Shape Classes 8 & 9: Medium and Large Plates	**3.3**	**7.9**	**5.0**	**3.5**
Unidentified Small Rims	15.4	9.4	3.5	9.2
Odd shapes	3.4	4.2	2.9	1.8
Tzec Rims	1.8	3.0	1.0	—
TOTAL RIM SHERDS	**387**	**329**	**101**	**55**

but serve a similar function. In sum, it is easy to distinguish Chuen Complex samples from those of earlier complexes on the basis of shapes. The disappearance of Tzec characteristic jar shapes is, by itself, an excellent indicator because jars are common in all samples. Similarly, the shift from plates to medium-diameter bowls and dishes with elaborated

rims is so strong that it should be detectable even in small samples.

The distinction of the Chuen Complex from later Preclassic Complexes is somewhat more difficult, but it is simplified by the fact that each of the later complexes has quite distinctive and relatively common marker shapes that do not appear in Chuen. The

TABLE 4.6 (part 3)
Shape Frequencies of the Chuen Complex

| Shape Class and Shape | Group 5D-9 | | | | | |
| | | | Civic-Ceremonial | | | |
	Sample Loc. 3-6	Sample Loc. 3-5	Sample Loc. 3-4	Sample Loc. 3-3	Sample Loc. 3-2	Sample Loc. 3-1
	%	%	%	%	%	%
1. Wide-mouth Jar (with Short Neck)	23.7	4.4	8.8	19.4	13.9	10.7
2. Narrow-mouth Jar (with Short Neck)	19.5	23.5	21.4	16.8	15.1	21.3
3. Very Large-diameter Jar	—	—	1.5	—	—	—
4. Widely Outcurving-side Bowl	—	3.2	3.7	0.7	5.9	2.0
4. Bucket	1.4	1.3	—	1.3	2.0	2.8
Total Shape Class 4: Large Capacity Bowls	**1.4**	**4.5**	**3.7**	**2.0**	**7.9**	**4.8**
5. Slightly Incurving to Round-side Bowl or Dish	16.7	22.2	8.1	12.8	8.5	3.9
5. Outflaring to Slightly Outcurving-side Bowl or Dish	15.4	15.2	24.9	10.9	21.2	21.4
5. Labial-flange Bowl or Dish	—	—	—	0.7	—	2.9
5. Recurving-side Bowl	—	1.9	1.5	2.7	—	—
5. Composite-silhouette Bowl or Dish	—	—	—	1.4	0.7	—
Total Shape Class 5: Medium Diameter Bowls and Dishes	**32.1**	**39.3**	**34.5**	**28.5**	**30.4**	**28.2**
6. Slightly Incurving to Round-side Bowl or Dish	9.8	8.9	9.5	10.8	14.0	11.6
6. Cuspidor	—	1.3	2.9	3.4	4.0	2.9
Total Shape Class 6: Small Diameter Bowls and Dishes	**9.8**	**10.2**	**12.4**	**14.2**	**18.0**	**14.5**
8. Outflaring-side Plate	—	—	—	—	—	—
9. Outflaring to Slightly Outcurving-side Plate	4.2	2.5	3.7	0.7	3.3	1.0
Total Shape Classes 8 & 9: Medium and Large Plates	**4.2**	**2.5**	**3.7**	**0.7**	**3.3**	**1.0**
Unidentified Small Rims	5.2	12.4	11.4	17.7	11.4	18.5
Odd shapes	4.1	1.9	1.9	0.7	—	—
Tzec Rims	—	1.3	0.7	—	—	1.0
TOTAL RIM SHERDS	**72**	**158**	**136**	**149**	**152**	**103**

Chuen Complex has fewer such "type fossils," but the outflaring to slightly outcurving-side bowl or dish with labial flange, and the use of bolstered lips on a variety of shapes serve fairly well as indicators of Chuen. None of these shapes appear in earlier collections and they either decline sharply or disappear completely from samples that postdate Chuen.

Chuen Shapes: Social Dimension

Chuen ceramics from seven locations were quantitatively analyzed for shapes. Three of the locations were inferred to be domestic from small structure groups (Locations 1, 4, and 7); three were thought to be civic-ceremonial (Locations 2, 3, and 6), and

TABLE 4.6 (part 4)
Shape Frequencies of the Chuen Complex

Shape Class and Shape	Gp. 6E-1 Small Structure Group Sample Loc. 4-1	Gp. 5D-10 Range Structure Group Sample Loc. 5-1	Gp. 5D-2 Civic-Ceremonial Sample Loc. 6-1	Gp. 2F-1 Small Structure Group Sample Loc. 7-1
	%	%	%	%
1. Wide-mouth Jar (with Short Neck)	22.4	8.7	11.2	13.6
2. Narrow-mouth Jar (with Short Neck)	7.5	7.6	11.2	18.3
3. Very Large-diameter Jar	—	—	—	—
4. Widely Outcurving-side Bowl	17.9	—	1.1	3.1
4. Bucket	1.5	—	1.1	—
Total Shape Class 4: Large Capacity Bowls	**19.4**	—	**2.2**	**3.1**
5. Slightly Incurving to Round-side Bowl or Dish	-	—	18.7	2.6
5. Outflaring to Slightly Outcurving-side Bowl or Dish	19.5	42.4	12.8	18.3
5. Labial-flange Bowl or Dish	—	—	—	2.6
5. Recurving-side Bowl	1.5	—	1.1	—
5. Composite-silhouette Bowl or Dish	—	—	0.5	—
Total Shape Class 5: Medium Diameter Bowls and Dishes	**21.0**	**42.4**	**33.1**	**23.5**
6. Slightly Incurving to Round-side Bowl or Dish	15.0	5.5	15.5	11.5
6. Cuspidor	1.5	2.2	2.7	2.1
Total Shape Class 6: Small Diameter Bowls and Dishes	**16.5**	**7.7**	**18.2**	**13.6**
8. Outflaring-side Plate	1.5	—	—	—
9. Outflaring to Slightly Outcurving-side Plate	—	—	11.8	5.8
Total Shape Classes 8 & 9: Medium and Large Plates	**1.5**	—	**11.8**	**5.8**
Unidentified Small Rims	5.7	21.5	3.2	19.5
Odd shapes	4.5	4.4	3.2	1.0
Tzec Rims	1.5	7.7	5.9	1.6
TOTAL RIM SHERDS	**67**	**92**	**187**	**191**

one (Location 5) was from the area of a Classic period elite range structure group, although it is unknown what kind of structures were present in the Preclassic. Although the frequencies of shapes vary considerably between samples, there are no consistent patterns that can be interpreted to represent social differences in the use of ceramics. Variations between individual samples from the same location and between different locations from the same inferred social context are as great as differences between samples from civic-ceremonial and residential locations. Since none of the Chuen deposits were in-situ, any social inferences presented below are questionable at best.

How are these results to be interpreted? Accepted at face value, they would suggest that there was little social differentiation in the use of ceramics during the Chuen period. However, most archaeological evidence suggests there was fairly strong class differentiation at Tikal by the time of the Chuen Complex, and it is unlikely that this differentiation would not be represented in material possessions such as ceramics. Secondly, solid conclusions for this time period are difficult because there seem to be too many possible sources of error in correlating ceramics with function and shape. In addition to the problems in assigning behavioral implications to locations and deciding whether samples actually represent associated activities, there is the additional complication that shape-sorting categories for the Chuen samples do not match easily with shape classes. The fact that a large number of the sorting categories cannot be assigned securely to a single shape class opens the possibility that differences that actually exist within the collections have gone undetermined.

In summary, then, it cannot be denied that vessel shape frequencies for the Chuen Complex samples fail to show consistent variation that can be interpreted as representing social variation in the use of ceramics. It seems more likely that problems in dealing with the analysis are responsible for these

results than that there was no social variation in the use of ceramics at this time.

Special Deposits of the Chuen Complex

Burials of the Chuen Complex

Only four Chuen Complex special deposits classified as burials included ceramic offerings (Table 4.7), and the total sample of vessels is only ten. All of the Chuen Complex burials were encountered in the stratigraphic cut through the North Acropolis, Gp. 5D-2, but none of them contained ceramics of the abundance and richness that characterized later burials from this location. It is difficult to determine whether the relative paucity of vessels and the lack of imported vessels in the Chuen burials is significant given the small sample size. There is no way of ruling out the possibility that the limited excavation at this stratigraphic level failed by chance to encounter more elaborate burials.

One burial included a single vessel; one burial included two vessels; one included three vessels, and one included four. Seven of the ten vessels are Sierra Red, and one is Polvero Black; two vessels of Repasto Black-on-red are the only decorated examples. All of the vessels seem to have been of local manufacture.

TABLE 4.7
Burials of the Chuen Complex

Burial No.	Op.SubOp./ Lot	Location Gp. Str.	Structure Group Type	TR. 25A Illustration	TR.	No. of Vessels
122	12P/153	North Acropolis Gp. 5D-2 Str. 5D-Sub.14-1st	Civic-Ceremonial	2b1–2	14	2
123	12P/158	North Acropolis Gp. 5D-2 Str. 5D-Sub.14-1st	Civic-Ceremonial	2c	14	1
126	12P/159	North Acropolis Gp. 5D-2 Str. 5D-Sub.14-1st	Civic-Ceremonial	2d1–2; 3a	14	3
164	12P/126, 129, 170	North Acropolis Gp. 5D-2 Plat. 5D-4-8th	Civic-Ceremonial	3b1–4	14	4

The large outflaring to slightly outcurving-side plate was the most commonly represented shape in Chuen burials. Three of the four burials included at least one example of the shape, and Bu. 122 and 123 contained only large plates. Slightly incurving to round-side dishes were included in two burials. Burial 164 proved to be slightly different from the other Chuen burials in that it did not include a large outflaring to slightly outcurving-side plate but did contain two narrow-mouth jars with short-neck, unrepresented in other Chuen burials. The pattern of offerings in Bu. 164 bears some resemblance to offerings in later Cauac burials, where jars were usually present.

Caches of the Chuen Complex

Three special deposits classified as caches contain ceramics from Chuen Complex stratigraphic levels in the North Acropolis (Table 4.8). The two earliest of these caches (Ca. 141 and Ca. 147) both contained a single vessel, in each case a cuspidor of Sierra Red. The third cache (Ca. 168) included two vessels, a small slightly incurving to round-side bowl of Polvero Black for which an outflaring to slightly outcurving-side dish of Sierra Red served as a cover. Since Ca. 168 is later in stratigraphic position than the other two caches, it is possible that the pattern of ceramic offerings changed from a single vessel to a set of vessels with one used as a cover. This possibility is strengthened by the fact that cache vessels in later Preclassic complexes typically consist of such sets (see Chapters 5 and 6).

Problematical Deposits of the Chuen Complex

Seven problematical deposits with ceramics (Table 4.9) were originally identified as containing Chuen Complex ceramics (TR. 25A); only five of these can be assigned securely to the Chuen Complex on either stratigraphic or typological grounds. All of the problematical deposits with secure stratigraphic assignment were from the main civic-ceremonial area of the site: PD. 83 and PD. 265 from the North Acropolis and three PD. 90, PD. 91, and PD. 97 from the Seven Temples Plaza. Six of the problematical deposits contained a single vessel and one contained two vessels. There are problems with the exact dating of two of the problematical deposits, PD. 93 from the Seven Temples Plaza and PD. 114 from Ch. 5G-7 in the small structure group that includes Str. 5G-18.

Five of these problematical deposits contained only a single vessel, four of which are Sierra Red, and one is Lechugal Incised. Problematical Deposits 83 and 265 were located in the lowest level of architecture in the North Acropolis. Most of these sherds are primarily Chuen ceramics, but some lots have a strong admixture of earlier material and there are fragments of early architecture in the area, some of which might conceivably predate the time of the Chuen Complex. The final decision about the date of the activities represented by the problematical deposits must be based on evidence from excavation. Problematical Deposit 83 was found in the same lot

TABLE 4.8
Caches of the Chuen Complex

Cache No.	Op.SubOp./ Lot	Location Gp. Str.	Structure Group Type	TR. 25A Illustration	TR.	No. of Vessels
141	12P/115	North Acropolis Gp. 5D-2 Plat. 5D-4-10th	Civic-ceremonial	99*b*	14	1
147	12P/136	North Acropolis Gp. 5D-2 Plat. 5D-4-10th	Civic-ceremonial	99*a*	14	1
168[1]	12P/184	North Acropolis Gp. 5D-2 Str. 5D-Sub.11	Civic-ceremonial	99*c*	14	2

[1] Chuen or Cauac

TABLE 4.9
Problematical Deposits of the Chuen Complex

PD. No.	Op.SubOp./ Lot	Location	Structure Group Type	TR. 25A Illustration	TR.	Est. No. of Vessels
108	71F/56,57	Gp. 5F-1 In quarry pit near Str. 5F-17, -18	Small Structure Group	142d1–d6; 143a1–a3	21	9–14
266	12P/144	Gp. 5D-2 Plat. 5D4-10		155e	14	1
267	12P/145	Gp. 5D-2 Plat. 5D4-10		155f	14	1
83	12P/118	North Acropolis Gp. 5D-2 Plat. 5D-4-10th	Civic-ceremonial	139a	14	1
90	64A/6–1	Seven Temples Plaza Gp. 5D-9 Plat. 5D-9	Civic-ceremonial	141a		1
91	64G/5–2	Seven Temples Plaza Gp. 5D-9 Plat. 5D-9	Civic-ceremonial	141b		2
931	64J/9–2	Seven Temples Plaza Gp. 5D-9 Plat. 5D-9	Civic-ceremonial	141c		1
97	64A//6–2	Seven Temples Plaza Gp. 5D-9 Plat. 5D-9	Civic-ceremonial	142a		1
114[1]	66X/29,30	Gp. 5G-18 Ch. 5G-7	Small Structure Group	144a	20	2
265	12P/137	North Acropolis Gp. 5D-2 Plat. 5D-4-10th	Civic-ceremonial	155d	14	1

[1] Chuen or Cauac

group in the North Acropolis, but, in this case, the single vessel is a Sierra Red outflaring to slightly outcurving side dish with concave base that is almost certainly of Chuen Complex affiliation.

Excavations in the Seven Temples Plaza produced four additional problematical deposits of which three (PD. 90, 91 and 97) are definitely of Chuen date, and PD. 93 that may date as late as the Cauac or Cimi Complex. Two of these (PD. 90 and 97) contain single Sierra Red vessels. Also from the Seven Temples Plaza, PD. 91 includes a Sierra Red bucket that was covered by a Repasto Black-on-red

slightly incurving to round-side dish or plate, a combination that was typical of late Chuen and Cauac Complex caches. Finally, PD. 114 of uncertain date (Chuen, Cauac, or Cimi) from Ch. 5G-7, in a small structure group that includes Str. 5G-18, contained two vessels, one a Sierra Red outflaring to slightly outcurving-side bowl and the other a Sapote Striated jar. Additionally, the three problematical deposits originally defined as Tzec (TR. 25A), PD. 108, PD. 266, and PD. 267 (see Table 3.8) are in fact a mix of Tzec and Chuen ceramics and should be considered Early Chuen.

In summary, the three typologically early single vessel problematical deposits from the North Acropolis and the two-vessel offering in PD. 91 are similar in content to caches of the Preclassic period at Tikal. The other problematical deposits are all of single vessels or of uncertain date, but are not shapes found in other known caches. It should be emphasized, that the sample of Preclassic caches recovered in the Tikal excavations is small and the contents far from rigidly standardized, thus any conclusions must be considered very tentative.

V

Cauac Ceramic Complex

Cauac Complex Collections

Introduction

The Cauac Ceramic Complex is represented by collections of good size that are associated with excellent architectural stratigraphy. In the total site collections, scatters of Cauac sherds mixed with other ceramics in frequencies too small for quantitative treatment occurred with about the same frequency as scatters of Chuen Complex ceramics. This suggests that the rapid growth of population that occurred between the Tzec and Chuen Complexes had moderated.

Four locations at Tikal provided quantifiable samples of Cauac Complex ceramics. The multiple lots (a total of six sample locations) that were large enough for individual quantification permitted checks of internal consistency within each level and comparison between levels. For the sake of larger samples, however, even lots that could be individually quantified were combined. The superb architectural stratigraphy of the North Acropolis excavations demonstrated the change from the Chuen Complex to the Cauac Complex, as well as the transition from Cauac to the succeeding Cimi Complex. In addition, the interrelated stratigraphy from the Great Plaza-North Terrace area was added to the ceramic record for the Cauac Complex. Two of the Cauac locations were within the major civic-ceremonial architectural complex of Gp. 5D-2 and may represent ceramic use in such contexts. The other two Cauac Complex samples came from small structure groups at some distance from the site center and can be presumed to represent commoner residential areas. Information on the Cauac locations is presented in Table 5.1. Cauac Complex ceramics occurred in association with six special deposits classified as burials, three special deposits classified as caches that were of either Cauac or Cimi date, and three problematical deposits. The burial record is enriched by the large ceramic offerings from three major burials in the North Acropolis.

CAUAC-CIMI LOCATION 1

The excavated areas of the North Terrace and adjacent sections of the Great Plaza have been designated Cauac-Cimi Location 1 (see TR. 14). The excavations revealed a series of floors and architectural developments that could be related to those of the North Acropolis sequence. Three architectural levels provided sealed samples dating from the Late and Terminal Preclassic. The two lowest samples contained no material later than Cauac Complex ceramics, while the uppermost levels included ceramics pertaining to the Cimi Complex.

Like the adjacent North Acropolis, the North Terrace-Great Plaza yielded sealed fill material associated with major construction activities. Consequently, all samples included a mixture of early ceramics combined with those current at the time of construction but were uncontaminated with later materials. Since the most likely source of fill material at the heart of the site would be debris from surrounding civic-ceremonial and elite residential

TABLE 5.1
Locations of Cauac Complex Samples

Sample #	Op.Sub-Op./Lot	Structure Group and Structure Number	Structure Group Type	Total Sherds-Types	Total Sherds-Shapes	Comments	TR.
Location 1 (Sample 1-1 is Cimi)	12E,G	North Acropolis Group 5D-2 Plat. 5D-4-6th, -7th	Civic-Ceremonial			Unspecified Lots	14
Sample 1-2	Combined sample of 7 lots			513	—	Construction levels above Sample 1-3	
Sample 1-3	Combined sample of 7 lots			1609	534	Lowest level of construction	
Location 2 (Samples 2-1 through 2-3 are Cimi)	12P	North Acropolis Group 5D-2	Civic-Ceremonial				14
Sample 2-4		Plat. 5D-4-6th and 5D-4-7th		299	—	Combined sample between the 10th and 11th floors of the North Acropolis	
Sample 2-5	Combined sample of 3 lots	Plat. 5D-4-6th and 5D-4-7th		1417	373	Combined sample sealed by the 11th floor of the North Acropolis	
Sample 2-6		Plat. 5D-4-6th and 5D-4-7th		427	37	Combined sample between the 13th and 14th floors of the North Acropolis	
Location 3	Residential group including Str. 5G-18	Intermediate Structure Group					
Sample 3-1	66X/6,9,24,26–32	Chultun 5G-7		181	233	Combined sample includes PD. 114 and PD. 125	
Location 4		Str. 6F-62 Locus	Small Structure Group				20A
Sample 4-1	72D/7–13,15,16,18	Chultun 6F-3, near Str. 6F-62		—	73	Combined sample includes PD. 115	
TOTAL SHERDS				4446	1250		

areas, the samples are assumed likely to represent upper-class activities.

Sample 1-1: Contains only Cimi Complex ceramics.

Cauac Sample 1-2: This sample was obtained from construction levels immediately above those that produced Cauac Sample 1-3. The sample included seven lots, with a combined total of 513 sherds, all of which were counted for types.

Cauac Sample 1-3: This sample was sealed beneath the lowest level of construction in the North Terrace-Great Plaza. Twenty-four excavation lots at this level included ceramics. Type counts were made for seven lots. A combined total of 1,609 sherds counted for types provided this sample. All lots were counted for vessel shapes, providing a combined total of 534 sherds.

CHUEN-CIMI LOCATION 2

This location consists of the massive cut through the construction levels of the North Acropolis (see TR. 14). Although the 10th through the 13th floors of the North Acropolis sequence were of Cauac date, the ceramic sample obtained was not particularly large. It should be noted that Cimi Sample 2-3, discussed in Chapter 6, is in fact a large sample that is transitional between the Cauac and Cimi Complexes, thus, providing a firm base for the end of the Cauac Complex.

Samples 2-1 through 2-3: These contained only Cimi Complex ceramics.

Cauac Sample 2-4: This sample was sealed between the 10th and 11th floors of the North Acropolis. It is a small sample consisting of several lots that provided 299 sherds for typological count. The sample contained too few rim sherds for quantification of vessel shapes.

Cauac Sample 2-5: This is the largest of the Cauac Complex samples from the North Acropolis. The sample was sealed by the 11th floor of the North Acropolis series, two floors above Cauac Sample 2-6. Cauac Sample 2-5 includes three lots. The combined sample from the three lots contained 1,417 sherds counted for types and 373 rims for shape quantification.

Cauac Sample 2-6: This sample was obtained from between the 13th and 14th floors of the North Acropolis sequence, immediately overlying the most recent of the Chuen Complex samples from the location. Too few sherds were obtained from material underlying the 12th Acropolis floor to permit quantification. Unfortunately, Cauac Sample 2-6 was small. It provided a total of only 427 sherds for typological counts and 37 rim sherds.

CAUAC LOCATION 3

Cauac Sample 3-1: This sample was procured from the excavation of Ch. 5G-7 and 5G-24, actually a single large, multi-chambered chultun located in the plaza between Str. 5G-18 to -21 (an intermediate structure group), about 1.5 km E of the Great Plaza. Although a number of lots were separated in the complex stratigraphy offered by the chultun, none was large enough for individual quantification and a total sample of all sherds had to be used for analysis. The counted sample included 181 sherds quantified for types and 233 sherds quantified for shapes. Because the structures near the chultun were all small, the sample is considered representative of commoner domestic activity.

CAUAC LOCATION 4

Cauac Sample 4-1: Cauac Location 4 was Ch. 6F-3, located beside the isolated small Str. 6F-62, about 1.5 km SE of the Great Plaza (see TR. 20A). All of the lots from the chultun excavation were combined into a single sample of 73 rim sherds quantified for shapes. Typological counts were not made. Because the nearest structure is a small mound, the material is probably the result of domestic activity. The chultun, however, is located just off the SE corner of the large platform of the Temple of the Inscriptions and it is possible that a center of Preclassic ceremonial activity might have been located in the vicinity.

Pastes of the Cauac Complex

Introduction

The most common pastes of the Cauac Complex are the same as those of the Chuen Complex: Coarse-carbonate Paste for unslipped types and Preclassic Monochrome Paste for slipped types. Cauac

Complex pottery, however, begins a trend in the increase of the finer paste, Preclassic Fine Paste, which reaches its peak frequencies in the succeeding Cimi Complex. Although many of the fine-paste examples show the carbonate inclusions that characterize both other pastes, the majority of fine-paste specimens do not include carbonate. In addition, volcanic ash inclusions often occur in fine-paste sherds.

Cauac Paste Descriptions

COARSE-CARBONATE PASTE

Identifying characteristics: In all regards except for color the same as the Chuen Complex (see Chapter 4 for complete description).

Color: The most common colors include various shades of brown and yellow (10YR 6/6 to 6/3; 5/8 to 5/3; 7.5YR 7/6, 6/6, 6/4; 5/6, 5/4, 4/4), however, there is not a red variety in the Chuen Complex.

PRECLASSIC MONOCHROME PASTE

Identifying characteristics: In all regards same as the Chuen Complex (see Chapter 4 for complete description).

PRECLASSIC FINE PASTE

Identifying characteristics: Unlike many of the other pastes used in the production of Preclassic slipped types, Preclassic Fine Paste cannot be distinguished from comparable pastes of the Classic Period. In the context of a Preclassic collection, the paste is identifiable because of its relatively fine texture and finely divided inclusions.

Color: A wide range of paste colors occurs in Preclassic Fine Paste. Most common are reddish yellow (5YR 6/6, 7/6; 7.5YR 6/6), yellowish brown (5YR 5/6), and strong brown (7.5YR 5/6). At one end of the Munsell scale, colors range to light brownish gray (2.5YR 6/2), light yellowish gray (2.5YR 6/4), and pale yellow (2.5YR 7/4). At the other end of the scale, examples of light gray (10YR 6/1), very pale brown (10YR 7/4, 8/4), and yellow (10YR 7/6) occur.

Texture: Fine.

Inclusions: A considerable variety of inclusions occurred in Preclassic Fine Paste, but no single kind of inclusion characterizes all examples of the paste type. Very finely divided carbonate particles that sparkle under a strong light are characteristic of many examples. Small white particles, small dark particles, and pinkish particles that are probably a second clay type also occur. Some examples contain volcanic ash. A subdivision of the paste type might be made into two subclasses, one characterized by carbonate without volcanic ash, the other characterized by ash in the absence of carbonate. The subclass of carbonate-containing sherds is considerably more common than the ash-tempered category.

Types: Preclassic Fine Paste occurred in all slipped types of the Late Preclassic complexes but is most common in the Cimi Complex.

Discussion

As was true for the Chuen Complex, the small number of paste types for the Cauac Complex masks a considerable degree of variability. All pastes are broadly defined and far from homogeneous.

Ceramic Types of the Cauac Complex

Introduction

The Cauac Ceramic Complex includes the 10 ceramic groups and 21 types (comprised of 29 varieties) listed in Table 5.2. With the typological stability characteristic of the Late Preclassic ceramic complexes at Tikal, all major types of the Chuen Complex continued to appear in the Cauac Complex. The only new types in Cauac were several important, but relatively rare, decorated types, a new monochrome red group (Cabro) and a new unslipped group (Morfin).

Cauac Type Descriptions

ACHIOTES CERAMIC GROUP

Achiotes Unslipped: Achiotes Variety

Established: Smith and Gifford (1966)

TABLE 5.2
Ceramic Groups and Types of the Cauac Complex

Culbert and Kosakowsky	Culbert (1993)
ACHIOTES CERAMIC GROUP	**ACHIOTES CERAMIC GROUP**
Achiotes Unslipped: Achiotes Variety	Achiotes Unslipped: Achiotes Variety
SAPOTE CERAMIC GROUP	**SAPOTE CERAMIC GROUP**
Sapote Striated: Sapote Variety	Sapote Striated: Sapote Variety
MORFIN CERAMIC GROUP	**MORFIN CERAMIC GROUP**
Morfin Unslipped: Morfin Variety	Morfin Unslipped: Morfin Variety
SIERRA CERAMIC GROUP	**SIERRA CERAMIC GROUP**
Sierra Red: Sierra Variety	Sierra Red: Sierra Variety
Laguna Verde Incised: Simple-incised Variety	Laguna Verde Incised: Simple-incised Variety
Laguna Verde Incised: Design-incised Variety	Laguna Verde Incised: Design-incised Variety
Laguna Verde Incised: Usulutan-style Variety	Laguna Verde Incised: Usulutan-style Variety
Alta Mira Fluted: Alta Mira Variety	Alta Mira Fluted: Alta Mira Variety
Lagartos Punctated: Lagartos Variety	Lagartos Punctated: Lagartos Variety
Repasto Black-on-red: Repasto Variety	Repasto Black-on-red: Repasto Variety
Hiabon Punctated: Hiabon Variety	Hiabon Punctated: Hiabon Variety
In Cabro Ceramic Group	Mut Red-on-brown: Mut Variety
In Cabro Ceramic Group	Correlo Incised-dichrome: Correlo Variety
CABRO CERAMIC GROUP	*Not identified*
Cabro Red: Cabro Variety	*Not identified*
Mut Dichrome: Mut Variety	*In Sierra Ceramic Group*
Correlo Incised-dichrome: Correlo Variety	*In Sierra Ceramic Group*
POLVERO CERAMIC GROUP	**POLVERO CERAMIC GROUP**
Polvero Black: Polvero Variety	Polvero Black: Polvero Variety
Lechugal Incised: Simple-incised Variety	Lechugal Incised: Simple-incised Variety
Lechugal Incised: Design-incised Variety	Lechugal Incised: Design-incised Variety
BACLAM CERAMIC GROUP	**BACLAM CERAMIC GROUP**
Baclam Red-orange: Baclam Variety	Baclam Orange: Baclam Variety
Cay Incised: Simple-incised Variety	Cay Incised: Simple-incised Variety
Cay Incised: Design-incised Variety	Cay Incised: Design-incised Variety
BOXCAY CERAMIC GROUP	**BOXCAY CERAMIC GROUP**
Boxcay Brown: Boxcay Variety	Boxcay Brown: Boxcay Variety
Xtabcab Incised: Simple-incised Variety	Xtabcab Incised: Simple-incised Variety
Xtabcab Incised: Design-incised Variety	Xtabcab Incised: Design-incised Variety
FLOR CERAMIC GROUP	**FLOR CERAMIC GROUP**
Flor Cream: Flor Variety	Flor Cream: Flor Variety
Accordian Incised: Simple-incised Variety	Accordian Incised: Simple-incised Variety
Accordian Incised: Design-incised Variety	Accordian Incised: Design-incised Variety
SACLUC CERAMIC GROUP	**SACLUC CERAMIC GROUP**
Caramba Red-on-orange: Chic Variety	Caramba Red-on-orange: Chic Variety
Sacluc Black-on-orange: Sis Variety	Sacluc Black-on-orange: Sis Variety
Metapa Trichrome: Itsul Variety	Metapa Trichrome: Itsul Variety

Group: Achiotes

Ware: Uaxactun Unslipped

Ceramic Complex: Cauac (Begins in Chuen and continues into Cimi)

Ceramic Sphere: Chicanel

Illustrations: Fig. 9.1–63; 13.20–22; 14.14. See TR. 25A: fig. 6*b–c*; 8*a*1; 11*a*2.

Principal identifying attributes: Unslipped only partially smoothed surfaces that reflect highly variable paste colors on wide-mouth jars.

Identifying characteristics and sorting problems: Both surface and paste are quite characteristic and overlap little with other types.

Paste: Characterized by Coarse-carbonate Paste. Most examples are of the brown to gray regular variety of Coarse-carbonate Paste, but some are of the red variety.

Firing: Many examples are darkened completely, but less than one-quarter show separable dark cores. Cores showing two or more shades of paste color are common. About half of the sherds show fireclouding of the surface.

Color: Highly variable, even on individual sherds. Light brown (7.5YR 6/4), strong brown (7.5YR 5/6), very pale brown (10YR 8/3), yellowish brown (10YR 5/4), and dark yellowish brown (10YR 4/4) all occur.

Surface finish: Most examples were carelessly finished and many sherds show smoothing marks and poor obliteration of coils; some examples are medium smooth.

Shapes: Almost entirely confined to the various wide-mouth jar shapes: wide-mouth jar with short neck and very large-diameter jar. There are occasional examples of outflaring to slightly outcurving-side unslipped dishes.

Temporal distribution: Begins in the Tzec Complex. After the Tzec Complex, the type becomes rare and although there is still a fairly abundant sherd-sorting category for Achiotes Unslipped, it contains mostly jar necks that may be from vessels that were actually striated.

Comments: Unslipped sherds made from Coarse-carbonate Paste that occur in Cauac Complex samples are mostly necks of jars that were probably Sapote Striated. Other unslipped sherds belong to the new type Morfin Unslipped.

Intersite comparisons: Achiotes Unslipped is used as the predominate unslipped type at Acanmul (Ball and Taschek 2015); Altar de Sacrificios (Adams 1971); Becan (Ball 1977); El Mirador (Forsyth 1989); El Perú/Waka' (Eppich 2011); Holmul (Callaghan 2008, 2016b); the Petexbatun (Foias and Bishop 2013); and Seibal (Sabloff 1975). In Belize there is some variation noted from the Achiotes Ceramic Group and Paila Unslipped is used in its place at Barton Ramie; (Gifford 1976); Blue Creek (Kosakowsky and Lohse 2003); Chan (Kosakowsky 2012); and La Milpa (Sagebiel 2005). Paila Unslipped is also used at Uaxactun (Smith and Gifford 1966) for the Late Preclassic. Richardson Peak Unslipped is used at Cerros (Robertson 2016); Cuello (Kosakowsky 1987; Pring 1977); and Colha (Valdez 1987).

SAPOTE CERAMIC GROUP

Sapote Striated: Sapote Variety

Established: Smith and Gifford (1966)

Group: Sapote [It is included in the Achiotes Group elsewhere]

Ware: Uaxactun Unslipped

Ceramic Complex: Cauac (Begins in Chuen and continues into Cimi)

Ceramic Sphere: Chicanel

Illustrations: Fig. 9.1–63; 13.1–19; 15.13. See TR. 25A: fig. 10*h*; 11*a*4; 144*a*1.

Principal identifying attributes: Unslipped surfaces with closely spaced striations only on the bodies of wide-mouth jars.

Paste: Coarse-carbonate Paste.

Firing: One-quarter to one-half of the sherds show dark cores. Many of the sherds without dark cores have a different paste color near the core than at the surface. Nearly half the sherds exhibit fireclouding of the surface.

Color: Highly variable, ranging from reddish tones (red, 10R 5/6, 2.5YR 5/6 to 4/8; light red, 2.5YR 6/6; reddish brown, 5YR 4/8) to brown (10YR 4/3, 5/3).

Surface finish and decoration: Striations are closely spaced, ranging from shallow to quite deep and from narrow to broad lines. Striations occur only on the bodies of jars.

Shapes: Almost entirely wide-mouth jars: wide-mouth jars with short neck and very large-diameter jars.

Temporal distribution: Occurs in late samples of the Tzec Complex in small quantities. Becomes common in the earliest Chuen Complex samples and continues unchanged until the end of the Preclassic. Thin-walled examples are less common than in the preceding Chuen Complex.

Comments: Sapote Striated continued to be an important type in the Cauac Complex as it did in the preceding Chuen Complex.

Intersite comparisons: Acanmul (Ball and Taschek 2015); Altar de Sacrificios (Adams 1971); Barton Ramie (Gifford 1976); Becan (Ball 1977); Blue Creek (Kosakowsky and Lohse 2003); Calakmul (Dominguez Carrasco 1994); Chan Chich (Valdez 1998, Valdez and Houk 2000); Cerros (Robertson-Freidel 1980); Colha (Valdez 1987); Cuello (Kosakowsky 1987); Holmul (Callaghan 2008, 2016b); El Pozito (Eppich 2000); El Mirador (Forsyth 1989); K'axob (Lopez Varela 1996); La Milpa (Sagebiel 2005); Naachtun (Walker and Reese-Taylor 2012); Nakbe (Forsyth 1993); Nohmul (Kosakowsky and Pring 2001); "Zapote" in the Petexbatun (Foias and Bishop 2013); Rio Azul (Adams 1999); Seibal (Sabloff 1975); Uaxactun (Smith and Gifford 1966); Yaxchilan (Lopez Varela 1989).

MORFIN CERAMIC GROUP
Morfin Unslipped: Morfin Variety

Established: Adams (1971)

Group: Morfin

Ware: Uaxactun Unslipped

Ceramic Complex: Cauac (Continues into Cimi)

Ceramic Sphere: Chicanel

Illustrations: Fig. 11.19–22. See TR. 25A: fig. 7*g*; 9*a*3; 12*f*, 35*a*2; 155*g*.

Principal identifying attributes: Unsmoothed unslipped surfaces that are frequently fireclouded. Only found on dish shapes.

Identifying characteristics and sorting problems: The combination of unslipped surfaces, dish shapes, and paste that is not coarse-carbonate is very distinctive.

Paste: Preclassic Fine Paste and Preclassic Monochrome Paste. It is important to note that unlike all other unslipped types in the Late Preclassic complexes, Morfin Unslipped is not made from Coarse-carbonate Paste.

Firing: Fireclouding is present in 56% of the examples. Of the fireclouded vessels, 62% exhibit fireclouding on the interior only, 21% show it on both interior and exterior, and only 8% show it on the exterior only. This is quite different from the distribution of fireclouding on other types in which exterior fireclouding predominates.

Color: Light brownish gray (10YR 6/2) to very pale brown (10YR 7/4).

Surface finish: The vessels are carelessly finished with the marks of the smoothing tool clearly visible on a number of sherds. A few examples are striated on the exterior. If one surface is better finished than the other, it is almost always the interior that shows greater care in finishing.

Shapes: Almost exclusively used for the production of small, unslipped dish shapes.

Temporal distribution: First appears at the beginning of the Cauac Complex, reaches a peak in very early Cimi lots, and continues until the end of the Cimi Complex. The type is not present in Chuen and is quite easily recognized. It is a good diagnostic for the Cauac and Cimi Complexes.

Comments: Whether the dishes made from Morfin Unslipped had a primary use as incensarios is a still unresolved question. The fact that many of the vessels were fireclouded on the interior, a characteristic generally uncommon in other vessel shapes, would suggest incensario use as it does to Adams (1971:18) for the same type at Altar de Sacrificios. On the other hand, almost half of the vessels do not show smudging or fireclouding on the interior, and, even where such smudging occurs, it is rarely associated with the heavy accumulations of soot that are characteristic of incensarios. Another possibly relevant characteristic is a very uneven distribution of the type within Tikal. In some lots, usually from the North Acropolis, the type is very common, but in many other lots the frequency is quite low. The best conclusion would seem to be that Morfin Unslipped had some special use or uses among which was use as an incensario, but that it was not primarily an incensario type.

Intersite comparisons: Altar de Sacrificios (Adams 1971) and Becan (Ball 1977).

SIERRA CERAMIC GROUP

Sierra Red: Sierra Variety

Established: Smith and Gifford (1966)

Group: Sierra

Ware: Paso Caballo Waxy

Ceramic Complex: Cauac (Begins in Chuen and continues into Cimi)

Ceramic Sphere: Chicanel

Illustrations: Fig. 10.24–27, 10.49, 10.51; 11.35, 11.45, 11.48; 12.3–5, 12.8–12, 12.39–45, 12.47–53, 12.55–58, 12.63–64, 12.67–73; 13.26–28, 13.32–38, 13.43–46, 13.48–50, 13.55–57, 13.60; 14.8–10, 14.16–21, 14.28; 15.10; 16.6, 16.8, 16.12, 16.21, 16.28, 16.31; 56.13, 56.28–29; 57.1. See TR. 25A: fig. 4*b–c*; 6*d–f*; 7*a–f*; 8*b1*; 9*a*2,4–5,*b*1; 10*a,c*,e–g; 11*a*5; 12*e*; 13*a,b,e,g*; 99*c,d*1–2,*e,f*; 141*c*; 144*a*2.

Principal identifying attributes: Monochrome red, thick, waxy slip that fireclouds to brown and black on round-side bowls and dishes.

Identifying characteristics and sorting problems: Because almost all whole vessels of Sierra Red include areas in which the color variegates to black or light brown, sherds from variegated areas may be difficult to attribute to a specific type. In non-variegated areas, the color range of Sierra Red is small and quite distinct from that of other monochrome types. There are some examples that are unslipped on the exterior (see Fig. 16.5 and TR. 25A fig. 9*a*2) that may be similar to Puletan Red-and unslipped in northern Belize (Kosakowsky 1987).

Paste: Preclassic Monochrome Paste.

Firing: Dark cores occur in about one-third of the sherds, usually in thicker sections. Fireclouding occurs on 30% to 45% of the sherds in individual lots, more frequently on jars than on bowls.

Slip: The slip is thick and tends to flake. In most cases the surface was not well polished before application of the slip.

Polish: Usually low to medium. Waxiness is common but by no means universal.

Color: Most sherds are red (10R 4/8 to 2.5YR 5/6); a few examples range to reddish yellow (7.5YR 6/6).

Surface finish and decoration: Monochrome red slip on well-smoothed surfaces. Slip is waxy and non-lustrous.

Shapes: Medium-diameter bowls and dishes are the most common shapes (68%) in Cauac samples (of which 14% have medial flanges or ridges), followed by narrow-mouth jars (20%), and fewer examples of small to large buckets, large diameter widely out-curving-side bowls, and small and medium-diameter slightly incurving to round-side bowls.

Comments: Sierra Red was the most common slipped type in the Cauac Complex. There are a few examples of Sierra Red that have unslipped exteriors and appliqué spikes attached but there are too few to name a separate variety.

Temporal distribution: Chuen Complex to the end of the Preclassic.

Intersite comparisons: Extremely widespread throughout lowland Maya sites in the Late Preclassic. Acanmul (Ball and Taschek 2015); Altar de Sacrificios (Adams 1971); Barton Ramie (Gifford 1976); Becan (Ball 1977); Blue Creek (Kosakowsky and Lohse 2003); Calakmul (Dominguez Carrasco 1994); Chan (Kosakowsky 2012); Chan Chich (Valdez 1998, Valdez and Houk 2000); Cerros (Robertson-Freidel 1980); Colha (Valdez 1987); Cuello (Kosakowsky 1987); Holmul (Callaghan 2008, 2016b); El Mirador (Forsyth 1989); El Perú/Waka' (Eppich 2011); El Pozito (Eppich 2000); Kichpanha (McDow 1997); La Milpa (Sagebiel 2005); Nakbe (Forsyth 1993); Nohmul (Kosakowsky and Pring 2001); the Petexbatun (Foias and Bishop 2013); Rio Azul (Adams 1999); Seibal (Sabloff 1975:77–81); Uaxactun (Smith and Gifford 1966, Smith 1955).

Laguna Verde Incised: Simple-incised Variety and Design-incised Variety

Established: Type named by Smith and Gifford (1966); varieties named by Culbert (1993 [TR. 25A])

Group: Sierra

Ware: Paso Caballo Waxy

Ceramic Complex: Cauac (Begins in Chuen and continues into Cimi)

Ceramic Sphere: Chicanel

Illustrations: Fig. 10.1–12, 10.28–31, 10.40, 10.47; 12.14, 12.34–36.

Principal identifying attributes: Sierra Red slip decorated secondarily with pre-slip groove incising around vessel exteriors.

Surface finish and decoration: The Simple-incised Variety is decorated with single or multiple lines encircling the vessels almost always on the exterior near the rim. Patterns of the Design-incised Variety are usually no more than curving lines or straight lines that cross. Very few sherds were large enough to demonstrate overall vessel patterns.

Shapes: Small-diameter bowls and dishes are the most common shape represented in all incised types. Large-diameter bowls or dishes, buckets, and narrow-mouth jars occur with somewhat lesser frequencies.

Temporal distribution: Begins and is most common during the Chuen Complex. Incising and grooving are considerably less common in the Sierra Group in the Cauac and Cimi Complexes.

Intersite comparisons: Varieties of Laguna Verde Incised are found at Acanmul (Ball and Taschek 2015); Altar de Sacrificios (Adams 1971); Becan (Ball 1977); Barton Ramie (Gifford 1976); Blue Creek (Kosakowsky and Lohse 2003); Calakmul (Dominguez Carrasco 1994); Cerros (Robertson-Freidel 1980); Chan (Kosakowsky 2012); Chan Chich (Valdez 1998, Valdez and Houk 2000); Colha (Valdez 1987); Cuello (Kosakowsky 1987); El Mirador (Forsyth 1989); El Perú/Waka' (Eppich 2011); El Pozito (Eppich 2000); Holmul (Callaghan 2008, 2016b); La Milpa (Sagebiel 2005); Nakbe (Forsyth 1993); Nohmul (Kosakowsky and Pring 2001); the Petexbatun (Foias and Bishop 2013); Rio Azul (Adams 1999); Seibal (Sabloff 1975); Uaxactun (Smith 1955; Smith and Gifford 1966).

Laguna Verde Incised: Usulutan-style Variety

[**Note:** Given the composite nature of the decoration that includes imitation Usulutan and incising, this type should have been named a composite according to the type: variety rules of nomenclature (Gifford 1976). However, the original type and variety names have been retained for ease of comparison with the prior publication of Tikal ceramics (TR. 25A).]

Established: Type named by Smith and Gifford (1966); variety named by Culbert (1993 [TR. 25A])

Group: Sierra

Ware: Paso Caballo Waxy

Ceramic Complex: Cauac (Continues into Cimi)

Ceramic Sphere: Chicanel

Illustrations: Fig. 14.2. See TR. 25A: fig. 8*b*2; 9*a*1; 12*d*2; 13*d*.

Principal identifying attributes: Sierra Red slip decorated secondarily with pre-slip groove incising around vessel exteriors, and imitation Usulutan multiple wavy lines.

Identifying characteristics and sorting problems: Quite distinctive.

Comments: Identical to Sierra Red except in the following categories:

Surface finish and decoration: Techniques of incising include light pre-fire scratching of the slip that lightens the slip color but does not penetrate to the clay, and post-fire incising. Designs consist of multiple parallel wavy (or sometimes straight) lines that are an obvious imitation of the Usulutan effect. Designs are perpendicular to the rim near the top of the vessel and become circles of wavy patterns on the interior base.

Shapes: Mostly medium-diameter bowls with medial flanges, and composite silhouette bowls. Large widely outcurving-side bowls also occur.

Temporal distribution: Cauac and Cimi Complexes only.

Comments: The imitation of Usulutan designs through incising is very common in Correlo Incised-dichrome and occurs rarely on occasional Lechugal and Accordian Incised sherds.

Intersite comparisons: Imitation Usulutan decoration occurs in the Sarteneja Ceramic Group at

Barton Ramie (Gifford 1976), and in the Sacluc Group (also found at Tikal) at Altar de Sacrificios (Adams 1971); Blue Creek (Kosakowsky and Lohse 2003; Kosakowsky, Robertson, and Walker 2016); El Mirador (Forsyth 1989); Nakbe (Forsyth 1993); Punta de Chimino (Bachand 2007); Seibal (Sabloff 1975); and possibly at La Milpa (Sagebiel 2005).

Alta Mira Fluted: Alta Mira Variety

Established: Smith and Gifford (1966)

Group: Sierra

Ware: Paso Caballo Waxy

Ceramic Complex: Cauac (Continues into Cimi)

Ceramic Sphere: Chicanel

Illustrations: See TR. 25A: fig. 6*c*; 9*b*2,3.

Principal identifying attributes: Monochrome red slip same as Sierra Red with the addition of pre-slip shallow, wide vertical fluting.

Comments: Identical to Sierra Red except for the addition of fluting.

Shapes: Medium and small buckets, though occurs less commonly on other shapes similar to Sierra Red. There is one example of a florero, originally called an urn jar (TR. 25A).

Temporal distribution: Begins in Cauac and continues into the Cimi Complex.

Intersite distribution: Altar de Sacrificios (Adams 1971); Barton Ramie (Gifford 1976); Blue Creek (Kosakowsky and Lohse 2003); Calakmul (Dominguez Carrasco 1994); Holmul (Callaghan 2008, 2016b); El Mirador (Forsyth 1989); El Pozito (Eppich 2000); El Perú/Waka' (Eppich 2011); Edzna (Forsyth 1983); La Milpa (Sagebiel 2005); Nakbe (Forsyth 1993); the Petexbatun (Foias and Bishop 2013); Piedras Negras (Muñoz 2006); Seibal (Sabloff 1975); Uaxactun (Smith and Gifford 1966).

Lagartos Punctated: Lagartos Variety

Established: Smith and Gifford (1966)

Group: Sierra

Ware: Paso Caballo Waxy

Ceramic Complex: Cauac (Begins in Chuen and continues into Cimi)

Ceramic Sphere: Chicanel

Principal identifying attributes: Monochrome red slip same as Sierra Red with the addition of secondary decoration of punctations on the exterior.

Comments: The type begins in the preceding Chuen Complex in small frequencies and continues in equally small quantities in Chuen Complex collections. In typological characteristics, the sherds are identical to Sierra Red and are too small to permit comments about the patterns of punctation.

Intersite comparisons: Lagartos Punctated is named as a type, or unnamed within the Sierra Red Group at Altar de Sacrificios (Adams 1971:46); Blue Creek (Kosakowsky and Lohse 2003); Cuello (Kosakowsky 1987); El Mirador (Forsyth 1989); El Pozito (Eppich 2000); Holmul (Callaghan 2008, 2016b); Seibal (Sabloff 1975); Uaxactun (Smith and Gifford 1966).

Repasto Black-on-red: Repasto Variety

Established: Smith and Gifford (1966)

Group: Sierra

Ware: Paso Caballo Waxy

Ceramic Complex: Cauac (Begins in Chuen)

Ceramic Sphere: Chicanel

Illustrations: Fig. 15.1–2.

Principal identifying attributes: Identical to Sierra Red with the addition of secondary decoration by means of black resist. This decoration is dots, patch-es, and irregular lines of black on red.

Identifying characteristics and sorting problems: The irregular boundaries between red and black areas are quite characteristic. Sherds of the type that do not include areas of black would be classified as Sierra Red, though fireclouding on Sierra Red can be mistaken for Repasto Black-on-red.

Slip: A standard Sierra Red slip is applied first. After the intended design areas have been covered with a protective coating, one or both sides of the vessel are coated with a black pigment.

Color: Red identical to that of Sierra Red. Black ranges from a good clear black to dark red (2.5YR 4/6) in areas where the black pigment is inadequate.

Surface finish and decoration: Irregular lines, dots, and patches of the base red color appear on sherds. Whole vessels show overall designs that usually divide the vessel into sections. Because control of the areas of application was poor, only broad-line patterns were attempted.

Shapes: Slightly incurving to round-side bowls and dishes are by far the dominant shape class. Narrow-mouth jars appear occasionally, while various other shapes occur in low frequencies.

Temporal distribution: Repasto Black-on-red begins in the Chuen Complex and is rare in the Cauac Complex

Comments: The resist technique and design patterns of Repasto Black-on-red are identical to those used in the Chuen Complex Ahchab Red-on-buff.

Intersite comparisons: Altar de Sacrificios (Adams 1971); Barton Ramie (Gifford 1976); Becan (Ball 1977); Blue Creek (Kosakowsky and Lohse 2003); Cerros (Robertson 2016); Edzna (Forsyth 1983); El Mirador (Forsyth 1989); Holmul (Callaghan 2008; 2016b); La Milpa (Sagebiel 2005); Nohmul (Kosakowsky and Pring 2001); Uaxactun (Smith and Gifford 1966, Smith 1955).

Hiabon Punctated: Hiabon Variety

[**Note:** The decoration includes unslipped areas of

the vessels as well as punctations, the type should have been described as a composite. However, the original name was retained in order to facilitate comparisons with the published vessels in Culbert (TR. 25A).]

Established: TR. 25A (Culbert 1993)

Group: Sierra

Ware: Paso Caballo Waxy

Ceramic Complex: Cauac (Continues into Cimi)

Ceramic Sphere: Chicanel

Principal identifying attributes: Sierra Red slip on portions of exterior of vessel with the remaining surface left unslipped and decorated secondarily with punctations.

Identifying characteristics and sorting problems: Completely distinctive.

Comments: Identical to Sierra Red except for the following categories:

Surface finish and decoration: Part of the vessel is red-slipped; the remainder is smoothed but unslipped. Small and shallow crescent-shaped or straight-line punctations cover all or most of the unslipped portions. The punctations occur randomly or are arranged in irregular, often double, rows. The line of separation between the red and unslipped/punctated sections is the break in curvature of a composite vessel. Slip and punctation are on the vessel exterior; the interior is unslipped.

Shapes: Almost all examples are from composite silhouette bowls. Sherds that are large enough to indicate total vessel shape all seem to be from "mushroom stands."

Temporal distribution: Occurs with very low frequency in the Cauac and Cimi Complexes.

Intersite comparisons: Mushroom stands have been identified as the Hongo Composite type at Altar de Sacrificios (Adams 1971); Becan (Ball 1977:114);

Colha (Valdez 1987); El Mirador (Forsyth 1989); El Pozito (Eppich 2000); El Perú/Waka' (Eppich 2011); La Milpa (Sagebiel 2005); Rio Azul (Adams 1999).

CABRO CERAMIC GROUP

Cabro Red: Cabro Variety

Established: Robertson-Freidel (1980)

Group: Cabro

Ware: Chunux Hard

Ceramic Complex: Cauac (Continues into Cimi)

Ceramic Sphere: Chicanel

Illustrations: Fig. 12.17–18; 14.5.

Principal identifying attributes: Double red slip, with outer thin slip that fires to a high luster with hard surfaces.

Identifying characteristics and sorting problems: The lustrous hard slip, which is unusual in the Cauac Complex, makes it easy to separate this type from the waxy non-lustrous and more common Sierra Red.

Paste: Preclassic Monochrome and Preclassic Fine Pastes, with the latter more common.

Firing: Fireclouding is uncommon and most examples are completely oxidized.

Slip: Monochrome red slip is hard and not easily scratched.

Polish: High

Color: Glossy, hard outer slip is usually red (10R4/6-8). The red underslip is a lighter red in color (2.5YR4/5-8) and only visible on eroded surfaces.

Surface finish and decoration: Surfaces of vessels are burnished and well smoothed, though when eroded the over-slip tends to flake off, and the surfaces are subject to rootlet marks. There is less fireclouding on this monochrome red type than in Sierra Red.

Shapes: Overlap with Sierra Red.

Temporal distribution: Restricted to the Cauac and Cimi Complexes.

Comments: Originally Cabro Red sherds were not identified in the Tikal collections (TR. 25A) and went unnoticed as slightly glossier sherds in the Sierra Group. However, upon reexamination it is clear that double slipped glossier red examples are better described as part of the Cabro Group.

Other Cabro Group: Three whole vessels (see Culbert TR. 25A: fig. 5*a,b*; 9*b*4) originally classified as Alta Mira Fluted have a glossy double monochrome red slip that is characteristic of Cabro Red, rather than Sierra Red. All three examples are urn jars, or floreros, from Cauac burials. Two examples may be Tuk Red-on-red Trickle (Fig. 14.4; 16.1) similar to examples from Cerros (Robertson-Freidel 1980).

Intersite distribution: Cabro Red was originally identified at the site of Cerros (Robertson-Freidel 1980). Sierra Red: Big Pond Variety at Cuello (Kosakowsky 1983; 1987) and Nohmul (Kosakowsky and Pring 2001) has been reclassified as Cabro Red. It is also present at Blue Creek (Kosakowsky and Lohse 2003); Chan (Kosakowsky 2012); El Pozito (Eppich 2000); and Naachtun (Walker and Reese-Taylor 2012).

Mut Dichrome: Mut Variety

Established: Type originally called Mut Red-on-brown Culbert (1993 [TR. 25A]). Renamed in this work.

Group: Cabro [originally in the Sierra Group (TR. 25A)]

Ware: Chunux Hard

Ceramic Complex: Cauac (Continues into Cimi)

Ceramic Sphere: Chicanel

Illustrations: Fig. 10.52; 11.27, 11.33.

Principal identifying attributes: Exterior surfaces are the same as Cabro Red and the interior surfaces are slipped a brown to reddish yellow color.

Identifying characteristics and sorting problems: Only sherds large enough to indicate clearly that the distinction in color between the two sides of the vessel was intentional rather than an accident of firing are counted as part of the type. Many small sherds that belong to the type were probably sorted into the variegated sorting category. Mut Dichrome also identical to Correlo Incised-dichrome except that it lacks incising.

Paste: Preclassic Fine Paste.

Comments: Identical to Cabro Red except as detailed below.

Color: Red is within the color range of Cabro Red. The interior "brown" is highly variable in color and includes brown (7.5YR 4/4, 5/4), reddish yellow (7.5YR 6/6), pink (7.5YR 7/4), and dark gray (10YR 4/1).

Surface finish and decoration: The two colors occur on opposite sides of the vessel, with red always on the exterior and brown on the interior.

Shapes: Outflaring to slightly outcurving-side bowls and dishes are most common, but a variety of other shapes also occur.

Temporal distribution: Identified in the Cauac and Cimi Complexes.

Intersite comparisons: None noted though Correlo Incised-dichrome is found at Blue Creek (Kosakowsky and Lohse 2003) and El Perú/Waka' (Eppich 2011) so there may be examples of Mut Dichrome sherds that lack incising that were misclassified as Correlo.

Correlo Incised-dichrome: Correlo Variety

Established: Smith and Gifford (1966)

Group: Cabro [originally in the Sierra Group (TR. 25A); identified as in the Cabro Group by Robertson (2016)]

Ware: Chunux Hard

Ceramic Complex: Cauac (Continues into Cimi)

Ceramic Sphere: Chicanel

Illustrations: Fig. 16.7.

Principal identifying attributes: Surfaces the same as Mut Dichrome with the addition of incised decoration.

Identifying characteristics and sorting problems: The combination of incising and the different colors on two sides makes the type easy to identify.

Paste: Preclassic Fine Paste.

Firing: Dark cores rare and fireclouded exteriors fairly common.

Slip: Medium.

Polish: Medium.

Color: The exterior surface is red and the interior cream to brown. Although these colors are within the range of seemingly unintentional fireclouding on Late Preclassic monochrome reds, it seems certain in this case that the two-color effect was intentionally created. The color ranges from red (10R 5/6, 5/8; 2.5YR 4/8) to dark red brown (2.5YR 2/4) and light red (2.5YR 6/8). The interior color is extremely variable and includes reddish yellow (5YR 6/6, 7/8), yellowish red (5YR 5/4), brown (7.5YR 4/4), and pink (7.5YR 8/4). Some examples fall within the color range of Flor Cream at light gray (2.5Y 7/2) and grayish brown (2.5Y 5/2).

Surface finish and decoration: The most common incised pattern is multiple parallel wavy lines on the vessel exterior that are an obvious imitation of the Usulutan style. A number of examples, however, show patterned incising that is fine-line crosshatched rectangles or triangles. The incising was usually done while the slip was still wet, but sometimes was done after firing.

Shapes: The most common shape is a composite silhouette bowl. Also occurs on medial-flange bowls.

Temporal distribution: Begins during the Cauac

Complex and seems to continue during the Cimi Complex.

Comments: The great similarity of small jars of Correlo Incised-dichrome between locations and at other sites makes the type a good temporal marker for the Cauac Complex. Whether the vessels were actually traded or the similarities are the result of copying is uncertain, and there is no reason to consider them trade items.

Intersite comparisons: Altar de Sacrificios (Adams 1971); Barton Ramie (Gifford 1976); Blue Creek (Kosakowsky and Lohse 2003; Kosakowsky, Robertson, and Walker 2016); Cerros (Robertson 2016); El Perú/Waka' (Eppich 2011); Uaxactun (Smith; 1955, Smith and Gifford 1966).

POLVERO CERAMIC GROUP
Polvero Black: Polvero Variety

Established: Smith and Gifford (1966)

Group: Polvero

Ware: Paso Caballo Waxy

Ceramic Complex: Cauac (Begins in Chuen and continues into Cimi)

Ceramic Sphere: Chicanel

Illustrations: Fig. 11.23, 11.36, 11.47; 12.1–2, 12.6, 12.13, 12.16, 12.61–62, 12.65–66, 12.74; 13.29–31, 13.41, 13.47, 13.51–54, 13.58–59, 13.61–63; 57.2–3. See TR. 25A: fig. 6*b,g*; 11*a*1,3; 99*c*.

Principal identifying attributes: Thick black, sometimes waxy slip, which tends to flake and craze and fireclouds to red and brown.

Identifying characteristics and sorting problems: Polvero Black is easily separated from the earlier Chunhinta Black by paste characteristics. The separation of small sherds of various monochrome types frequently presents sorting problems because of the poor control of color and firing in all types.

Paste: Preclassic Monochrome Paste.

Firing: Darkening of the paste beneath the surface indicates firing in a reducing atmosphere. Completely darkened paste bodies or separate dark cores are common.

Slip: Medium to relatively thick slip, that tends to craze and flake.

Polish: Low to medium. Most, but not all, sherds have a waxy feel.

Color: Color ranges from black (5YR 2.5/1, 7.5YR 2.5/1, 10YR 2/1, 2.5Y 2.5/1) to dark reddish brown (5YR 2.5/2). Control of the reduction process was not good, and few vessels are completely black. Blemishes are reddish and gray to tan.

Shapes: In Cauac samples, narrow-mouth jars are by far the most common shape represented in Polvero Black (58% of rim sherds). Slightly incurving to round-side bowls and dishes (18%) and medial-flange, z-angle, and composite silhouette bowls (13%) are fairly common and a variety of other shapes including outflaring to outcurving-side bowls and dishes occur in low frequencies.

Temporal distribution: The Polvero Variety is fully established by the preceding Chuen Complex and continues until the end of the Preclassic with little change.

Intersite comparisons: Altar de Sacrificios (Adams 1971); Barton Ramie (Gifford 1976); Becan (Ball 1977); Blue Creek (Kosakowsky and Lohse 2003); Calakmul (Dominguez Carrasco 1994); Chan (Kosakowsky 2012); Chan Chich (Valdez 1998, Valdez and Houk 2000); Colha (Valdez 1987); Cuello (Kosakowsky 1987); Edzna (Forsyth 1983); El Peru/Waka' (Eppich 2011); El Pozito (Eppich 2000); Holmul (Callaghan 2008, 2016b); El Mirador (Forsyth 1989); La Milpa (Sagebiel 2005); Naachtun (Walker and Reese-Taylor 2012); Nakbe (Forsyth 1983); Nohmul (Kosakowsky and Pring 2001); the Petexbatun (Foias and Bishop 2013); Piedras Negras (Muñoz 2006); Seibal (Sabloff 1975); Uaxactun (Smith and Gifford 1966, Smith 1955); Yaxchilan (Lopez Varela 1989).

Lechugal Incised: Simple-incised Variety and Design-incised Variety

Established: Type named by Smith and Gifford

(1966); Varieties named by Culbert (1993 [TR. 25A])

Group: Polvero

Ware: Paso Caballo Waxy

Ceramic Complex: Cauac (Begins in Chuen and continues into Cimi)

Ceramic Sphere: Chicanel

Illustrations: Fig. 15.11–12.

Principal identifying attributes: Monochrome black slip same as Polvero Black decorated with fine line incising in simple designs.

Comments: See Polvero Black above. In typological characteristics, Lechugal is indistinguishable from Polvero Black. The same comments on decoration and shape made for Laguna Verde Incised in the Sierra Group apply to Lechugal Incised.

Temporal distribution: All incised types are rare in Cauac Complex samples. Incised types are more common in the preceding Chuen Complex.

Intersite comparisons: Lechugal Variety used at Calakmul (Dominguez Carrasco 1994); Holmul (Callaghan 2008, 2016b); La Milpa (Sagebiel 2005); and Uaxactun (Smith and Gifford 1966; Smith 1955). Unspecified Variety used at Altar de Sacrificios (Adams 1971); Blue Creek (Kosakowsky and Lohse 2003); Chan (Kosakowsky 2012); El Mirador (Forsyth 1989); Seibal (Sabloff 1975). Macaw Bank Variety is used at Barton Ramie (Gifford 1976), Chan Chich (Valdez 1998; Valdez and Houk 2000), and Colha (Valdez 1987). Grooved-incised Variety used at Cuello (Kosakowsky 1987) and Nohmul (Kosakowsky and Pring 2001); Gouged-incised Variety used at Edzna (Forsyth 1983).

BACLAM CERAMIC GROUP

Baclam Red-orange: Baclam Variety

Established: Originally called Baclam Orange Culbert (1993 [TR. 25A]). Renamed Baclam Red-orange in this work.

Group: Baclam

Ware: Paso Caballo Waxy

Ceramic Complex: Cauac (Begins in Chuen and continues into Cimi)

Ceramic Sphere: Chicanel

Illustrations: Fig. 11.34; 13.23–25, 13.42, 13.64–65.

Principal identifying attributes: Slightly waxy monochrome red-orange slip that overlaps with Sierra Red on the extreme and is difficult to sort from Sierra Red.

Identifying characteristics and sorting problems: Surface color is the sole identifying characteristic of the type. The range of color grades continuously into that of Sierra Red, so there are many borderline examples. Only the most clearly red-orange examples were classified in sorting as Baclam Red-orange.

Paste: Preclassic Monochrome Paste.

Slip: Usually medium thickness. On some examples, the clay surfaces were well polished before application of the slip. In these examples, the slip tends to flake off, revealing sections of light clay.

Polish: Low to medium. Waxiness variable.

Color: The most typical examples are reddish yellow (2.5YR 6/8), but the range of colors includes red (2.5YR 6/8) and overlaps with Sierra Red.

Shapes: Outflaring to slightly outcurving-side bowls and dishes, slightly incurving to round-side bowls and dishes, and large widely outcurving-side bowls common shapes.

Temporal Distribution: A low frequency of Baclam Red-orange sherds occurs in all Late Preclassic complexes, however, it occurs in greater frequencies in the preceding Chuen Complex.

Comments: Because Baclam Red-orange is the end of a continuum in color shared with Sierra Red, it is impossible to say whether prehistoric potters deliberately produced red-orange pottery or whether the examples so classified represent color variants due to firing or other chance circumstances.

Intersite comparisons: El Perú/Waka' (Eppich 2011). It is probable that some red-orange examples are sorted with Sierra Red at other sites.

Cay Incised: Simple-incised Variety and Design-incised Variety

Established: TR. 25A (Culbert 1993)

Group: Baclam

Ware: Paso Caballo Waxy

Ceramic Complex: Cauac (Begins in Chuen and continues into Cimi)

Ceramic Sphere: Chicanel

Principal identifying attributes: Slightly waxy monochrome red-orange slip same as Baclam Red-orange that overlaps with Sierra Red on the extreme and is difficult to sort from Sierra Red, decorated secondarily with incising.

Comments: A few red-orange slipped sherds show uncomplicated incised decoration. The sample was too small to permit a full typological characterization, but in all observable features the sherds are identical to Baclam Red-orange. Patterns and shapes cannot be determined from the sample available.

Intersite comparisons: None noted; however, at other sites red-orange examples are likely included in the Sierra Red Group, Laguna Verde Incised type.

BOXCAY CERAMIC GROUP

Boxcay Brown: Boxcay Variety

Established: TR. 25A (Culbert 1993)

Group: Boxcay

Ware: Paso Caballo

Ceramic Complex: Chuen (Begins in Chuen and continues into Cimi)

Ceramic Sphere: Chicanel

Illustrations: Fig. 11.44, 11.46; 13.52–54.

Principal identifying attributes: Slightly lustrous rather than waxy monochrome brown slip that exhibits crazing,

Identifying characteristics and sorting problems: Because the color of Boxcay Brown ranges into the colors of Polvero Black and Flor Cream, separation is not always clear. Boxcay Brown can be easily separated from the earlier Boolay Brown on the basis of paste.

Paste: Preclassic Monochrome Paste.

Firing: Dark cores occur in half of the sample. Better than half of the sherds show fireclouding.

Slip: Medium thickness.

Polish: Low to medium; waxiness not common.

Color: Ranges from dark yellowish brown (10YR 4/4) to olive brown (2.5Y 4/4).

Shapes: Slightly incurving to round-side bowls and dishes and narrow mouth jars with short necks.

Temporal distribution: Boxcay Brown continues to exist as a rare type in the Cauac Complex. The type continues until the end of the Preclassic period.

Comments: The separation of this type on the basis of surface color from among the highly variegated monochromes may be simply an artifact of sorting. Because a few large sherds show only brown color, there is a possibility that the production of brown pottery was intentional.

Intersite comparisons: Holmul (Callaghan 2008, 2016b) and Piedras Negras (Muñoz 2006).

Xtabcab Incised: Simple-incised Variety and Design-incised Variety

Established: TR. 25A (Culbert 1993)

Group: Boxcay

Ware: Paso Caballo

Ceramic Complex: Cauac (Begins in Chuen and continues into Cimi)

Ceramic Sphere: Chicanel

Illustrations: Fig. 16.9.

Principal identifying attributes: Same as Boxcay Brown with the addition of simple incised decoration.

Comments: The few examples of brown-slipped incised sherds in Cauac Complex collections do not give enough information to allow full description of the type.

Intersite comparisons: None noted with incising but see Boxcay Brown above.

FLOR CERAMIC GROUP

Flor Cream: Flor Variety

Established: Type named by Smith and Gifford (1966)

Group: Flor

Ware: Paso Caballo Waxy

Ceramic Complex: Cauac (Begins in Chuen and continues into Cimi)

Ceramic Sphere: Chicanel

Illustrations: Fig. 11.24, 11.32, 11.37, 11.41; 12.7, 12.37–38, 12.59. See TR. 25A: fig. 10*b*; 13*f*.

Principal identifying attributes: Lustrous, slightly waxy, cream, slip that is variable in color.

Identifying characteristics and sorting problems: Except for a slight overlap with the color range of Boxcay Brown, Flor Cream presents few sorting problems.

Paste: Preclassic Fine Paste predominates, but Preclassic Monochrome Paste is also represented.

Firing: Dark cores and fireclouding occur.

Slip: Thick slip that adheres better and shows less tendency to flake or craze than other Preclassic monochrome slips.

Polish: Light to high, but all examples are polished.

Color: Slip color of Flor Cream is extremely variable. Very pale brown (10YR 8/3), pale brown (10YR 6/3), brown (10YR 5/3), and light yellowish brown (10YR 6/4) are most common, but white (10YR 8/1, 8/2; 2.5Y 8/2), gray (10YR 6/1; 5Y 5/1), and very pale brown (10YR 7/3) to pale yellow (2.5Y 8/4) also occur. It is common for sherds to show patches of two different colors.

Shapes: Medial-flange and z-angle bowls, and out-flaring to slightly outcurving-side bowls and dishes.

Temporal distribution: Some examples of the Flor Variety appear as early as the Chuen Complex, but the peak frequency of the variety occurs in Cimi lots.

Comments: The Flor Variety of Flor Cream increases in frequency in the Cauac Complex but is not as common as in the succeeding Cimi Complex. Although Cauac samples of the variety are too small for good quantitative estimates, a greater variety of vessel shapes seem to be represented in the Flor Variety in Cauac rather than in Cimi. The Cozom Variety originally identified by Culbert (TR. 25A) has been subsumed in the Flor Variety in this work because of the great degree of overlap between the two varieties.

Intersite comparisons: Altar de Sacrificios (Adams 1971); Barton Ramie (Gifford 1976); Becan (Ball 1977); Blue Creek (Kosakowsky and Lohse 2003); Chan Chich (Valdez 1998; Valdez and Houk 2000); Colha (Valdez 1987); Cuello (Kosakowsky 1987); El Perú/Waka' (Eppich 2011); El Mirador (Forsyth 1989); Holmul (Callaghan 2016b); La Milpa (Sagebiel 2005); Nakbe (Forsyth 1993); Piedras Negras (Muñoz 2006); Nohmul (Kosakowsky and Pring 2001); Seibal (Sabloff 1975); Uaxactun (Smith 1955; Smith and Gifford 1966). It is an Unspecified Variety at Chan (Kosakowsky 2012); Edzna (Forsyth 1983); K'axob (Lopez Varela 1996); the Petexbatun (Foias and Bishop 2013); Yaxchilan (Lopez Varela 1989).

Accordian Incised: Simple-incised Variety and Design-incised Variety

Established: Type named Smith and Gifford (1966); varieties named Culbert (1993 [misspelled as Accordion in TR. 25A])

Group: Flor

Ware: Paso Caballo Waxy

Ceramic Complex: Cauac (Begins in Chuen and continues into Cimi)

Ceramic Sphere: Chicanel

Illustrations: Fig. 12.46.

Principal identifying attributes: Monochrome cream slip similar to Flor Cream: Flor Variety with the addition of incised decoration on the exterior of vessels.

Comments: Typologically, sherds of Accordian Incised are identical to sherds of Flor Cream with the addition of incising. The sherds of incised cream pottery in the Cauac Complex collections are too rare to permit adequate characterization.

Intersite comparisons: Identified as the Accordian Variety at Holmul (Callaghan 2008, 2016b); and Uaxactun (Smith and Gifford 1966). It is an Unspecified Variety at Barton Ramie (Gifford 1976); Becan (Ball 1997); and Edzna (Forsyth 1983); and called Acordeon Incised in the Petexbatun (Foias and Bishop 2013). There are unnamed examples at Seibal (Sabloff 1975).

SACLUC CERAMIC GROUP

Caramba Red-on-orange: Chic Variety

Established: Type named by Adams (1971); Variety named by Culbert (1993 [TR. 25A]).

Group: Sacluc [in the Caramba Group at El Mirador (Forsyth 1989)]

Ware: Paso Caballo Waxy

Ceramic Complex: Cauac (Continues into Cimi)

Ceramic Sphere: Chicanel

Illustrations: Fig. 10.38; 14.11; 15.3–9. See TR. 25A: fig. 4*a*; 8*b*1; 9*b*5; 10*d*; 11*a*6–7; 12*a*; 13*c*.

Principal identifying attributes: Red-orange slip on interiors and exteriors of vessels with red slip applied over base and then wiped off to create a Usulutan-like decoration.

Identifying characteristics and sorting problems: The type is quite distinctive and overlaps only with other types in the Usulutan-related series.

Paste: Both Preclassic Monochrome Paste and Preclassic Fine Paste are represented.

Firing: About half of the examples show dark cores and one-quarter show two-tone cores with a different color in the center than near the surface. Fireclouding is rare.

Slip: Medium to thick.

Polish: Low to medium.

Color: The background color is usually reddish yellow (5YR 6/8, 7/8). Variants include strong brown (7.5YR 5/8), red (2.5YR 5/8), and pink (7.5YR 7/4). The darker stripes are red (10R 4/6, 4/8 to 2.5YR 5/8) with some examples ranging to reddish brown (5YR 4/8).

Surface finish and decoration: Although the decorative patterns are obviously related to those of Usulutan Ware, Caramba Red-on-orange: Chic Variety was not produced by a resist technique, but by at least two other techniques. The more common was a "wipe-off" technique in which a slip was applied and then partially wiped off in some areas to produce lighter stripes. The second technique was positive painting with a second coat of the original slip or one of a different color. Although for many sherds the technique of production cannot be determined, those that do permit determination suggest a correlation between the wipe-off technique and Preclassic Fine Paste and between positive painting and

Preclassic Monochrome Paste. Decoration consists of multiple parallel lines, sometimes executed with a multipronged instrument. On the vessel exteriors, the lines are only gently curved and run vertically. They start in the same vertical fashion at the top of vessel interiors, giving way to wavy lines and circles on the interior.

Shapes: Composite silhouette bowls are most common, as well as z-angle bowls. There are a cuspidor and a narrow-mouth jar with tall neck and spout in special deposits.

Temporal distribution: The North Acropolis stratigraphy demonstrates that Caramba Red-on-orange begins at the start of the Cauac Complex and continues until the end of the Cimi Complex.

Intersite comparisons: Altar de Sacrificios (Adams 1971); Becan (Ball 1977); Blue Creek (Kosakowsky and Lohse 2003; Cerros (Robertson 2016); Edzna (Forsyth 1983); El Mirador (Forsyth 1989); El Perú/Waka' (Eppich 2011); Holmul (Callaghan 2008, 2016b); and the Petexbatun (Foias and Bishop 2013).

Sacluc Black-on-orange: Sis Variety

Established: Type named by Adams (1971); Variety named by Culbert (1993 [TR. 25A])

Group: Sacluc

Ware: Paso Caballo Waxy

Ceramic Complex: Cauac (Continues into Cimi)

Ceramic Sphere: Chicanel

Illustrations: Fig. 15.15, 15.18–24.

Principal identifying attributes: Light orange slip overpainted with a black or brownish-black slip in multiple parallel wavy lines.

Identifying characteristics and sorting problems: The Usulutan-related types are easy to distinguish from all other types by the multiple parallel-line decoration.

Paste: Both Preclassic Monochrome Paste and Preclassic Fine Paste are represented.

Firing: Half of the examples have dark cores. Fire-clouding is rare.

Slip: Thin to medium.

Polish: Low to medium.

Color: The background color may be reddish yellow (5YR 6/8), red (2.5YR 6/8), or light red (7.5YR 6/8). The black stripes are produced by a black-firing pigment rather than by reduction firing.

Surface finish and decoration: Like Caramba Red-on-orange, Sacluc Black-on-orange: Sis Variety is produced by both wipe-off and positive painting techniques. In Sacluc Black-on-orange, positive painting is slightly more common than wipe-off. Decoration consists of quite broad lines of medium curvature well separated from each other.

Shapes: Composite silhouette bowls and outflaring to slightly outcurving-side bowls and dishes.

Temporal distribution: The type appears at the start of the Cauac Complex and continues to appear through the Cimi Complex.

Intersite comparisons: Altar de Sacrificios (Adams 1971); Blue Creek (Kosakowsky and Lohse 2003; Kosakowsky, Robertson and Walker 2016); El Mirador (Forsyth 1989); Nakbe (Forsyth 1993); Punta de Chimino (Bachand 2007); Seibal (Sabloff 1975); and possibly at La Milpa (Sagebiel 2005).

Metapa Trichrome: Itsul Variety

Established: Type named by Adams (1971); Variety named by Culbert (1993 [TR. 25A])

Group: Sacluc

Ware: Paso Caballo Waxy

Ceramic Complex: Cauac (Continues into Cimi)

Ceramic Sphere: Chicanel

Illustrations: Fig. 12.15; 14.1; 16.2–4, 16.13–14, 16.24, 16.29–30.

Principal identifying attributes: Light orange slip overpainted with a black or brownish-black slip in multiple parallel wavy lines. Additional decoration includes areas of red slip on the upper exterior of composite silhouette vessels.

Comments: Identical to Sacluc Black-on-orange: Sis Variety except in the following characteristics as detailed below.

Color: The background color is usually reddish yellow (5YR 6/6, 6/8) or yellowish red (5YR 5/8), but ranges to light red (2.5YR 6/8). The stripes are black and the areas of red are 10R 5/8.

Surface finish and decoration: The designs are multiple wavy line patterns in black on orange. The red occurs as a separate section on the lip or on the upper exterior of the vessel.

Shapes: Composite silhouette bowls, medial-flange bowls. There is a tall-neck jar with spout in a special deposit.

Temporal distribution: Begins in the Cauac Complex and may continue in small frequencies in the succeeding Cimi Complex.

Intersite comparisons: Altar de Sacrificios (Adams 1971) and Punta de Chimino (Bachand 2007).

Cauac Types: Chronological Change

Type frequency counts for the Cauac Complex were calculated for only six samples, from two locations: Gp. 5D-2 (civic-ceremonial) and Ch. 5G-7 (small structure group). The two most common types of the Cauac Complex were Sierra Red and Sapote Striated. Sierra Red constituted between one-quarter and one-third of the sherds in most samples, while Sapote Striated made up about one-quarter. Polvero Black, ranging in frequency between 10% and 15%, was the next most common type. Cabro Red, Boxcay Brown, Flor Cream, and Baclam Red-orange followed in that order, usually in frequencies between 2% and 5%. Unslipped types in total ranged from 3% to 5%,

TABLE 5.3
Ceramic Type Frequencies of the Cauac Complex

Ceramic Groups/Types	Civic-ceremonial			Civic-ceremonial			Small Structure Group
	Sample Loc. 1-3 Gp. 5D-2	Sample Loc. 1-2 Gp. 5D-2	Sample Loc. 2-6 Gp. 5D-2	Sample Loc. 2-5 Gp. 5D-2	Sample Loc. 2-4 Gp. 5D-2		Sample Loc. 3-1 Ch. 5G-7
	%	%	%	%	%		%
Achiotes Group and Morfin Group[1]	5.7	3.1	1.6	5.1	5.0		4.8
Sapote Group	14.2	27.1	24.6	26.3	36.1		21.7
Sierra Group[2]	35.6	32.6	28.0	27.0	17.0		30.4
Laguna Verde Incised: Simple- and Design-incised Variety	0.1	0.2	—	—	—		0.2
Repasto Black-on-red: Repasto Variety	0.6	0.4	—	0.1	0.3		—
Polvero Group	13.4	10.3	11.7	14.7	7.3		21.5
Flor Group	3.1	2.4	2.5	1.5	1.3		1.0
Baclam Group	2.8	2.2	1.4	0.8	—		1.7
Boxcay Group	1.9	2.7	4.5	6.3	6.0		9.2
Sacluc Group	0.4	0.2	0.2	1.0	0.7		1.7
Unclassified and Rare Types	6.9	4.2	3.3	8.7	3.9		2.4
Weathered	15.3	14.6	22.2	8.5	22.4		5.4
Number of Sherds	1609	513	427	1417	299		414

[1] All unslipped unstriated examples were originally classified together.

[2] Cabro Red was not differentiated in the original frequency sorting.

but many of the sherds sorted into these types were jar necks that would probably have been Sapote Striated had body sections of the vessels been present. Decorated types were uncommon in the Cauac Complex: incised types, Repasto Black-on-red and the Usulutan-related Sacluc Ceramic Group occurred in most samples, but frequencies are usually lower than 1%.

In keeping with the stability of ceramics during the Late Preclassic, there are few typological changes between the Chuen and Cauac Complexes. Almost all Chuen types seem to continue into Cauac, although the upward mixing of earlier sherds in the North Acropolis may blur the disappearance of old types. Three new ceramic groups are added in Cauac: Morfin, Cabro and Sacluc. The three types of the Sacluc Ceramic Group and the Usulutan-style variety of Laguna Verde Incised in the Sierra Group use the multiple parallel-line designs that characterize the Usulutan Design Style. The Cabro Group utilizes a double slip which becomes more common in the Late Preclassic and leading into the Early Classic, as well as a hard-fired more lustrous surface that is uncommon in preceding time periods. The other new type is Morfin Unslipped, the first unslipped type used for bowl and dish shapes. Although these new types are distinctive and easily recognized, they are all rare and do not necessarily appear in small collections of the Cauac Complex.

There are frequency changes in some types between the Chuen and Cauac Complexes (see Tables 4.3 and 5.3). Sapote Striated seems to have increased in frequency; it is almost always more than 25% of Cauac samples (with one exception of about 14%) as compared to 10–20% frequencies in Chuen collections. Several of the minor monochrome types show slight changes in frequency between the Chuen and Cauac Complexes, although the frequency differences between individual samples within a given complex vary more than the changes between complexes. The frequency of Flor Cream increases slightly in Cauac. Boxcay Brown shows a similar slight increase, while Baclam Red-orange is less common in Cauac samples than in Chuen. These changes involve no more than one or two percentage points among types for which even the highest frequencies remain below 5% of total sherds, so these minor changes do not serve as good markers of chronological change between the Chuen and Cauac Complexes.

Information about chronological change within the time span represented by the Cauac Complex is weak because the key North Acropolis stratigraphic sequence contains only one large sample of Cauac date, while the other two samples are too small to give reliable information about gradual change.

Cauac Types: Social Dimension

Cauac Complex samples provide very little information about social variation related to ceramic use within Tikal. Two of the sample locations (1 and 2) are from civic-ceremonial contexts and the other 2 samples (3 and 4) are from small structure groups, a likely residential context. Cauac Sample 3-1 differs in ways that contradicts expectations. Sample 3-1 includes PD. 125, which may represent a relocated, possibly desecrated burial, also included human skull fragments and censer fragments. The presence of this special deposit may explain why Sapote Striated, a likely utility ware, is less common in Sample 3-1, a small structure group, than in samples from some civic-ceremonial locations, and the slightly higher frequencies of Polvero Black and the Usulutan-related decorated types. These differences are probably not significant ones and it appears that typological variations are not good indices of social variation in Preclassic complexes.

Vessel Shapes of the Cauac Complex

Introduction

Seven shape classes and twenty-one shapes, listed in Table 5.4, occur in the Cauac Complex. Several relatively common new shapes, especially the medial-flange bowl or dish, appear for the first time in the Cauac Complex. Because typological changes between the Chuen and Cauac Complexes are minor, these new shapes are useful to distinguish between the two complexes.

Cauac Shape Descriptions

SHAPE CLASS 1: WIDE-MOUTH JARS

Wide-mouth Jar with Short Neck

Illustrations: Fig. 7.9–10, 7.69; 9.1–18, 9.21–23;

TABLE 5.4
Shape Classes and Shapes of the Cauac Complex

1. **Wide-mouth Jars**

   Wide-mouth Jar (with Short Neck)

2. **Narrow-mouth Jars**

   Narrow-mouth Jar (with Short Neck)

   Narrow-mouth Jar (with Tall Neck and Spout)

   Florero

3. **Very Wide-mouth Jars**

   Very Large-diameter Jar

4. **Large Capacity Bowls**

   Widely Outcurving-side Bowl

   Bucket

   Cuspidor

5. **Medium Diameter Bowls and Dishes**

   Slightly Incurving to Round-side Bowl or Dish

   Outflaring to Slightly Outcurving-side Bowl or Dish

   Bucket

   Outflaring-side Vase

   Medial-flange Bowl

   Z-angle Bowl

   Composite Silhouette Bowl

6. **Small Diameter Bowls and Dishes**

   Slightly Incurving to Round-side Bowl or Dish

   Bucket

   Outflaring to Slightly Outcurving-side Unslipped Dish

   Slightly Incurving to Round-side Unslipped Dish

11. **Miniature Vessels**

    Miniature Jar

    Miniature Bowl

13.1–19, 13.21–22; 14.14; 15.3. See TR. 25A: fig. 8*a*1; 10*h*.

Identifying characteristics and sorting problems: Easy to distinguish on the basis of short neck, large lip diameter, and unslipped surface.

Base and body: No whole examples, but body seems to have been globular.

Neck-body juncture: Usually rounded but well defined.

Orientation of neck: Medium to wide outflare.

Neck: Outcurves in varying degrees.

Rim: Direct.

Lip: Usually rounded to pointed; a few examples are beveled or flattened.

Surface: Striated below neck-body juncture; variable care in finishing.

Types: Usually Sapote Striated; rarely, Achiotes Unslipped.

Lip diameter: Range 10–24 cm; median 20 cm.

Neck height: Range 1.4–4.6 cm; median 2.8 cm.

Lip diameter/neck height ratio: Range 4.8–12.8; median 7.4.

Shape class: 1, wide-mouth jars.

Temporal Distribution: Common in the Late Preclassic Chuen, Cauac, and Cimi Complexes.

Comments: Considerable variability occurs in the shape, but it is not distinctive enough to allow meaningful subdivision. Examples with thinner walls seem slightly more common in the Chuen Complex than in later complexes.

SHAPE CLASS 2: NARROW-MOUTH JARS

Narrow-mouth Jar with Short Neck

Illustrations: Fig. 7.47, 7.62, 7.65; 8.20, 8.33–34; 13.23–65; 14.21, 14.43–46; 15.10, 15.12. See TR. 25A: fig. 6*b–g*; 8*a*2; 11*a*1–7; 144*a*1.

Identifying characteristics and sorting problems: For sherds that do not show the neck-body juncture, it is often difficult to distinguish narrow-mouth jars from interior-slipped jars. The short neck makes it fairly easy to distinguish this jar from earlier and later shapes.

Base and body: The few complete examples have globular bodies of small size, but these examples, all from special deposits, may not be representative.

Neck-body juncture: Usually well marked; most frequently angular but sometimes rounded.

Orientation of neck: Medium outflare.

Neck: Ranges from medium outcurve to nearly straight.

Rim: Usually direct; a subclass has sharp to rounded eversion of the rim.

Lip: Rounded or pointed; some examples of the everted rim subclass have flattened lips.

Surface: Slipped on exterior and on interior of neck; remainder of interior unslipped. Care in finishing varies.

Types: Cauac samples show a much higher frequency of Sierra Red than samples from either the Chuen or Cimi Complexes. In Cauac, about 75% of the jars are Sierra Red and about 17% are Polvero Black, followed by small quantities of Boxcay Brown.

Diameter: Range 10–30 cm; median 14 cm. There is some indication of a secondary peak of diameters in the 20–26 cm range.

Neck Height: Range 1.2–4.0 cm; median 2.4 cm.

Lip diameter/neck height ratio: Range 3.6–11.7; median 5.8. The ratio shows a wide distribution with little central tendency; it seems unlikely that the ratio was of much significance to the users.

Shape class: 2, narrow-mouth jars.

Temporal distribution: Common in the Chuen, Cauac, and Cimi Complexes. The frequency of the shape is quite stable, both through time and between lots at the same time range.

Narrow-mouth Jar (with Tall Neck and Spout)

Illustrations: See TR. 25A: fig. 4*c,d*; 9*b*5.

Identifying characteristics and sorting problems: Identified by spout. Often called a "chocolate pot."

Base and Body: The body has a marked angle between upper and lower sections. The base is flat.

Neck-body juncture: Usually well marked and angular.

Orientation of neck: Medium to wide outflare.

Neck: Outcurving except for one straight example.

Rim: Usually everted, often strongly everted; one example is direct.

Lip: A variety of lip shapes include rounded, thickened, and beveled; sometimes there is a groove inside the lip.

Spout: The spout leaves the body near the midpoint and extends upward vertically to the height of the lip. Spout cross section is round. There are few spouted vessels in Late Preclassic collections at Tikal.

Types: Whole vessels include Sierra Red; two others are Usulutan types, as well as Caramba Red-on-orange and Metapa Trichrome.

Maximum diameter of body (3 examples): Range 18–30 cm.

Height of body to neck (3 examples): Range 12–21 cm.

Diameter of lip (5 examples): Range 13–21 cm; median 14 cm.

Height of neck (5 examples): Range 4.4 to 8.8 cm; median 6.5 cm.

Lip diameter/neck height ratio (5 examples): Range 1.8–3.2; median 2.4.

Shape class: 2, narrow-mouth jars.

Comments: The shape is rare in sherd collections, and the majority of recognized examples come from burials. One (see TR. 25A: fig. 4d) is an effigy form with the spout serving as tail, a small head on the opposite side, roughly outlined legs, and four small feet.

Florero

Illustrations: See TR. 25A: fig. 5*a*,*b*; 9*b*4; 11*b*.

Identifying characteristics and sorting problems: The overall shape is completely distinctive. Although lip sections might be sorted as outflaring-side bowls, the junctures between the three parts of the vessel are easily noticeable from sherds. Originally called an urn jar (TR. 25A).

Base: Three examples are flat; one rounded and slightly concave.

Comments: This shape is composed of three sections: a widely outflaring neck, a narrow but long section below the neck, and a short, broader basal section.

Orientation of side: The neck section is widely outflaring, the central section slopes inward from the basal section to the neck, and the basal section is widely outflaring at about the same angle as the neck.

Side: The neck is straight to slightly outcurving; the central section is incurving or (in one example) straight and insloping; the basal section is rounded or straight.

Rim: Sharply everted in three examples, slightly everted in the fourth.

Lip: Pointed or rounded.

Junctures and proportions: On three of the vessels, a tall neck leads to a well-defined juncture with the central section that is marked by a large flange with triangular cross section. The fourth example has a very short neck section that might simply be considered a broadly everted rim. Instead of a flange, this vessel has handles between the lip and the juncture between the neck and central sections. The central section of floreros leads down to another juncture with the basal section. The juncture is marked by a

clear ridge on the vessel exterior of three of these vessels, and on the fourth vessel the juncture is rounded. The basal section in all examples is too short to add substantially to the capacity of the vessel.

Types: Three are Other Cabro Group (unnamed type), and the fourth is stuccoed over a black fluted unnamed type.

Diameter: Range (4 examples) 25–36 cm.

Height: Range (4 examples) 31–41 cm.

Diameter/height ratio: Range (4 examples) 0.7–0.9.

Shape class: 12, narrow-mouth jars.

Temporal distributions: The shape occurs in burials from the Cauac Complex and there may be a few sherds of this shape in Cauac and Cimi lots.

Comments: The rarity of such an easily identifiable shape in the large sherd collections suggests specialized use, probably in burials.

SHAPE CLASS 3: VERY WIDE-MOUTH JARS

Very Large-Diameter Jar

Illustrations: Fig. 9.19–20.

Identifying characteristics and sorting problems: The diameter is so large that the shape stands far apart from other jars. It is not certain, however, whether some of the taller fragments without neck-body juncture might be bowls.

Base and body: No information available.

Neck-body juncture: Vague in the few instances where present.

Orientation of neck: Outflaring.

Neck: Slight Outcurve.

Rim: Direct.

Lip: Rounded, very thick.

Surface: Unslipped.

Type: Either Achiotes Unslipped or Sapote Striated, though more commonly Sapote Striated.

Lip diameter: Range 40–50 cm; median 44 cm.

Neck height: Range 1.7–3.2 cm; median 2.7 cm.

Lip diameter/neck height ratio: Range 15.3–26.7; median 18.2.

Shape class: 3, very wide-mouth jars.

Temporal distribution: Occurs in low frequencies in all Preclassic complexes.

Shape Class 4: Large Capacity Bowls

Widely Outcurving-side Bowl

Illustrations: Fig. 10.1–10; 11.28, 11.37–38; 12.19, 12.31–33; 14.36–38, 14.40–42; 15.7–9, 15.19. See TR. 25A: fig. 8*b*1; 9*a*2; 12*d,e,f*; 13*a*.

Identifying characteristics and sorting problems: The identifying features are the broad lip grooves combined with the widely outflaring side.

Base: Flat.

Orientation of side: Medium to wide outflare at lip.

Side: Outcurving.

Rim: Direct or rounded eversion that may be pronounced. The entire rim section is often thickened.

Lip: Rounded, usually thickened. There may be one to three broad grooves on interior of the lip.

Surface: Usually slipped on the interior and exterior. Interior carefully finished; exterior less carefully done.

Types: The majority of the examples are Sierra Red. Baclam Red-orange and various incised types also occur. There are also examples of Laguna Verde Incised: Usulutan-style Variety and Morfin Unslipped.

Diameter: Range 24–58 cm; median 38.0 cm. The median has little meaning because of a split distribution between a group of smaller vessels with diameters between 24 and 42 cm and a group of larger vessels with diameters between 44 and 58 cm.

Height: Range 5–39 cm. There is a clear division of the height measurements into three groups: 5–10 cm; 14–18 cm; and greater than 21 cm.

Diameter/height ratio: Again, there is a wide range from 1.4 and 5.0.

Shape class: 4, large-capacity bowls.

Temporal distribution: The shape first appears in the Chuen Complex. Frequency increases in the Chuen Complex and peaks in samples from the Cauac and early Cimi Complexes.

Bucket

Illustrations: Fig. 10.45; 11.30. See TR. 25A: fig. 99*d*1, *e*(bottom), *f*(bottom).

Identifying characteristics and sorting problems: This shape is separated from the other outflaring-side shapes of the Late Preclassic by the higher walls and rim eversion, though in sherd samples difficult to differentiate from outflaring to slightly outcurving-side bowls or dishes. This shape was originally included in outcurving-side bowls (TR. 25A).

Base: Probably flat.

Orientation of side: Medium to wide outflare.

Side: Medium to wide outcurve.

Rim: Direct, although the rim section sometimes accentuates the outcurve of the side.

Lip: Rounded, often thickened.

Surface: Slipped on both interior and exterior.

Types: Four-fifths of the examples are Sierra Red, followed by Baclam Red-orange and Polvero Black.

Diameter: Range 30–42 cm.

Height: 20.0–26.0 cm.

Diameter/height ratio: 1.4–1.6.

Shape class: 4, large capacity bowls.

Temporal distribution: The shape first appears in the Chuen Complex. Frequency increases throughout the Late Preclassic and peaks in samples from the Cauac and early Cimi Complexes.

Cuspidor

Illustrations: Fig. 10.46; 14.20, 14.22–23. See TR. 25A: fig. 8*b*1(bottom); 12*a*.

Identifying characteristics and sorting problems: Although lip sections would be sorted as widely outcurving-side bowls with grooved lips or outflaring-side bowls with sharply everted rims, the overall shape is distinctive, and the characteristic lower wall section would be apparent in sherd collections. Originally called an urn bowl (TR. 25A).

Comments: Known primarily from three intact examples, the shape has two sections, a deep upper section and a short lower section that angles to the base.

Base: Flat.

Orientation of side: Upper section nearly vertical; middle section straight to slightly outcurving; lower section is straight.

Side: Upper section straight to slightly outcurving; lower section is straight.

Rim: Wide eversion; either angled or rounded.

Lip: Flattened, pointed, or rounded and thickened, with a deep groove or grooves on the interior.

Juncture between sections: In two examples, the juncture between the sections makes an angular composite silhouette. The third example lacks a composite silhouette, but the juncture is marked by a flange.

Types: Two examples; both are Caramba Red-on-orange.

Diameter: Range 33–43 cm.

Height: Range 23–27 cm.

Diameter/height ratio: Range 1.4–1.6.

Shape class: 4, large-capacity bowls.

Temporal distribution: The vessels occur in burials from the Cauac Complex and in rare sherds from Cauac and Cimi lots.

Comments: The relationship to floreros is obvious, but the capacity of the urn bowl is much larger. It is probably a specialized shape for burial offerings.

SHAPE CLASS 5: MEDIUM DIAMETER BOWLS AND DISHES

Slightly Incurving to Round-Side Bowl or Dish

Illustrations: 11.26, 11.33–35, 11.47; 12.39–45, 12.55–77; 14.26, 14.28; 15.11; 16.4–5, 16.8, 16.12, 16.17. See TR. 25A: fig. 4*b*; 10*d,e*; 13*e,f*; 99*d*2.

Identifying Characteristics and Sorting Problems: Includes examples with both direct and incurved rims.

Base: Usually flat.

Side: Rounded, low to high curvature.

Rim: Direct or incurving. Just below the lip, the side curves inward either in a rounded curve accentuating curvature of the side or with a more abrupt break.

Lip: Round, pointed, or occasionally a flattened bevel that comes close to a labial flange. Some examples have a thickened lip.

Surface: Well-finished interior and exterior. Occasionally exterior is less well-finished than the interior, especially near the base, and a few examples are unslipped on the exterior.

Types: As in the Chuen Complex, the majority of the Cauac examples were Sierra Red. The next most common types were Baclam Red-orange and Boxcay Brown (both about 8%). Polvero Black declined in frequency compared with the Chuen Complex, and a few examples of Repasto Black-on-red, as well as incised varieties.

Diameter: Range 14–58 cm (most examples 20–40 cm); median 30 cm.

Height: (11 examples) range 4.8–10.0 cm; median 6.0 cm.

Diameter/height ratio: (11 examples) range 3.2–6.4; median 4.2.

Shape class: 5, medium-diameter dishes.

Temporal distribution: Slightly incurving to round-side bowls and dishes occur in all ceramic complexes but are most frequent in the Chuen Complex. In Cauac and Cimi, incurved rims are more common than in Chuen.

Outflaring to Slightly Outcurving-side Bowl or Dish

Illustrations: 10.16–30, 10.36–44, 10.52; 11.31; 12.47–53; 14.8–9, 14.11, 14.16, 14.24, 14.39; 15.5–6, 15.20; 16.15–16, 16.18–19, 16.21–23. See TR. 25A: fig. 99e(top), f(top); 139a.

Identifying characteristics and sorting problems: The flattened lip is the identifying feature. Some examples are close to the dimensions of medium to large plates.

Base: Flat to concave.

Orientation of side: Slight to medium outflare.

Side: Straight to slight outcurve.

Rim: Usually direct, but sometimes everted.

Lip: Rounded or flattened and extended outward to give a flat upward surface, occasionally grooved.

Surface: Slipped on both interior and exterior.

Types: Mostly Sierra Red (80%); Polvero Black makes up 10% of the sample; occasional examples of Flor Cream and Baclam Red-Orange.

Diameter: Range 18–32.0 cm; median 30.0 cm.

Height: 8.0–16.0 cm.

Diameter/Height Ratio: 1.4–4.2

Shape class: 5, medium-diameter bowls and dishes

Temporal distribution: Some examples that could be sorted into the shape occur in all Late Preclassic complexes. This shape occurs occasionally in the Cauac Complex but reaches higher frequencies in Cimi Complex samples than in those from earlier complexes.

Bucket

Illustrations: Fig. 11.9, 11.23–25, 11.27, 11.48; 14.15. See TR. 25A: fig. 9b1,3.

Identifying characteristics and sorting problems: This shape is separated from the other outflaring to slightly outcurving-side shapes of the Late Preclassic by the higher walls and rim eversion, though in sherd samples difficult to differentiate from outflaring to slightly outcurving-side bowls or dishes. This shape was originally included in both the outcurving-side bowl and the outflaring-side bowl or dish with gradual everted rim (TR. 25A).

Base: Flat.

Orientation of Side: Slight to medium outflare.

Side: Outcurving to nearly straight in upper section. Some large sherds and whole vessels suggest that some examples have recurved to rounded sides in lower sections of the vessel.

Rim: Everted with a rounded eversion that does not make a sharp break with the side of the vessel. The everted section is broad.

Lip: Rounded or pointed, frequently thickened.

Surface: Slipped on both interior and exterior.

Types: Sierra Red and Alta Mira Fluted.

Diameter: Range 20.0–25.0 cm; median 22.0 cm.

Height: Range 18.0–21.0 cm.; median 15 cm.

Diameter/Height Ratio: median 1.2.

Shape class: 5, medium diameter bowls and dishes

Temporal Distribution: Medium buckets are found throughout the Late Preclassic.

Outflaring-side Vase

Illustrations: See TR. 25A: fig. 5*c–e*; 6*a*; 12*b*.

Identifying characteristics and sorting problems: The brown-black incised type used to produce this imported shape is the key identifying characteristic. Any common locally produced shapes in the Preclassic complexes do not duplicate this shape, although it is similar to medium buckets, but lacking the everted rim. The only examples of this shape occur in two Cauac burials (Bu. 85 and Bu. 167). [Note: A fifth example of this imported type in Bu. 167 is an outflaring to slightly outcurving-side dish (see TR. 25A: fig. 12c).]

Base: Flat.

Orientation of Side: Slight to medium outflare.

Side: Straight-to-slight outcurve.

Rim: Direct.

Lip: Round or rounded bevel.

Surface: On four of the five examples, three ridges encircle the exterior of the vessel, one just below the lip, one at midpoint, and one just above the base. These ridges divide the exterior into two horizontal panels for decoration. The final example has ridges at lip and base only.

Types: All examples are of an incised brown-black ware, probably imported from highland Guatemala.

Diameter: Range 16.8–24.8 cm (5 examples); median 18.0 cm.

Height: median 15 cm.

Diameter/Height Ratio: median 1.2 cm.

Shape class: 5, medium diameter bowls and dishes

Temporal distribution: Found only in Cauac Complex burials.

Comments: Despite ease of recognition, the shape (and type) does not occur in sherd collections.

Medial-flange Bowl

Illustrations: Fig. 12.1–5, 12.8–11, 12.13–15, 12.34–36; 14.1, 14.4, 14.47–48; 15.3, 15.14, 15.16–17; 16.31. See TR. 25A: fig. 7*a–e*; 8*b*2; 9*a*1; 10*a–c*.

Identifying characteristics and sorting problems: This particular shape is identified by the combination of an unrestricted orifice and incurving side with or without a break at a medial flange. Occasionally the flange is narrow enough to be considered a ridge. The position of the flange is quite distinctive.

Base: Flat. Two examples (see TR. 25A: fig. 8*b*2; 9*a*1) have small nubbin feet.

Orientation of side: Slight to medium outflare.

Side: Nearly straight above flange, straight to slightly rounded below, with or without break of curvature on the inside of the vessel at the flange. Slight to marked angle on the interior at the position of the flange when there is a break in curvature.

Rim: Direct.

Lip: The wall is almost always thicker above the flange than below. The lip is most frequently rounded and somewhat thickened but is sometimes pointed or a reverse rounded bevel. There is one unusual example (see TR. 25A: fig. 141*c*) with an incurving rim and bolstered lip that may pertain either to the Cauac or Cimi Complex.

Flange: The flange is located medially on the vessel. It is most frequently pointed in cross section, occasionally rounded. Usually, the flange is quite narrow, and could even be called a ridge, but there are also a few examples of broad lip flanges. Flanges are sometimes modified by scalloping, modeling, or the addition of handles occurring between the flange and the lip.

Surface: Slipped on both interior and exterior. Carefully finished on the interior and the exterior above the flange. Often carelessly finished outside below the flange.

Types: Nearly three-quarters Sierra Red; followed by Polvero Black and Flor Cream. There are also examples of Laguna Verde Incised: Usulutan-style Variety and other decorated types.

Diameter: Range 20–38 cm; median 28 cm.

Height: Range 3.6–9.0 cm.

Diameter/height ratio: Range 3.2–4.3 cm.

Shape class: 5, medium-diameter bowls and dishes.

Temporal distribution: All of the medial-flange bowls and dishes are excellent time markers. In the sealed deposits from the North Acropolis, not a single example of a medial-flange bowl or dish appears before the Cauac Complex levels. They reach a peak frequency in the Cauac samples and continue to appear in Cimi.

Z-angle Bowl

Illustrations: Fig. 11.43–45; 12.7, 12.12, 12.17–18, 12.37–38; 14.2, 14.7, 14.49; 16.1–3, 16.10, 16.24, 16.27, 16.29. See TR. 25A: fig. 7*f.* [See also fig. 4*a.*]

Identifying characteristics and sorting problems: The restricted orifice and z-angle make the shape easy to identify, with only a few examples that are intermediate between this shape and the medial-flange (or ridge) bowl, especially those with

a break at the flange or ridge. There is one Caramba Red-on-orange unusual example that has both a rounded angle and nubbin feet (see TR. 25A: fig. 4*a*).

Base: Usually flat.

Orientation of side: Vertical to slightly restricted, giving a distinct composite silhouette.

Side: Upper section, straight; lower section, straight to slightly rounded. Usually there is a sharp break in the angle of the side between the two sections that almost always corresponds to the point of the Z-angle.

Rim: Usually direct; a few examples everted.

Lip: This shape demonstrates considerable variety of lip and upper section shapes. A variant where the upper section is short has a pointed lip in which wall thickness decreases continually between the flange and the lip. Another common variant has a thickened upper section with a reverse rounded bevel lip.

Z-angle: Sharp z-angle in which the exterior of the lower section continues without break to form a triangular cross section that makes a pronounced angle with the upper section of the wall on the vessel exterior.

Types: Mostly Sierra Red; some examples of Polvero Black and Flor Cream.

Diameter: Range 18–44 cm; median 28 cm.

Height: Range 6.5–9.8 cm.

Diameter/height ratio: 3.0–3.4.

Shape class: 5, medium-diameter bowls and dishes.

Temporal Distribution: Z-angle bowls begin in the Chuen Complex and continue into Cimi. In the Early Classic Manik Complex, they occur on different types.

Composite Silhouette Bowl

Illustrations: Fig. 11.45–46; 14.5–6, 14.13, 14.17, 14.50–52; 15.22–23; 16.6–7, 16.9, 16.11, 16.13–

14, 16.20, 16.25–26, 16.30. See TR. 25A: fig. 9*a*4–5; 13*b–d*.

Identifying characteristics and sorting problems: The composite silhouette is the identifying feature. Some bowls with small lateral ridges rather than flanges may overlap with this shape. In sorting, rim sherds too short to show the break between sections would be sorted into other categories.

Base: Flat to slightly concave.

Side: The upper section of the side is generally short and vertical to either slightly outcurving or incurving. The lower section is rounded.

Rim: Direct or everted.

Lip: Thickened and rounded.

Surface: Slipped on both interior and exterior.

Types: Sierra Red and Polvero Black, with a few examples of Laguna Verde Incised: Usulutan-style Variety and Caramba Red-on-orange. Other decorated types represented infrequently.

Diameter: Range 18–28 cm; median 24 cm.

Shape class: 5, medium-diameter bowls and dishes

Temporal distribution: This shape occurs throughout the Late Preclassic but is more common in Cimi than in Cauac.

SHAPE CLASS 6: SMALL DIAMETER BOWLS AND DISHES

Slightly Incurving to Round-side Bowl or Dish

Illustrations: Fig. 11.31; 12.47–53; 14.3, 14.9. See TR. 25A: fig. 99*d*2.

Identifying characteristics and sorting problems: There is some overlap with examples that have a more restricted orifice that necessitated frequent difficult decisions.

Temporal distribution: Occurs sporadically through the Late Preclassic complexes.

Base: Flat or slightly rounded.

Side: Rounded; usually high curvature.

Rim: Direct.

Lip: Usually rounded; usually slightly thickened.

Surface: Well-finished both inside and out. This was a favorite form for incised decoration, which invariably occurs on the exterior, usually as a line or lines on the upper part of the vessel.

Types: Occurs in low frequencies on all monochrome slipped types.

Diameter: Range 18–30 cm; median 20 cm.

Height: median 8 cm.

Diameter/Height ratio: median 2.0

Shape class: 6, small-diameter bowl.

Temporal distribution: The shape occurs in low frequencies in the Chuen, Cauac, and Cimi Complexes.

Bucket

Illustrations: See TR. 25A: fig. 6*c*(top); 9*b*2; 144*a*2.

Identifying characteristics and sorting problems: The eversion of the rim and outflaring sides are the identifying characteristics. Sherds from this shape form a continuum with those from the outflaring-side bowl with gradual everted rim and the outflaring-side bowl with flattened lip. Some examples are small enough that they could be classified as cups, or miniatures.

Base: Probably flat.

Orientation of side: Medium to wide outflare.

Side: Straight to slightly outcurving.

Rim: Sharply everted, usually to horizontal, with broad everted section.

Lip: Rounded or pointed, often thickened.

Surface: Slipped on both interior and exterior.

Types: Sierra Red (including Alta Mira Fluted), Baclam Red-orange, Polvero Black, and various incised types.

Diameter: Range 10–20 cm. Some examples are small and close to being miniature in size.

Height: 7.0–12.0 cm.

Diameter/Height Ratio: 1.4–1.6.

Shape class: 6, small-diameter bowls and dishes

Temporal distribution: Occurs in all Preclassic complexes.

Outflaring to Slightly Outcurving-side Unslipped Dish

Illustration: Fig. 11.19–22; 14.29–35. See TR. 25A: fig. 6*b*(top); 7*g*; 35*a*2; 155*g*.

Identifying characteristics and sorting problems: This class of unslipped dishes sort clearly, as most are Morfin Unslipped.

Base: Flat or slightly concave.

Orientation of side: Medium to wide outflare.

Side: Straight to medium outcurve.

Rim: Direct or slight rounded eversion; occasional examples with a more widely everted rim.

Lip: Rounded, flattened, or beveled. Occasionally thickened or grooved.

Surface: Smoothing is carelessly done leaving smoothing marks on many examples. Finishing on interior is more careful than on the exterior; on some examples the exterior is left unsmoothed.

Type: Mostly Morfin Unslipped; there a few examples of Achiotes Unslipped.

Diameter: Range 14–32 cm; median 20 cm. Some examples might be considered within the range of medium-diameter bowls and dishes, but most are in the small range, as is the median.

Height: Range 4.0–7.9 cm.

Diameter/height ratio: Range 3.1–4.5.

Shape class: 6, small-diameter bowls and dishes.

Temporal distribution: The shape does not appear in any of the Chuen Complex samples. The first appearance is in early Cauac samples from the North Acropolis. It increases in frequency in later Cauac samples and reaches a peak frequency in early Cimi Complex samples. The shape is a good marker for the Cauac and Cimi Complexes when it is present, but its distribution is spotty; some lots have high frequencies of the shape, but it is totally absent from other lots in the same time-range. It is more common in Cimi than in Cauac.

Comments: About half of the examples are smudged on the interior of the vessel; far less are smudged on the exterior. It is uncertain whether the smudging results from firing or from use of the vessel. The use of an unslipped surface as an identifying characteristic of the shape violates general principles for the separation of shapes, but the combination of shape and restricted type is in this case so useful and diagnostic that utility outweighs the virtue of consistency.

Slightly Incurving to Round-side Unslipped Dish

Illustrations: See TR. 25A: fig. 9*a*3.

Identifying characteristics and sorting problems: The unslipped surface and rounded side are quite distinctive and there are almost no sorting problems.

Base: Probably flat.

Orientation of side: Medium to wide outflare.

Side: Rounded, low curvature.

Rim: Direct or slightly everted.

Lip: Rounded, pointed, and beveled lips are all common.

Surface: Carelessly finished.

Types: Morfin Unslipped.

Diameter: Range 14–30 cm; median 20 cm. Some examples might be considered within the range of medium-diameter bowls and dishes, but most are in the small range, as is the median.

Height: Range 4.5–5.0 cm.

Diameter/height ratio: Range 3.1–4.2

Shape class: 6, small-diameter bowls and dishes.

Temporal distribution: This shape first appears in the Cauac Complex at Tikal and continues into the Cimi Complex.

SHAPE CLASS 11: MINIATURE VESSELS

There are two examples of miniature bowls and one miniature jar from burials (Bu. 166 and Bu. 167) that may pertain to the Cauac Complex.

Miniature Jar

Illustration: See TR.25A: fig. 13*g*.

Shapes: Short-necked narrow-mouth jar.

Types: Sierra Red.

Diameter: 4 cm.

Height: 6 cm.

Diameter/Height Ratio: 0.7

Shape class: 11, miniature vessels

Miniature Bowl

Illustrations: Fig. 56.13, 56.28–29; 57.3. See TR. 25A: fig. 10*f,g*.

Shapes: Slightly incurving to round-side bowls and composite silhouette bowls.

Types: Sierra Red, Polvero Black.

Diameter: 2–4 cm.

Height: 4 cm.

Diameter/Height ratio: 0.5

Shape class: 11, miniature vessels

The median dimensions of Cauac shapes are presented in Table 5.5, when sample sizes are large enough to calculate them.

Cauac Shapes: Chronological Change

Several new and important vessel shapes first appeared during the time of the Cauac Complex. In addition, frequency changes in some shapes and shape classes help separate the Cauac Complex from the preceding Chuen Complex. Given the relatively insignificant typological changes between the two complexes, they are more easily distinguished by a consideration of vessel shape along with type. The frequency distributions of vessel shapes across contexts are so divided that no shape classes or shapes predominate in the Cauac collections. Jars, both wide-mouth and narrow-mouth, are among the more common shapes, along with slightly incurving to round-side dishes bowls and dishes and medial-flange bowls (see Table 5.6).

The most notable diagnostic for the beginning of the Cauac Complex was the appearance of medial-flange and z-angle bowls. In all except the very small Cauac Sample 2-6, medial-flange and z-angle bowls occur in frequencies greater than 8% to as much as 20%, making them a good "type fossil" for distinguishing even small Cauac (or Cimi) collections from Chuen collections. In addition, medial-flange bowls are easily distinguished from labial-flange bowls, the only flanged shape of the Chuen Complex. The two unslipped dish shapes also appear for the first time in the Cauac Complex. They are not as good a diagnostic as medial-flange bowls because unslipped dishes occurred in less than half the Cauac samples and are more common during the Cimi Complex. Plates (shape classes 8 and 9) are

TABLE 5.5
Shape Dimensions of the Cauac Complex

Shape Class and Shape	Median Diameter or Range (cm)	Median Height or Range (cm) (Neck Height for Jars)	Median Diameter/ Height Ratio or Range (cm)
1. Wide-mouth Jar (with Short Neck)	20.0	2.8	7.4
2. Narrow-mouth Jar (with Short Neck)	14.0	2.4	5.8
2. Narrow-mouth Jar (with Tall Neck and Spout)	14.0	6.5	2.4
2. Florero	25.0–36.0	31.0–41.0	0.7–0.9
3. Very Large-diameter Jar	44.0	2.7	18.2
4. Widely Outcurving-side Bowl	24.0–58.0	5.0–39.0	1.4–5.0
4. Bucket	30.0–42.0	20.0–26.0	1.4–1.6
4. Cuspidor	33.0–43.0	23.0–27.0	1.4–1.6
5. Slightly Incurving to Round-side Bowl or Dish	30.0	6.0	4.2
5. Outflaring to Slightly Outcurving-side Bowl or Dish	30.0	8.0–16.0	1.4–4.2
5. Bucket	22.0	15.0	1.2
5. Outflaring-side Vase	18.0	15.0	1.2
5. Medial-flange Bowl	28.0	3.6–9.0	3.2–4.3
5. Z-angle Bowl	28.0	6.5–9.8	3.0–3.4
5. Composite Silhouette Bowl	24.0	—	—
6. Slightly Incurving to Round-side Bowl or Dish	20.0	8.0	2.0
6. Bucket	10.0–20.0	7.0–12.0	1.4–1.6
6. Outflaring to Slightly Outcurving-side Unslipped Dish	20.0	4.0–7.9	3.1–4.5
6. Slightly Incurving to Round-side Unslipped Dish	20.0	4.5–5.0	3.1–4.2
11. Miniature Bowl	2.0–4.0	4.0	0.5
11. Miniature Jar	4.0	6.0	0.7

present in low frequencies in most Chuen samples and virtually disappear in the Cauac Complex.

In summary, the changes in vessel shape that separate the Chuen and Cauac Complexes are significant enough so that the two complexes can be easily distinguished, largely because of the appearance of new and distinctive shapes in the Cauac Complex. Nevertheless, the differences in shapes between Chuen and Cauac are not so profound as the differences between Tzec and Chuen shapes and, as we move to the succeeding Cimi Complex, the rate of change continues to diminish.

Cauac Shapes: Social Dimension

Three of the five Cauac samples came from civic-ceremonial architectural complexes adjacent to the Great Plaza. Although all of these samples were obtained from fill, it seems likely that the ceramics represent material used somewhere within the general area and are attributable to civic-ceremonial activities. The other two samples came from small and intermediate structure groups in areas of the site where nothing larger than small mounds are known. The ceramics probably originated from

TABLE 5.6
Shape Frequencies of the Cauac Complex

Shape Class and Shape	Civic-ceremonial			Small Structure Groups	
	Sample Loc. 1-3 Gp. 5D-2	Sample Loc. 2-6 Gp. 5D-2	Sample Loc. 2-5 Gp. 5D-2	Sample Loc. 3-1 Ch. 5G-7	Sample Loc. 4-1 Ch. 6F-3
	%	%	%	%	%
1. Wide-mouth Jar (with Short Neck)	16.1	5.4	18.4	15.9	19.2
Total Shape Class 1: Wide-mouth Jars	**16.1**	**5.4**	**18.4**	**15.9**	**19.2**
2. Narrow-mouth Jar (with Short Neck)	16.7	13.5	14.4	12.8	9.6
Total Shape Class 2: Narrow-mouth Jars	**16.7**	**13.5**	**14.4**	**12.8**	**9.6**
3. Very Large-diameter Jar	1.1	—	—	0.7	—
Total Shape Class 3: Very Wide-mouth Jars	**1.1**	**—**	**—**	**0.7**	**—**
4. Widely Outcurving-side Bowl	2.4	10.8	4.0	4.6	2.7
4. Large Bucket	2.8	10.8	1.3	5.0	1.4
Total Shape Class 4: Large Capacity Bowls	**5.2**	**21.6**	**5.3**	**9.6**	**4.1**
5. Slightly Incurving to Round-side Bowl or Dish	14.3	10.8	12.5	9.9	20.5
5. Outflaring to Slightly Outcurving-side Bowl or Dish	7.6	—	5.3	3.2	—
5. Medium Bucket	0.7	—	1.8	5.3	2.7
5. Medial-flange and Z-angle Bowls	8.8	2.7	15.6	16.7	20.6
5. Composite Silhouette Bowl	3.2	10.8	1.6	5.7	1.4
Total Shape Class 5: Medium Diameter Bowls and Dishes	**34.6**	**24.3**	**36.8**	**40.8**	**45.2**
6. Slightly Incurving to Round-side Bowl or Dish	7.9	13.5	1.9	4.9	4.1
6. Small Bucket	0.9	2.7	—	—	—
6. Outflaring to Slightly Outcurving-side Unslipped Dish	0.2	—	6.1	—	—
6. Slightly Incurving to Round-side Unslipped Dish	—	—	0.8	—	—
Total Shape Class 6: Small Diameter Bowls and Dishes	**9.0**	**16.2**	**8.8**	**4.9**	**4.1**
Unidentified Small Rims	5.9	10.9	6.1	8.3	9.6
Odd shapes	11.4	8.1	10.2	7.0	8.2
TOTAL RIM SHERDS	534	37	374	282	73

residential activities of households of low social status.

The most pronounced difference between samples from the two contexts is that the average frequency of medial-flange and z-angle bowls is slightly higher in the small structure group samples than in those from the civic-ceremonial contexts. These results are somewhat surprising in that this category of well finished and frequently decorated vessels seems to fall within the category of vessels that might be assumed to associate with elite status, though as noted previously, PD. 125 in Sample 3-1 likely skews the results. If, however, food service was a more important use for medial-flange and z-angle bowls than ceremonial activity, the distribution may simply be indicative of a relative lack of food service among the activities in the site center. A second consistent difference in vessel shapes between domestic small and intermediate structure groups, and a civic-ceremonial context is that the narrow-mouth jar is less common in the domestic context than in the civic-ceremonial context. This result is also the reverse of what would have been anticipated. The narrow-mouth jar probably functioned primarily for the transportation of water, an activity that might be more characteristic of domestic routines rather than of civic-ceremonial activities. The distribution of unslipped dish shapes is easier to explain. All of these shapes are completely absent in samples from small-structure groups and appear consistently, although in very low frequencies, in the Great Plaza civic-ceremonial contexts. Since it is possible that all of these shapes may have been used as incensarios, their distribution can be explained as a result of ceremonial activity in the site center that lacked a counterpart in the small structure groups.

All in all, although there are a few differences in the frequencies of vessel shapes between samples from the center of Tikal and those from peripheral small and intermediate structure groups, they are not large enough to be surely indicative of social differentiation in the use of ceramics. All the problems with social interpretation outlined for the Chuen Complex continue to hold true for the Cauac Complex. With the existence of so many unresolved issues that could interfere with interpretation, it is difficult to infer meaning from relatively small differences in shape frequencies.

Special Deposits of the Cauac Complex

Burials of the Cauac Complex

The sample of burial vessels from the Cauac Complex was considerably larger than that from the Chuen Complex. Although only five of the Cauac special deposits classified as burials included ceramic offerings, the total sample of vessels was seventy, a seven-fold increase from the number of Chuen burial vessels. The Cauac burial sample showed a great range in the number of vessels per burial. Burial 37 contained no vessels and Bu. 124 only two, but Bu. 128, 167, 166, and 85 included eight, fourteen, twenty, and twenty-five vessels respectively. The range of social contexts was comparably great. Two burials came from Small Structure Groups 4F-1 and 6E-1, one from the Seven Temples Plaza (Gp. 5D-9), and three were major chamber burials from the North Acropolis (Gp. 5D-2).

Sierra Red, with twenty-nine examples, is by far the most common type represented among the burial vessels. Nevertheless, the Sierra Red frequency of 41% is considerably lower than it would have been for a comparable sample of vessels from general sherd collections. The decorative message in Cauac Complex burials is carried by Usulutan-style types. Nine examples of Usulutan-style types of the Sacluc Ceramic Group occur among the burial vessels, a frequency (13%) far higher than among the general sherd collections. If the four examples of Laguna Verde Incised: Usulutan-style Variety are added to this, the impact of Usulutan decoration in Cauac burial ceramics is considerable. Cauac burials included three examples of Alta Mira Fluted, a type very rare in the general sherd collections. Five of the burial vessels are of imported types, a matter to be discussed in more detail below. Unslipped types are more common among Cauac burial offerings than anticipated, with six examples of Achiotes Unslipped, two of Sapote Striated, and one of Morfin Unslipped. Although this frequency of unslipped types is not high in relation to the frequency in sherd collections, it contrasts markedly with the obvious avoidance of such plain ceramics in Classic Period burials. Monochrome types other than Sierra Red are underrepresented in the burial offerings. Of special interest is the fact that Flor Cream, is represented in Cauac burials by only two examples.

TABLE 5.7
Burials of the Cauac Complex

Burial No.	Op.SubOp./ Lot	Location Gp. Str.	Structure Group Type	TR. 25A Illustration	TR.	No. of Vessels
37	20H/31–2	Gp. 4F-1 Str. 4F-8	Small Structure Group	—	19	1
85	12P/78	North Acropolis Gp. 5D-2 Str. 5D-Sub.2-2nd	Civic-ceremonial	4–7	14	25
124	64J/9, 10, 11	Seven Temples Plaza Gp. 5D-9 Plat. 5D-9	Civic-ceremonial	8a	23D	2
128	68I/27	Gp. 6E-1 Plat. 6E-1	Small Structure Group	8b,9a	20A	8
166	12P/177	North Acropolis Gp. 5D-2 Str. 5D-Sub.11	Civic-ceremonial	9b–11a	14	20
167	12P/179	North Acropolis Gp. 5D-2 Str. 5D-Sub.10-1st	Civic-ceremonial	11b–13	14	14

Vessel shapes in Cauac burials also differ substantially from frequencies in sherd collections. Medial-flange bowls and narrow-mouth jars account for 23% and 20% respectively of the burial sample, large widely outcurving-side bowls with grooved lips are 9% of the sample, and slightly incurving to round-side bowls and dishes comprise 7%. These shapes are common in sherd collections. But unusual shapes that fall outside of those normally encountered in sherd samples make up nearly a third of the burial sample.

Details of shapes in the burial sample are best discussed by reference to individual burials. Burial 124, encountered near the surface in the Seven Temples Plaza (Gp. 5D-9), was accompanied by a fragmentary narrow-mouth jar and a wide-mouth jar of Achiotes Unslipped, the charred condition of which suggests possible use as a cooking vessel before it was placed in the burial. The location of the burial close to the surface and the unprepossessing nature of the offering in an area that must have had considerable ceremonial significance may suggest some special meaning for this burial. The grave included the almost complete skeleton of an adult (probably male).

The remaining four Cauac burials were from a Small Structure Group (Bu. 128 in Plat. 6E-1, Gp. 6E-1; see TR. 20A) and from major chamber burials in the North Acropolis (Bu. 85, 166, and 167 in Gp. 5D-2). As might be expected, the contents are much richer, and a great variety of vessel shapes are represented. Nevertheless, there are common patterns that give some unity to the vessel sets that accompanied the burials. Each of the burials contained either three or six medial-flange or z-angle bowls, although the size and specific shapes of the vessels varied both between and within burials. Each burial contained either one or two floreros or cuspidors. As mentioned previously, cuspidors and floreros are special shapes intended for burial offerings at Tikal because they were common in such offerings, but almost totally absent from the large sherd samples from other contexts. A few slightly incurving to round-side bowls and dishes occurred in each burial, but the number and specific shapes differed from one burial to the next. Large-capacity bowls were another common component of the offerings but vary even more between burials. Burial 167 was well stocked with such vessels, while the large offering with Bu. 85

completely lacked examples of these largest capacity vessels. Narrow-mouth jars tended to occur in large sets (Bu. 85 and 166 had six and seven respectively) or to be scarce (none in Bu. 167 and one in Bu. 128). In the burials where large sets of narrow-mouth jars occurred, they were accompanied by one or two examples of narrow-mouth jars with tall neck and spouts, a shape that is rare in sherd collections. Thus, although there is some patterning in the kinds of vessels that accompanied the richer burials of the Cauac Complex, there is no indication of the rigidly standardized sets of vessels of carefully controlled shapes and sizes that accompanied the elite burials of the Classic Period.

Six vessels in the Cauac burial sample were definitely imports to Tikal, probably from a place of origin in the Guatemalan Highlands. They appear similar to Arenal Phase pottery from the site of Kaminaljuyu (Kidder, Jennings, and Shook 1946; Shook and Kidder 1952). All these vessels are of the same black-brown incised type, with five of the six showing very similar vertical bands of incised design. A perfectly matched set of three deep outflaring-side vases from Bu. 85 is similar to a single vessel from Bu. 167 that is slightly shorter but of quite similar design. A fourth imported vessel in Bu. 85 is a

slightly different shape and has simple horizontal bands of incision but is enough alike in type so that it seems likely to have been from the same source. A second import from Bu. 167 has a very similar kind of decoration to the set from Bu. 85 but is a shallow dish rather than an outflaring-side vase. Aside from these six vessels, none of the other vessels from Cauac burials is different enough from the local tradition to be sure that it represents a trade ware. Some of the Usulutan-related pieces might be from outside Tikal, but most were probably of local origin. All in all, the number and variety of sources represented by trade vessels is much lower in the Cauac Complex than in the Early Classic. It should be noted, however, that this comment applies only to the ceramic content of burial offerings, as a rich diversity of exotic materials and trade goods was represented in non-ceramic offerings in the same burials.

Caches of the Cauac Complex

A total of four special deposits classified as caches contain Cauac ceramics. One of these caches (Ca. 168), from the deep trench into the North Acropolis, was more likely stratigraphically datable to the Chuen Complex and is briefly discussed in

TABLE 5.8
Caches of the Chuen Complex

Cache No.	Op.SubOp./ Lot	Location Gp. Str.	Structure Group Type	TR. 25A Illustration	TR.	No. of Vessels
24[2]	11D/19	North Acropolis Gp. 5D-2 Plat. 5D-1-4th	Civic-ceremonial	99d	14	2
168[1]	12P/184	North Acropolis Gp. 5D-2 Str. 5D-Sub.11	Civic-ceremonial	99c	14	2
205[2]	90C/4	Lost World Pyramid Gp. 5C-11 Str. 5C-54	Civic-ceremonial	99e	23C	2
209[2]	90B/1	Lost World Pyramid Gp. 5C-11 Str. 5C-54	Civic-ceremonial	99f	23C	2

1. Chuen or Cauac

2. Cauac or Cimi

Chapter 4. Cache 168 could be late Chuen or early Cauac. The remaining three caches did not have stratigraphic locations that could be related to a specific ceramic complex period. Stylistically, these latter caches are probably either Cauac or Cimi.

These three other, probably later, caches of Preclassic date are all from major civic-ceremonial locations. Cache 24 was from the North Terrace of the North Acropolis (Gp. 5D-2, Plat. 5D-1), while Ca. 205 and 209 were from Gp. 5C-11, Str. 5C-54 (the Lost World Pyramid). Although no clear stratigraphic date was indicated, they would probably be equivalent to the Cauac or Cimi Complexes. Each cache contains a two-vessel set with a large vessel of a cuspidor covered by an outflaring to slightly outcurving-side bowl or dish. This pattern of large-capacity vessels with bowls or dishes used as covers in cache offerings continues into the Early Classic Manik Complex, although at that time it is elaborated by special shapes for caches and the inclusion of large sets of such vessels in most caches.

Ceramic offerings in Tikal Preclassic caches are very different from ceramic burial offerings. The pattern of a large vessel with bowls or dishes used as covers that characterizes all except the two earliest caches occurs with certainty only once in burials, one such set in Bu. 167. There is much greater ceramic variety in both types and shapes in burials than in caches. Nine of the ten Preclassic cache vessels

are Sierra Red and the tenth is an undistinguished Polvero Black. In burials, decorated and exotic types are considerably more common. The same lack of variety is evident in shapes, where a very few shapes in the caches can be compared to a great variety of shapes in burial offerings.

Problematical Deposits of the Cauac Complex

Three problematical deposits containing ceramics are probably of Cauac Complex date. The most certainly dated is PD. 268, a single-vessel problematical deposit of undeniable Cauac stratigraphic placement in the North Acropolis. The vessel, an outflaring to slightly outcurving-side unslipped dish of Morfin Unslipped, is an unusual offering because such vessels are never found in any other caches and are rare as part of burial offerings. The second problematical deposit attributed to the Cauac Complex is PD. 93, which was encountered in excavations in the Seven Temples Plaza. The single vessel in the problematical deposit, a medial-flange bowl, is typologically either Cauac or Cimi, but a Cauac date is preferred because there were almost no Cimi ceramics in this location. The final problematical deposit of possible Cauac affiliation is PD. 114, containing two vessels encountered during the excavation of Ch. 5G-7. The vessels, a fragmentary wide-mouth jar of

TABLE 5.9
Problematical Deposits of the Chuen Complex

PD. No.	Op.SubOp./ Lot	Location Gp. Str.	Structure Group Type	TR. 25A Illustration	TR.	Est. No. of Vessels
93[1]	64J/9–2	Seven Temples Plaza Gp. 5D-9 Plat. 5D-9	Civic-ceremonial	141*c*	23D	1
114[2]	66X/29,30	Str. 5G-18 Ch. 5G-7	Small Structure Group	144*a*		3
268	12P/60	North Acropolis Gp. 5D-2 Plat. 5D-4-6th	Civic-ceremonial	155*g*	14	1

1. Chuen or Cauac

2. Cauac or Cimi

Sapote Striated and a small bucket of Sierra Red, are not temporally diagnostic and they are tentatively assigned to the Cauac Complex because Cauac ceramics predominate in associated lots. These two vessels are unlikely to be a cache and would be more at home among Preclassic burial vessels. Additionally, there is a fragment of an imported Sarteneja Usulutan spouted animal effigy jar. Like PD. 125 from the same chultun, PD. 114 may also represent the remains of a relocated, possibly desecrated burial.

VI

Cimi Ceramic Complex

Cimi Complex Collections

Introduction

The Cimi Complex continues the excellent record of Preclassic ceramics at Tikal. In fact, in terms of collections usable for quantitative analysis, the data for Cimi are the best for the entire period. Large multiple-lot collections were available and the superb architectural stratigraphy of the North Acropolis covered the period thoroughly. Unfortunately, no special deposits classified as burials pertaining to the Cimi Complex were discovered at Tikal, although three caches of possible Cauac or Cimi date, and three problematical deposits are of this date, as well two additional problematical deposits that contain possible Cimi ceramics.

Cimi Complex ceramics are difficult to distinguish from those of the Cauac Complex. All of the ceramic markers of Cimi are items that occur with relatively low frequencies, and the rest of Cimi ceramics are identical to those of the Cauac Complex. It was, however, important to make Cimi a separate complex. The material covers a critical period of time and establishes, in the light of the information on the beginning of the Manik Complex gathered by the Proyecto Nacional Tikal in the Mundo Perdido Group (Hermes 1993; Laporte and Fialko 1987, 1990 1995), a superb understanding of the transition between the Terminal Preclassic and the Early Classic.

Site-wide minor occurrences of Cimi ceramics occur with slightly lesser frequency than those for the preceding Chuen and Cauac Complexes, but this does not necessarily indicate a decline in population. It is likely that some small samples of Cimi date lacked the identifying markers of Cimi and were classified as Cauac.

Five locations at Tikal provided seven Cimi ceramic samples (Table 6.1). Two of these locations are from civic-ceremonial construction in the North Acropolis where the stratigraphic record demonstrates the transition between the Cauac and Cimi Complexes. The other three locations are in outlying areas of the site, two from chultuns not associated with visible contemporary structures, and one from a quarry.

CAUAC-CIMI LOCATION 1

The excavated areas of the North Terrace and adjacent sections of the Great Plaza have been designated Cauac-Cimi Location 1 (see TR. 14). The excavations revealed a series of floors and architectural developments that could be related to those of the North Acropolis sequence. Three architectural levels provided sealed samples dating from the Late and Terminal Preclassic. The Cimi sample came from a single level from the uppermost Preclassic level in the excavations. Two levels of Cauac Complex samples underlie the Cimi sample, so there is continuity with earlier material. Above this level, however, there are only badly mixed collections of much later date, so there is no evidence of the transition from the Preclassic to the Early Classic.

TABLE 6.1
Locations of Cimi Complex Samples

Sample #	Op.Sub-Op./Lot	Structure Group and Structure Number	Structure Group Type	Total Sherds-Types	Total Sherds-Shapes	Comments	TR.
Location 1		**North Acropolis Group 5D-2**	**Civic-Ceremonial**			**Unknown lot assignments**	14
Sample 1-1	12B,E,G	Plat. 5D-4-4th and 5D-4-5th		568	102	Combined sample	
Location 2		**North Acropolis Group 5D-2**	**Civic-Ceremonial**			**Unknown lot assignments**	14
Sample 2-1	12P: 7 lots quantified for types and 4 lots for shapes	North Acropolis Plat. 5D-4-4th		1946	223	Sample from between the 7th and 8th floors	
Sample 2-2	12P: 12 lots quantified for types and 8 lots for shapes	North Acropolis Plat. 5D-4-4th		2884	590	Sample from between the 8th and 9th floors	
Sample 2-3	12P: 7 lots quantified for types and 5 for shapes	North Acropolis Plat. 5D-4-4th		4780	735	Sample from between the 9th and 10th floors	
Location 3		**Near Str. 5C-39 to 57**	**Small Structure Group**				**20A**
Sample 3-1	26 A-H/all lots	Chultun 5C-8		—	687	No associated structures	
Location 4		**Group 4F-1**	**Small Structure Group**				19
Sample 4-1	20H/4–6, 8	Chultun 6F-3, near Str. 6F-62		—	73		
Location 5		**Group 5B-1 Locus**	**Small Structure Group**				18[†]
Sample 5-1	66K/4, 5, 20, 21	Chultun 5B-10		—	83	No associated structures	
	TOTAL SHERDS			**10178**	**2849**		

[†] Forthcoming

Cimi Sample 1-1: This sample came from the uppermost Preclassic level in Gp. 5D-2, the North Terrace-Great Plaza. It consisted of a total of 10 lots. The combined sample from all lots consisted of 568 sherds counted for types and 102 rims counted for shapes.

CHUEN-CIMI LOCATION 2

Chuen-Cimi Location 2 included all Preclassic floors and architecture encountered in the trench that sectioned the North Acropolis (see TR. 14). Control of architectural stratigraphy was superb and construction levels were sealed so that no material later than the sealing date could have been intruded into the deposits. Consequently, there was a splendid sequence of "points of introduction" in which the first appearances of ceramic features could be fitted into the sequence of North Acropolis floors. Most of the material recovered was structural fill, which included both ceramics contemporaneous with construction and material derived from the destruction of earlier units. The "upwelling" of early sherds blurred quantitative patterns of change.

The Chuen levels are described in Chapter 4, the Chuen Complex, and the Cauac levels are described in Chapter 5, the Cauac Complex. Three levels of Cimi date were encountered, sealed by the 7th, 8th, and 9th floors of Platform 5D-4 of the North Acropolis in Gp. 5D-2. All provided excellent samples of large size, each consisting of multiple lots that were large enough for individual quantification, which permitted checks of internal consistency within each level and comparison between levels. For the sake of larger samples, even lots that could be individually quantified were combined. The samples provide good documentation for the transition between the Cauac and Cimi Complexes, and the uppermost level shows trends toward the Early Classic Manik Complex.

Cimi Sample 2-1: This sample included sherds from between the 7th and 8th floors of the North Acropolis. The ceramics show trends toward the development of Early Classic characteristics. Sample size was good and a total of seven individual lots were quantified for type and four lots quantified for shape, which were combined into a single sample that included 1,946 sherds quantified for types and 223 sherds quantified for shapes.

Cimi Sample 2-2: This was a very large sample sealed by the 8th floor of the Acropolis sequence and almost entirely overlying the 9th floor. The material is typical Cimi. Twelve lots were large enough for type counts and eight lots for shape counts, providing an excellent basis for intersample comparison. In all, the combined total sample contains 2,884 sherds quantified for types and 590 sherds quantified for shapes.

Cimi Sample 2-3: This sample was sealed by the 9th floor of the North Acropolis sequence. Stratigraphy was complex in this section of the North Acropolis, so that some lots were confined to the area between the 9th and 10th floors, but many others, although sealed by the 9th floor, penetrated to deeper levels and contained significant quantities of ceramics of somewhat earlier date. Markers of the Cimi Complex occurred in a number of the lots of Sample 2-3, so that ceramics of the complex had clearly started by the time the 9th floor was laid. But many lots in Sample 2-3 contained no Cimi sherds and the quantitative distribution of the whole sample is close to that shown by Cauac samples. Cimi Sample 2-3 included seven lots that could be quantified for types and five lots that could be quantified for shapes. The combined sample consists of 4,780 sherds quantified for types including 735 sherds quantified for shapes.

CIMI LOCATION 3

This sample came from excavation of Ch. 5C-8, a large multichambered chultun located in an area without visible surface structures about 0.5 km W and slightly S of the Great Plaza (see TR. 20A), which may be associated with Str. 5C-57 (see TR. 19:149).

Cimi Sample 3-1: The large collection provided excellent examples of typical Cimi ceramics, but there was a mixture of both earlier and later material. Several subsamples, divided by chultun room and by depth within room, were separated during excavation, but there were no consistent differences between the subsamples, and frequent fits of broken sherds between lots suggest that the chultun was filled in a single dumping operation. Consequently, the sample is used here as a single combined sample that includes 687 sherds quantified for shapes. The social context seems most likely to have been lower class residential. The chultun is off the edge of the very large platform of Gp. 5C-11 on which are located Str. 5C-39 through -57 and it is possible that the chultun might contain refuse from these ceremonial-elite structures.

CIMI LOCATION 4

This sample was obtained during excavation of Gp. 4F-1, a small-structure group slightly less than 1 km NE of the Great Plaza (see TR. 19). The Cimi Sample came from a deep pit underlying later construction and was not associated with any identifiable construction.

Cimi Sample 4-1: Although there were a number of stratigraphic levels that contained Cimi sherds, the samples from individual levels were too small to permit quantitative comparison, and the sample was treated as a single sample containing 429 sherds quantified for shapes. Typological counts were not made. The sample most likely represents commoner domestic activity.

CIMI LOCATION 5

This sample came from Ch. 5B-10 in Gp. 5B-1, located about 1 km W and slightly S of the Great Plaza in an area with no visible surface structures (see TR. 18 forthcoming). The sample contained enough Cimi ceramics to indicate a Cimi date, but was aberrant in frequencies and may have a heavy component of Chuen ceramics as well. The total sample was small, consisting of only 83 sherds quantified for shapes. Type counts were not made. A commoner domestic context is assumed because of the absence of large structures in the vicinity.

Pastes of the Cimi Complex

Introduction

The most common pastes of the Cimi Complex are the same as those that characterize the Chuen and Cauac Complexes: Coarse-carbonate Paste for unslipped ceramic types and Preclassic Monochrome Paste for slipped types. Preclassic Fine Paste is more common in the Cimi Complex than in the earlier complexes. In Cimi Sample 2-1, the uppermost Preclassic level in the North Acropolis, the frequency

of Preclassic Fine Paste increases considerably, but even in this sample the paste accounts for only about 10% of the total sherds.

Cimi Paste Descriptions

COARSE-CARBONATE PASTE

Identifying characteristics: In all regards the same as the Chuen Complex (see Chapter 4 for complete description).

PRECLASSIC MONOCHROME PASTE

Identifying characteristics: In all regards the same as the Chuen Complex (see Chapter 4 for complete description). This quite variable paste continued to be the paste from which most monochrome types were produced during the Cimi Complex.

PRECLASSIC FINE PASTE

Identifying characteristics: In all regards the same as the Cauac Complex (see Chapter 5 for complete description). Preclassic Fine Paste is more common in the Cimi Complex than in the preceding Cauac Complex.

Discussion

As in the preceding Chuen and Cauac Complexes, a relatively small number of paste types in the Cimi Complex masked a considerable variety in paste characteristics. A broad range of colors, textures, and inclusions combined in nearly random fashion in Cimi ceramics suggesting considerable freedom of choice in the manner in which individual potters used their materials, as well as a population increase resulting in new and more potters.

Ceramic Types of the Cimi Complex

Introduction

The Cimi Ceramic Complex includes the ten ceramic groups and twenty-five types (comprised of thirty-two varieties) listed in Table 6.2. Types and type frequencies vary even less between the Cauac and Cimi Complexes than between the Chuen and Cauac Complexes. All of the important earlier types persist in Cimi in about the same frequencies as in Cauac. The Cimi Complex can be identified typologically only by the appearance of several new but relatively rare types and varieties of the Sacluc Ceramic Group.

TABLE 6.2 (part 1)
Ceramic Groups and Types of the Cimi Complex

Culbert and Kosakowsky	Culbert (1993)
ACHIOTES CERAMIC GROUP	**ACHIOTES CERAMIC GROUP**
Achiotes Unslipped: Achiotes Variety	Achiotes Unslipped: Achiotes Variety
SAPOTE CERAMIC GROUP	**SAPOTE CERAMIC GROUP**
Sapote Striated: Sapote Variety	Sapote Striated: Sapote Variety
MORFIN CERAMIC GROUP	**MORFIN CERAMIC GROUP**
Morfin Unslipped: Morfin Variety	Morfin Unslipped: Morfin Variety
SIERRA CERAMIC GROUP	**SIERRA CERAMIC GROUP**
Sierra Red: Sierra Variety	Sierra Red: Sierra Variety
Laguna Verde Incised: Simple-incised Variety	Laguna Verde Incised: Simple-incised Variety
Laguna Verde Incised: Design-incised Variety	Laguna Verde Incised: Design-incised Variety
Laguna Verde Incised: Usulutan-style Variety	Laguna Verde Incised: Usulutan-style Variety
Alta Mira Fluted: Alta Mira Fluted	Alta Mira Fluted: Alta Mira Fluted
Lagartos Punctated: Lagartos Variety	Lagartos Punctated: Lagartos Variety
Hiabon Punctated: Hiabon Variety	Hiabon Punctated: Hiabon Variety
In Cabro Ceramic Group	Mut Red-on-brown: Mut Variety
In Cabro Ceramic Group	Correlo Incised-dichrome: Correlo Variety
CABRO CERAMIC GROUP	*Not identified*
Cabro Red: Cabro Variety	*Not identified*
Mut Dichrome: Mut Variety	*In Sierra Ceramic Group*
Correlo Incised-dichrome: Correlo Variety	*In Sierra Ceramic Group*
POLVERO CERAMIC GROUP	**POLVERO CERAMIC GROUP**
Polvero Black: Polvero Variety	Polvero Black: Polvero Variety
Lechugal Incised: Simple-incised Variety	Lechugal Incised: Simple-incised Variety
Lechugal Incised: Design-incised Variety	Lechugal Incised: Design-incised Variety
BACLAM CERAMIC GROUP	**BACLAM CERAMIC GROUP**
Baclam Red-orange: Baclam Variety	Baclam Orange: Baclam Variety
Cay Incised: Simple-incised Variety	Cay Incised: Simple-incised Variety
Cay Incised: Design-incised Variety	Cay Incised: Design-incised Variety
BOXCAY CERAMIC GROUP	**BOXCAY CERAMIC GROUP**
Boxcay Brown: Boxcay Variety	Boxcay Brown: Boxcay Variety
Xtabcab Incised: Simple-incised Variety	Xtabcab Incised: Simple-incised Variety
Xtabcab Incised: Design-incised variety	Xtabcab Incised: Design-incised variety

TABLE 6.2 (part 2)
Ceramic Groups and Types of the Cimi Complex

Culbert and Kosakowsky	Culbert (1993)
FLOR CERAMIC GROUP	**FLOR CERAMIC GROUP**
Flor Cream: Variety	Flor Cream: Variety
Accordian Incised: Simple-incised Variety	Accordian Incised: Simple-incised Variety
Accordian Incised: Design-incised Variety	Accordian Incised: Design-incised Variety
SACLUC CERAMIC GROUP	**SACLUC CERAMIC GROUP**
Caramba Red-on-Orange: Chic Variety	Caramba Red-on-Orange: Chic Variety
Sacluc Black-on-orange: Sis Variety	Sacluc Black-on-orange: Sis Variety
Sacluc Black-on-orange: Xux Variety	Sacluc Black-on-orange: Xux Variety
Metapa Trichrome: Itsul Variety	Metapa Trichrome: Itsul Variety
Cayetano Trichrome: Cayetano Variety	Cayetano Trichrome: Cayetano Variety
Cayetano Trichrome: Xnuk Variety	Cayetano Trichrome: Xnuk Variety
Mojara Orange Polychrome: Mojara Variety	Mojara Orange Polychrome: Mojara Variety
MANIK COMPLEX GROUP	**AGUILA CERAMIC GROUP**
Manik Complex Type	Aguila Orange: Aguila Variety
Manik Complex Type	Xacin Black-on-orange: Xacin Variety
Manik Complex Type	Xacin Black-on-orange: Xacnal Variety
MANIK COMPLEX GROUP	**DOS ARROYOS CERAMIC GROUP**
Manik Complex Type	San Blas Red-on-orange: San Blas Variety

Cimi Type Descriptions

ACHIOTES CERAMIC GROUP

Achiotes Unslipped: Achiotes Variety

Established: Smith and Gifford (1966)

Group: Achiotes

Ware: Uaxactun Unslipped

Ceramic Complex: Cimi (Begins in Chuen and continues into Cauac and Cimi)

Ceramic Sphere: Chicanel

Illustrations: Fig. 9.1–63; 13.20–22; 14.14.

Principal identifying attributes: Unslipped only partially smoothed surfaces that reflect highly variable paste colors on wide-mouth jars.

Identifying characteristics and sorting problems: Both surface and paste are quite characteristic and overlap little with other types.

Paste: Characterized by Coarse-carbonate Paste. Most examples are of the brown to gray regular variety of Coarse-carbonate Paste, similar to the Chuen and Cauac Complexes, but some are of the red variety that first appears in the Eb and Tzec Complexes.

Firing: Many examples are darkened completely, but less than one-quarter show separable dark cores. Cores showing two or more shades of paste color are common. About half of the sherds show fireclouding of the surface.

Color: Highly variable, even on individual sherds. Light brown (7.5YR 6/4), strong brown (7.5YR 5/6), very pale brown (10YR 8/3), yellowish brown (10YR 5/4), and dark yellowish brown (10YR 4/4) all occur.

Surface finish: Most examples were carelessly finished and many sherds show smoothing marks and poor obliteration of coils; some examples are medium smooth.

Shapes: Almost entirely confined to the various wide-mouth jar shapes: wide-mouth jar with short neck and very large-diameter jar.

Temporal distribution: Begins in the Tzec Complex. After the Tzec Complex, the type becomes rare and although there is still a fairly abundant sherd-sorting category for Achiotes Unslipped, it contains mostly jar necks that may be from vessels that were actually striated.

Comments: Although counts of unslipped sherds ran to several percent in Cimi samples, the majority of the examples are jar necks that probably came from vessels of Sapote Striated.

Intersite comparisons: Achiotes Unslipped is used as the predominate unslipped type at Acanmul (Ball and Taschek 2015); Altar de Sacrificios (Adams 1971); Becan (Ball 1977); El Mirador (Forsyth 1989); El Perú/Waka' (Eppich 2011); Holmul (Callaghan 2008, 2016b); the Petexbatun (Foias and Bishop 2013); and Seibal (Sabloff 1975). In Belize, there is some variation noted from the Achiotes Ceramic Group and Paila Unslipped is used in its place at Barton Ramie; (Gifford 1976); Blue Creek (Kosakowsky and Lohse 2003); Chan (Kosakowsky 2012); and La Milpa (Sagebiel 2005). Paila Unslipped is also used at Uaxactun (Smith and Gifford 1966) for the Late Preclassic. Richardson Peak Unslipped is used at Cerros (Robertson 2016); Cuello (Kosakowsky 1987; Pring 1977); Colha (Valdez 1987).

SAPOTE CERAMIC GROUP

Sapote Striated: Sapote Variety

Established: Smith and Gifford (1966)

Group: Sapote [It is included in the Achiotes Group elsewhere]

Ware: Uaxactun Unslipped

Ceramic Complex: Cimi (Begins in Chuen and continues into Cauac and Cimi)

Ceramic Sphere: Chicanel

Illustrations: Fig. 9.1–63; 13.1–19; 15.13. See TR. 25A: fig. 144*a*1.

Principal identifying attributes: Unslipped surfaces with closely spaced striations only on the bodies of wide-mouth jars.

Paste: Coarse-carbonate Paste.

Firing: Dark cores are present on 25% to 50% of sherds. Many sherds without dark cores have different paste color near the core than at the surface. Nearly half the sherds exhibit fireclouding of the surface.

Color: Highly variable, and ranges from reddish tones (red, 10R 5/6, 2.5YR 5/6 to 4/8; light red, 2.5YR 6/6; reddish brown, 5YR 4/8) to brown (10YR 4/3, 5/3).

Surface finish and decoration: Striations are closely spaced, ranging from shallow to quite deep and from narrow to broad lines. Striations occur only on the bodies of jars.

Shapes: Almost entirely wide-mouth jars: wide-mouth jar with short neck and very large-diameter jar.

Temporal distribution: Becomes common in the earliest Chuen Complex samples and continues unchanged until the end of the Preclassic. Thin-walled examples are less common than in the preceding Chuen Complex.

Comments: This long-lasting type continued to be as important a type in the Cimi Complex as it did in the preceding Preclassic complexes and remains unchanged.

Intersite comparisons: Acanmul (Ball and Taschek 2015); Altar de Sacrificios (Adams 1971); Barton Ramie (Gifford 1976); Becan (Ball 1977); Blue Creek (Kosakowsky and Lohse 2003); Calakmul (Dominguez Carrasco 1994); Chan Chich (Valdez 1998, Valdez and Houk 2000); Cerros (Robertson-Freidel 1980); Colha (Valdez 1987); Cuello (Kosakowsky 1987); Holmul (Callaghan 2008, 2016b); El Pozito (Eppich 2000); El Mirador (Forsyth 1989); K'axob

(Lopez Varela 1996); La Milpa (Sagebiel 2005); Naachtun (Walker and Reese-Taylor 2012); Nakbe (Forsyth 1993); Nohmul (Kosakowsky and Pring 2001); "Zapote" in the Petexbatun (Foias and Bishop 2013); Rio Azul (Adams 1999); Seibal (Sabloff 1975); Uaxactun (Smith and Gifford 1966); Yaxchilan (Lopez Varela 1989).

MORFIN CERAMIC GROUP

Morfin Unslipped: Morfin Variety

Established: Adams (1971)

Group: Morfin

Ware: Uaxactun Unslipped

Ceramic Complex: Cimi (Begins in Cauac)

Ceramic Sphere: Chicanel

Illustrations: Fig. 14.29–35. See TR. 25A: fig. 35*a*2; 148*d*1.

Principal identifying attributes: Unsmoothed unslipped surfaces that are frequently fireclouded. Only found on dish shapes.

Identifying characteristics and sorting problems: The combination of unslipped surface, dish shape, and paste that is not coarse-carbonate is very distinctive.

Paste: Preclassic Fine Paste and Preclassic Monochrome Paste. It is important to note that unlike all other unslipped types in the Late Preclassic complexes, Morfin Unslipped is not made from Coarse-carbonate Paste.

Firing: Fireclouding is present on 56% of the examples. Of the fireclouded vessels, 62% exhibit fireclouding on the interior only, 21% show it on both interior and exterior, and only 8% show it on the exterior only. This is quite different from the distribution of fireclouding on other types in which exterior fireclouding predominates.

Color: Light brownish gray (10YR 6/2) to very pale brown (10YR 7/4).

Surface finish and decoration: The vessels are carelessly finished with the marks of the smoothing tool clearly visible on a number of sherds. A few examples are striated on the exterior. If one surface is better finished than the other, it is almost always the interior that shows greater care in finishing.

Shapes: Almost exclusively used for the production of the small unslipped dish shapes with outflaring to slightly outcurving sides or slightly incurving to round sides.

Temporal distribution: First appears at the beginning of the Cauac Complex, reaches a peak in very early Cimi lots and continues until the end of the Cimi Complex. Because the type is not present in Chuen and is quite easily recognized, it is a good diagnostic for the Cauac and Cimi Complexes.

Comments: Whether the dishes made from Morfin Unslipped have a primary function, as incensarios is a still unresolved question. The fact that many of the vessels were fireclouded on the interior, a characteristic generally uncommon in other vessel shapes, would suggest incensario use as it does to Adams (1971:18) for the same type at Altar de Sacrificios. On the other hand, almost half of the vessels do not show smudging or fireclouding on the interior, and, even where such smudging occurs, it is rarely associated with the heavy accumulations of soot that are characteristic of incensarios. Another possibly relevant characteristic is a very uneven distribution of the type within different contexts at Tikal. In some lots, usually from the North Acropolis, the type is very common, but in many other lots the frequency is quite low. The best conclusion would seem to be that Morfin Unslipped had some special use or uses among which may have included functioning as incensarios, but that it was not primarily an incensario type.

Intersite comparisons: Altar de Sacrificios (Adams 1971) and Becan (Ball 1977).

SIERRA CERAMIC GROUP

Sierra Red: Sierra Variety

Established: Smith and Gifford (1966)

Group: Sierra

Ware: Paso Caballo Waxy

Ceramic Complex: Cimi (Begins in Chuen and continues into Cauac and Cimi)

Ceramic Sphere: Chicanel

Illustrations: Fig. 13.26–28, 13.32–38, 13.43–46, 13.48–50, 13.55–57, 13.60; 14.3, 14.8–10, 14.13, 14.16–21, 14.43–46, 14.48–52; 15.10; 16.28, 16.31; 17.14. See TR. 25A: fig. 99*e,f*; 139*b*3–6; 140*a–j,l*; 141*c*.

Principal identifying attributes: Monochrome red, thick, waxy slip that fireclouds to brown and black on round-side bowls and dishes.

Identifying characteristics and sorting problems: Because almost all whole vessels of Sierra Red include areas in which the color variegates to black or light brown, sherds from variegated areas may be difficult to attribute to a specific type. In non-variegated areas, the color range of Sierra Red is small and quite distinct from that of other monochrome types.

Paste: Preclassic Monochrome Paste.

Firing: Dark cores occur in about one-third of the sherds, usually in thicker sections. Fireclouding occurs on 30% to 45% of the sherds in individual lots, more frequently on jars than on bowls.

Slip: The slip is thick and tends to flake. In most cases the surface was not well polished before application of the slip.

Polish: Usually low to medium. Waxiness is common but by no means universal.

Color: Good control of color. Most sherds are red (10R 4/8 to 2.5YR 5/6); a few examples range to reddish yellow (7.5YR 6/6).

Comments: Sierra Red is the most common slipped type in the Cimi Complex collections. Characteristics of the type remain the same throughout the Preclassic except in the frequency of vessel shapes represented.

Shapes: The Cimi Complex vessel shape distribution of Sierra Red returns to frequencies very similar to those that characterize the Chuen Complex. The most common group of Cimi shapes in the type is outflaring to slightly outcurving-side bowls and dishes that make up about one-third of the sample. Slightly incurving to round-side dishes and narrow-mouth jars each account for about one-sixth of the Sierra Red examples while the remainder of the sample is distributed among a variety of other shapes. There are some examples of Sierra Red that are red and unslipped (see TR. 25A: fig. 140*k*) and may be similar to vessels of the Puletan Red-and-unslipped type identified in northern Belize (Kosakowsky 1987). There are other examples of Sierra Red that have unslipped exteriors and appliqué spikes attached but there are too few to name a separate variety. Vessels with appliquéd spikes are traditionally classified as incensarios in Maya Lowland ceramics. In the present case, there seems to be nothing besides this tradition to support such a functional assignment. The slipped interior and the lack of any significant amount of smudging on the vessels would suggest some other use of these spiked vessels.

Temporal distribution: Chuen Complex to the end of the Preclassic.

Intersite comparisons: Extremely widespread throughout lowland Maya sites in the Late Preclassic. Acanmul (Ball and Taschek 2015); Altar de Sacrificios (Adams 1971); Barton Ramie (Gifford 1976); Becan (Ball 1977); Blue Creek (Kosakowsky and Lohse 2003); Calakmul (Dominguez Carrasco 1994); Chan (Kosakowsky 2012); Chan Chich (Valdez 1998, Valdez and Houk 2000); Cerros (Robertson-Freidel 1980); Colha (Valdez 1987); Cuello (Kosakowsky 1987); Holmul (Callaghan 2008, 2016b); El Mirador (Forsyth 1989); El Perú/Waka' (Eppich 2011); El Pozito (Eppich 2000); Kichpanha (McDow 1997); La Milpa (Sagebiel 2005); Nakbe (Forsyth 1993); Nohmul (Kosakowsky and Pring 2001); the Petexbatun (Foias and Bishop 2013); Rio Azul (Adams 1999); Seibal (Sabloff 1975:77–81); Uaxactun (Smith and Gifford 1966, Smith 1955).

Laguna Verde Incised: Simple-incised Variety and Design-incised Variety

Established: Type named by Smith and Gifford (1966); varieties named by Culbert (1993 [TR. 25A])

Group: Sierra

Ware: Paso Caballo Waxy

Ceramic Complex: Cimi (Begins in Chuen and continues into Cauac and Cimi)

Ceramic Sphere: Chicanel

Illustrations: Fig. 14.7, 14.21, 14.23–24, 14.37–38, 14.41–42; 16.16–19; 17.1,34. See TR. 25A: fig. 35*a*5.

Principal identifying attributes: Sierra Red slip decorated secondarily with pre-slip groove incising around vessel exteriors.

Surface finish and decoration: The Simple-incised Variety is decorated with single or multiple lines encircling the vessels almost always on the exterior near the rim. Patterns of the Design-incised Variety are usually no more than curving lines or straight lines that cross. Very few sherds were large enough to demonstrate overall vessel patterns.

Shapes: Small-diameter bowls and dishes are the most common shape represented in all incised types. Medium-diameter bowls or dishes, large capacity bowls, and narrow-mouth jars occur with somewhat lesser frequencies.

Temporal distribution: Begins and is most common during the Chuen Complex. Incising and grooving are considerably less common in the Late Preclassic than in the prior Middle Preclassic Tzec Complex..

Intersite comparisons: Varieties of Laguna Verde Incised are found at Acanmul (Ball and Taschek 2015); Altar de Sacrificios (Adams 1971); Becan (Ball 1977); Barton Ramie (Gifford 1976); Blue Creek (Kosakowsky and Lohse 2003); Calakmul (Dominguez Carrasco 1994); Cerros (Robertson-Freidel 1980); Chan (Kosakowsky 2012); Chan Chich (Valdez 1998, Valdez and Houk 2000); Colha (Valdez 1987); Cuello (Kosakowsky 1987); El Mirador (Forsyth 1989); El Perú/Waka' (Eppich 2011); El Pozito (Eppich 2000); Holmul (Callaghan 2008, 2016b); La Milpa (Sagebiel 2005); Nakbe (Forsyth 1993); Nohmul (Kosakowsky and Pring 2001); the

Petexbatun (Foias and Bishop 2013); Rio Azul (Adams 1999); Seibal (Sabloff 1975); Uaxactun (Smith 1955; Smith and Gifford 1966).

Laguna Verde Incised: Usulutan-style Variety

[**Note:** Given the composite nature of the decoration that includes imitation Usulutan and incising this type should have been named a composite according to the type: variety rules of nomenclature (Gifford 1976). However, the original type and variety names have been retained for ease of comparison with the prior publication of Tikal ceramics (TR. 25A).]

Established: Type named by Smith and Gifford (1966); variety named by Culbert (1993 [TR. 25A])

Group: Sierra

Ware: Paso Caballo Waxy

Ceramic Complex: Cimi (Begins in Cauac)

Ceramic Sphere: Chicanel

Illustrations: Fig. 14.2, 16.25.

Principal identifying attributes: Sierra Red slip decorated secondarily with pre-slip groove incising around vessel exteriors, and imitation Usulutan multiple wavy lines.

Identifying characteristics and sorting problems: None. It is quite distinctive.

Comments: The imitation of the Usulutan style of design by incising is more common in Cimi collections than other incised designs. Identical to Sierra Red except in the following categories:

Surface finish and decoration: Techniques of incising include light pre-fire scratching of the slip that lightens the slip color but does not penetrate to the clay, and post-fire incising. Designs consist of multiple parallel wavy (or sometimes straight) lines that are an obvious imitation of the Usulutan effect. Designs are perpendicular to the rim near the top of the vessel and become circles of wavy patterns on the interior base.

Shapes: Mostly medial-flange bowls and dishes and widely outcurving-side large capacity bowls, often with a grooved-hooked lip.

Temporal distribution: Cauac and Cimi Complexes only.

Comments: The imitation of Usulutan designs through incising is very common in Correlo Incised-dichrome and occurs rarely in Lechugal and Accordian Incised.

Intersite comparisons: The decoration on this type at Tikal bears some similarities to Usulutan-like decoration in the Sarteneja Group at Barton Ramie (Gifford 1976) and Uaxactun (Smith 1955) and an unnamed group at Seibal (Sabloff 1975). There are also some decorative similarities to the Caramba Red-on-red-orange type at Tikal and elsewhere.

Alta Mira Fluted: Alta Mira Variety

Established: Smith and Gifford (1966)

Group: Sierra

Ware: Paso Caballo Waxy

Ceramic Complex: Cauac (Begins in Cauac)

Ceramic Sphere: Chicanel

Principal identifying attributes: Monochrome red slip same as Sierra Red with the addition of pre-slip shallow, wide vertical fluting.

Comments: Identical to Sierra Red except for the addition of fluting.

Shapes: Outflaring to slightly outcurving-side bowls and dishes are most common, though occurs on other shapes similar to Sierra Red less commonly.

Temporal distribution: Begins in Cauac and continues into the Cimi Complex.

Intersite distribution: Altar de Sacrificios (Adams 1971); Barton Ramie (Gifford 1976); Blue Creek (Kosakowsky and Lohse 2003); Calakmul (Dominguez Carrasco 1994); Holmul (Callaghan 2008, 2016b); El Mirador (Forsyth 1989); El Pozito (Eppich 2000); El Perú/Waka' (Eppich 2011); Edzna (Forsyth 1983); La Milpa (Sagebiel 2005); Nakbe (Forsyth 1993); the Petexbatun (Foias and Bishop 2013); Piedras Negras (Muñoz 2006); Seibal (Sabloff 1975); Uaxactun (Smith and Gifford 1966).

Lagartos Punctated: Lagartos Variety

Established: Smith and Gifford (1966)

Group: Sierra

Ware: Paso Caballo Waxy

Ceramic Complex: Cimi (Begins in Chuen and continues into Cauac and Cimi)

Ceramic Sphere: Chicanel

Principal identifying attributes: Monochrome red slip same as Sierra Red with the addition of secondary decoration of punctations on the exterior.

Comments: The type begins in the Chuen Complex in small frequencies and continues throughout the Preclassic in equally small frequencies. In typological characteristics, the sherds are identical to Sierra Red, and are too small to permit comments about the patterns of punctation.

Intersite comparisons: Lagartos Punctated is named as a type, or unnamed within the Sierra Red Group at Altar de Sacrificios (Adams 1971:46); Blue Creek (Kosakowsky and Lohse 2003); Cuello (Kosakowsky 1987); El Mirador (Forsyth 1989); El Pozito (Eppich 2000); Holmul (Callaghan 2008, 2016b); Seibal (Sabloff 1975); Uaxactun (Smith and Gifford 1966).

Hiabon Punctated: Hiabon Variety

[**Note:** Given the decoration that includes unslipped areas of the vessels as well as punctations, the type should have been described as a composite. However, the original name was retained in order to facilitate comparisons with the published vessels in Culbert (TR. 25A).]

Established: TR. 25A (Culbert 1993)

Group: Sierra

Ware: Paso Caballo Waxy

Ceramic Complex: Cimi (Begins in Cauac)

Ceramic Sphere: Chicanel

Illustrations: None

Principal identifying attributes: Sierra Red slip on portions of exterior of vessel with the remaining surface left unslipped and decorated secondarily with punctations.

Identifying characteristics and sorting problems: Completely distinctive.

Comments: Identical to Sierra Red except for the following categories except as follows below.

Surface finish and decoration: Part of the vessel is red-slipped; the remainder is smoothed but unslipped. Small and shallow crescent-shaped or straight-line punctations cover all or most of the unslipped portions. The punctations occur randomly or are arranged in irregular, often double, rows. The line of separation between the red and unslipped/punctated sections is the break in curvature of a composite vessel. Slip and punctation are on the vessel exterior; the interior is unslipped.

Shapes: Almost all examples are from composite silhouette vessels. Sherds that are large enough to indicate total vessel shape all seem to be from "mushroom stands."

Temporal distribution: Occurs with very low frequency in the Cauac and Cimi Complexes.

Intersite comparisons: Mushroom stands have been identified as the Hongo Composite type at Altar de Sacrificios (Adams 1971); Becan (Ball 1977:114); Colha (Valdez 1987); El Mirador (Forsyth 1989); El Pozito (Eppich 2000); El Perú/Waka' (Eppich 2011); La Milpa (Sagebiel 2005); Rio Azul (Adams 1999).

CABRO CERAMIC GROUP

Cabro Red: Cabro Variety

Established: Robertson-Freidel (1980)

Group: Cabro

Ware: Chunux Hard

Ceramic Complex: Cimi (Begins in Cauac)

Ceramic Sphere: Chicanel

Illustrations: Fig. 14.4.

Principal identifying attributes: Double red slip, with outer thin slip that fires to a high luster with hard surfaces.

Identifying characteristics and sorting problems: The lustrous hard slip, which is unusual in the Cauac Complex, makes it easy to separate this type from the waxy non-lustrous and more common Sierra Red. There is one example of a probable Cabro Red vessel with black trickle (see TR. 25A: fig. 140*a*) and two examples that may be Tuk Red-on-red Trickle (Fig. 14.4; 16.1) similar to examples from Cerros (Robertson-Freidel 1980).

Paste: Preclassic Monochrome and Preclassic Fine Pastes, with the latter more common.

Firing: Fireclouding is uncommon and most examples are completely oxidized.

Slip: Monochrome red slip is hard and not easily scratched.

Polish: High

Color: Glossy, hard outer slip is usually red (10R4/6-8). The red underslip is a lighter red in color (2.5YR4/5-8) and only visible on eroded surfaces.

Surface finish and decoration: Surfaces of vessels are burnished and well smoothed, though when eroded the over-slip tends to flake off, and the surfaces are subject to rootlet marks. There is less fireclouding on this monochrome red type than in Sierra Red.

Shapes: Overlaps with Sierra Red.

Temporal distribution: Restricted to the Cauac and Cimi Complexes.

Comments: Originally Cabro Red sherds were not identified in the Tikal collections (TR. 25A) and went unnoticed as slightly glossier sherds in the Sierra Group. However, upon reexamination it is clear that double slipped glossier red examples are better described as part of the Cabro Group.

Intersite distribution: Cabro Red was originally identified at the site of Cerros (Robertson-Freidel 1980). Sierra Red: Big Pond Variety at Cuello (Kosakowsky 1983; 1987) and Nohmul (Kosakowsky and Pring 2001) has been reclassified as Cabro Red. It is also present at Blue Creek (Kosakowsky and Lohse 2003); Chan (Kosakowsky 2012); El Pozito (Eppich 2000); and Naachtun (Walker and Reese-Taylor 2012).

Mut Dichrome: Mut Variety

Established: Originally called Mut Red-on-brown by Culbert (1993 [TR. 25A]). Renamed in this work.

Group: Cabro [originally in the Sierra Group (TR. 25A)]

Ware: Chunux Hard

Ceramic Complex: Cimi (Begins in Cauac)

Ceramic Sphere: Chicanel

Illustrations: Fig. 16.26–27.

Principal identifying attributes: Exterior surfaces are the same as Sierra Red and the interior surfaces are slipped a brown to reddish yellow color.

Identifying characteristics and sorting problems: Only sherds large enough to indicate clearly that the distinction in color between the two sides of the vessel was intentional rather than an accident of firing are counted as part of the type. Many small sherds that belong to the type were probably sorted into the variegated sorting category. Mut Dichrome

is also identical to Correlo Incised-dichrome except that it lacks incising.

Comments: Identical to Sierra Red except in the following categories except as follows below.

Color: Red is within the color range of Sierra Red. The interior "brown" is highly variable in color and includes brown (7.5YR 4/4, 5/4), reddish yellow (7.5YR 6/6), pink (7.5YR 7/4), and dark gray (10YR 4/1).

Surface finish and decoration: The two colors occur on opposite sides of the vessel, with red always on the exterior and brown on the interior.

Shapes: Outflaring to slightly outcurving-side bowls are most common, but a variety of other shapes also occurs.

Temporal distribution: Probably occurred throughout the Late Preclassic, but only identified in the Cauac and Cimi Complexes.

Comments: Sherds that are large enough to make it clear that they were intentionally decorated in two colors occur rarely in most Cimi samples. Among the sherds in each lot classified as variegated, some were probably Mut Dichrome, but the number is impossible to judge because the two colors also occur frequently as unintentional variations due to firing.

Intersite comparisons: None noted though Correlo Incised-dichrome is found at Blue Creek (Kosakowsky and Lohse 2003) and El Perú/Waka' (Eppich 2011) so there may be sherds of Mut Dichrome that lack incising that were misclassified as Correlo.

Correlo Incised-dichrome: Correlo Variety

Established: Smith and Gifford (1966)

Group: Cabro [Originally in the Sierra Group (TR. 25A); identified in the Cabro Group by Robertson (2016).]

Ware: Chunux Hard

Ceramic Complex: Cimi (Begins in Cauac)

Ceramic Sphere: Chicanel

Illustrations: Fig. 16.7.

Principal identifying attributes: Surfaces the same as Mut Dichrome with the addition of incised decoration.

Identifying characteristics and sorting problems: The combination of incising and the different colors on two sides makes the type easy to identify.

Paste: Preclassic Fine Paste.

Firing: Dark cores rare; fireclouded exteriors fairly common.

Slip: Medium.

Polish: Medium.

Color: The exterior surface is red and the interior cream to brown. Although these colors are within the range of seemingly unintentional color variation in Sierra Red, it seems certain in this case that the two-color effect was intentionally created. The color ranges from red (10R 5/6, 5/8; 2.5YR 4/8) to dark red brown (2.5YR 2/4) and light red (2.5YR 6/8). The interior color is extremely variable and includes reddish yellow (5YR 6/6, 7/8), yellowish red (5YR 5/4), brown (7.5YR 4/4), and pink (7.5YR 8/4). Some examples fall within the color range of Flor Cream at light gray (2.5Y 7/2) and grayish brown (2.5Y 5/2).

Surface finish and decoration: The most common incised pattern is multiple parallel wavy lines on the vessel exterior that are an obvious imitation of the Usulutan style. A number of examples show patterned incising that is fine-line crosshatched rectangles or triangles. The incising was usually done while the slip was still wet, but sometimes was done after firing.

Shapes: The most common shape is a composite silhouette bowl, as well as medial-flange bowls.

Temporal distribution: Begins during the Cauac Complex and seems to continue during the Cimi Complex.

Comments: This rare decorated type continues to appear occasionally in Cimi collections.

Intersite comparisons: Altar de Sacrificios (Adams 1971); Barton Ramie (Gifford 1976); Blue Creek (Kosakowsky and Lohse 2003; Kosakowsky, Robertson, and Walker 2015); Cerros (Robertson 2016); El Perú/Waka' (Eppich 2011); Uaxactun (Smith; 1955, Smith and Gifford 1966).

POLVERO CERAMIC GROUP

Polvero Black: Polvero Variety

Established: Smith and Gifford (1966)

Group: Polvero

Ware: Paso Caballo Waxy

Ceramic Complex: Cimi (Begins in Chuen and continues into Cauac and Cimi)

Ceramic Sphere: Chicanel

Illustrations: Fig. 13.29–31, 13.41, 13.47, 13.51–54, 13.58–59, 13.61–63; 14.15, 14.27; 56.2; 57.2. See TR. 25A: fig. 140*m–o*; 148*d3*.

Principal identifying attributes: Thick black, sometimes waxy slip, which tends to flake and craze and fireclouds to red and brown.

Identifying characteristics and sorting problems: Polvero Black is easily separated from the earlier Chunhinta Black by paste characteristics. The separation of small sherds of various monochrome types frequently presents sorting problems because of the poor control of color and firing in all types.

Paste: Preclassic Monochrome Paste.

Firing: Darkening of the paste beneath the surface indicates firing in a reducing atmosphere. Completely darkened paste bodies or separate dark cores are common.

Slip: Medium to relatively thick slip, that tends to craze and flake.

Polish: Low to medium. Most, but not all, sherds have a waxy feel.

Color: Color ranges from black (5YR 2.5/1, 7.5YR 2.5/1, 10YR 2/1, 2.5Y 2.5/1) to dark reddish brown (5YR 2.5/2). Control of the reduction process was not good, and few vessels are completely black. Blemishes are reddish and gray to tan.

Shapes: Slightly more than half of the Cimi examples of Polvero Black are narrow-mouth jars, followed by slightly incurving to round-side bowls and dishes with a frequency of 18%. The remainder of the sample is divided among a number of other shapes, none of which occurs with a frequency greater than 5%. This distribution is almost identical to that for the Cauac Complex except that flanged bowls of Polvero Black are less common in Cimi than in Cauac.

Temporal distribution: The Polvero Variety is fully established by the Chuen Complex and continues until the end of the Preclassic with little change.

Intersite comparisons: Altar de Sacrificios (Adams 1971); Barton Ramie (Gifford 1976); Becan (Ball 1977); Blue Creek (Kosakowsky and Lohse 2003); Calakmul (Dominguez Carrasco 1994); Chan (Kosakowsky 2012); Chan Chich (Valdez 1998, Valdez and Houk 2000); Colha (Valdez 1987); Cuello (Kosakowsky 1987); Edzna (Forsyth 1983); El Perú/ Waka' (Eppich 2011); El Pozito (Eppich 2000); Holmul (Callaghan 2008, 2016b); El Mirador (Forsyth 1989); La Milpa (Sagebiel 2005); Naachtun (Walker and Reese-Taylor 2012); Nakbe (Forsyth 1983); Nohmul (Kosakowsky and Pring 2001); the Petexbatun (Foias and Bishop 2013); Piedras Negras (Muñoz 2006); Seibal (Sabloff 1975); Uaxactun (Smith and Gifford 1966, Smith 1955); Yaxchilan (Lopez Varela 1989).

Lechugal Incised: Simple-incised Variety and Design-incised Variety

Established: Type named by Smith and Gifford (1966); varieties named by Culbert (1993 [TR. 25A])

Group: Polvero

Ware: Paso Caballo Waxy

Ceramic Complex: Cimi (Begins in Chuen and continues into Cauac and Cimi)

Ceramic Sphere: Chicanel

Illustrations: Fig. 17.4.

Principal identifying attributes: Monochrome black slip same as Polvero Black decorated with fine line incising in simple designs.

Comments: See Polvero Black above. In typological characteristics, Lechugal is indistinguishable from Polvero Black. The same comments on decoration and shape made for Laguna Verde Incised apply to Lechugal Incised.

Temporal distribution: Occurs throughout the Late Preclassic but is more common in the Chuen Complex.

Intersite comparisons: Lechugal Variety used at Calakmul (Dominguez Carrasco 1994); Holmul (Callaghan 2008, 2016b); La Milpa (Sagebiel 2005); and Uaxactun (Smith and Gifford 1966; Smith 1955). Unspecified Variety used at Altar de Sacrificios (Adams 1971); Blue Creek (Kosakowsky and Lohse 2003); Chan (Kosakowsky 2012); El Mirador (Forsyth 1989); Seibal (Sabloff 1975). Macaw Bank Variety used at Barton Ramie (Gifford 1976), Chan Chich (Valdez 1998; Valdez and Houk 2000), Colha (Valdez 1987). Grooved-incised Variety used at Cuello (Kosakowsky 1987); Nohmul (Kosakowsky and Pring 2001) and Gouged-incised Variety used at Edzna (Forsyth 1983).

BACLAM CERAMIC GROUP

Baclam Red-orange: Baclam Variety

Established: Named Baclam Orange by Culbert (1993 [TR. 25A]). Renamed Baclam Red-orange in this work.

Group: Baclam

Ware: Paso Caballo Waxy

Ceramic Complex: Cimi (Begins in Chuen and continues into Cauac and Cimi)

Ceramic Sphere: Chicanel

Illustrations: Fig. 13.23–25, 13.42, 13.64–65.

Principal identifying attributes: Slightly waxy monochrome red-orange slip that overlaps with Sierra Red on the extreme, and is difficult to sort from Sierra Red.

Identifying characteristics and sorting problems: Surface color is the sole identifying characteristic of the type. The range of color grades continuously into that of Sierra Red, so there are many borderline examples. Only the most clearly red-orange examples were classified in sorting as Baclam Red-orange.

Paste: Preclassic Monochrome Paste.

Slip: Usually medium thickness. On some examples, the clay surface was well polished before application of the slip. In these examples, the slip tends to flake off, revealing sections of light clay.

Polish: Low to medium. Waxiness variable.

Color: The most typical examples are reddish yellow (light red 2.5YR 6/8), but the slip color overlaps with Sierra Red on the Munsell chart: red (2.5YR 5/8).

Shapes: Narrow-mouth jars with short necks and outflaring to slightly outcurving-side bowls and dishes.

Temporal Distribution: A low frequency of Baclam Red-orange sherds occurs in all Preclassic complexes beginning with Tzec.

Comments: Because Baclam Red-orange is the end of a continuum in color shared with Sierra Red, it is impossible to say whether prehistoric potters deliberately produced red-orange pottery or whether the examples so classified represent color variants due to firing or other chance circumstances. There is considerable overlap in color with both Sierra Red and the more red-orange examples of the later Aguila Orange.

Intersite comparisons: El Perú/Waka' (Eppich 2011). It is probable that some red-orange examples are sorted with Sierra Red at other sites.

Cay Incised: Simple-incised Variety and Design-incised Variety

Established: TR. 25A (Culbert 1993)

Group: Baclam

Ware: Paso Caballo Waxy

Ceramic Complex: Cimi (Begins in Chuen and continues into Cauac and Cimi)

Ceramic Sphere: Chicanel

Principal identifying attributes: Slightly waxy monochrome red-orange slip that overlaps with Sierra Red on the extreme, and is difficult to sort from the incised Sierra Red type, Laguna Verde Incised, with which it shares similar incising.

Comments: A few red-orange slipped sherds show uncomplicated incised decoration. The sample was too small to permit a full typological characterization, but in all observable features the sherds are identical to Baclam Red-orange.

Intersite comparisons: None noted, however at other sites red-orange examples are likely included in the Sierra Red Group, Laguna Verde Incised type.

BOXCAY CERAMIC GROUP

Boxcay Brown: Boxcay Variety

Established: TR. 25A (Culbert 1993)

Group: Boxcay

Ware: Paso Caballo

Ceramic Complex: Cimi (Begins in Chuen and continues into Cauac and Cimi)

Ceramic Sphere: Chicanel

Illustrations: Fig. 13.39–40. See TR. 25A: fig. 140*p*; 148*d*2.

Principal identifying attributes: Slightly lustrous rather than waxy monochrome brown slip that exhibits crazing.

Identifying characteristics and sorting problems: Because the color of Boxcay Brown ranges into the colors of Polvero Black and Flor Cream, separation is not always clear. Boxcay Brown can be easily separated from the earlier Boolay Brown that has a fine paste with few inclusions.

Paste: Preclassic Monochrome Paste.

Firing: Dark cores occur in half of the sample. Better than half of the sherds show fireclouding.

Slip: Medium thickness.

Polish: Low to medium; waxiness not common.

Color: Ranges from dark yellowish brown (10YR 4/4) to olive brown (2.5Y 4/4).

Shapes: Slightly more than half of the Cimi examples are narrow-mouth jars, and about one-quarter are slightly incurving to round-side dishes. The remainder of the sample is divided among a variety of other shapes, each present in low frequency. There are two examples of miniature jars.

Temporal distribution: Boxcay Brown continues to exist as a rare type in the Cimi Complex.

Comments: Boxcay Brown occurs with low frequency in all Cimi samples except for the large Cimi Sample 3-1 in which it accounts for about 10% of total sherds.

Intersite comparisons: Holmul (Callaghan 2008, 2016b) and Piedras Negras (Muñoz 2006).

Xtabcab Incised: Simple-incised Variety and Design-incised Variety

Established: TR. 25A (Culbert 1993)

Group: Boxcay

Ware: Paso Caballo

Ceramic Complex: Cimi (Begins in Chuen and continues into Cauac and Cimi)

Ceramic Sphere: Chicanel

Illustrations: Fig. 16.9.

Principal identifying attributes: Same as Boxcay Brown with the addition of simple incised decoration.

Comments: The few examples of brown-slipped incised sherds in Cimi Complex collections do not give enough information to allow full description of the type.

Intersite comparisons: None noted with incising but see Boxcay Brown above.

FLOR CERAMIC GROUP

Flor Cream: Flor Variety

Established: Smith and Gifford (1966)

Group: Flor

Ware: Paso Caballo Waxy

Ceramic Complex: Cimi (Begins in Chuen and continues into Cauac and Cimi)

Ceramic Sphere: Chicanel

Illustrations: Fig. 14.22, 14.47; 16.1, 16.10–11, 16.20, 16.22–23. See TR. 25A: fig. 139*b*2.

Principal identifying attributes: Lustrous, slightly waxy, cream slip that is variable in color.

Identifying characteristics and sorting problems: Except for slight overlap with the color range of Boxcay Brown, Flor Cream presents few sorting problems.

Paste: Preclassic Fine Paste predominates, but Preclassic Monochrome Paste is also represented.

Firing: Dark cores and fireclouding are rare.

Slip: Thick slip that adheres better and shows less tendency to flake or craze than other Preclassic monochrome slips.

Polish: Low to medium.

Color: Slip color of Flor Cream is extremely variable. Very pale brown (10YR 8/3), pale brown (10YR 6/3), brown (10YR 5/3), and light yellowish brown (10YR 6/4) are most common, but white (10YR 8/1, 8/2; 2.5Y 8/2) and gray (10YR 6/1; 5Y 5/1) also occur. It is common for sherds to show patches of two different colors.

Shapes: By far the most common shape (61% of the sample) represented in Cimi samples of Flor Cream is the slightly incurving to round-side bowl or dish, usually with an incurved rim. Because this shape rarely occurs in Flor Cream samples from the Chuen and Cauac Complexes, it is a good diagnostic for Cimi. The rest of the Cimi sample of Flor Cream is divided between a number of shapes of which composite silhouette and medial-flange bowls (11%), and narrow-mouth jars (8%) are the next most common.

Temporal distribution: Some examples of the Flor Variety appear as early as the Chuen Complex, but the peak frequency of the variety occurs in Cimi lots.

Intersite comparisons: Altar de Sacrificios (Adams 1971); Barton Ramie (Gifford 1976); Becan (Ball 1977); Blue Creek (Kosakowsky and Lohse 2003); Chan Chich (Valdez 1998; Valdez and Houk 2000); Colha (Valdez 1987); Cuello (Kosakowsky 1987); El Perú/Waka' (Eppich 2011); El Mirador (Forsyth 1989); Holmul (Callaghan 2016b); La Milpa (Sagebiel 2005); Nakbe (Forsyth 1993); Piedras Negras (Muñoz 2006); Nohmul (Kosakowsky and Pring 2001); Seibal (Sabloff 1975); Uaxactun (Smith 1955; Smith and Gifford 1966). It is an Unspecified Variety at Chan (Kosakowsky 2012); Edzna (Forsyth 1983); K'axob (Lopez Varela 1996); the Petexbatun (Foias and Bishop 2013); Yaxchilan (Lopez Varela 1989).

Accordian Incised: Simple-incised Variety and Design-incised Variety

Established: Type named Smith and Gifford (1966); varieties named by Culbert (1993 [misspelled as Accordion in TR. 25A])

Group: Flor

Ware: Paso Caballo Waxy

Ceramic Complex: Cimi (Begins in Chuen and continues into Cauac and Cimi)

Ceramic Sphere: Chicanel

Illustrations: Fig. 16.15.

Principal identifying attributes: Monochrome cream slip similar to Flor Cream: Flor Variety with the addition of incised decoration on the exterior of vessels.

Comments: Typologically, sherds of Accordian Incised are identical to sherds of Flor Cream with the addition of incising. The sherds of incised cream pottery in the Cimi Complex collections are too rare to permit adequate characterization.

Intersite comparisons: Identified as the Accordian Variety at Holmul (Callaghan 2008, 2016b, 2016c) and Uaxactun (Smith and Gifford 1966). It is an Unspecified Variety at Barton Ramie (Gifford 1976); Becan (Ball 1997); and Edzna (Forsyth 1983); and called Acordeon Incised in the Petexbatun (Foias and Bishop 2013). There are unnamed examples at Seibal (Sabloff 1975).

SACLUC CERAMIC GROUP
Caramba Red-on-orange: Chic Variety

Established: Type named by Adams (1971); variety named by Culbert (1993 [TR. 25A])

Group: Sacluc [in the Caramba Group at El Mirador (Forsyth 1989)]

Ware: Paso Caballo Waxy

Ceramic Complex: Cimi (Begins in Cauac)

Ceramic Sphere: Chicanel

Illustrations: Fig. 17.5, 17.23–25, 17.30–31. See TR. 25A: fig. 35*a*1.

Principal identifying attributes: Red-orange slip on interiors and exteriors of vessels with red slip applied over base and then wiped off to create the Usulutan-like decoration.

Identifying characteristics and sorting problems: The type is quite distinctive and overlaps only with other types in the Usulutan-related series.

Paste: Both Preclassic Monochrome Paste and Preclassic Fine Paste are represented.

Firing: About half of the examples show dark cores and one-quarter show two-tone cores with a different color in the center than near the surface. Fire-clouding is rare.

Slip: Medium to thick.

Polish: Low to medium.

Color: The background color is usually reddish yellow (5YR 6/8, 7/8). Variants include strong brown (7.5YR 5/8), red (2.5YR 5/8), and pink (7.5YR 7/4). The darker stripes are red (10R 4/6, 4/8 to 2.5YR 5/8) with some examples ranging to reddish brown (5YR 4/8).

Surface finish and decoration: Although the decorative patterns are obviously related to those of Usulutan Ware, Caramba Red-on-orange: Chic Variety was not produced by a resist technique, but by at least two other techniques. The more common was a "wipe-off" technique in which a slip was applied and then partially wiped off in some areas to produce lighter stripes. The second technique was positive painting with a second coat of the original slip or one of a different color. Although for many sherds the technique of production cannot be determined, those that do permit determination suggest a correlation between the wipe-off technique and Preclassic Fine Paste and between positive painting and Preclassic Monochrome Paste. Decoration consists of multiple parallel lines, sometimes executed with a multi-pronged instrument. On the vessel exteriors, the lines are only gently curved and run vertically. They start in the same vertical fashion at the top of vessel interiors, giving way to wavy lines and circles on the interior.

Shapes: Composite silhouette bowls are common shapes, followed by narrow-mouth jars and tetrapod bowls.

Temporal distribution: The North Acropolis stratigraphy demonstrates that Caramba Red-on-orange begins at the start of the Cauac Complex and continues to be an important decorated type until the end of the Cimi Complex.

Intersite comparisons: Altar de Sacrificios (Adams 1971); Becan (Ball 1977); Blue Creek (Kosakowsky and Lohse 2003; Kosakowsky, Robertson, and Walker 2015); Edzna (Forsyth 1983); El Mirador (Forsyth 1989); El Perú/Waka' (Eppich 2011); Holmul (Callaghan 2008, 2016b); and the Petexbatun (Foias and Bishop 2013).

Sacluc Black-on-orange: Sis Variety

Established: Type named by Adams (1971); variety named by Culbert (1993 [TR. 25A])

Group: Sacluc [in the Caramba Group at El Mirador (Forsyth 1989)]

Ware: Paso Caballo Waxy

Ceramic Complex: Cimi (Begins in Cauac)

Ceramic Sphere: Chicanel

Illustrations: Fig. 17.18–21, 17.32.

Principal identifying attributes: Light orange slip overpainted with a black or brownish-black slip in multiple parallel wavy lines.

Identifying characteristics and sorting problems: The Usulutan-related types are easy to distinguish from all other types by the multiple parallel-line decoration.

Paste: Both Preclassic Monochrome Paste and Preclassic Fine Paste are represented.

Firing: Half of the examples have dark cores. Fire-clouding is rare.

Slip: Thin to medium.

Polish: Low to medium.

Color: The background color may be reddish yellow (5YR 6/8), red (2.5YR 6/8), or light red (7.5YR 6/8). The black stripes are produced by a black-firing pigment rather than by reduction firing.

Surface finish and decoration: Like Caramba Red-on-orange, Sacluc Black-on-orange: Sis Variety is produced by both wipe-off and positive painting techniques. In Sacluc Black-on-orange, positive painting is slightly more common than wipe-off. Decoration consists of quite broad lines of medium curvature well separated from each other.

Shapes: Composite silhouette and tetrapod bowls.

Temporal distribution: The type appears at the start of the Cauac Complex and continues to appear through the Cimi Complex.

Intersite comparisons: Altar de Sacrificios (Adams 1971); Blue Creek (Kosakowsky and Lohse 2003; Kosakowsky, Robertson, and Walker 2015); El Mirador (Forsyth 1989); Nakbe (Forsyth 1993); Punta de Chimino (Bachand 2007); Seibal (Sabloff 1975); and possibly at La Milpa (Sagebiel 2005).

Sacluc Black-on-orange: Xux Variety

Established: Type named by Adams (1971); variety named by Culbert (1993 [TR. 25A])

Group: Sacluc

Ware: Paso Caballo Waxy

Ceramic Complex: Cimi

Ceramic Sphere: Chicanel

Illustrations: Fig. 15.14, 15.17; 17.2, 17.6–8, 17.10, 17.16–17; 17.26–28. See TR. 25A: fig. 139*b*1.

Principal identifying attributes: Light orange slip overpainted with a true black slip that is wiped off in multiple parallel wavy lines to reveal the underlying orange slip.

Paste: Three-quarters of the examples are of Preclassic Fine Paste; the remainder is Preclassic Monochrome Paste.

Firing: One-third of the sherds have dark cores. Fireclouding is rare.

Slip: Thin.

Polish: Medium.

Surface: A thin, very liquid, black slip was applied over the first orange slip and a multipronged instrument used to wipe off sections of the black slip revealing the underlying orange.

Color: The orange is usually reddish yellow (5YR 6/8, 7/8), ranging to light red (2.5YR 6/8) and red (2.5YR 5/8). The black is true black.

Surface finish and decoration: The black slip is applied to quite large areas and then wiped through with multiprong tools to create wavy zigzag patterns with sharp turns and many closely spaced lines. The edges of the black areas show two very characteristic features. One is a splashing of the thin slip in rayed patterns over the surrounding underslip. The second is the carrying of some slip by the wiping tools into surrounding areas where thin black lines are created along the edges of the tool.

Shapes: Widely outcurving-side bowls with grooved-hook lip are most common. A variety of other shapes also occur.

Temporal distribution: The type begins in the preceding Cauac Complex, but in a different variety. Xux Variety is confined to the Cimi Complex.

Intersite comparisons: Type is found at Altar de Sacrificios (Adams 1971); Blue Creek (Kosakowsky and Lohse 2003; Kosakowsky, Robertson, and Walker 2015); El Mirador (Forsyth 1989); Nakbe (Forsyth 1993); Punta de Chimino (Bachand 2007); Seibal (Sabloff 1975); and possibly at La Milpa (Sagebiel 2005).

Metapa Trichrome: Itsul Variety

Established: Type named by Adams (1971); variety named by Culbert (1993 [TR. 25A])

Group: Sacluc

Ware: Paso Caballo Waxy

Ceramic Complex: Cimi (Begins in Cauac)

Ceramic Sphere: Chicanel

Illustrations: Fig. 16.2–4, 16.24, 16.29–30; 16.13–14; 17.11–12.

Principal identifying attributes: Light orange slip overpainted with a black or brownish-black slip in multiple parallel wavy lines. Additional decoration includes areas of red slip on the upper exterior of composite silhouette vessels.

Comments: Identical to Sacluc Black-on-orange: Sis Variety except in the following characteristics.

Color: The background color is usually reddish yellow (5YR 6/6, 6/8) or yellowish red (5YR 5/8), but ranges to light red (2.5YR 6/8). The stripes are black and the areas of red are 10R 5/8.

Surface finish and decoration: The designs are multiple wavy line patterns in black on orange. The red occurs as a separate section on the lip or on the upper exterior of the vessel.

Shapes: Vessels of composite silhouette are most common, as well as medial-flange bowls, and narrow-mouth jars.

Temporal distribution: Begins in the Cauac Complex, but occurs in small quantities in the Cimi Complex.

Intersite comparisons: Altar de Sacrificios (Adams 1971) and Punta de Chimino (Bachand 2007).

Cayetano Trichrome: Cayetano Variety

Established: TR. 25A (Culbert 1993)

Group: Sacluc

Ware: Paso Caballo Waxy

Ceramic Complex: Cimi

Ceramic Sphere: Chicanel

Illustrations: Fig. 17.3, 17.9, 17.15, 17.29, 17.33, 17.35.

Principal identifying attributes: Double slipped with a red slip over an orange, which is wiped off creating wavy Usulutan decoration. Additionally decorated with a black slip that is also wiped off to create wavy Usulutan decoration.

Identifying characteristics and sorting problems: The type is very easy to recognize from the style of decoration. It is likely that the counts for Cayetano Trichrome are underrepresented because sherds in which the final black coat is predominate may not show the underlying red-on-orange and would be counted as the Xux Variety of Sacluc Black-on-orange.

Paste: Mostly Preclassic Fine Paste and a few examples of Preclassic Monochrome Paste.

Firing: Dark cores and fireclouding rare.

Slip: Thin.

Polish: Medium.

Color: The base coat ranges from light red (2.5YR 6/8) to reddish yellow (5YR 6/8, 7/8; 7.5YR 6/6) to yellow (10YR 7/6). The second slip is red (2.5YR 4/8, 5/8; 10R 4/8, 5/8). The final slip is black.

Surface finish and decoration: An orange slip was applied first and then covered with either a second reddish slip or a second coat of the initial slip. The second slip was then wiped off in sections to create red-on-orange Usulutan-style patterns typical of Caramba Red-on-orange. A very thin liquid black slip was then applied to sections of the vessel and again wiped through to create more wavy-line patterns as in the Xux Variety of Sacluc Black-on-orange.

Shapes: Medial flange and composite silhouette bowls.

Temporal distribution: Cimi Complex only.

Comments: Since Cayetano Trichrome and the related Xux Variety of Sacluc Black-on-orange are easily recognized and occur only in the Cimi Complex these two types serve as the best typological markers for the complex.

Intersite comparisons: Blue Creek (Kosakowsky, Robertson, and Walker 2015).

Cayetano Trichrome: Xnuk Variety

Established: TR. 25A (Culbert 1993)

Group: Sacluc

Ware: Paso Caballo Waxy

Ceramic Complex: Cimi

Ceramic Sphere: Chicanel

Illustrations: Fig. 17.13.

Principal identifying attributes: Double slipped with a red slip over an orange, which is wiped off creating wavy Usulutan decoration. Additionally decorated with a black band at the lip.

Comments: Identical to Cayetano Trichrome: Cayetano Variety except for the following characteristics.

Decoration: Designs are in red-on-orange as in Caramba Red-on-orange and black is added only as a band at the lip.

Intersite comparisons: None noted for this variety although the type is also identified at Blue Creek (Kosakowsky, Robertson, and Walker 2015).

Mojara Orange Polychrome: Mojara Variety

Established: Adams (1971)

Group: Sacluc

Ware: Paso Caballo Waxy

Ceramic Complex: Cimi

Ceramic Sphere: Chicanel

Illustrations: Fig. 17.22.

Principal identifying attributes: Decoration by red and black on orange using a Usulutan wavy multi-lined pattern.

Paste: Mostly Preclassic Fine Paste.

Firing: Dark cores and fireclouding rare.

Slip: Thin.

Polish: Medium.

Color: The base coat ranges from light red (2.5YR 6/8) to reddish yellow (5YR 6/8, 7/8; 7.5YR 6/6) to yellow (10YR 7/6). The second slip is red (2.5YR 4/8, 5/8; 10R 4/8, 5/8) to dark red (7.5R3/6, 4/6). The black decoration is 2.5YR2/10.

Comments: Only a few sherds of Mojara Orange Polychrome were recovered at Tikal. They seem to fall within the range of the type as described by Adams (1971:36). It should be noted that the characterizing feature of the type is the combination of Usulutan wavy-line designs with other, usually geometric, designs.

Intersite comparisons: Altar de Sacrificios (Adams 1971).

Cimi Types: Chronological Change

Sierra Red and Sapote Striated are the most common types in Cimi samples (see Table 6.3). Data on type frequencies were only available for four sample locations from Gp. 5D-2 (civic-ceremonial) so comparisons between the Cauac and Cimi Complexes are incomplete at best. Sierra Red frequencies range from 23% to almost 36% in individual samples, while Sapote Striated frequencies vary even more widely, from 14% to 27%. Polvero Black is the third most common type in most lots, with frequencies between 10% and almost 17%. Boxcay Brown occurs in most samples in frequencies of 2% to 4%. The unslipped types, Achiotes Unslipped and Morfin Unslipped, which had not been separated at the time

TABLE 6.3
Ceramic Type Frequencies of the Cimi Complex

Ceramic Types/ Groups	Civic-ceremonial			
	Sample Loc. 1-1 Gp. 5D-2	Sample Loc. 2-3 Gp. 5D-2	Sample Loc. 2-2 Gp. 5D-2	Sample Loc. 2-1 Gp. 5D-2
	%	%	%	%
Achiotes Group & Morfin Group[1]	5.1	7.6	5.3	3.2
Sapote Group	13.7	27.0	23.7	16.2
Sierra Group[2]	35.9	28.5	27.0	22.8
Laguna Verde Incised: Usulutan Style Variety	0.2	Trace	—	—
Polvero Group	9.7	16.7	15.9	9.7
Flor Group	1.4	1.2	2.1	2.0
Baclam Group	2.6	Trace	1.0	1.1
Boxcay Group	2.3	3.9	4.2	3.0
Sacluc Group	0.2	0.6	1.6	1.1
Chuen/Cauac Types	0.5	—	—	—
Early Classic Types	2.1	0.8	1.2	3.3
Rare or Unclassified Types	6.0	7.0	8.2	6.3
Weathered	20.2	6.6	9.8	31.3
TOTAL SHERDS	568	5515	3474	2169

[1] All unslipped unstriated examples were originally classified together.

[2] Cabro Red was not differentiated in the original frequency sorting.

of typological counts, average around 5%, but most of the sherds are jar necks that had probably been parts of Sapote Striated whole vessels. Flor Cream and Baclam Red-orange occur in most samples in frequencies that are almost always lower than 3%. The Usulutan-like Sacluc Ceramic Group appears in comparably low, but consistent, frequencies. Typological differences between the Cauac and Cimi Complexes are minimal. The only real difference between the complexes is the fact that several new, but relatively rare, types and varieties are added in the Cimi Complex. All major types from the Cauac Complex continue into Cimi and in frequencies that are similar enough so that a seriational separation between type samples from the two complexes is not really possible. This low degree of typological change was the factor that originally led to the designation of Cimi as a facet of the Cauac Complex rather than as a complex in its own right (Willey, Culbert, and Adams 1967).

Ultimately it was decided to identify Cimi as a full complex not because typological distinctions have become clearer, but because new types are added to the assemblage. Additionally, the time segment incorporated within Cimi is long enough, and the period is of enough cultural importance in the Maya Lowlands, that not to use even the minimal distinctions between the complexes to the fullest might make interpretations more difficult.

The new types and varieties that mark the Cimi Complex are associated with the Sacluc Ceramic Group. The Xux Variety of Sacluc Black-on-orange and the related Cayetano Trichrome are both easy to recognize and the North Acropolis stratigraphy makes it clear that both appear together at the start of the Cimi Complex. Together the two account for less than 2% of total sherds so they might not appear in small lots. Mojara Orange Polychrome is another new member of the group in Cimi, but is so rare that it is not a dependable diagnostic.

There are no consistent differences between Cauac and Cimi samples in type frequencies. Sapote Striated is somewhat less common in most Cimi samples than in Cauac samples. Boxcay Brown shows a similar distribution: on average lower in most Cimi samples than in Cauac. In general, frequencies of most types show greater variation in the Cimi samples than in those from Cauac, and it is not certain that any of the differences in frequency have chronological meaning.

Cimi Types: Social Dimension

Four of the seven Cimi type samples come from two locations in Gp. 5D-2 in the North Acropolis and probably represent the remains of civic-ceremonial activity in the central area of the site. The remaining samples resulted from excavations near small structure groups at some distance from the site center. The best guess is that these samples were the result of commoner domestic activity.

Substantial frequency differences exist [complete frequency data counts are unfortunately missing] in the ceramic types represented across these two broad social dimensions. Sapote Striated and Boxcay Brown sherds are present in the commoner domestic activity loci in the small structure groups in considerably higher frequencies than in the North Acropolis civic-ceremonial contexts. Sierra Red and other monochrome and decorated types, on the other hand, are present in greater amounts in the civic-ceremonial samples. Because Sapote Striated is entirely associated with the production of large-mouth jars and Boxcay Brown correlates with narrow-mouth jars, it seems not unlikely that the differences may be attributable to an expectably high frequency in the use of jars in a residential context and greater use of bowls and dishes in civic-ceremonial elite activity. It should be noted, however, that exactly the reverse of these expectations was found in the shape distributions of the preceding Cauac Complex.

Vessel Shapes of the Cimi Complex

Introduction

There are seven shape classes and sixteen vessel shapes, listed in Table 6.4, that occur in the Cimi Ceramic Complex. The large widely outcurving-side bowl, especially examples with a grooved hooked lip, appears for the first time in small numbers in the late Cauac Complex, but becomes a common diagnostic for the Cimi Complex. There are changes in vessel shape frequencies that help distinguish Cauac and Cimi samples quantitatively.

Cimi Shape Descriptions

SHAPE CLASS 1: WIDE-MOUTH JARS

Wide-mouth Jar (with Short Neck)

Illustrations: 13.1–19, 13.21–22; 14.14; 15.3.

Identifying characteristics and sorting problems: Easy to distinguish on the basis of short neck, large lip diameter, and unslipped surface.

Base and body: No whole examples, but body seems to have been globular.

Neck-body juncture: Usually rounded but well defined.

Orientation of neck: Medium to wide outflare.

Neck: Outcurves in varying degrees.

Rim: Direct.

Lip: Usually rounded to pointed; a few examples are beveled or flattened.

Surface: Striated below neck-body juncture; variable care in finishing.

Types: Usually Sapote Striated; rarely, Achiotes Unslipped.

Lip diameter: Range 10–24 cm; median 20 cm.

Neck height: Range 1.4–4.6 cm; median 2.8 cm.

Lip diameter/neck height ratio: Range 4.8–12.8; median 7.4.

Shape class: 1, wide-mouth jars.

TABLE 6.4
Shape Classes and Shapes of the Cimi Complex

1. Wide-mouth Jars

Wide-mouth Jar (with Short Neck)

2. Narrow-mouth Jars

Narrow-mouth Jar (with Short Neck)

Narrow-mouth Jar (with Tall Neck and Spout)

3. Very wide-mouth Jar

Very Large-diameter Jar

4. Large Capacity Bowls

Widely Outcurving-side Bowl

5. Medium Diameter Bowls and Dishes

Slightly Incurving to Round-side Bowl or Dish

Outflaring to Slightly Outcurving-side Bowl or Dish

Medial-flange Bowl

Z-angle Bowl

Composite Silhouette Bowl

Tetrapod Bowl or Dish

6. Small Diameter Bowls and Dishes

Slightly Incurving to Round-side Bowl or Dish

Outflaring to Slightly Outcurving-side Bowl or Dish

Outflaring to Slightly Outcurving-side Unslipped Dish

Slightly Incurving to Round-side Unslipped Dish

11. Miniature Vessels

Miniature Jar

Temporal Distribution: Common in the Late Preclassic Chuen, Cauac, and Cimi Complexes.

Comments: This stable and long-lasting shape continues to be common in the Cimi Complex, although it disappears by the succeeding Manik Complex.

SHAPE CLASS 2: NARROW-MOUTH JARS

Narrow-mouth Jar (with Short Neck)

Illustrations: Fig. 13.23–65; 14.21, 14.43–46; 15.10, 15.12; 16.5. See TR. 25A: fig. 148*d*3.

Identifying characteristics and sorting problems: For sherds that do not show the neck-body juncture, it is often difficult to distinguish narrow-mouth jars from interior-slipped jars. The short neck makes it fairly easy to distinguish this jar from earlier and later shapes.

Base and body: The few complete examples have globular bodies of small size, but these examples, all from special deposits, may not be representative.

Neck-body juncture: Usually well marked; most frequently angular but sometimes rounded.

Orientation of neck: Medium outflare.

Neck: Ranges from medium outcurve to nearly straight.

Rim: Usually direct; a subclass has sharp to rounded eversion of the rim.

Lip: Rounded or pointed; some examples of the everted rim subclass have flattened lips.

Surface: Slipped on exterior and on interior of neck; remainder of interior unslipped. Care in finishing varies.

Types: Sierra Red is the most common type represented (52%), followed by Polvero Black (22%), Baclam Red-orange (7%), and small quantities of Boxcay Brown and Flor Cream. These frequencies show less Sierra Red than in the Cauac samples and a higher frequency of red-orange than in any of the other Preclassic complexes.

Diameter: Range 10–30 cm; median 14 cm. There is some indication of a secondary peak of diameters in the 20–26 cm range.

Neck height: Range 1.2–4.0 cm; median 2.4 cm.

Lip diameter/neck height ratio: Range 3.6–11.7; median 5.8. The ratio shows a wide distribution with little central tendency; it seems unlikely that the ratio was of much significance to the users.

Shape class: 2, narrow-mouth jars.

Temporal distribution: This common and long-lived shape ends in the Cimi Complex.

Narrow-mouth Jar (with Tall Neck and Spout)

Illustrations: See TR. 25A: fig. 9b5.

Identifying characteristics and sorting problems: Identified by spout.

Base and Body: The body has a marked angle between upper and lower sections. The base is flat.

Neck-body juncture: Usually well marked and angular.

Orientation of neck: Medium to wide outflare.

Neck: Outcurving except for one straight example.

Rim: Usually everted, often strongly everted; one example is direct.

Lip: A variety of lip shapes include rounded, thickened, and beveled; sometimes there is a groove inside the lip.

Spout: The spout leaves the body near the midpoint and extends upward vertically to the height of the lip. Spout cross section is round.

Types: Sierra Red.

Maximum diameter of body: Range 18–30 cm.

Height of body to neck: Range 12–21 cm.

Diameter of lip: Range 13–21 cm; median 14 cm.

Height of neck: Range 4.4–8.8 cm; median 6.5 cm.

Lip diameter/neck height ratio: Range 1.8–3.2; median 2.4.

Shape class: 2, narrow-mouth jars.

Temporal distribution: This rare shape occurs occasionally in Cimi Complex collections.

SHAPE CLASS 3: VERY WIDE-MOUTH JARS

Very Large-diameter Jar

Identifying characteristics and sorting problems: The diameter is so large that the shape stands far apart from other jars. It is not certain, however, whether some of the taller fragments without neck-body juncture might be bowls.

Base and body: No information available.

Neck-body juncture: Vague in the few instances where present.

Orientation of neck: Outflaring.

Neck: Slight Outcurve.

Rim: Direct.

Lip: Rounded, very thick.

Surface: Unslipped. None of the fragments are large enough to indicate whether the body was striated like other unslipped jars.

Type: Either Achiotes Unslipped and Sapote Striated, although more commonly Sapote Striated.

Lip diameter: Range 40–50 cm; median 44 cm.

Neck height: Range 1.7–3.2 cm.; median 2.7 cm.

Lip diameter/neck height ratio: Range 15.3–26.7; median 18.2.

Shape class: 3, very wide-mouth jars.

Temporal distribution: Occurs in low frequencies in all Preclassic complexes.

SHAPE CLASS 4: LARGE CAPACITY BOWLS

Widely Outcurving-side Bowl

Illustrations: Fig. 14.36–38, 14.40–42; 15.7–9, 15.19; 17.9, 17.18–21, 17.23–29.

Identifying characteristics and sorting problems: Deep bowl with widely outcurving sides.

While the general shape begins in the Chuen Complex, it is only at the end of the Cauac Complex that examples with a hooked rim and broad lip grooves begin and the shape becomes a diagnostic marker for the Cimi Complex. The lip shape is the chief identifying characteristic and is distinctive enough so that there are few sorting problems.

Base: Flat.

Orientation of side: Medium to wide outflare at lip.

Side: Outcurving.

Rim: Rounded eversion that may be pronounced. The entire rim section is often thickened.

Lip: Rounded, usually thickened. One to three broad grooves on the interior of the lip. The grooves are made on the interior of the lip in a manner that results in a bump on the exterior of the lip. This lip shape is very characteristic and is one of the key features that relates the Usulutan-derived types of Tikal to true Usulutan vessels from Salvador.

Surface: Interior carefully finished; exterior less carefully done. Most decoration occurs on the interior of the vessel.

Types: Examples in the Cauac Complex are generally Sierra Red, however, in the Cimi Complex the shape usually occurs on Usulutan related types.

Diameter: Range 24–58 cm; median 35 cm. The median has little meaning because of a split distribution between a group of smaller vessels with diameters between 24 and 42 cm and a group of larger vessels with diameters between 44 and 58 cm.

Height: Height: Range 5–39 cm. There is a clear division of the height measurements into three groups: 5–10 cm; 14–18 cm; and greater than 21 cm.

Diameter/height ratio: 1.4–5.0.

Shape class: 4, Large Capacity Bowls

Temporal distribution: Begins in late Cauac. This shape is one of the best diagnostics of the Cimi Complex.

SHAPE CLASS 5: MEDIUM DIAMETER BOWLS AND DISHES

Slightly Incurving to Round-side Bowl or Dish

Illustrations: Fig. 14.26, 14.28; 15.11; 16.4–5, 16.8, 16.12, 16.17; 17.20–22. See TR. 25A: fig. 140*b,l–o*.

Identifying Characteristics and Sorting Problems: This shape is distinguished from the round-side dish with incurved rim only by the rim shape. Although rim shape overlaps between the two, most examples can be sorted without difficulty. There is also an overlap between the round-side dish and small round-side bowl with the two shapes differentiated by size and wall thickness.

Base: Flat or slightly concave.

Orientation of side: Medium to wide outflare.

Side: Rounded, medium to low curvature.

Rim: Direct or just below the lip, the side curves inward either in a rounded curve accentuating curvature of the side or with a more abrupt break, sometimes marked by a slight groove on the interior.

Lip: Rounded, pointed.

Surface: Well-finished interior and exterior; exterior sometimes less carefully done.

Types: In the Cimi samples of round-side dishes, Sierra Red makes up 56% of the examples and Flor Cream examples increase to provide 20%. The increase is dramatic enough so that the shape in Flor Cream is a good marker for the Cimi Complex. Other types include Polvero Black (11%) and Baclam Red-orange and the Sacluc Ceramic Group accounting for an additional 9%. Boxcay Brown and Cabro Red occur in rare examples.

Diameter: Range 14–58 cm (most examples 20–40 cm); median 30 cm.

Height: Range 4.8–10.0 cm; median 6.0 cm.

Diameter/height ratio: Range 3.2–6.4; median 4.2.

Shape class: 5, medium-diameter dishes.

Temporal distribution: Slightly incurving to round-side bowls and dishes occur in all ceramic complexes.

Outflaring to Slightly Outcurving-side Bowl or Dish

Illustrations: Fig. 14.8–9, 14.11, 14.16, 14.24, 14.39; 15.5–6, 15.20; 16.15–16, 16.18–19, 16.21–23; 17.1–2, 17.4, 17.6–8, 17.10–11, 17.13. See TR. 25A: fig. 140*a–k*; 141*d*2–3.

Identifying characteristics and sorting problems: This is a very simple shape, examples of which occur in all complexes. The most distinctive Cimi Complex examples, have beveled or rounded beveled lips, are relatively distinctive and do not occur with frequency in earlier Preclassic complexes, although they presage forms that are even more common in the Early Classic Manik Complex.

Base: Flat to slightly concave

Orientation of side: Medium outflare.

Side: Straight.

Rim: Direct.

Lip: Although the shape itself is a common one that occurs in all Tikal ceramic complexes, the lips present on the shape in the Cimi Complex are frequently flattened and beveled or rounded beveled. Rounded, pointed, and bolstered lips also occur with less frequency.

Surface: Slipped on both interior and exterior.

Types: Sierra Red is the most common type, followed by Polvero Black, Usulutan-derived types, and Baclam Red-orange. Flor Cream and various incised types make up the rest of the sample. Although the shape is simple and does not stand out from that in other Preclassic complexes, the distribution of types produced in the shape is unusual in the high frequency of types other than Sierra Red.

Diameter: range 18–60 cm; median 30–32 cm.

Height: range 6.8–17.2; median 12.0.

Diameter/height ratio: range 1.0–5.5 cm; median 3.2 cm.

Shape class: 5, medium-diameter bowls and dishes.

Temporal distribution: This shape occurs with low frequencies in all Preclassic complexes, with minor peaks in frequency in late Chuen Complex samples and again in the Cimi Complex. This shape is quite common in the Cimi Complex.

Comments: There is a clear bimodal distribution in both vessel diameter and vessel height between the small and medium-diameter examples in this shape that makes a separation of two sizes. Because the diameter bimodality is the clearest, diameter was used as the criterion for attributing a vessel to the different classes. The diameter/height ratios overlap considerably, indicating that the basic proportions remain the same in spite of differences in size. These vessels, characteristic of the Early Classic Manik Complex, first appear during the Cimi Complex. The Cimi examples are identical to those in the Manik Complex, except that they are of Sierra Red with a few examples of Polvero Black.

Medial Flange Bowl

Illustrations: Fig. 14.1, 14.4, 14.47–48; 15.3, 15.14, 15.16–17; 16.31; 17.12. See TR. 25A: fig. 123*f*.

Identifying characteristics and sorting problems: This particular shape is identified by the combination of an unrestricted orifice, and incurving side with or without a break at a medial flange. Occasionally the flange is narrow enough to be considered a ridge. The position of the flange is quite distinctive.

Base: Flat.

Orientation of side: Medium outflare.

Side: Nearly straight above flange, straight to slightly rounded below, with or without break of curvature on the inside of the vessel at the flange. Slight to marked angle on the interior at the position of the flange when there is a break in curvature.

Rim: Direct.

Lip: Rounded or Pointed. The lip section is often thickened. There is one unusual example (see TR. 25A: fig. 141*c*) with an incurving rim and bolstered lip that may pertain either to the Cauac or Cimi Complex.

Flange: The flange is located just medially on the vessel. It is most frequently pointed in cross section, occasionally rounded. Usually, the flange is quite narrow and could even be called a ridge, but there are also few examples of broad lip flanges.

Surface: Slipped on both interior and exterior. Carefully finished on the interior and the exterior above the flange. Often carelessly finished outside below the flange.

Types: Sierra Red, Cabro Red, Polvero Black, and Flor Cream. There are also examples of Laguna Verde Incised: Usulutan-style Variety and incised types.

Diameter: Range 20–38 cm; median 28 cm.

Height: Range 3.6–9.0 cm.

Diameter/height ratio: Range 3.2–6.8.

Shape class: shape class 5, medium-diameter bowls and dishes.

Temporal distribution: All of the medial-flange dishes are excellent time markers. In the sealed deposits from the North Acropolis, not a single example of a medial-flange dish appears before the Cauac Complex levels. The dishes reach a peak frequency in the Cauac samples and continue to appear in Cimi.

Z-angle Bowl

Illustrations: Fig. 14.2, 14.7, 14.49; 16.1–3, 16.10, 16.24, 16.27, 16.29.

Identifying characteristics and sorting problems: The restricted orifice and z-angle make the shape easy to identify, with only a few examples that are intermediate between this shape and the medial-flange (or ridge) bowl, especially those with a break at the flange or ridge.

Base: Usually flat.

Orientation of side: Vertical to slightly restricted, giving a distinct composite silhouette.

Side: Upper section, straight; lower section, straight to slightly rounded. Usually there is a sharp break in the angle of the side between the two sections that almost always corresponds to the point of the Z-angle.

Rim: Usually direct; a few examples everted.

Lip: This shape demonstrates considerable variety of lip and upper section shapes. A variant where the upper section is short has a pointed lip in which wall thickness decreases continually between the flange and the lip. Another common variant has a thickened upper section with a reverse rounded bevel lip.

Z-angle: Sharp z-angle in which the exterior of the lower section continues without break to form a triangular cross section that makes a pronounced angle with the upper section of the wall on the vessel exterior.

Types: Mostly Sierra Red; some examples of Polvero Black and Flor Cream.

Diameter: Range 18–28 cm; median 24 cm.

Height: Range 6.5–9.8 cm.

Diameter/height ratio: 3.0–3.4.

Shape class: 5, medium-diameter bowls and dishes.

Temporal Distribution: Z-angle bowls begin in the Chuen Complex and continue unchanged into Cimi. In the Early Classic Manik Complex, they occur on different types.

Composite Silhouette Bowl

Illustrations: Fig. 14.5–6, 14.13, 14.17, 14.50–52; 15.22–23; 16.6–7, 16.9, 16.11, 16.13–14, 16.20, 16.25–26, 16.30; 17.7, 17.22, 17.34.

Identifying characteristics and sorting problems: The composite silhouette is the identifying feature. In sorting, rim sherds too short to show the break between sections would be sorted into other categories, however, the bolster lip and nearly vertical side of the upper wall are the identifying characteristics.

Base: Flat.

Orientation of side: Upper wall vertical to slightly insloping.

Side: Slightly rounded, straight or slightly outcurving.

Rim: Direct.

Lip: Flattened bolster.

Types: Sierra Red accounts for one-half of the sample and Flor Cream makes up one-fifth. A variety of additional monochrome and decorated types are also represented including a few examples of Laguna Verde Incised: Usulutan-style Variety, Caramba Red-on-orange, and other decorated types in small frequencies.

Diameter: Range 18–28 cm; median 24 cm.

Shape class: 5, medium-diameter bowls and dishes.

Temporal distribution: This shape occurs in low frequencies in the Cauac and Cimi Complexes. It is more common in the Cimi Complex than in Cauac.

Tetrapod Bowl or Dish

Illustrations: Fig. 14.25; 15.21, 15.24; 17.30–31. See TR.25A: fig. 139*b*1–6.

Identifying characteristics and sorting problems: The presence of hollow mammiform (or occasionally hollow conical) tetrapod supports is characteristic of this shape. In the absence of the feet, small sherds might be sorted as slightly outcurving or round-side bowls and dishes.

Base: Frequently, perhaps always, mammiform tetrapod.

Orientation of side: Medium to wide outflare or slightly rounded.

Side: Medium outcurve.

Rim: Direct or everted.

Lip: Rounded, flattened or occasionally exteriorly bolstered.

Surface: Well finished and slipped on both the interior and exterior. The base and feet may be less well finished and unslipped on some examples.

Types: The most frequent type in which the shape occurs is Sierra Red, but there are a substantial number of examples made from Usulutan-derived types. Rare examples of other monochrome types also occur, including Sacluc Black-on-orange and Flor Cream.

Diameter: Range 18–36 cm; median 30 cm.

Height: Without feet: Range 6.0–12.0 cm. With feet: Range 10.0–4.0 cm.

Diameter/height ratio: 2.8–4.1; median 3.1.

Shape class: 5, medium-diameter bowls and dishes.

Temporal distribution: This shape, with mammiform supports, occurs only in the Cimi Complex and is a good temporal marker for the complex.

SHAPE CLASS 6: SMALL DIAMETER BOWLS AND DISHES

Slightly Incurving to Round-side Bowl or Dish

Illustrations: Fig. 14.3, 14.9; 17.14, 17.32–33.

Identifying characteristics and sorting problems: There is some overlap with examples that have a more restricted orifice, and the range of vessel diameters overlaps with medium-diameter bowls and dishes.

Base: Flat in the few examples that show complete sections, although the sides may be rounded to the base.

Side: Rounded; usually high curvature.

Rim: Direct; occasionally the rim is slightly everted producing a recurving profile, but there are too few examples to create a separate shape.

Lip: Usually rounded; occasionally thickened.

Surface: Well-finished both inside and out. This was a favorite form for incised decoration, which invariably occurs on the exterior, usually as a line or lines on the upper part of the vessel.

Types: Occurs in low frequencies on slipped types, and incised varieties as well.

Diameter: median 20 cm.

Height: median 8 cm.

Diameter/Height ratio: median 2.0.

Shape class: 6, small-diameter bowl.

Temporal distribution: Occurs sporadically through the Late Preclassic complexes.

Outflaring to Slightly Outcurving-side Bowl or Dish

Illustrations: Fig. 17.35. See TR. 25A: fig. 140*a,d,e, g–k*; 141*d*1.

Identifying characteristics and sorting problems: Originally classified as an Outflaring-side Cache Vessel: Small Variety (TR. 25A), as the shape was first recognized as whole vessels in caches or burials. However, these vessels were not manufactured as a specialized set for special deposits and overlap with the same shape found in middens and other contexts. The vessels cannot be distinguished from outflaring to outcurving-side bowls and dishes unless a large section of the vessel is present and small sherds may be overlooked as they overlap with the outflaring or outcurving upper vessel wall sections of other shapes.

Base: Flat or slightly concave.

Side: Straight-to-medium outcurve.

Orientation of side: Medium outflare.

Rim: Direct.

Lip: Usually rounded, some flattened or beveled.

Surface: Slipped on both interior and exterior except that the exterior base is usually left unslipped.

Types: Sierra Red and rarely Polvero Black.

Diameter: range 11–27 cm; median 18 cm.

Height: range 3.0–10.8 cm; median 6.0 cm.

Diameter/height ratio: range 2.3–6.3 cm; median 3.6 cm.

Shape classes: 6, small-diameter bowls and dishes.

Temporal Distribution: While outflaring to slightly outcurving-side bowls or dishes occur in all Preclassic Complexes, their primary use in burials and caches is restricted to the Cimi Complex. In the succeeding Manik Complex, the same shape is also used in burials and caches but on different types.

Comments: There is a clear bimodal distribution in both vessel diameter and vessel height between the small and medium-diameter examples in this shape that makes a separation of two sizes. Because the diameter bimodality is the clearest, diameter was used as the criterion for attributing a vessel to the different classes. The diameter/height ratios overlap considerably, indicating that the basic proportions remain the same in spite of differences in size. These vessels, characteristic of the Early Classic Manik Complex, first appear during the Cimi Complex. The Cimi examples are identical to those in the Manik Complex, except that they are of Sierra Red with a few examples of Polvero Black.

Outflaring to Slightly Outcurving-side Unslipped Bowl or Dish

Illustrations: See TR. 25A: fig. 35*a*2; 148*d*1.

Identifying characteristics and sorting problems: This class of unslipped dishes sort clearly, as most are Morfin Unslipped.

Base: Flat or slightly concave.

Orientation of side: Medium to wide outflare.

Side: Straight to medium outcurve.

Rim: Direct or more commonly everted, either angular or rounded. The everted section is broad and usually presents a flat interior surface.

Lip: Rounded, flattened, or beveled. Occasionally thickened.

Surface: Smoothing is carelessly done leaving smoothing marks on many examples. Finishing on interior is more careful than on the exterior; on some examples the exterior is left unsmoothed.

Type: Morfin Unslipped.

Diameter: Range 14–32 cm; median 20 cm.

Height: 4.0–7.9 cm; median 5.5 cm.

Diameter/height ratio: Range 3.1–4.5.

Shape class: 6, small-diameter bowls and dishes.

Temporal distribution: The shape does not appear in any of the Chuen Complex samples. The first appearance is in early Cauac samples from the North Acropolis. It increases in frequency in later Cauac samples and reaches a peak frequency in early Cimi Complex samples. The shape is a good marker for the Cauac and Cimi Complexes when it is present, but its distribution is spotty; some lots have high frequencies of the shape, but it is totally absent from other lots in the same time-range. This shape with a beveled lip is present in the Cauac Complex but becomes more common in Cimi.

Comments: About half of the examples are smudged on the interior of the vessel; far less are smudged on the exterior. It is uncertain whether the smudging results from firing or from use of the vessel. The use of an unslipped surface as an identifying characteristic of the shape violates general principles for the separation of shapes, but the combination of shape and restricted type is in this case so useful and diagnostic that utility outweighs the virtue of consistency.

Slightly Incurving to Round-side Unslipped Bowl or Dish

Illustrations: Same form as the Cauac Complex; see TR. 25A: fig. 9a3.

Identifying characteristics and sorting problems: The unslipped surface and rounded side are quite distinctive and there are almost no sorting problems.

Base: Probably flat.

Orientation of side: Medium to wide outflare.

Side: Rounded, low curvature.

Rim: Direct or slightly everted.

Lip: Rounded, pointed, and beveled lips are all common.

Surface: Carelessly finished.

Types: Morfin Unslipped.

Shape class: 6, small-diameter bowls and dishes.

Diameter: Range 14–30 cm; median 20 cm. Some examples might be considered within the range of medium-diameter bowls and dishes but most are in the small range.

Height: Range 4.5–5.0 cm.

Diameter/height ratio: Range 3.1–4.2.

Temporal distribution: This shape first appears in the Cauac Complex at Tikal and continues into the Cimi Complex.

SHAPE CLASS 11: MINIATURE VESSELS

Miniature Jar

Illustration: Fig. 56.2. See TR. 25A: fig. 140p; 148d2.

There are three examples of miniature jars that may pertain to the Cimi Complex. Two are Boxcay Brown and one is Polvero Black.

Diameter: 2 cm.

Height: 4 cm.

Diameter/Height ratio: 0.5 cm.

Shape class: 11, miniature vessels

Median measurements for all shapes are presented in Table 6.5.

Cimi Shapes: Chronological Change

As was true for the Cauac Complex, the distribution of Cimi vessel shapes includes a great deal of rim and lip modifications on a limited number of different shapes, none of them in very high frequencies (see Table 6.6). Wide-mouth jars are the most common shape, accounting for 10–25% of the examples in individual samples. Narrow-mouth jars are the next most common shape in frequencies between 8% and 16%. However, as a group, medium-diameter bowls and dishes comprise the greatest frequency at all locations, ranging from 24–32%.

Because typological changes between the Cauac and Cimi Ceramic Complexes are minimal, vessel shapes provide the best key to distinguishing samples from the two complexes. Only one lip modification, the grooved-hooked lip, on the widely outcurving-side bowl, increases in use in the Cimi Complex (there is a single example in a Cauac deposit; see TR. 25A: fig. 12*d*). Because the lip is easily recognizable even from small lip fragments, it is a good type fossil for Cimi. The addition of tetrapod bowls to the Cimi Complex is another good marker as these vessels shapes are absent in the preceding Late Preclassic complexes.

In addition, however, there are a few frequency differences in a number of vessel shapes between Cauac and Cimi that make possible a fairly easy quantitative separation of the complexes. Wide-mouth jars, narrow-mouth jars and large-capacity bowls (shape classes 1, 2, and 4) all remain at about the same average frequencies between the two complexes, and all show substantial variation between individual samples within each complex. Medial-flange bowls are relatively more common in Cauac than in Cimi, although the frequencies overlap.

Small-diameter bowls and dishes (shape class 6) average slightly higher in frequency in the Cimi samples than in Cauac, but there is a great deal of variation in frequency between individual samples. The increase can be attributed to a sharp rise in the number of unslipped bowls in Cimi. The frequency of unslipped bowls and dishes in individual Cimi samples is extremely variable, however, ranging from total absence in the single sample from the North Terrace/Main Plaza to a high of more than 17% of total shapes in the North Acropolis. The unslipped bowls seem to have been most common at the start of the Cimi Complex and to have declined by the end of the complex, although it is possible that the vessels had some special use that gives their frequency a significance that is not chronological.

In summary, the distinction between the Cauac and Cimi Complexes in vessel shapes is marked by the appearance of a new and easily identified lip shape, as well as tetrapod bowls, and a series of small frequency changes that combine to make a pattern for Cimi shape distributions that is distinguishable from Cauac distributions.

Cimi Shapes: Social Dimension

Four of the seven Cimi Complex samples came from within two locations in the main civic-ceremonial precinct at the center of Tikal and can be assigned a most likely origin in ceremonial-elite activities. The remaining three samples came from outlying areas of the site well away from monumental architecture and near small structure groups. These latter samples are probably best assigned a commoner residential function, although two of the three came from chultuns unassociated with visible structures, a context that makes any functional assignment open to question.

If one compares average shape frequencies from the civic-ceremonial context with those from the small structure groups, there are quite a few differences (see Table 6.6). The comparison of averages, however, may not be a very meaningful procedure because many shapes show substantial variation in frequency from sample to sample within each of the two major contexts.

Given this caveat, the shape frequency differences between the civic-ceremonial and small

TABLE 6.5
Shape Dimensions of the Cimi Complex

Shape Class and Shape	Median Diameter or Range (cm)	Median Height or Range (cm)	Median Diameter/ Height Ratio or Range (cm)
1. Wide-mouth Jar (with Short Neck)	20.0	2.8	7.4
2. Narrow-mouth Jar (with Short Neck)	14.0	2.4	5.8
2. Narrow-mouth Jar (with Tall Neck and Spout)	14.0	6.5	2.4
3. Very Large-diameter Jar	44.0	2.7	18.2
4. Widely Outcurving-side Bowl	24.0–58.0	5.0–39.0	1.4–5.0
5. Slightly Incurving to Round-side Bowl or Dish	30.0	6.0	4.2
5. Outflaring to Slightly Outcurving-side Bowl or Dish	30.0–32.0	12.0	3.2
5. Medial-flange Bowl	28.0	3.6–9.0	3.2–6.8
5. Z-angle Bowl	24.0	6.5–9.8	3.0–3.4
5. Composite Silhouette Bowl	24.0	—	—
5. Tetrapod Bowl or Dish	30.0	6.0–12.0 (without feet) 10.0–14.0 (with feet)	3.1
6. Slightly Incurving to Round-side Bowl or Dish	20.0	8.0	2.0
6. Outflaring to Slightly Outcurving-side Bowl or Dish	18.0	6.0	3.6
6. Outflaring to Slightly Outcurving-side Unslipped Dish	20.0	5.5	3.1–4.5
6. Slightly Incurving to Round-side Unslipped Dish	20.0	4.5–5.0	3.1–4.2
11. Miniature Jar	2.0	4.0	0.5

structure group samples from the Cimi Complex will be considered here. A starting point is to ask whether shapes that varied in frequency between social contexts in the Cauac Complex continued to do so in the Cimi samples, because patterns that are repeated in two sequent complexes seem more likely to represent real differences in the use of ceramics. The most notable difference between civic-ceremonial and small structure group residential contexts in the Cauac samples was a higher frequency of medial-flange bowls in the residential samples. This difference fails to appear in Cimi. The average frequency in the two contexts is almost identical and individual samples show a pattern of variation that

seems to be random. The other differences in frequencies between contexts noted in the Cauac collections continue to appear in Cimi. Narrow-mouth jars are generally more common in Cimi civic-ceremonial contexts, however, they overlap in part with small structure group residential contexts.

In addition to these patterns that occur in both the Cauac and the Cimi samples, there are a number of differences in average shape frequencies between civic-ceremonial and small structure group contexts that characterize the Cimi samples, but do not appear in the Cauac analysis. The most noticeable of these differences is that wide-mouth jars were slightly more common in small structure groups

TABLE 6.6
Shape Frequencies of the Cimi Complex

Shape Class and Shape	Civic-ceremonial				Chultun	Small Structure Group	Chultun
	Sample Loc. 1-1	Sample Loc. 2-3	Sample Loc. 2-2	Sample Loc. 2-1	Sample Loc. 3-1	Sample Loc. 4-1	Sample Loc. 5-1
	%	%	%	%	%	%	%
1. Wide-mouth Jar (with Short Neck)	16.7	10.5	14.9	16.7	19.2	24.7	13.2
Total Shape Class 1: Wide-mouth Jars	**16.7**	**10.5**	**14.9**	**16.7**	**19.2**	**24.7**	**13.2**
2. Narrow-mouth Jar (with Short Neck)	15.7	15.9	10.8	15.3	16.5	8.6	8.4
Total Shape Class 2: Narrow-mouth Jars	**15.7**	**15.9**	**10.8**	**15.3**	**16.5**	**8.6**	**8.4**
3. Very Large-diameter Jar	1.0	—	0.5	1.8	1.4	0.5	—
Total Shape Class 3: Very Wide-mouth Jars	**1.0**	—	**0.5**	**1.8**	**1.4**	**0.5**	—
4. Widely Outcurving-side Bowl	4.9	7.4	8.2	4.5	11.2	14.0	3.6
Total Shape Class 4: Large Capacity Bowls	**4.9**	**7.4**	**8.2**	**4.5**	**11.2**	**14.0**	**3.6**
5. Slightly Incurving to Round-side Bowl or Dish	12.8	12.8	15.4	17.6	9.5	14.7	14.4
5. Outflaring to Slightly Outcurving-side Bowl or Dish	12.7	4.8	10.3	5.4	5.2	2	6
5. All Medial-flange, Z-angle, and Tetrapod Bowls	5.9	7.0	5.0	2.7	4.2	9.8	-
5. Composite Silhouette Bowl	1.0	1.5	1.5	0.8	6.6	2.3	3.6
Total Shape Class 5: Medium Diameter Bowls and Dishes	**32.4**	**26.1**	**32.2**	**26.5**	**25.5**	**28.8**	**24.0**
6. Slightly Incurving to Round-side Bowl or Dish	5.9	1.7	2.7	1.3	2.3	1.8	10.8
6. Outflaring to Slightly Outcurving-side Bowl or Dish	3.0	3.2	6.1	3.7	2.0	4.0	1.2
6. Outflaring to Slightly Outcurving-side Unslipped Dish	—	16.2	5.4	13.5	6.7	0.4	1.2
6. Slightly Incurving to Round-side Unslipped Dish	—	5.2	0.8	0.4	1.4	—	—
Total Shape Class 6: Small Diameter Bowls and Dishes	**8.9**	**26.3**	**15.0**	**18.9**	**12.4**	**6.2**	**13.2**
Unidentified Small Rims	8.8	4.3	7.9	6.3	5.5	7.7	26.4
Odd shapes	11.6	9.5	10.5	10.0	9.3	10.3	11.2
TOTAL RIM SHERDS	**102**	**735**	**590**	**222**	**709**	**429**	**83**

than in samples from civic-ceremonial contexts, although there is some degree of overlap. Because this class of jar would probably have had storage and cooking functions, its association with residential small structure group samples is not surprising.

Differences in average frequency in vessel shapes between the two main inferred contexts are more common in the Cimi samples than they were in Cauac, while the Cauac samples show more differences than those from the earlier Chuen Complex. One might be tempted to infer greater differentiation in the use of ceramics through time in Preclassic Tikal. Such an interpretation would show a lamentable lack of caution. It is far more likely that the same problems occur in the social interpretation of shapes that occurred with the social interpretation of ceramic types in Preclassic samples at Tikal, and the large variability within samples from each of the contexts makes it better to conclude that it is simply impossible, given present archaeological data, to say anything much about social variation in ceramic use for this time period.

Special Deposits of the Cimi Complex

Burials of the Cimi Complex

No special deposits classified as burials that included Cimi Complex ceramics were encountered during the excavations at Tikal.

Caches of the Cimi Complex

Three special deposits classified as caches contained Cimi ceramics, however, they did not have stratigraphic locations that could be related to a specific period. Stylistically, these caches are probably either Cauac or Cimi and are from major civic-ceremonial locations. Cache 24 was from the Great Plaza, Platform 5D-1-4th, while Ca. 205 and Ca. 209 were from Str. 5C-54, the Lost World Pyramid. Although no clear stratigraphic date was indicated, they would probably be equivalent to the Cauac or Cimi Complexes. Each cache contains a two-vessel set with a large cuspidor covered by a dish. The pattern of large-capacity vessels with covers as cache offerings continues into the Early Classic Manik Complex, although at that time it is elaborated by special shapes for caches and the inclusion of large sets of such vessels in some caches.

Ceramic offerings in Tikal Preclassic caches are very different from ceramic burial offerings. The pattern of a large vessel with cover that characterizes all except the two earliest caches occurs with certainty only once in burials, one such set in Bu. 167 that dates to the Cauac Complex. There is much greater ceramic variety in both types and shapes in burials than in caches. Nine of the ten cache vessels are Sierra Red and the tenth is an undistinguished Polvero Black. In burials, decorated and exotic types are considerably more common. The same lack of variety is evident in shapes, where a very few shapes in the caches can be compared to a great variety of shapes in burial offerings.

TABLE 6.7
Caches of the Cimi Complex

Cache No.	Op.SubOp./Lot	Str.	Structure Group Type	TR. 25A Illustration	TR.	No. of Vessels
24[1]	11D/19	Gp. 5D-2, Great Plaza (Plat. 5D-1-4th)	Civic-ceremonial	99d	14	2
205[1]	90C/4	Gp. 5C-11, Lost World Pyramid Str. 5C-54	Civic-ceremonial	99e	23C	2
209[1]	90B/1	Gp. 5C-11, Lost World Pyramid Str. 5C-54	Civic-ceremonial	99f	23C	2

[1] Cauac or Cimi

Problematical Deposits of the Cimi Complex

Three problematical deposits (PD. 2, PD. 87, and PD. 157) were recovered from stratigraphically certain Cimi locations in the North Acropolis. Two other problematical deposits (PD. 93 and PD. 114) are of uncertain date and described in previous chapters. One of the Cimi problematical deposits, PD. 2, contained only a single vessel, a tripod bowl of Cayetano Trichrome. This single-vessel problematical deposit is comparable to single vessels in Chuen and Cauac problematical deposits, but since the vessel is fragmentary it is also possible that it is a chance, rather than meaningful, find. The other two Cimi problematical deposits are considerably more interesting. Problematical deposit 157, which was deliberately intruded through earlier North Acropolis floors at a time late in the period of the Cimi Complex, contains three vessels. One is a fragmentary narrow-mouth jar of Polvero Black. The second is a Boxcay Brown miniature jar, and the third is an outflaring to slightly outcurving-side dish of Morfin Unslipped. The narrow-mouth jar is a common component of Preclassic burials, but the unslipped dish is rare in burials and never found in caches. Miniature vessels are very rare in Preclassic ceramic complexes and do not occur in caches and only rarely in burials. Together, the three vessels make a unique collection unlike any other burial or cache offerings of the Preclassic.

The final Cimi problematical deposit, PD. 87, is of even greater significance because it contains a much larger number of vessels (twenty-three) and because of the lack of burials of Cimi date. The problematical deposit was obtained from lots between the seventh and eighth floors of the North Acropolis, Str. 5D-22-4th, the most recent of the Cimi levels at that location. It includes twenty-three vessels: fourteen are Sierra Red, three are Polvero Black, and there are one vessel each of Flor Cream, Sacluc Black-on-orange, Boxcay Brown, an unnamed type with red slip on one side and unslipped striations on the other that may be similar to the type identified as Puletan Red-and-unslipped in northern Belize (Kosakowsky 1987), and a polished red-slipped vessel decorated with black paint in a trickle design that is likely in the Cabro Group, as well as one unidentified vessel nubbin foot. Six of the vessels are bowls with mammiform tetrapod feet, one is a fragmentary

TABLE 6.8
Problematical Deposits of the Cimi Complex

PD No.	Op.SubOp./Lot	Location	Structure Group Type	TR. 25A Illustration	TR.	Est. No. of Vessels
2	12P/19	Gp. 5D-2, North Acropolis, Str. 5D-26-4th	Civic-ceremonial	121	14	1
87	12R	Gp. 5D-2, North Acropolis, Str. 5D-22-4th	Civic-ceremonial	139b, 140	14	23
93[1]	64J	Gp. 5D-9, Seven Temples Plaza Plat. 5D-9	Civic-ceremonial	141c	23D	1
114[2]	66X	Gp. of Str. 5G-18, Ch. 5G-7	Small Structure Group	144a		2
157	12P/187	Gp. 5D-2, North Acropolis, Plat. 5D-4-4th	Civic-ceremonial	148d	14	3

[1] Cauac or Cimi

[2] Chuen, Cauac or Cimi

miniature jar, and the remaining sixteen are outflaring to slightly outcurving-side vessels identical or close to the shape of later Manik Complex cache vessels. Because the vessels are Sierra Red, their shape is not indicative of a mixture in the deposit.

Because there is a possibility that the vessels in PD. 87 might be from a redeposited Cimi Complex cache or burial, it is important to consider whether they match the ceramics typical of either burials or caches in the preceding Cauac Complex or the following Manik Complex. The vessels from PD. 87 do not prove a good match for burial offerings of either the Cauac or Manik Complexes. They lack the variety of decorated and exotic types that occur in large burial offerings in both complexes. Even more notably, the vessel shapes represented in PD. 87 show a much more restricted range than in burials of either the Cauac or the Manik Complexes. On the other hand, the few vessel shapes with mammiform feet bear a certain resemblance to vessels in the Manik 2 burials from the Mundo Perdido. Perhaps more importantly, PD. 87 contained human remains (TR. 14:345–6). The PD. 87 assemblage is an even worse match for Cauac Complex caches that invariably consist of only a single pair of vessels, one a deep bowl, and the other a plate that serves as a cover. The number of vessels in PD. 87 is far too large for a Preclassic cache and does not show the matched sets of deep bowls and covers that typify caches. Among known burial and cache patterns, the contents of PD. 87 are closest to the ceramics of the Early Classic. Even here, however, the match is not very good. The Early Classic assemblages and PD. 87 share the characteristic of including a substantial number of outflaring- to slightly outcurving-side cache vessels. But PD. 87 lacks the covered cylindrical cache vessels that are usually found in Early Classic caches and there is no counterpart in Manik for the mammiform tetrapod vessels that are part of the Cimi problematical deposit. All in all, PD. 87 seems to be a unique assemblage that does not correspond directly to any known offertory pattern, but may be a Cimi Complex relocated burial.

Preclassic Problematical Deposits

Consideration of the ceramic contents of problematical deposits through the full range of the Preclassic Period at Tikal indicates neither significant patterns nor any trend of change through time. The majority of the Preclassic problematical deposits contain only a single vessel. These single vessels might be appropriate as offerings in caches for the Chuen Complex or in simple burials at any time, but unless there is evidence from excavation or from other associated artifacts, there seems no reason to conclude that any specific problematical deposit necessarily has cache or burial significance. The problematical deposits, with larger numbers of vessels, do not match burial or cache patterns, nor do they reveal other patterning, because each differs significantly from the others. It is not unexpected that the material from problematical deposits should fail to pattern because the reasons for defining a problematical deposit in the process of excavation were many and varied. It does seem certain, however, that no underlying unitary sort of special deposit is inherent in Preclassic problematical deposits.

VII

Manik Ceramic Complex

The Preclassic–Early Classic Ceramic Transition

Ceramic change between the Terminal Preclassic and the Early Classic was massive and affected almost the entire ceramic inventory. Typologically, the most obvious change was the replacement of Usulutan-related decorated ceramics by polychromes. Aguila Orange replaced Sierra Red, the dominant monochrome type of the Late and Terminal Preclassic. Only the striated types of the two periods demonstrated no noticeable change.

In Early Classic vessel shapes, the necks of both unslipped and slipped jars became taller than they had been in the Preclassic. Large bowls underwent changes in wall configuration, and serving-vessel shapes were completely different except for the simplest shapes such as slightly incurving to round side and outflaring to slightly outcurving-side bowls and dishes. Supports, which had been rare in the Terminal Preclassic, became common in Early Classic serving vessels.

Despite the profundity of the changes, they were by no means sudden. Some typical Early Classic types and shapes occurred well back in the Terminal Preclassic. The combined data of the Penn Museum Tikal Project and the Proyecto Nacional Tikal provide superb information on the details and timing of the changes. The deep trench through the North Acropolis excavated by the Museum produced three very large samples of the Cimi Complex that were completely sealed by floors and in a stratigraphic sequence. These large samples give conclusive evidence of vessel types and forms that were not present in Cimi times and evidence of the points at which some features typical of the Early Classic appeared in the Terminal Preclassic. It is these North Acropolis levels that demonstrate conclusively which of the types and shapes characteristic of the Early Classic appeared in the Cimi Complex. Red-orange sherds of the Baclam Ceramic Group overlap with some examples of the Aguila Ceramic Group. Not a single polychrome of Early Classic types appears in the large Cimi collections. The type called "Mojara Orange Polychrome" is, in fact, within the range of Usulutan style decorations and can be termed a polychrome only because some simple two-color decorations appear in addition to the dominant Usulutan wavy-line patterns. Also, appearing in Cimi levels are annular bases, which become more frequent in the Early Classic. Bowls and dishes with sharp z-angles appear in Cimi and become one of the most common decorated shapes at the beginning of the Early Classic. Basal flanges, however, do not occur in the Cimi deposits.

Vessel supports are rare in the Late Preclassic, although a few solid nubbin feet occur which, in Bu. 85 (TR. 25A: fig. 4–7), are demonstrated to be from a tetrapodal vessel. Similar tetrapods increase in frequency in the Cimi Complex. Small, hollow, mammiform supports also occur in low frequency in Cimi contexts and in PD. 87 (TR. 25A: fig. 139b, 140), which is of Cimi date.

The research of the Proyecto Nacional Tikal in the Mundo Perdido Complex (Laporte and Fialko

1987) provided information about the earliest parts of the Early Classic, which were poorly represented in the Penn Museum collections. The evidence for the beginnings of the Manik Complex came from collections, especially in the Mundo Perdido Group that had both excellent stratigraphic control and a series of burials with spectacular ceramic contents.

Manik 1, the earliest of the Early Classic subphases, does not appear in most of the Penn Museum collections and is not well represented in Mundo Perdido. By the time of Manik 2, which is abundantly represented in Mundo Perdido, the changes that differentiate the Early Classic from the Preclassic had occurred. Aguila Orange had become the dominant monochrome type and polychromes had appeared, as had the Early Classic shapes. It is important to note that Usulutan style decoration no longer occurred, so that the temporal distributions of Usulutan style decoration and polychromes are mutually exclusive.

Manik Complex Collections

Introduction

Samples of Manik Complex ceramics that were large enough for quantitative analysis were relatively rare at Tikal considering the lengthy period of time during which the ceramics were in use. On the other hand, unmixed samples of the complex too small for reliable quantification were not uncommon and admixture of some Manik materials in the fill of later structures was considerably more frequent than admixture of Preclassic ceramics had been. This suggests that Manik occupation of central Tikal was both larger and more evenly distributed than the Preclassic occupation.

Manik samples large enough to permit quantitative analysis occurred at 18 locations. In these locations, 22 samples were quantified for types and 36 for shapes. As was true for other complexes, vessel shapes were the most temporally sensitive ceramic variables.

Chronological subdivision of the Manik Complex proved extremely difficult. This was due in part to the great ceramic stability of the period, which is manifest at sites throughout the Petén (Willey, Culbert, and Adams 1967:310). At Tikal, it is also due to the nature of the ceramic collections and their stratigraphic contexts. The long architectural sequences in Early Classic locations failed to provide ceramic collections large enough for quantitative treatment and there were only two cases in which temporally differing samples could be related to a controlled stratigraphic sequence. Middens covering a long enough period to exhibit detectable ceramic change were equally scarce, with only one location providing superposition of temporally differentiated samples. Faceting of the complex was provided by the seriation of a series of short time-span deposits from various sources, but even this procedure was difficult because of the relative scarcity of housemound debris, the best source of appropriate samples. After the initial division of Manik (TR. 25A) into Early (Manik 1), Middle (Manik 2), and Late (Manik 3) facets on the basis of sherd seriation, Coggins (1975) achieved a more successful division into Manik 1, 2, 3A, and 3B on the basis of decorated vessels (see Table 7.1). The work of the Proyecto Nacional Tikal provided more detailed ceramic information on Manik, especially in the definition of Manik 2 on the basis of discoveries in the Mundo Perdido Group (Iglesias Ponce de Leon 1988, 1996; Laporte 1995, 2000; Laporte and Fialko 1987, 1990, 1995; Laporte et al. 1992).

TABLE 7.1
Correlation between TR. 25A (Culbert 1993) and TR. 25B Facets

TR. 25A	Coggins (1975); Laporte (1989); Moholy-Nagy (2016):Table 1	Calendar Date
Late Facet	Manik 3B	c. AD 480–550
Middle Facet	Manik 3A	c. AD 380–480
Early Facet	Manik 2	c. AD 300–380
	Manik 1	c. AD 250–300

While the chronology might appear to imply a gap in occupation in Manik 1 (c. AD 250–300) on the basis of sherd collections, this is not the case. In part, late Cimi pottery may extend in use until AD 300, and this 50-year period probably represents a time when Cimi ceramics were falling out of favor and were replaced by Manik types and forms that took hold by c. AD 300.

The three facets of the Manik Complex were not equally represented in the collections. Manik 2 appeared at only two locations at Tikal. Manik 3A was better represented, occurring at seven locations, although not usually in large quantities. Manik 3B was found at 12 locations, several of which produced very large quantities of sherds. The terminology identifying facets of the Manik Complex (TR. 25A) has been dropped in favor of the Coggins (1975) divisions in keeping with other Tikal Project research and publications.

The Manik Complex was well represented in special deposits (see TR. 25A). A total of twenty-six special deposits classified as burials provided 128 whole vessels of the complex, however, two of the Manik burials, Bu. 107 and Bu. 206, are excluded from the sample because of uncertain dates. A total of forty-five special deposits classified as caches contained ceramics. Manik Complex ceramics occurred in twenty-three deposits classified as problematical.

Among the locations that produced Manik collections, five are from large civic-ceremonial groups, four are from range structure groups, four are from intermediate structure groups, three are from small structure groups, one is from the Madeira Reservoir, and one is from the area north of Str. 7C-12 to 20, the last two of which were not associated with structures. The specialized nature of the Madeira Reservoir sample leaves little doubt that it derived from activities associated with the reservoir. The abundance of collections from major architectural groups can be attributed to the fact that exploration of the early histories of large Late Classic structures revealed prior Early Classic structures with Manik fill samples.

There exist the usual insecurities about whether the sherds in any given location actually represent activity at the locus. For the Manik material, which is not infrequently overlain by Late Classic deposits, there is the additional possibility that a particular locus might have changed its primary function between the Early Classic and Late Classic. Particularly for large ceremonial units, the assumption of ceremonial nature is often based on Late Classic architecture preserved on the surface. Although the frequently demonstrated pattern of continuity of a single activity through long periods of time would support this assumption, it is obviously not an infallible principle. The special deposits associated with structure groups, i.e., the burials, caches, and problematical deposits, do hint at social changes (e.g., in the Twin Pyramid Complex Gp. 5C-1 and the residential groups 4F-1, 6E-1, and 7F-1).

The following section describes the archaeological context of Manik locations and the samples recovered from them. The collections are summarized in Table 7.2.

MANIK LOCATION 1

This collection was located in the southwest Perdido quadrant of the site about 50 m N of the group containing Str. 7C-12 to 20, in an area designated as the Str. 7C-62 Locus in TR. 27B. It was first noted because of an unusually heavy concentration of sherds on the surface, although the state of preservation was poor. The depth of the deposit originally provided hope that stratigraphy showing ceramic change might be present, but the ceramics were essentially homogeneous within each test pit and all dated to Manik 3B. Two parallel columns of 20 cm levels were excavated that provided ten samples with an additional sample from another excavation pit. The material represents domestic debris from residential occupation somewhere near this locus.

Manik Sample 1-1: This sample of 151 rim sherds came from the 20–40 cm level in Column 1, the original excavated column. The top 20 cm level was not analyzed.

Manik Sample 1-2: This sample of 132 rim sherds came from the 40–60 cm level in Column 1.

Manik Sample 1-3: This sample of 162 rims and 501 total sherds came from the 60–80 cm level in Column 1.

Manik Sample 1-4: This sample of 106 rims and 446 total sherds came from the 80–100 cm level in Column 1.

TABLE 7.2 (part 1)
Locations of Manik Complex Samples

Sample #	Op.Sub-Op./Lot	Structure Group and Structure Number	Structure Group Type	Total Sherds-Types	Total Sherds-Shapes	Facet	Comments	TR.
Location 1	**39F,G,H**	**Str. 7C-62 Locus**	**No Structures**			Manik 3B	Includes PD.274	20A
Sample 1-1	39F/2	No Structures		None	151			
Sample 1-2	39F/3	No Structures		None	132			
Sample 1-3	39F/4	No Structures		501	162			
Sample 1-4	39F/5	No Structures		446	106			
Sample 1-5	39F/7	No Structures		None	149			
Sample 1-6	39F/8	No Structures		268	127			
Sample 1-7	39F/9	No Structures		374	178			
Sample 1-8	39F/10–13	No Structures		None	177			
Sample 1-9	39F/10	No Structures		289	None			
Sample 1-10	39F/11	No Structures		305	None			
Sample 1-11	39G	No Structures		413	177			
Location 2	**3C**	**Gp. 7F-1**	**Intermediate Structure Group**			Manik 3B		22
Sample 2-1	3C/4–5	Chultun 7F-8		816	165		Above and into chultun	
Sample 2-2	3C/6	Chultun 7F-8		None	277		Top 40 cm in chultun	
Sample 2-3	3C/7	Chultun 7F-8		843	155		Below 3C/6 to floor	
Location 3	**12L**	**Gp. 5D-2, North Acropolis**	**Civic-Ceremonial**			Manik 3A		14
Sample 3-1	12L/13	Str. 5D-33-1st		None	108			
Sample 3-2	12L/16	Str. 5D-33-1st		None	154			
Sample 3-3	12L/28	Str. 5D-33-1st		None	117			
Location 4	**22I**	**N. of North Acropolis**	**Civic-Ceremonial**			Manik 3A		17
Sample 4-1	22I	No Structures		None	152			

TABLE 7.2 (part 2)
Locations of Manik Complex Samples

Sample #	Op.Sub-Op./Lot	Structure Group and Structure Number	Structure Group Type	Total Sherds-Types	Total Sherds-Shapes	Facet	Comments	TR.
Location 5	**23I**	**N. of West Plaza, Gp. 5D-10**	**Range Structure Group**			Manik 2 & 3A		17
Sample 5-1	23I/3	No Structures		None	117			
Sample 5-2	23I/4	No Structures		None	164			
Sample 5-3	23I/5	No Structures		291	101			
Sample 5-4	23I/6	No Structures		None	88			
Sample 5-5	23I/7	No Structures		None	86			
Sample 5-6	23I/8	No Structures		452	164			
Sample 5-7	23I/9–10	No Structures		378	73			
Location 6	**33A/51**	**Gp. 4H-1**	**Intermediate Structure Group**			Manik 2		21
Sample 6-1	33A/51	Chultun 4H-9		1105	113			
Location 7	**36P,Q**	**Gp. 7E-6**	**Intermediate Structure Group**			Manik 3B		20A
Sample 7-1	36P/4–6	7E-6 platform		564	159			
Sample 7-2	36Q	7E-6 platform		None	189			
Location 8	**37C**	**Gp. 6D-4**	**Intermediate Structure Group**			Manik 3B		
Sample 8-1	37C/1–3	6D-4 platform		566	227			
Location 9	**37H**	**No Group (Map Square 6D)**	**Madeira Reservoir**			Manik 3B		
Sample 9-1	37H/9–13	No Structures		None	180			
Location 10	**37P**	**Gp. 5D-9, 7 Temples**	**Civic-Ceremonial**			Manik 3B		23A
Sample 10-1	37P	Str. 5D-91		None	124		Below	
Sample 10-2	37P/9	Str. 5D-91		249	None		Above	

TABLE 7.2 (part 3)
Locations of Manik Complex Samples

Sample #	Op.Sub-Op./Lot	Structure Group and Structure Number	Structure Group Type	Total Sherds-Types	Total Sherds-Shapes	Facet	Comments	TR.
Location 11	43D	Gp. 5C-1	Twin Pyramid Complex			Manik 3A		18[†]
Sample 11-1	43D/8, 11	Str. 5C-14		None	80			
Location 12	45G	Gp. 5D-11, Central Acropolis	Range Structure Group			Manik 3A & 3B		15[†]
Sample 12-1	45G/10	Str. 5D-50		None	235			
Sample 12-2	45G/25	Str. 5D-50		None	196			
Sample 12-3	45G/28	Str. 5D-50		None	99		Not worked completely	
Sample 12-4	45G/9	Str. 5D-50		548	None			
Location 13	67A	Gp. 6C-1	Small Structure Group			Manik 3A & 3B		20A, 20B
Sample 13-1	67A/44	Str. 6C-45		None	99			
Sample 13-2	67A/49–51	Str. 6C-45		None	466			
Sample 13-3	67A/52–55	Str. 6C-45		None	207			
Sample 13-4	67A/58–60	Str. 6C-45		None	176			
Sample 13-5	67A/18	Str. 6C-45		None	189			
Sample 13-6	67A/35	Str. 6C-45		None	102			
Sample 13-7	67A/49, 50	Str. 6C-45		799	None		Includes PD. 275	
Sample 13-8	67A/51–55	Str. 6C-45		1719	None		Includes PD. 275	
Sample 13-9	67A/58	Str. 6C-45		289	None		Includes PD. 275	
Sample 13-10	67A/40	Str. 6C-45		86	None			

TABLE 7.2 (part 4)
Locations of Manik Complex Samples

Sample #	Op.Sub-Op./Lot	Structure Group and Structure Number	Structure Group Type	Total Sherds-Types	Total Sherds-Shapes	Facet	Comments	TR.
Location 14	68I, K	Gp. 6E-1	Small Structure Group			Manik 3B		20A, 20B
Sample 14-1	68I	6E-1 platform		None	169			
Sample 14-2	68K	6E-1 platform		None	372			
Sample 14-3	68K/13	6E-1 platform		152	None			
Sample 14-4	68K/14	6E-1 platform		115	None			
Sample 14-5	68K/16	6E-1 platform		240	None			
Location 15	78O	Gp. 5D-3, East Plaza	Civic-Ceremonial			Manik 3B		16
Sample 15-1	78O	No Structures		None	267			
Location 16	97H/8	Gp. 5D-11, Central Acropolis	Range Structure Group					15[†]
Sample 16-1	97H/8	Str. 5D-55		None	242			
Location 17	98B	Gp. 5D-11, Central Acropolis	Range Structure Group			Manik 3B		15[†]
Sample 17-1	98B	Str. 5D-46		None	94			
Sample 17-2	98B/14	Str. 5D-46		353	None			
Sample 17-3	98B/15	Str. 5D-46		323	None			
Sample 17-4	98B/16	Str. 5D-46		153	None			
Location 18	119B, vacant terrain	Gp. 5F-2, "vacant" terrain	Small Structure Group			Manik 3A		20A
Sample 18-1	119B	10m N. of Str. 5F-2 and 5F-4		None	195			
	TOTAL SHERDS			12637	7460			

[†] Forthcoming

Manik Sample 1-5: This sample of 149 rim sherds came from the 20–40 cm level in Column 2.

Manik Sample 1-6: This sample of 127 rims and 268 total sherds came from the 40–60 cm level in Column 2.

Manik Sample 1-7: This sample of 178 rims and 374 total sherds came from the 60–80 cm level in Column 2.

Manik Sample 1-8: This combined sample of 177 rim sherds came from the 80–140 cm levels in Column 2.

Manik Sample 1-9: This sample of 289 sherds counted for types came from 80–100 cm level in Column 2.

Manik Sample 1-10: This sample of 305 sherds counted for types came from 100–120 cm level in Column 2.

Manik Sample 1-11: The sample of 177 rims and 413 total sherds came from the 40–60 cm level in a pit immediately N of the pit that yielded the preceding samples. Although much of this location was defined as PD. 274 because of the inclusion of human remains and monument fragments, there is nothing unusual about the ceramic content.

MANIK LOCATION 2

Excavations in Gp. 7F-1 (see TR. 22) provided a long and well-controlled architectural sequence that was associated, in its lower levels, with large and well-preserved samples of Manik ceramics and with Manik Bu. 160 and 162. Although the temporal range of individual samples extended from the early to the middle parts of Manik 3B, samples of different date could not be stratigraphically related. The samples provided interesting features in polychrome and incised types that probably have social rather than chronological meaning.

Culturally, the samples provide an example of a collection associated with an intermediate structure group, with possible elite status. Within the group, attribution of samples to structures of specific function is difficult because some samples may have been used as fill material while others were encountered in deep trenches or tunnels where definite architectural associations are difficult to define.

Manik Sample 2-1: This sample, from a pit in front of the W stair of Str. 7F-31, was below the floor and included the lowest deposits above Chultun 7F-8 in bedrock and those from the top 30 cm within the pit. The sample included 165 rims counted for shapes and 816 sherds counted for types.

Manik Sample 2-2: This sample of 277 rim sherds included the 30–70 cm level within the pit noted in the preceding sample.

Manik Sample 2-3: This sample of 155 rims and 843 total sherds included material from the lowest level of deposits within the pit. Bu. 162 and PD. 223, which included human remains, came from the same lot.

MANIK LOCATION 3

Manik Location 3 comprises Str. 5D-33-1st (see TR. 14). Excavation of the structure provided large quantities of well-preserved sherds. Because the samples are from the fill of a temple substructure erected in early Late Classic times, their stratigraphic position is meaningless and the sample of Manik material had to be obtained by typological separation from associated Preclassic and Late Classic sherds. It is interesting, therefore, that the samples all seriated nicely as Manik 3A. Because the samples came from different large blocks of fill in Str. 5D-33-1st, their homogeneity suggests that some major deposit of Manik 3A material was used during the filling operation. Although, there are always problems in attributing an origin to the fill of a major structure, it is assumed here that the majority of fill samples from around the Great Plaza originated from activities in the heart of the civic-ceremonial area.

Manik Sample 3-1: This sample of 108 rim sherds came from a fill compartment defined by retaining walls in the center of the third body (from the top) of Str. 5D-33-1st. It is from the W half of the compartment.

Manik Sample 3-2: This sample of 154 rims came from the E half of the same fill compartment described for Sample 3-1.

Manik Sample 3-3: This sample of 117 rims was fill from the fourth body of Str. 5D-33-1st below the preceding samples.

MANIK LOCATION 4

This location was one tested in the early days of the Tikal Project with the hope of revealing deep midden stratigraphy that would provide evidence of gradual change. Although the location tested, on the steep slope N of the North Acropolis (see TR. 17), yielded 13 levels of materials, the quantity of sherds in most levels was small and only a single combined sample from three levels could be quantified. The sample dated to Manik 3A. The assumption has been made that the sample results from activities somewhere within the main ceremonial center, possibly fill from the collapse of a structure on the North Acropolis.

Manik Sample 4-1: This sample of 152 rim sherds was from a column of 25 cm stratigraphic levels. Sample 4-1 combined material from the eighth, ninth, and tenth levels below the surface.

MANIK LOCATION 5

This was another location excavated by the midden test-pitting project early in the history of the Tikal Project (see TR. 17). Its location, on the slope below Str. 5D-14 in the West Plaza, Group 5D-10, makes a West Plaza origin likely because there is no other nearby group. The 3.7 m of deposits began with scanty Late Preclassic material in levels 11–13, above which are 8 levels (lumped into 7 levels for quantitative purposes) of Manik ceramics extending from Manik 2 through 3B, and by two levels of surface debris. Ceramics in the Manik levels were fairly abundant although not particularly well preserved. The collections from Location 5 were critical for Manik chronology because it was the only occurrence of a deep stratified midden demonstrating patterns of ceramic change, and one of the few examples in Tikal Project collections of Manik 2. The samples were from a column of 25 cm levels with Sample 5-1 the level between 50 and 75 cm from the surface and each succeeding sample 25 cm deeper, except that Sample 5-7 combines the data from two levels. All samples were quantified for shapes, but only three were quantified for types. Both excavation and ceramic data support the conclusion that the samples are debris discovered in the location in which it accumulated. The assumption that the sample originated

from activities in the main ceremonial center seems acceptable because of the isolation of the location from other groups.

Manik Sample 5-1: This sample of 117 rim sherds came from 50–75 cm below the surface. It is Manik 3A.

Manik Sample 5-2: This sample of 164 rim sherds came from 75–100 cm below the surface. It is Manik 3A.

Manik Sample 5-3: This sample of 101 rims and 291 total sherds came from 100–125 cm below the surface. It is Manik 3A.

Manik Sample 5-4: This sample of 88 rim sherds came from 125–150 cm below the surface. It is Manik 2.

Manik Sample 5-5: This sample of 86 rim sherds came from 150–175 cm below the surface. It is Manik 2.

Manik Sample 5-6: This sample of 164 rims and 452 total sherds came from 175–200 cm below the surface. It is Manik 2.

Manik Sample 5-7: This combined sample of 73 rims and 378 total sherds came from 200–250 cm below the surface. It is Manik 2.

MANIK LOCATION 6

Manik Sample 6-1: Excavation in Str. 4H-4 (see TR. 21), Manik Location 6, produced a sample of 113 Manik 2 rim sherds and 1,105 total sherds. Culturally, the material provides an example of debris from an intermediate structure group.

MANIK LOCATION 7

Two test pits on the platform that supports Str. 7E-42 and 44 provided samples (see TR. 20A). Culturally, the samples are from an intermediate structure group, Gp. 7E-6.

Manik Sample 7-1: Several small lots from the lowest levels in a test pit in front of Str. 7E-44 were combined to give a single Manik 3B sample of 159 rims and 564 total sherds.

Manik Sample 7-2: Two small lots from the lowest levels in a test pit in front of Str. 7E-42 were combined to give a single Manik 3B sample of 189 rims.

MANIK LOCATION 8

A test pit, on the large platform sustaining Str. 6D-52 and 53 (Gp. 6D-4), provided three levels of Manik 3B material (see TR. 20A). The group is a residential intermediate structure group.

Manik Sample 8-1: Three individual lots were large enough for quantification, but, in spite of considerable variation in content, there were no patterns indicating consistent chronological differentiation between lots. Consequently, the lots were combined as a single sample of 227 rims and 566 total sherds.

MANIK LOCATION 9

This location was a test pit in the southwest interior corner of the bottom of the dry Madeira Reservoir. The reservoir is located somewhat east of the small structure Gp. 6D-1. The pit was abandoned at a depth of 3.25 m without reaching bedrock. Thirteen 25 cm levels provided small quantities of poorly preserved sherds. The samples seem to be generally Manik 3B with no indication of chronological change.

Manik Sample 9-1: The ninth through thirteenth level were combined in a single total sample of 180 rim sherds. The vessel shape frequencies, especially the very high frequencies of slipped jars, differentiate these samples strongly from other Manik samples. This suggests functional specificity related to the use of the reservoir as a water source. This sample also included PD. 271 (lots 37H/9–13, 15, 17), which included human remains and domestic and status goods.

MANIK LOCATION 10

A ceramic test pit on the large platform near Str. 5D-91 produced 14 levels of cultural debris, the lowest 10 of which are relatively pure Manik samples (see TR. 23A). The platform is a southwesterly extension of Group 5C-11, the Mundo Perdido. Individual lots were too small for meaningful quantitative studies of vessel shapes, however, and the entire group was combined into a single Manik 3B

sample in the shape seriation charts. The combined sample fits the chart well and inspection of individual lots provided no indication of change from top to bottom of the deposit. A sample from one level was also counted for types. The samples are considered to represent activities from an important civic-ceremonial group, but since they may well be the result of intentional filling in the construction of the platform, the attribution should be accepted with caution.

Manik Sample 10-1: Eleven small lots were combined into a single sample of 124 rim sherds.

Manik Sample 10-2: The ninth level in the test pit provided a type sample of 249 total sherds.

MANIK LOCATION 11

Excavation within Str. 5C-14, the pyramid on the west side of the Twin Pyramid Complex, Gp. 5C-1 near Temple IV, provided two lots of Manik sherds from structure fill (see forthcoming TR. 18). The lots were architecturally separated, and the stratigraphically earlier lot may be somewhat earlier in ceramic frequencies. Both lots are Manik 3A, however, and they were combined to provide a sufficiently large sample for use to seriate the facet based on vessel shapes. The classification of the sample as ceremonial-elite is particularly suspect for two reasons. First, there are nearby sources from which a non-elite sample could have been obtained for use as fill. Second, because Twin Pyramid complexes are a Late Classic phenomenon, there is no solid evidence that the location need have been ceremonial or elite during the Early Classic.

Manik Sample 11-1: A lot from fill below the W stairs of the Str. 5C-14 was combined with a lot from fill in a tunnel to the E to give a sample of 80 rim sherds.

MANIK LOCATION 12

Manik Location 12 was within early levels of construction under Str. 5D-50 in the Central Acropolis, Gp. 5D-11, which were sampled by tunneling (see TR. 15). The location provided three shape samples at different depths that ranged from Manik 3A–B.

Manik Sample 12-1: This sample of 235 rim sherds was from fill of an earlier range structure under Str. 5D-50. The sample is Manik 3A.

Manik Sample 12-2: This sample of 196 rims was from an earlier fill level than that for Sample 12-1. It dates to Manik 3A.

Manik Sample 12-3: This sample of 99 rims was from the earliest level of Manik Complex fill under Str. 5D-50. It is Manik 3A.

Manik Sample 12-4: This sample of 548 sherds counted for types was from the same level of fill as Sample 12-1.

MANIK LOCATION 13

The excavation of Str. 6C-45, one of a group of four housemounds in Gp. 6C-1, was Manik Location 13 (see TR. 20A, 20B). The location yielded an unusually large sample of Manik ceramics that provided six samples quantified for shapes and four samples quantified for types. This location included Manik 3B PD. 275, lots 67A/49–60, associated with Str. 6C-45-4th. There was complex architectural stratigraphy at the site to which samples could be tied. The fact that some stratigraphically late samples seriate earlier than lower samples is not a matter of great concern. In fill situations, inverted stratigraphy is not surprising. Excavation evidence suggests differences in function between the series of structures found superimposed at this location, but all structures would fall within the category of commoner small structure residential groups on the basis of size and general architecture.

Manik Sample 13-1: This Manik 3A sample of 99 rim sherds came from mixed fill of Str. 6C-45-3rd, 4th, and 5th.

Manik Sample 13-2: This Manik 3B combined sample of 466 rims came from three lots of mixed fill of Str. 6C-45-4th.

Manik Sample 13-3: This Manik 3B combined sample of 207 rims came from four lots of fill of Str. 6C-45-4th.

Manik Sample 13-4: This Manik 3B combined sample of 176 rims came from three lots of fill of Str. 6C-45-4th.

Manik Sample 13-5: This Manik 3A sample of 189 rims came from fill of Str. 6C-45-4th that probably originated as midden material from Str. 6C-45-5th.

Manik Sample 13-6: This Manik 3A sample of 102 rims came from fill of Str. 6C-45-4th that probably originated as midden material from Str. 6C-45-5th.

Manik Sample 13-7: This combined sample of 799 sherds counted for types came from two lots of fill of Str. 6C-45-4th.

Manik Sample 13-8: This combined sample of 1,319 sherds counted for types came from five lots of fill of Str. 6C-45-4th.

Manik Sample 13-9: This sample of 289 sherds counted for types came from sealed fill of Str. 6C-45-4th.

Manik Sample 13-10: This sample of 86 sherds counted for types came from sealed fill of Str. 6C-45-4th.

MANIK LOCATION 14

Manik Location 14 was the result of extensive excavations in Plat. 6E-1, the platform that serves as a base for Str. 6E-25 and 26 in Gp. 6E-1 (see TR. 20A, 20B). Location 14 provided two samples quantified for shapes and three samples quantified for types. This is a small structure group.

Manik Sample 14-1: Two lots of Manik material were obtained from within Plat. 6E-1, in an area between Str. 6E-Sub 1 and 6E-Sub 3. The frequencies for the two lots were similar and they were combined into a single Manik 3B sample of 169 rims.

Manik Sample 14-2: Nine lots beneath and behind U. 8 were combined into a single sample of 372 rims that dated to Manik 3B.

Manik Sample 14-3: This sample of 152 sherds counted for types came from fill behind U. 8.

Manik Sample 14-4: This sample of 115 sherds counted for types came from fill behind U. 8.

Manik Sample 14-5: This sample of 240 sherds counted for types came from brown earth below U. 8.

MANIK LOCATION 15

This location was a deep pit through the floor of the East Plaza, Gp. 5D-3 (see TR. 16). At a depth between 3 and 4 m below the present surface, the excavation encountered a Manik 3B midden. The material undoubtedly derives from within a major civic-ceremonial group that included Tikal's central marketplace during Late Classic times.

Manik Sample 15-1: Six stratigraphic levels between 3 and 4 m below the surface in Location 15 gave Manik 3B samples. Because they were similar in content, they were combined into a single sample of 267 rim sherds for the seriation.

MANIK LOCATION 16

Manik Location 16 was a trench on the central axis, E side of Str. 5D-55 in the Central Acropolis, Gp. 5D-11 (see TR. 15). The context is a major elite residential range structure group.

Manik Sample 16-1: A single sample of 242 Manik 3B rim sherds was obtained from the tunnel.

MANIK LOCATION 17

Manik Location 17 consisted of Manik Complex material obtained from a tunnel within Str. 5D-46, an elite range structure residential group, in the Central Acropolis, Gp. 5D-11 (see TR. 15). The location provided one sample counted for vessel shapes and three samples counted for types.

Manik Sample 17-1: Three samples of fill from Str. 5D-46 were combined into a single Manik 3B sample of 94 rim sherds.

Manik Sample 17-2: This type sample of 353 sherds came from a band of construction fill of Str. 5D-46 that overlay the two samples that follow.

Manik Sample 17-3: This type sample of 323 sherds came from construction fill that underlay Manik Sample 17-2.

Manik Sample 17-4: This type sample of 153 sherds was obtained from the fill of the cap over Ca.

197 and 198. Cache 198 is the important cache that contains a Urita Gouged-incised vessel that names the ruler Chak Tok Ich'aak I (Jaguar Paw).

MANIK LOCATION 18

Manik Location 18 was a part of the testing of areas of "vacant" land in the southeastern quadrant of Tikal 10 m N of Str. 5F-2 and 5F-4, Op. 119B (see TR. 20A). The testing resulted in the discovery of a series of small mounds invisible on the surface and a single sample of sherds quantified for shapes. The cultural context is domestic residence.

Manik Sample 18-1: Eight small samples were combined into a single Manik 3A sample of 195 rim sherds.

Pastes of the Manik Complex

Introduction

As in other parts of the Tikal sequence, paste composition in the Manik Complex maintained enough independence from other typological considerations to demand study in its own right. A system of paste categories was established on the basis of kind and size of inclusions, while paste color was studied as an independent cross-cutting variable.

The primary feature in the separation of paste categories was the presence or absence of carbonate (presumably calcite) inclusions. A second distinction was based on the size and abundance of inclusions, yielding coarse and fine groups. A final separation was made within the fine-carbonate category on the basis of presence or absence of a gray amorphous carbonate that is unique to the Manik Complex as an alternative or addition to the more common white or translucent crystalline carbonate.

Manik Paste Descriptions

COARSE-CARBONATE PASTE

Identifying characteristics: In all regards except for color the same as the Chuen Complex (see Chapter 4 for complete description).

Color: The paste is marked by a broad range of colors, often within single sherds. The most common colors include dark brown (7.5YR 4/4), some very pale brown (10YR 7/3, 7/4); light red (2.5YR 6/6), or light brownish gray (2.5Y 6/2).

Comments: Identical to the paste used in all Late Preclassic and Classic Complexes for striated and unslipped types.

STANDARD-CARBONATE PASTE

Identifying characteristics: Contains carbonate, but lacks gray carbonate.

Color: Most common colors are yellow (10YR 7/6), very pale brown (10YR 7/4), brownish yellow (10YR 6/6), light yellowish brown (10YR 6/4), and yellowish brown (10YR 5/6). Reddish yellow (7.5YR 7/8, 6/8, 6/6) also occurs.

Texture: Very fine to fine.

Inclusions: High to medium amounts of very fine, carbonate particles that give a sparkly appearance in strong light. Small to medium amounts of medium-size translucent or white crystalline carbonates are present.

Comments: The most typical examples of this paste that have large amounts of sparkly particles are quite characteristic of the Manik Complex, but many examples would be equally at home in other Tikal complexes.

GRAY-CARBONATE PASTE

Identifying characteristics: Particles of gray, amorphous carbonate.

Color: A range of yellowish colors occurs: pale yellow (2.5Y 7/4), light yellow (2.5Y 6/4), yellow (10YR 7/6), very pale brown (10YR 7/4), and reddish yellow (7.5YR 7/6; 5YR 6/8).

Texture: Medium to fine.

Inclusions: Small to medium amounts of fine to medium powdery gray carbonate; small amounts of very fine sparkly material.

Comment: The kind of gray carbonate that characterizes this paste is rarely found in sherds of other complexes and is, therefore, a reasonably good diagnostic for Manik.

NON-CARBONATE PASTE

Identifying characteristics: Does not contain carbonate.

Color: A range of yellowish colors occurs: yellow (10YR 7/6), brownish yellow (10YR 6/8, 6/6), light yellow brown (10YR 6/4), reddish yellow (7.5YR 7/6, 6/6; 5YR 6/6), and pink (5YR 7/4).

Texture: Medium to fine.

Inclusions: Low to high amounts of very fine particles and some medium particles of white glassy material; some medium translucent crystalline particles; golden mica; shiny black particles; no carbonate.

Comments: There is a considerable range of variation in texture and amount of inclusions in this paste, but no useful subdivisions could be made. The paste could easily be duplicated in other Tikal complexes and is, consequently, not an identifying characteristic for Manik.

Discussion of Manik Pastes

Paste studies with Tikal ceramics were restricted in scope. Analysis and sorting were done by visual inspection with a binocular microscope used only occasionally as an aid in description. Dilute hydrochloric acid was used to test for the presence of carbonates. Counts of paste types by ceramic type (presented in Tables 7.3 to 7.7) were made on a restricted number of lots more for the purpose of a broad temporal comparison than for detailed intrasite analysis. The potential for gaining useful information about patterns of ceramic manufacture and trade by using available techniques of technological analysis is very good, and collections that would permit such studies are in storage at Tikal.

There are some correlations between pastes and types. The most obvious is the almost exclusive use of Coarse-carbonate Paste in the production of Triunfo Striated, a manifestation of the correlation between unslipped types and heavy calcite tempering throughout the Tikal sequence. Otherwise, Coarse-carbonate Paste occurs rarely in Manik ceramics and seems never to have been used in some of the thin-walled decorated types such as Lucha Incised and Urita Gouged-incised.

TABLE 7.3
Frequency of Coarse Carbonate Paste in Manik Pottery

	Aguila Orange	Balanza Black	Lucha Incised	Triunfo Striated	Polychromes
Manik 3B	19.0	6.0	0.0	99.0	2.0
Manik 3A	2.0	5.0	0.0	99.0	3.0
Manik 2	5.0	4.0	0.0	99.0	0.0

TABLE 7.4
Frequency of Standard Carbonate Paste in Manik Pottery

	Aguila Orange	Balanza Black	Lucha Incised	Triunfo Striated	Polychromes
Manik 3B	18.0	47.0	58.0	Trace	16.0
Manik 3A	18.0	64.0	0.00	Trace	12.0
Manik 2	15.0	61.0	0.00	Trace	26.0

TABLE 7.5
Frequency of Gray Carbonate Paste in Manik Pottery

	Aguila Orange	Balanza Black	Lucha Incised	Triunfo Striated	Polychromes
Manik 3B	28.0	27.0	9.0	Trace	12.0
Manik 3A	44.0	25.0	0.0	Trace	24.0
Manik 2	55.0	32.0	0.0	Trace	34.0

TABLE 7.6
Frequency of Non-Carbonate Paste in Manik Pottery

	Aguila Orange	Balanza Black	Lucha Incised	Triunfo Striated	Polychromes
Manik 3B	34.0	20.0	31.0	0.0	70.0
Manik 3A	36.0	6.0	0.0	0.0	61.0
Manik 2	25.0	3.0	0.0	0.0	41.0

TABLE 7.7
Frequency of Red Paste in Manik Pottery

	Aguila Orange	Balanza Black	Lucha Incised	Triunfo Striated	Polychromes
Manik 3B	8.0	24.0	14.0	3.0	5.0
Manik 3A	4.0	18.0	0.0	Trace	5.0
Manik 2	4.0	10.0	0.0	0.0	3.0

The highly distinctive Gray-carbonate Paste is strongly associated with Aguila Orange. This paste, however, may actually have occurred with considerably higher frequencies in Balanza Black than those reported in Table 7.5. Identification of the paste depends on the ability to note the color of the particles, and many sherds of Balanza Black have dark paste that hindered identification. Polychrome types and Triunfo Striated have unquestionably lower frequencies of Gray-carbonate Paste than does Aguila Orange.

Standard-carbonate Paste occurs as a minor paste class in all except the black types where the problems of classification discussed above probably resulted in some upward distortion of the frequencies.

Non-carbonate Paste shows an interesting distribution. Polychrome types were more frequently made from Non-carbonate Paste than other types. The difference between Balanza Black as compared with Lucha Incised and Urita Gouged-incised is interesting because it suggests that decorated and undecorated black types may have had different sources or processes of manufacture.

In general, all of the major types for which quantified paste analyses were run have characteristic frequencies of pastes. This would suggest that either the tradition of pottery making dictated differential use of clays or tempering materials depending on anticipated surface treatment, or that several centers of pottery manufacture are represented. I would favor the latter alternative because Late Classic data, particularly from the Sustaining Area Project (Fry 1979), suggests a number of manufacturing centers.

There is some chronological variation in paste frequencies. Gray-carbonate Paste seems to decline in frequency between Manik 2 and Manik 3A, while Non-carbonate Paste increases in frequency. However, the changes are not striking enough to be of use as a chronological marker.

The only variation in paste colors is between pastes of reddish tones and pastes of other colors. Reddish paste color is rare in all except the black-slipped types where it runs to frequencies as high as 24%. It seems likely that paste color is related to firing conditions rather than to paste composition. The firing necessary to produce the black surface may have contributed to the frequency of reddish paste.

The analysis of Manik Complex pastes demonstrates considerable variety in materials and production processes. There are correlations between paste characteristics and types, but the two are by no means coterminous. Gray-carbonate Paste and the more typical examples of Standard-carbonate Paste are distinctive enough to serve as markers for the Manik Complex, but paste changes are too poorly marked to contribute to an internal subdivision of the complex. The diversity of pastes and the way in which they combine suggests that further and more technological analysis might provide useful information about ceramic production and distribution, but to use the present scanty data to form or test hypotheses would be a dubious procedure.

Ceramic Types of the Manik Complex

Introduction

The Manik Ceramic Complex includes the 10 ceramic groups and 22 ceramic types (comprised of 23 varieties) listed in Table 7.8. In general, all major groups listed for Uaxactun (Smith and Gifford 1966) occur at Tikal and types are closely parallel. Types that are new at Tikal and do not appear at Uaxactun are all relatively minor and may simply be the result of different ways of looking at the variables involved.

Perhaps the most striking characteristic of Manik Complex typology is the monolithic stability of the types and varieties. There was almost no discernible change over time and little meaningful variation between samples from different contexts. Consequently, the primary utility of the Manik typology is its differentiation from preceding and following complexes, but it contributes little to knowledge of change within the three centuries that the complex remained in use. Similarly, Manik type frequencies show little variation that related to contextually indicated differences in social structure.

Manik Type Descriptions

QUINTAL CERAMIC GROUP

Quintal Unslipped: Quintal Variety

Established: Smith and Gifford (1966)

Group: Quintal

TABLE 7.8
Ceramic Groups and Types of the Manik Complex

QUINTAL CERAMIC GROUP

Quintal Unslipped: Quintal Variety

TRIUNFO CERAMIC GROUP

Triunfo Striated: Triunfo Variety

MAAX CERAMIC GROUP

Maax Red-striated: Maax Variety

AGUILA CERAMIC GROUP

Aguila Orange: Aguila Variety

Aguila Orange: Matte-red Variety

Pita Incised: Pita Variety

San Clemente Gouged-incised: San Clemente Variety

BALANZA CERAMIC GROUP

Balanza Black: Balanza Variety

Lucha Incised: Lucha Variety

Urita Gouged-incised: Urita Variety

Delirio Plano-relief: Delirio Variety

Paradero Fluted: Paradero Variety

Positas Modeled: Positas Variety

PUCTE CERAMIC GROUP

Pucte Brown: Pucte Variety

FAMA CERAMIC GROUP

Fama Buff: Fama Variety

DOS ARROYOS CERAMIC GROUP

Dos Arroyos Orange Polychrome: Dos Arroyos Variety

Cochol Orange Polychrome: Cochol Variety

San Blas Red-on-orange: San Blas Variety

Caldero Buff Polychrome: Caldero Variety

San Bartolo Red-on-buff: San Bartolo Variety

Yaloche Cream Polychrome: Yaloche Variety

MOC CERAMIC GROUP

Moc Orange Polychrome: Moc Variety

JAPON CERAMIC GROUP

Japon Resist: Japon Variety

Ware: Uaxactun Unslipped

Ceramic Complex: Manik

Ceramic Sphere: Tzakol

Illustrations: Fig. 18.1–51, 18.54–55; 19.46; 56.33; 57.4. See TR. 25A: fig. 21*b–j*; 33*b*3; 36*a*5; 38*c*1–2,*c*4; 100*a*1–3,*b–e*; 101*a*1–3,*b*2,*d*; *102e*; 103*b*; 108*a*; 129*f,n*; 137*g*; 138*c,g,i–j m–n.*

Principal identifying attributes: Unslipped well-smoothed surfaces on mostly jars and some bowls.

Paste: All Manik pastes represented in proportions similar to those of slipped types. In paste, then, Quintal Unslipped differs radically from Triunfo Striated.

Firing: Dark cores rare. Fireclouding is common, but it is uncertain whether it results from firing conditions or from use.

Color: Most common, various shades of brown (5YR 5/4 to l0YR 6/2); some red to light red (2.5YR 5/8, 6/6).

Surface finish: Usually well smoothed except that the exterior of some vessels and the interior of cache vessels are left unsmoothed.

Shapes: Wide-mouth jars 42%; slightly incurving to round-side bowls 32%; large recurving-side bowls 26%. Cylindrical cache vessels and their covers were frequently made in Quintal Unslipped, but they do not occur as sherds. Quintal Unslipped was also commonly used in the production of censers (Ferree 1972) and may include examples of Candelario Appliquéd identified at Uaxactun (Smith and Gifford 1966) and originally identified at Tikal (misprinted as Candelaria in TR. 25A). The sample is too small to adequately describe a complete type, so all examples are included in the Quintal Group. There are also two examples with impressed appliqué rims that may be examples of Cubierta Impressed (see Fig. 18.52–53) and a body sherd with an appliqué button (Fig. 57.4).

Temporal distribution: Present throughout the Manik Complex.

Comments: Originally Quintal Unslipped was considered an unstriated version of Triunfo Striated. It became increasingly clear that in paste and the shapes represented, Quintal is more closely related to the slipped types than to Triunfo Striated. Sherd counts, unfortunately, were completed while still counting unslipped jar necks as Quintal Unslipped, even though it is virtually certain that most of them would have showed striations had the body sections been present. The sherd counts, therefore, reflect more of such jars than of Quintal Unslipped as now defined.

Intersite Comparisons: Blue Creek (Kosakowsky and Lohse 2003); Calakmul (Dominguez Carrasco 1994); Chan (Kosakowsky 2012); Holmul (Callaghan 2008, 2016d); Edzná (Forsyth 1983); El Mirador (Forsyth 1989); El Pozito (Eppich 2000); La Milpa (Sagebiel 2005); the Petexbatun (Foias and Bishop 2013); Seibal (Sabloff 1975); Uaxactun (Smith and Gifford 1966); Yaxchilan (Lopez Varela 1998). Maybe related to Hewlett Bank Unslipped at Barton Ramie (Gifford 1976); Chan Chich (Valdez and Houk 2000); and Colha (Valdez 1987).

TRIUNFO CERAMIC GROUP

Triunfo Striated: Triunfo Variety

Established: Smith and Gifford (1966)

Group: Triunfo

Ware: Uaxactun Unslipped

Ceramic Complex: Manik

Ceramic Sphere: Tzakol

Illustrations: Fig. 18.1–51, 18.54–55; 19.40–42, 19.47–48. See TR. 25A: fig. 32*b*1; 33*d*3; 34*b–d*; 126*e–n*; 138*a–b,e*. See also Cubierta Impressed now included in Triunfo Striated because of small sample size: TR. 25A: fig. 138*l,p*.

Principal identifying attributes: Unslipped striated jars with narrow deep striations that begin below the neck body juncture.

Identifying Characteristics and Sorting Problems: The striations and lack of slip identify the type. There are no typological characteristics that differentiate Triunfo Striated from striated types of the preceding and following complexes.

Paste: Almost exclusively Coarse-carbonate Paste.

Firing: Dark cores rare. More than half of the sherds show fireclouding, with interior and exterior fireclouding equally common.

Color: Most commonly various shades of brown (5YR 5/4 to l0YR 6/2); some red to light red (2.5YR 5/8, 6/6).

Surface and finish and decoration: Striations are usually deep, narrow, close together, and quite regular. There is a range to broader and more widely spaced striations. Striations cover the bodies, but not the necks of jars. Occasionally, clay pellets were appliquéd to the upper bodies of jars and then grooved or indented. The same vessels with appliquéd pellets frequently have a row of indentations at the top of the striated section. Other jars show the indentations, but not the appliquéd pellets. Lips are occasionally indented in a piecrust effect.

Shapes: Almost 100% of the vessels produced from Triunfo Striated are wide-mouth jars. Some incensarios would also fall within the defining characteristics of the type, but are covered in a separate report (see Ferree 1972).

Temporal distribution: Equally common in all Manik facets.

Comments: Subsumed within Triunfo Striated lip-and-neck are impressed examples that would be called Cubierta Impressed in the Uaxactun sample (Smith and Gifford 1966) and the few jars with appliquéd knobs are included simply as a decorative variant of Triunfo Striated.

Intersite Comparisons: Altar de Sacrificios (Adams 1971); Becan (Ball 1977); Blue Creek (Kosakowsky and Lohse 2003); Calakmul (Dominguez Carrasco 1994:114–117); Chan (Kosakowsky 2012); El Mirador (Forsyth 1989); Holmul (Callaghan 2008, 2016d); K'axob (Lopez Varela 2006); La Milpa (Sagebiel 2005); Nohmul (Kosakowsky and Pring 2001);

the Petexbatun (Foias and Bishop 2013); Seibal (Sabloff 1975); Uaxactun (Smith and Gifford 1966); Yaxchilan (Lopez Varela 1989). Possibly related to Mopan Striated at Barton Ramie (Gifford 1976); Chan Chich (Valdez 1998; Valdez and Houk 2000); and Colha (Valdez 1987), and to Socotz Striated also used at Barton Ramie (Gifford 1976) and Colha (Valdez 1987).

MAAX CERAMIC GROUP

Maax Red-striated: Maax Variety

Established: TR. 25A (Culbert 1993)

Group: Maax

Ware: Unspecified

Ceramic Complex: Manik 3B

Ceramic Sphere: Tzakol

Illustrations: See TR. 25A: fig. 32*a*2; 34*a*; 101*e*; 154*b,d*.

Principal identifying attributes: Striation and a matte red slip on narrow-mouth jars.

Identifying characteristics and sorting problems: The matte red slip on unslipped striated surfaces is easily distinguishable from the other unslipped types.

Paste: Standard-carbonate Paste is most common, with some Gray-carbonate Paste. The inclusions are finely ground and the paste texture fine.

Firing: Dark cores and fireclouding are rare.

Slip: Thin slip that adheres well.

Polish: Matte finish.

Color: Usually red (l0R 5/6; 2.5YR 5/8).

Surface and finish and decoration: Striations are of medium depth, narrow and well separated. The vessels were striated before application of the slip.

Shapes: Always narrow-mouth jars.

Temporal distribution: Maax Red-striated is characteristic of the Manik 3A and B.

Comments: This is one of the few types that served as a temporal diagnostic for facets within the Manik Complex. Although not abundant, the type is highly distinctive and, thus, a good time-marker.

Intersite Comparisons: None noted.

AGUILA CERAMIC GROUP

Aguila Orange: Aguila Variety

Established: Smith and Gifford (1966)

Group: Aguila

Ware: Petén Gloss

Ceramic Complex: Manik

Ceramic Sphere: Tzakol

Illustrations: Fig. 19.1–3, 19.5–17, 19.20–22, 19.24–26, 19.32–36, 19.38–39; 20.19–29, 20.31–32, 20.34–42; 21.1–16, 21.18–19, 21.21–22, 21.26, 21.32–51; 28.8, 28.11–21, 28.23–24, 28.26; 29.3, 29.6–10, 29.12; 37.21, 37.23, 37.26, 37.28–30; 38.1–4, 38.9, 38.32; 56.44; 57.6–7, 57.13. See TR. 25A: fig. 17*b–e*; 27*a*5; 28*a*2–3; 28*b*1; 29*a–j*; 32*b*2,*c,d*; 33*b*1–2; 34*e*; 35*b*1–3; 37*d–e*; 38*c*3,*e*1; 100*f*; 101*c*2; 101*b*1,3,*c,d*; 102*a*1–3,*b-c,d*1–2,*e,f*1–2; 103*a*17; 104*a*1–5,*b*1–3; 105*a–g*; 106*a*–3; 107*a*1–11,*c*; 108*a–b*; 109*b,m*; 114*d*1–2; 123*e,g*; 124*d–f,j–k*; 127*h*1; 130*f–j,l–o*; 134*j*; 138*o*; 154*a*.

Principal identifying attributes: Glossy orange to reddish orange or reddish yellow slip most commonly on bowl forms.

Paste: Gray-carbonate Paste predominates followed by Non-carbonate and Standard-carbonate Pastes. The occurrence of Coarse-carbonate Paste is sporadic, usually quite low, but high in some individual lots.

Firing: Dark cores and two-color cores are rare (less than 10%); fireclouding occurs in about one-fifth of the sherds, about equally on interiors and exteriors.

Slip: Thin, adheres well.

Polish: Usually medium, sometimes high.

Color: Ranges from reddish yellow (5YR 6/8, 5/6) to red (2.5YR 4/6, 5/8; l0R 4/6, 5/8, 6/8), with fire-clouding to strong brown (7.5YR 5/8).

Surface and finish and decoration: The color is usually streaky or blotchy.

Shapes: Slightly incurving to round-side bowls 32%; outflaring to slightly outcurving-side bowls or dishes 26%; large recurving-side bowls 16%; narrow-mouth jars 9%; z-angle bowls 6%; tripod dishes 4%; scutate lids 2%; basal-flange bowls 2%; cylindrical vessels 1%; other shapes, less than 1%. Aguila Orange also is common in outflaring to slightly outcurving-side cache vessels.

Temporal distribution: Present in high frequency throughout the Manik Complex.

Comments: A few examples of orange slipped pottery with fingernail impressions occur in the Manik Complex. They seem to be nothing more than a variant of Aguila Orange. They are identified as Milpa Impressed at Uaxactun (Smith and Gifford 1966) and were originally included as a separate type at Tikal as well (TR. 25A), however the sample from Tikal is too small to describe completely a separate type and they have been included in the Aguila Orange type. There are also a few examples with modeling but again the sample size is too small to identify a separate variety.

Intersite Comparisons: Altar de Sacrificios (Adams 1971); Barton Ramie (Gifford 1976); Becan (Ball 1977); Blue Creek (Kosakowsky and Lohse 2003); Calakmul (Dominguez Carrasco 1994); Chan (Kosakowsky 2012); Chan Chich (Valdez 1998, Valdez and Houk 2000); Colha (Valdez 1987); Holmul (Callaghan 2008, 2016d); El Mirador (Forsyth 1989); El Perú/Waka' (Eppich 2011); El Pozito (Eppich 2000); La Milpa (Sagebiel 2005); Nakbe (Forsyth 1993); Nohmul (Kosakowsky and Pring 2001); the Petexbatun (Foias and Bishop 2013); Uaxactun (Smith and Gifford 1966). Local varieties are identified at Edzná (Forsyth 1983) and Piedras Negras (Muñoz 2006).

Aguila Orange: Matte-red Variety

Established: TR. 25A (Culbert 1993)

Group: Aguila

Ware: Petén Gloss

Ceramic Complex: Manik

Ceramic Sphere: Tzakol

Illustrations: Fig. 20.1–8, 20.10–18.

Principal identifying attributes: Red orange matte rather than glossy slip that overlaps with Aguila Orange: Aguila Variety on jar forms.

Identifying characteristics and sorting problems: Sherds that overlap in color with some examples of Aguila Orange also appear in Cimi Complex levels in the North Acropolis in the Baclam Ceramic Group.

Paste, firing, and slip: Like Aguila Orange: Aguila Variety.

Polish: Unpolished to low polish. Temper particles project through the slip and provide foci for erosion on weathered examples.

Color: Mostly red (10R 5/4, 5/6); some range toward orange (2.5YR 5/6).

Shapes: Better than three-quarters of the sherds of this variety come from narrow-mouth jars; most of the remainder are from large recurving-side bowls.

Temporal distribution: Present throughout the Manik Complex.

Comments: Although this variety overlaps with the Aguila Variety, the typical examples differ enough from the most common examples of the Aguila Variety to make a separation useful.

Intersite Comparisons: Found at La Milpa (Sagebiel 2005). The redder slightly more matte slip is reminiscent of Dos Hermanos Red at Barton Ramie (Gifford 1976) and Holmul (Callaghan 2008, 2016d) and the Dos Hermanos Variety of Aguila Orange at El Mirador (Forsyth 1989).

Pita Incised: Pita Variety

Established: Smith and Gifford (1966)

Group: Aguila

Ware: Petén Gloss

Ceramic Complex: Manik

Ceramic Sphere: Tzakol

Illustrations: Fig. 22.6, 22.12, 22.24, 22.33; 23.2, 23.15, 23.21; 28.22, 28.24; 38.19–20, 38.37. See TR. 25A: fig. 36*a*3,*a*6–9; 115*j*1–2; 134*d,j*.

Principal identifying attributes: Surface finish and color same as Aguila Orange with the addition of pre-slip fine line incising.

Color: Ranges from light red (2.5YR 6/8) through reddish yellow (5YR 6/8) to strong brown (7.5YR 5/8).

Temporal Distribution: Present throughout the Manik Complex in small quantities.

Comments: In all characteristics, except color, the small group of sherds that can be classified as Pita Incised are identical to Lucha Incised. In fact, a large number of Lucha Incised sherds show areas that are mottled to the colors mentioned above. It is not certain whether there were vessels intentionally made in orange incised or whether this small sherd group represents misfiring of what were intended to be Lucha Incised.

Intersite Comparisons: Barton Ramie (Gifford 1976); Becan (Ball 1977); Blue Creek (Kosakowsky and Lohse 2003); Calakmul (Dominguez Carrasco 1994); Chan (Kosakowsky 2012); El Mirador (Forsyth 1989); El Pozito (Eppich 2000); Holmul (Callaghan 2008, 2016d); La Milpa (Sagebiel 2005); Uaxactun (Smith and Gifford 1966); Yaxchilan (Lopez Varela 1989). Buj Incised identified at Altar

de Sacrificios (Adams 1971) and Piedras Negras (Muñoz 2006) appear to be the same.

San Clemente Gouged-incised: San Clemente Variety

Established: Smith and Gifford (1966)

Group: Aguila

Ware: Petén Gloss

Ceramic Complex: Manik

Ceramic Sphere: Tzakol

Illustrations: Fig. 23.22; 24.11; 25.10, 25.15; 26.6; 38.35, 38.60; 56.10. See TR. 25A: fig. 20*a*–*b*; 25*b*–*e,g*; 33*c*; 134*a*; 135*j,m*.

Principal identifying attributes: Surface finish and color same as Aguila Orange with the addition of post-slip gouge incising.

Color: Ranges from light red (2.5YR 6/8) through reddish yellow (5YR 6/8) to strong brown (7.5YR 5/8). Mottling to black not uncommon.

Comments: In all characteristics except color, San Clemente Gouged-incised is identical to Urita Gouged-incised. Because there are some whole vessels that are almost entirely orange, it seems that the type was intentional.

Temporal Distribution: Present throughout the Manik Complex in small quantities.

Intersite Comparisons: Becan (Ball 1977) and Uaxactun (Smith and Gifford 1966).

BALANZA CERAMIC GROUP

Balanza Black: Balanza Variety

Established: Smith and Gifford (1966)

Group: Balanza

Ware: Petén Gloss

Ceramic Complex: Manik

Ceramic Sphere: Tzakol

Illustrations: Fig. 19.19, 19.29–31, 19.37, 19.43–45; 20.30; 21.2, 21.23–25, 21.27, 21.29–31; 28.2–10, 28.27–32; 29.1–2, 29.4–5, 29.11, 29.20, 29.22; 37.40, 37.46, 37.47; 38.5–8, 38.11, 38.14–17, 38.21–25, 38.28–31, 38.34, 38.38–47, 38.49, 38.53–59, 38.61–70. See TR. 25A: fig. 25*j*; 27*a*2–4; 29*k–n*; 31*b–h*; 32*a*1; 33*b*4, *d*2; 35*a*4; 36*a*2,*a*4,*a*10; 37*a*2, *b*1–2; 100*f*; 101*b*1,3,*c*1,*d*; 102*a*1–3,*b–c*,*d*1–2,*e*,*f*1–2; 102*a*17; 104*a*1–2, *b*1–3; 105*a–g*;106*a*1–3; 107*a*1–11,*c*; 108*a–b*; 109*b*; 114*d*1–2; 123*e*,*g*; 124*d–f*,*j–k*; 127*h*1; 130*f–j*,*l–o*; 134*j*; 138*o*; 154*a*; 134*h*.

Principal identifying attributes: Glossy, hard black slip that fireclouds to red or brown on various bowl forms.

Paste: Standard-carbonate Paste predominates, although the dark paste in many sherds makes it difficult to identify gray carbonate particles. Non-carbonate Paste is used much less frequently than in other types, particularly in Manik 2 and 3A samples of Balanza.

Firing: The black slip color is a result of reduction firing that usually leaves only a thin penetration below the surface, except in the one-third of examples that show darkened cores.

Slip: Thin, hard, and adheres well.

Polish: Usually highly polished, some medium polish. Degree of polish relates to thickness of walls, with thinner vessels being more highly polished.

Color: Uneven; many sherds show spots in which the black fades to red (2.5YR 5/6) or brown (10YR 4/2).

Shapes: Tripod dishes 26%; outflaring to slightly outcurving-side bowls or dishes 25%; incurving to slightly round-side bowls 17%; cylindrical vessels 14%; narrow-mouth jars 6%; large recurving-side bowls 5%; basal-flange bowls 4%; scutate lids 3%; z-angle bowls 2%; other shapes less than 1%.

Special Shape: Cache cylinders are found only in caches with lids. These vessels have the same surface color as Balanza Black: Balanza Variety but they are less well finished and restricted to poorly made cylinders. Originally they were identified as a separate variety from Balanza Black (TR. 25A), however naming a variety on the basis of a vessel shape violates type: variety nomenclature (see Gifford 1976). Completely dark cores are common on this shape and smudging on the interior of many vessels suggests that burning may have been involved in their use. The majority of the vessels show a lack of care in shaping and finishing. It is this carelessness, particularly in firing to a good black surface, which makes these vessels worth noting. The shape is a specific designation for sorting purposes at Tikal, however, as noted above for Balanza Black, the type is found throughout the Maya Lowlands, and better made cylinders are common as well. There are examples of tripod cylinders with coffee bean appliqué around the base, as well as other shapes with appliqué and modeling that are not separated from the Balanza Variety of Balanza Black. (See TR. 25A: fig. 134*g*,*h*. Note: The example illustrated in Fig. 134g is misidentified as Pita Incised.)

Temporal distribution: Present throughout the Manik Complex. Many sherds are indistinguishable from examples of Late/Terminal Preclassic and Late Classic black types.

Comments: The few examples of Maroma Impressed identified at Uaxactun (Smith and Gifford 1966) and listed in Culbert (TR. 25A) are now included in Balanza Black because the sample was too small to completely describe a separate type.

Intersite Comparisons: Identified as Balanza Variety or an Unspecified Variety at Altar de Sacrificios (Adams 1971); Barton Ramie (Gifford 1976); Becan (Ball 1977); Blue Creek (Kosakowsky and Lohse 2003); Calakmul (Dominguez Carrasco 1994); Chan (Kosakowsky 2012); Chan Chich (Valdez 1998, Valdez and Houk 2000); Colha (Valdez 1987:173); Edzná (Forsyth 1983); El Mirador (Forsyth 1989); El Perú/Waka' (Eppich 2011); El Pozito (Eppich 2000); Holmul (Callaghan 2008, 2016d); K'axob (Lopez Varela 2004); La Milpa (Sagebiel 2005); Nohmul (Kosakowsky and Pring 2001); the

Petexbatun (Foias and Bishop 2013); Piedras Negras (Muñoz 2006); Seibal (Sabloff 1975); Uaxactun (Smith and Gifford 1966); Yaxchilan (Lopez Varela 1989).

Lucha Incised: Lucha Variety

Established: Smith and Gifford (1966)

Group: Balanza

Ware: Petén Gloss

Ceramic Complex: Manik

Ceramic Sphere: Tzakol

Illustration: Fig. 22.1–5, 22.7–11, 22.13–23, 22.25–32; 23.1, 23.3–14, 23.16–20; 24.2–5, 24.12–19, 24.24–26; 25.1, 25.11–12, 25.16; 26.1–3, 26.5, 26.7–8, 26.12, 26.14–15; 27.1–7, 27.10–11, 27.18–20, 27.22; 29.24, 29.26; 37.24, 37.31–32, 37.37–38, 37.42, 37.44; 38.10, 38.13, 38.26, 38.33, 38.48. See TR. 25A: fig. 38*b*; 125*b–c*; 134*b*; 135*a,c–f,h,n*.

Principal identifying attributes: Same as Balanza Black with the addition of pre-slip fine line incising in geometric designs.

Paste: Standard-carbonate Paste predominates, followed by Non-carbonate Paste and Gray-carbonate Paste. The paste frequencies of Lucha Incised differ from those of Balanza Black in the considerably greater frequency of Non-carbonate Paste in Lucha Incised.

Firing: As in Balanza Black.

Slip: Thin, adheres well.

Polish: Medium to high.

Color: Black color somewhat better controlled than in Balanza Black, but mottling to red-brown and red still common.

Surface and finish and decoration: Incising was usually done after the slip was applied. The incisions cover a wide range of variation in width and depth. They were usually done with care to keep lines straight and make meetings between lines accurate, but there are some examples of very sloppy execution.

Designs: Usually simple geometric designs.

Shapes: Slightly incurving to round-side bowls or dishes 40%; basal-flange bowls 21%; cylindrical vessels 11%; apron covers 9%; scutate covers 8%; tripod dishes 6%; outflaring to slightly outcurving-side bowls or dishes 5%.

Temporal distribution: Occurs throughout the Manik Complex.

Intersite Comparisons: Identified as Lucha Variety or an Unspecified Variety at Altar de Sacrificios (Adams 1971); Barton Ramie (Gifford 1976); Becan (Ball 1977); Blue Creek (Kosakowsky and Lohse 2003); Calakmul (Dominguez Carrasco 1994); Chan (Kosakowsky 2012); Chan Chich (Valdez 1998; Valdez and Houk 2000); Colha (Valdez 1987); El Mirador (Forsyth 1989); El Perú/Waka' (Eppich 2011); El Pozito (Eppich 2000); Holmul (Callaghan 2008, 2016d); La Milpa (Sagebiel 2005); Nohmul (Kosakowsky and Pring 2001); the Petexbatun (Foias and Bishop 2013); Piedras Negras (Muñoz 2006); Seibal (Sabloff 1975); Uaxactun (Smith and Gifford 1966).

Urita Gouged-incised: Urita Variety

Established: Smith and Gifford (1966)

Group: Balanza

Ware: Petén Gloss

Ceramic Complex: Manik

Ceramic Sphere: Tzakol

Illustrations: Fig. 23.23–26; 24.1,6–10, 24.20–23; 25.2–9, 25.13–14, 25.17; 26.4, 26.9–11, 26.13, 26.16–17; 27.9, 27.12–17, 27.21; 37.25, 37.33, 37.35–36, 37.39, 37.41, 37.43, 37.45; 38.12, 38.27. See TR. 25A: fig. 30*a*; 31*a*; 37*b*5; 102*b*; 108*d*; 124*a–b*; 125*a*; 134*c,e–f*; 135*g,i,k–l*; 153*f*3.

Principal identifying attributes: Same as Balanza Black with the addition of post-slip gouge-incising.

Paste: Standard-carbonate Paste predominates, followed by Non-carbonate Paste and Gray-carbonate Paste. Paste frequencies differ considerably from Balanza Black in the higher frequency of Non-carbonate Paste in Urita Gouged-incised. Generally, the paste and temper particles are finer than in Balanza Black or Lucha Incised.

Firing: As in Balanza Black.

Slip: Thin, adheres well.

Polish: Usually high.

Color: Usually mottled to orange, red or brown, same as Balanza Black.

Surface and finish and decoration: Gouging contrasts with incising by having lines that are deeper and broader than incised lines. In fact, however, most vessels demonstrate lines of a variety of depths and widths within the same design so the distinction between gouging and incising is not a simple one of mutually exclusive alternatives. The surface was modified with unusually complex designs after the slip was applied.

Shapes: Apron cover 52%; cylindrical tripods 24%; basal-flange bowls 11%; slightly incurving to round-side bowls 5%; outflaring to slightly outcurving-side bowls or dishes 5%; scutate lids 2%.

Temporal distribution: Occurs throughout the Manik Complex, but there is weak evidence that the type is uncommon in Manik 1 and 2 and increases thereafter.

Comments: Urita Gouged-incised differs from both Balanza Black and Lucha Incised in features such as paste, designs, and vessel shapes.

Intersite Comparisons: Altar de Sacrificios (Adams 1971); Colha (Valdez 1987); Holmul (Callaghan 2008, 2016d); the Petexbatun (Foias and Bishop 2013); Piedras Negras (Muñoz 2006); Seibal (Sabloff 1975); Uaxactun (Smith and Gifford 1966).

Delirio Plano-relief: Delirio Variety

Established: Smith and Gifford (1966)

Group: Balanza

Ware: Petén Gloss

Ceramic Complex: Manik

Ceramic Sphere: Tzakol

Illustrations: Fig. 27.8. See TR. 25A: fig. 25*f.*

Principal identifying attributes: Same as Balanza Black with the addition of post-slip, pre-firing, low relief and gouge-incised decoration.

Identifying Characteristics and Sorting Problems: This is a low-frequency type in the Tikal collections. Based on the small sample available, it closely resembles Urita Gouged-incised except for the following features.

Surface and finish and decoration: A thin layer of clay was removed from the surface of the vessel to leave major design areas in low relief. The background from which clay was removed is left with a striated appearance. Major designs are then usually executed in the gouged-incised technique of Urita Gouged-incised.

Shapes: Only slightly incurving to round-side bowls were represented in the sample.

Intersite Comparisons: Becan (Ball 1977); Uaxactun (Smith and Gifford 1966). May be similar to examples of San Roman Plano-relief at Altar de Sacrificios (Adams 1971).

Paradero Fluted: Paradero Variety

Established: Smith and Gifford (1966)

Group: Balanza

Ware: Petén Gloss

Ceramic Complex: Manik 3B

Ceramic Sphere: Tzakol

Illustrations: Fig. 29.25, 29.27. See TR. 25A: fig. 124*i*; 131*i*.

Principal identifying attributes: Slip color and finish the same as Balanza Black with the addition of pre-slip vertical fluting on vessel exteriors.

Paste: All of the finer pastes represented. There is a tendency to fine texture and temper.

Firing: Dark cores rare.

Slip: Thin, adheres well.

Polish: Highly polished.

Color: Firing usually gives good black, although some examples have areas that range to brown or orange.

Surface and finish and decoration: Secondary decoration on exterior of vessels that is almost always pre-slip, pre-polish fluting. There is a range from very broad flutes with little raised areas to what might be called deep grooves.

Shapes: Sample too small for quantitative analysis, but slightly incurving to round-side dishes, cylindrical tripods, apron covers, outflaring to slightly out-curving-side bowls or dishes, and small jars occur.

Temporal distribution: Possibly only in Manik 3B, but the sample is too small to make temporal conclusions meaningful.

Comments: In its surface color and finish, Paradero Fluted is more like Lucha Incised and Urita Gouged-incised than like Balanza Black.

Intersite Comparisons: Altar de Sacrificios (Adams 1971); Becan (Ball 1977); Blue Creek (Kosakowsky and Lohse 2003); Calakmul (Dominguez Carrasco 1994); El Mirador (Forsyth 1989); El Pozito (Eppich 2000); La Milpa (Sagebiel 2005); Uaxactun (Smith and Gifford 1966). May be the same as the Oakburn Variety at Barton Ramie (Gifford 1976) and Colha (Valdez 1987).

Positas Modeled: Positas Variety

Established: Smith and Gifford (1966)

Group: Balanza

Ware: Petén Gloss

Ceramic Complex: Manik 3A–B

Ceramic Sphere: Tzakol

Illustrations: Fig. 38.18, 38.36, 38.50–51, 38.71. See TR. 25A: fig. 20*c*; 25*a*; 26*b–c*; 30*b*; 135*b*.

Principal identifying attributes: Surface finish and color same as Balanza Black with modeled heads on vessel covers.

Comments: Occurs as only a few intact examples in large burials. Mostly, the examples consist of modeled heads on apron covers used with cylindrical tripod vessels. There is one modeled head on a scutate cover for a basal-flange bowl and one effigy vessel both in Bu. 22. The type seems more closely related to Urita Gouged-incised than to other types of the Balanza Group.

Temporal Distribution: Small sample size suggests Manik 3A to 3B.

Intersite Comparisons: Blue Creek (Kosakowsky and Lohse 2003); Holmul (Callaghan 2008, 2016d); La Milpa (Sagebiel 2005); Uaxactun (Smith and Gifford 1966).

PUCTE CERAMIC GROUP

Pucte Brown: Pucte Variety

Established: Smith and Gifford (1966)

Group: Pucte

Ware: Petén Gloss

Ceramic Complex: Manik

Ceramic Sphere: Tzakol

Illustrations: Fig. 19.4, 19.18, 19.23; 20.9, 20.33; 21.17, 21.28. See TR. 25A: fig. 21*k*, 37*c*.

Principal identifying attributes: Glossy brown slip that fireclouds to reddish brown.

Identifying characteristics and sorting problems: All features are the same as Balanza Black except the following:

Color: Reddish brown (5YR 4/4) through brown (7.5YR 5/4, 5/6) to yellowish brown (l0YR 4/4, 5/4). Color on most sherds is blotchy and variable.

Shapes: The sample was too small to permit quantitative treatment, but it is clear that the majority of vessels were narrow-mouth jars with occasional examples of large recurving-side bowls, z-angle bowls, and tripod dishes.

Comments: In many cases, the brown surface color seems to be an unintentional firing variant of Balanza Black. Some sherds, however, are almost entirely brown and suggest that the color was intentional. There are two examples of incised Pucte Brown covers (a scutate and an apron cover), but given the small sample a separate incised type was not defined.

Intersite Comparisons: Altar de Sacrificios (Adams 1971); Barton Ramie (Gifford 1976); Becan (Ball 1977); Calakmul (Dominguez Carrasco 1994); Chan (Kosakowsky 2012); Colha (Valdez 1987); El Pozito (Eppich 2000); La Milpa (Sagebiel 2005); Uaxactun (Smith and Gifford 1966).

FAMA CERAMIC GROUP

Fama Buff: Fama Variety

Established: Smith and Gifford (1966)

Group: Fama Buff

Ware: Petén Gloss

Ceramic Complex: Manik

Ceramic Sphere: Tzakol

Illustrations: See TR. 25A: fig. 38*d*; 137*f*.

Principal identifying attributes: Light brown to buff slip that fireclouds to reddish yellow.

Identifying characteristics and sorting problems: Slip color of the monochrome types occasionally ranges on some parts of the vessels to reddish-yellow (7.5YR 6/6, 7/6), yellowish-brown (10YR 5/4, 5/6), light yellowish brown (10YR 6/4), and brownish yellow (10YR 6/6, 6/8). Fama Buff may not be an actual type, but one that occurred as an intended variation of monochrome orange and brown. The same may be true at Uaxactun, because the only vessel illustrated that is attributed to this type (Smith and Gifford 1966:158; Smith 1955, vol. 2: fig. 23*b*4) is referred to in text (Smith 1955, vol. 1:154) as variegated.

Intersite Comparisons: Uaxactun (Smith and Gifford 1966).

DOS ARROYOS CERAMIC GROUP

Dos Arroyos Orange Polychrome: Dos Arroyos Variety

Established: Smith and Gifford (1966)

Group: Dos Arroyos

Ware: Petén Gloss

Ceramic Complex: Manik

Ceramic Sphere: Tzakol

Illustrations: Fig. 20.43; 28.1, 28.33–48; 29.13–15, 29.18–19; 30.1–26; 31.1–2, 31.6–15, 31.18; 32.1–7, 32.9, 32.11, 32.15–18, 32.20–22; 33.1–11, 33.15–16, 33.18–22; 34.1–4, 34.9–13, 34.17, 34.19–22, 34.26–27, 34.29; 35.1–7, 35.10–12, 35.16–17, 35.19–21, 35.23–26; 36.3, 36.5, 36.7, 36.10–14, 36.16–17; 37.2, 37.4, 37.6–7, 37.9, 37.14, 37.16–17, 37.22; 57.10–11. See TR. 25A: fig. 22*a–c*; 23*a*; 28*b*2; 33*a*; 34*f*; 36*a*1; 37*a*; 123*c*; 129*c*; 133*a*1–2; 136*d,g–h,k–m*; 143*c*; 149*a*; 154*c*.

Principal identifying attributes: Red and black designs, usually geometric or naturalistic, on a glossy orange slip, predominantly on bowl forms.

Paste: Non-carbonate Paste predominates by a considerable margin. Gray-carbonate Paste and Standard-carbonate Paste also occur.

Firing: Dark cores and fireclouding rare.

Polish: Polish and care of application may vary considerably, even on different surfaces of the same vessel.

Color: There is considerable variation in the color of the orange background. Generally, the color is a good clear orange (reddish yellow 5YR 6/8; 7.5YR 6/8; yellowish red 5YR 5/8; a number of examples exceed /8 in chroma); the range of color includes some examples of reddish tones (light red 2.5YR 6/8; red 2.5YR 5/8). Red is applied over the orange base and often has a streaky appearance. Two coats of red slip are apparent on some examples. Color of the red is quite well controlled (red 10R 4/8, 5/8; 7.5YR 4/8). Black slip is also applied over the background color and is usually faded, with the hue of the background color showing through. An intentional gray color (10YR 6/1) was used that contrasts clearly with the faded sections of black.

Surface and finish and decoration: Simple combinations of red and black-on-orange are by far the most common. There are no examples of intentional use of multiple shades of red or orange. The use of gray is rare. There are infrequent examples with modeling and stucco as additional decoration.

Shapes: Outflaring to slightly outcurving-side sherds 56% (probably most were basal-flange bowls but broken above the flange); slightly incurving to round-side bowls and dishes 19%; narrow-mouth jars 1%.

Temporal Distribution: Occurs throughout the Manik Complex.

Intersite Comparisons: Identified as both Dos Arroyos Variety or an Unspecified Variety at Altar de Sacrificios (Adams 1971); Barton Ramie (Gifford 1976); Becan (Ball 1977); Blue Creek (Kosakowsky and Lohse 2003); Calakmul (Dominguez Carrasco 1994); Chan (Kosakowsky 20120); Chan Chich (Valdez 1998; Valdez and Houk 2000); Col-

ha (Valdez 1987); Edzná (Forsyth 1983); El Mirador (Forsyth 1989); El Perú/Waka' (Eppich 2011); El Pozito (Eppich 2000); Holmul (Callaghan 2008, 2016d); La Milpa (Sagebiel 2005); Nakbe (Forsyth 1993); Nohmul (Kosakowsky and Pring 2001); the Petexbatun (Foias and Bishop 2013); Piedras Negras (Muñoz 2006); Uaxactun (Smith and Gifford 1966); Yaxchilan (Lopez Varela 1989). Actuncan Orange Polychrome is undifferentiated from Dos Arroyos Orange Polychrome at Seibal (Sabloff 1975).

Cochol Orange Polychrome: Cochol Variety

Established: TR. 25A (Culbert 1993)

Group: Dos Arroyos

Ware: Petén Gloss

Ceramic Complex: Manik

Ceramic Sphere: Tzakol

Illustrations: Fig. 35.33–37, 35.39–43.

Principal identifying attributes: Red and black curvilinear designs on an orange to yellow brown surface that appears to be made on a local paste different from Dos Arroyos Orange Polychrome.

Paste: Paste seems to be local with Non-carbonate Paste predominating.

Firing: Dark cores very rare.

Polish: Usually low.

Color: Base colors on the exterior cover a range of orange and brown shades that contrast with the range of interior color. Most common on the exterior are reddish yellow (7.5YR 6/6, 6/8, 7/6; 5YR 6/6, 6/8) followed by strong brown (7.5YR 5/6) and yellowish red (5YR 5/6). A few examples are very pale brown (10YR 7/4). Interior color is a clear orange (light red 2.5YR 6/8; reddish yellow 5YR 7/8, 6/8; 7.5YR 7/6). The red lip band is streaky and varies over red shades (10R 4/6, 4/8; 2.5YR 5/8, 4/8). Designs on the exterior are executed in black that tends to allow base color to show through.

Surface and finish and decoration: Orange on the interior, with designs in black on reddish yellow on the exterior. Red lip band(s) are on both the exterior and the interior. Complex curvilinear designs done in fairly broad lines.

Shapes: Slightly incurving to round-side bowl. Other shapes are very rare.

Temporal Distribution: Occurs throughout Manik.

Comments: The execution of designs in only two colors, the restriction of motifs to complex curvilinear elements, and the fact that the exterior base color differs in range from the orange of other polychromes seem sufficient to designate this a separate type. The paste, however, indicates that the type is of local origin.

Intersite Comparisons: None noted.

San Blas Red-on-orange: San Blas Variety

Established: Smith and Gifford (1966)

Group: Dos Arroyos

Ware: Petén Gloss

Ceramic Complex: Manik

Ceramic Sphere: Tzakol

Illustrations: Fig. 35.9, 35.13, 35.18.

Principal identifying attributes: Glossy orange slipped surfaces with simple red lips and bands.

Paste: Non-carbonate Paste greatly predominates with a few examples of Standard-carbonate Paste.

Firing: Dark cores rare.

Polish: Medium.

Color: The background orange color tends to be variable from sherd to sherd and shows some tendency to streakiness. Color is yellowish red (5YR 5/8, 5/6) to reddish yellow (7.5YR 6/8; 5YR 6/8). The overpainted red is usually evenly applied, although in places it is thin enough to let the underlying base color show through. Color is consistently red (10R 4/8; 2.5YR 4/8).

Surface and finish and decoration: All examples are simple banded designs, usually a red band around the lip.

Shapes: Almost entirely slightly incurving to round-side bowls with a few examples of outflaring to slightly outcurving-side vessels.

Temporal Distribution: Occurs throughout Manik.

Intersite Comparisons: Becan (Ball 1977); El Mirador (Forsyth 1989); El Perú/Waka' (Eppich 2011); El Pozito (Eppich 2000); La Milpa (Sagebiel 2005); Uaxactun (Smith and Gifford 1966).

Caldero Buff Polychrome: Caldero Variety

Established: Smith and Gifford (1966)

Group: Dos Arroyos

Ware: Petén Gloss

Ceramic Complex: Manik

Ceramic Sphere: Tzakol

Illustrations: Fig. 31.3–5, 31.16–17; 32.8, 32.12–14, 32.19; 33.12–14, 33.17; 34.5–8, 34.14–16, 34.18, 34.23–25, 34.28; 35.15, 35.29, 35.38; 36.6, 36.9; 37.8, 37.19. See TR. 25A: fig. 23*b*; 24*a–c*; 26*a*; 28*c*; 32*e*, 37*b*3–4; 123*a–c*; 149*a*.

Principal identifying attributes: Red and black painted designs on polished buff surfaces.

Indentifying characteristics and sorting problems: This type is identical to Dos Arroyos Orange Polychrome in all features except background color. In Caldero Buff Polychrome, the background varies widely and includes very pale brown (10YR 8/3, 7/3, 7/4), light yellowish brown (10YR 6/4), reddish yellow (7.5YR 6/6, 7/6), and pink (7.5YR 7/4). In some cases the background seems to be simply the smoothed clay of the vessel. In others, it is a thin slip or wash. The buff is used both as general background and, by reserve space technique, as an integral part of design. On most vessels of Caldero Buff Polychrome, orange is still used as the base color on either the interior or exterior. The presence of even a small area of buff was used as a criterion for classification as Caldero Buff Polychrome.

Intersite Comparisons: Altar de Sacrificios (Adams 1971); Barton Ramie (Gifford 1976); Edzná (Forsyth 1983); El Pozito (Eppich 2000); El Perú/Waka' (Eppich 2011); Holmul (Callaghan 2008, 2016d); Uaxactun (Smith and Gifford 1966).

San Bartolo Red-on-buff: San Bartolo Variety

Established: Smith and Gifford (1966)

Group: Dos Arroyos

Ware: Petén Gloss

Ceramic Complex: Manik

Ceramic Sphere: Tzakol

Illustrations: Fig. 19.28; 35.22; 37.27. See TR. 25A: fig. 33*d*1.

Principal identifying attributes: Buff surfaces similar to Caldero Buff Polychrome with the addition of simple red lip bands.

Paste: Mostly Non-carbonate Paste; some Standard-carbonate and Gray-carbonate. The paste color is always buff to tan with no examples of reddish pastes. This is probably due to the firing conditions necessary to produce the buff surface color.

Firing: Dark cores extremely rare.

Slip: The red is a thin slip that adheres well; the buff may be either the smoothed natural clay surface or a thin wash.

Polish: Medium polish on red surfaces; the buff has a matte finish.

Color: The red is a true red (10R 4/8 to 2.5YR 5/8). The buff ranges from light brown (7.5YR 6/4) to reddish yellow (7.5YR 6/6).

Surface and finish and decoration: The only designs noted are simple bands of red, usually around the lips of vessels.

Shapes: Mostly slightly incurving to round-side bowls with some scutate lids.

Temporal distribution: Sample too small to be certain.

Intersite Comparisons: Uaxactun (Smith and Gifford 1966).

Yaloche Cream Polychrome: Yaloche Variety

Established: Smith and Gifford (1966)

Group: Dos Arroyos

Ware: Petén Gloss

Ceramic Complex: Manik

Ceramic Sphere: Tzakol

Illustrations: Fig. 31.19; 32.10; 33.1; 35.27–28, 35.30–32; 36.1, 36.4, 36.8, 36.15, 36.18; 37.1–3, 37.5, 37.10–13, 37.15, 37.18, 37.20, 37.34.

Principal identifying attributes: Glossy cream base slip decorated with red and black geometric designs.

Identifying characteristics and sorting problems: There was a gradual gradation in background color between light brown and pure white that made a realistic distinction between Caldero Buff Polychrome and Yaloche Cream Polychrome difficult. Consequently, the term Yaloche Cream Polychrome is arbitrarily assigned to examples in which the background color is classified as white on the Munsell scale (10YR 8/1, 8/2). So defined, the type is rare and seems to be identical to Caldero Buff Polychrome except for background color. There is one example of modeling as a secondary decoration that includes gadrooning to simulate a squash.

Temporal distribution: Sample too small to be certain.

Intersite Comparisons: Barton Ramie (Gifford 1976); Becan (Ball 1977); Blue Creek (Kosakowsky and Lohse 2003); Calakmul (Dominguez Carrasco 1994); El Pozito (Eppich 2000); La Milpa (Sagebiel 2005); Uaxactun (Smith and Gifford 1966).

MOC CERAMIC GROUP

Moc Orange Polychrome: Moc Variety

Established: TR. 25A (Culbert 1993)

Group: Moc

Ware: Petén Gloss

Ceramic Complex: Manik

Ceramic Sphere: Tzakol

Illustrations: Fig. 29.16–17, 29.21. See TR. 25A: fig. 18*a*.

Principal identifying attributes: Black and red decoration on a bright orange slip, with a cream to pink underslip.

Identifying characteristics and sorting problems: Because Moc Orange Polychrome has a paste that differs from local pastes, it is described here.

Paste color: Usually reddish (red 2.5YR 5/8); a few examples are brown (strong brown 7.5YR 5/6).

Texture: fine.

Inclusions: Medium amounts of small to medium particles that include whitish calcite, occasional hematite and possible quartz. A few examples do not contain calcite.

Firing: Dark cores seem to be common (about 40% in a small sample).

Slip: A cream to pinkish underslip was applied before painting.

Polish: Highly polished.

Surface and finish and decoration: The background color is a clear bright orange (reddish yellow 5YR 6/8; yellowish red 5YR 5/8). Red is a consistent color (l0R 4/6, 4/8; 2.5YR 4/8) except where it is applied thinly and the base color shows through. Black paint is generally thin, showing base color underneath. Only red, orange, and black used; all incorporated as a part of the designs.

Shapes: Mostly basal-flange bowls; some slightly incurving to round-side bowls.

Comments: Moc Orange Polychrome differs consistently from other polychromes in almost all characteristics. The best identifying criteria are the paste, the brightness of colors (probably due to the use of an underslip), and the unusual shape features of the basal-flange bowls, distinguished from other basal-flange bowls by beveled or everted lip-rim, thin sides, and exaggerated flange. Beveled or everted rims and wider flanges are more common on Actuncan Orange Polychrome (Altar de Sacrificios [Adams 1971]; Barton Ramie [Gifford 1976]; Blue Creek [Kosakowsky and Lohse 2003]; Holmul [Callaghan 2008, 2016d]; Seibal [Sabloff 1975]). Moc Orange Polychrome is the "Polychrome A" from Mounds A and B at Kaminaljuyu discussed by Kidder, Jennings, and Shook (1946:178–179, 236–237) who correctly identified it as different from their single "Polychrome B" that is of Petén derivation. Moc Orange Polychrome is certainly imported to Tikal, probably from some still unidentified location in the southeastern Petén.

Temporal distribution: Sample too small to be certain.

Intersite Comparisons: None noted though due to its unusual paste and similarity to examples from highland Guatemala this is likely an import.

JAPON CERAMIC GROUP

Japon Resist: Japon Variety

Established: Smith and Gifford (1966)

Group: Japon

Ware: Petén Gloss

Ceramic Complex: Manik 3B

Ceramic Sphere: Tzakol

Illustrations: See TR. 25A: fig. 21*a*, 27*a*, 137*a–b*.

Principal identifying attributes: Black resist designs on a reddish brown to buff slip.

Identifying characteristics and sorting problems: The combination of the resist techniques and the use of multiple small dots of light color are completely distinctive.

Comments: The fact that all the examples were from special deposits made them inaccessible for observations of the paste and detailed color readings that are usually parts of type descriptions. The type is so rare and so unusual that it seems certain that it must have been imported from an unknown source.

Slip: A lighter-colored base slip was applied, then covered with the resist agent and a second darker slip applied that appears in areas not protected by the resist agent.

Color: Color of the original slip seems to have been variable because observations suggest a range from buff through orange to golden brown. Elsewhere the most common base color is either a monochrome red (2.5YR4/8) or a monochrome yellowish brown (10YR 6/3, 7/6) over which a resist agent is applied and black designs result. The second slip is always black.

Surface and finish and decoration: The resist technique was far better controlled than in the Preclassic resist types and could be used for quite complex designs. Most characteristic was the use of very small light dots that outlined other designs or filled areas between designs.

Shapes: In Bu. 10 and 22, tripod cylinders with apron covers were found. In PD. 74, two examples of slightly incurving to round-side bowls occurred. The examples from Uaxactun (Smith 1955) were also cylindrical tripods.

Temporal distribution: All examples are Manik 3B.

Intersite Comparisons: Holmul (Callaghan 2008, 2016d) and Uaxactun (Smith and Gifford 1966). Noted as an Unspecified Variety at Altar de Sacrificios (Adams 1971).

UAXACTUN TYPES NOT IDENTIFIED AT TIKAL

Dos Hermanos Red: Dos Hermanos Variety

Comments: From the descriptions and illustrations listed by Smith and Gifford (1966) in reference to Smith's Uaxactun material (1955), there does not seem to be any striking characteristic that distinguishes this type aside from slip color. Because red-orange is within the color range of Aguila Orange at Tikal, the name Dos Hermanos Red is not used in reference to Tikal

Balanza Black: Pantan Variety

Comments: At Uaxactun (Smith and Gifford 1966), this is a shape-defined variety consisting of everted-rim, flaring-side tripod dishes. This shape occurs frequently in black slip at Tikal, but because shape varieties are not a useful means of recording variation, the variety designation is not used in this report.

Thin Black Ware (Discordia Black and Catzim Incised)

Comments: This ware, defined by Smith (1955) at Uaxactun, is not used at Tikal. The distinguishing criterion for the ware and its associated types seems to be thin walls, although the "cream pitcher" shape would seem, from the Smith and Gifford (1966) key to Uaxactun types, to be an auxiliary criterion. Although identical vessels occur in the Tikal collections, the thin-walled samples are simply at one extreme of wall thickness of types of the Balanza group and do not differ in other aspects. Consequently, separation of a specific ware to cover the otherwise identical extremes of wall thickness seems to be unnecessary.

Actuncan Orange Polychrome: Actuncan Variety

Comments: The primary identifying characteristic of this type as used at Uaxactun seems to be the appearance of rows of dots in association with geometric motifs. This motif with dots appears in a number of examples in the Tikal collections. It occurs more frequently, however, on buff polychrome than on orange polychrome and does not associate with other features, such as color and shape, which would help to distinguish it from the general range of polychromes. To preserve the designation Actuncan Orange Polychrome would elevate one specific motif out of a large number of motifs to typological status. Consequently, the term "Actuncan Orange Polychrome" will not be used and the examples will be considered as Dos Arroyos Orange Polychrome or Caldero Buff Polychrome. However, the beveled lip and wider flanges on many examples of Actuncan Orange Polychrome are more similar in form to Moc Orange Polychrome as noted above.

Manik Types: Chronological Change

The stability of ceramic types throughout the period of the Manik Complex is remarkable. Analyses of stratigraphic columns and seriation arrangements failed to produce meaningful patterns and, had chronology been dependent on types and varieties alone, it would have been impossible to identify facets within the complex. Unfortunately, the original data with complete type frequencies for the Manik Complex are missing and only the general summary presented below exists in the Tikal files.

Given a known chronological ordering of samples, there are a few changes in frequency that might have temporal significance. One is an increase in the frequency of Triunfo Striated between Manik 2 and Manik 3. The median frequency of Triunfo Striated in all quantified Manik 2 samples is 10% as compared to a median of 25% for Manik 3 samples. Samples with 21% to 42% Triunfo Striated are common in Manik 3, while the maximum frequency in a Manik 2 sample is 20%. Maax Red-striated is a second type with possible chronological significance. The type is always rare, but it appears most consistently and in highest frequencies in Manik 3 samples. The type certainly existed during Manik 2, but the only Manik 1 examples are a few dubious sherds from one lot.

Manik Types: Social Dimension

To analyze ceramic variability along a social axis, a sub-set of the samples was analyzed. The samples were divided into three sets based on the size of the architectural group from which they were obtained. This subset included six samples from small structure groups, ten samples from groups of intermediate size, and seven from civic-ceremonial groups. One additional sample obtained from a test pit at the bottom of the Madeira Reservoir was considered separately because it was both functionally and typologically specialized and had no associated structures.

Temporally, the sample from small structure groups was equally divided between Manik 2 and 3, with Manik 1 unrepresented. The intermediate structure group collections were almost all Manik 3, while the samples from the civic ceremonial groups contained material from all facets, with Manik 3 predominating slightly. Because most type frequencies did not vary significantly through time, the analysis of social variation should not be seriously affected by the temporal differences between the sample groups.

The results of the comparison show some differentiation in type frequencies between architectural groups, but the degree of variation is not pronounced. Two unslipped types, Quintal Unslipped and Triunfo Striated, are less common in samples from large architectural groups than in those from medium and small groups. Because these two types probably had a strictly utilitarian function, it is predictable that they would have been less used in the elite-ceremonial contexts represented by major architectural groups. In fact, it is surprising that the frequency differences are as slight as they are, because the social differences in the distribution of unslipped types are considerably more marked in the Late Classic. Aguila Orange: Aguila Variety shows a reverse distribution trend, being most common in samples from major architectural groups and less common in the other smaller architectural groups.

Maax Red-striated and the associated Mattered Variety of Aguila Orange increase in general frequency from small to larger size mound groups. Because these ceramics are composed almost completely of narrow-mouth jars, it may be either that the combination of form and type had a special function or that the Maax Red-striated jars were more highly valued than examples of the shape made from other types.

Perhaps as significant as this social variation between types is the lack of variation in the distributions of decorated types. Both polychrome types and Lucha Incised are uniformly distributed throughout the site, while Urita Gouged-incised is actually somewhat less common in larger groups than in smaller groups. These results, strikingly at variance with those for Late Classic decorated pottery, may suggest relatively equal access to this pottery by members of all social classes. Burial and cache pottery does, of course, demonstrate special features and reflect social status, but these collections will be discussed in a later section.

The ceramic samples from the test pit at the bottom of the Madeira Reservoir merit separate discussion because they depart radically from type frequencies of samples from other locations in a manner that relates to the use of the reservoir. A series of eight superimposed samples obtained from depths ranging from two to four meters below the modern surface of the reservoir bottom were quantitatively analyzed. In most typological characteristics these samples are fairly homogeneous. They are marked by unusually low frequencies of Triunfo Striated and high frequencies of the Matte-red Variety of Aguila Orange and Maax Red-striated. These frequencies may be explained in terms of the vessel shapes with which these types are usually associated. Triunfo Striated occurs almost entirely in wide-mouth jars, a shape usually far too large to be carried to a water source, while the other two types are associated with the smaller and more portable narrow-mouth jar shape. Maax Red-striated was absent from the lowest two levels in the Madeira Reservoir pit, a fact most likely explained by temporal variation of this probably late type. The type frequencies support the inference that the ceramics from the Madeira Reservoir represent a specialized collection associated with water procurement. [Note: Original quantitative data on type frequencies in different contexts is missing.]

Vessel Shapes of the Manik Complex

Introduction

Vessel shapes in the Manik Complex prove to be considerably variable, both temporally and socially (see Table 7.9). Shape analysis confirmed the division of the Manik Complex into three facets, first by a traditional seriation procedure that was later verified and refined by factor and discriminant analyses [Note: The original quantitative data for these analyses are missing.] The changes between facets are largely in vessel frequencies, although there are a few shapes that were not in production throughout the phase. Socially, also, vessel shapes tend to be unevenly distributed between contexts from groups of different sizes and presumably relate to differential patterns of activity. The Manik Complex is composed of 10 vessel shape classes and 24 shapes (see Table 7.9).

Manik Shape Descriptions

SHAPE CLASS 1: WIDE-MOUTH JARS

Wide-mouth Jar (with Tall Neck)

Illustrations: Fig. 18.1–55; 19.40–42, 19.47–48. See TR. 25A: fig. 32*b*1; 33*b*3,*d*3; 34*a*–*d*; 126*e*–*n*; 129*g*; 138*a*–*c,e,l,p*.

Identifying characteristics and sorting problems: The combination of unslipped pottery, large-neck diameter, and tall neck height is distinctive. The height of the neck is strikingly greater than that of Late Preclassic unslipped jars. After the Manik Complex, the shape continues essentially unchanged until the end of the Tikal sequence.

Base and Body: Probably rounded, but few whole vessels are present.

Neck-body juncture: Well defined. A ridge on the body interior frequently marks the point where neck and body have been joined.

Orientation of neck: Slight to medium outflare.

Neck: Ranges from nearly straight to medium outcurve.

Rim: Direct except for a few cases in which the lip is tilted outward in association with an exterior bolster.

Lip: Features that occur with frequency are an exterior bolster, flattening of the upper lip surface, and grooving of upper or interior lip surface. A few

TABLE 7.9
Shape Classes and Shapes of the Manik Complex

1. Wide-mouth Jars

Wide-mouth Jar (with Tall Neck)

2. Narrow-mouth Jars

Narrow-mouth Jar (with Medium to Tall Neck)

Very Short Neck Jar

4. Large Capacity Bowls

Large Recurving-side Bowl

5. Medium Diameter Bowls and Dishes

Z-angle Bowl

Basal-flange Bowl

Slightly Incurving to Round-side Bowl

Tripod Bowl

Outflaring to Slightly Outcurving-side Bowl or Dish

6. Small Diameter Bowls and Dishes

Slightly Incurving to Round-side Bowl

Outflaring to Slightly Outcurving-side Bowl or Dish

Tripod Bowl or Dish

7. Cylindrical Vessels

Cylinder

Tripod Cylinder

Pitcher

10. Specialized Burial and Cache Vessels and Covers

Cache Cylinder

Cylindrical Cache Vessel Cover

11. Miniature Vessels

Miniature Jar

Miniature Bowl or Cylinder

12. Covers

Scutate Cover

Apron Cover

Small Flat or Slightly Rounded Cover

13. Effigy Vessels

Effigy Jar

Two-part Effigy

examples show an indented "piecrust" effect. The aforementioned features occur in numerous combinations with simple, rounded lips rare.

Surface: Always unslipped. Neck is usually smoothed, but coarse temper leaves pits and drag marks. Bodies usually, perhaps always, striated with striations running nearly horizontal.

Types: Triunfo Striated and some Quintal Unslipped.

Diameter of lip: Range 12–42 cm; median 26 cm.

Height of neck: Range 4.5–13.0 cm; median 8.0 cm.

Diameter of lip/neck height ratio: Range 2.3–4.0; median 3.2.

Shape class: 1, wide-mouth jars.

Comments: Although the measurements for neck height show a distribution with three peaks, the lip diameter/neck height ratio gives a smooth curve suggesting that a single neck shape is represented, although there is considerable diversity in size.

SHAPE CLASS 2: NARROW-MOUTH JARS

Narrow-mouth Jar (with Medium to Tall Neck)

Illustration: Fig. 19.1–27, 19.32–39, 19.43–45; 24.14; 36.1–7. See TR. 25A: fig. 21*k*; 25*g*; 28*b*1; 32*a*2; 33*d*1; 36*a*10; 101*c*2,*e*; 102*f*2; 121*e*; 126*a,c,d,o–p*; 129*g*; 138*d,f,h–k,m,n*; 154*a–e*; 155*c*1–2.

Identifying characteristics and sorting problems: The neck diameter and height are the defining characteristics. There is some overlap with the tall-neck Late Classic narrow-mouth jars, but little with the short-neck narrow mouth of the Late Preclassic.

Base: Rounded, flat, concave or low ring base.

Body: From a sample of nine whole vessels from burials, the jar body seems usually to have had a slightly ovoid shape with the broadest point either at the mid-line or slightly above. There are some completely rounded bodies.

Neck-body juncture: Well defined and angular; may be right angle or somewhat greater than a right angle on the exterior resulting in an inward-sloping lower neck section.

Orientation of neck: Usually a slight outflare, though occasionally a slight inslope.

Neck: Straight to slightly outcurved.

Rim: Direct, slightly everted, or markedly everted.

Lip: Rounded to slightly pointed; a few flat lips.

Appendages: There are a few jars with spouts of a type formed with a strip of clay so that part of the interior of the spout is the body and neck of the jar. One or two examples of tiny lug handles occur.

Surface: The finish tends to be carelessly done. A single incised line below the lip on either interior or exterior is not uncommon.

Types: Aguila Orange: Aguila Variety 48%; Aguila Orange: Matte-red Variety 24%; Balanza Black 7%; Pucte Brown 2%; polychrome types 1%, and small quantities of Maax Red-striated.

Diameter of lip: Range 8–24 cm; median 16 cm.

Total Height: Range 14.7–36.8 cm; median 17.5 cm.

Height of Neck: Range 2.7–6.2 cm; a few examples have extremely high necks, as tall as 11 cm. median 4.2 cm; median 5.5 cm.

Diameter of lip/neck height ratio: Range 1.5–5.3; median 2.8.

Shape class: 2 narrow-mouth jars.

Comments: The burial vessels have the same general dimensions as sherds.

Very Short-neck Jar

Illustration: Fig. 19.29–31; 26.17; 29.25; 30.6. See TR. 25A: fig. 33*d*2.

Identifying characteristics and sorting problems: The rudimentary neck is very distinctive.

Base: Unknown.

Body: Probably globular.

Neck-body Juncture: Rounded.

Neck-rim: The neck consists of little more than an outcurved rim section.

Lip: Rounded.

Surface: Usually slipped on both interior and exterior; one example has unslipped interior.

Types: Mostly Balanza Black; rare examples of Aguila Orange and polychromes.

Diameter (Lip): Range 12–22 cm.

Height (Neck): Range 0.8–2.8 cm.

Diameter/height ratio: Range 6.4–9.5.

Shape class: 2 narrow-mouth jars.

SHAPE CLASS 4: LARGE CAPACITY BOWLS

Large Recurving-side Bowl

Illustration: Fig. 20.1–25. See TR. 25A: fig. 125*e*; 137*d–f.*

Identifying characteristics and sorting problems: No problems exist because all sherds have a distinct rounded recurved side.

Base: Possibly annular (no whole vessels in sample).

Orientation of side: Upper portion of wall is outflared to slightly outcurved.

Side: Straight to slight outcurve on upper vessel wall, rounded below.

Rim: Direct.

Lip: Beveled predominates; beveled with exterior

bolster, flattened exterior bolster alone, and rounded also occur.

Surface: Although some examples are well polished, rather careless slipping and low to medium polishing predominate. The exterior base is unslipped and unslipped areas on the lower part of the exterior wall are common.

Types: Aguila Orange (mostly matte-red) 86%; Balanza Black 5%; Quintal Unslipped 4%; other types rare.

Diameter: Range 22–60 cm; median 40 cm.

Height: No complete examples available.

Shape class: Probably 4, large-capacity bowls.

SHAPE CLASS 5: MEDIUM DIAMETER BOWLS AND DISHES

Z-angle Bowl

Illustration: Fig. 20.26–43; 21.32–51; 28.45; 30.25; 33.1; 34.20–21, 34.25, 34.27; 36.14, 36.16–17. See TR. 25A: fig. 114*b*2; 133*a*3; 143*c*.

Identifying characteristics and sorting problems: The shape is generally marked by the sharp z-angle. However, there are some examples that are rounded to the base.

Base: Usually, perhaps always, annular.

Base-wall juncture: The z-angle is formed by the continuation of the basal section beyond the point at which the wall is attached. The z-angle is differentiated from the basal flange by the fact that the z-angle is a continuation of the base without break in curvature while the basal flange stands out from both the base and the wall. The ridge made by the angle is sometimes faceted. The angle of juncture of the base and wall is marked by a slight groove on the interior of the vessel.

Side: Straight to slight outcurve above z-angle; slightly rounded below.

Orientation of side: Medium outflare.

Rim: Direct; a few examples show a slight inward rounding just at the lip.

Lip: Rounded, flattened, or beveled.

Surface: Well finished except that the exterior of the basal section is carelessly slipped or left unslipped.

Types: Aguila Orange 83%; polychromes 9%; Balanza Black 5%; other types less than 1%.

Diameter: Range 20–40 cm; median 26 cm.

Length of upper section: Range 4.4–6.2 cm.

Height: median 7.3 cm.

Diameter/Height ratio: median 3.8.

Shape class: 5, medium-diameter bowls and dishes.

Basal-flange Bowl

Illustration: Fig. 22.14, 22.18, 22.27; 23.1–2, 23.8, 23.16; 24.15–16, 24.18–20, 24.24; 28.1, 28.33–44, 28.46–48; 29.1–19, 29.21; 30.1–4, 30.6–17, 30.23–24, 30.26; 31.1–19; 32.1–4, 32.7–22; 33.2–22; 34.1–19, 34.22–24, 34.26, 34.28, 34.29; 36.8–10, 36.12, 36.15–16, 36.18. See TR. 25A: fig. 18*a*; 22; 23*b*; 24; 25*a*; 28*b*2,*c*; 29*a*; 32*b*2,*d*1,*e*; 34*e,f*; 36*a*1; 37*a*1,*b*3–4; 114*b*1; 123*a–c*; 129*c*; 133*a*1–2; 136*a,b,d*; 144*f*1; 149*a*.

Identifying characteristics and sorting problems: The basal flange identifies the shape.

Base: Usually annular; some tripod with hollow feet; rare examples have a flat base.

Base-wall juncture: Ranges from sharp to very slight break in curvature. A slight groove often marks the point of juncture on the interior of most examples, even those in which the break in curvature is slight.

Orientation of Side: Slight to wide outflare.

Side: Usually straight; sometimes a slight outcurve with a few examples slightly rounded above flange; rounded below flange.

Rim: Direct or rounded eversion.

Lip: Rounded or flattened; some beveled.

Wall thickness: Thickened at flange and lip; very thin in center of wall.

Flange: Exterior edge rounded; cross section ranges from triangular to parallel-sided. The angle between the flange and wall is well marked. The angle between the flange and base is usually abrupt. Examples are both narrow and wide.

Feet: Occasional examples with tripod feet that are large, hollow, and of nearly cylindrical shape.

Spouts: A few examples have a single gutter spout.

Surface: Well-finished on the interior and on the exterior down to the flange. Exterior section below flange is unslipped or carelessly slipped

Types: Aguila Orange 45%; polychrome types 35%; Balanza Black 20%.

Diameter: Range 18–40 cm; median 28 cm.

Length between lip and flange: Range 3.0–6.5 cm; median 4.7 cm.

Height of vessel alone: (13 examples from burials) Range 6.4–15.0 cm; median 8.5 cm.

Diameter/height ratio: (13 examples from burials) Range 2.3–4.8; median 3.3.

Shape class: 5, medium-diameter bowls and dishes.

Comments: In the analysis of the whole vessels that appear in TR. 25A, originally a distinction was made between two variants of the basal-flange shape: a high-side variant and an open-side variant. As is obvious from the names, the variants are distinguished primarily by the orientation of the side. The high-side variant has an orientation that ranges from very slight outflare to nearly vertical. In addition the break on the interior between the upper and lower sections is sharp. In the open-side variant, the orientation of the side is medium to wide outflare and the

break on interior between the upper and lower sections is usually less well marked. The distinction between the variants was not used in counting sherds, but is maintained in the illustrations. In addition, there is one example among the whole vessels and a few in illustrations of a round-side variant in which the vessels are nothing more than standard round-side bowls with a flange on the exterior. However, many examples overlap and the decision was made not to maintain this distinction in this publication.

Slightly Incurving to Round-side Bowl

Illustrations: Fig. 21.1–11, 21.15–19, 21.22–30; 22.24; 23.5, 23.9–11, 23.13, 23.15, 23.17–19, 23.24–26; 25.11, 25.14–15, 25.17; 29.20; 35.15, 35.19–20, 35.31–33. See TR. 25A: fig. 15; 16; 17*a–d*; 27*b,c*3; 29*h–n*; 33*a,b*1; 35*b*3–4; 36*a*3–4; 37*d*; 38*a,c*1; 125*c*; 129*i,j*; 135*a*; 136*j–m*; 137*a–c*; 153*f*1–3.

Identifying characteristics and sorting problems: The round side is the identifying feature. Otherwise, there is a great deal of variety that would not yield meaningful subdivisions.

Base: Usually annular; some examples are flat.

Orientation of Side: Varies from very open mouth to slightly restricted orifice.

Side: Rounded; considerable variation, from very slight to strong curvature.

Rim: Direct, except for a few everted examples.

Lip: Rounded.

Surface: Usually well finished on both interior and exterior; examples slipped on interior only also occur.

Unusual features: Appendages such as tabs, bumps, "screwheads" or effigy heads on the vessel exterior occur occasionally.

Types: Aguila Orange 78%; Balanza Black 8%; polychrome 8%; Quintal Unslipped 2%; other types less than 1%.

Diameter: Sherds: Range 12–44 cm; median 28 cm. Whole vessels (26 examples): range 7.9–33.4 cm; median 21.1 cm.

Height of flat base examples: range 4.2–4.0 cm; median 7.6 cm.

Height including annular base: range 5.8–16.0 cm; median 7.4 cm.

Diameter/height ratio: Annular or flat-base burial vessels: range 1.0–5.1; median 2.7.

Shape class: 5, medium-diameter bowls and dishes.

Comments: The sherd sample demonstrates a great deal of variation in size and gross shape. All attempts to achieve a consistent subdivision were fruitless, and it seems best to lump all examples in a single category. Intact vessels from burials suggest that vessels with flat or annular bases cover a comparably broad range of sizes, but the vessels with tripod supports are of a more standardized size with median dimensions larger than those of vessels without feet.

Tripod Bowl

Illustrations: Fig. 21.31; 29.18; 30.17; 32.7. See TR. 25A: fig. 25*b*; 29*b–g*; 32*c*; 36*a*2; 121*c*; 125*f–g*; 129*d–e*.

Identifying characteristics and sorting problems: The round side is the identifying feature, along with large, rounded, hollow tripod feet.

Base: Flat to slightly rounded with tripod feet.

Orientation of Side: Varies from very open mouth to slightly restricted orifice.

Side: Rounded; considerable variation, from very slight to strong curvature.

Rim: Direct, except for a few everted examples.

Lip: Rounded.

Feet: Large, rounded, hollow feet.

Surface: Usually well finished on both interior and exterior; examples slipped on interior only also occur.

Types: Almost always Aguila Orange; occasional examples of Balanza Black.

Diameter: (9 examples): range 25.6–31.6 cm; median 28.4 cm.

Height of vessel not including feet: Tripod burial vessels: range 6.8–10.2 cm; median 8.8 cm.

Height including feet: Tripod burial vessels: range 6.0–10.7 cm; medium 10.0 cm.

Diameter/height ratio: Tripod burial vessels: range 2.8–4.1; median 3.1.

Shape class: 5, medium-diameter bowls and dishes.

Outflaring to Slightly Outcurving-side Bowl or Dish

Illustrations: Fig. 22.9, 22.12, 22.15, 22.19–20, 22.22, 22.26, 22.28–33; 23.3–4; 25.1–5, 25.8, 25.10, 25.15, 25.17; 26.1–2, 26.14–15; 27.11–14, 27.17; 28.2–32; 29.23; 35.26; 36.8–10. See TR. 25A: fig. 17*e*; 25*f*; 38*e*1–2; 103*a*4; 108*f–g*; 114*e*1–2; 115*i*,*j*3–4; 123*h*; 124*j*; 127*d*,*f*; 148*c*1–3; 149*c–f*; 150*a–j*; 151*a*1–3.

Identifying characteristics and sorting problems: This is a simple shape that is often found in caches and burials and is usually Aguila Orange. Originally, when this shape was encountered in caches or burials, it was called an Outflaring-side Cache Vessel: Large Variety (TR. 25A), however, it is the same basic shape found in all contexts and is combined into a single shape in this work.

Base: Flat to concave; occasional examples have three solid nubbin feet.

Orientation of side: Slight to medium outflare.

Side: Slight to medium outcurve.

Rim: Usually direct; occasionally, the curvature increases near the top.

Lip: Most common, rounded; some flattened; less often beveled.

Surface: Usually well-finished on both interior and exterior, although unslipped on the exterior of the base.

Types: Aguila Orange 63%; polychrome types 17%; Balanza Black 14%; Lucha Incised and Urita Gouged-incised 3%.

Diameter: Range 32–55 cm; median, 30–32 cm. There is a bimodal distribution of medium and slightly larger diameter examples, but the shape has been classified in shape class 5, Medium Diameter Bowls and Dishes, because most examples are on the medium side.

Height: range 2.4–6.4 cm on the smaller examples and 6.8–17.2 cm on the larger examples.

Diameter/height ratio: range 1.0–6.7; median 3.2.

Shape class: 5, medium-diameter bowls and dishes.

Comments: There is a clear bimodal distribution in both vessel diameter and vessel height of this shape. Because the diameter bimodality is the clearest, diameter was used as the criterion for attributing a vessel to this shape class. The diameter/height ratios overlap considerably, indicating that the basic proportions remain the same in spite of differences in size. This shape occurs primarily in caches, although it is also found in some burials. The data for actual frequency counts in all contexts is not available, however, the shape is infrequent outside of burial and cache contexts.

SHAPE CLASS 6: SMALL DIAMETER BOWLS AND DISHES

Slightly Incurving to Round-side Bowl

Illustrations: Fig. 21.12–14, 21.20–21; 22.1–6, 22.10–11, 22.25; 23.6, 23.20–21; 24.1–5, 24.25–26; 25.6, 25.9; 26.2–3, 26.8, 26.13, 26.16–17; 27.4–6, 27.10, 27.15; 29.25; 34.4; 35.2–14, 35.16–17, 35.21–25, 35.27–30, 35.34–43; 36.11, 36.13. See TR. 25A: fig. 30*a*; 32*d*3; 36*a*6–7; 37*b*1; 102*b*; 124*k*; 135*e*.

Identifying characteristics and sorting problems: This shape was described as a barrel when found in burials and caches (TR. 25A), although in sherd samples, barrels were counted as slightly incurving to round-side bowls, and the two shapes have been combined in this work. Small incurving bowls are not common in the Manik Complex, and, in particular, the barrel shape is more common in Ik and Imix.

Base: Flat, annular (occasionally only a hint of a ring base), or short pedestal.

Orientation of side: Restricted orifice.

Side: Rounded.

Rim: Direct.

Lip: Rounded.

Surface: Usually well finished and slipped on both interior and exterior; some of the examples with a strongly restricted orifice have unslipped interiors.

Types: Most commonly Balanza Black 33% and Aguila Orange 29%; less common are Lucha Incised 14%; Urita Gouged-incised 14%; and polychromes 10%.

Diameter: Range 6–32 cm; median 16 cm.

Height (total): 9.4–9.9 cm.

Diameter/height ratio: 1.3–4.5.

Shape class: 5, small diameter bowls and dishes.

Comments: Two examples, both from Bu. 160 (see TR. 25A: fig. 36*a*6–7), are unusual examples with round covers.

Outflaring to Slightly Outcurving-side Bowl or Dish

Illustrations: Fig. 22.16–17; 23.14; 24.7, 24.13; 26.4; 27.7–9, 27.16, 27.21–22; 30.18–22; 35.1, 35.39–41. See TR. 25A: fig. 17*e*; 25*d–e*; 100*a*2; 101*d*; 102*a*4; 103*a*1–3,5–16,*b*; 106*b*1–6; 107*b*1–10; 108*c*; 114*a,c*; 115*b,d,f–h*; 127*a–c*; 130*a–e*; 133*a*4; 142*c*1–3; 143*b*; 144*e,f*2; 149*b*; 153*a,e*.

Identifying characteristics and sorting problems: Whole vessels with these characteristics are usually found in burials and caches and were originally classified as Outflaring-side Cache Vessel: Small Variety. This shape was less common in refuse contexts.

Base: Flat or slightly concave.

Orientation of side: Slight to medium out flare.

Side: Straight-to-medium outflare or outcurve.

Rim: Direct

Lip: Usually rounded; some flattened or beveled.

Surface: Usually well finished. Slipped on both interior and exterior except that the exterior base is usually left unslipped.

Types: Aguila Orange 60%; polychrome types 23%; Balanza Black 10%; Lucha Incised or Urita Gouged-incised 4%; incised types 1%; other types rare.

Dimensions: These figures are based on the relatively small samples included in burials.

Diameter: Range 11–27 cm; median 18 cm.

Height: Range 3.0–10.8 cm; median 7 cm.

Diameter/height ratio: 1.5–6.3; median 3.2.

Shape class: 6, small-diameter bowls and dishes.

Comments: The shape is the same as the medium diameter examples but with a smaller diameter.

Tripod Bowl or Dish

Illustrations: Fig. 29.22; 35.3. See TR. 25A: fig. 35*b*1–2; 37*b*2; 124*f–g,i.*

Identifying characteristics and sorting problems: This is another simple shape characterized by the outflaring to slightly outcurving-side, eversion of the rim, and tripod nubbin feet.

Base: Flat; some, perhaps all, have three nubbin feet.

Orientation of side: Slight outflare.

Side: Straight or slight to medium outcurve.

Rim: Most examples have a sharp, angular eversion with a ridge on the interior at the point of change in curvature. Some examples have a rounded, but well-marked eversion of the rim. The everted section of the rim is usually of medium length.

Lip: Rounded or pointed.

Feet: Small, solid feet.

Surface: Well finished on both interior and exterior.

Types: Balanza Black 51%; Aguila Orange 33%; Lucha Incised or Urita Gouged-incised 5%; polychrome types 3%; weathered 3%.

Diameter: Range 12–34 cm; median 20 cm.

Height excluding feet: Range 3.5–6.6 cm; median 5.2 cm.

Height including feet: Range 4.4–7.2 cm.

Diameter/height ratio: Range, 3.0–4.1; median 3.6.

Shape class: 6, small-diameter bowls and dishes.

SHAPE CLASS 7: CYLINDRICAL VESSELS

Cylinder

Illustrations: Fig. 19.43–45; 23.22–23; 26.5, 26.7, 26.9–12, 26.16; 27.1–2. See TR. 25A: fig. 27*c*1–2; 33*b*4; 127*h*1.

Identifying characteristics and sorting problems: This shape is easily identified in whole vessels. Its general dimensions are about the same as the smaller examples of cylindrical cache vessels, from which it is distinguished by the rounding to the base, more careful monochrome slipped finish, and lack of cover.

Base: Flat, but sides round to base.

Orientation of side: Vertical.

Side: Straight.

Rim: Direct.

Lip: Rounded

Features: One example has a double base with rattle.

Surface: Variable.

Types: Balanza Ceramic Group (including Balanza Black, Lucha Incised, Paradero Fluted, and Urita Gouge-incised; Aguila Orange; Japon Resist.

Diameter: Range 6–12 cm.

Height: Range 6–13 cm.

Diameter/ height ratio: Range 0.9–1.1.

Shape class: 7, cylindrical vessels.

Tripod Cylinder

Illustrations: Fig. 38.1–4, 38.7–11, 38.14–17, 38.19, 38.21–25, 38.29–34, 38.41, 38.43–44, 38.46–47, 38.53–58, 38.60–65, 38.67–69. See TR. 25A: fig. 19*a–c*; 20*a–c,e*; 21*a*; 26*c*; 27*a*1–4; 30*b*; 31*a–h*; 36*a*8–9; 37*b*5,*c*; 124*a*; 128*a,b*; 129*a,b*; 134*c,j.*

Identifying characteristics and sorting problems: When a section complete to base is present, the shape is unmistakable.

Base: Flat to very slightly rounded or slightly concave.

Juncture of base and side: The base is continued outward somewhat past the wall to give a ridge at the vessel exterior. The top of the ridge is rounded upward to join the vessel side.

Side: Straight to slightly outcurved. Examples range from hourglass to straight-vertical sides.

Orientation of Side: Very slight outflare at lip.

Rim: The outcurve of the side sometimes increases slightly just below the lip.

Lip: Rounded or pointed.

Feet: Hollow slab most common; sometimes hollow cylindrical, open at base; some solid slab.

Surface: Very carefully finished except that exterior base is unslipped and unsmoothed.

Types: Balanza Black 62%; Aguila Orange 25%; Lucha Incised and Urita Gouged-incised 8%; polychrome types 3%; incised types 1%; other types rare.

Diameter: Sherds calculated as continuous distribution; range 12–38 cm; median 22 cm. Sherds calculated as bimodal distribution: lower mode, range 12–24 cm; median 20 cm; upper mode, range 26–38 cm; median 30 cm. Burial vessels (24 examples) range 10.1–18.0 cm; median 13.7 cm.

Height including feet: (sample of 24 burial vessels): range 11.2–17.2 cm; median 18.1 cm.

Height excluding feet: (sample of 24 burial vessels): range 8.4–13.4 cm; median 10.4 cm.

Diameter/height ratio: (sample of 24 burial vessels) range 0.9–1.8; median 1.2.

Shape class: 7, cylindrical vessels.

Comments: In the absence of complete rim to base profiles sherds are difficult to sort with certainty and this may be reflected in the large range of sizes included in this shape.

Pitcher

Illustrations: See TR. 25A: fig. 123*g.*

Comments: It is not completely certain what shape the sherds in this class represent, but they seem to bear a general resemblance to the pitchers and vases reported by Smith (1955:154, fig. 12r, 17c16, 23b3) at Uaxactun. Other sherds of this shape may well have been sorted as cylindrical tripods, which they closely resemble in lip silhouette. Pitchers are also identified at Kaminaljuyu (Kidder, Jennings, and Shook 1946: fig. 67p,q, 69f,g, 70l,m) but they all have handles and pedestal bases.

Base: Unknown.

Orientation: Slightly outflaring.

Side: Straight to slightly outcurving.

Rim: Usually rounded outward below lip; one sharply everted.

Lip: Rounded.

Surface: Well finished on exterior; interior may be finished or left unslipped.

Types: Balanza Black.

Diameter: Range 8–10 cm.

Shape class: 7, cylindrical vessels.

SHAPE CLASS 10: SPECIALIZED BURIAL AND CACHE VESSELS AND COVERS

Cache Cylinder

Illustrations: See TR. 25A: fig. 21*b–j*; 32*a*1; 100*a*1,*b–f*; 101*a*1–3,*b*1–3,*c*1,*d*; 102*a*1–3,*c*,*d*1–3,*f*; 103*a*17; 104*a*1–5,*b*1–3; 105*b–g*; 106*a*1–3; 107*a*1–11,*c*; 108*a–b,d,e*; 109*b*; 115*a,j*1–2; 130*f–o*.

Identifying characteristics and sorting problems: The cylindrical shape and slightly rounded side are the identifying features of this variety. The majority of the examples are poorly finished Balanza Black or Quintal Unslipped, and they are specialized vessels found paired with dishes that serve as covers in caches. There are two examples (see TR. 25A: fig. 28*a*1; 36*b*) of possible Candelario Appliquéd (in the Quintal Ceramic Group) found in burials that were originally called urns (TR. 25A) but are now included this shape.

Base: Flat.

Base-wall juncture: Wall rounds inward to base, or angled to base.

Side: Straight to slightly curved.

Orientation of side: Vertical to slightly outflaring.

Rim: Direct or slightly everted.

Lip: Usually rounded; some flattened, beveled or grooved.

Surface: Carelessly slipped on exterior wall; exterior base and interior usually unslipped and poorly finished. On a few examples, the slip extends part of the way down the vessel interior. On unslipped examples, the exterior wall is slightly smoothed.

Types: Balanza Black and Quintal Unslipped. There is one example of a Balanza Black cache vessel that is slightly rectangular with four hollow feet (see TR. 25A: fig. 105*b*).

Diameter: Range 10–30 cm; median 15 cm.

Height: Range 7–33 cm; median 13 cm.

Diameter/height ratio: Range 0.4–1.8.

Shape class: 10, Specialized Burial and Cache Vessels and Covers

Cylindrical Cache Vessel Cover

Illustrations: See TR. 25A: fig. 21*b–j*; 32*a*1; 100*b–f*; 101*a*1–3,*b*1–3; 102*a*1–3,*c*,*d*1–2,*e,f*; 103*a*17; 104*a*1–5,*b*1–3; 105*a–g*; 106*a*1–3; 107*a*1–10,*c*; 108*a,b,d,e*; 109*b*; 115*j*1–2; 127*h*1; 130*f–1*.

Top: Usually flat or concave; a few rounded.

Orientation of side: Usually slightly outflaring; a few vertical.

Side: Mostly straight; some slightly rounded or slightly outcurving.

Rim: Direct.

Lip: Rounded, flattened or grooved; a few examples have an exterior bolster.

Surface: Carelessly slipped on exterior; interior usually unslipped. If unslipped, exterior is usually smoothed.

Types: Balanza Black and Quintal Unslipped. There is one example of a Balanza Black cover that is slightly rectangular, found in Ca. 119 (see TR. 25A: fig. 105*a*).

Diameter: Range 10–24 cm; median 14 cm.

Height: Range 1.5–7.8 cm; median 3.2 cm.

Diameter/height ratio: Range 0.5–8.0; median 3.8. The sample is spread widely over the range and there may actually be two peaks, one at about 3.5 and the other about 6.0.

Shape Class: 10, Specialized Burial and Cache Vessels and Covers

Comments: Covers with concave tops tend to associate with more vertical-side cylinders, and those with flat tops associate with cylinders with walls that are slightly curved.

SHAPE CLASS 11: MINIATURE VESSELS

Miniature Jar

Illustrations: Fig. 19.46; 56.33. See TR. 25A: fig. 129*f.*

Identifying characteristics and sorting problems: The small size makes these unmistakable.

Base: Rounded.

Body: Globular.

Neck-body juncture: Rounded break in curvature.

Orientation of neck: Slightly outflaring.

Neck: Outcurving.

Rim: Direct.

Lip: Rounded.

Surface: Carelessly smoothed.

Type: Quintal Unslipped.

Diameter (Neck): Range 3–5 cm; body diameter (one example) 7.5 cm.

Height (Total): one example 5.6 cm.

Height (Neck): Range 0.7–1.1 cm.

Diameter/height ratio: Range 4.3–5.1.

Shape Class: 11, miniature vessels

Miniature Bowl or Cylinder

Illustrations: Fig. 56.9–10, 56.35, 56.44.

Identifying characteristics and sorting problems: The small size makes these unmistakable.

Shapes: Incurving to round-side bowls; composite silhouette bowls; tripod cylinder.

Types: Aguila Orange and Balanza Black.

Diameter: 2–4 cm.

Height: 4 cm.

Diameter/Height ratio: 0.5

Comments: There are also possible examples of two miniature cups, one of a Quintal Unslipped and the other Aguila Orange. There is one example of a possible miniature tripod cylinder, Balanza Black (Fig. 56.25) from PD. 275, and another of an unknown type from PD. 231 (Fig. 56.18).

Shape Class: 11, miniature vessels

SHAPE CLASS 12: COVERS

Scutate Cover

Illustrations: Fig. 24.17, 24.21–23; 25.12–13, 25.16; 27.18–20; 37.1–37; 57.11. See TR. 25A: fig. 22; 23*a,b*; 24; 25*a,b*; 136*f–i*; 149*a.*

Identifying characteristics and sorting problems: Identified as a cover by the general shape and exterior decoration.

Top: There may either be an opening from the cover interior into the handle or a small flattened section of the cover top to which the handle is appliquéd.

Side: Slightly rounded or straight.

Orientation of side: Widely outflaring.

Rim: Usually direct; sometimes everted upward near lip; usually fairly wide.

Lip: Usually rounded; sometimes flattened or beveled; a few examples have a slight exterior bolster.

Interior flange: Triangular in cross section; a few rare examples of the same general shape that do not have an interior flange are also included as scutate lids; these always have an everted rim.

Handle: Usually effigy, sometimes cylindrical. Included among the effigy characterizations are bird, jaguar, human, and possibly were-jaguar.

Surface: Exterior well finished; interior usually unslipped; occasionally careless monochrome slip on interior.

Types: Aguila Orange 51%; polychrome types 17%; Lucha Incised and Urita Gouged-incised 13%; Balanza Black 12%; Pucte Brown Incised 3%; other types rare. Actually if the sherds on which these figures are based included handles, they would probably all have been of the corresponding modeled types because handles seem in all cases to have been modeled.

Diameter: Range 12–42 cm; median 30 cm.

Height (including handle): (6 examples) range 9.5–19.0 cm.

Height (excluding handle): (6 examples) range 5.7–11.0 cm.

Diameter/height ratio: (6 examples) range 3.1–5.0.

Shape Class: 12, covers.

Comments: In the examples from burials in which scutate lids are associated with particular vessels, they are usually associated with basal-flange bowls.

Apron Cover

Illustrations: Fig. 23.7; 24.6, 24.9–11; 25.7; 37.38–47; 38.5–6, 38.12–13, 38.18, 38.20, 38.26–29, 38.32–33, 38.35–40, 38.42, 38.45, 38.48–52, 38.59, 38.66, 38.70–71. See TR. 25A: fig. 19*a–c*; 20*a–e*; 21*a*; 26*c*; 27*a*1,5; 30*b*; 31*a*; 124*b*; 135*g,i–n*.

Identifying characteristics and sorting problems: The unslipped interior marks these as covers even for small sherds. No other problems in recognition.

Top: The handle is attached to a small flat area at the apex of the lid.

Orientation of side: Widely outflaring.

Side: A very short vertical section near the rim gives way to a straight or concave section sloping upward to the top.

Rim: Turned downward at a right angle to fit over top of vessel.

Lip: Rounded or pointed.

Handle: Human-head effigy is most common; also bird effigy, cylindrical, and wheel. The interior is open to the effigy in about half the cases, while in the others the interior is closed and the handle is appliquéd on the exterior.

Surface: Well finished on exterior; interior unslipped but usually smoothed.

Types: Aguila Orange 44%; Balanza Black 29%; Lucha Incised/Urita Gouged-incised 16%; Pucte Brown Incised 11%.

Diameter: Range 10–34 cm; median 20 cm.

Height (including handle): (9 burial vessels) Range

4.5–13.0 cm; median 8.0 cm.

Height (excluding handle): (11 burial vessels) Range 1.6–3.3 cm; median 2.4 cm.

Diameter/height ratio: (11 burial vessels) Range 2.8–7.5; median 5.6.

Shape Class: 12, covers.

Comments: In the limited examples from burials where apron covers are associated with specific vessels, they are always associated with cylindrical tripods.

Small Flat or Slightly Rounded Cover

Illustrations: See TR. 25A: fig. 26*a*; 36*a*6,7.

Comments: There are only three examples of these small unusual covers. Two, slightly rounded, Pita Incised, come from Bu. 160 where they were covers for slightly incurving to round-side bowls that are unusual shapes for Tikal. The flat cover, a Caldero Buff Polychrome, was found in Bu. 22, where it covered a short-neck, thin-walled jar of Aguila Orange.

Surface: Well finished.

Lip Diameter: (three examples) 10.2, 11.1, and 11.4 cm.

Height (including handle): (three examples) 5.4, 6.6, and 6.2 cm.

Diameter/height ratio: (three examples) 3.9; 3.0, 1.8.

Shape Class: 12, covers.

SHAPE CLASS 13: EFFIGY VESSELS

Effigy Jars

Comments: Only two examples, both from rich burials (Bu. 10 and 22).

Illustrations: See TR. 25A: fig. 18*b*; 26*b*.

Base: Concave.

Body: Globular.

Neck-body juncture: Vague.

Orientation of neck: Slightly insloping.

Neck: Slightly outcurving.

Top: The head of the figure is appended to the top of the neck; in both examples the head is hollow but has no opening to the exterior.

Spout: The spout leaves the body slightly above the midpoint at the back of the effigy and proceeds upwards. It is bridged to the back of the head by a solid piece that makes the spout serve as a handle. There is a hole in the back of the effigy under the spout that presumably was used to fill the vessel.

Effigy: One effigy is a bird, possibly a parrot; the second is a grotesque human. Details of the bodies are appliquéd to the body of the jar.

Surface: Carefully finished and decorated.

Types: One example is Positas Modeled; the other is stuccoed over a buff slip and is probably a trade piece.

Maximum diameter: 16 and 15.8 cm.

Total height: 21.5 and 19.0 cm.

Shape Class: 13, effigy vessels.

Comments: Some of the stray, modeled sherds may have come from effigy jars, but it is impossible to say with assurance. Certainly the shape was rare at Tikal.

Two-part Effigy

Illustrations: See TR. 25A: fig. 14.

Shape Class: 13, effigy vessels.

Comments: There is only a single example of this class of vessel, the effigy of the Old God from Bu. 10. The bottom part of the vessel, which includes the legs and the lower torso of the figure, is a cylinder with the lower third slightly expanded to a globular shape. The supports of the vessel are a tripod modeled as long bones. The upper part of the vessel that fits over the lower part has a lower section that is of a slightly larger diameter than the lower cylinder; this is surmounted by the head, which is hollow, and opens into the lower part of the top. The mouth of the figure opens to the inside of the top. The vessel is carefully painted in polychrome that is probably an imported type. Total height is 37.2 cm and maximum diameter of the vessel itself, excluding appliquéd decoration, is about 10 cm. Although the effigy is often spoken of as an incensario, there is no indication of burning on either the exterior or interior.

Median measurements of all Manik shape classes and shapes are presented in Table 7.10.

Manik Shapes: Chronological Change

The first attempt made to separate chronological facets of the Manik Complex was based on sherd collections using a seriation of vessel-shape frequencies in 58 samples. Initial clues to chronological changes were noted in a few key stratigraphic columns and in lots seriated by Rathje (1967) and Cheek (1970) for decorated types. Additional samples were added and arranged in an order based on a few key shape frequencies in a typical seriation procedure. The establishment of three facets was an arbitrary procedure. A small group of samples that constituted Manik 2 were well set off from other samples. The remainder of the collections formed a continuous series without any obvious place for a dividing line, but with too much variation between extremes to make them a single unit. Choosing to divide the continuous series

TABLE 7.10
Shape Dimensions of the Manik Complex

Shape Class and Shape	Median Diameter or Range (cm)	Median Height or Range [Median height of neck for Jars] (cm)	Median Diameter/ Height Ratio or Range
1. Wide-mouth Jars (with Tall Neck)	26.0	8.0	3.2
2. Narrow-mouth Jar (with Medium to Tall Neck)	16.0	5.5	2.8
2. Very Short-neck Jar	12.0–22.0	0.8–2.8	6.4–9.5
4. Large Recurving-side Bowl	40.0	—	—
5. Z-angle Bowl	26.0	7.3	3.8
5. Basal-flange Bowl	28.0	8.5	3.3
5. Slightly Incurving to Round-side Bowl	28.0	7.6	2.7
5. Tripod Bowl	28.4	8.8 (without feet) 10.0 (with feet)	3.1
5. Outflaring to Slightly Outcurving-side Bowl or Dish	30.0–32.0	6.8–17.2	3.2
6. Slightly Incurving to Round-side Bowl	16.0	9.4–9.9	1.3–4.5
6. Outflaring to Slightly Outcurving-side Bowl or Dish	18.0	7.0	3.2
6. Tripod Bowl or Dish	20.0	5.2 (without feet) 4.4–7.2 (with feet)	3.6
7. Cylinder	6.0–12.0	6.0–13.0	0.9–1.1
7. Tripod Cylinder (whole vessels only)	13.7	18.1	1.2
11. Miniature Vesssels	5.0	7.0	(4.3–5.1)

into facets gives a three-part subdivision comparable to the division of Tzakol at Uaxactun (Smith 1955).

Using the three temporal divisions obtained from the seriation of vessel shapes, an attempt was made to validate and refine the temporal arrangement by means of discriminant analysis. The analysis provided a clear separation between Manik 2 samples and those for Manik 3A and 3B. Manik 3A and 3B samples were arranged in a continuous distribution, the extremes of which were quite distinct from each other, although the order of adjacent samples was open to all the possible rearrangements common in a seriation by traditional means.

Coggins (1975) achieved considerably greater success in subdividing the complex based on an analysis of decorated sherds and burials. Her divisions of Manik 1, 2, and 3 were the starting point on which the current faceting of the Manik Complex was based. The situation was greatly clarified by the very detailed analysis of Manik materials made possible by the excavations of the Proyecto Nacional Tikal, especially in the Mundo Perdido Complex (Laporte and Fialko 1987, 1990, 1995). The Guatemalan Project produced large samples with excellent architectural stratigraphy and rich burials.

The changes in vessel shapes that characterize the three facets of the Manik Complex are mainly quantitative, although a few shapes seem to have had temporal distributions that did not persist through the entire time of the complex [Note: The original quantitative data for shape frequencies in the Manik Complex are missing.] Manik 2 is characterized by high frequencies of the z-angle bowl. The z-angle frequency, between 12 and 30% in Manik 2 samples, is the most striking feature of this facet and the frequency range for the shape shows no overlap with Manik 3A frequencies. The presence of scutate lids is a good marker for both Manik 2 and 3A, but the shape is a relatively rare one.

Manik 2 is also characterized by negative characteristics. Cylindrical tripods and their associated covers were probably not manufactured at this time because the two samples that contain them could well be mixed with later material. Slightly incurving to round-side bowls are present in frequencies that are strikingly low in comparison with an increase in Manik 3A and 3B. Footed vessels are also present in average frequencies in Manik 2, lower than those of Manik 3A and B, but the range of individual samples overlaps that of later samples.

The ranges of frequencies of basal-flange bowls and wide-mouth jars in Manik 2 are very large, probably due to the small size of several samples. Of these two shapes, basal-flange bowl frequencies are temporally significant in the later facets and might be so for Manik 2 if more and larger samples were available. Wide-mouth jars are not temporally diagnostic for any of the Manik facets.

Manik 3A is intermediate, both qualitatively and quantitatively, between Manik 2 and Manik 3B. Important additions to the Manik 3A shape repertory are cylindrical tripods and apron covers that are present in the samples in small but consistent quantities.

The most striking increase in shape frequencies for Manik 3A samples is in slightly incurving to round-side bowls that show a modal frequency of 15–20% for Manik 3A compared to only 5–10% for Manik 2. The basal-flange bowl probably reached its peak of popularity during Manik 3A, although the extremely variable frequency of the shape in Manik 2 samples makes its history rather unclear. The modal frequency of feet in Manik 3A also increases over that for Manik 2, although the frequency ranges are about the same for the two facets.

Z-angle bowls, a characteristic shape of Manik 2, decrease sharply in frequency in Manik 3A. Outflaring to slightly outcurving-side vessels also show an average decrease in frequency. Scutate lids, on the other hand, continue unchanged in general frequency range and modal frequency.

Manik 3B culminates trends that appear in the preceding facets. There are no new additions to the shape inventory at the time, while several shapes characteristic of Manik 2 seem to have dropped from production. The most frequent shape in the great majority of Manik 3B samples continues to be slightly incurving to round-side bowls. Modal frequencies of this shape increase to 30–35% as compared to a modal frequency of 15–20% in Manik 3A. Cylindrical tripods and covers also reach peak frequencies in Manik 3B as do footed vessels.

Z-angle and outflaring to slightly outcurving-side bowls or dishes continue in frequencies that are about the same as those in Manik 3A. Basal-flange bowls, on the other hand, decrease in frequency between Manik 3A and 3B, with a decline in modal frequency from 15–20% to 5–10%. Although outflaring-side bowls or dishes from the two facets show the same modal frequency (10–15%), the overall frequency distribution and mean frequency are lower in Manik 3B than in Manik 3A. Z-angle bowls and scutate lids, both characteristic shapes of Manik 2, are absent from most Manik 3B samples and were probably no longer being produced.

Manik Shapes: Social Dimension

The Manik Complex offers the earliest set of Tikal collections large enough and varied enough to allow a serious investigation of variation that may have arisen from social rather than temporal causes and a subset of the samples was analyzed to examine possible social variation in Manik shapes. This subset included twenty samples from small structure groups, twelve samples from intermediate structure groups, and twenty-four samples from larger range structure or civic-ceremonial groups.

There are, however, some features of the sample sets that might tend to obscure social variability. First, there is not a completely random representation of temporal facets within the context sets. The small structure group set contains no Manik 2 samples, thirteen Manik 3A samples, and seven Manik 3B samples. The figures for the intermediate structure group set are one Manik 2, four Manik 3A, and seven Manik 3B, while those for the large civic-ceremonial and range structure group set are six Manik 2, twelve Manik 3A, and six Manik 3B. Therefore, frequencies of vessel shapes that vary temporally may be skewed within the context sets, a factor that must be taken into account in interpreting the results.

A second factor that may interfere with the correct interpretation of results is uncertainty about context in locations where Early Classic levels were not completely investigated. This factor would not be a problem in small structure group contexts, because the tiny mounds of later levels could hardly hide larger groups of different social contexts from early periods. Similarly, it is not a problem in areas like those near the Great Plaza where there has been enough digging to be certain of continuity in the ceremonial-elite functions of the location as far back as the Preclassic. In other cases, however, assignment of context rests on the assumption of continuity when

there is little evidence from excavation that such continuity existed. A good case in point is provided by two Manik samples recovered from underneath the Late Classic Twin Pyramid complexes. Because the Twin Pyramid Complex is a Late Classic ceremonial innovation built after almost complete razing of earlier structures, it is uncertain whether these locations were occupied by earlier structures of a similar ceremonial-elite character. In all, six intermediate structure group samples and four large civic-ceremonial and range structure group samples must be classified as likely rather than certain contexts.

Finally, although the number of samples from each context is fairly high, the number of locations represented is not great. When a single location provides a high percentage of the samples from a context there is a danger that peculiarities of that location may seem to be true of the context as a whole.

The first point that had to be investigated in examining potential relationships between social factors and ceramics is whether the contexts in which samples were finally deposited were actually at or near the loci where the ceramics were originally used. This point was raised in the introductory discussion on archaeological contexts and is a matter that should be tested rather than assumed, particularly when dealing with collections recovered from the fill of large structures. The Manik collections provide the first chance in the Tikal collections to test the hypothesis that the final archaeological contexts of samples did, in general, relate to the loci of use. If this hypothesis is correct, the following predictions would follow: (1) Large civic-ceremonial and range structure groups should contain high frequencies of better-finished "serving vessels" of shapes appropriate for ceremonial/elite use. (2) Small structure groups should contain high frequencies of vessels usable for domestic activities. Intermediate structure groups do not lead to a prediction because they include both residential and ceremonial structures. (3) The frequencies characteristic of the larger size structure groups should not occur in other kinds of contexts because there are few situations that would lead to the movement of refuse from large groups to groups of smaller size. (4) Samples with frequencies characteristic of small structure groups might be expected to occur in groups of larger size, especially where the demand for fill material was high and might have resulted in importing fill material from nearby domestic groups. (5) Samples characteristic of intermediate structure groups should occasionally occur in larger groups for the same reason. But such material should be rare in small structure groups. (6) The null hypothesis in all cases would be that samples do not relate to the groups in which they were found and that consequently the ceramic frequencies would not vary consistently in relation to group size.

The first two tests depend on consistent differences between the samples from large civic-ceremonial and range structure groups and those from small structure groups. Two methods were used to test these hypotheses. First, a simple comparison of the range in median vessel frequencies from large and small groups was made. Second, a discriminant analysis was run using the size of mound groups as the criterion for the separation of samples. Both tests provided comparable results indicating consistent differences between samples from large- and small-structure groups in shape frequencies. The vessel shape that shows the highest consistent difference between small and large groups is the wide-mouth jar that is more abundant in almost all small-group samples than in any large group. The most likely function of this shape was water storage, although other storage and cooking uses are also possible. Any of these functions would be compatible with the commoner domestic activities postulated for small structure groups. Rounded z-angle bowls also show higher mean and modal frequencies in small structure groups than in large structure groups, but this is largely a result of consistently very high frequencies for these shapes in samples from Manik Location 1. Samples from other small structure groups are quite similar to those from large structure groups in rounded z-angle bowl frequencies. Because this shape is a large-capacity vessel with inferred storage functions, it would have been expected to be more common in small structure groups than in large structure groups.

Large structure groups are distinguishable from small structure groups by high frequencies of a series of small bowls and dishes, including outcurving-side bowls, outflaring-side bowls or dishes, z-angle bowls, basal-flange bowls, and scutate lids. All of these shapes fall in the category of serving vessels. In addition, they were the most common shapes in burial offerings suggesting that they had ritual and/

or status connotations. In general terms, the first two predictions based on the hypothesis that samples from large civic-ceremonial and range structure groups and small structure groups represent differential activities from the two contexts are confirmed by the data.

It was impossible to predict the vessel shapes that should predominate in samples from mound groups of intermediate size because the groups include both domestic and ceremonial precincts and there was no way to deduce what kinds of activities would be most represented in the ceramic samples. The results suggest that collections from groups of intermediate size are similar to collections from small structure groups rather than to those from large civic-ceremonial or range structure groups. Shape frequencies from intermediate structure groups resemble those from small structure groups in six cases while they are similar to large structure groups only in the case of showing a low frequency of rounded z-angle bowls. Intermediate structure groups differ from both large structure and small structure groups in the frequencies of only three shape categories, and none of the differences appears to be very significant. Frequencies of outcurving-side bowls and dishes in intermediate structure groups are intermediate between frequencies in samples from large structure and small structure groups, and also shows lower frequencies of everted-rim dishes and annular bases than either large structure or small structure groups. In summary, it appears that vessel shape frequencies from groups of intermediate structure size are so close to those from groups of small structure size that it is likely that the samples obtained from them were the result of the same kinds of domestic activities posited for small structure groups.

One final set of predictions remains—testing the hypothesis that ceramic samples represent activities that took place at or near the locations in which the samples were discovered. This test involves samples that show shape frequencies that are aberrant from those that would be deemed characteristic of the size of the group to which the samples belong. For this test, the discriminant analysis and canonical variants program is crucial because it gives a mapped representation of group means and sample distributions. One prediction is that samples with the frequencies characteristic of large structure groups will occur rarely in small structure or intermediate structure groups because there is no reason to move debris from large groups to smaller groups. This prediction is confirmed, because the samples from large groups form a consistent cluster around the group mean that does not include any samples from groups of smaller size. A second prediction is that samples found in large structure groups will occasionally show frequencies characteristic of small structure groups because some fill samples in the large structure group may consist of material imported from small structure groups. Again the prediction is confirmed because one sample from a large structure group falls within the distribution of small structure groups and one sample falls within the distribution of intermediate structure groups.

A prediction that samples from intermediate structure groups would sometimes show frequencies characteristic of small structure groups while the reverse would not be true was not confirmed. Three samples from groups of intermediate structure groups fall within the range of frequencies characteristic of small structure groups, while two small structure group samples fit well with the intermediate structure group distribution in the canonical variants mapping. Because, as discussed above, it seems unlikely that the differences between small and intermediate groups are of real significance, a genuine separation could hardly have been expected. In summary, it seems that the separation between groups of different sizes is good and, particularly, that the amount of aberrant samples encountered in large structure groups was less than might have been expected. It appears that in most cases the Maya located enough material in local contexts to supply the need for fill.

One Manik sample, Location 9, was separated as potentially representing a specialized activity. This is the sample recovered from the deep deposits at the bottom of the Madeira Reservoir. The shape frequencies confirm the predicted specialized character of the sample. The sample shows an extremely high frequency of narrow-mouth jars (the vessel used to transport water). The frequency of 40% for this shape in the reservoir lots far exceeds the frequency in any other Manik lot. The only other shape that appears with considerable frequency is the round-side bowl, which might be used to dip water from the reservoir. Large shapes that would be difficult to transport, such as wide-mouth jars and rounded z-angle bowls, show particularly low frequencies.

These results demonstrate quite conclusively that the Madeira Reservoir was, in fact, used as a reservoir during the time of the Manik Complex and that considerable silting of the reservoir took place at this time.

The analyses designed to investigate social variation in Manik ceramics produced several useful results. First, the viability of comparisons between groups of different sizes, a point in question because of the frequent movement of refuse material by the ancient Maya, was confirmed when the predictions based on the hypothesis that the samples do represent activities at the locus at which they were found were substantiated.

The ceramics used in large civic-ceremonial or range structure groups differ from those used in smaller structure groups in about the way that would have been predicted on the basis of inferred function. Inhabitants of large structure groups used more of the well-made smaller vessels and less large storage vessels than did the inhabitants of small structure groups. Perhaps more significant than this result, however, is the fact that the variation between the groups is smaller than it is in the Late Classic, possibly suggesting a less strongly stratified society in Early Classic times. Groups of intermediate structure size do not differ significantly in ceramic use from small structure groups, another bit of evidence that would tend to support a less stratified society than that which characterized Late Classic Tikal.

Special Deposits of the Manik Complex

Burials of the Manik Complex

Twenty-six special deposits classified as burials at Tikal contained Manik Complex ceramics (see Table 7.11) however two burials (Bu. 107 and 206) are excluded from the sample because of uncertain dates based on the pottery contained as grave goods. Four were from the civic-ceremonial epicenter of Tikal, Gp. 5D-2. Four were from elite residential range structure groups, Gps. 5D-1 and 5D-11. Eleven were from Intermediate Structure Groups scattered throughout the city. Five came from Small Structure Groups. One each came from the outlying Minor Centers of Uolantun and Navajuelal.

A total of 128 vessels occurred in these burials. It should be noted that when vessel covers occurred as part of a burial offering, they were not counted separately, but were considered to be part of the same vessel they covered. The exception to this rule is that outflaring-side cache vessels were counted separately, even when they occurred as lip-to-lip pairs with one vessel covering the other. The reason for this decision is that outflaring-side cache vessels sometimes occurred separately and obviously could have served as individual vessels. It should also be noted that the vessels in Bu. 107 were not included in the following analysis. Burial 107 included both Terminal Preclassic and Early Classic vessels as well as many large sherds. It seems likely that some of the pieces may have been incidental to the burial and not a part of the grave goods. Bu. 107 is best considered as a problematical deposit that includes human remains. In addition, Bu. 206, described as possibly of Manik date in TR. 25A: fig. 38e, was not included in the analysis because the date is very uncertain.

In the Manik Complex, mortuary offerings of one or two vessels were by far the most common, represented by ten and four cases respectively. There was one burial that included three vessels, three with four vessels, and one burial each with five and six vessels. Four rich burials had considerably larger ceramic offerings that included 10, 17, 27, and 30 vessels. These four burials included more vessels (84) than the total of the other twenty burials combined (44).

For the total sample of all burials, Aguila Orange is the type most frequently represented with a frequency of 28%, followed by Balanza Black with 23%, polychrome group types and Quintal Unslipped, both at 11%, and unusual types at 6%. No other type comprises more than 4% of the sample. Total frequencies, however, are biased by the fact that the four richest burials include nearly twice as many vessels as all other burials combined, and differ significantly from other burials in the types represented. The richest burials have a much higher frequency of Balanza Black, a lower frequency of Aguila Orange, and only half as many polychromes (8% in comparison to 16%). It might be argued that the difference is temporal and that polychromes became less common in Manik 3B. It is more probable, however, that the differences are due to the fact that cylindrical tripod vessels were usually produced in types of the Balanza Group and were the vessels of highest status in Manik 3A and 3B.

There is a similar disparity between the vessel shapes represented in the four largest burials and the remainder. In the total sample of 128 vessels from Manik burials, round-side bowls are most common (27%), followed by cylindrical tripods (21%), basal-flange bowls (12%), and unusual shapes (11%). Cylindrical cache vessels (8%), straight-side bowls (6%), narrow-mouth jars (5%), and a variety of shapes at less than 5% frequency round out the sample. In the sample from the largest burials, cylindrical tripods are far more common than in simple burials—29% of the sample against only 7% in the simple burials. Conversely, basal-flange bowls, straight-side vessels, and unusual shapes are more common in the sample from simple burials. Cylindrical cache vessels occur only in the sample from the richest chamber burials, while wide-mouth jars appear only in the sample from other burials.

The types of vessels included in burials differ greatly between one-vessel and two-vessel offering sets. Among the burials that contained only a single vessel, three include a vessel of Aguila Orange and two are weathered. The other five vessels are of relatively rare types, but not a single polychrome vessel is included unless a polychrome was among the weathered examples. On the other hand, four of the eight vessels in two-vessel sets are polychromes, two are Aguila Orange, one is Balanza Black, and one is Triunfo Striated.

There are also strong differences in shapes between one-vessel and two-vessel offerings. When only a single vessel was included as an offering, it is most frequently (seven of ten cases) a round-side or outflaring-side bowl or dish. In burials with two vessels, one vessel is invariably a basal-flange bowl. The second vessel of the set is not highly standardized. In two cases, the second vessel is a jar, while a round-side dish and a cylindrical tripod occur once each.

Burial 162 deserves special mention. It was located in Ch. 7F-8 of Gp. 7F-1, sealed by the fill for Plat. 7F-3-2nd and Haviland (TR. 22:52–54) suggests that it might have been the burial of Lady of Tikal (Lady "Ix" Kaloomte). A single unusual vessel was included in the burial. It is a large red cache cylinder with an appliquéd decoration on the exterior. Coggins (1975:233–235) suggests that the appliquéd design, much of which is missing, "may

TABLE 7.11

Burials of the Manik Complex

Burial No.	Op.SubOp./Lot	Str.	Structure Group Type	TR. 25A Illustration	TR.	No. of Vessels
10	12C/34	5D-34, Dedic.	Civic-Ceremonial	14–21	14	30
17	20A/47	4F-43, under	Small Structure Group	38*a*	19	1
22	12H/18	5D-26, 1st	Civic-Ceremonial	22–27*a*	14	17
33	20H/9	Quarry 4F-1	Small Structure Group	27*b*	19	1
34	20H/10	Quarry 4F-1	Small Structure Group	38*b*	19	1
35	20H/21	Quarry 4F-1	Small Structure Group	54*a*	19	6
47	12O/12	5D-26-1st North side	Civic-Ceremonial	28*b*	14	2
48	12K/22	Plat. 5D-4-3rd	Civic-Ceremonial	28*c*–32*a*	14	27
73	27L/4	Chultun 5G-19	Intermediate Structure Group	32*b*	21	2
74	27G/14	Plat. 5G-1, North wall	Intermediate Structure Group	32*c*	21	1
84	30A/5	4G-9, bedrock	Intermediate Structure Group	32*d*	21	3
94	33A/20	4H-4	Intermediate Structure Group	32*e*, 33*a*	21	2
95	33A/21	4H-4	Intermediate Structure Group	33*b*	21	4
101	33A/31	4H-4	Intermediate Structure Group	33*c*	21	1
107	33A/38, 48–51	4H-4	Intermediate Structure Group	33*d*, 34, 35*a*	21	Excluded problematical deposit
115	27A/21	5G-8	Intermediate Structure Group	38*c*	21	4
152	68G/20	0.0	Small Structure Residential	35*b*		4
160	3B/18	7F-30	Intermediate Structure Group	36*a*	22	10
162	3C/7	Chultun 7F-8	Intermediate Structure Group	36*b*	22	1
169	76B/5	5D-7	Range Structure Group	37*a*	20A&B	2
177	87A/6	5D-71, in front, below court	Range Structure Group	37*b*	15[†]	5
182	98D/9	5D-46 E stair	Range Structure Group	38*d*	15[†]	1
187	112B/6	3H-3	Intermediate Structure Group	37*c*		1
206	129D/8–9	SE(S)-430	Minor Center	38*e*		Excluded uncertain date
213	135A/110	SE-486	Minor Center	37*d*		1
217	45G/13	5D-50	Range Structure Group	37*e*	15[†]	1

[†] Forthcoming

have represented a frontal skeletal long-nosed head without lower jaw." A similar vessel was included in Bu. 35, to be discussed shortly.

Burials with offerings of between three and six vessels show almost no patterning. These burials show a de-emphasis of decorated types and higher frequency of monochromes, especially Aguila Orange. Round-side and outflaring-side bowls and dishes are the shapes most frequently present. There are only three examples of basal-flange bowls and only a single cylindrical tripod.

As noted above, Bu. 35 deserves special discussion. The burial was located in small-mound Group 4F-1 east of a deep pit designated Quarry 4F-1. It may have been dedicatory to a possible shrine, Str. 4F-8, although the structure showed no surviving architecture (TR 19:134–135). Four of the six vessels in the burial are very unusual. One is a cache cylinder with red-appliquéd decoration similar to the vessel in Bu. 162, discussed earlier. Two more are gouged-incised vessels with scroll designs. One of these is a unique cream type; the second is weathered, but has a paste that is not local. It seems likely that both were imported. The final vessel is a cylinder with hollow rattle base of a weathered grooved type. This vessel may be local but is outside the usual range of Tikal vessels. It is very surprising to find a collection of such unusual vessels, some imported, in a small structure group. Considered together with the three caches found nearby, these special deposits indicate a change in social status between Early and Late Classic times.

The sequence of the four richest Manik Complex burials, the chamber burials of Tikal's rulers, is well established by stratigraphy and/or Long Count dates. There can be little doubt that Bu. 22 was the earliest. The ceramic contents suggest a position at about the time of transition between Manik 2 and Manik 3A, and the stratigraphic position should be slightly earlier than that of Bu. 10. Because the burial was entered and possibly looted in the Late Classic, the full contents remain unknown. Burial 10 is generally accepted to be that of the Ruler Yax Nuun Ayiin I (Curl Nose). The inscriptions do not give a secure death date for Yax Nuun Ayiin I, but it was obviously before AD 411 when his successor, Siyaj Chan K'awiil II (Stormy Sky), took the throne. Burial 48 was almost certainly that of Siyaj Chan K'awiil II, fixed by a Long Count date of AD 457

painted on the wall of the tomb. This is about a year after the ruler's recorded death date in AD 456, a not unreasonable time for final rites and preparation of the tomb.

Burial 160, of Manik 3B date, was the only one of the four richest Manik burials not located in the North Acropolis. It was located in Gp. 7F-1 and was probably dedicatory to Str. 7F-30-5th. Originally hypothesized as the burial for the ruler Chak Tok Ich'aak II (Jaguar Paw Skull), it has since been concluded this is not the case, though clearly the individual interred in Bu. 160 was someone of importance based on the quantity and quality of grave goods. For a detailed discussion of the burial and its contents see TR. 22:49–52.

Ceramic offerings from these four burials show a considerable degree of variability. A few vessel shapes occurred in all tombs. These are basal-flange bowls or dishes, round-side bowls, narrow-mouth jars, and cylindrical tripods. The ceramic offerings are large because each tomb contained sets of vessels of one or two shapes. Burial 22 contained four basal-flange bowls and four cylindrical tripods. Burial 10 included seven round-side bowls, nine cylinder tripods, and nine cylindrical cache vessels, while Bu. 48 contained ten round-side bowls and nine cylindrical tripods. The smaller offering in Bu. 160 did not include any large sets.

There are seventeen vessels and nine covers in Bu. 22, including 5 cylindrical tripods. Two of the cylindrical vessels have apron covers, and a third cover was not associated with any vessel and is of a different type. There are four basal-flange bowls, all with scutate lids. Two outflaring-side cache vessels, a round-side tripod dish with scutate lid, an effigy vessel, an outcurving-side dish, a narrow-mouth jar, and an unusual jar with spout and small cover complete the assemblage. The types represented (including covers) include seven Dos Arroyos Group, seven Balanza Black, seven Aguila Orange, three Positas Modeled, and two Japon Resist.

The primary decorative message in Bu. 22 comes from three Manik 2 polychrome basal-flange bowls with scutate lids that are probable heirlooms. A jaguar body is modeled on one of the lids with the head serving as a handle. A second lid has a were-jaguar handle that combines human and jaguar characteristics. A fourth basal-flange scutate lid in black has a human head as the handle. The scutate lids are an indication of an earlier date than that for Bu. 10 and 48, because this type of cover disappeared from the ceramic repertory of Tikal early during Manik 3 times. Of the five cylindrical tripods, one is Japon Resist; the others are Balanza Black. One of the Balanza tripods has a human head as a handle for the cover and is stuccoed and painted with glyphic cartouches. The vessel is nearly identical to three stuccoed cylinders in Bu. 10, even in its glyphs. The designs on all the vessels are typically "Maya" and the only indication of Teotihuacan influence in the tomb is the shape of the cylindrical tripods. A black effigy jar of a monkey is the only other vessel worth noting. Moreover, none of the vessels with the possible exception of the effigy jar and the Japon Resist cylindrical tripod seems to be imported.

Manik 3A Bu. 10 of the ruler Yax Nuun Ayiin I included 30 vessels, not counting the extra cover. There is a set of nine cylindrical cache vessels with covers and a set of eight cylindrical tripods (although the inclusion of an extra apron cover suggests there may have been nine cylindrical tripods originally). There are seven round-side bowls or dishes, two outflaring-side cache vessels, two effigies, one basal-flange bowl, and one narrow-mouth jar. Typologically, Quintal Unslipped is the most frequent because of the nine cylindrical cache vessels with covers. The great majority of the remaining vessels and covers are decorated. Six vessels and five covers are stuccoed and painted. Three vessels and four covers are of gouged-incised types. There is one Japon Resist vessel and cover, and only one polychrome vessel, that of the imported Moc Orange Polychrome type, that corresponds to Polychrome A at Kaminaljuyú (Kidder, Jennings, and Shook 1946:fig. 182a–e and 183a–d).

Burial 10 marks the peak of Teotihuacan ceramic influence in Tikal. In the burial, the burden of painted decoration falls to stuccoed and painted vessels. Three round-side bowls, two with round-side covers and effigy handles, fall into this class. All have designs that were obviously influenced by Teotihuacan. Although it is likely the Mexican designs on these vessels were painted in the Maya area, the vessels and their covers are not of local types. The designs of incised lines and dots that underlie the stucco on two of the vessels echo motifs that commonly occur in Thin Orange Ware at Teotihuacan, but whether this indicates a Central Mexican origin or copying

elsewhere is a question that must be resolved by technical analysis. Three of the eight cylindrical tripods with apron covers, that have mold-made handles shaped like human heads, also have painted stucco decoration. The designs are clearly "Maya" in inspiration and have brief hieroglyphic inscriptions on the covers. The vessels are so similar in size and shape, and the glyphs are so alike, it seems that they may be the work of the same workshop or artist. These vessels are likely to have been of local origin. Three cylindrical tripods with apron covers and a fourth cover without associated vessel have gouged-incised designs in cartouches. These are variations on what seems to be the same generally Mayoid motif, although Coggins (1975:153) notes that in one case this motif takes the form of a serpent head in Mexican style. Unlike the previously mentioned cylindrical tripods, this group comes from different locations and is of quite distinct workmanship. The fact that an apron cover without vessel occurred in the burial opens the possibility that Bu. 10, like Bu. 22, may have been re-entered by the Maya at some later time. One of these tripods and lid and the unmatched lid without vessel are surely from the Tiquisate region on the Pacific coast of Guatemala. The designs in cartouches on both vessels are nearly identical to the designs on gouged-incised tripods, which are almost surely from the Petén. This suggests that the vessels may have been fashioned specifically to match the vessels found in Bu. 10 or, as Coggins (1975:157–158) suggests, the carving of the vessels may have been done after they arrived in Tikal. The seventh cylindrical tripod is a highly polished black with the partially broken diving figure as the handle. The eighth cylindrical tripod is Japon Resist, a type that is rare at Tikal and may have been of non-local origin, although its origins are unknown. The only basal-flange vessel in the burial is the Moc Orange Polychrome example that is also non-local.

Two effigy vessels in Bu. 10 are also imported types. These are mold-made, common in Teotihuacan style pottery. One is the famous Old God effigy based on the Mexican Old God. The second is a bird effigy that was stuccoed and painted, although the stucco is too fragmentary to indicate designs. Eight of the vessels and five of the covers in Bu. 10 were imported to Tikal, a far greater number than in any other Early Classic burial.

A set of nine cylindrical cache vessels with covers is another feature of Bu. 10. The vessels are unslipped and poorly shaped, suggesting that it was their contents rather than the vessels themselves that were of significance.

Manik 3A Bu. 48 of the ruler Siyaj Chan K'awiil II included twenty-seven vessels. There are nine cylindrical tripods, seven round-side bowls with annular or flat bases, six round-side tripod bowls or dishes, two basal-flange bowls, a barrel, a cylindrical cache vessel, and a narrow-mouth jar. The vessels, however, lack the exuberance of decoration and the abundance of obviously imported examples that occurred in Bu. 10. Among decorated types, there is only one stuccoed vessel with lid, two Urita Gouged-incised vessels, one with a lid, and one Caldero Buff Polychrome. Twenty-two of the remaining vessels are either Aguila Orange or Balanza Black.

Only a few of the vessels from Bu. 48 are noteworthy for their style or beauty. The most interesting is the cylindrical tripod with apron cover that was stuccoed and painted. The tripod shows a very Mexican motif of skulls dripping blood and stars. In addition, the vessel is shorter and of greater diameter than is common among cylindrical tripods at Tikal. The painting on the cover is related, as Coggins (1975:194) notes, to Mexican butterfly symbolism. The colors and painting style of the cover, however, differ from those on the tripod, and it seems possible that the cover was decorated by a different artist than the vessel itself. The modeled head on the cover also lacks the delicacy of heads on the apron covers in Bu. 10 and wears a different headdress. The tripod vessel with gouged-incised bird designs and apron cover with modeled bird handle is of spectacular workmanship. The design on the tripod seems more Maya than Mexican, although the birds carved on the side panel have speech scrolls in Mexican fashion. In addition, the style of feet on the vessel is not a common one for Tikal, although it also occurs as single examples in Bu. 10 and in PD. 50, the smashed, burned, and redeposited remains of the burial of an individual of very high rank with many indications of Mexican influence. The modeled bird on the handle of the cover is outside the range of such handles at Tikal, but similar examples occur in Guatemalan museum collections. The seven other cylindrical tripods in the burial are monochrome black and lack covers. The black gouged-incised barrel with pedestal base is a spectacular piece of art. The cartouches carry Maya designs, but the shape and especially the

pedestal are outside the normal range for Tikal. At a guess, it is a Maya lowlands piece, but not made at Tikal. The rest of the vessels from Bu. 48 are routine, almost surely local products, and though Siyaj Chan K'awiil II was a ruler of great significance, he did not choose to display his wealth in the ceramic offerings in his tomb.

Although Manik 3B Bu.160 from beneath Str. 7F-30 in Group 7F-1 includes the presence of two sacrificed adolescents and considerable richness in non-ceramic material (TR. 22:49–52), the ceramic contents are undistinguished. There are ten vessels in the burial: two cylindrical tripods without covers, two unusual small jars with covers, three small bowls and dishes, a basal-flange tripod dish, a round-side tripod dish, and a narrow-mouth jar. Except for simple incised lines on several vessels, the only decorated vessel is a polychrome basal-flange bowl. Aside from the presence of cylindrical tripods, there is no indication of Mexican influence. An instrumental neutron activation analysis of samples from the whole vessels from Bu. 10, Bu. 48, and PD. 50 to determine place of production proved inconclusive (Reents-Budet and Bishop 2003).

Caches of the Manik Complex

A total of 45 Manik special deposits classified as caches contained ceramics (Table 7.12). Thirty were from Gp 5D-2, associated with the temples and stone stelae of the Great Plaza and North Acropolis; one from the Mundo Perdido, Gp. 5C-11, four from Gp. 5D-11, the Central Acropolis; one each from the East Plaza, Gp. 5D-3, and West Plaza, Gp. 5D-10; one (Ca. 85) from a small structure group that was redeposited in late Late Classic times, and seven from outlying Minor Centers including six from Uolantun and one from Navajuelal.

The total number of vessels counted was 164, but a decision had to be made in the manner in which vessels were counted. A cache cylinder and cover were counted as a single vessel, while lip-to-lip bowls were counted as two vessels, producing a total of 152 vessels. The reason for this decision is that outflaring-side cache vessels sometimes occur singly, while a cylindrical cache vessel cover never appears alone.

The number of vessels in Manik caches ranged from 1 to 22. Twenty caches contained only a single

TABLE 7.12 (part 1)
Caches of the Manik Complex

Cache No.	Op.SubOp./Lot	Str.	Structure Group Type	TR. 25A Illustration	TR.	No. of Vessels
10	12A/3	Plat. 5D-4-3rd	Civic-Ceremonial	100*a*	14	2
13	12B/3	near St. P1	Civic-Ceremonial	100*b*	14	2
41	12B/14	near St. P9	Civic-Ceremonial	100*c*	14	1
43	12C/23	Str. 5D-34	Civic-Ceremonial	108*a*	14	1
58	12G/4	Plat. 5D-4-3rd	Civic-Ceremonial	114*a*	14	1
65	12G/14	Str. 5D-22	Civic-Ceremonial	100*d*	14	1
74	12E/4	Str. 5D-25	Civic-Ceremonial	104*a*	14	6
79	12J/4	Str. 5D-26	Civic-Ceremonial	100*e*	14	1
81	12K/12	Str. 5D-33	Civic-Ceremonial	108*b*	14	1
85[1]	20B/49	Str. 4E-31	Small Structure Group	115*b*	19	2
86	12M/17	Str. 5D-23	Civic-Ceremonial	100*f*	14	1
93	12O/8	Str. 5D-26	Civic-Ceremonial	101*a*	14	3
98	12K/19	Str. 5D-33	Civic-Ceremonial	104*b*	14	14
102	12O/15–17	Str. 5D-26	Civic-Ceremonial	101*b*	14	3
108	12M/28,30	Str. 5D-23	Civic-Ceremonial	114*c*	14	2
109	12O/18	Str. 5D-26	Civic-Ceremonial	115*a*	14	1
110	12J/10,13,14	Str. 5D-26	Civic-Ceremonial	103*a*	14	20
119	12J/20	Str. 5D-26	Civic-Ceremonial	105,106	14	22
120	12J/22	Str. 5D-26	Civic-Ceremonial	101*c*	14	2
130	12G/41	Plat. 5D-4-3rd	Civic-Ceremonial	114*d*	14	2
132	12R/6	Str. 5D-22	Civic-Ceremonial	103*b*	14	2
134	12K/29,33,34	Str. 5D-33	Civic-Ceremonial	109*b*	14	1
136	12R/12	Str. 5D-22	Civic-Ceremonial	107*a,b*	14	21
138	12R/14	Str. 5D-22	Civic-Ceremonial	108*c*	14	2
140	12R/15,16	Str. 5D-22	Civic-Ceremonial	101*d,e*	14	2
142	12R/18	Str. 5D-22	Civic-Ceremonial	102*a,b*	14	7
143	12R/22	Str. 5D-22	Civic-Ceremonial	107*c*	14	1
144	12R/21	Str. 5D-22	Civic-Ceremonial	114*e*	14	2
159	12K/60	Str. 5D-33	Civic-Ceremonial	No Illustration	14	1
167	42F/19	Str. 5D-15	Range Structure Group	102*e*	17	1
186	12R/28	Str. 5D-22	Civic-Ceremonial	102*f*	14	2
188	78M/26	Str. 5D-sub 16	Civic-Ceremonial	102*c*	16	1
196	98B/10	Str. 5D-46	Range Structure Group	108*f*	14	2
197	98B/12	Str. 5D-46	Range Structure Group	102*d*	15[†]	2
198	98B/13	Str. 5D-46	Range Structure Group	108*d*	15[†]	1
206	90C/4	Str. 5C-54	Civic-Ceremonial	108*g*	23C	2
214	135A/54	Str. SE-486	Minor Center	115*e*		1
215	129F/5,7–12	Str. SE-430	Minor Center	115*j*		4

TABLE 7.12 (part 2)
Caches of the Manik Complex

Cache No.	Op.SubOp./Lot	Str.	Structure Group Type	TR. 25A Illustration	TR.	No. of Vessels
218	135A/82	Str. SE-486	Minor Center	115*i*		2
219	135A/84	Str. SE-486	Minor Center	115*d*		2
221	135C/23	Str. SE-486	Minor Center	115*f*		1
222	135A/85	Str. SE-486	Minor Center	115*g*		1
224	144C/1	MS.131 pit	No Structures	No Illustration		1
228	98X/16	Court 5D-6	Range Structure Group	108*e*	15[†]	1
232	135B/119	Str. SE-486	Minor Center	115*h*		1

[1] Contents of Ca. 85 are of Manik date but cache was placed in Imix times.

[†] Forthcoming

vessel; sixteen contained 2 vessels; two caches contained 3 vessels, and seven caches included more than 3 vessels. The numbers in the additional caches were 4, 7, 14, 18, 20, 21, and 22. All of the large caches were from the area of the Great Plaza. Except for the caches with seven vessels and multiples of seven, there was no pattern of including vessels that represented sacred Maya numbers.

There was a very restricted repertoire in the ceramics included in Manik caches. Three types, Balanza Black, Aguila Orange, and Quintal Unslipped account for 96% of the vessels. Two shapes, the cylindrical cache vessel and outflaring-side cache vessels, make up 94% of the shapes.

The overwhelming majority of cylindrical cache vessels were Balanza Black with a minority Quintal Unslipped. The Balanza Black used for the cylinders originally was designated a different variety (the Cache-cylinder Variety) than the Balanza Variety. The decision to make a separate variety was based on the fact that the cache vessels were carelessly done. Unlike the generally careful control of firing in the Balanza Variety, almost all examples of the Cache-cylinder Variety were mottled to include areas of red, orange, and brown. In addition, the vessels were poorly shaped with walls of uneven thickness and sometimes bases that made the vessels sit at an angle. This carelessness in producing cache cylinders suggests that it was the contents rather than the vessels themselves that were of ceremonial concern. On the other hand, the Aguila Orange used for almost all the outflaring-side cache vessels

was no different from the same type as it occurred in other vessels.

Both cylindrical cache vessels and outflaring-side cache vessels were separated into two shape varieties. Cylindrical cache vessels were divided into straight-side and round-side varieties. The round-side variety was by no means hemispherical in shape, but included only a slight rounding. The outflaring-side vessels were divided by size of lip diameter into large and small varieties.

Caches tended to contain vessels of only a single shape. Fourteen caches included only outflaring-side cache vessels and nineteen were limited to cylindrical cache vessels. Among the caches with outflaring-side cache vessels, five contained a single vessel and nine two vessels. The caches with only cylindrical vessels included 1 vessel in fourteen cases, 3 vessels in two cases, and 14 vessels in one case (Ca. 98). A mixture of more than one vessel shape occurred most frequently in caches with a large number of vessels, but the ratio between different vessel shapes was variable. Cache 74 contained 2 outflaring-side cache vessels and 16 cylindrical cache vessels. Cache 110 contained 19 outflaring-side cache vessels and 1 cylindrical cache vessel. Cache 119 included 12 outflaring-side cache vessels and 8 cylindrical cache vessels as well as a rectangular cache vessel. Cache 136 contained 10 outflaring-side cache vessels and 11 cylindrical cache vessels.

In summary, aside from the limited range in types and shapes of vessels included in Manik caches, there were no obvious patterns. The only cache in which a cache vessel itself seems to have had great significance is Ca. 198 from beneath the stairs of Str. 5D-46 in the Central Acropolis (see TR. 25A: fig. 108*d*). The Urita Gouged-incised cylinder and cover bears an inscription that names the ruler Chak Tok Ich'aak I.

Problematical Deposits of the Manik Complex

Twenty-three special deposits defined as problematical included pottery of the Manik Complex (Table 7.13). There are additional problematical deposits that contain Manik ceramics, however, they date to other time periods. Because many of the problematical deposits included sherds and fragmentary vessels, only an estimated count can be made of the number of vessels included.

There is also no clear pattern to the kinds of vessel shapes included in the Manik problematical deposits or the number of vessels. Twelve of the problematical deposits consisted almost entirely of outflaring-side cache vessels of Aguila Orange, while an almost equal number (eleven) did not consist primarily of cache vessel shapes. Seven problematical deposits included only a single vessel; eight included two vessels each, usually found as lip-to-lip pairs. One problematical deposit contained three vessels, and one contained nine vessels. Problematical Deposit 170 consisted of thirty-three vessels, thirty-two of which were outflaring-side cache vessels that contained human skulls. Because the pattern, especially of lip-to-lip pairs is identical to Manik caches, it seems likely that many of these problematical deposits were actually caches.

Three problematical deposits that are distinguished either by the number of vessels included or the special character of their contents deserve special consideration. One, PD. 22, was encountered in front of Str. 5D-26 in the North Acropolis. The thirty-eight mostly incomplete vessels in PD. 22 included many of the same kinds of vessels that were encountered in the North Acropolis Early Classic chamber burials, but lacked the stuccoed and painted vessels found in those tombs. A beautiful Urita Gouged-incised cylindrical tripod with apron cover is the single vessel with strong Mexican affiliation and was almost surely an imported piece. A Urita Gouged-incised outflaring-side dish carved

with brief panels of glyphs is the second vessel of particular interest. Although the bulk of the vessels are of types and shapes that occur in burials, there were also ten wide-mouth unslipped jars that are not typical burial furniture. The material included human remains, status and domestic goods, cache material, lithic debitage, and fragments of stone monuments, including much of Stela 32 (TR. 14:324–327), however, the total amount of material seems unlikely to be burial goods, though some of the decorated pieces may have been.

Problematical Deposit 50, found in a dump just west of the North Acropolis, contained ceramics very similar to those discovered in the rich Early Classic chamber burials of the North Acropolis and includes at least twenty-six vessels, of which six are pairs of covered cache cylinders. The ceramics are closest in content to those of Bu. 10. Both the burial and problematical deposit included nine cylindrical cache vessels with covers. Both contained outflaring-side cache vessels (two in Bu. 10 and five in PD. 50), one basal-flange polychrome bowl, and one slipped jar. Both contained several round-side vessels. The most significant vessels in both Bu. 10 and PD. 50 are cylindrical tripods, eight in Bu. 10 and four in PD. 50. All the tripods in Bu. 10 were decorated in either gouged-incised decoration or painted stucco. Two of the vessels in PD. 50 were gouged-incised, one including the famous scene of Mexicans parading to a Maya temple, and the other a design of entwined serpents. Both these vessels were clearly of Mexican inspiration. A third cylindrical tripod had a simple incised scroll decoration. All of the tripods in Bu. 10 had apron covers, and there were no covers with those in PD. 50. Lacking in PD. 50 was the stuccoed and painted decoration that was so important in Bu. 10. Similar to Bu. 10, PD. 50 also included a number of imported vessels. All of the cylindrical tripods in the problematical deposit were almost surely imported. It has been suggested that the material in PD. 50 might have been derived from an important Early Classic chamber burial. The ceramic contents are strongly suggestive of such an origin. In addition, the material included human remains (Moholy-Nagy, pers. comm. 2016).

An unusually large deposit of Manik Complex ceramics was encountered as PD. 74 near the location of the later Str. 5C-15, the southern structure of

TABLE 7.13
Problematical Deposits of the Manik Complex

PD. No.	Op.SubOp./Lot	Location	Structure Group Type	TR. 25A Illustration	TR.	Est. No. of Vessels
22	12J/17,23–29	Gp. 5D-2 Str. 5D-26-1st	Civic-Ceremonial	123–126	14	38
23	20H/342	Gp. 4F-1 Quarry 4F-1	Small Structure Group	127*a*	19	2
24	20H/34-3	Gp. 4F-1 Quarry 4F-1	Small Structure Group	127*b*	19	2
25	20H/35	Gp. 4F-1 Quarry 4F-1	Small Structure Group	127*c*	19	2
27	12H/28–35	Gp. 5D-2 Str. 5D-26	Civic-Ceremonial	127*d*	14	1
40	12M/5	Gp. 5D-2 Str. 5D-23	Civic-Ceremonial	127*f*	14	1
50	10E/2	Gp. 5D near St. 29	No structures	128–130		>26
64[1]	24C/71	Gp. 2G-1 Str. 2G-59	Small Structure Group	132*a*	20A&B	1
67	27G/9	Gp. 5G-1 Plat. 5G-1	Intermediate Structure Group	133*a*	21	4
74	43F/17,18	Gp. 5C-1 under Str. 5C-15	Civic-Ceremonial	134–138	18	>71
99	67C/10	Gp. 7C-1 Str. 7C-4	Small Structure Group	142*c*	20	3
109	67F/9	Gp. 3F-3 Str. 3F-12	Small Structure Group	143*b*	20	2
111	66P/9–11	Chultun 5C-1 Tozzer Causeway	No structures	143*c*		1
124	76B/13	Gp. 5D-1 Str. 5D-7	Small Structure Group	144*e*	20A&B	2
129	90B/6	Gp. 5C-11 Str. 5C-53	Civic-Ceremonial	144*f*	23C	2
147	45G/22	Gp. 5D-11 Str. 5D-50	Range Structure Group	148*a*	15[†]	1
152	12T/60	Gp. 5D-2 Str. 5D-22	Civic-Ceremonial	148*c*	14	3
167	3E/25	Gp. 7F-1 Str. 7F-29	Intermediate Structure Group	None	22	1
170	53C/9	Gp. 6F-27G Chultun 6F-6	Civic-Ceremonial	149–151*a*	23B	33
227	129B/21	SE-001 Str. SE-430	Minor Center	153*e*	24B	1
231	66H/5–16	Gp. 6C-5 Chultun 6C-11	Small Structure Group	153*f*, 154	20	9
233	3D/4	Gp. 7F-1 Plat. 7F-1	Intermediate Structure Group	155*a*	22	2
263	72C/5	Gp. 7G-1 Chultun 7G-4	Small Structure Group	155*c*	20	2

[1] Late Manik or Early Ik

[†] Forthcoming

Twin Pyramid Complex, Gp. 5C-1, near Temple IV. Its contents included human remains, domestic and status goods, lithic debitage, and many (>71) sherds of incomplete vessels. The collection dates largely to Manik 3B, but there is an admixture of earlier Manik as well. The contents feature a large number of decorated cylindrical tripods and apron covers. Some of the tripods have coffee-bean decoration in Mexican style, but no incised or painted Mexican design elements are present. Very large quantities of such domestic shapes as unslipped and slipped jars are present. Totally lacking are vessels typical of large Manik burials, such as cylindrical and outflaring-side cache vessels. Ceramically, the material seems to represent refuse over a period of time, perhaps from an elite residential area.

VIII

Ik Ceramic Complex

The Early Classic–Early Late Classic Ceramic Transition

The ceramic changes between the Early Classic and Early Late Classic at Tikal were as profound as those that separated the Preclassic from the Early Classic. The only segment of the ceramic inventory that remained almost unchanged was the unslipped striated types and the wide-mouth jar shape class with which they were associated.

Tinaja Red, the new type that predominated among Late Classic monochromes differs quite strongly from Aguila Orange of the Early Classic. At Uaxactun, Smith and Gifford (1966:171–172) identified three different monochrome red types in the Late Classic. The Tepeu I, Ik Complex, equivalent was called Tasital Red, the Tepeu 2, Imix Complex, equivalent was called Nanzal Red, and the Tepeu 3, Eznab Complex, equivalent was named Tinaja Red. While some have been able to differentiate among the Late Classic monochrome reds, it was felt that the Tikal sample overlapped too much to separate into separate types or varieties, so all Late and Terminal Classic monochrome reds were classified within the Tinaja Ceramic Group. Of the two shape classes produced from Tinaja Red, narrow-mouth jars differ less between the Early and Late Classic than large-capacity bowls. Narrow-mouth jar necks are slightly taller and thicker in the Late Classic than in the Early Classic, but there is some overlap. The large-capacity bowls of the Late Classic are very different from those of the Early Classic and serve as a reliable horizon marker of the period across most of the Maya lowlands. Once Tinaja Red and the utilitarian shapes associated with it became established at the start of the Ik Complex, they continued with little change through the Imix and Eznab Complexes.

Decorated types changed significantly between the Early and Early Late Classic. The highly decorated black types of the Early Classic Balanza Group had no major counterparts throughout the Late Classic when black types became rare. The painted types, especially polychromes, of the Late Classic are quite different from those of the Early Classic. Additionally, throughout the Late Classic, there was a much stronger correlation between types and serving vessel shapes. In the Early Classic, serving vessels had been produced in monochrome types, decorated black types, and polychromes. In the Late Classic, nearly 100% of serving vessels were of one of the polychrome groups.

There were also major changes in some of the serving vessel shapes. Simple shapes such as slightly incurving to round-side and outflaring to slightly outcurving-side bowls and dishes changed little between the two periods. On the other hand, the diagnostic basal-flange bowls of the Early Classic disappeared and laterally ridged tripod plates became the type fossil for the Ik Complex. Unlike striated or monochrome shapes, serving vessel shapes changed rapidly in the Late and Terminal Classic. For this time interval, there was no evidence comparable to the superb North Acropolis stratigraphic sequence to demonstrate the timing of the ceramic changes.

Pastes of the Ik Complex

Introduction

There were major changes in pastes between the Manik and Ik Complexes. Tinaja Paste, used for Late Classic monochromes, differs significantly from the pastes used for monochromes in the Manik Complex. The appearance of Tinaja Paste in the Ik Complex establishes a tradition that continues through the Terminal Classic Eznab Complex. Saxche Paste, used for Ik Complex polychromes, is also characteristic and a single-complex marker because it is replaced by a different polychrome paste in the Imix Complex. The long-lived Coarse-carbonate Paste continued to be used for striated jars as it had been since the Preclassic.

The limited variety in pastes, the relatively strong homogeneity within each paste, and the very strong correlation between pastes and ceramic groups indicate a high degree of standardization in Ik Complex ceramics. One is tempted to think of a greater specialization in Ik ceramic production than is suggested by the distinctly less homogeneous Manik pastes, but it is a suggestion that would need considerably more sophisticated studies for verification.

Ik Complex Collections

Introduction

Ceramics of the Ik Complex are very widely distributed at Tikal and were encountered in the majority of operations (Table 8.1). Nevertheless, the number of pure Ik samples of a size that permitted quantitative analysis was not large. Ik/Imix Location 2, the area of extensive excavations in small-mound Gp. 4F-1 and 4F-2 (see TR. 19), provided the key to the chronology of both complexes. This location produced a large number of quantifiable samples, most of which represented relatively brief time spans. The samples were seriated into a sequence that was supported by numerous cases of both architectural and midden stratigraphy within the groups. As a result, the information about ceramic change during the time of the Ik and Imix Ceramic Complexes is far more detailed than that for other complexes. Samples from other Ik locations

fitted well into the seriation charts obtained from Location 2, but did not offer any additional stratigraphic confirmation.

Ik locations represented a range of social contexts. Two locations were in the area of the Great Plaza (Group 5D-2) and provided samples that probably originated in ceremonial-elite activities; one was in an Intermediate Structure Group (Group 7F-1), and the remaining three were in Small Structure Groups (Groups 4F-1, 4F-2, and 7E-3), presumably commoner residential contexts. Twenty-one special deposits classified as burials of Ik date contained ceramics, ranging from chamber burials within the site center to burials intruded in housemounds. Six special deposits classified as caches of Ik date included ceramics, as did ten problematical deposits.

IK-IMIX LOCATION 1

This location includes areas from Group 7F-1 that supplied quantifiable samples from the Ik and Imix Complexes. All of the samples came from the western edge of the group around Str. 7F-32, 34, 35, and 36 (see TR. 22). Both architectural and metric stratigraphy was used during excavation, however, the size of samples was relatively small. Group 7F-1 contains intermediate-size architecture and the sherds may consequently be assigned to an intermediate social status.

Ik Sample 1-3: A series of lots from the fill of Str. 7F-32 was combined to obtain a single sample of 146 rim sherds quantified for shapes. The sample dated to the Ik Complex, but was too mixed to attribute to a specific segment of the time range.

Ik Samples 1-4 through 1-10: Of these seven samples, six, totaling 1758 sherds, all from various parts of the fill of Str. 7F-32, were counted for types.

IK-IMIX LOCATION 2

Ik-Imix Location 2 was the area of Group 4F-1 and 4F-2, small structure groups located about 1 km NE of the Great Plaza (see TR. 19). The groups were extensively excavated during the early seasons of the Tikal Project and provided huge samples of ceramics with very detailed stratigraphic control. Because the preservation of sherd surfaces was very poor, the samples were not useful for typological analysis, but they provided the key to an excellent sequence of

TABLE 8.1 (part 1)
Locations of Ik Samples

Sample #	Op.Sub-Op./Lot	Structure Group and Structure Number	Structure Group Type	Total Sherds-Types	Total Sherds-Shapes	Ceramic Complex	Comments	TR.
Location 1		**Group 7F-1**	**Intermediate Structure Group**				**Around Str. 7F-32, 34, 35, and 36**	**22**
Sample 1-3	3G	Str. 7F-32		—	146	Ik	Combined with Samples 1-1, 1-2	
Sample 1-4	3G/6	Str. 7F-32		257	—	Ik	Unsealed fill	
Sample 1-5	3G/7	Str. 7F-32		—	—	Ik	Unsealed fill	
Sample 1-6	3G/10	Str. 7F-32		287	—	Ik	Sealed fill	
Sample 1-7	3G/11	Str. 7F-32		136	—	Ik	Sealed fill	
Sample 1-8	3G/12	Str. 7F-32		472	—	Ik	Sealed fill	
Sample 1-9	3G/17	Str. 7F-32		159	—	Ik	Sealed fill lower level	
Sample 1-10	3H/2	Plat. 7F-2		447	—	Ik	Fill	
Location 2		**Groups 4F-1 and 4F-2**	**Small Structure Groups**					**19**
Sample 2a-2	20B/31, 42, 47, 50, 53, 56, 57, 59, 61, 70, 81	Str. 4E-31		231	110	Ik	Sealed in substructure	
Sample 2a-3	20B/45, 55, 63	Str. 4E-31		310	145	Ik	Lower fill in structure	
Sample 2b-6	20D/19, 22, 29, 30, 31, 33, 34, 35, 36, 38, 41, 49, 50, 51, 53, 54, 57, 68	Str. 4F-3-2nd-B		265	—	Early Ik	Fill of Str. 4F-3-2nd-B	
Sample 2c-3	20E/20, 30, 31, 35, 36, 37, 44	Str. 4F-4		169	145	Early Ik	Unsealed fill of Str. 4F-4	
Sample 2e-1	20M/1, 3, 12, 14, 15, 17, 20, 21, 22, 25, 26, 31, 33, 36, 37, 44, 27, 28, 39	Str. 4F-6		324	145	Late Ik	Surface to bedrock east of Str. 4F-6	
Sample 2e-2	20M/29, 40, 41, 45, 47	Str. 4F-6-B		332	137	Late Ik	Unsealed fill Str. 4F-6-B	
Sample 2e-3	20M/24, 30, 34, 35, 42, 43, 46, 48	Str. 4F-6-B		236	101	Late Ik	Unsealed fill Str. 4F-6-B	
Sample 2f-2	20L/7, 8, 10, 14, 16, 26, 31, 34	Str. 4F-7		371	101	Early Ik	Unsealed fill of lowest level Str. 4F-7	

TABLE 8.1 (part 2)
Locations of Ik Samples

Sample #	Op.Sub-Op./Lot	Structure Group and Structure Number	Structure Group Type	Total Sherds-Types	Total Sherds-Shapes	Ceramic Complex	Comments	TR.
Sample 2g-1	20K/1, 4, 6, 8, 10, 12, 14, 17, 19, 22, 24, 30, 34, 35, 40, 43, 45, 50, 51, 55, 56, 62	Str. 4F-10		309	118	Late Ik	Surface to top of walls outside of Str. 4F-10	
Sample 2g-2	20K/3, 5, 7, 9, 11, 13, 15, 18, 20, 23, 25, 31, 36, 42, 46, 47, 48, 49, 52, 57, 63	Str. 4F-10		582	220	Late Ik	Top to base of walls outside Str. 4F-10	
Sample 2g-3	20K/21, 26, 27, 28, 29, 32, 33, 37, 41, 53, 54, 58, 73, 77, 78, 93	Str. 4F-10-A and 4F-10-B		207	59	Late Ik	Mixed fill from Str. 4F-10-A and 4F-10-B	
Sample 2g-4	20K/60, 61, 64, 65, 66, 67, 68, 69, 70, 71, 72, 79, 80, 82, 86, 87, 91	Str. 4F-10-B		635	172	Early Ik	Unsealed and sealed fill of Str. 4F-10-B	
Sample 2i-2	20A/6, 12, 42, 43, 49, 52, 53, 68, 81	Plat. 4F-7		224	104	Early Ik	Area between Str. 4F-13 and Plat. 4F-7	
Sample 2i-3	20A/27, 50, 63, 64, 65, 67, 71, 72, 76, 82, 91	Str. 4F-13		276	86	Early Ik	Fill of Str. 4F-13	
Sample 2j-1	20A/11, 29	Str.4F-15-1st-A		351	126	Late Ik	Surface of Str. 4F-15-1st-A	
Sample 2j-2	20A/58, 84	Str. 4F-15-1st-B		200	73	Early Ik	Unsealed fill of Str. 4F-15-1st-B	
Sample 2k-1	20A/16, 17, 33, 34, 57	Str. 4F-16-1st-C		211	91	Late Ik	Unsealed fill of Str. 4F-16-1st-C	
Sample 2l-1	20A/24	Str. 4F-42		191	—	Early Ik	Above Floor 1 of Str. 4F-42	
Sample 2m-1	20A/30, 56	Plat. 4F-1		206	76	Late Ik	Above surface of Plat. 4F-1	

TABLE 8.1 (part 3)
Locations of Ik Samples

Sample #	Op.Sub-Op./Lot	Structure Group and Structure Number	Structure Group Type	Total Sherds-Types	Total Sherds-Shapes	Ceramic Complex	Comments	TR.
Location 3		**Group 5D-2**	**Civic-Ceremonial**					14
Sample 3-1	12L/16, 28, 31, 34	Str. 5D-33-1st		—	388	Early Ik	Combined sample from fill of Str. 5D-33-1st	
Location 4		**Group 7E-3**	**Small Structure Group**					20A
Sample 4-1	36U	Group platform in front of Str. 7E-9		—	167	Early Ik	Group platform in front of Str. 7E-9	
Location 5		**Group 5D-11 Central Acropolis**	**Range Structure Group**					15[†]
Sample 5-1	97A/19	Str. 5D-54		423	—	Ik	Inside SW room of Str. 5D-54, 3rd story in debris	
Sample 5-2	97A/13	Str. 5D-54		224	—	Ik	Inside SW room of Str. 5D-54, 3rd story on floor	
	TOTAL SHERDS			8035	2564			

[†] Forthcoming

vessel shapes that is at the heart of the Ik and Imix chronology.

As was typical at Tikal, deep midden deposits representing long periods of in situ accumulation were lacking at the location. Instead, evidence from excavation and from fits between sherds from different deposits clearly indicated that refuse was accumulated for brief periods of time and was then used as fill for whatever construction happened to be in progress. This meant that Ik-Imix Location 2 provided, from both structure fill and those middens still in place at the time of excavation, a large set of short time-span samples amenable to seriation. Because most structures in the groups showed reconstructions, remodeling, or additions that could be related by architectural stratigraphy, there were multiple instances of short stratigraphic sequences to test the seriation. The ceramic results from Ik-Imix Location 2, supplemented by samples from other locations at Tikal, provided a very detailed picture of ceramic change covering the span of the Ik and Imix Complexes.

In the following description of sub-locations and samples from Ik-Imix Location 2, only samples pertaining to the Ik Complex are discussed at this point. Samples pertaining to the Imix Complex are discussed in Chapter 9 on the Imix Complex.

IK-IMIX LOCATION 2A

This location was Str. 4E-31, the largest structure in Group 4F-1. Two samples from fills of construction units dated to the late part of the Ik Complex. Seriational order of the two samples did not match the architectural sequence in detail, although it is clear that both were of Ik date. There is good stratigraphic and temporal separation between the Ik fill samples and the Imix Complex sample from occupation and surface levels outside the structure.

Ik Sample 2a-2: This sample of 231 sherds quantified for types and 110 sherds quantified for shapes came from the sealed fill of the supplementary platform alone.

Ik Sample 2a-3: This sample of 310 sherds quantified for types and 145 sherds quantified for shapes came from the sealed fill of the supplementary platform and the hard-packed gray stratum above bedrock.

IK-IMIX LOCATION 2B

Str. 4F-3, Ik-Imix Location 2b, provided one early Ik Complex sample from structure fill that preceded five Imix Complex samples encountered on the living surface outside structure walls.

Ik Sample 2b-6: This sample of 265 sherds quantified for shapes came from the fill of Str. 4F-3-2nd-B. It is early Ik.

IK-IMIX LOCATION 2C

Str. 4F-4, Ik-Imix Location 2c, provided an excellent stratigraphic series of three levels. Only the earliest member of the series pertains to the Ik Complex. It is followed by an early Imix sample from later fill and a late Imix sample from surface lots.

Ik Sample 2c-3: This sample of 169 sherds quantified for types and 145 sherds quantified for shapes came from the fill of Str. 4F-4-B. It pertains to the early part of the Ik Complex.

IK LOCATION 2E

Structure 4F-6 was Ik Location 2e. All three samples from the location were late Ik. One sample was from the earliest construction and a pre-construction level; one was from fill of later construction; and one was from outside of and above the structure.

Ik Sample 2e-1: This sample of 324 sherds quantified for types and 145 sherds quantified for shapes came from excavation from the surface to bedrock outside of the structure. It is late Ik.

Ik Sample 2e-2: This sample of 332 sherds quantified for types and 137 sherds quantified for shapes came from the unsealed fill of Str. 4F-6-B, and dates to late Ik.

Ik Sample 2e-3: This sample of 236 sherds quantified for types and 101 sherds quantified for shapes came from fill of the earliest construction at the locus and the pre-construction level of earth below the structure. The sample was late Ik.

IK-IMIX LOCATION 2F

A sample from the fill of Str. 4F-7, Ik-Imix Location 2f, dated from the Ik Complex. A stratigraphically later sample from the location dated to the Imix Complex.

Ik Sample 2f-2: This sample of 371 sherds quantified for types and 101 sherds quantified for shapes came from the lowest level of fill within Str. 4F-7. It dates to early Ik.

IK LOCATION 2G

Excavations at Ik Location 2g, Str. 4F-10, provided four quantified samples all dating to the Ik Complex. Several sequent levels of construction and occupation yielded samples. The earliest construction unit, a hard-packed stratum of gray earth, was added to provide a level surface before structures were built. A sample from this stratum dated to early Ik and seriated earliest although it was too small for reliable quantification. A fill sample from Str. 4F-10-B dated to early Ik but seriated somewhat later than the gray earth sample. A sample containing mixed fill from Str. 4F-10-B and the final Str. 4F-10-A was later and dated to late Ik. Material from outside the structure was separated into two samples by metric stratigraphy. Both samples were late Ik, but the lower sample actually seriated marginally later than the upper sample. Such stratigraphic reversals are not uncommon in small-structure excavations where the chance for samples to include varying amounts of fill slumped from structure platforms is high.

Ik Sample 2g-1: This sample of 309 sherds quantified for types and 118 sherds quantified for shapes came from excavation of all lots outside the structure, between ground surface to the level of the top of the walls of Str. 4F-10. It dated to late Ik.

Ik Sample 2g-2: This sample of 582 sherds quantified for types and 220 sherds quantified for shapes came from excavation of all lots below those of Sample 2g-1 between the level of the top of the walls of Str. 4F-10 to bedrock. It dated to late Ik but seriated later than the preceding sample.

Ik Sample 2g-3: This sample of 207 sherds quantified for types and 59 sherds quantified for shapes came from mixed fill of Str. 4F-10-A and 4F-10-B. It dated to late Ik.

Ik Sample 2g-4: This early Ik sample of 635 sherds

quantified for types and 172 sherds quantified for shapes came from unsealed fill of Str. 4F-10-B. It dated to early Ik.

IK LOCATION 2I

Structure 4F-13, Ik Location 2i, provided two quantified samples dated to the Ik Complex. A fill sample, too small for reliable quantification, from the structure fill was early Ik and seriated earlier than the two quantified samples. A sample from above the structure floors seriated slightly later, but was still early Ik, as was a sample from an area outside the structure.

Ik Sample 2i-2: This sample of 224 sherds quantified for types and 104 sherds quantified for shapes came from the area between Str. 4F-13 and Plat. 4F-7. Stratigraphically unrelated to the other samples, it dated to early Ik.

Ik Sample 2i-3: This sample of 276 sherds quantified for types and 86 sherds quantified for shapes came from the fill of Str. 4F-13. It dated to early Ik.

IK-LOCATION 2J

Two Ik Complex samples were encountered at Str. 4F-15, Location 2j. A sample from fill of the penultimate structure at the location dated to early Ik, while a sample from the surface above the latest structure was late Ik.

Ik Sample 2j-1: This sample of 351 sherds quantified for types and 126 sherds quantified for shapes from the surface of Str. 4F-15-1st-A was late Ik.

Ik Sample 2j-2: This sample of 200 sherds quantified for types and 73 sherds quantified for shapes from unsealed fill of Str. 4F-15-1st-B dated to early Ik.

IK LOCATION 2K

Structure 4F-16, Ik Location 2k, provided only a single sample large enough for analysis.

Ik Sample 2k-1: This sample of 211 sherds quantified for types and 91 sherds quantified for shapes comes from the fill of Str. 4F-16-lst-C and is dated to late Ik.

IK LOCATION 2L

Str. 4F-42, Ik Location 2l, provided only a single Ik Complex sample from above the floor of the structure.

Ik Sample 2l-1: This sample of 191 sherds quantified for types came from above Floor 1 of Str. 4F-42 and is dated to Early Ik.

IK LOCATION 2M

Plat. 4F-1, Ik Location 2m, provided a single Ik Complex sample from above the plaza.

Ik Sample 2m-1: This sample of 206 sherds quantified for types and 76 sherds quantified for shapes from above the surface of the plaza dated to late Ik.

IK LOCATION 3

This location included lots from the fill of Str. 5D-33-1st at the northern edge of the Great Plaza (of Group 5D-2), a civic-ceremonial context (see TR. 14). In the process of construction, the builders used a number of partitioning walls, presumably to keep fill from slumping. The divisions created by the walls provided a series of separate "bins" of fill material. Samples from different bins were carefully segregated in the process of excavation to see whether they would differ significantly. Ik Complex ceramics predominated in all of the fill samples, but were always mixed with substantial amounts of Manik Complex material and some material from Preclassic complexes. To quantify the Ik material in the samples demanded typological separation of Ik sherds from those of earlier complexes, a separation that is possible only for certain categories of shapes. Serving vessels, large bowls, and narrow-mouth jars of the Ik Complex are distinctive enough to separate from earlier sherds in mixed samples, but wide-mouth jars of the Ik Complex are so like those of the Manik Complex that separation is impossible. Consequently, only partial sherd counts for fill samples from Str. 5D-33 were possible, but quantification of serving vessel and large bowl classes was possible. The first significant result of the analysis was to demonstrate that there were no substantial differences between samples from different bins of fill.

Ik Sample 3-1: Given the general homogeneity of the fill from different bins, all fill sherds from Str. 5D-33 were lumped into a single Ik Complex sample of 388 rims quantified for shapes that had serving vessel and large bowl decoration frequencies typical of the early part of the Ik Complex. Although fill material is difficult to assign to a specific origin, it seems likely that most of the material would have been obtained from ceremonial-elite activity somewhere near the site center.

IK LOCATION 4

Ik Sample 4-1: This location included a series of excavations just to the S of Str. 7E-11, the largest of Small Structure Group 7E-3, slightly more than 1 km S and slightly E of the Great Plaza (see TR. 20A). Although a fair depth of deposit and some floors were encountered in the excavations, samples were so small that they had to be combined into a single, somewhat mixed, early Ik Complex sample that included 167 rim sherds counted for shape. The context was almost certainly commoner residential from a small structure group.

IK LOCATION 5

Ik Location 5 was Group 5D-11, the Central Acropolis, is a Range Structure Group (see TR. 15). The Ik Complex samples were two lots recovered in the excavation inside the SW room. Because such early material cannot have been from occupation in the room, it must represent debris from the collapse of the vault of the structure. Preservation of the material was excellent, so that type counts were possible, but there were not enough rim sherds for shape counts. In this area of the site an elite residential source for the material would be most likely.

Ik Sample 5-1: This sample of 423 sherds quantified for types came from above-floor debris in the SW room of the third story of Str. 5D-54.

Ik Sample 5-2: This sample of 224 sherds quantified for types came from on-floor debris in the SW room of the third story of Str. 5D-54.

Ik Paste Descriptions

COARSE-CARBONATE PASTE

Identifying characteristics: In all regards except for color the same as the Chuen Complex (see Chapter 4 for complete description).

Color: A broad range of colors, often within single sherds, marks the paste. The most common colors in the Ik Complex sherds include light yellow brown (7.5YR6/4; 10YR6/4), reddish yellow (7.5YR 7/6, 6/6), and yellowish brown (10YR5/4).

Comments: Identical to the paste used in all Late Preclassic and Classic complexes for striated and unslipped types.

TINAJA PASTE

Identifying characteristics: The most typical examples of Tinaja Paste combine a sandy feel of the paste surface and a reddish-yellow color that are quite distinctive. The paste is unique enough so that it can be used as a diagnostic for recognizing Late/Terminal Classic sherds.

Color: The most common and characteristic color is reddish yellow (5YR 7/6, 7/8; 6/6, 6/8; 7.5YR 7/6, 7/8; 6/6, 6/8). Other colors that appear include brownish yellow (10YR 6/4), yellowish brown (10YR 5/4, 5/6), dark yellowish brown (10YR 4/4), very pale brown (10YR 7/4), yellow (10YR 7/6), and pink (7.5YR 7/4).

Texture: Fine to medium; quite porous.

Inclusions: Small to medium amounts of small white particles and occasional flecks of golden mica are visible macroscopically. Magnification by 30X shows very large quantities of glassy particles that are almost certainly volcanic ash, quite large quantities of black shiny material, occasional lumps of white to cream powdery material, and golden mica. Carbonate inclusions occur in a small fraction of the sherds.

Types: Types of the Tinaja and Maquina Groups are made from Tinaja Paste, as are the rare Ucum Unslipped vessels, and a few polychrome vessels.

Temporal distribution: The paste first appears at the beginning of the Ik Complex and continues until the end of the Eznab Complex.

SAXCHE PASTE

Identifying characteristics: The primary identifier is the red to reddish-yellow color of the paste. Saxche Paste also has a finer texture and less visible inclu-

sions than the polychrome pastes of other complexes.

Color: Reddish yellow (5YR 6/6, 6/8; 7/6, 7/8; 7.5YR 6/8), yellowish red (5YR 4/8; 5/6, 5/8), red (2.5YR 5/8), or light red (2.5YR 6/6, 6/8). Thicker sections sometimes show a core color of grayish brown (2.5Y 5/2) or light yellowish brown (10YR 6/4).

Texture: Fine.

Inclusions: Only occasional white particles are visible macroscopically. Under 30X magnification, about half the examples show large amounts of very fine, glassy particles (probably volcanic ash) and the remainder shows much smaller amounts of the same material. Also present occasionally are shiny black particles and hematite lumps.

Types: Strongly associated with the Saxche Polychrome Group and rarely used with monochrome types.

Temporal distribution: Confined to the Ik Complex.

Ceramic Types of the Ik Complex

Introduction

The Ik Ceramic Complex includes the 9 ceramic groups and 19 types listed in Table 8.2. In general, all major groups listed for Uaxactun (Smith and Gifford 1966) occur at Tikal and types are closely parallel. There were, however, significant changes in naming types. The Uaxactun custom of adopting new type names for each complex was abandoned in cases where the types were indistinguishable between complexes. Thus, for example, the name Tinaja Red is used for the Ik, Imix, and Eznab Complexes rather than having three separate red types (and groups) as was done at Uaxactun.

Because many Ik Complex samples came from contexts in which surface preservation is very poor, only eight lots from two locations were utilized to examine type frequencies, as shown in Table 8.3. In these contexts, the total of unslipped types (Encanto Striated and Cambio Unslipped) ranges between 13% and 44% with a median of 37%. The Tinaja

TABLE 8.2
Ceramic Groups and Types of the Ik Complex

CAMBIO CERAMIC GROUP

Cambio Unslipped: Cambio Variety

ENCANTO CERAMIC GROUP

Encanto Striated: Encanto Variety

UCUM CERAMIC GROUP

Ucum Unslipped: Ucum Variety

Kokob Carved: Kokob Variety

TINAJA CERAMIC GROUP

Tinaja Red: Tinaja Variety

Cameron Incised: Cameron Variety

Chinja Impressed: Chinja Variety

Chinja Impressed: Appliquéd Variety

Rosa Punctated: Rosa Variety

VERACAL CERAMIC GROUP

Veracal Orange: Veracal Variety

Kau Incised: Kau Variety

MAQUINA CERAMIC GROUP

Maquina Brown: Maquina Variety

ZACEC CERAMIC GROUP

Zacec Black: Zacec Variety

Chilar Fluted: Chilar Variety

UZ CERAMIC GROUP

Uz Buff: Uz Variety

SAXCHE CERAMIC GROUP

Saxche Orange Polychrome: Saxche Variety

Desquite Red-on-orange: Desquite Variety

Uacho Black-on-orange: Uacho Variety

Jama Red Polychrome: Jama Variety

Sibal Buff Polychrome: Sibal Variety

Red Group, the second most common group, shows a range between 18% and 43% with a median of 29%. The Saxche Group ranges between 5% and 22% with a median of 14%. Maquina Brown appears consistently in low frequencies that are usually between 6% and 9%. Zacec Black and Veracal Orange occur in all lots in low frequencies. There is considerable lot-to-lot variation in ceramic group frequencies, a matter that does not obviously relate to chronology or social context.

Ik Type Descriptions

CAMBIO CERAMIC GROUP

Cambio Unslipped: Cambio Variety

Established: Smith and Gifford (1966)

Group: Cambio

Ware: Uaxactun Unslipped

Ceramic Complex: Ik (Continues into Imix and Eznab)

Ceramic Sphere: Tepeu 1–3

Illustrations: Fig. 39.1–19; 39.25–29; 39.39–53; 56.34, 56.37. See TR. 25A: fig. 133c1.

Principal Identifying Attributes: Unslipped surfaces on large wide-mouth jars.

Identifying characteristics and sorting problems: Unslipped sherds without striations are otherwise identical to Encanto Striated. Because most of them are jar necks that are not decorated with striations, many examples may be Encanto Striated and they are difficult to sort from striated jars.

Paste: Coarse-carbonate Paste.

Firing: Dark cores are common and over one-third of the sherds show fireclouding. Because the fireclouding is more often on the interior than on the exterior, it is probably due to the original firing rather than to smudging from use.

Color: There is a wide range of color, even on a single sherd or vessel. The most common colors range from strong brown (7.5YR 5/6) to pale brown (10YR 7/3; 6/3). There are occasional light gray (10YR 7/2) and some light red brown (5YR 6/4) tones.

Surface finish and decoration: The nature of the paste and coarse inclusions made smoothing of vessel surfaces difficult.

TABLE 8.3
Ceramic Type Frequencies of the Ik Complex

| Ceramic Group | Intermediate Structure Group | | | | | | Range Structure Group | |
| | Location 1 | | | | | | Location 5 | |
	Sample 1-4 Op. 3G/6 Group 7F-1 Str. 7F-32	Sample 1-6 Op. 3G/10 Group 7F-1 Str. 7F-32	Sample 1-7 Op. 3G/11 Group 7F-1 Str. 7F-32	Sample 1-8 Op. 3G/12 Group 7F-1 Str. 7F-32	Sample 1-9 Op. 3G/17 Group 7F-1 Str. 7F-32	Sample 1-10 Op. 3H/2 Group 7F-1 Str. 7F-32	Sample 5-1 Op. 97A/19 Str. 5D-54, Central Acropolis	Sample 5-2 Op. 97A/13, Str. 5D-54, Central Acropolis
	%	%	%	%	%	%	%	%
Cambio Group	35.8	18.1	14.0	27.1	28.3	32.9	20.6	10.3
Encanto Group	4.7	24.0	5.9	10.6	6.3	4.0	4.0	2.7
Tinaja Group	22.6	26.5	43.4	29.4	18.2	24.8	30.0	34.8
Zacec Group	3.1	7.7	1.5	3.8	1.9	5.4	12.3	10.3
Maquina Group	3.1	5.9	8.8	8.1	5.0	9.4	9.5	8.0
Veracal Group	3.9	0.3	—	1.7	3.1	5.4	3.3	3.6
Saxche Group	19.5	5.6	14.0	4.9	20.1	12.8	14.9	22.3
Total Unslipped	40.5	42.1	19.9	37.7	34.6	36.9	24.6	12.9
Total Slipped	52.2	46.0	67.7	47.9	48.3	57.8	70.0	79.0
Unclassified & Rare Types	0.4	—	—	—	—	—	0.5	—
Weathered	7.0	11.8	12.5	14.4	17.0	5.4	5.0	8.0
Number of Sherds	257	287	136	472	159	447	423	224

Shapes: Almost entirely wide-mouth jars with tall necks.

Temporal distribution: Begins at the start of the Ik Complex and continues through the Eznab Complex.

Intersite comparisons: The Cambio Unslipped type is used at Altar de Sacrificios (Adams 1971); Becan (Ball 1977); Calakmul (Dominguez Carrasco 1994); El Mirador (Forsyth 1989); Holmul (Callaghan 2008, 2016e); La Milpa (Sagebiel 2005); Piedras Negras (Muñoz 2004); Seibal (Sabloff 1975); Uaxactun (Smith and Gifford 1966); and Yaxchilan (Lopez Varela 1989). The similar Cayo Unlipped type is used at Barton Ramie (Gifford 1976); Chan (Kosakowsky 2012); and Colha (Valdez 1987). Both Zibal Unslipped and Cambio Unslipped are used at Blue Creek (Kosakowsky and Lohse 2003). An Impressed Variety occurs in the Petexbatun (Foias and Bishop 2013). At Xunantunich the Cambio Group is used for censer forms only (LeCount 1996).

ENCANTO CERAMIC GROUP

Encanto Striated: Encanto Variety

Established: Smith and Gifford (1966)

Group: Encanto

Ware: Uaxactun Unslipped

Ceramic Complex: Ik (Continues into Imix and Eznab)

Ceramic Sphere: Tepeu 1–3

Illustrations: Fig. 39.1–19, 39.25–29, 39.39–53.

Principal Identifying Attributes: Unslipped striated surfaces on wide-mouth jars. Crisscross striations occur on bodies of jars and end at the neck.

Identifying characteristics and sorting problems: Striated types are almost identical throughout the Tikal sequence and can only be separated on features of shape.

Paste: Coarse-carbonate Paste.

Firing: Dark cores are common and over one-third of the sherds show fireclouding. Because the fireclouding is more often on the interior than on the exterior, it is probably due to the original firing rather than to smudging from use.

Color: There is a wide range of color, even on a single sherd or vessel. The most common colors range from strong brown (7.5YR 5/6) to pale brown (10YR 7/3; 6/3). There are occasional light gray (10YR 7/2) and some light red brown (5YR 6/4) tones.

Surface finish and decoration: The nature of the paste and coarse inclusions made smoothing difficult. Striations are variable, ranging from fine to heavy. Striations cease abruptly at the necks of vessels, which they approach either vertically or obliquely. Crisscross striations on bodies are common. Bottoms of the rounded bases are often unstriated.

Shapes: Almost entirely wide-mouth jars with tall necks.

Temporal distribution: Begins at the start of the Ik Complex and continues through the Eznab Complex.

Intersite Comparisons: The Encanto Striated type is used at Altar de Sacrificios (Adams 1971); Becan (Ball 1977); Calakmul (Dominguez Carrasco 1994); El Mirador (Forsyth 1989); Holmul (Callaghan 2008, 2016e); La Milpa (Sagebiel 2005); Piedras Negras (Muñoz 2004); Seibal (Sabloff 1975); Uaxactun (Smith and Gifford 1966); and Yaxchilan (Lopez Varela 1989). The similar Tu-tu Camp Striated type is used at Barton Ramie (Gifford 1976); Chan (Kosakowsky 2012); Colha (Valdez 1987); and Xunantunich (LeCount 1996). Tu-tu Camp Striated and Encanto Striated are used interchangeably at Blue Creek (Kosakowsky and Lohse 2003).

UCUM CERAMIC GROUP

Ucum Unslipped: Ucum Variety

Established: TR. 25A (Culbert 1993)

Group: Ucum

Ware: Uaxactun Unslipped

Ceramic Complex: Ik (Continues into Imix)

Ceramic Sphere: Tepeu 1–2

Illustrations: See TR. 25A: fig. 45; 47*d*; 49*b*2; 110*a*2,*b–c*; 146*e*.

Principal Identifying Attributes: Unslipped or highly well smoothed weathered surfaces on a Tinaja Paste. Occurs in only specialized contexts on restricted shapes (see description of shapes below).

Identifying characteristics and sorting problems: The location in Special Deposits and the unusual shapes make identification easy. In sherd collections, although the use of Tinaja Paste for an unslipped type is a good marker, many sherds could have been misidentified as other unslipped types or weathered.

Paste: Tinaja Paste.

Surface: Usually little smoothed.

Color: No data available.

Shapes: The shapes represented are either specialized cache vessels or aberrant examples of standard shapes. They include outflaring-side cache vessels; cache cylinders; rectangular cache vessels; miniature jars with covers; a small jar of unusual shape; outcurving-side bowls with aberrant features of shape; and an unusual round-side dish. The only vessels that fall within normal shape patterns are cylinders and barrels.

Temporal distribution: Begins in the Ik Complex and becomes more common in the Imix Complex.

Comments: This is a specialized type that occurs almost entirely in burials and caches. The type occurs in three Ik Complex burials, four Imix Complex burials, three Ik Complex caches, six Imix Complex caches, and in one problematical deposit that contains largely Ik Complex ceramics.

Intersite comparisons: None noted.

Kokob Carved: Kokob Variety

Established: TR. 25A (Culbert 1993)

Group: Ucum

Ware: Uaxactun Unslipped

Ceramic Complex: Ik

Ceramic Sphere: Tepeu 1

Illustrations: See TR. 25A: fig. 45.

Principal Identifying Attributes: Unslipped or highly well smoothed weathered surface on a Tinaja Paste with carved designs.

Comments: A single whole vessel of Kokob Carved was located in Ik Bu. 132 (TR. 25A:fig. 45). The vessel is an outflaring-side cache vessel that served as a cover for a second cache vessel, which contained a large offering primarily of marine materials. The bottom vessel is Ucum Unslipped, the special unslipped type used primarily for burials and caches in the Ik and Imix Complexes. The fabric of the Kokob Carved vessel is the same as Ucum Unslipped. The carving consists of a central complex design on the top of the cover and five medallions around the side of the vessel. Coggins (1975:236–247, 317–319) believes that the vessel was actually of Manik date and had been part of a Manik cache discovered and reused in Ik times in Bu. 132. Because some of the few contexts in which Kokob Carved sherds were discovered are pure Ik deposits, the type is more likely of Ik date.

Intersite comparisons: None noted.

TINAJA CERAMIC GROUP

Tinaja Red: Tinaja Variety

Established: Smith and Gifford (1966)

Group: Tinaja

Ware: Petén Gloss

Ceramic Complex: Ik (Continues into Imix and Eznab)

Ceramic Sphere: Tepeu 1–3

Illustrations: Fig. 50.1, 50.3–5, 50.10, 50.17, 50.19, 50.32, 50.34–36, 50.38–39, 50.41–42, 50.44–45, 50.47, 50.52; 51.1–7, 51.12–14, 51.16–22, 51.24–25, 51.28, 51.30–31, 51.33, 51.36, 51.46, 51.48–49, 51.53; 56.6, 56.27, 56.30. See TR. 25A: fig. 41*b*3–4; 50*a*,*c*; 109*c*1–2; 110*a*1.

Principal Identifying Attributes: Light to medium polished monochrome red surfaces on jars and large bowls. Paste is characteristically a pale yellow.

Identifying characteristics and sorting problems: The combination of Tinaja Paste and the shapes produced from it is very characteristic.

Paste: Tinaja Paste.

Firing: Dark cores and fireclouding are rare.

Slip: Thin to medium slip applied to a surface that has received little attention; the slip wears easily.

Polish: There is a great range of polish. Most examples show low to medium polish, but there are a few highly polished examples.

Color: Most common color is red (10R 4/6, 4/8; 5/6, 5/8; 2.5YR 5/6, 5/8). Occasional weak red (10R 4/4), light red (2.5YR 6/6, 6/8), reddish yellow (5YR 6/6, 6/8), and yellowish red (5YR 5/8) occur.

Shapes: Narrow-mouth jars and large-capacity bowls. Jars and large-capacity bowls were quantified separately in sherd counting. Originally two varieties of Tinaja Red were identified on the basis of vessel form in TR. 25A, but this varietal distinction is not maintained here because separating varieties based on shape violates type: variety nomenclature (see Gifford 1976). Also occurs on slightly incurving to round-side bowls and the occasional cylinder.

Temporal distribution: Begins at the start of the Ik Complex and continues through the Eznab Complex.

Comments: San Julio Modeled was originally identified at Tikal (TR. 25A) in the Ik Complex, however, the sample is too small to adequately describe the type so examples are included in the Tinaja Group.

Intersite comparisons: Tinaja Red is used throughout Tepeu (1–3) at Altar de Sacrificios (Adams 1971); Chan Chich (Valdez 1998; Valdez and Houk 2000); Holmul (Callaghan 2008, 2016e); Nakbe (Forsyth 1993); and Rio Azul (Adams 1999; Adams and Jackson-Adams 1991). Tinaja Red: Nanzal Variety is used for the Ik equivalent at El Mirador (Forsyth 1989) and in the Petexbatun (Foias and Bishop 2013). At Uaxactun, the Ik equivalent is called Tasital Red (Smith and Gifford 1966). In Belize, type names from Barton Ramie (Gifford 1976) are utilized for the Tepeu 1 monochrome red at Blue Creek (Kosakowsky and Lohse 2003); Chan (Kosakowsky 2012); La Milpa (Sagebiel 2005); and Nohmul (Kosakowsky and Pring 2001). Elsewhere Tinaja Red is used as a type only for the Tepeu 2–3 monochrome red.

Cameron Incised: Cameron Variety

Established: Smith and Gifford (1966)

Group: Tinaja

Ware: Petén Gloss

Ceramic Complex: Ik (Continues into Imix and Eznab)

Ceramic Sphere: Tepeu 1–3

Illustrations: Fig. 50.40, 50.50; 51.9–11, 51.15, 51.26–27, 51.32, 51.35, 51.37–38, 51.43, 51.46, 51.56. TR. 25A: fig. 144*d*4.

Principal Identifying Attributes: Surface finish and paste similar to Tinaja Red, with the addition of a single incised groove on the exterior of large capacity bowls.

Identifying characteristics and sorting problems: Cameron Incised is identical to Tinaja Red: Tinaja Variety in all characteristics except that it is limited to large-capacity bowls (with incurved or bolstered lips) with a single groove below the lip on the exterior. Originally called Large Bowl Variety by Culbert (TR. 25A).

Intersite comparisons: Similar to Altar de Sacrificios (Adams 1971); Holmul (Callaghan 2008,

2016e); Seibal (Sabloff 1975); and Uaxactun (Smith and Gifford 1966). See intersite comparison discussion for Tinaja Red for more detailed information.

Chinja Impressed: Chinja Variety

Established: Smith and Gifford (1966)

Group: Tinaja

Ware: Petén Gloss

Ceramic Complex: Ik (Continues into Imix and occasionally Eznab)

Ceramic Sphere: Tepeu 1–2 (occasionally 3)

Illustrations: Fig. 50.6, 50.8–9, 50.12–13, 50.15–16, 50.18, 50.20–22, 50.28, 50.30–31, 50.43, 50.48–49, 50.51; 51.8, 51.23, 51.29, 51.47, 51.50, 51.54–55, 51.57, 51.59–62. TR. 25A: fig. 49*c*; 122*a*; 144*d*3.

Principal Identifying Attributes: Surface finish and paste similar to Tinaja Red, with the addition of a single row of finger impressions on the exterior of large capacity bowls.

Identifying characteristics and sorting problems: Chinja Impressed: Chinja Variety is identical to Tinaja Red: Tinaja Variety except for the characteristics noted below. Originally called Simple-impressed variety by Culbert (TR. 25A).

Surface Finish and Decoration: Large-capacity bowls have a row of impressions encircling the vessel exterior below the lip. The impressions were made directly on the vessel wall. The impressions were usually made with fingernails but, in a few examples, were made with a hollow circular tool (and these latter examples should be reclassified as Rosa Punctated).

Shapes: Large capacity bowls.

Temporal distribution: Chinja Impressed: Chinja Variety occurs in about equal quantities in Ik and Imix collections and is rare in Eznab collections.

Intersite comparisons: Chinja Impressed identified in later time periods at Calakmul (Dominguez Carrasco 1994); El Mirador (Forsyth 1989:86–89); La Milpa (Sagebiel 2005); Nakbe (Forsyth 1993); and in the Nanzal Group at Uaxactun (Smith and Gifford 1966). It is similar to Chaquiste Impressed at Altar de Sacrificios (Adams 1971); Holmul (Callaghan 2008, 2016e); and Seibal (Sabloff 1975). It is similar to Pascua Impressed, Gloria Impressed, and Kaway Impressed at Barton Ramie (Gifford 1976), and to Kaway Impressed at Xunantunich (LeCount 1996). In form it is similar to Subin Red at Altar de Sacrificios (Adams 1971) and San Jose IV and V monochrome red bowls (Thompson 1939).

Chinja Impressed: Appliquéd Variety

Established: Smith and Gifford (1966)

Group: Tinaja

Ware: Petén Gloss

Ceramic Complex: Ik (Continues into Imix)

Ceramic Sphere: Tepeu 1–2

Illustrations: Fig. 50.2, 50.7, 50.14, 50.23–27, 50.33; 51.39, 51.42, 51.51, 51.58. TR. 25A: fig. 147*d*.

Principal identifying attributes: Surface finish and paste similar to Tinaja Red, with the addition of an impressed fillet that is appliquéd on the exterior of large capacity bowls.

Identifying characteristics and sorting problems: Chinja Impressed: Appliquéd Variety is identical to Chinja Impressed: Chinja Variety except for the characteristics noted below:

Surface Finish and Decoration: A fillet of clay was added to the exterior of large-capacity bowls. The fillet has a row of impressions encircling the vessel exterior below the lip. The impressions were usually made with fingernails but in a few examples were made with a textured tool, perhaps a piece of rope or a corncob.

Temporal distribution: Chinja Impressed: Appliquéd Variety is considerably more common in Ik than in Imix collections and does not appear in Eznab collections. Because it is easily recognizable and temporally restricted, it is a good type fossil for the Ik Complex.

Intersite comparisons: See above for Chinja Impressed: Chinja Variety. Examples that possess an appliqué fillet are often included in the Chinja Variety alongside those without at other sites.

Rosa Punctated: Rosa Variety

Established: Smith and Gifford (1966)

Group: Tinaja

Ware: Petén Gloss

Ceramic Complex: Ik (Continues into Imix and occasionally Eznab)

Ceramic Sphere: Tepeu 1–2 (occasionally 3)

Illustrations: Fig. 50.11, 50.29, 50.37, 50.46; 51.34, 51.40–41, 51.52.

Principal identifying attributes: Surface finish and paste similar to Tinaja Red, with the addition of a single row of punctated impressions made with a hollow tool on the exterior of large capacity bowls.

Identifying characteristics and sorting problems: The occasional examples of large-capacity bowls with a row of impressions made with a hollow circular tool that are noted under the description of Chinja Impressed are technically Rosa Punctated.

Temporal Distribution: See Chinja Impressed.

Intersite comparisons: For general comparisons see Chinja Impressed. Examples with punctuated fillets are often included in the Chinja Variety at other sites.

VERACAL CERAMIC GROUP

Veracal Orange: Veracal Variety

Established: Smith and Gifford (1966)

Group: Veracal

Ware: Petén Gloss

Ceramic Complex: Ik (Continues into Imix)

Ceramic Sphere: Tepeu 1–2

Illustrations: TR. 25A: fig. 42*b*4; 46*a*2.

Principal Identifying Attributes: Slightly polished monochrome orange surfaces on small bowls, dishes, and possibly jars.

Identifying characteristics and sorting problems: Overlaps in color with Tinaja Red, but shapes and paste indicate separate status.

Paste: Fine paste with medium amounts of very fine white inclusions. Paste color brownish yellow (10YR 6/6) to yellowish red (5YR 6/6).

Polish: Medium.

Color: Reddish yellow (7.5YR 6/8) to yellowish red (5YR 6/6).

Shapes: The two whole vessels in burials are a cylinder rounded to base and an unusual widely outcurving-side bowl. Sherds suggest jars, and small bowls or dishes.

Temporal distribution: Ik and Imix Complexes, but considerably more common in Ik.

Intersite comparisons: Naachtun (Walker and Reese-Taylor 2012); Uaxactun (Smith and Gifford 1966).

Kau Incised: Kau Variety

Established: TR. 25A (Culbert 1993)

Group: Veracal

Ware: Petén Gloss

Ceramic Complex: Ik

Ceramic Sphere: Tepeu 1

Illustrations: Fig. 56.49. TR. 25A: fig. 43*d*.

Principal Identifying attributes: Highly polished surfaces similar to Veracal Orange in color with the addition of post-slip incising.

Identifying characteristics and sorting problems: A small sherd sample seems to fit within the range of variation of Veracal Orange except in the following categories:

Polish: High.

Surface finish and decoration: Incising is usually post-slip and post-polish, mostly glyph or pseudo-glyph band with a few examples of geometric elements.

Shapes: Almost all examples are cylinders.

Comments: The only whole vessel that may be Kau Incised is the splendid cylinder from Bu. 81 with an incised design of birds with long beaks.

Intersite comparisons: Veracal Orange at Uaxactun (Smith and Gifford 1966), but no other incised examples noted.

MAQUINA CERAMIC GROUP

Maquina Brown: Maquina Variety

Established: Smith and Gifford (1966)

Group: Maquina

Ware: Petén Gloss

Ceramic Complex: Ik (Continues into Imix and Eznab)

Ceramic Sphere: Tepeu 1–3 (most common in 3)

Principal identifying attributes: Monochrome brown surfaces that overlap at the extremes with fireclouded Tinaja Red on narrow-mouth jars and large-capacity bowls.

Color: A wide range of colors exists within Maquina Brown without a clustering around any central color. Examples include dark reddish brown (2.5YR 3/4), reddish brown (5YR 4/4, 5/4), brown (7.5YR 5/4), light brown (7.5YR 6/4), grayish brown (10YR 5/2), light brownish gray (10YR 6/2), light yellowish brown (10YR 6/4), and dark yellowish brown (10YR 4/4). These colors range around the edges of the more central reddish shades of Tinaja Red, a fact that increases the probability that many examples called Maquina Brown may be nothing more than misfiring of Tinaja Red.

Shapes: Most examples of Maquina Brown are large-capacity bowls with either incurved lip or restricted orifice. These two shapes were separated as varieties of the type for counting and in TR. 25A, however, naming varieties on the basis of vessel shape violates the rules of nomenclature in type: variety (Gifford 1976) so both shapes are now included in the Maquina Variety.

Temporal distribution: Maquina Brown sherds occur in all Late Classic complexes. They have a higher frequency of occurrence in the Eznab Complex than in Ik and Imix, but it is possible that this may be an artifact of the better preservation of the Eznab samples.

Intersite Comparisons: Calakmul (Dominguez Carrasco 1994); El Perú/Waka' (Eppich 2011); Holmul (Callaghan 2008, 2016e); Rio Azul (Adams 1999; Adams and Jackson-Adams 1991) and Uaxactun (Smith and Gifford 1966). Some overlap with the Tepeu 2 Tialipa Brown at Barton Ramie (Gifford 1976) and Uaxactun (Smith and Gifford 1966).

ZACEC CERAMIC GROUP

Zacec Black: Zacec Variety

Established: TR. 25A (Culbert 1993)

Group: Zacec

Ware: Petén Gloss

Ceramic Complex: Ik (Continues into Imix)

Ceramic Sphere: Tepeu 1–2

Illustrations: Fig. 57.19, 57.24. See TR. 25A: fig. 46c1; 50b; 52c–d.

Principal identifying attributes: Highly polished thin black monochrome slips that are well fired.

Paste: Saxche Paste.

Firing: Dark cores rare. The fact that the black does not penetrate the paste indicates that a pigment that fired black in an oxidizing atmosphere was used.

Surface: A thin black slip characterizes the type.

Polish: Polish is usually high.

Color: The black is well controlled with only rare examples of dark grayish brown (10YR 3/2).

Shapes: Sherds give little indication of shapes although some may be small jars. Of four whole vessels in burials, two were cylinders rounded to base and two were unusual small cups.

Temporal distribution: Zacec Black occurs with low frequency in the Ik collections, but is quite rare in Imix.

Comments: Monochrome Black sherds of the Late Classic are difficult to sort and differentiate at Tikal and there is some degree of continuity throughout Tepeu 1, 2, and 3. Originally Molino Black was the name used for Tepeu 1, Infierno Black for Tepeu 2, and Achote Black for Tepeu 3 at Uaxactun (Smith and Gifford 1966). While the decision was made to create a new monochrome black group for the Ik and Imix types at Tikal, at most other lowland Maya sites the type Molino Black is used for Tepeu 1 (Smith and Gifford 1966), or Achote Black is used for the entirety of the Late and Terminal Classic (Callaghan 2008, 2016e). There are a few examples with modeling.

Intersite comparisons: Molino Black is used at Barton Ramie (Gifford 1976); Becan (Ball 1977); Blue Creek (Kosakowsky and Lohse 2003); El Perú/Waka' (Eppich 2011); La Milpa (Sagebiel 2005); Nohmul (Kosakowsky and Pring 2001); Uaxactun (Smith and Gifford 1966). Infierno Black is used at El Mirador (Forsyth 1989); El Perú/Waka' (Eppich 2011).

Chilar Fluted: Chilar Variety

Established: Smith and Gifford (1966)

Group: Zacec (TR. 25A)/Achote (Smith and Gifford 1966)

Ware: Petén Gloss

Ceramic Complex: Ik (Continues into Imix)

Ceramic Sphere: Tepeu 1–2

Illustrations: See TR. 25A: fig. 40c–f; 41a1–4.

Principal identifying attributes: Monochrome black slip similar to Zacec Black at Tikal and Achote Black at Uaxactun (Smith and Gifford 1966) with additional decoration in the form of pre-slip vertical, horizontal, or oblique grooves or flutes.

Identifying characteristics and sorting problems: Chilar Fluted occurs in both Ik and Imix burials and very rarely in sherd collections. Too few sherds of Chilar Fluted were recovered to permit description, so the following entries are based on the sample in burials. Because it was impossible to see sections of the vessels, no information on pastes or frequency of dark cores is available.

Color: In some examples the black was well controlled. In others, the black shades into areas of reddish brown. This suggests that a pigment firing black in oxidizing conditions was used in some examples and that other examples were fired in a reducing atmosphere.

Surface finish and decoration: The type would be better described as "fluted-grooved" than as "fluted" because there is a range between the broad shallow depressions traditionally called fluting and the deeper depressions called grooving. The flutes/grooves usually are vertical and occasionally diagonal. In all examples except one, there are between one and three horizontal grooves above the fluted/grooved area. There are sometimes horizontal grooves below and sometimes the flutes/grooves run all the way to the vessel base.

Shapes: In the burial sample, there are sixteen cylinders and five outflaring to slightly outcurving-side bowls. The cylinders, except for a single cylinder in Bu. 193, occur as sets: a set of eight is present in Ik Bu. 23. There is great variety within the sets in size, color, and style of decoration. It must be concluded that the sets were made by different potters or centers rather than made together by a single potter.

Temporal distribution: Chilar Fluted occurs in both Ik and Imix burials.

Comments: Chilar Fluted is a type that is described in the Achote Ceramic Group at Uaxactun (Smith and Gifford 1966), although placed in the Zacec Ceramic Group at Tikal (TR. 25A). At other sites it is more common in Tepeu 2 and 3.

Intersite comparisons: It is similar to Jojoba Channeled (Molino Group) at Becan (Ball 1977). Chilar Fluted is used for Tepeu 2/3 at Barton Ramie (Gifford 1976); Blue Creek (Kosakowsky and Lohse 2003); Calakmul (Dominguez Carrasco 1994); La Milpa (Sagebiel 2005); Seibal (Sabloff 1975), and Uaxactun (Smith and Gifford 1966). At El Mirador, there is an "other Infierno Group: Fluted" (Forsyth 1989). At Río Azul "Glossy Rippled Black" is used (Adams and Jackson-Adams 1991).

UZ CERAMIC GROUP

Uz Buff: Uz Variety

Established: TR. 25A (Culbert 1993)

Group: Uz

Ware: Petén Gloss

Ceramic Complex: Ik (Continues into Imix)

Ceramic Sphere: Tepeu 1–2

Principal identifying attributes: Well smoothed light brown to buff surfaces on small bowls and dishes.

Paste: Fine to very fine paste with medium amounts of very fine white inclusions. Paste color most commonly reddish yellow (7.5YR 6/6).

Polish: Surface well smoothed, but does not take high polish.

Color: Light yellowish brown (10YR 6/4); pink (7.5YR 7/4); brown (7.5YR 5/4).

Shapes: The few sherds that indicate shape are small bowls and dishes too fragmentary to determine specific shapes.

Temporal distribution: Occurs rarely in the Ik and Imix Complexes; slightly more common in Imix.

Intersite comparisons: None noted.

SAXCHE CERAMIC GROUP

Saxche Orange Polychrome: Saxche Variety

Established: Smith and Gifford (1966)

Group: Saxche

Ware: Petén Gloss

Ceramic Complex: Ik

Ceramic Sphere: Tepeu 1

Illustrations: Fig. 40.1–6, 40.8–9, 40.11–19, 40.21–23; 41.1–12, 41.14–16; 42.1–4, 42.7–11, 42.14–19, 42.21, 42.23–27, 42.30. See TR. 25A: fig. 42*c*; 43*b–c*; 44*a*2,*b*3–4,*c*1–2; 46*a*1,*c*2–4; 47*b–c*; 48*c*; 49*a*1,*b*1; 50*d–f*; 51; 131*c*; 142*b*;146*a–d*; 147*a*; 148*e–f*.

Principal Identifying Attributes: Glossy red and black designs on orange slipped plates, bowls, and dishes.

Paste: Saxche Paste

Firing: Dark cores and fireclouding rare.

Slip: A thin orange slip serves as the background color, then red and black are overpainted, leaving exposed areas in orange.

Polish: The orange slip does not take a high polish. Red and black are more highly polished.

Color: The most typical colors: orange (reddish yellow 7.5YR 7/8; 5YR 6/8) and red (10R 5/8) are quite distinctive, but there is a considerable range of variation. The orange background can include reddish yellow (7.5YR 8/6, 6/8; 5YR 6/6, 6/8, 7/8) and sometimes red (2.5YR 5/8). Red is red (10R 4/10; 7.5R 4/10, 4/8). Occasionally, small well-controlled areas of gray (5YR 5/1) occur.

Surface finish and decoration: Designs are usually done in black on orange; red is used as bands or panels.

Shapes: Almost half the samples are large tripod plates with ridges; one-quarter are barrels. Out-flaring to slightly outcurving-side bowls or dishes, slightly incurving to round-side bowls, cylinders, and an occasional small jar also occur.

Temporal distribution: Almost entirely confined to the Ik Complex.

Intersite comparisons: Common throughout most Maya Lowland sites with Tepeu 1 occupation. Altar de Sacrificios (Adams 1971); Barton Ramie (Gifford 1976); Becan (Ball 1977); Blue Creek (Kosakowsky and Lohse 2003); Calakmul (Dominguez Carrasco 1994); Colha (Valdez 1987); El Perú/Waka' (Eppich 2011); Holmul (Callaghan 2008, 2016e); Nohmul (Kosakowsky and Pring 2001); Rio Azul (Adams 1999; Adams and Jackson-Adams 1991); Uaxactun (Smith and Gifford 1966). Saxche/Palmar is used at Seibal (Sabloff 1975).

Desquite Red-on-orange: Desquite Variety

Established: Smith and Gifford (1966)

Group: Saxche

Ware: Petén Gloss

Ceramic Complex: Ik

Ceramic Sphere: Tepeu 1

Illustrations: Fig. 40.10; 42.5,6. See TR. 25A: fig. 41*b*5; 42*b*1–3.

Principal Identifying Attributes: Surface finish similar to Saxche Orange Polychrome, however, decoration includes only red-on-orange and no black.

Identifying characteristics and sorting problems: It is usually impossible to determine which sherds belonged to this type because small sherds with only red and orange may have had additional colors on missing sections. On the basis of whole vessels and the few sherds that seem likely to be Desquite Red-on-orange, the type seems identical to Saxche Orange Polychrome except it lacks black decoration.

Surface finish and decoration: On three of the four whole examples, red appears only as a band at the lip. One vessel shows red lip bands on both the interior and exterior and a simple, partly eroded design in red on the exterior. On sherds, simple curvilinear designs executed in thin red lines predominate.

Shapes: Two whole examples are slightly incurving to round-side bowls; two are large tripod plates with ridges. On sherds fourteen of fifteen examples have designs on the exterior suggesting that they were barrels or round-side vessels.

Temporal distribution: Confined to the Ik Complex.

Intersite comparisons: Uaxactun (Smith and Gifford 1966)

Uacho Black-on-orange: Uacho Variety

Established: Smith and Gifford (1966)

Group: Saxche

Ware: Petén Gloss

Ceramic Complex: Ik

Ceramic Sphere: Tepeu 1

Illustrations: Fig. 40.7, 42.29. See TR. 25A: fig. 44*b*2, 49*a*2, 155*b*.

Principal Identifying Attributes: Surface finish similar to Saxche Orange Polychrome, however decoration includes only black-on-orange and no red.

Identifying characteristics and sorting problems: It is usually impossible to determine which sherds belonged to this type because small sherds with only black and orange may have had additional colors on missing sections. On the basis of whole vessels and the few sherds that seem likely to be Uacho Black-on-orange, the type seems identical to Saxche Orange Polychrome except it lacks red decoration.

Surface finish and decoration: Two of the whole vessels have only black rim bands both inside and out and otherwise have only the background orange; the third has black rim bands on both interior and exterior and a glyph band on the exterior. The sherds show relatively simple geometric designs except for two with glyph bands: one on the exterior of a barrel, the other near the rim on the interior of a lateral-ridge tripod plate.

Shapes: The whole vessels are a slightly incurving to round-side bowl, a barrel, and a cylinder rounded to base. On the sherds, two-thirds show exterior decoration on what were probably barrels or round-side vessels and one-third are on the interiors of what were almost surely lateral-ridge tripod plates.

Temporal distribution: Confined to the Ik Complex.

Intersite Comparisons: Barton Ramie (Gifford 1976); El Pozito (Eppich 2000); Uaxactun (Smith and Gifford 1966). A similar variety is present at Altar de Sacrificios (Adams 1971).

Jama Red Polychrome: Jama Variety

Established: Smith and Gifford (1966)

Group: Saxche

Ware: Petén Gloss

Ceramic Complex: Ik

Ceramic Sphere: Tepeu 1

Illustrations: See TR. 25A: fig. 39*a,b*; 40*a*.

Principal Identifying Attributes: Polychrome vessels with black and white on a red slip

Identifying characteristics and sorting problems: Three nearly identical large tripod plates with ridges in Bu. 23 provide the majority of examples. Because they were stored in the Tikal Museum, they could not be examined for all characteristics.

Paste: No data available.

Surface finish and decoration: The base color is red with overpainted designs in black and white. Munsell readings are not available. In all cases the designs include four Ahau glyph on the interior walls and an Ahau on the interior base. Numbers associated with the Ahau symbols vary (see Coggins 1975:374–379). While Smith and Gifford (1966:158) included Jama Red Polychrome in the Saxche Group given the base slip that is more red than orange, it might be more appropriate to place this type in its own ceramic group. However, the sample size at Tikal is so small that the original group placement has been maintained.

Temporal distribution: Confined to the Ik Complex.

Comments: The color combinations are unusual as are some of the shape features of the plates. There seems a good chance that the vessels were imported.

Intersite Comparisons: El Perú/Waka' (Eppich 2011) and Uaxactun (Smith and Gifford 1966).

Sibal Buff Polychrome: Sibal Variety

Established: Smith and Gifford (1966)

Group: Saxche

Ware: Petén Gloss

Ceramic Complex: Late Ik

Ceramic Sphere: Tepeu 1

Illustrations: Fig. 40.20; 41.13, 41.17; 42.12–13, 42.20, 42.22, 42.28. See TR. 25A: fig. 41*b*2; 43*a*; 46*b*; 48*a–b*; 52*b*1–3; 122*d*; 131*b*; 144*d*1–2.

Principal Identifying Attributes: Monochrome black and red designs similar to Saxche Orange Polychrome on a buff slip.

Identifying characteristics and sorting problems: Identical to Saxche Orange Polychrome except for a buff rather than an orange base surface color.

Color: The buff covers a variety of colors in the 7.5YR hue. These include pink (7.5YR 7/4), reddish yellow (7.5YR 7/6; 6/8, 6/6), light brown (7.5YR 6/4), and strong brown (7.5YR 5/6). Yellow (10YR 7/6) also occurs. Other colors are the same as those in Saxche Orange Polychrome.

Shapes: Cylinders, barrels, and slightly outflaring to outcurving-side bowls or dishes each account for about one-fifth the examples; slightly incurving to round-side bowls or dishes, one-eighth; large tripod plates with ridges, about one-tenth. A few other bowl or dish shapes occur.

Temporal distribution: The relative scarcity of lateral-ridge or lateral-flange tripod plates in comparison with Saxche Orange Polychrome and the higher frequency of cylinders and slightly outcurving-side bowls or dishes suggest that Sibal Buff Polychrome may have been common towards the end of the Ik Complex and transitional to Zacatel Cream Polychrome of the Imix Complex.

Comments: Juleki Cream Polychrome was originally identified in the Tikal Collections (TR. 25A) but it was felt that the few examples were a better fit for the Sibal Buff Polychrome type and they have been included with them.

Intersite comparisons: Barton Ramie (Gifford 1976); Uaxactun (Smith and Gifford 1966).

Ik Types: Chronological Change

The major changes that separate Manik Complex types from those of the Ik Complex have been reviewed at the start of this chapter. Because few samples could be quantified for types and changes seemed random, there is no indication of gradual change during the time of the Ik Complex. The only change at the end of the Ik Complex is that types of the Saxche Ceramic Group gave way to those of the Palmar Ceramic Group.

Ik Types: Social Dimension

The only two Ik Complex contexts quantified for types were from the intermediate structure Group 7F-1 and the Central Acropolis range structure Group 5D-11. The two samples from the Central Acropolis showed lower frequencies of unslipped types and higher frequencies of black and polychromes types than the most common frequencies in Group 7F-1 (see Table 8.3).

Vessel Shapes of the Ik Complex

Introduction

Vessel shapes changed almost completely between the Manik and Ik Complexes. Only the wide-mouth jar with tall neck remained essentially unchanged between the two complexes. Narrow-mouth jars in the Ik Complex are distinguished from those of Manik by having taller and more outcurving necks. Large bowls in Ik establish the pattern of rounded sides and thickened lips that mark the Late and Terminal Classic across the Maya lowlands. The Ik Complex is composed of seven major shape classes, and ten shapes, as well as two specialized shape classes (caches and miniatures) comprised of three shapes (Table 8.4).

The serving-vessel class in the Ik Complex is mostly characterized by relatively simple shapes, which are not distinctive. The large tripod plate with ridge, however, is a very characteristic shape that is common enough in Ik collections so that it appears in even relatively small collections.

Shape Quantification for the Late and Terminal Classic Complexes

For the Ik, Imix, and Eznab Complexes, a different and more minutely subdivided system of shape quantification was used than for earlier complexes. The use of this system was made possible by the fact that collections were large enough so that there were sufficient sherds even within subclasses for

TABLE 8.4
Shape Classes and Shapes of the Ik Complex

1. Wide-mouth Jars

Wide-mouth Jar (with Tall Neck)

2. Narrow-mouth Jars

Narrow-mouth Jar (with Tall Neck)

Small Jar

4. Large Capacity Bowls

Large Incurving-side Bowl

6. Small Diameter Bowls and Dishes

Outflaring to Slightly Outcurving-side Bowl or Dish

Slightly Incurving to Round-side Bowl

7. Cylindrical Vessels

Barrel

Cylinder

8. Medium Plates

Outflaring to Slightly Outcurving-side Tripod Plate

9. Large Plates

Large Tripod Plate with Ridge

10. Specialized Cache Vessels and Covers

Cache Cylinder

Cylindrical Cache Vessel Cover

Outflaring to Slightly Outcurving-side Cache Vessel

11. Miniature Vessels

Miniature Jar with Cover

Miniature Bowl or Cylinder

quantitative treatment. The primary division into four major shape categories: wide-mouth jars, narrow-mouth jars, large-capacity bowls, and serving vessels continued in use for the Late and Terminal Classic. The frequency of each of these major categories was calculated as a percentage of total rim sherds.

Next, each major category was subdivided in ways discussed below and the total of rim sherds in that category used as the basis to calculate frequencies of the particular features selected. In the category of wide-mouth jars, subdivision was based on lip shapes, a feature that proved to have chronological significance. No subdivisions were made for narrow-mouth jars because none of the features

examined proved to vary significantly either temporally or by social context. The category of large-capacity bowls was subdivided in two different ways that had chronological significance. One was a separation of five individual shapes based on rim features and lip shape, the second was an independent division based on decoration by surface manipulation. Details of these subdivisions are presented later. Both the shape and decoration subdivisions proved to have temporal significance in separating the Late and Terminal Classic complexes. The final category, serving vessels, contains a large number of different shapes, some of which show strong changes through time. These are discussed in sections dealing with chronological change of vessel shapes.

Seriation of Late Classic Shapes

Separation of the Ik and Imix Complexes provides an example of the way in which techniques of investigation must be fitted to the collections and contexts available. Burials provided an initial key to differentiation of the two complexes. Decorated types of the Saxche and Palmar groups were quite distinct. In addition, several key serving-vessel shapes differed between the Ik and Imix Complexes, but because utilitarian vessels were rarely included in burials, there was little indication of whatever sequence might exist for utilitarian shapes. For these shapes, a sequence had to be derived from the sherd collections.

To provide this record, an old-fashioned hand seriation was done by arranging bar graphs of shape frequencies in the traditional manner. Samples to use in the seriation were determined using two criteria. The first was that samples should be large enough to provide reliable quantification. The second criterion was that samples should be relatively "pure"; i.e., primarily confined in content to one of the two complexes. Information from burials that provided the characteristic shapes associated with Ik and Imix was used as a guide to determine the degree of mixing in samples.

Twenty-four samples were used in the seriation. The majority of the samples (13) came from Gp. 4F-1 and 2 excavated by Haviland (TR. 19) as Op. 20. The heavy reliance on this operation resulted from the fact that samples were very large and there were occasional small bits of architectural stratigraphy.

On the other hand, because preservation of sherd surfaces was very poor, counts of types could rarely be made. The remaining samples in the seriation covered a wide range of social contexts throughout the site, as indicated in discussion of the collections for the Ik and Imix Complexes.

The seriation was considerably more successful than that done for the Manik Complex. It confirmed the sequence of serving-vessel shapes already evident from burials and showed changes over time in other vessel shapes and modes. A four-part division of the samples was made with the first two sections pertaining to the Ik Complex and the last two to Imix. Differences between the sections were usually quantitative rather than the sharp qualitative differences seen in the burial sample. The quantitative nature of change may reflect both gradual development and the fact that many of the samples may have been subject to some mixing.

Ik Shape Descriptions

SHAPE CLASS 1: WIDE-MOUTH JARS

Wide-mouth Jar (with Tall Neck)

Illustrations: Fig. 39.1–53.

Identifying characteristics and sorting problems: The combination of unslipped types, large-neck diameter, and tall-neck height is distinctive, but the shape is nearly identical through the Early, Late, and Terminal Classic.

Base: Probably rounded.

Body: Globular.

Neck-body juncture: Vague.

Orientation of neck: Most commonly wide outflare; sometimes medium to slight outflare.

Neck: Usually widely outcurving, but ranges to slightly outcurving or straight.

Rim: Usually direct, though a minority of about 10% have a sharp angular eversion.

Lips: The two major lip shapes are rounded/roll and flat/grooved. In the Ik Complex, rounded/roll lips predominate, making up one-half to three-quarters of the examples. A quantitative difference in lip shapes is the only distinction between the wide-mouth jars of the Late Classic and Terminal Classic complexes.

Types: Cambio Unslipped and Encanto Striated.

Diameter of lip: Range 12–42 cm; median 26 cm.

Height of neck: Range 4.5–13.0 cm; median 8.0 cm.

Diameter of lip/neck height ratio: Range 2.3–4.0; median 3.2.

Temporal distribution: Common in all Late and Terminal Classic complexes.

Shape class: 1, wide-mouth jars.

SHAPE CLASS 2: NARROW-MOUTH JARS

Narrow-mouth Jar (with Tall Neck)

Illustrations: See TR. 25A: fig. 50c.

Identifying characteristics and sorting problems: The shape is distinguished by the tall, outcurving neck with small diameter, aided by paste and red slip. There is relatively little overlap with the narrow-mouth jar with medium neck of the Manik Complex. If paste and slip characteristics are used in identification, there is little danger of confusion with wide-mouth unslipped jars.

Base: Both rounded and flat bases occur, but the data are not sufficient to indicate which predominates.

Body: Globular.

Neck-body juncture: Angular and well marked.

Orientation of neck: Medium to wide outflare.

Rim: Usually direct, but a minority show either rounded or angular eversion.

Lip: Rounded or pointed.

Surface: Slipped on entire exterior and on interior of neck.

Types: Invariably Tinaja Red.

Lip diameter: Range 10–28 cm; median 16 cm.

Neck height: Range 3.0–8.4 cm; median 5.6 cm.

Lip diameter/neck height ratio: Range 1.5–4.9; median 2.9.

Temporal distribution: Common in all Late and Terminal Classic complexes.

Shape class: 2, narrow-mouth jars.

Small Jar

Illustrations: Fig. 40.19; 42.14, 42.30.

Identifying characteristics and sorting problems: This is a diverse group unified only by the very short neck, small diameter of lip, and the fact that the majority are not of Tinaja Red. The neck dimensions and frequency of decoration set the shape apart from the narrow-mouth jar with tall neck and suggest that the two shapes had different functions.

Base and body: Unknown.

Neck-body juncture: Usually well marked but ranges to rounded and poorly defined.

Orientation of neck: Usually vertical to slightly outflaring, but some examples widely outflaring.

Neck: Usually straight to slightly outflaring; some examples widely outflaring.

Rim: Usually direct, but some examples of various degrees of eversion occur.

Lip: Rounded or pointed.

Types: The Saxche Ceramic Group is most common followed by Zacec Black. There are only a few Tinaja Red.

Lip diameter: Range 6–18 cm; median 12 cm.

Neck height: Range 2.2–4.6 cm; median 3.5 cm.

Lip diameter/neck height ration: Range 2.4–5.4; median 3.2.

Shape class: 2, narrow-mouth jars.

Temporal distribution: The small jar is a rare shape that always occurs with low frequency. It is somewhat more common in the Ik Complex than in Imix.

SHAPE CLASS 4: LARGE CAPACITY BOWLS

Large-capacity bowls (shape class 4) are an important component of Late and Terminal Classic complexes. All examples within the shape class share the features of large size and monochrome (usually red) decoration. In other characteristics there is considerable variety that forms a continuum along several axes of variation. The continuous character of variation makes subdivision into separate shapes a difficult procedure that, no matter how it is done, leaves many intermediate examples that provide sorting difficulties. Nevertheless, the information makes important contributions to temporal separation of the complexes. Before a description of the individual shapes, some comment on the range of variation in several different characteristics will be useful.

Orientation of side: The large-capacity bowls range from quite open to restricted orifice.

Rim: Many vessels have rims that incurve sharply, making a distinct angular break with the curvature of the vessel wall. Again there is a continuous range of variation from these sharply angled incurves through more gradual incurves to some examples in which the rim simply continues the curvature of the side.

Lip: Most examples display some thickening of the lip, although there is a minority of cases in which the lip is the same thickness as the vessel wall.

Decoration: Decoration of large-capacity bowls also shows significant variation. Because decoration is not a shape characteristic it was handled in a separate analysis from the subdivision of the shape class. The four kinds of decoration are: (1) undecorated except for slip; (2) grooved, featuring a single grooved line just below the lip on the exterior; (3) impressed, with a row of impressions at the same location; and (4) fillet-impressed, which has impressions on a strip of clay appliquéd to the vessel exterior rather than directly on the vessel wall. The type of decoration proved temporally diagnostic with impressed-fillet decoration almost entirely confined to the Ik and Imix Complexes, but almost entirely absent from Eznab, and plain and grooved examples present in all Late Classic complexes but of higher frequency in the Eznab Complex, as all kinds of impressed decoration disappeared. Ik examples are more likely to have impressed or fillet-impressed decoration than later examples.

Large Incurving-side Bowl

Illustrations: Fig. 50.1–52; 51.1–62. See TR. 25A: fig. 49*c*; 109*c*1,2; 122*a*; 144*d*3–4; 147*d*.

Identifying characteristics and sorting problems: The shape class of Late and Terminal Classic large-capacity bowls is easily separable from shapes of earlier complexes. The most exaggerated examples are even easier to recognize, many with an incurved rim.

Base: Flat.

Orientation of side: Medium to slight restriction of orifice.

Side: Rounded.

Rim: Direct or thickened. The rim bends inward, usually leaving a distinct angle on the exterior. When direct it simply continues the curvature of the side to an increased curve that gives a rounded incurve. When thickened it is usually at the point at which the rim bends inward, and a few examples are slightly more everted or incurving just at the lip.

Lip: Rounded or pointed, and occasionally rounded and beveled inward. On many Ik examples there is a defining "bolster" lip, thickened on the exterior, but rounded on the interior and originally called a bump-lip in TR. 25A.

Surface: Slipped on both interior and exterior, although the area near the exterior base is usually poorly finished and may be unslipped in spots.

Decoration: Decoration occurs on the exterior slightly below the lip and may consist of a single groove, or a row of impressions on an appliquéd fillet of clay. The bowls with bolster lips have a higher frequency of impressions and appliquéd impressions than the other large incurving-side examples and are more common in the Ik Complex.

Types: The most common type is Cameron Incised, followed by Tinaja Red. Chinja Impressed and Maquina Brown occur in low frequencies.

Diameter: 22–60 cm (mostly 26–46 cm); median 36 cm. The shape has a broad range of diameter sizes with little tendency to cluster.

Height: 4.6 to 9.0 cm.; median 6.8 cm.

Diameter/height ratio: 3.3–3.5; median 3.4

Shape class: 4, large-capacity bowls.

Temporal distribution: Occurs in all Late/Terminal Classic complexes. The bolster lip (formerly called a bump-lip) is a good quantitative diagnostic for the Ik Complex because it occurs among large bowls in Ik collections with a much higher frequency than in other complexes.

SHAPE CLASS 6: SMALL DIAMETER BOWLS AND DISHES

Outflaring to Slightly Outcurving-side Bowl or Dish

Illustrations: Fig. 41.5; 42.5, 42.7–10, 42.12–13, 42.24. See TR. 25A: fig. 43*c*; 49*a*1; 52*a*3,*b*2; 133*c*2.

Identifying characteristics and sorting problems: The shape overlaps with the short cylinder, originally identified as a separate shape in TR. 25A but included now in this shape.

Base: Flat or slightly concave.

Orientation of side: Straight to medium outflare or outcurve.

Rim: Direct.

Lip: Pointed or rounded or flat bevel.

Surface: Interior usually has simple bands of color although there are a few more complex designs. Major decoration is on the exterior, consisting of one or more bands of color near lip and base. Between these bands may be broader bands of designs. On some examples, the exterior is divided into vertical panels of color.

Types: Usually Saxche Ceramic Group.

Diameter: Range 10–32 cm, median 18 cm.

Height: Range 4–14 cm; mostly 6–8.6 cm.

Diameter/height ratio: Range 1.0–6.5 (mostly 2.0–4.4).

Shape class: 6, small-diameter bowls and dishes.

Temporal distribution: Shape is present in most ceramic complexes, however the combination of shape and type (Saxche) are easy to identify as pertaining to the Ik Complex when surfaces are not weathered.

Slightly Incurving to Round-side Bowl or Dish

Illustrations: Fig. 40.1; 42.2, 42.4, 42.11, 42.17–18, 42.27–28. See TR. 25A: fig. 41*b*2–3; 42*b*1–2; 44*b*2; 50*a*,*d*; 53*d*2; 54*b*3,*d*3; 77*c*2; 131*c*; 142*b*.

Identifying characteristics and sorting problems: The rounded side is the diagnostic characteristic. There is a nearly continuous overlap with barrels and a diameter/height ratio of 1.5 was chosen as the separation point between the two. There is a clear bimodal distribution of diameter/height ratios for the two shapes indicating that they are distinct. Among sherds, where the diameter/height ratio cannot be calculated, those with restricted orifice were considered barrels.

Base: Flat or slightly concave.

Orientation of side: Slightly open to slightly restricted orifice.

Side: Rounded, medium curvature.

Rim: Direct.

Lip: Usually pointed; sometimes rounded.

Surface: Interior slipped, sometimes with bands of color at lip. Major decoration is always on the exterior but is usually simple, either several bands of alternating colors or a simple banded design that is occasionally glyphic.

Types: Usually Saxche Ceramic Group.

Diameter: Range 10–32 cm, mostly 14–26 cm; median 20 cm.

Height: Range 4–15 cm; median 8 cm.

Diameter/height ratio: Range 1.4–2.8; median 2.0.

Shape class: 6, small-diameter bowls and dishes.

SHAPE CLASS 7: CYLINDRICAL VESSELS

Barrel

Illustrations: Fig. 41.2, 41.6; 42.3, 42.19–23, 42.25–26, 42.29. See TR. 25A: fig. 41*b*1; 42*c*; 44*b*1,*c*1; 46a1–2,*b*,*c*2–3; 47*b*; 48*b*; 49*a*2,*b*1; 52*a*,*b*1,*h*2; 109*a*; 131*b*; 146*a*–*e*; 148*e*–*f*.

Identifying characteristics and sorting problems: The relatively thin walls and restricted orifice are the best diagnostics of the shape. There is a nearly continuous overlap with slightly incurving to round-side bowls with the two shapes separated on the basis of diameter/height ratio; ratio below 1.5 considered to denote barrel. Among sherds, where the diameter/height ratio cannot be calculated, those with restricted orifice were considered barrels.

Base: About equally divided between flat and slightly concave.

Orientation of side: Slightly restricted orifice.

Side: Rounded, medium curvature.

Rim: Direct.

Lip: Usually pointed; sometimes rounded.

Surface: Interior usually a single color and carelessly finished. Exterior a lip band (usually black) occurs on most examples. The most frequent additional decoration is a band of motifs at mid-point or above on the exterior. Overall exterior decoration also occurs. Glyphs may occur as part of single-band decoration or above additional decoration. In most cases, glyphic inscriptions are meaningful.

Types: Invariably Saxche Ceramic Group.

Diameter: Range 8–20 cm; median 14 cm.

Height: Range 8–14 cm; median 12 cm.

Diameter/height ratio: Range 0.7–1.5; median 1.2.

Shape class: 7, cylindrical vessels.

Temporal distribution: Some barrels occur in the Manik Complex. The shape becomes considerably more frequent in the Ik Complex. Barrels appear in low frequency in Imix and become somewhat more common again in Eznab. Although barrels are by no means confined to the Ik Complex, their frequency in Ik samples is a good temporal marker, especially when the characteristic banded decoration occurs.

Cylinder

Illustrations: Fig. 41.14–17; 42.1,6. See TR. 25A: fig. 40*b–f*; 41*a*1–4; 43*d*; 44*a*3; 48*a*; 50*b*.

Identifying characteristics and sorting problems: The straight, vertical side identifies the shape well. There is a minor overlap between the barrel shape and the shape called Cylinder Rounding to Base by Culbert in TR. 25A. The latter are now included in the cylinder shape.

Base: Usually flat to slightly concave. Some examples have a distinct rounding of the wall as it approaches the base. See TR. 25A: fig. 41*b*4; 46*c*1; 155*b*.

Orientation of side: Vertical or nearly so.

Side: Straight to very slightly outcurving.

Rim: Direct.

Lip: Usually rounded; rarely pointed, rounded, bevel or nearly flat.

Comments: Cylinders occur in the Ik Complex, although they are less common than in Imix. The cylinder rounding to base is a variation of the cylinder shape characteristic of the Ik Complex, but it can be recognized only with complete sections. The types represented in the Ik Complex examples differ from those in later complexes.

Types: Among cylinders in the Ik whole vessel collections, polychrome types are less common than among Imix cylinders. In the Ik collections, Chilar Fluted is the most common type, accounting for nearly half the examples. Polychrome and dichrome types make up less than a quarter of the examples and the reminder are a variety of monochrome and incised types. Cylinders rounding to base include both monochrome (Tinaja Red and Zacec Black) and dichrome/polychrome types.

Diameter: Range 6–28 cm; median 12 cm.

Height: Range 8–30 cm; median 18 cm.

Diameter/height ratio: Range 0.4–1.0; median 0.6.

Shape class: 7, cylindrical vessels.

Temporal distribution: More common in the Imix Complex. Cylinders rounding to base are confined to the Ik Complex except for two Manik Complex examples.

SHAPE CLASS 8: MEDIUM PLATES

Outflaring to Slightly Outcurving-side Tripod Plate

Illustrations: Fig. 40.5–18, 40.20–23; 42.15–16.

Identifying characteristics and sorting problems: The entire set of characteristics is very diagnostic. Even for sherds, the beveled lip makes recognition easy. Some examples are less shallow than others and might be classified as a dish.

Base: Usually flat; a few examples slightly rounded.

Orientation of side: Medium outflare; rarely wide outflare.

Side: Most common is slight outcurve; some wide outcurve; rarely straight. The wall is thicker than in most other Ik Complex shapes.

Rim: Usually direct. Some examples have a lip extended outward to resemble eversion.

Lip: Flat bevel and some rounded bevel.

Feet: Cylindrical, usually flat bottom, although some slightly rounded bottoms occur.

Type: Saxche Ceramic Group

Diameter: Range 20–50 cm; median 30 cm.

Height (without feet): Range 3.2–10.3 cm, usually 4–7 cm; median 5.0 cm.

Diameter/height ratio: Range 3.8–9.5; median 6.0.

Shape class: 8, medium plates.

Temporal distribution: Some examples in Ik but mostly Imix and Eznab Complexes.

Comments: This shape is missing from some of the earliest Ik samples, but most samples contain a few examples.

SHAPE CLASS 9: LARGE PLATES

Large Tripod Plate with Ridge

Illustrations: Fig. 40.2–4; 41.1, 41.3–4, 41.7–13. See TR. 25A: fig. 39*a–b*; 40*a*; 41*b*5; 42*b*3; 43*a,b*; 44*a*2,*b*3–4,*c*2; 46*c*4; 47*c*; 48*c–d*; 50*e,f*; 51; 122*d*; 123*d*; 147*a*.

Identifying characteristics and sorting problems: The combination of widely outflaring side,

unslipped or poorly slipped exterior, and the ridge or flange make this one of the most easily recognized of Tikal shapes.

Base: Rounded. A few examples have rudimentary annular bases.

Juncture of base and side: Almost equal distributions of continuous curve, slight break, and a pronounced angular break.

Orientation of side: Wide outflare.

Side: Below the flange is rounded, but with low curvature. Above the flange/ridge is straight, slightly outcurving, or slightly rounded.

Rim: Usually direct, but some examples are everted just below the lip.

Lip: Rounded or rounded bevel; sometimes flat bevel.

Flange or ridge: Most common are very small lateral ridges, but some are larger. About one-third of the larger ridges are notched. There is a continuum in size between flanges (present in the Early Classic Manik Complex) and ridges; intermediate examples occur that are not easy to classify. A flange is usually associated with a slight break at the base in the curvature of the side on both interior and exterior of the vessel. Some examples show a sharp break in curvature at this point. A ridge is most commonly correlated with a rounded side that does not show a break in curvature.

Feet: The feet have rounded sides and come to a rounded, pointed, or flattened bottom. Feet are general smaller and more rounded than the feet of Imix Complex tripod plates.

Surface: The exterior is often unslipped below the ridge. Above it is often carelessly slipped. A few examples have decoration of colored bands on the exterior. On the interior, the upper section characteristically shows bands of solid colors that enclose a band of decoration that is often glyphic. The major decoration is on the interior base and is usually a single composition such as a dancer. Some examples have a simpler interior decoration consisting of bands of color or simple geometric designs.

Types: Almost invariably Saxche Ceramic Group.

Diameter: Range 26–44 cm; median 35 cm.

Height (excluding feet): Range 4.4–7.4 cm; median 6.0 cm.

Diameter/height ratio: Range 4.4–6.6; median 5.8.

Shape class: 9, large plates.

Temporal distribution: Only Ik Complex.

Comments: The frequent occurrence and very easy recognition make this shape an excellent type fossil for the Ik Complex.

SHAPE CLASS 10: SPECIALIZED CACHE VESSELS AND COVERS

Cache Cylinder

Illustrations: See TR. 25A: fig. 110*a*1.

Identifying characteristics and sorting problems: The unusual lip and unslipped surface make the shape very distinctive.

Base: Flat to slightly concave.

Orientation of side: Vertical.

Side: Straight, but often uneven.

Rim: Direct. On the exterior side below the lip a "shelf" is formed by gradual thickening of the side, which was then cut back to make the shelf resulting in a thinned rim that was designed to support a cover.

Lip: Rounded or flat.

Comments: A single example of the shape was found in the Ik Complex.

Type: Tinaja Red

Shape class: 10, specialized cache vessels and covers

Outflaring to Slightly Outcurving-side Cache Vessel

Illustrations: See TR. 25A: fig. 45.

Identifying characteristics and sorting problems: Recognized only when present in caches or burials. The context defines the shape, and, lacking contextual information, sherds of this vessel shape found in middens or fills may have been misidentified or overlooked.

Base: Flat or very slightly concave.

Side: Straight-to-medium outcurve.

Orientation of side: Medium outflare.

Rim: Direct.

Lip: Usually rounded, some flattened or beveled.

Surface: Unslipped

Types: Ucum Unslipped and Kokob Carved.

Comments: Vessels are indistinguishable in shape from the outflaring-side cache vessel of the Manik Complex in Bu. 132 and occur occasionally as sherds in Ik collections as well.

Shape class: 10, specialized cache vessels and covers.

Cylindrical Cache Vessel Cover

Illustration: See TR. 25A: fig. 109*a*; 110*a*1.

Top: Usually flat or concave; a few rounded.

Orientation of side: Usually slightly outflaring; a few vertical.

Side: Mostly straight; some slightly rounded or slightly outcurving.

Rim: Direct.

Lip: Rounded, flattened, or grooved; a few examples have an exterior bolster.

Surface: Carelessly slipped on exterior; interior usually unslipped.

Comments: The single Late Classic example of a cache cylinder with cover occurs in Ik Ca. 131. The shape is identical to that described for cylindrical cache vessel covers in the Manik Complex.

Shape class: 10, specialized cache vessels and covers.

SHAPE CLASS 11: MINIATURE VESSELS

Miniature Jar

Illustrations: Fig. 56.34, 56.37. See TR. 25A: fig. 110*a*2,*b*,*c*.

Identifying characteristics and sorting problems: The shape is easy to identify based on size.

Base: Flat.

Body: Globular.

Orientation of neck: Vertical.

Neck: Straight.

Rim: Direct.

Lip: Rounded.

Types: Cambio Unslipped, Tinaja Red, Ucum Unslipped.

Lip diameter: Range 5.0–8.1 cm.

Neck height: Range 2.8–3.0 cm.

Lip diameter/neck height ratio: Range 1.8–2.9.

Total height: Range 7.3–9.8 cm.

Shape class: 11, miniature vessels.

Comments: Ucum Unslipped miniature jars occurred only in special deposits, although the other types are found in other contexts.

Miniature Jar Cover

Illustrations: See TR. 25A: fig. 110*a*2,*b*,*c*.

Identifying characteristics and sorting problems: The shape is unique.

Top: Flat.

Orientation of side: Slight outflare.

Rim: Direct.

Lip: Flattened.

Types: Ucum Unslipped.

Lip diameter: Range (three examples) 6.5–10.0 cm.

Height: Range (three examples) 3.1–4.0 cm.

Diameter/height ration: Range (three examples) 1.9–3.2.

Shape class: 11, miniature vessels.

Temporal distribution: In Late Classic, only Ik Complex.

Miniature Bowl or Cylinder

Illustrations: Fig. 56.1, 56.6, 56.27, 56.49; 57.24.

Identifying characteristics and sorting problems: The small size makes these unmistakable.

Shapes: Slightly incurving to round-side bowls and cylinders (short).

Types: Tinaja Red, Kau Incised, Zacec Black.

Diameter: 2–4 cm.

Height: 4–6 cm.

Diameter/Height ratio: 0.5

Shape class: 11, miniature vessels.

Comments: The cylinders are not true straight-sided cylinders, but have slightly curving sides. The median dimensions of all major shapes are presented in Table 8.5.

Ik Shapes: Chronological Change

Many of the shapes that are most prevalent in the Ik Complex are simple ones that occur occasionally throughout the sequence and do not serve as good "type fossils" that unmistakably mark the complex. But in the four-part seriation discussed earlier, there are a number of shapes that show strong quantitative trends over time. In the four-part seriation, the earliest section is considered early Ik and the second is late Ik. The remaining two sections of the seriation are considered early and late Imix. In the following discussion, the frequencies referred to are median frequencies from all the samples in each section.

Among wide-mouth jars, lip shapes proved to be the only temporally diagnostic marker. Round and/or bolstered lips were by far the most common in early Ik (66% of lip shapes), while most of the remainder were the flat and/or grooved lips that proved characteristic of the Imix Complex. In late Ik, the round and/or bolstered lips declined to a median of 54%, and then continued to decline in early Imix to reach a low in late Imix.

Among the large-capacity bowls, both the vessel shape and types of decoration proved temporally diagnostic. The large-capacity bowl with bolster lip was highly diagnostic for early Ik, with median frequency slightly above 60% of examples. The frequency of the shape declined to 30% in late Ik and continued regular decline in the Imix Complex. In decoration, impressions, with or without an appliquéd fillet of clay, were predominant. In early Ik, they accounted for a median of 66%, although samples from individual lots were small and highly variable. Impressions on appliquéd fillets accounted for about 25% of the sample. In late Ik, where samples were larger, the frequencies of both total impressions and impressions on fillets declined to 30% and 14%. Although total impressions continued to be fairly strong in Imix, appliquéd fillets all but disappeared. Because impressions on a fillet are very distinctive and do not occur in any other context, they are a type fossil for the Ik Complex.

TABLE 8.5
Shape Dimensions of the Ik Complex

Shape Class and Shape	Median Diameter	Median Height	Median Diameter/ Height Ratio
1. Wide-mouth Jar with Tall Neck	26.0	8.0	3.2
2. Narrow-mouth Jar with Tall Neck	16.0	5.6	2.9
2. Small Jar	12.0	3.5	3.2
4. Large Incurving-side Bowl	36.0	6.8	3.4
6. Outflaring to Slightly Outcurving-side Bowl or Dish	18.0	6.0–8.6	2.0–2.4
6. Slightly Incurving to Round-side Bowl	20.0	8.0	2.0
7. Barrel	14.0	12.0	1.2
7. Cylinder	12.0	18.0	0.6
8. Outflaring to Slightly Outcurving-side Tripod Plate	30.0	5.0	6.0
9. Large Tripod Plate with Ridge	35.0	6.0	5.8
10. Outflaring to Slightly Outcurving-side Cache Vessel	28.0	5.0	5.6
11. Miniature Jar with Cover	6.6	2.9	2.6
11. Miniature Bowl or Cylinder	2.0–4.0	4.0–6.0	0.5

In the serving-vessel category, the simple shapes of slightly incurving to round-side and outflaring to slightly outcurving-side bowls and dishes are most common. Although which of the two shapes is more common varies in individual samples, and the total of the two shapes makes up more than half of the serving vessels in early Ik and still one-third in late Ik.

The large tripod plate with ridge is next most common with a median frequency of 14% in early Ik and 10% in late Ik before a drastic decline in Imix. The large tripod plate with ridge is an excellent type fossil for the Ik Complex because the shape is very common. The barrel shape proves transitional between Ik and Imix because it reaches 11 to 12% in late Ik and early Imix.

Ik Shapes: Social Dimension

The vast majority of Ik Complex samples came from commoner residential contexts in small structure groups. Because there was a wide range of shape frequencies in these contexts and because there were almost no samples from other social contexts, no meaningful conclusions can be drawn about the social variation of Ik Complex shapes.

Special Deposits of the Ik Complex

Burials of the Ik Complex

Twenty-one special deposits classified as burials of Ik Complex date included ceramic offerings (Table 8.6). Seventy vessels were included in these burials. Eight of the Ik burials are from the central part of the site: three each from the North Acropolis and the Central Acropolis, and two from the ball courts in the Seven Temples Group. Nine burials come from groups of intermediate size, five of which are from Gp. 7F-1. The remaining four burials are from small structure groups in outlying parts of the site.

Only three burials included six or more vessels. In the remaining sample, one and four vessels are most common while two and three vessels occur with less frequency.

The most obvious characteristic of Ik Complex burial ceramics is that utilitarian vessels are extremely rare. There are no vessels of the utilitarian unslipped

or striated types (the type Ucum Unslipped is a completely different type with some specialized, probably ceremonial significance). In the entire sample of seventy vessels, there is only one large-capacity bowl and two jars, one of which is of an unusual and non-utilitarian shape. Tinaja Red, the type most commonly used in the production of these utilitarian shapes, is correspondingly underrepresented as well, although it is occasionally used for some vessels of the serving-vessel category.

Saxche Orange Polychrome (31%) is by far the most common type, and the Saxche Ceramic Group amounts to almost half of the sample. No other type exceeds a frequency of 10%. The only noteworthy characteristic of the way in which types occur in burials is that there seems to have been an emphasis on variety. Of the 14 burials that include at least two vessels, only one (Bu. 130 with two Saxche Orange Polychrome vessels) does not have at least two different types represented. In addition, at least one Saxche Orange Polychrome vessel occurs in all burials except for two of the burials with only a single vessel, and Bu. 58 that includes three vessels of the closely related Desquite Red-on-orange type. There are no other consistencies in the way types are combined in the burial offerings.

Three vessel shapes dominate the burial sample. Cylinders and large tripod plates with ridge occur with a frequency of 27%. For the cylinder shape, however, it should be noted that nine of the seventeen cylinders in the sample occur as a set in Bu. 23, so that in other burials cylinders are less frequent than tripod plates. Barrels occur with a frequency of 19%. Slightly incurving to round-side bowls occur with a frequency of 13% as do "odd" vessel shapes that fall outside the range of usual Tikal shapes. Outflaring to slightly outcurving-side bowls make up only 2% of the sample, considerably lower than their frequency in sherd samples of the Ik Complex. Cylinders, tripod plates, and barrels occur with considerably higher frequency in the burial sample than in sherd samples of the decorated category. When only the Ik sherd samples from elite-ceremonial contexts are considered, however, they do not differ very significantly, and there seems no basis for arguing that the burial sample differed significantly from the vessel shapes of ceramics in use in such elite contexts.

As with types, there seems to have been an emphasis on variety in choosing shapes to be included

TABLE 8.6
Burials of the Ik Complex

Burial No.	Op.SubOp./Lot	Str.	Structure Group Type	TR. 25A Illustration	TR.	No. of Vessels
23	12K/13	Gp. 5D-2 Str. 5D-33 1st Ded.	Civic-Ceremonial	39–41a	14	12
24	12K/18	Gp. 5D-2 Str. 5D-33-2nd Intr	Civic-Ceremonial	41b, 42a	14	6
40	20L/30	Gp. 4F-1 Str. 4F-7	Small Structure Group	52a	19	1
54	24C/125	Gp. 2G-1 Str. 2G-59-2nd	Small Structure Group	52b	20A&B	3
58	24C/138	Gp. 2G-1 Str. 2G-59-2nd	Small Structure Group	42b	20A&B	4
72	27A/18	Gp. 5G-1 Str. 5G-8	Intermediate Structure Group	42c	21	1
81	30A/2	Gp. 4G-1 Str. 4G-9	Intermediate Structure Group	43	21	4
83	30A/4	Gp. 4G-1 Str. 4G-9	Intermediate Structure Group	44a	21	3
96	33A/22	Gp. 4H-1 Str. 4H-4	Intermediate Structure Group	44b	21	4
130	68I/31	Gp. 6E-1 Plat. 6E-1	Intermediate Structure Group	44c	20A&B	2
132	3B/4	Gp. 7F-1 Str. 7F-30	Intermediate Structure Group	45, 46a	22	4
134	3B/8	Gp. 7F-1 Str. 7F-30	Intermediate Structure Group	46b	22	1
140	3B/14	Gp. 7F-1 Str. 7F-30	Intermediate Structure Group	46c	22	4
150	3B/17	Gp. 7F-1 Str. 7F-30	Intermediate Structure Group	47	22	4
159	3C/9	Gp. 7F-1 Str. 7F-31	Intermediate Structure Group	48	22	4
173	84A/9	Gp. 5D-9 Str. 5D-80	Civic-Ceremonial	52c	23D	1
174	84B/11	Gp. 5D-9 Str. 5D-79	Civic-Ceremonial	52d	23D	1
183	98D/14	Gp. 5D-11 Str. 5D-46, east stair	Range Structure Group	49a	15[†]	2
184	98D/18	Gp. 5D-11 Str. 5D-46, east stair	Range Structure Group	49b	15[†]	2
185	98D/22	Gp. 5D-11 Str. 5D-46, east stair	Range Structure Group	49c	15[†]	1
195	12U/27	Gp.5D-2 Str. 5D-32 Ded.	Civic-Ceremonial	50, 51	14	6

[†] Forthcoming

as burial offerings. Except for single vessel offerings, every burial includes at least two different shapes, and all burials with three or more vessels include at least three different shapes. There are no consistent combinations of different shapes that suggest rules on the formation of vessel sets. In effect, then, the rules for vessel selection for Ik burial offerings seem to be only that one should choose an assortment (of both types and shapes) of vessels from the serving-vessel category. The Maya mind was undoubtedly subtle and symbolic, but does not seem to have wasted such subtle symbolism upon ceramic funeral offerings in Ik times.

Two burials merit individual discussion. One is the set of vessels included in Bu. 23. The vessels included three large tripod plates with ridges, all decorated with Ahau signs, a cylinder of Saxche Orange Polychrome (or perhaps a similar trade type), and eight Chilar Fluted cylinders. This set of vessels is unlike any other Ik burial and is reminiscent of the contents of highly elite burials of the Imix Complex. It is possible that the burial dates to the end of the Ik Complex. The Saxche Orange Polychrome cylinder in both shape and design looks as though it may be transitional to Imix. It is also possible that this is the only Ik burial encountered of social status high enough to merit the full display of royal (or upper elite) ceramic offerings.

The final Ik burial to be discussed, Bu. 150, contains a mixture of Ik and Imix Complex characteristics. Three of the four vessels, a barrel and large tripod plate with ridge, both Saxche Orange Polychrome, and an Ucum Unslipped outflaring-side dish, are typically Ik Complex. The remaining set, a cylinder and lid, are of Palmar Orange Polychrome and Zacatel Cream Polychrome, types that are characteristic of the Imix Complex. One might explain this mixture of vessels as a combination of later pieces with heirlooms saved from earlier days. It is equally likely that the vessels are contemporaneous and represent a time at which older and newer ceramic traditions coexisted at the transition between Ik and Imix. The cylindrical vessel also exhibits an anomalous mix of features. The shape of the cylinder, rounding to the base, is typical of Ik cylinders and the band of glyphs is also an Ik characteristic. However, both the colors of the polychrome and the red bar design are clearly Imix characteristics. Although a cover for a vessel is very rare in either the Ik or Imix Complexes, the design and colors are typical of Zacatel Cream Polychrome.

Caches of the Ik Complex

There were six special deposits classified as caches with Ik Complex ceramics (Table 8.7). Five of the caches came from major civic-ceremonial structures: four from the area of the Great Plaza in Gp. 5D-2, and one from Str. 4D-32 in Twin Pyramid Complex, Group 4D-1, of the North Zone. One cache came from Str. 7F-30 in the intermediate structure Gp. 7F-1, which also included an unnumbered cache in Bu. 132. Four of the caches contained a single vessel and two included two vessels.

Most common in Ik caches were Ucum Unslipped miniature jars with covers. Two of the single-vessel caches were such jars, and, in the third, the jar was paired with a Tinaja Red cache cylinder with cover. A single-vessel cache from the Great Plaza area consisted of a weathered barrel with cover. The two-vessel cache from the North Zone contained two large bowls of Tinaja Red. The inclusion of such utilitarian vessels in a cache was unusual. More unusual yet was Ca. 201 from Str. 5D-33-1st. This cache included a cylinder that was stuccoed over an imported incised white type. In addition, a stuccoed piece of limestone served as a cover for the cylinder.

Problematical Deposits of the Ik Complex

Ik Complex vessels occurred in eleven problematical deposits, of which three (PD. 3, 54, and 76)

TABLE 8.7
Caches of the Ik Complex

Cache No.	Op.SubOp./Lot	Str.	Structure Group Type	TR. 25A Illustration	TR.	No. of Vessels
53	12B/31	Gp. 5D-2 St. 3 Locus	Civic-Ceremonial	109*a*	14	1
131	13F/5	Gp. 5D-2 Str. 5D-22	Civic-Ceremonial	110*a*	14	2
161	3B/7	Gp. 7F-1 Str. 7F-30	Intermediate Structure Group	110*b*	22	1
174	12L/8	Gp. 5D-2 Str. 5D-33	Civic-Ceremonial	110*c*	14	1
178	56G/5	Gp. 4D-1 Str. 4D-32	Civic-Ceremonial	109*c*	18[†]	2
201	12L/27	Gp. 5D-2 Str. 5D-33 1st	Civic-Ceremonial	114*d*	14	1

[†] Forthcoming

TABLE 8.8
Problematical Deposits of the Ik Complex

PD No.	Op.SubOp./ Lot	Str.	Structure Group Type	TR. 25A Illustration	TR.	No. of Vessels
3[1]	27A/6	Gp. 5G-1 Str. 5G-8	Small Structure Group	122a	21	1
19	12H/15	North Acropolis Gp. 5D-2 Str. 5D-26	Civic-Ceremonial	122d	14	1
54[2]	12C	North Acropolis Gp. 5D-2 Str. 5D-34	Civic-Ceremonial	131	14	2(Ik) 5(Imix)
762	43C/26	Gp. 5C-1 Str. 5C-17	Civic-Ceremonial	133c	18[†]	2
98	3B/3	Gp. 7F-1 Str. 7F-3	Intermediate Structure Group	142b	22	1
126	76B/11	Gp. 5D-1 Str. 5D-7	Small Structure Group	144d	20A&B	4
134[3]	12T	North Acropolis Gp. 5D-2 Str. 5D-22	Civic-Ceremonial	146, 147	14	10
158	98D/17	Central Acropolis Gp. 5D-11 Str. 5D-46	Range Structure Group	148e	14	1
160[4]	12T/73,78,79	North Acropolis Gp. 5D-2 Str. 5D-22	Civic-Ceremonial	148f	14	1
1654	12T/82,86	North Acropolis Gp. 5D-2 Str. 5D-22	Civic-Ceremonial	None	14	1
235	12K/8	North Acropolis Gp. 5D-2 Str. 5D-33	Civic-Ceremonial	155b	14	1

[1] Uncertain date: Ik or Imix

[2] Includes Imix Complex vessels

[3] Includes Eznab Complex vessels

[4] Many fits between PD. 160 & PD. 165

[†] Forthcoming

also may date to the Imix Complex, and one (PD. 134) includes possible Eznab ceramics (Table 8.8). Seven were discovered in the central area of the site: six in the North Acropolis and one in the Central Acropolis. One each was found in Twin Pyramid Group 5C-1, Intermediate Structure Group 7F-1, and Range Structure Group 5D-1, and there were two from Small Structure Groups 5G-1 and 5D-1. Seven problematical deposits included only a single vessel, two had two vessels, one had four vessels, and one had ten vessels.

There were twenty-five vessels in the sample. Typologically, the majority was of decorated types, including eleven Saxche Orange Polychrome vessels, and four Sibal Buff Polychrome vessels. Four vessels were of the Tinaja Ceramic Group, one was Ucum Unslipped and two were unusual types. In terms of vessel shapes, serving vessels are predominant (seventeen examples): nine barrels; two cylinders; two outflaring to slightly outcurving-side bowls; two large tripod plates with ridges; and two slightly incurving to round-side bowls. There were four large-capacity bowls, one narrow-mouth jar, and one unusual shape.

Ik Complex problematical deposits differed very significantly from those of the Manik Complex. In Manik, half of the problematical deposits consisted almost entirely of outflaring-side cache vessels and seem likely to have been caches. In Ik, the preponderance of decorated serving vessels occurred in all sherd deposits, and also in burials. However, there were not as many large tripod plates with ridges in Ik problematical deposits as in burials, and not many showed the elaborate designs common in burials.

Except for PD. 134, to be discussed below, there seems no good reason to believe that the vessels were derived from burials.

Only a few of the Ik problematical deposits merit extended comments. Problematical Deposit 54 included both Ik and Imix vessels. Only the two Ik vessels are noted here, and the five Imix vessels are discussed in the Imix Complex section. Three of the problematical deposits with single vessels (PD. 3, 158, and 160) include only large sherds that may not have any special significance. By far the most interesting Ik problematical deposit was PD. 134. This included the contents of a chamber burial, Bu. 200 (Coggins 1975:360–369) intruded into Str. 5D-22 in the North Acropolis. The burial was looted in Eznab times and the ceramics from the Ik burial were dumped into the fill covering an Eznab burial, Bu. 201. The ten vessels included several pieces with designs and composition that were outside the usual range of Tikal ceramics. Five barrels including two that depicted monkeys and one "melon" bowl, designs that are not typical at Tikal and that Coggins (1975:367) suggests may have an origin to the SE of Tikal. The fourth barrel has an eroded inscription around the rim and an eroded design band below. The fifth barrel is Ucum Unslipped, a type that otherwise would not be used in an important burial. A large tripod plate with ridge with a glyphic or pseudo-glyphic band on the interior and an eroded central base design is typical of Tikal. A fragmentary polychrome cylinder with figural design using specular hematite paint also points to an origin to the SE. Finally, a large-capacity bowl and a narrow-mouth jar of Tinaja Red are utility vessels that usually do not occur in other large Ik Complex burials.

IX

Imix Ceramic Complex

Imix Complex Collections

Introduction

Late Late Classic Imix Complex ceramics are very common at Tikal and were encountered in the majority of excavations. Pure Imix samples large enough for quantitative analysis were also quite common because the complex represented the last occupation at most Tikal structures. Ten separate locations yielded Imix collections usable in the analysis. As was the case for the Ik Complex, Ik-Imix Location 2 (Gp. 4F-1 and 4F-2) provided the basis for the chronology. This location provided twelve Imix Complex samples. The Imix samples from other locations could be fitted into the seriation charts derived from Location 2, but did not add very substantially to the stratigraphic confirmation of the chronology.

There was a well-balanced representation of different social contexts among the Imix Complex locations. Two locations were civic-ceremonial and two from range structure groups in major ceremonial-elite precincts; three were from intermediate structure groups, and three were from small structure groups. Seventy-one special deposits classified as burials, seventeen as caches, and twelve as problematical deposits included Imix Complex ceramics. Table 9.1 presents information on Imix Complex locations.

IK-IMIX LOCATION 1

This location is Gp. 7F-1, an intermediate structure group located 1.5 km SE of the Great Plaza (see TR. 22). The group provided one shape sample and one type sample pertaining to the Imix Complex.

Imix Sample 1-1 : This sample came from two lots that represented debris from the occupation of Str. 7F-35, north of the structure. Combined, the lots provided a sample of 232 rim sherds quantified for shapes that dates to late Imix.

Imix Sample 1-2: This sample of 407 sherds counted for types came from above living levels outside Room 2 of Str. 7F-32.

IK-IMIX LOCATION 2

Ik-Imix Location 2 was the area of Gp. 4F-1, a small structure group located about 1 km NE of the Great Plaza (see TR. 19). There were fewer Imix Complex samples than Ik Complex samples.

IK-IMIX LOCATION 2A

Imix Sample 2a-1: In Location 2a (Str. 4E-31), an Imix Complex sample from occupation and surface levels outside the structure was superimposed over two Ik samples from structure fill. This was a combined sample of 200 sherds quantified for type and 68 sherds quantified for shape partly from lots S of Str. 4E-31 on the presumed occupation surface, and

TABLE 9.1 (part 1)
Locations of Imix Samples

Sample #	Op.Sub-Op./Lot	Structure Group and Structure Number	Structure Group Type	Total Sherds-Types	Total Sherds-Shapes	Ceramic Complex	Comments	TR.
Location 1		Group 7F-1	Intermediate Structure Group			Imix		22
Sample 1-1	3F/2, 4	Str. 7F-35		—	232		N of structure	
Sample 1-2	3G/32	Str. 7F-32		407	—		Above living level outside Rm. 2	
Location 2		Group 4F-1	Small Structure Group					19
Sample 2a-1	20B/1, 3, 5, 6, 7, 9, 11, 14, 15, 18, 28, 30, 32, 33, 34, 35, 40, 41, 48, 54, 64, 66, 73, 78, 87	Str. 4E-31		200	68	Imix	South of Str. 4E-31; mixed occupation and fill	
Sample 2b-1	20D/18, 21, 26, 32, 40, 44 20J/1–10, 21–25	Str. 4F-3		604	221	Imix	North of Str. 4F-3, surface to 1m.	
Sample 2b-2	20D/11, 13, 14, 42, 43, 56, 58, 59, 64, 65, 66; 20D/2, 15, 27, 46, 47, 48, 61	Str. 4F-3		401	153	Imix	East of Str. 4F-3, surface to 1m.	
Sample 2b-3	20D/32	Str. 4F-3		310	—	Imix	South of Str. 4F-3, surface to 1m.	
Sample 2b-4	20D/42	Str. 4F-3		572	—	Imix	West of Str. 4F-3, surface to 1m.	
Sample 2b-5	20D/63	Str. 4F-3		168	—	Imix	Surface above floor of Str. 4F-3	
Sample 2c-1	20E/18, 42, 48, 49, 50; 20E/9, 10, 14, 15, 16	Str. 4F-4		710	264	Imix	Surface to living level north and south of Str. 4F-3	
Sample 2c-2	20E/1, 2, 5, 7, 12, 13, 19, 51, 55	Str. 4F-4		380	110	Early Imix	Unsealed fill west side Str. 4F-4 and from Plat. 4F-4-A	

TABLE 9.1 (part 2)
Locations of Imix Samples

Sample #	Op.Sub-Op./Lot	Structure Group and Structure Number	Structure Group Type	Total Sherds-Types	Total Sherds-Shapes	Ceramic Complex	Comments	TR.
Sample 2d-1	20G/8, 12, 15, 40, 41, 42, 43, 61, 62, 63; 20G/11, 16, 23, 24, 29, 30, 32, 39; 20G/25, 26, 28, 31, 33, 34, 35, 36, 37; 20G/18, 20, 21, 22	Str. 4F-5		227	94	Imix	Combined samples from around Str. 4F-5	
Sample 2f	20L/2, 4, 11, 3, 6, 9, 15, 19, 12, 17, 24, 25	Str. 4F-7		476	165	Early Imix	Outside Str. 4F-7	
Sample 2h-1	20F/13, 14, 15, 7, 8, 11, 33, 1, 3, 4, 5, 6, 35, 10, 12	Str. 4F-2		291	96	Early and Late Imix	Outside Str. 4F-2	
Sample 2h-2	20F/2, 9, 16, 17, 18, 19, 20, 21, 22, 23, 24, 25, 26, 27, 28, 29, 30, 31, 32	Str. 4F-2		448	185	Late Imix	Unsealed fill Str. 4F-2-1st	
Location 3	**All lots of midden-quality Imix ceramics obtained from excavations in the West Plaza and Central Acropolis**	**Groups 5D-10 and 5D-11**	**Range Structure Groups & Civic-Ceremonial**			**Late Imix**		15[†], 17
Sample 3-1	Various lots in suboperations from Ops. 19, 41, and 100.			247	175		Op. 19 is various contexts in Gp. 5D-10 (West Plaza); Op. 41 is Str. 5D-11 in Gp. 5D-10; Op. 100 is various contexts in Gp. 5D-11 (Central Acropolis)	
Location 4		**Group 5D-3**	**Civic-Ceremonial**			**Late Imix**		16
Sample 4-1	22O/1–20	Between Str. 5E-29, -30		275	203		Use of Platform 5D-2-1st	
Sample 4-2	22O/21–42	Between Str. 5E-29, -30		381	281		Use of Platform 5D-2-1st	

TABLE 9.1 (part 3)
Locations of Imix Samples

Sample #	Op.Sub-Op./Lot	Structure Group and Structure Number	Structure Group Type	Total Sherds-Types	Total Sherds-Shapes	Ceramic Complex	Comments	TR.
Location 5	Op. 33F[1]	Group 4H-1	**Intermediate Structure Group**			Late Imix		21
Sample 5-1	33F/3, 7, 8, 9, 12, 13, 29, 30, 32, 33, 39, 40, 46, 47A, 50, 51			683	369		Mixed sample from trenches 30–90 cm. below surface	
Sample 5-2	33F/11, 14–16, 19–23, 34–36, 43			515	332		Mixed sample from trenches 90–140 cm. below surface	
Location 6		Group 5C-1	Civic-Ceremonial			Late Imix		18[†]
Sample 6-1	43D/15	Str. 5C-14		185	129		North stairs Gp. 5C-1, post construction debris	
Sample 6-2	43E/9	Str. 5C-16		126	98		West stairs Gp. 5C-1, post construction debris	
Sample 6-3	43E/6	Str. 5C-16		132	78		Northwest corner, post construction debris	
Location 7		Str. 5C-26 Locus	Small Structure Group			Early Imix		20A
Sample 7-1	49A/4	Str. 5C-56		238	127		Above living surface west of Str. 5C-56	
Location 8		Group 6E-1	Small Structure Group			Imix		20A, 20B
Sample 8-1	68G/5; 68L	Str. 6E-26		342	156		East and north of Str. 6E-26	

TABLE 9.1 (part 4)
Locations of Imix Samples

Sample #	Op.Sub-Op./Lot	Structure Group and Structure Number	Structure Group Type	Total Sherds-Types	Total Sherds-Shapes	Ceramic Complex	Comments	TR.
Location 9		**Group 5D-11**	**Range Structure Group**			Late Imix		15[†]
Sample 9-1	100B/2	Str. 5D-48		240	—		Ravine below Str. 5D-48	
Sample 9-2	100N/1, 2	Str. 5D-48		113	—		Midden and ravine east of Str. 5D-48	
Sample 9-3	104A/1, 2, 3, 4	Palace Reservoir		124	—		Palace Reservoir excavation	
Location 10		**Group 3H-1**	**Intermediate Structure Group**			Imix		21
Sample 10-1	112A and 112B			280	—		mixed sample	
Sample 10-2	112A/1			149	—			
Sample 10-3	112A/2			411	—			
Sample 10-4	112A/3			146	—			
Sample 10-5	112A/5			138	—			
Sample 10-6	112B/2			477	—			
Sample 10-7	112B/3			208	—			
	TOTAL SHERDS			**10604**	**3536**			

[1] May not include all the lots used in the analyss

[†] Forthcoming

partly from surface debris that included mixed occupation and fill. The total sample was Imix, but too mixed to specify what part of the complex.

IK-IMIX LOCATION 2B

This location yielded four Imix samples from outside the walls of Str. 4F-3. The samples had no stratigraphic relationship to each other.

Imix Sample 2b-1: The sample, of 604 sherds quantified for types and 221 sherds quantified for shapes, came from above the living level N of the structure, from the surface to 1.0 m. It was marginal between early and late Imix.

Imix Sample 2b-2: The sample of 401 sherds quantified for types and 153 sherds quantified for shapes was a combined sample that came from above the living levels E of the structure. It was marginal between early and late Imix.

Imix Sample 2b-3: This sample of 310 total sherds counted for types came from above the living level S of Str. 4F-3.

Imix Sample 2b-4: This sample of 572 total sherds counted for types came from above the living level W of Str. 4F-3.

Imix Sample 2b-5: This sample of 168 total sherds counted for types came from the surface above the floor of Str. 4F-3.

IK-IMIX LOCATION 2C

Structure 4F-4 was Ik-Imix Location 2c. The location provided an excellent stratigraphic series of three levels. The earliest (Ik Sample 2c-3) from the fill of Str. 4F-4-B pertains to the Ik Complex (early Ik). It is followed by fill from Str. 4F-4-A (Sample 2c-2) dating to the transition between the Ik and Imix Complexes. A combined sample from surface to living levels (2c-1) dates to the transition between the early and late sections of Imix.

Imix Sample 2c-1: This combined sample of 710 sherds quantified for type and 264 sherds quantified for shapes from the surface to the living levels N and S of Str. 4F-4-A dates to the transition between early and late Imix.

Imix Sample 2c-2: This sample of 380 sherds quantified for types and 110 sherds quantified for shapes came from unsealed fill on the west side of Str. 4F-4, from Plat. 4F-4-A and was early Imix.

IK-IMIX LOCATION 2D

Imix Sample 2d-1: A single Imix sample of 227 quantified for types and 94 sherds quantified for shapes was obtained from the surface to the living and floor levels above and outside of Str. 4F-5. It was temporally later than Ik Complex sherds from the fill of the structure.

IK-IMIX LOCATION 2F

Structure 4F-7 was Ik-Imix Location 2f. One sample from early fill dated to the Ik Complex. A sample from outside the structure dated from early Imix.

Imix Sample 2f-1: This sample of 476 sherds quantified for types and 165 sherds quantified for shapes from excavations S and E of Str. 4F-7 dated to early Imix.

IMIX LOCATION 2H

Structure 4F-2 was Ik-Imix Location 2h. The structure provided no Ik Complex samples and only two Imix Complex samples were large enough for quantitative analysis.

Imix Sample 2h-1: This sample of 291 sherds quantified for types and 96 sherds quantified for shapes came from surface to bedrock outside N, W, and S walls of the structure. It was transitional between early and late Imix.

Imix Sample 2h-2: This sample, of 448 sherds quantified for types and 185 sherds quantified for shapes came from the unsealed fill of Str. 4F-2-1st. It dated to late Imix. This is another case of reverse stratigraphy involving a sample from outside structure walls.

IMIX LOCATION 3

Imix Sample 3-1: Imix Location 3 includes all lots of midden-quality Imix ceramics obtained from excavations in Gp. 5D-10, the West Plaza, and Gp. 5D-11, the Central Acropolis (see TR. 15 and 17). Most of the sherds in the sample came from deposits at the N and S sides of Str. 5D-11, the pyramidal structure at the W side of the Gp. 5D-10 plaza. A combined sample of 247 sherds quantified for types and 175 sherds quantified for shapes from a number of small lots dated to the late part of the Imix Complex. Because the material almost certainly came from activities within the plaza, it can be described as a range structure group context as well as civic-ceremonial.

IMIX LOCATION 4

Imix Location 4 was an excavation at the bottom of the steep N wall of the East Plaza just E of the stairway that exits from the plaza between Str. 5E-29 and 30, Gp. 5D-3 (see TR. 16). Although the excavators report that construction fill was laid at the bottom of the excavated area, it was never topped by construction. The total depth of deposit in Location 4 exceeded 2 m. Despite the separation of a series of metric levels, the samples showed no indication of temporal change from top to bottom of the deposit. The deposits were combined into two samples for quantification. Both samples dated to late Imix. Because the location is a likely dumping area for the East Plaza, the sample probably represents ceremonial-elite activities. The East Plaza was the site of a possible market structure, so the material may include market debris, but there are many other structures in the plaza that might also have been the source of the sample.

Imix Sample 4-1: This sample included a total of 275 sherds quantified for types and 203 sherds quantified for shapes from lots 1–20.

Imix Sample 4-2: This sample included a total of 381 sherds quantified for types and 281 sherds quantified for shapes from lots 21–42.

IMIX LOCATION 5

Imix Location 5 was Str. 4H-8, a small mound in Gp. 4H-1 more than 2 km E and N of the Great Plaza (see TR. 21). A deep deposit of material was excavated in a number of stratigraphic levels and the material was separated into two levels depending on depth below surface. There was no significant difference between the levels and both dated to late Imix. The context of the sample was an Intermediate Structure Group. The recovery of large quantities of some unusual kinds of ceramics and a high frequency of serving-vessel shapes make it seem likely that the location was the site of a ceramic manufacturing center, probably for the production of specialty items and polychromes (Becker 1973; TR. 21).

Imix Sample 5-1: This sample of 683 sherds quantified for types and 369 types quantified for shapes was from levels located at 30–90 cm below the surface.

Imix Sample 5-2: This sample of 515 sherds quantified for types and 332 sherds quantified for shapes was from levels located at 90–140 cm below the surface.

IMIX LOCATION 6

This location is Twin Pyramid Gp. 5C-1 (Complex N) immediately in front of Temple IV, which includes Str. 5C-14 through 16 (see TR. 18 forthcoming). The location provided three Imix Complex samples, all of them associated with the two pyramids in the group. The context is civic-ceremonial. Both the artifactual material and ceramics are unusual and may represent workshops. The material overlies secondary modifications of the group and certainly postdates by some years Stela 16 dedicated 9.14.0.0.0 (AD 711; see TR. 33A), a date that would fit the likely late Imix attribution of the samples. The ceramic samples all have unusually high frequencies of tripod plates with beveled lips that suggest they may have resulted from some specialized activity different from those that produced most Imix samples.

Imix Sample 6-1: This sample came from post-construction debris recovered in the excavation of the N stairway of Str. 5C-14, the E Pyramid of Complex N. The sample included 185 sherds quantified for types, 129 sherds quantified for shapes, and probably dated to the late part of the Imix Complex.

Imix Sample 6-2: This sample included post-construction refuse from around the W stairway of Str. 5C-16. The sample provided both a type count of 126 sherds and a shape sample of 98 sherds probably dating to late Imix.

Imix Sample 6-3: This sample included post-construction debris encountered in excavation at the NW corner of Str. 5C-16, the pyramid at the W side of Gp. 5C-1. The sample included 132 type sherds and 78 sherds quantified for shapes that probably dated to the late segment of the Imix Complex.

IMIX LOCATION 7

Imix Sample 7-1: This location consisted of excavations in the area of Ch. 5C-5 in an area without visible surface structures, about 0.5 km W and slightly S of the Great Plaza (see TR. 20A). In the process of excavation, the unmapped low Str. 5C-56 was discovered and a midden that provided Imix Sample 7-1. The sample of 238 sherds quantified for types and 127 quantified for shapes came from above the living level W of the structure. It dated to early Imix. The sample probably was associated with the small structure group, but the location is also close to the edge of the high platform at the W edge of Gp. 5C-11 on which Str. 5C-39 through 54 are located, so the possibility cannot be ruled out that dumping from this area might have occurred in the location.

IMIX LOCATION 8

Imix Sample 8-1: This location includes all excavations at Plat. 6E-1, a small but relatively high platform surmounted by Str. 6E-25 and 26 in Gp. 6E-1, located about 600 m SE of the Great Plaza (see TR. 20A, 20B). Extensive excavation of the platform revealed a lengthy and complex architectural sequence culminating in several rebuildings of Str. 6E-25 and 26. Midden-quality ceramics of the Imix Complex were all associated with Str. 6E-26 and provided a sample of 342 sherds quantified for types and 156 sherds quantified for shapes, but impossible to assign to a specific part of Imix. The cultural context is a small structure group.

IMIX LOCATION 9

Imix Sample 9-1: This sample resulted from excavations in the steep ravine behind Str. 5D-48 that leads down from the Central Acropolis to the Palace Reservoir. No construction was evident at the location and it seems likely that the material was dumped from Str. 5D-48 or other structures in the Central Acropolis (see TR. 15). It is considered to represent an elite-residential context. The sample was of 240 sherds quantified for types and dated to the late part of the Imix Complex.

Imix Sample 9-2: This sample resulted from excavations in the ravine and midden to the east of Str. 5D-48 and produced 113 sherds quantified for types.

Imix Sample 9-3: This sample resulted from excavation in the Palace reservoir near Str. 5D-48 and produced 124 sherds quantified for types.

IMIX LOCATION 10

Imix Sample 10-1: This location is an Intermediate Structure Group, Gp. 3H-1 off the detailed site map in Sq. 3H, beyond the end of the Tikal airstrip more than 2 km E and N of the Great Plaza (see TR. 21). To obtain a sample large enough for shape quantification, lots obtained from excavation around Str. 3H-2 were combined with lots obtained in excavating Str. 3H-3. The sample of 280 rim sherds was predominantly Imix, but there was a substantial admixture of Ik Complex ceramics.

Imix Samples 10-2 through 10-7: These were samples from Location 10 that were counted for types. Samples 10-2 through 10-5 were from various locations around Str. 3H-3, while Samples 10-6 and 10-7 came from Str. 3H-2. The samples were not stratigraphically related to each other and type counts varied randomly with no apparent relationship to location within the group. Total sherds counted for types in each sample were Sample 10-2: 149 sherds; Sample 10-3: 411 sherds; Sample 10-4: 146 sherds; Sample 10-5: 138 sherds; Sample 10-6: 477 sherds; Sample 10-7: 208 sherds.

Pastes of the Imix Complex

Introduction

The basic pastes for the Late and Terminal Classic complexes were established at the beginning of the Ik Complex. For the Imix Complex, only the substitution of Zacatel Paste for Saxche Paste for decorated types and the appearance of the type fossil Tinaja Pink Paste were significant changes.

Imix Paste Descriptions

COARSE-CARBONATE PASTE

Identifying characteristics: In all regards identical to the Ik Complex (see Chapter 8).

TINAJA PASTE

Identifying characteristics: In all regards identical to the Ik Complex (see Chapter 8). Tinaja Paste continues as the standard paste for monochrome types in the Imix Complex, however, the rare Tinaja Pink Paste also appears.

TINAJA PINK PASTE

Identifying characteristics: The buff to pinkish color of the paste differs significantly from the color of Tinaja Paste.

Color: Most common are pink (7.5YR 8/4, 7/4; 5YR 8/4), very pale brown (10YR 8/3, 7/3), and pale brown (10YR 7/4, 6/3). White (10YR 8/2), yellow (10YR 7/6), light gray (10YR 7/2), and brown (10YR 5/3) also occur.

Texture: Medium.

Inclusions: Small to medium amounts of fine to medium particles. Fluffy white inclusions most common; some pinkish particles occur.

Types: Tinaja Red.

Temporal distribution: Confined to the Imix Complex.

Comments: The paste is relatively rare, but occurs in collections from all parts of Tikal. The initial supposition that the paste was from a different production center than other Imix pastes was confirmed by X-ray fluorescence studies in which the elemental composition stood well apart from that of Tinaja Paste (Schwalbe and Culbert 1987). Tinaja Pink Paste also occurs in pottery from the area of Yaxha and there seems a possibility that examples at Tikal were imported from there.

ZACATEL PASTE

Identifying characteristics: The primary identifier is a large quantity of finely divided inclusions.

Color: The most common colors are brownish yellow (10YR 6/6), light yellowish brown (10YR 6/4), yellowish brown (10YR 5/8, 5/6), reddish yellow (7.5YR 6/8, 6/6; 5YR 6/8), and strong brown (7.5YR 5/6). Some examples extend to neighboring readings on all sides of these central colors. A few sherds have cores that are gray (7.5YR 7/0).

Texture: Fine to medium.

Inclusions: Medium to large amounts of medium to very finely divided clear to white particles that may be volcanic ash. Shiny black particles and golden mica appear occasionally.

Types: Used for all Palmar Group types.

Temporal distribution: Occurs occasionally in the Ik Complex, but is most common in the Imix Complex. Also used for rare examples of polychromes in the Eznab collections.

Ceramic Types of the Imix Complex

Introduction

The Imix Ceramic Complex includes the 10 ceramic groups and 23 types (and 26 varieties) listed in Table 9.2. Because many Imix Complex samples came from contexts in which surface preservation was very poor, only ten lots from three operations could be counted for types (see Table 9.3). There was a great deal of variation in the frequencies of types, often between different lots from the same context. The total of unslipped groups (Encanto Striated and Cambio Unslipped) shows the highest average frequency, but the range in frequency extends from 18% to 63% with a median between 35% and 43%. The next most common group is Tinaja Red with a range of frequency between 22% and 56% and a median of 32%. The only other group that usually exceeds 10% is Palmar Orange Polychrome that ranges in frequency between 4% and 19% with a median of 11%.

Imix Type Descriptions

CAMBIO CERAMIC GROUP

Cambio Unslipped: Cambio Variety

Established: Smith and Gifford (1966)

TABLE 9.2
Ceramic Groups and Types of the Imix Complex

CAMBIO CERAMIC GROUP

Cambio Unslipped: Cambio Variety

ENCANTO CERAMIC GROUP

Encanto Striated: Encanto Variety

UCUM CERAMIC GROUP

Ucum Unslipped: Ucum Variety

TINAJA CERAMIC GROUP

Tinaja Red: Tinaja Variety

Cameron Incised: Cameron Variety

Chinja Impressed: Chinja Variety

Chinja Impressed: Appliqued Variety

Rosa Punctated: Rosa Variety

VERACAL CERAMIC GROUP

Veracal Orange: Veracal Variety

Salada Fluted: Salada Variety

MAQUINA CERAMIC GROUP

Maquina Brown: Maquina Variety

ZACEC CERAMIC GROUP

Zacec Black: Zacec Variety

Chilar Fluted: Chilar Variety

UZ CERAMIC GROUP

Uz Buff: Uz Variety

Paap Fluted: Paap Variety

PALMAR CERAMIC GROUP

Palmar Orange Polychrome: Palmar Variety

Palmar Orange Polychrome: Red-bar Variety

Zacatel Cream Polychrome: Zacatel Variety

Zacatel Cream Polychrome: Red-bar Variety

Chinos Black-on-cream: Chinos Variety

Naranjal Red-on-cream: Naranjal Variety

Chantuori Black-on-orange: Chantuori Variety

Yuhactal Black-on-red: Yuhactal Variety

Mex Composite: Mex Variety

Paixban Buff Polychrome: Paixban Variety

KANALCAN CERAMIC GROUP

Kanalcan Gouged-incised: Kanalcan Variety

Group: Cambio

Ware: Uaxactun Unslipped

Ceramic Complex: Imix

Ceramic Sphere: Tepeu 1–3

Illustrations: Fig. 39.1–53; 55.1–9, 55.11–19; 56.34, 56.37–38. See TR. 25A: fig. 111*d*4–5; 133*c*1; 144*b*2.

Principal identifying attributes: Unslipped surfaces on large wide-mouth jars.

Identifying characteristics and sorting problems: Unslipped sherds without striations are otherwise identical to Encanto Striated. Because most of them are jar necks that are not decorated with striations, many examples may be Encanto Striated and they are difficult to sort from striated jars.

Paste: Coarse-carbonate Paste.

Firing: Dark cores are common and over one-third of the sherds show fireclouding. Because the fireclouding is more often on the interior than on the exterior, it is probably due to the original firing rather than to smudging from use.

Color: There is a wide range of color, even on a single sherd or vessel. The most common colors range from strong brown (7.5YR 5/6) to pale brown (10YR 7/3; 6/3). There are occasional light gray (10YR 7/2) and some light red brown (5YR 6/4) tones.

Surface finish and decoration: The nature of the paste and coarse inclusions made smoothing difficult. Striations are variable, ranging from fine to heavy. Striations cease abruptly at the necks of vessels, which they approach either vertically or obliquely. Crisscross striations on bodies are common. Bottoms of the rounded bases are often unstriated.

Shapes: Almost entirely wide-mouth jars with tall necks.

Temporal distribution: Begins at the start of the Ik Complex and continues through the Eznab Complex.

TABLE 9.3
Ceramic Type Frequencies of the Imix Complex

Ceramic Group	Small Structure Group			Intermediate Structure Group						
	Sample Loc. 2b-3 Gp. 4F-1 Str. 4F-3	Sample Loc. 2b-4 Gp. 4F-1 Str. 4F-3	Sample Loc. 2b-5 Gp. 4F-1 Str. 4F-3	Sample Loc. 1-2 Gp. 7F-1 Str.7F-32	Sample Loc. 10-2 Gp. 3H-1 Str. 3H-3	Sample Loc. 10-3 Gp. 3H-1 Str. 3H-3	Sample Loc. 10-4 Gp. 3H-1 Str. 3H-3	Sample Loc. 10-5 Gp. 3H-1 Str. 3H-3	Sample Loc. 10-6 Gp. 3H-1 Str. 3H-2	Sample Loc. 10-7 Gp. 3H-1 Str. 3H-2
	%	%	%	%	%	%	%	%	%	%
Cambio Group	44.8	43.4	22.0	31.9	12.8	37.7	20.5	40.6	30.8	23.1
Encanto Group	9.0	19.2	6.5	2.7	4.7	5.4	8.2	7.2	15.1	8.2
Tinaja Group	24.2	24.3	32.1	30.2	55.7	32.4	43.2	34.8	22.0	42.3
Zacec Group	1.0	0.9	—	1.5	1.3	0.2	—	0.7	—	1.9
Maquina Group	—	—	4.8	6.9	—	0.7	2.1	—	0.8	0.5
Palmar Group	16.5	10.4	19.0	11.5	9.4	6.6	19.8	4.3	13.4	11.1
Total Unslipped	53.8	62.6	28.5	34.6	17.5	43.1	28.7	47.8	45.9	31.3
Total Slipped	41.7	35.6	55.9	50.1	66.4	39.9	65.1	39.8	36.2	55.8
Unclassified & Rare Types	1.3	1.8	—	—	—	—	—	—	—	—
Weathered	3.2	—	15.6	15.3	16.1	17.0	6.2	12.4	17.9	12.9
Number of Sherds	310	572	168	407	149	411	146	138	477	208

Comments: Unslipped sherds without striations are otherwise identical to Encanto Striated. They are difficult to sort from striated jars because most of them are jar necks and may be Encanto Striated, which lacks striations on the jar necks as well. This type continues unchanged from the preceding Ik Complex.

Intersite comparisons: The Cambio Unslipped type is used at Altar de Sacrificios (Adams 1971); Becan (Ball 1977); Calakmul (Dominguez Carrasco 1994); El Mirador (Forsyth 1989); Holmul (Callaghan 2008, 2016e); La Milpa (Sagebiel 2005); Piedras Negras (Muñoz 2004); Seibal (Sabloff 1975); Uaxactun (Smith and Gifford 1966); and Yaxchilan (Lopez Varela 1989). The similar Cayo Unlipped type is used at Barton Ramie (Gifford 1976); Chan (Kosakowsky 2012); and Colha (Valdez 1987). Both Zibal Unslipped and Cambio Unslipped are used at Blue Creek (Kosakowsky and Lohse 2003). An Impressed Variety occurs in the Petexbatun (Foias and Bishop 2013). At Xunantunich the Cambio Group is used for censer forms only (LeCount 1996).

ENCANTO CERAMIC GROUP

Encanto Striated: Encanto Variety

Established: Smith and Gifford (1966)

Group: Encanto

Ware: Uaxactun Unslipped

Ceramic Complex: Imix

Ceramic Sphere: Tepeu 1–3

Illustrations: Fig. 39.1–53.

Principal identifying attributes: Unslipped striated surfaces on wide-mouth jars. Crisscross striations occur on bodies of jars and end at the neck.

Identifying characteristics and sorting problems: Striated types are almost identical throughout the Tikal sequence and can only be separated on features of shape.

Paste: Coarse-carbonate Paste.

Firing: Dark cores are common and over one-third of the sherds show fireclouding. Because the fireclouding is more often on the interior than on the exterior, it is probably due to the original firing rather than to smudging from use.

Surface treatment: The nature of the paste and coarse inclusions made smoothing difficult. Striations are variable, ranging from fine to heavy. Striations cease abruptly at the necks of vessels, which they approach either vertically or obliquely. Crisscross striations on bodies are common. Bottoms of the rounded bases are often unstriated.

Color: There is a wide range of color, even on a single sherd or vessel. The most common colors range from strong brown (7.5YR 5/6) to pale brown (10YR 7/3; 6/3). There are occasional light gray (10YR 7/2) and some light red brown (5YR 6/4) tones.

Shapes: Almost entirely wide-mouth jars with tall necks.

Temporal distribution: Begins at the start of the Ik Complex and continues through the Eznab Complex without change.

Intersite Comparisons: The Encanto Striated type is used at Altar de Sacrificios (Adams 1971); Becan (Ball 1977); Calakmul (Dominguez Carrasco 1994); El Mirador (Forsyth 1989); Holmul (Callaghan 2008, 2016e); La Milpa (Sagebiel 2005); Piedras Negras (Muñoz 2004); Seibal (Sabloff 1975); Uaxactun (Smith and Gifford 1966); and Yaxchilan (Lopez Varela 1989). The similar Tu-tu Camp Striated type is used at Barton Ramie (Gifford 1976); Chan (Kosakowsky 2012); Colha (Valdez 1987); and Xunantunich (LeCount 1996). Tu-tu Camp Striated and Encanto Striated are used interchangeably at Blue Creek (Kosakowsky and Lohse 2003).

UCUM CERAMIC GROUP

Ucum Unslipped: Ucum Variety

Established: TR. 25A (Culbert 1993)

Group: Ucum

Ware: Uaxactun Unslipped

Ceramic Complex: Imix

Ceramic Sphere: Tepeu 1–2

Illustrations: See TR. 25A: fig. 47*d*; 77*a*5–6; 81*d*; 96*c*; 111*b*1–2,*e1*; 112*b*1,*c*1,*e*4.

Principal identifying attributes: Unslipped or highly well smoothed weathered surfaces on a Tinaja Paste. Occurs in only specialized contexts on restricted shapes (see description of shapes below).

Identifying characteristics and sorting problems: The location in Special Deposits and the unusual shapes make identification easy. In sherd collections, although the use of Tinaja Paste for an unslipped type is a good marker, many sherds could have been misidentified as other unslipped types or weathered.

Paste: Tinaja Paste

Surface: Usually little smoothed.

Color: No data available.

Shapes: The shapes represented are either specialized cache vessels or aberrant examples of standard shapes. They include one outflaring-side cache vessel; four flanged cache cylinders; one rectangular cache vessel; three miniature jars with covers; one small jar of unusual shape; three outcurving-side bowls with aberrant features of shape; and one unusual round-side dish. The only vessels that fall within normal shape patterns are two cylinders and one barrel.

Temporal distribution: Begins in the Ik Complex and becomes more common in the Imix Complex. Two Imix examples, from Ca. 4 and 123, are dated to 9.17.0.0.0 (AD 771) and 9.19.0.0.0 (AD 810) respectively.

Comments: This is a specialized type that occurs almost entirely in burials and caches. The type occurs in three Ik Complex burials, four Imix Complex burials, three Ik Complex caches, six Imix Complex caches, and in one problematical deposit that contains largely Ik Complex ceramics.

Intersite comparisons: None noted.

TINAJA CERAMIC GROUP

Tinaja Red: Tinaja Variety

Established: Smith and Gifford (1966)

Group: Tinaja

Ware: Petén Gloss

Ceramic Complex: Imix

Ceramic Sphere: Tepeu 1–3

Illustrations: Fig. 50.1, 50.3–5, 50.10, 50.17, 50.19, 50.32, 50.34–36, 50.41–42, 50.44–45, 50.47, 50.52; 51.1–7, 51.12–14, 51.16–22, 51.24–25, 51.28, 51.30–31, 51.36, 51.44–45, 51.47, 51.48–49, 51.53; 56.6, 56.14, 56.19, 56.27, 56.30. See TR. 25A: fig. 56*b*2; 144*b*1.

Principal identifying attributes: Light to medium polished monochrome red surfaces on jars and large bowls. Paste is characteristically a pale yellow.

Identifying characteristics and sorting problems: The combination of Tinaja Paste and the shapes produced from it is very characteristic.

Paste: Tinaja Paste.

Firing: Dark cores and fireclouding are rare.

Slip: Thin to medium slip applied to a surface that has received little attention; the slip wears easily.

Polish: There is a great range of polish. Most examples show low to medium polish, but there are a few highly polished examples.

Color: Most common color is red (10R 4/6, 4/8; 5/6, 5/8; 2.5YR 5/6, 5/8). Occasional weak red (10R 4/4), light red (2.5YR 6/6, 6/8), reddish yellow (5YR 6/6, 6/8), and yellowish red (5YR 5/8) occur.

Shapes: Almost entirely narrow-mouth jars and large-capacity bowls. Jars and bowls were quantified separately in sherd counting. Originally two varieties of Tinaja Red were identified on the basis of vessel form in TR. 25A, but this varietal distinction is not maintained here because separating varieties based on shape violates type: variety nomenclature (see Gifford 1976).

Temporal distribution: Begins at the start of the Ik Complex and continues through the Eznab Complex.

Comments: The few examples of San Julio Modeled originally identified in the Tikal collections (TR. 25A) are too few to describe completely and are included in the Tinaja Group.

Intersite comparisons: Tinaja Red is used throughout Tepeu (1–3) at Altar de Sacrificios (Adams 1971); Chan Chich (Valdez 1998; Valdez and Houk 2000); Holmul (Callaghan 2008, 2016e); Nakbe (Forsyth 1993); and Rio Azul (Adams 1999; Adams and Jackson-Adams 1991). Tinaja Red: Nanzal Variety is used for the Ik equivalent at El Mirador (Forsyth 1989) and in the Petexbatun (Foias and Bishop 2013). At Uaxactun, the Ik equivalent is called Tasital Red (Smith and Gifford 1966). In Belize, type names from Barton Ramie (Gifford 1976) are utilized for the Tepeu 1 monochrome red at Blue Creek (Kosakowsky and Lohse 2003); Chan (Kosakowsky 2102); La Milpa (Sagebiel 2005); and Nohmul (Kosakowsky and Pring 2001). Elsewhere, Tinaja Red is used as a type only for the Tepeu 2–3 monochrome red.

Cameron Incised: Cameron Variety

Established: Smith and Gifford (1966)

Group: Tinaja

Ware: Petén Gloss

Ceramic Complex: Imix

Ceramic Sphere: Tepeu 1–3

Illustrations: Fig. 50.40, 50.50; 51.9–11, 51.14, 51.26–27, 51.32, 51.35, 51.37–38, 51.43, 51.46, 51.56.

Principal identifying attributes: Surface finish and paste similar to Tinaja Red, with the addition of a single incised groove on the exterior of large capacity bowls.

Identifying characteristics and sorting problems: Cameron Incised is identical to Tinaja Red: Tinaja Variety in all characteristics except that it is limited to large-capacity bowls with a single groove below the lip on the exterior. Originally called Large Bowl Variety by Culbert (TR. 25A).

Intersite comparisons: Similar to Altar de Sacrificios (Adams 1971); Holmul (Callaghan 2008, 2016e); Seibal (Sabloff 1975); and Uaxactun (Smith and Gifford 1966). See intersite comparison discussion for Tinaja Red for more detailed information.

Chinja Impressed: Chinja Variety

Established: Smith and Gifford (1966)

Group: Tinaja

Ware: Petén Gloss

Ceramic Complex: Imix

Ceramic Sphere: Tepeu 1–2 (occasionally 3)

Illustrations: Fig. 50.6, 50.8–9, 50.12–13, 50.15–16, 50.20–22, 50.28, 50.30–31, 50.43, 50.48–49, 50.51; 51.8, 51.23, 51.29, 51.47, 51.50, 51.54–55, 51.57, 51.59–62. See TR. 25A: fig. 122a.

Principal identifying attributes: Surface finish and paste similar to Tinaja Red, with the addition of a single row of fingernail impressions on the exterior of large capacity bowls.

Identifying characteristics and sorting problems: Chinja Impressed: Chinja Variety is identical to Tinaja Red: Tinaja Variety except for the characteristics noted below. Originally called Simple-impressed variety by Culbert (TR. 25A).

Surface Finish and Decoration: Large-capacity bowls have a row of impressions encircling the vessel exterior below the lip. The impressions were made directly on the vessel wall. The impressions were usually made with fingernails, but in a few examples were made with a hollow circular tool (and these latter examples should be reclassified as Rosa Punctated).

Temporal distribution: Chinja Impressed: Chinja Variety occurs in about equal quantities in Ik and Imix collections and is rare in Eznab collections.

Intersite comparisons: Chinja Impressed identified in later time periods at Calakmul (Dominguez Carrasco 1994); El Mirador (Forsyth 1989:86–89); La Milpa (Sagebiel 2005); Nakbe (Forsyth 1993); and in the Nanzal Group at Uaxactun (Smith and Gifford 1966). It is similar to Chaquiste Impressed at Altar de Sacrificios (Adams 1971) and Seibal (Sabloff 1975). It is similar to Chinja Impressed: Floresas Variety at Holmul (Callaghan 2008, 2016e); to Pascua Impressed, Gloria Impressed, and Kaway Impressed at Barton Ramie (Gifford 1976), and to Kaway Impressed at Xunantunich (LeCount 1996). In form it is similar to Subin Red at Altar de Sacrificios (Adams 1971) and San Jose IV and V monochrome red bowls (Thompson 1939).

Chinja Impressed: Appliquéd Variety

Established: Smith and Gifford (1966)

Group: Tinaja

Ware: Petén Gloss

Ceramic Complex: Imix

Ceramic Sphere: Tepeu 1–2

Illustrations: Fig. 50.2, 50.7, 50.14, 50.23–27, 50.33; 51.39, 51.42, 51.51, 51.58.

Principal identifying attributes: Surface finish and paste similar to Tinaja Red, with the addition of an impressed fillet that is appliquéd on the exterior of large capacity bowls.

Identifying characteristics and sorting problems: Chinja Impressed: Appliquéd Variety is identical to Chinja Impressed: Chinja Variety except for the characteristics noted below:

Surface Finish and Decoration: A fillet of clay was added to the exterior of large-capacity bowls. The fillet has a row of impressions encircling the vessel exterior below the lip. The impressions were usually made with fingernails but in a few examples were made with a textured tool, perhaps a piece of rope or a corncob.

Temporal distribution: Chinja Impressed: Appliquéd Variety is considerably more common in Ik than in Imix collections and does not appear in Eznab collections.

Intersite comparisons: See above for Chinja Impressed: Chinja Variety. Examples that possess an appliqué fillet are often included in the Chinja Variety alongside those without at other sites.

Rosa Punctated: Rosa Variety

Established: Smith and Gifford (1966)

Group: Tinaja

Ware: Petén Gloss

Ceramic Complex: Imix

Ceramic Sphere: Tepeu 1–2 (occasionally 3)

Illustrations: Fig. 50.11, 50.29, 50.37, 50.46; 51.34, 51.40–41, 51.52.

Principal identifying attributes: Surface finish and paste similar to Tinaja Red, with the addition of a single row of punctuated impressions made with a hollow tool on the exterior of large capacity bowls.

Identifying characteristics and sorting problems: The occasional examples of large-capacity bowls with a row of impressions made with a hollow circular tool that are noted under the description of Chinja Impressed are technically Rosa Punctated.

Temporal Distribution: See Chinja Impressed.

Intersite comparisons: For general comparisons see Chinja Impressed. Examples with punctuated fillets are often included in the Chinja Variety at other sites.

VERACAL CERAMIC GROUP

Veracal Orange: Veracal Variety

Established: Smith and Gifford (1966)

Group: Veracal

Ware: Petén Gloss

Ceramic Complex: Imix

Ceramic Sphere: Tepeu 1–2

Principal identifying attributes: Slightly polished monochrome orange surfaces on small bowls, dishes, and possibly jars.

Identifying characteristics and sorting problems: Overlaps in color with Tinaja Red, but shapes and paste indicate separate status.

Paste: Fine paste with medium amounts of very fine white inclusions. Paste color brownish yellow (10YR 6/6) to yellowish red (5YR 6/6).

Polish: Medium.

Color: Reddish yellow (7.5YR 6/8) to yellowish red (5YR 6/6).

Shapes: The two whole vessels in burials are a barrel and an unusual everted-rim bowl. Sherds suggest jars and small bowls or dishes.

Temporal distribution: Ik and Imix Complexes, but considerably more common in Ik.

Comments: It was originally thought that Kau Incised, the incised type in the Veracal Orange Group, which begins in the Ik Complex continued into Imix (TR. 25A). However it is currently felt that the type is restricted to Ik and not found in Imix contexts.

Intersite comparisons: Naachtun (Walker and Reese-Taylor 2012); Uaxactun (Smith and Gifford 1966).

Salada Fluted: Salada Variety

Established: Smith and Gifford (1966)

Group: Veracal

Ware: Petén Gloss

Ceramic Complex: Imix

Ceramic Sphere: Tepeu 2

Illustrations: See TR. 25A: fig. 60*d*4.

Principal identifying attributes: Slightly polished monochrome orange surfaces on a single miniature jar.

Comments: A single vessel of Salada Fluted was found in Bu. 87. The vessel is a miniature jar, slipped orange on the exterior with vertical flutes extending from just below the neck to the base.

Intersite comparisons: Veracal Orange is found at Naachtun (Walker and Reese-Taylor 2012) and Uaxactun (Smith and Gifford 1966) but fluted decoration not noted elsewhere.

MAQUINA CERAMIC GROUP

Maquina Brown: Maquina Variety

Established: Smith and Gifford (1966)

Group: Maquina

Ware: Petén Gloss

Ceramic Complex: Imix

Ceramic Sphere: Tepeu 1–3; most common in Tepeu 3

Principal identifying attributes: Monochrome brown surfaces that overlap at the extremes with fireclouded Tinaja Red on narrow-mouth jars and large-capacity bowls.

Color: A wide range of colors exists within Maquina Brown without a clustering around any central color. Examples include dark reddish brown (2.5YR 3/4), reddish brown (5YR 4/4, 5/4), brown (7.5YR 5/4), light brown (7.5YR 6/4), grayish brown (10YR 5/2), light brownish gray (10YR 6/2), light yellowish brown (10YR 6/4), and dark yellowish brown (10YR 4/4). These colors range around the edges of the more central reddish shades of Tinaja Red, a fact that increases the probability that many examples called Maquina Brown may be nothing more than misfiring of Tinaja Red.

Shapes: Most examples of Maquina Brown are either narrow-mouth jars or large-capacity bowls with either incurved lip or restricted orifice. These two shapes were separated as varieties of the type for counting and in TR. 25A, however naming varieties on the basis of vessel shape violates the rules of nomenclature in type: variety (Gifford 1976) so both shapes are now included in the Maquina Variety.

Temporal distribution: Maquina Brown sherds occur in all Late Classic complexes. They have a higher frequency of occurrence in the Eznab Complex than in Ik and Imix, but it is possible that this may be an artifact of the better preservation of the Eznab samples.

Comments: Maquina Brown occurs in all Late and Terminal Classic complexes, but is somewhat more common in the Eznab Complex.

Intersite Comparisons: Calakmul (Dominguez Carrasco 1994); El Perú/Waka' (Eppich 2011); Holmul (Callaghan 2008, 2016e); Rio Azul (Adams 1999; Adams and Jackson-Adams 1991), and Uaxactun (Smith and Gifford 1975). Some overlap with the Tepeu 2 Tialipa Brown at Barton Ramie (Gifford 1976) and Uaxactun (Smith and Gifford 1966).

ZACEC CERAMIC GROUP

Zacec Black: Zacec Variety

Established: TR. 25A (Culbert 1993)

Group: Zacec

Ware: Petén Gloss

Ceramic Complex: Imix

Ceramic Sphere: Tepeu 1–2

Illustrations: Fig. 57.20–22, 57.24. See TR. 25A: fig. 57*a*1; 68*a*; 91*a*; 92*c*.

Principal identifying attributes: Highly polished thin black monochrome slips that are well fired.

Paste: Highly variable. Some examples show Zacatel Paste; others have a fine tan to brown paste with small amounts of medium-gray powdery particles.

Firing: Dark cores rare. The black penetrates into the paste suggesting firing in a reducing atmosphere. This is surprising because a pigment that fired black in an oxidizing atmosphere was used for polychromes, and because that was the pigment used for Zacec Black in the Ik Complex.

Surface: On some examples, the white underslip characteristic of the Palmar Group was used. Others show a thin black slip applied directly to the clay.

Polish: Polish is medium to high.

Color: The black surface sometimes shows areas of reddish brown (5YR 5/3) or dark grayish brown (10YR 3/2).

Shapes: The few sherds that indicate shape include tripod plates with beveled lips and round-side bowls or dishes. Of four whole vessels in burials, two are cylinders that are stuccoed and painted; two are slightly outcurving-side bowls with unusual features of shape. There are a few examples with modeling.

Temporal distribution: Zacec Black is quite rare in Imix collections.

Comments: The difference in Zacec Black between the Ik and Imix Complexes is surprising, but is not consistent enough to merit separation as two varieties.

Intersite comparisons: Infierno Black is used for Tepeu 2 at Calakmul (Dominguez Carrasco 1994); El Mirador (Forsyth 1989); Naachtun (Walker and Reese-Taylor 2012); Seibal (Sabloff 1975); Uaxactun (Smith and Gifford 1966). Achote Black is used for Tepeu 2 at Altar de Sacrificios (Adams 1971); Becan (Ball 1977); Blue Creek (Kosakowsky and Lohse 2003); Holmul (Callaghan 2008, 2016e); La Milpa (Sagebiel 2005); Nakbe (Forsyth 1993); Rio Azul

(Adams 1999; Adams and Jackson-Adams 1991). At Barton Ramie, Meditation Black and Achote Black are used for Spanish Lookout/Tepeu 2-3 (Gifford 1976). At Chan Chich, Teakettle Bank Black and Achote are used for Tepeu 1/2 and only Achote is used for Tepeu 3 (Valdez and Houk 2000). At Colha, Teakettle Bank Black is used for Tepeu 1/2 (Valdez 1987) and Meditation Black and Achote are used for Tepeu 2/3 (Valdez 1987).

Chilar Fluted: Chilar Variety

Established: Smith and Gifford (1966)

Group: Zacec (TR. 25A)/Achote (Smith and Gifford 1966)

Ware: Petén Gloss

Ceramic Complex: Imix

Ceramic Sphere: Tepeu 1–2

Illustrations: See TR. 25A: fig. 77*a*3; 82*a*5; 83*b*2; 91*b–h*; 92*d–e,g*.

Principal identifying attributes: Monochrome black slip similar to Zacec Black at Tikal and Achote Black at Uaxactun (Smith and Gifford 1966) with additional decoration in the form of pre-slip vertical, horizontal, or oblique grooves or flutes.

Identifying characteristics and sorting problems: Too few sherds of Chilar Fluted were recovered to permit description, so the following entries are based on the sample in burials. Because it was impossible to see sections of the vessels, no information on pastes or frequency of dark cores is available.

Color: In some examples, the black was well controlled. In others, the black shades into areas of reddish brown. This suggests that a pigment firing black in oxidizing conditions was used in some examples and that other examples were fired in a reducing atmosphere.

Surface finish and decoration: The type would be better described as "fluted-grooved" than as "fluted" because there is a range between the broad shallow depressions traditionally called fluting and the deeper depressions called grooving. The flutes/grooves usually are vertical and occasionally diagonal. In all examples except one, there are between one and three horizontal grooves above the fluted/grooved area. There are sometimes horizontal grooves below and sometimes the flutes/grooves run all the way to the vessel base.

Shapes: In the burial sample, there are 16 cylinders and 5 slightly outcurving-side bowls. The cylinders, except for a single cylinder in Bu. 193, occur as sets: a set of eight in Ik Bu. 23 and a set of seven in Imix Bu. 196. There is great variety within the sets in size, color, and style of decoration. It must be concluded that the sets were made by different potters or centers rather than made together by a single potter.

Temporal distribution: Chilar Fluted occurs in both Ik and Imix burials.

Comments: Chilar Fluted is a type that is described in the Achote Ceramic Group at Uaxactun (Smith and Gifford 1966), although placed in the Xacec Ceramic Group at Tikal (TR. 25A). At other sites it is more common in Tepeu 2 and 3.

Intersite comparisons: It is similar to Jojoba Channeled (Molino Group) at Becan (Ball 1977). Chilar Fluted is used for Tepeu 2/3 at Barton Ramie (Gifford 1976); Blue Creek (Kosakowsky and Lohse 2003); Calakmul (Dominguez Carrasco 1994); La Milpa (Sagebiel 2005); Seibal (Sabloff 1975), and Uaxactun (Smith and Gifford 1966). At El Mirador, there is an "other Infierno Group: Fluted" (Forsyth 1989). At Río Azul "Glossy Rippled Black" is used (Adams and Jackson-Adams 1991).

UZ CERAMIC GROUP

Uz Buff: Uz Variety

Established: TR. 25A (Culbert 1993)

Group: Uz

Ware: Petén Gloss

Ceramic Complex: Imix

Ceramic Sphere: Tepeu 2

Illustrations: Fig. 56.43.

Principal identifying attributes: Well smoothed light brown to buff surfaces on small bowls and dishes.

Paste: Fine to very fine paste with medium amounts of very fine white inclusions. Paste color most commonly reddish yellow (7.5YR 6/6).

Polish: Surface well smoothed, but does not take high polish.

Color: Light yellowish brown (10YR 6/4); pink (7.5YR 7/4); brown (7.5YR 5/4).

Shapes: The few sherds that indicate shape are small bowls and dishes too fragmentary to determine specific shapes. There is one miniature jar (Fig. 56.43).

Temporal distribution: Occurs rarely in the Ik and Imix Complexes; slightly more common in Imix.

Intersite comparisons: None noted.

Paap Fluted: Paap Variety

Established: TR. 25A (Culbert 1993)

Group: Uz

Ware: Petén Gloss

Ceramic Complex: Imix

Ceramic Sphere: Tepeu 2

Illustrations: See TR. 25A: fig. 80*a*2.

Principal identifying attributes: Well smoothed light brown to buff surfaces with secondary decoration by means of diagonal fluting on a cylinder.

Comments: A single vessel of Paap Fluted was found in Bu. 157 (TR. 25A: fig. 80*a*2). The vessel is a cylinder the color of Uz Buff. On the vessel exterior, diagonal fluting extends from a point slightly

below two horizontal grooved lines to the base. The fluting is comparable to that of Chilar Fluted.

Intersite comparisons: None noted though similar fluted decoration occurs on coeval monochrome black pottery.

PALMAR CERAMIC GROUP

Palmar Orange Polychrome: Palmar Variety

Established: Smith and Gifford (1966)

Group: Palmar

Ware: Petén Gloss

Ceramic Complex: Imix (Continues into Eznab)

Ceramic Sphere: Tepeu 2–3

Illustrations: Fig. 43.3–4, 43.7, 43.9, 43.16–17; 44.1–8, 44.20–23; 45.1, 45.4, 45.6, 45.9–10, 45.13, 45.18; 46.33. See TR. 25A: fig. 47*a*; 53*c*,*d*1,*e*; 54*a*1–2; 55*b*3; 56*b*3; 57*b*4,*c*2; 58*a*; 59*a*3,*b*1; 60*d*2–3; 61*a*1–3,*b*1–2,*c*1,3; 62*a*1–3,*d*1,3,*e*; 63*a*2,*b*1–2,*c*,*f*2; 64*a*1,*b*; 72*a*; 73; 74*a*–*b*; 75*a*; 76*a*1,*c*2–3; 77*a*2; 78*a*1–2,*b*1; 79*a*2,*b*3,*c*2,*d*; 80*b*3,*c*2,*d*1,3; 81*a*,*c*; 82*a*2,*b*1; 85*a*; 91*i*; 92*a*–*b*,*h*–*i*; 93; 94*a*–*b*; 95*a*–*c*; 96*a*–*c*; 97*b*3; 151*b*2,*c*1.

Principal identifying attributes: Glossy orange slip on a white underslip decorated with red and black designs.

Identifying characteristics and sorting problems: The most easily recognized characteristic is the white background color even though it is overpainted; other colors separate the type from the Saxche Polychrome Group as do many of the shapes involved.

Paste: Zacatel Paste.

Firing: Dark cores and fireclouding rare.

Surface: As in Zacatel Cream Polychrome, a whitish coat was first applied over all surfaces to be decorated. This underslip was then completely covered with the colors noted below.

Polish: Highly polished on well-preserved examples.

Color: The background color is orange (reddish yellow 5YR 7/8, 6/8; light red 2.5YR 6/8; red 2.5YR 5/8). Additional colors are red (red 10R 4/8, 4/6; 7.5R 4/8, 5/8; 5R 5/8; dark red 7.5R 3/8), and black. The black pigment used fires black in an oxidizing atmosphere.

Shapes: Distribution of shapes in the sherd sample were tripod plate with beveled lip 31%; cylinder 24%; slightly outcurving-side bowl or dish 20%; straight-side bowl or dish 11%; barrel 9%; widely outcurving-side plate 4%. Shapes in the sample of burial vessels were cylinder 40%; tripod plate with beveled lip 31%; slightly outcurving-side bowl or dish 22%; short cylinder 2%; barrel 2%; straight-side bowl or dish 2%; others 2%. The burial sample is biased by multiple examples of some shapes in rich burials.

Temporal distribution: A few examples occur in Ik collections. The presence in the sherd sample of such typical Ik forms as barrels and widely outcurving-side plates may indicate that Palmer Orange Polychrome appeared slightly earlier than Zacatel Cream Polychrome. The great majority of the examples occur in Imix and a few examples continue to occur in Eznab.

Intersite comparisons: Altar de Sacrificios (Adams 1971); Barton Ramie (Gifford 1976); Becan (Ball 1977); Blue Creek (Kosakowsky and Lohse 2003); Calakmul (Dominguez Carrasco 1994); Chan (Kosakowsky 2012); Chan Chich (Valdez 1998; Valdez and Houk 2000); Colha (Valdez 1987); El Mirador (Forsyth 1989); Holmul (Callaghan 2008, 2016e); El Peru/Waka' (Eppich 2011); La Milpa (Sagebiel 2005); Naachtun (Walker and Reese-Taylor 2012); Nakbe (Forsyth 1993); Nohmul (Kosakowsky and Pring 2001); Piedras Negras (Muñoz 2004); Rio Azul (Adams 1999; Adams and Jackson-Adams 1991); Uaxactun (Smith and Gifford 1966); Xunantunich (LeCount 1996). At Seibal Palmar is lumped with Saxche (Sabloff 1975) and in the Petexbatun it is lumped with Zacatel (Foias and Bishop 2013).

Palmar Orange Polychrome: Red-bar Variety

Established: Type named by Smith and Gifford (1966). Variety named by Culbert (1993 [TR. 25A]).

Group: Palmar

Ware: Petén Gloss

Ceramic Complex: Imix

Ceramic Sphere: Tepeu 2

Illustrations: Fig. 44.24–25; 45.20; 46.15, 46.21, 46.24, 46.29; 47.1; 49.7, 49.12.

Principal identifying attributes: Glossy orange slip on a white underslip decorated with red and darker orange bars.

Identifying characteristics and sorting problems: This variety is identical to the Palmar Variety except that the Red-bar Variety has alternating bands of red and darker orange on parts of the vessels. The only characteristic that needs separate comment is the shapes represented.

Shapes: Sherds provided too few examples for meaningful quantification. In the small sample of burial vessels (N=15), the percentages were slightly outcurving-side bowl or dish 53%; tripod plate with beveled lip 40%; and straight-side bowl or dish 7%.

Comments: In the burial sample, 21% of Palmar Orange Polychrome vessels were of the Red-bar Variety, less than for Zacatel Cream Polychrome.

Intersite comparisons: See Palmar Orange Polychrome: Palmar Variety. Generally decoration of this type is included in the Palmar Variety at other sites.

Chantuori Black-on-orange: Chantuori Variety

Established: Smith and Gifford (1966)

Group: Palmar

Ware: Petén Gloss

Ceramic Complex: Imix (Continues into Eznab)

Ceramic Sphere: Tepeu 2–3

Illustrations: Fig. 45.2–3, 45.7–8, 45.11–12; 46.31. See TR. 25A: fig. 57b3,c1.

Principal identifying attributes: Glossy orange slip similar to Palmar Orange Polychrome with the addition of monochrome black decoration.

Identifying characteristics and sorting problems: Type is misprinted as "Chantouri" in Culbert (TR. 25A). It is usually impossible to determine which sherds belonged to this type because small sherds with only black and orange may have had additional colors on missing sections. No sherds that are undeniably of the type were detected. On the basis of whole vessels, there is no reason to suggest any difference from Palmar Orange Polychrome except for the fact that only two colors were used. One of the burial vessels is a cylinder with an orange background on the exterior and horizontal black bands at lip, base, and slightly above midpoint. Between the midpoint and basal bands are broad black diagonal stripes. The other burial vessel is a tripod plate with beveled lip that has black bands at the top and base of the exterior on an orange background. Because the interior is weathered, it is likely that the vessel would probably have been a polychrome.

Intersite comparisons: Uaxactun (Smith and Gifford 1966).

Zacatel Cream Polychrome: Zacatel Variety

Established: Smith and Gifford (1966)

Group: Palmar [Note: Others (Callaghan 2016e) have suggested placing the Zacatel Cream Polychrome type and its associated varieties in the separate Zacatel Group.]

Ware: Petén Gloss

Ceramic Complex: Imix (Continues into Eznab)

Ceramic Sphere: Tepeu 2–3

Illustrations: Fig. 43.1–2, 43.5,–6, 43.8, 43.11–15, 43.18–19; 44.9–11, 44.13–18; 45.5, 45.14–17, 45.19, 45.21, 45.26–32; 46.1–4, 46.16–18, 46.20, 46.23, 46.25–28, 46.30, 46.32; 47.2, 47.6–9, 47.14–15; 48.1–4, 48.7–8, 48.11, 48.13–14; 49.4–6, 49.8–10, 49.13. See TR. 25A: fig. 47a; 53f; 57b2; 58b–c; 59b2; 60a–b,d1; 61b3; 62b,c2,d2; 63b3,d–e,f1; 64a2,c2–3; 65b; 66; 67; 69; 70; 71; 72b; 75b–c; 76b,d1–2; 77a4; 78c; 79a1,b2,c1,3; 80a1,c3; 81b; 82a1,4,b2; 83b1; 85b; 91j–l; 97a,b1,c,e; 131a,d,f–g; 148b;151b1,e.

Principal identifying attributes: White to cream glossy slip that matches the underslip on Palmar Orange Polychrome, decorated secondarily with red, black and red-orange designs.

Identifying characteristics and sorting problems: The most easily recognized characteristic is the white slip that underlies all other colors, a characteristic that is not found in the Saxche Polychrome Group; other colors separate the type from the Saxche Group as do many of the shapes involved.

Paste: Zacatel Paste.

Firing: Dark cores and fireclouding rare.

Surface: A whitish coat was first applied over all surfaces to be decorated. Additional colors were painted over this coat, leaving some areas uncovered to use the whitish layer as part of the design.

Polish: Highly polished on well-preserved examples.

Color: The initial layer is not cream but white (10YR 8/1, 8/2; 2.5Y 8/2), pale brown (10YR 8/3), or pinkish white (5YR 8/2). The most common additional colors are red (red 10R 4/8, 4/6; 7.5R 4/8, 5/8; 5R 5/8; dark red 7.5R 3/8), orange (reddish yellow 5YR 7/8, 6/8; light red 2.5YR 6/8; red 2.5YR 5/8), and black. A weak red (10R 5/4) or pale red (10R 6/4) that is clearly intentional is used in small areas on some examples. The black pigment used fires black in an oxidizing atmosphere.

Shapes: Present in the sherd sample were tripod plate with beveled lip 44%; cylinder 17%; straight-side dish 17%; slightly outcurving-side bowl or dish 14%; outcurving-side bowl or dish 3%; round-side bowl or dish 2%; others 3%. In the sample of burial vessels were slightly outcurving-side bowl or dish 39%; cylinder 27%; tripod plate with beveled lip

12%; others 22%. The burial sample is small and biased by multiple examples of some shapes in rich burials.

Comments: While Zacatel Cream Polychrome shares the color of the Palmar Orange Polychrome underslip and was, therefore, grouped together with it, subsequent researchers have chosen to place the Zacatel type in a separate group which is more closely aligned with type: variety nomenclature, that is based on surface color and characteristics (Gifford 1976).

Temporal distribution: A few examples occur in Ik collections, although they may be due to mixing. The great majority of the examples occur in Imix and a few examples continue to occur in Eznab.

Intersite comparisons: Altar de Sacrificios (Adams 1971); Barton Ramie (Gifford 1976); Becan (Ball 1977); Blue Creek (Kosakowsky and Lohse 2003); Colha (Valdez 1987); La Milpa (Sagebiel 2005); Nakbe (Forsyth 1993); Nohmul (Kosakowsky and Pring 2001); the Petexbatun (Foias and Bishop 2013); Rio Azul (Adams 1999; Adams and Jackson-Adams 1991); Uaxactun (Smith and Gifford 1966); Xunantunich (LeCount 1996). At Seibal, it is part of the Saxche/Palmar Group (Sabloff 1975). At El Mirador (Forsyth 1989) and Holmul (Callaghan 2008, 2016e), it is placed in the separate Zacatel Group.

Zacatel Cream Polychrome: Red-bar Variety

Established: Smith and Gifford (1966)

Group: Palmar

Ware: Petén Gloss

Ceramic Complex: Imix

Ceramic Sphere: Tepeu 2

Illustrations: Fig. 43.10; 44.24–25; 45.20; 46.15, 46.21, 46.24, 46.29; 49.7, 49.12.

Principal identifying attributes: White to cream glossy slip that matches the underslip on Palmar Or-

ange Polychrome, decorated secondarily with alternating bands of red and red-orange.

Identifying characteristics and sorting problems: The red bar designs are very distinctive.

Comments: This variety is identical to the Zacatel Variety except for the following characteristics. Color combinations: In addition to design features like those of the Zacatel Variety, the Red-bar Variety has alternating bands of red and orange on parts of the vessels. The red is overpainted in bars over an original coat of orange. Application of the colors tends to be streaky. Red bars occur on areas of the vessel that are not used for major designs: e.g., on the exterior of a vessel where the major design is on the interior. Most often the bars are vertical and usually are wavy rather than straight. On bases of vessels the bars make swirling patterns around the center of the base.

Shapes: For the sherd sample were slightly outcurving-side bowl or dish 38%; straight-side bowl or dish 31%; tripod plate with beveled lip 29%; barrel 2%. Although the sample is small (N=48), the absence of cylinders is significant. An even smaller sample of vessels from special deposits classified as burials shows the same general distribution of shapes and cylinders are again absent.

Temporal distribution: The fact that the Red-bar Variety occurs in such late burials as Bu. 77 and Bu. 196 and that it associates strongly with the late Muan Feather design suggests that it may be a late characteristic of the Imix Complex.

Comments: Although initially hesitant to make the presence of the red bar designs the basis for a varietal distinction, the fact that shape distributions differ so strongly from those of the Zacatel Variety seems a significant reason for doing so. In the burial sample, 37% of the examples of Zacatel Cream Polychrome were of the Red-bar Variety, but in the sherd sample 25% were of the Red-bar Variety.

Intersite comparisons: See Zacatel Cream Polychrome: Zacatel Variety. Generally vessels with these decorations are included in the Zacatel Variety at other sites.

Chinos Black-on-cream: Chinos Variety

Established: Smith and Gifford (1966)

Group: Palmar

Ware: Petén Gloss

Ceramic Complex: Imix (Continues into Eznab)

Ceramic Sphere: Tepeu 2–3

Illustrations: Fig. 45.22–25; 46.19, 46.22. See TR. 25A: fig. 65a; 97b2; 127h2.

Principal identifying attributes: Glossy white slip decorated with black designs.

Identifying characteristics and sorting problems: It is usually impossible to determine which sherds belonged to this type because small sherds with only black and white may have had additional colors on missing sections. As with Zacatel "Cream" Polychrome, the background color is actually white. On the basis of whole vessels and the few sherds that seem likely to be Chinos Black-on-cream, the type seems identical to Zacatel Cream Polychrome except there is no red decoration.

Surface finish and decoration: On the basis of sherds and the three intact vessels, the designs seem to cover the same range from simple to complex that is seen in Zacatel Cream Polychrome.

Shapes: In shape as well as decoration the small sample available seems to cover the same range as Zacatel Cream Polychrome.

Intersite comparisons: Becan (Ball 1977) and Uaxactun (Smith and Gifford 1966). At El Mirador (Forsyth 1989), it is placed in the Zacatel Group.

Naranjal Red-on-cream: Naranjal Variety

Established: Smith and Gifford (1966)

Group: Palmar

Ware: Petén Gloss

Ceramic Complex: Imix (Continues into Eznab)

Ceramic Sphere: Tepeu 2–3

Illustrations: See TR. 25A: fig. 144b; 152c.

Principal identifying attributes: Glossy white to cream slip decorated secondarily with monochrome red designs.

Identifying characteristics and sorting problems: It is usually impossible to determine which sherds belonged to this type because small sherds with only red and cream may have had additional colors on missing sections. No sherds of the type were detected. On the basis of whole vessels, there is no reason to suggest any difference from Zacatel Cream Polychrome except for the fact that only two colors were used. The only whole vessel of Imix date is a miniature jar with a red lip band on cream.

Intersite comparisons: Uaxactun (Smith and Gifford 1966).

Yuhactal Black-on-red: Yuhactal Variety

Established: Smith and Gifford (1966)

Group: Palmar

Ware: Petén Gloss

Ceramic Complex: Imix (Continues into Eznab)

Ceramic Sphere: Tepeu 2–3

Illustrations: Fig. 56.8, 56.22. See TR. 25a: fig. 64c1.

Principal identifying attributes: Glossy monochrome red surface over a white underslip, and secondary decoration with black lines.

Paste: Zacatel Paste.

Surface: The same white underslip that characterizes the Palmar Group was applied first, then overpainted with black and red.

Colors: Colors cover the same range as typical for the Palmar Group.

Surface finish and decoration: A red background with broad black horizontal or diagonal bands also occurs as do narrow lines of black on red. No complex designs appear in the small sample. Decoration also consists of a red lip band or bands with the rest of the vessel entirely black.

Shapes: Slightly over half the examples are tripod plates with beveled lips. The remainder consists of a variety of standard Imix shapes.

Intersite comparisons: Barton Ramie (Gifford 1976); Becan (Ball 1977); Mayapan (Smith 1971); Uaxactun (Smith and Gifford 1966).

Mex Composite: Mex Variety

Established: Chase (1984)

Group: Palmar

Ware: Petén Gloss

Ceramic Complex: Imix

Ceramic Sphere: Tepeu 2

Illustrations: Fig. 44.19. See TR. 25A: fig. 54*d*1; 55*b*1; 56*b*1,*c*1; 57*b*1,*c*3; 76*c*1,*d*3; 77*a*1; 80*d*2; 92*f*; 111*e*4; 112*a*1,*e*3,5; 133*b*2.

Principal identifying attributes: Surface finish and decoration same as Palmar Orange Polychrome with the addition of vertical or diagonal fluting.

Identifying characteristics and sorting problems: Mex Composite adds fluting to polychrome vessels of the Palmar Group. The fluting is unmistakable, but completely eroded examples cannot be distinguished from monochrome fluted types.

Comments: The following description is based largely on sixteen whole vessels. The paste and white underslip characteristic of the Palmar Ceramic Group also occurs in Mex Composite. Of the twenty-six whole vessels, nine are too eroded to be cer-

tain of colors; four are Palmar Orange Polychrome colors; two are red-on-orange, and one is back on red. No examples are of Zacatel Cream Polychrome colors.

Surface and decoration: The diagnostic feature of Mex Composite is the use of fluted or deeply grooved lines. The lines are vertical or diagonal and are often outlined by grooves above and/or below the fluting. Three examples include sets of quatrefoils painted on top of the fluting. One example has a red lip band on orange without further painted design. Other examples are too eroded to determine whether painted designs were present.

Shapes: Eleven of the 16 examples are cylinders; 2 are straight-side dishes; 1 is a slightly outcurving-side tripod bowl; 1 is a plate with beveled lip but without feet.

Temporal distribution: All identified examples are Imix Complex.

Intersite comparisons: Tayasal Region (Chase 1984).

Paixban Buff Polychrome: Paixban Variety

Established: Smith and Gifford (1966)

Group: Palmar

Ware: Petén Gloss

Ceramic Complex: Imix

Ceramic Sphere: Tepeu 2

Illustrations: Fig. 44.12; 45.33; 47.3, 47.5, 47.10–11, 47.13. See TR. 25A: fig. 131*e*.

Principal identifying attributes: Similar to Zacatel Cream Polychrome but with a buff base slip.

Comments: Very few examples of Paixban Buff-polychrome could be identified. The only difference from Zacatel Cream Polychrome seems to be that the underlying original coat tends more toward buff (Munsell readings not available) than the cream (white) of Zacatel.

Intersite comparisons: Acanmul (Ball and Taschek 2015); Barton Ramie (Gifford 1976); El Perú/Waka' (Eppich 2011); Nakbe (Forsyth (1993); Uaxactun (Smith and Gifford 1966).

KANALCAN CERAMIC GROUP

Kanalcan Gouged-incised: Kanalcan Variety

Established: TR. 25A (Culbert 1993)

Group: Kanalcan

Ware: Petén Gloss

Ceramic Complex: Imix

Ceramic Sphere: Tepeu 2

Illustrations: See TR. 25A: fig. 68*b*; 86–90.

Principal identifying attributes: Streaky brown surfaces decorated with painted stucco.

Comments: Kanalcan Gouged-incised occurred only in two major burials at Tikal. A single cylinder of the type was found in Bu. 116 (TR. 25A: fig. 68*b*), and a set of 13 cylinders was located in Bu. 196 (TR. 25A: fig. 86–90). The examples are nearly identical in major features, although there is considerable variety in details. Because no examples were found in the sherd collections, no information is available on paste or Munsell readings for colors.

Surface finish and decoration: A streaky brown-black paint that seems intended to imitate wood was applied to both the exterior and interior of the vessels. In the Bu. 196 set, a band of pseudo-glyphs that in some examples is no more than a series of concentric circles was carved, gouged-incised, or incised below the lip on the exterior. On the exterior body of the vessel, two panels are gouged-incised or incised with the head of a long-nosed deity (Coggins 1975:562–266). A red pigment, probably cinnabar, was rubbed into the pseudo-glyph band and the entire exterior except for the band and panels is covered with stucco painted with red and green. A couple of examples have pink-painted stucco on the exterior base. The vessels are extremely similar in size and shape, but the designs were done by a number of different hands. The best designs are not exceptional art, and a number are what might best be termed "amateurish or childlike." In addition, the brown-black paint and stucco were very carelessly applied and often fail to cover or go outside of the intended areas. One would conclude that a skilled potter, probably by a single person, shaped all the vessels at one time. Several individuals, many of who had little or no artistic training or ability, however, did the designs. In this, they resemble a set of ten painted cylinders in Bu. 116, where the vessels themselves were well made, but different hands of varying skill executed the designs. The single Kanalcan Gouged-incised cylinder in Bu. 116 is very similar except that the pseudo-glyphs are in vertical panels between the deity and the designs are better executed. In addition, this cylinder is not covered by stucco.

Intersite comparisons: None noted.

Imix Complex Types: Chronological Change

The only obvious change in types at the beginning of the Imix Complex was the replacement of the Saxche Ceramic Group by the Palmar Ceramic Group. A few rare types, mostly from burials that appeared in the Ik Complex, did not occur in Imix, however, a few new rare types appeared for the first time in Imix.

Imix Complex Types: Social Dimension

The degree of variation within each location of samples of Imix types was too high to allow any analysis of social variation. Because there is such a strong correlation between vessel shapes and types, the comments about the social dimension of Imix shapes that follow would almost surely be true for types.

Vessel Shapes of the Imix Complex

Introduction

The Imix Ceramic Complex includes 7 major shape classes and 11 shapes, as well as two specialized shape classes (cache vessels and miniatures) composed of four shapes, listed in Table 9.4. There was relatively little change in shapes between the Ik and Imix Complexes, except in the serving-vessel class. See the section below on "Imix Complex Shapes: Chronological Change" for details.

Imix Shape Descriptions

SHAPE CLASS 1: WIDE-MOUTH JARS

Wide-mouth Jar (with Tall Neck)

Illustrations: Fig. 39.1–53.

Identifying characteristics and sorting problems: The combination of unslipped types, large-neck diameter, and tall-neck height is distinctive, but the shape is nearly identical through the Early, Late, and Terminal Classic.

Base: Probably rounded.

Body: Globular.

Neck-body juncture: Vague.

Orientation of neck: Most commonly wide outflare; sometimes medium to slight outflare.

Neck: Usually widely outcurving, but ranges to slightly outcurving or straight.

Rim: Usually direct, though a minority of about 10% have a sharp angular eversion.

Lips: The two major lip shapes are rounded/roll and flat/grooved. In the Ik Complex, rounded/roll lips predominate, making up one-half to three-quarters of the examples. A quantitative difference in lip shapes is the only distinction between the wide-mouth jars of the Late Classic and Terminal Classic complexes. The flat and grooved lips become most common in Imix.

Types: Cambio Unslipped and Encanto Striated.

Diameter of lip: Range 12–42 cm; median 26 cm.

Height of neck: Range 4.5–13.0 cm; median 8.0 cm.

TABLE 9.4
Shape Classes and Shapes of the Imix Complex

1. **Wide-mouth Jars**
   Wide-mouth Jar (with Tall Neck)
2. **Narrow-mouth Jars**
   Narrow-mouth Jar (with Tall Neck)
4. **Large Capacity Bowls**
   Large Incurving-side Bowl
6. **Small Diameter Bowls and Dishes**
   Outflaring to Slightly Outcurving-side Bowl or Dish
   Small Outcurving-side Bowl
   Slightly Incurving to Round-side Bowl
   Recurving-side Bowl
7. **Cylindrical Vessels**
   Barrel
   Cylinder
8. **Medium Plates**
   Outflaring to Slightly Outcurving-side Tripod Plate
9. **Large Plates**
   Large Tripod Plate with Ridge
10. **Specialized Cache Vessels and Covers**
    Cache Cylinder
    Rectangular Cache Vessel
11. **Miniature Vessels**
    Miniature Jar
    Miniature Bowl or Cylinder

Diameter of lip/neck height ratio: Range 2.3–4.0; median 3.2.

Temporal distribution: Common in all Late and Terminal Classic complexes.

Shape Class: 1, wide-mouth jars.

Comments: This shape is common in the Late and Terminal ceramic complexes. In the Imix collections, the frequency of lip shapes varies from the preceding Ik Complex.

SHAPE CLASS 2: NARROW-MOUTH JARS

Narrow-mouth Jar with Tall Neck

Illustrations: Fig. 43.18; 45.6; 48.15–16. See TR. 25A fig. 56*b*2; 147*e*.

Identifying characteristics and sorting problems: The shape is distinguished by the tall, outcurving neck with small diameter, aided by paste and red slip.

Base: Both rounded and flat bases occur, but the data are not sufficient to indicate which predominates.

Body: Globular.

Neck-body juncture: Angular and well marked.

Orientation of neck: Medium to wide outflare.

Rim: Usually direct, but a minority show either rounded or angular eversion.

Lip: Rounded or pointed.

Surface: Slipped on entire exterior and on interior of neck.

Types: Tinaja Red.

Lip diameter: Range 10–28 cm; median 16 cm.

Neck height: Range 3.0–8.4 cm; median 5.6 cm.

Lip diameter/neck height ratio: Range 1.5–4.9; median 2.9.

Temporal distribution: Common in all Late and Terminal Classic complexes.

Shape class: 2, narrow-mouth jars.

SHAPE CLASS 4: LARGE CAPACITY BOWLS

Large Incurving-side Bowl

Illustrations: Fig. 50.1–52; 51.1–62. See TR. 25A: fig. 112*b*2–3; 122*a*.

Identifying characteristics and sorting problems: The combination of shape and type makes it easy to identify.

Base: Flat.

Side: Incurving to Rounded.

Rim: The rim either curves gradually inward, or bends more sharply inward, leaving a distinct angle on the exterior. The rim is usually thickened at the point at which the rim bends inward.

Lip: Pointed or rounded. Bolstered examples are less common in Imix than they are in the preceding Ik Complex.

Surface: Slipped on both interior and exterior, although the area near the exterior base is usually poorly finished and may be unslipped in spots.

Types: About 60% of the examples are Cameron Incised and one-third are Tinaja Red. Chinja Impressed and Maquina Brown occur in low frequencies.

Diameter: 22–60 cm (mostly 26–46 cm); median 36 cm.

Height: Two examples: 4.6 and 9.0 cm, median 6.0 cm.

Diameter/height ratio: Two examples: 3.3 and 3.5, median 3.4.

Temporal distribution: Occurs in all Late Classic complexes, but is most common in Imix.

Shape class: 4, large-capacity bowls.

SHAPE CLASS 6: SMALL DIAMETER BOWLS AND DISHES

Outflaring to Slightly Outcurving-side Bowl or Dish

Illustrations: Fig. 43.3, 43.21; 44.4–5, 44.9, 44.12–13, 44.16, 44.19, 44.21–22, 44.24–25; 45.1–4, 45.15, 45.17, 45.19–21, 45.32; 46.1–4, 46.7–9, 46.12, 46.14–15, 46.17–18, 46.20–21,

46.23–24, 46.27; 47.2–3, 47.5, 47.9; 48.1–3, 48.5–6, 48.8–9, 48.11; 49.6–7, 49.11. See TR. 25A: fig. 53*a*1–2,*b*1–2,*d*3,*e*,*h*,*i*3; 54*a*3,*b*2,*c*3,*d*1–2; 55*a*2–3,*b*1–2,*c*3;56*b*3,*c*3,*d*2–4; 57*a*1–3,*b*2; 58*c*; 59*a*2–3; 60*a*,*c*4; 61*a*2–3,*b*1,*c*2,4; 61*b*2; 62*a*2–3,*b*1,*c*2; 62*a*2–3,*b*,*c*1,*d*1–2,*e*; 63*a*1,*b*1–2,3,*c*–*e*,*f*–1; 64*a*2,*b*,*c*2–3; 76*a*,*b*,*c*2–3,*d*1–2; 77*a*3–6,*b*; 78*a*2,*b*2; 79*a*1–2,*b*2,*c*3; 80*a*1,*b*1,*c*2–3,*d*2; 81*b*; 82*a*4–5,*b*1; 91*j*–*l*; 92*a*–*g*; 97*a*; 99*c*; 111*a*,*c*2,*d*1,*e*2–3; 112*a*3; 113*a*2,4,*b*2,*c*,*d*1; 131*e*; 133*b*1–2,*c*2; 144*d*1–2; 148*b*; 153*d*1–2.

Identifying characteristics and sorting problems: Originally divided into three separate shapes (TR. 25A): outflaring-side bowl or dish, slightly outcurving-side bowl or dish, and straight-side bowl or dish (also referred to as a short cylinder), however, these shapes overlap and have been combined into a single shape. In sherds, some examples are hard to distinguish from cylinders.

Base: Flat or slightly concave.

Orientation of side: Slight to medium outflare or outcurve.

Side: Usually slightly outcurving or outflaring; some are medium outcurve. Walls are relatively thin. Some examples are almost straight.

Rim: Direct.

Lip: Pointed or rounded or flat bevel.

Surface: The interior is slipped and most frequently has a single band of additional color near the lip, although there are a few more complex designs. Multiple lip bands, or red-on-orange vertical bars are other variants. The exterior usually has one or more bands of color near the lip and base. Between the bands, the major design space is filled with either overall designs such as checkerboards or triangles, or repeating single or alternating motifs such as Muan Bird Feathers or quatrefoils. Occasionally, the exterior is decorated by vertical fluting or grooving. Interior usually has simple bands of color.

Types: Most commonly Palmar Ceramic Group. Some examples of monochrome fluted or grooved types, in particular Chilar Fluted.

Diameter: Range 10–44 cm, (mostly 10–28 cm); median 18 cm.

Height: Range 4–14 cm ; median 8.6 cm.

Diameter/height ratio: Range 1.0–6.5 (mostly 2.0–4.4).

Temporal distribution: Similar shapes occur in all complexes, but, in the Late and Terminal Classic, the shape is most frequent in the Imix Complex.

Shape class: 6, small-diameter bowls and dishes.

Small Outcurving-side Bowl

Illustrations: Fig. 43.2; 45.12, 45.14, 45.18, 45.26; 46.5, 45.10–11, 45.16, 45.29, 45.31, 45.33; 47.7–8, 47.10, 47.13–14; 48.4; 49.13.

Identifying characteristics and sorting problems: The shape was identified only on the basis of the whole vessel sample. It is distinguished by the small size, although somewhat larger than miniature vessels, and the fact that the wall is more outcurving than in the slightly outflaring to outcurving-side bowl. Among sherds, examples would have been sorted as slightly outcurving-side bowls or dishes.

Base: Flat or slightly concave.

Orientation of side: Medium outflare.

Side: Medium outcurve.

Rim: Direct or slightly everted,

Lip: Usually pointed, sometimes rounded.

Types: The small sample available includes Ucum Unslipped, Zacec Black, and Tinaja Red. Even in this small sample, the absence of types of the Palmar Ceramic Group is significant.

Diameter: Range 10–13 cm; median 12 cm.

Height : Range 4–7 cm; median 6 cm.

Diameter/height ratio: Range 1.6–2.6; median 1.9–21.

Temporal distribution: Although this was identified as a separate shape only in the Imix Complex collections, the shape is so simple that it would undoubtedly have occurred in a few examples in all Tikal ceramic complexes.

Shape class: 6, small-diameter bowls or dishes.

Slightly Incurving to Round-side Bowl or Dish

Illustrations: Fig. 43.1; 44.8, 44.17, 44.20; 45.9, 45.11, 45.22–23, 45.27–28, 45.30–31; 48.10, 48.12. See TR. 25A: fig. 53*d*2; 54*b*3,*d*3; 77*c*2.

Identifying characteristics and sorting problems: The rounded side is the diagnostic characteristic. There is a nearly continuous overlap with barrels and a diameter/height ratio of 1.5 was chosen as the separation point between the two. There is a clear bimodal distribution of diameter/height ratios for the two shapes indicating that they are distinct. Among sherds, where the diameter/height ratio cannot be calculated, those with restricted orifice were considered barrels.

Base: Flat or slightly concave. One example has small tripod feet (see TR. 25A: fig. 113*a*1).

Orientation of side: Slightly open to slightly restricted orifice.

Side: Rounded, medium curvature.

Rim: Direct.

Lip: Usually pointed; sometimes rounded.

Surface: Interior slipped, sometimes with bands of color at lip. Major decoration is always on the exterior but is usually simple, either several bands of alternating colors or a simple banded design that is occasionally glyphic.

Types: Usually Palmar Ceramic Group.

Diameter: There are two different size ranges.

Range 10–32 cm, mostly 14–26 cm; median 20 cm.

Height: Range 4–15 cm; median 8.0 cm.

Diameter/height ratio: Range 1.4–2.8; median 2.0.

Comments: This shape is less common in Imix than in the Ik Complex.

Shape class: 6, small-diameter bowls and dishes.

Recurving-side Bowl

Illustrations: Fig. 43.20; 49.12. See TR. 25A: fig. 60*c*2.

Identifying characteristics and sorting problems: The composite silhouette is the identifying characteristic. The shape can be recognized only if most of the wall is preserved.

Base: Usually rounded; two examples have double base with pellets of clay between two bases.

Side: Slightly above the base, the outcurving upper section of the side makes a composite silhouette where it joins the lower section.

Types: In the small sample, there is considerable variety with the Palmar Ceramic Group, Zacec Black, and unusual incised and composite types represented.

Shape Class: 6, small diameter bowls and dishes.

Comments: This is an unusual shape in Imix samples and some may be imported vessels.

SHAPE CLASS 7: CYLINDRICAL VESSELS

Barrel

Illustrations: Fig. 45.29; 46.28; 48.19. See TR. 25A: fig. 53*h*2; 60*b*; 78*b*1; 83*a*; 97*d*2; 111*c*1.

Identifying characteristics and sorting problems: The relatively thin walls and restricted orifice are the best diagnostics of the shape. There is a nearly continuous overlap with round-side bowls with the two shapes separated on the basis of diameter/height ratio with ratio below 1.5 considered to denote barrel. Among sherds, where the diameter/height ratio cannot be calculated, those with restricted orifice were considered barrels.

Base: About equally divided between flat and slightly concave.

Orientation of side: Slightly restricted orifice.

Side: Rounded, medium curvature.

Rim: Direct.

Lip: Usually pointed; sometimes rounded.

Surface: Interior is usually a single color and carelessly finished. On the exterior, a lip band (usually black) occurs on most examples. The most frequent additional decoration is a band of motifs at midpoint or above on the exterior. Overall exterior decoration also occurs. Glyphs may occur as part of single-band decoration or above additional decoration. In most cases, glyphic inscriptions are meaningful.

Types: Palmar Ceramic Group.

Diameter: Range 8–20 cm; median 14 cm.

Height: Range 8–14 cm; median 12 cm.

Diameter/height ratio: Range 0.7–1.5; median 1.2.

Temporal distribution: Some barrels occur in the Manik Complex. The shape becomes considerably more frequent in the Ik Complex. This shape occurs with less frequency in the Imix Complex than in the Ik or Eznab Complexes.

Shape class: 7, cylindrical vessels.

Cylinder

Illustrations: Fig. 43.1, 43.11, 43.13, 43.17, 43.19; 44.2–3, 44.6, 44.9–11, 44.18–19; 45.5, 45.7, 45.24–25; 46.13, 46.19, 46.30; 47.11, 47.15; 48.17, 48.20–22; 49.5. See TR. 25A: fig. 53*d*1,*i*1; 54*a*1,*b*1,*c*2; 55*a*1,*b*3,*c*1–2,*d*; 56*a*,*b*1,*c*1,*d*1; 57*a*4,*b*1,*c*1–3;59*a*4,*b*1; 60*c*1,*d*3; 61*a*1,*b*3,*c*3; 62*a*1,*d*3; 63*a*2,*f*2; 64*c*1; 68*a*,*b*; 69; 70; 71; 72*a*,*b*; 73; 74*a*,*b*; 75*a*–*c*; 76*c*1,*d*3; 77*a*1,*c*3; 79*b*1,*c*1–2; 80*a*2,*b*3,*c*1,*d*1; 81*c*,*d*; 82*a*3; 83*b*2,*c*; 85*a*,*b*; 86*a*,*b*; 87*a*–*c*; 88*a*–*c*; 89*a*–*c*; 90*a*,*b*; 91*a*–*i*; 111*b*1,*e*4; 112*a*1–2,*d*,*e*2–3,5; 114*g*; 131*a*.

Identifying characteristics and sorting problems: The straight, vertical side identifies the shape well. There is a minor overlap with the barrel shape.

Base: Flat to slightly concave. One example is similar to the Ik shape with a rounded base (See TR. 25A: fig. 47*a*).

Orientation of side: Vertical or nearly so.

Side: Straight to very slightly outcurving.

Rim: Direct.

Lip: Usually rounded; rarely pointed, rounded, bevel or nearly flat.

Decorations: The interior usually has a red lip band on orange although a few examples have multiple bands of red, orange, and black. The major design is on the exterior. It usually involves some kind of banded design below the lip with the major design below the banding. The major design is most frequently a continuous design such as a checkerboard. Sometimes the design is more complex with alternating motifs. Fluting and grooving, usually vertical, sometimes diagonal, occur occasionally. Fluted/grooved examples are usually delimited at top by one or more grooves, but not delimited at bottom. Figural scenes on cylinders occur only in major tomb burials.

Types: Most commonly Palmar Ceramic Group. There are a few examples of monochrome grooved or fluted types, such as Chilar Fluted and Paap Fluted, especially in caches.

Diameter: Range 6–28 cm; median 12 cm. The distribution of diameter measurements is weakly bimodal with a smaller and more common cylinder ranging between 6 and 14 cm in diameter and a larger ranging from 16 to 28 cm. Among whole vessels most of the larger cylinders occur in Bu. 116.

Height: Range 8–30 cm; median 18 cm. The large-diameter group ranges from 22 to 30 cm in height, while the smaller group ranges from 8 to 24 cm.

Diameter/height ratio: Range 0.4–1.0; median 0.6. The large and small groups do not differ significantly in diameter/height ratio.

Shape class: 7, cylindrical vessels.

Temporal distribution: Most characteristic of the Imix Complex, but quite common in Ik and especially Eznab.

SHAPE CLASS 8: MEDIUM PLATES

Outflaring to Slightly Outcurving-side Tripod Plate

Illustrations: Fig. 43.4, 43.6–8, 43.12, 43.14–16; 44.1, 44.7, 44.14, 44.23; 45.8, 45.10, 45.13, 45.16, 45.33; 46.6, 46.25–26, 46.32; 47.1, 47.4, 47.6, 47.12; 48.7, 48.13, 48.23; 49.1–3, 49.8–10. See TR. 25A: fig. 131*d*.

Identifying characteristics and sorting problems: The sides of these vessels, while generally more outcurving than examples of outflaring to slightly outcurving-side dishes or bowls, present a sorting problem in cases where there is overlap. Some examples may also be closer in dimensions to dishes rather than plates.

Base: Usually flat; a few examples slightly rounded.

Orientation of side: Medium to wide outflare.

Side: Medium to wide outcurve.

Rim: Usually direct. Some examples everted just below the lip.

Lip: Rounded or pointed.

Feet: No feet were found intact on the examples, but some had foot scars. It seems likely that some vessels were tripods while others lacked feet.

Decoration: Preservation is poor on most examples, but major decoration was probably on the interior.

Types: Mostly Palmar Ceramic Group, but grooved or fluted examples are more common than in other outcurving-side vessels.

Diameter: Range 18–36 cm; median 28 cm.

Height: Range 3.2–7.8 cm; median 5.6 cm.

Diameter/height ratio: Range 3.2–7.8; median 5.0. The median and about three-quarters of the examples fall within the range of plates, but the remainder are scattered at ratios well within the range of dishes.

Shape class: 8, medium plates, although some examples fall within the range of shape class 5, medium dishes.

Temporal distribution: Occurs in Late and Terminal Classic complexes, but is most common in the Imix Complex.

SHAPE CLASS 9: LARGE PLATES

Large Tripod Plate with Ridge

Illustrations: Fig. 43.5,10. See TR. 25A: fig. 53*f,g,h*1,*i*2; 54*a*2,*c*1; 56*c*2; 57*b*3–4; 58*a,b*; 59*a*1,*b*2; 60*c*3,*d*1–2; 61*c*1; 64*a*1; 65*b*; 66; 67; 76*a*2; 77*a*2,*c*1; 78*a*1,*b*3,*c*; 79*b*3,*d*; 80*b*2,*d*3; 81*a*; 82*a*1–2,*b*2; 92*h*–1; 93; 94*a,b*; 95*a–c*; 96*a,b*; 131*f*.

Identifying characteristics and sorting problems: The entire set of characteristics is very diagnostic. Even for sherds, the beveled lip makes recognition easy. In the Imix collections, examples that are similar but lack the beveled lip were separated as outcurving-side plates. This separation on the basis of lip shape alone may not be significant, but it helps maintain an undiluted category for beveled lip examples that cuts down on overlap with other plate shapes.

Base: Usually flat; a few examples slightly rounded.

Orientation of side: Medium outflare; rarely wide outflare.

Side: Most common is slight outcurve; some wide outcurve; rarely straight. The wall is thicker than in most other Imix Complex shapes.

Rim: Usually direct. Some examples have a lip extended outward to resemble eversion.

Lip: Flat bevel and some rounded bevel.

Feet: Cylindrical, usually flat bottom, although some slightly rounded bottoms occur. Feet are general larger and more cylindrical than the feet of Ik Complex tripod plates.

Surface: The exterior wall usually has decoration consisting either of the red-on-orange vertical stripes of the Red-bar Variety, bands of color near the lip alone, or bands near both the lip and base. More complicated exterior decoration is infrequent, although there are some examples of checkerboards or repeated motifs. Rarely, the exterior base is decorated as well, but it is usually left unslipped. Major decoration is on the interior, usually on the interior base. Sometimes this decoration consists of a central figure, e.g., a dancer or large Ahau. Sometimes the base decoration consists of a repeated motif, usually geometric. Examples from burials more often have a major central design on the interior base, while sherds are more likely to have repeated motifs. Interior walls are decorated with simple banding or repeated motifs.

Types: Palmar Ceramic Group and Zacec Black.

Diameter: Range 20–50 cm; median 30 cm.

Height (without feet): Range 3.2–10.3 cm, usually 4–7 cm; median 5.0 cm.

Diameter/height ratio: Range 3.8–9.5; median 6.0.

Temporal distribution: Some examples in Ik but mostly Imix and Eznab Complexes.

Comments: The frequent occurrence and easy recognition make this shape an excellent type fossil for the Imix and Eznab Complexes.

Shape class: 9, large plates.

*SHAPE CLASS 10: SPECIALIZED CACHE
VESSELS AND COVERS*

Cache Cylinder

Illustrations: See TR. 25A: fig. 111*b*2,*e1*; 112*e*4.

Identifying characteristics and sorting problems: The flange and unslipped surface make the shape very distinctive.

Base: Flat to slightly concave.

Orientation of side: Vertical.

Side: Straight, but often uneven.

Rim: Direct. On the exterior side below the lip a "shelf" is formed by gradual thickening of the side, which was then cut back to make the shelf resulting in a thinned rim that was designed to support a cover.

Lip: Rounded or flat.

Surface: Unslipped.

Types: Ucum Unslipped. One example was made with a very coarse paste and a matte red slip carelessly applied to the surface of an Ucum Unslipped vessel.

Diameter: Range: 14–36 cm.

Height: Range 16–22 cm.

Diameter/height ratio: 0.8–1.7.

Temporal distribution: Two early examples occurred in Manik caches, one in Ik, and three in Imix. The shape is confined to caches.

Shape class: 10, specialized cache vessels and covers.

Rectangular Cache Vessel

Illustrations: See TR. 25A: fig. 111*d*2–5; 112*b*1,*c*1–2; 113*b*1; 133*c*1.

Identifying characteristics and sorting problems: The rectangular shape is completely distinctive.

Base: Flat.

Orientation of side: Vertical to slightly outflaring or slightly restricted.

Side: Usually rounded, but sometimes straight or slightly outcurving. Shaping of the vessels is careless and sides very uneven.

Rim: Direct. On the exterior side below the lip a "shelf" is formed by gradual thickening of the side, which was then cut back to make the shelf resulting in a thinned rim that was designed to support a cover.

Lip: Rounded or flattened.

Feet: One example has four solid slab feet.

Surface: Unslipped and carelessly finished.

Types: Cambio Unslipped or Ucum Unslipped.

Diameter: Long axis: range 16–24 cm; median 20 cm. Short axis: range 10–12 cm; median 10 cm.

Height: Range 7.4–14.6 cm; median 9.0 cm.

Shape class: 10, specialized cache vessels and covers.

Temporal distribution: One example was found in Manik Ca. 119; all other examples (10) are Imix Complex.

Comments: The shape is confined to caches and problematical deposits.

SHAPE CLASS 11: MINIATURE VESSELS

Miniature Jar

Illustrations: Fig. 56.30, 56.34, 56.37–38. See TR. 25A: fig. 144*b*1–2,4.

Identifying characteristics and sorting problems: The shape is easy to identify based on size, however, those with globular bases overlap with rounded feet from tripod plates in both size and shape.

Body: Globular.

Neck-body juncture: Outcurving.

Orientation of neck: Vertical.

Neck: Straight.

Rim: Direct.

Lip: Rounded.

Types: Tinaja Red and Cambio Unslipped.

Lip diameter: Range (three examples) 2.8–3.2 cm.

Neck height: Range (three examples) 1.0–2.0 cm.

Total height: Range (three examples) 4.0–6.0 cm.

Shape class: 11, miniature vessels.

Miniature Bowl or Cylinder

Illustrations: Fig. 56.1, 56.6, 56.27; 57.24.

Identifying characteristics and sorting problems: The small size makes these unmistakable.

Shapes: Slightly incurving to round-side bowls and cylinders (short).

Types: Tinaja Red, Zacec Black.

Diameter: 2–4 cm.

Height: 4–6 cm.

Diameter/Height ratio: 0.5

Shape class: 11, miniature vessels.

Comments: The cylinders are not true straight-sided cylinders, but have slightly curving sides.

There are two additional fragmentary pieces (see TR. 25A: fig. 144*b*3,5) that could be the bases of other miniature vessels, either bowls or jars, but they may also be broken feet from tripod plates.

Median dimensions of all shapes are presented in Table 9.5.

Imix Shapes: Chronological Change

The distinction between shapes of the Ik and Imix Complexes was more quantitative than qualitative with few shapes that were totally confined to either complex.

TABLE 9.5
Shape Dimensions of the Imix Complex

Shape Class and Shape	Median Diameter	Median Height	Median Diameter/ Height Ratio
1. Wide-mouth Jar (with Tall Neck)	26.0	8.0	3.2
2. Narrow-mouth Jar (with Tall Neck)	16.0	5.6	2.9
4. Large Incurving-side Bowl	36.0	6.8	3.4
6. Outflaring to Slightly Outcurving-side Bowl or Dish	18.0	8.6	2.0–4.4
6. Small Outcurving-side Bowl	12.0	6.0	1.9–2.1
6. Slightly Incurving to Round-side Bowl or Dish	20.0	8.0	2.0
7. Barrel	14.0	12.0	1.2
7. Cylinder (small)	12.0	18.0	0.6
7. Cylinder (large)	22.0	26.0	0.6
8. Outflaring to Slightly Outcurving-side Tripod Plate	28.0	5.6	5.0
9. Large Tripod Plate with Ridge	30.0	5.0	6.0
10. Cache Cylinder	22.0	17.5	0.8–1.7
10. Rectangular Cache Vessel	Long: 20.0 Short: 10.0	9.0	—
11. Miniature Jar	2.8–3.2	1.0–2.0	4.0–6.0
11. Miniature Bowl or Cylinder	2.0–4.0	4.0–6.0	0.5

In the Imix Complex, lip shapes of wide-mouth jars continued to change from a prevalence of round and/or bolstered lips to a predominance of flat and/or grooved lips. In early Imix, the two major shapes occurred in approximately equal quantities but, in late Imix, flat and/or grooved lips outnumbered round and/or bolstered ones by 64% to 36%.

In the Imix Complex, the large capacity in-curving-side bowl continues as an important shape. Large-capacity bowls with no decoration except for slip became most common in late Imix, increasing to 45% from 31% in early Imix. Grooved examples remained steady at 36% to 38% in the two sections. Impressions declined notably, accounting for 14% of vessels in late Imix in comparison with 37% in early Imix. Decoration with impressions on an appliquéd fillet was nearly nonexistent in Imix.

Among serving vessels, the trends from the Ik Complex continued in the Imix Complex. By late Imix, the outflaring to slightly outcurving-side tripod plate (or dish) was very common, with a median frequency of 28% of the collection in late Imix, up from a median frequency of 17% in early Imix. The cylinder was the second most common shape at a median frequency of 24%, up from a median frequency of 15% in early Imix. The total of simple shapes, slightly incurving to round-side and slightly outflaring to outcurving-side bowls and dishes, was still common in Imix: a median frequency of 22% in early Imix and a median frequency of 16% in late Imix. Slightly outflaring to outcurving-side bowls and dishes made up median frequencies of 12% and 9% in the two temporal facets of Imix. The large tripod plate with ridge, the hallmark of the Ik Complex, was rare (4%) in early Imix and almost nonexistent by late Imix.

Imix Shapes: Social Dimension

A correlation reflecting variation in the use of vessels in different social contexts was a strong differentiation in the frequencies of two (wide-mouth jars and large-capacity bowls) of the three shape categories generally considered to be "utilitarian" or "domestic" in function and the general category of "serving vessels."

Serving vessels correlated strongly with size of group, occurring with median frequencies of 34% in small structure groups, 54% in intermediate structure groups, and 68% in larger civic-ceremonial and range structure groups. Wide-mouth jars varied in reverse order, occurring with median frequencies of 30% in small structure groups, 19% in intermediate structure groups, and 10% in large civic-ceremonial and range structure groups. Large-capacity bowls showed a pattern similar to that of wide-mouth jars with median frequencies of 22% in small structure groups, 19% in intermediate structure groups, and 14% in large civic-ceremonial and range structure groups. Only narrow-mouth jars failed to correlate with group size, with median frequencies of 7% to 9% unrelated to group size.

Special Deposits of the Imix Complex

Burials of the Imix Complex

Seventy-one special deposits classified as burials of Imix Complex date included ceramic offerings, by far the most burials of any complex (Table 9.6). Surprisingly, considering the large number of burials, only three are from the central part of the site: two from the Great Plaza and one from the West Plaza. Twenty-one come from intermediate structure groups, and the remaining forty-seven burials are from small-structure groups in widely scattered locations throughout the site.

More than two hundred vessels were included in these burials. Figures on the number of vessels per burial are provided in Table 9.6. Even a brief inspection of the data makes it obvious that the choices about the number of vessels to include as burial offerings were strongly patterned in Imix. There was a strong preference for three vessels. This pattern held for contexts of small and intermediate groups throughout the site (Culbert 2003:78). It also contrasts with burial customs of the Ik Complex when there was a preference for offerings of four vessels and an almost complete lack of three-vessel offerings.

In the total sample of burial vessels, nearly 75% are from the Palmar Ceramic Group that includes as primary components Palmar Orange Polychrome and Zacatel Cream Polychrome and their associated types. There are 6% weathered, and about 5% each of Chilar Fluted and Kanalcan Gouged-incised. These figures were biased, however, by the inclusions in the two large burials (Bu. 116 and 196) of large sets of Chilar Fluted and Kanalcan Gouged-incised vessels. With the figures from the two large burials removed, the frequency of Palmar Group increases to 82%, but was actually probably over 90% because it is likely that the majority of weathered vessels were also Palmar Group. No other type accounts for more than 3% of the sample. The avoidance of utilitarian types is indicated by the fact that in the total sample of vessels there is only one Tinaja Red vessel.

Among vessel shapes represented in the total sample, 34% are cylinders, 32% outflaring to slightly outcurving-side bowls, and 20% are outflaring to slightly outcurving-side tripod plates (or dishes); 6% of the sample are unusual shapes, and no other shape accounts for as much as 4% of the sample. Once again, the sample from the two large burials skews the total sample because of very large sets of cylinders that amounted to 57% of the shapes from these burials. Subtracting these two burials from the totals resulted in a distribution among other burials in which outflaring to slightly outcurving-side bowls are predominant with 38% of the sample, followed by 25% cylinders, 20% outflaring to slightly outcurving-side tripod plates (or dishes), and 6% unusual shapes. No other shape accounts for more than 5% of this sample.

There are also patterns among the choices of vessels to include in the offering sets of three vessels. Among the thirty-four examples of three-vessel sets, the most common (ten examples) is a set that includes an outflaring to slightly outcurving-side bowl, a cylinder, and a outflaring to slightly outcurving-side tripod plate (or dish). The next most common set (six examples) includes two outflaring to slightly outcurving-side bowls and a cylinder. The remainder of the sets shows no strong pattern with various combinations of all standard serving-vessel shapes. It may be significant, however, that no set includes three identical vessels.

Cylinders are predominant in the two major chamber burials of the Imix Complex (Bu. 116 and

TABLE 9.6 (part 1)
Burials of the Imix Complex

Burial No.	Op.SubOp./Lot	Str.	Structure Group Type	TR. 25A Illustration	TR.	No. of Vessels
12	20A/95	Gp. 4F-2 Plat. 4F-1	Small Structure Group	52, 53	19	1
14	20A/93	Gp. 4F-2 Str. 4F-15	Small Structure Group	53*a*	19	3
16	20A/97	Gp. 4F-2 Str. 4F-15	Small Structure Group	53*b*	19	2
18	20A/55	Gp. 4F-2 Plat. 4F-1	Small Structure Group	53*c*	19	1
21	20A/59	Gp. 4F-2 Str. 4F-15	Small Structure Group	53*d*	19	3
26	20B/58,59,62	Gp. 4F-1 Str. 4E-31	Small Structure Group	53*e*	19	1
27	20B/67	Gp. 4F-1 Str. 4E-31	Small Structure Group	53*f*	19	1
28	20B/69	Gp. 4F-1 Str. 4E-31	Small Structure Group	53*g*	19	1
30	20B/84	Gp. 4F-1 Str. 4E-31	Small Structure Group	53*h*	19	3
31	20D/37	Gp. 4F-1 Str. 4F-3	Small Structure Group	53*i*	19	3
38	20H/49	Gp. 4F-1 Str. 4F-7	Small Structure Group	54*a*	19	3
39	20L/29	Gp. 4F-1 Str. 4F-7	Small Structure Group	54*b*	19	3
42	20L/33	Gp. 4F-1 Str. 4F-7	Small Structure Group	54*c*	19	3
45	24B/1	Gp. 4F-6 Str. 4F-26	Small Structure Group	54*d*	20A	3
49	24C/69	Gp. 2G-1 Str. 2G-59-1st	Small Structure Group	55*a*	20A	3
50	24C/70	Gp. 2G-1 Str. 2G-25-2nd	Small Structure Group	55*b*	20A	3
52	24C/104	Gp. 2G-1 Str. 2G-59-2nd	Small Structure Group	55*c*	20A	3
53	24C/114	Gp. 2G-1 Str. 2G-59	Small Structure Group	55*d*	20A	1
56	24C/135	Gp. 2G-1 Str. 2G-59-2nd	Small Structure Group	56*a*	20A	1
66	24R/17	Gp. 3F-1 Str. 3F-24-3rd	Small Structure Group	56*b*	20A	3
68	24T/24	Gp. 3F-2 Str. 3F-26	Small Structure Group	56*c*	20A	3
69	24T/20	Gp. 3F-2 Str. 3F-26	Small Structure Group	—	20A	1
70	24W/8	Gp. 3F-2 Plat. 3F-2, near Str. 3F-27	Small Structure Group	56*d*	20A	4
71	27E/7	Gp. 5G-1 Str. 5G-7	Intermediate Structure Group	57*a*	21	4
75	28B/14	Gp. 5G-2 Str. 5G-11	Intermediate Structure Group	57*b*	21	4
77	41F/4	Gp. 5D-10 Str. 5D-11, Dedic.	Range Structure Group	57*c*, 58	17	6
78	31A/2	Gp. 4H-4 Str. 4H-16	Intermediate Structure Group	59*a*	21	4
80	28B/24	Gp. 5G-2 Str. 5G-11	Intermediate Structure Group	59*b*, 60*a*	21	3
82	31A/4	Gp. 4H-4 Str. 4H-16	Intermediate Structure Group	60*b*	21	1
86	30B/7	Gp. 4G-1 Str. 4G-10	Intermediate Structure Group	60*c*	21	4
87	32A/7	Gp. 4H-5 Str. 4H-18, bedrock	Intermediate Structure Group	60*d*	21	4
88	33A/9	Gp. 4H-1 Str. 4H-4	Intermediate Structure Group	61*a*	21	3
89	33A/12	Gp. 4H-1 Str. 4H-4	Intermediate Structure Group	61*b*	21	3
90	33A/13	Gp. 4H-1 Str. 4H-4	Intermediate Structure Group	61*c*	21	3
91	33A/16	Gp. 4H-1 Str. 4H-4	Intermediate Structure Group	62*a*	21	3
92	33A/17	Gp. 4H-1 Str. 4H-4	Intermediate Structure Group	62*b*	21	1

TABLE 9.6 (part 2)
Burials of the Imix Complex

Burial No.	Op.SubOp./Lot	Str.	Structure Group Type	TR. 25A Illustration	TR.	No. of Vessels
93	33A/19	Gp. 4H-1 Str. 4H-4	Intermediate Structure Group	62c	21	2
97	33A/23	Gp. 4H-1 Str. 4H-4	Intermediate Structure Group	62d	21	3
99	33A/28	Gp. 4H-1 Str. 4H-4	Intermediate Structure Group	62e, 63a	21	3
100	33A/30	Gp. 4H-1 Str. 4H-4	Intermediate Structure Group	63b	21	3
102	33F/17	Gp. 4H-1 Plat.4H-1	Intermediate Structure Group	63c	21	1
103	33A/32	Gp. 4H-1 Str. 4H-4	Intermediate Structure Group	63d	21	1
104	33A/37	Gp. 4H-1 Str. 4H-4	Intermediate Structure Group	63e	21	1
105	33A/36	Gp. 4H-1 Str. 4H-4	Intermediate Structure Group	63f, 64a	21	4
113	33F/46	Gp. 4H-1 Str. 4H-8	Intermediate Structure Group	64b	21	1
116	4P/2	Gp. 5D-2, Str. 5D-1 Dedic.	Civic-Ceremonial	64c–75	14	20–21?
118	35C/5	Gp. 6E-14 Plat. 6E-14	Small Structure Group	76a	20A	2–3?
133	70A/3	Gp. 3H-1 Str. 3H-3 1st	Intermediate Structure Group	76b	21	1
135	70C/3	Gp. 6C-4 Str. 6C-41	Intermediate Structure Group	76c	21	3
137	70C/5	Gp. 6C-4 Str. 6C-41	Intermediate Structure Group	76d	21	3
139	70C/6	Gp. 6C-4 Str. 6C-41	Intermediate Structure Group	77a	21	6
141	70D/3	Gp. 3G-2 Str. 3G-20	Intermediate Structure Group	77b	21	1
142	70D/4	Gp. 3G-2 Str. 3G-20	Intermediate Structure Group	77c	21	3
147	70F/4	Gp. 6B-9 Str. 6B-9	Intermediate Structure Group	78a	21	2
149	70F/6	Gp. 6B-9 Str. 6B-9	Intermediate Structure Group	78b	21	3
154	70G/3	Gp. 3C-1 Str. 3C-15	Intermediate Structure Group	78c, 79a	21	1
155	70G/4	Gp. 3C-1 Str. 3C-15	Intermediate Structure Group	79b	21	3
156	70G/5	Gp. 3C-1 Str. 3C-15	Intermediate Structure Group	79c	21	3
157	70F/11	Gp. 6B-9 Str. 6B-9	Intermediate Structure Group	79d, 80a	21	3
186	112B/2	Gp. 3H-1 Str. 3H-3	Intermediate Structure Group	80b		3
188	112B/7	Gp. 3H-1 Str. 3H-3	Intermediate Structure Group	80c		3
189	103C/5	Gp. 4G-3 Str. 4G-7	Small Structure Group	80d	20A	3
190	3B/19	Gp. 7F-1 Str. 7F-30	Intermediate Structure Group	81	22	4
191	3B/21	Gp. 7F-1 Str. 7F-30	Intermediate Structure Group	82a	22	5
192	3E/27	Gp. 7F-1 Str. 7F-29	Intermediate Structure Group	82b, 83a	22	3
193	3C/10	Gp. 7F-1 Str. 7F-30	Intermediate Structure Group	83b	22	2
196	117A/36	Gp. 5D-2 Str. 5D-73, Dedic.	Civic-Ceremonial	83c–96	14	48
204	128A/10,11,15	SE-001 Navajuelal SE-423	Minor Center	—		1
212	140A/1	Str. 4C-34 Locus Str. 4C-34	Small Structure Group	—	20A	3
216	112C/1	Gp. 3H-1	Intermediate Structure Group	—		3
218	72D/4	Str. 6F-62 Locus Plat. 6F-1	Small Structure Group	—	20A	1

196). The ceramic centerpiece in Bu. 116 of Ruler A (*Jasaw Chan K'awiil*) is a set of ten painted cylinders that show scenes of individuals seated on thrones. Attendants, usually kneeling before the throne, appear on five of these cylinders; on the remainder, the person on the throne appears alone. The striking thing about these cylinders is the poor quality of much of the work. None of the scenes could be called great masterpieces and some are amateurish. It seems clear that highly skilled artisans did not do the painting. Coggins (1975) agrees with the conclusion, that the vessels may have been painted by other rulers, or their emissaries, as a special mark of respect for Ruler A. Also in Bu. 116 was an additional cylinder on which a throne scene was painted after the vessel had been stuccoed (a rare process for Imix). This scene is, indeed, a splendid piece of art. There was also a carved cylinder portraying the head of a long-nosed god, a theme that reappeared in Bu. 196. The remainder of the decorated vessels in Bu. 116 are non-figural: an unusual tripod plate in the shape of a half conch shell has a glyph in its central base that refers to soot and, by extension, black paint for writing and painting (Simon Martin, pers. comm. 2017); three tripod plates; an outflaring to slightly outcurving-side bowl decorated with Muan Bird feathers; an outflaring to slightly outcurving-side bowl decorated with Mexican year signs and *ahau* glyphs; and a simple banded black-on-red cylinder.

Burial 196 was considerably richer in ceramics, both in quantity and variety, than Bu. 116. Of the forty-eight vessels in the burial, twenty-five are cylinders. Three superb painted cylinders show a ruler on a throne accompanied by attendants. One, the "Hummingbird Pot," mentions the name of Ruler B (*Yik'in Chan K'awiil*). Although various suggestions have been made about the occupant of Bu. 196 (Coggins 1975), it seems quite clear that it was a very important individual but not Ruler B. It may be the burial of the son of *Yik'in Chan K'awiil*, the otherwise obscure 28th ruler of Tikal (Martin and Grube 2000) but this is only a supposition, or the burial of an older brother of Ruler B, who died early and did not succeed his father (William Haviland, pers. comm. 2018). Thirteen carved cylinders featuring the head of a long-nosed god show the same huge range of variation in execution and talent as the throne scenes in Bu. 116 and may also be posited to have been the work of non-artists. A set of nine cylinders, seven fluted, completes the list of cylinders. There are ten tripod plates that feature Muan Bird feathers as a theme, but differ considerably in other details. Ten small bowls and dishes of considerable variety, two unslipped bowls, and an unusual jar complete the inventory. One of the unslipped bowls and the jar are almost surely imports.

The paucity of meaningful inscriptions in Imix burials is striking. The stuccoed vessel from Bu. 116 has an important, although largely illegible text. Most of the seeming texts on the throne scene vessels in the burial, however, are pseudo-glyphs, rather than meaningful (Simon Martin, pers. comm. 2017). In Bu. 196, the Hummingbird pot has a text and the throne scene with the dancing figure has captions that probably identify the individuals involved. Otherwise, only two additional burials (Bu. 78 and 190) have texts. It seems probable that the many, looted cylinders with Primary Standard Sequence texts that have appeared in collections in recent years did not come from Tikal.

Caches of the Imix Complex

Seventeen special deposits classified as caches included ceramics of the Imix Complex (Table 9.7). All of the caches were associated with stelae. Only three of the stelae were carved (St. 11, 21, and 24), and the remainder were plain. An additional cache (Ca. 85) described in Chapter 7, contained Early Classic Manik ceramics but was placed in Imix times (see TR. 19).

The total number of vessels was forty-three, but there was no pattern in the number of vessels included in individual caches. There were four caches with a single vessel; seven with two vessels; two with three vessels; one with four vessels; and three with five vessels.

Twenty-eight of the forty-three vessels were too weathered to determine type. Six were of the Palmar Ceramic Group and, because the weathered vessels were of shapes that were traditionally polychrome in Imix times, it is likely that the majority of cache vessels were of the Palmar Group. Six unweathered cache vessels were of unslipped types. Only one vessel was Tinaja Red, but two more were probably this type based on their shapes.

Twenty-two of the forty-three vessels were in the serving-vessel category, with ten outflaring to

TABLE 9.7
Caches of the Imix Complex

Cache No.	Op.SubOp./Lot	Str.	Structure Group Type	TR. 25A Illustration	TR.	No. of Vessels
3	7A/9	Gp. 4E-4 (Twin Pyramid Gp.) St. P64	Civic-Ceremonial	111*a*	18[†]	1
4	7A/10	Gp. 4E-4 (Twin Pyramid Gp.) St. P65	Civic-Ceremonial	111*b*	18[†]	2
12	12A/7	Gp. 5D-2 St. P4	Civic-Ceremonial	111*c*	14	2
15	11D/11,12	Gp. 5D-2 St. 11	Civic-Ceremonial	111*d*	14	5
30	[1]	Str. 6F-27 Gp. (T.VI) St. 21	Civic-Ceremonial	115*c*	23B	1
31	[1]	Gp. 5D-2 St. P10	Civic-Ceremonial	None	14	1
42	11D/37	Gp. 5D-2 St. P20	Civic-Ceremonial	111*e*	14	4
45	11F/6	Gp. 5D-2 St. P29	Civic-Ceremonial	112*a*	14	3
50	11D/49	Gp. 5D-2 St. P15	Civic-Ceremonial	112*b*	14	3
56	11G/2	Gp. 5D-2 St. P83	Civic-Ceremonial	112*c*	14	2
121	11D/57	Gp. 5D-2 St. P27	Civic-Ceremonial	112*d*	14	1
123	8B/10	Str.. 5D-3 Gp. (T.III) St. 24	Civic-Ceremonial	112*e*	23B	5
150	61A/7	Gp. 3D-2 (Twin Pyramid Gp.) St. P54	Civic-Ceremonial	113*a*	18[†]	5
151	53A/1	Str. 6F-27 Gp. (T.VI) St. P74	Civic-Ceremonial	None	23B	2
154	61A/8	Gp. 3D-2 (Twin Pyramid Gp.) St. P50	Civic-Ceremonial	113*b*	18[†]	2
155	7A/13	Gp. 4E-4 (Twin Pyramid Gp.) St. P72	Civic-Ceremonial	113*c*	18[†]	2
203	5B/2	Str. 5C-4 Gp. (T.IV) St. P43	Civic-Ceremonial	113*d*	23B	2

[1] Previously looted. Reconstructed by W.R. Coe.

[†] Forthcoming

slightly outcurving-side vessels and nine cylinders predominating. Although these were the serving-vessel shapes that were most common in burials and sherd collections, tripod plates—the third important component of the burial assemblage—were completely absent. There were two specialized cache vessels that did not appear in other contexts: the rectangular cache vessel (nine Imix examples) and the cache cylinder (three Imix examples). Cache cylinders also occurred in the Manik and Ik Complexes. No jars occurred in Imix caches and two large capacity bowls were the only examples of "utilitarian" shapes.

There are clear differences between Imix Complex caches and the preceding Ik Complex caches that should be noted. Virtually all Ik caches that included pottery vessels were structure caches and all those of Imix were stela caches. The miniature jars that were a hallmark of Ik caches were absent in Imix, and the typical serving-vessel shapes and probable polychrome decoration that were characteristic of Imix caches were absent from Ik caches.

Problematical Deposits of the Imix Complex

Imix Complex vessels occurred in twelve problematical deposits (Table 9.8). Six were discovered in the central area of the site: four in the North Acropolis, one each in the West Plaza and a twin pyramid group, while the others were in small-structure groups (and one in the minor center of Uolantun). Four problematical deposits included only a single vessel, four had two vessels, one had three vessels, and two had five vessels. One problematical deposit from the minor center of Uolantun contained a Manik Complex vessel, though stratigraphically dated to the Imix Complex.

There were a total of twenty-four Imix vessels in problematical deposits. Typologically, the great majority (sixteen) were of the Palmar Ceramic Group.

TABLE 9.8
Problematical Deposits of the Imix Complex

PD. No.	Op.SubOp./ Lot	Str.	Structure Group Type	TR. 25A Illustration	TR.	No. of Vessels
6	20E/34-2	Gp. 4F-1 Str. 4F-4	Small Structure Group	122*b*	19	1
44[1]	19C, 41G	Gp. 5D-10 Str. 5D-11	Range Structure Group	127*h*	17	1(Imix) 1(Manik)
54[2]	12C	Gp. 5D-2 Str. 5D-34	Civic-Ceremonial Group	131	14	5(Imix) 2(Ik)
71	28B/6	Gp. 5G-2 Str. 5G-11	Intermediate Structure Group	133*b*	21	2
76[2]	43C/26	Gp. 5C-1 (Twin Pyramid Gp.) Str. 5C-17	Civic-Ceremonial Group	133*c*	18[†]	3
116	66X/20	Gp. 5G-18 Ch. 5G-7	Small Structure Group	144*b*	20	5
151	12T/59	Gp. 5D-2 Str. 5D-22 1st	Civic-Ceremonial Group	148*b*	14	1
179	12H/54A	Gp. 5D-2 Str. 5D-26 1st	Civic-Ceremonial Group	151*b*	14	2
181	120A/5	Gp. 5C-11 Str. 5C-49	Civic-Ceremonial Group	151*c*	23C	2
184	12U/15	Gp. 5D-2 Str. 5D-32 1st	Civic-Ceremonial Group	151*e*	14	1
199[1]	135C/23	Uolantun SE-486	Minor Center	153*a*		1(Manik)
221	140A/2	Str. 4C-34 Locus Str. 4C-34	Small Structure Group	153*d*	20A & B	2

[1] Includes ceramics from the Manik Complex

[2] Includes Ik Complex vessels

[†] Forthcoming

There were two Cambio Unslipped, one each of Zacec Black and Tinaja Red, and four weathered vessels. In terms of vessel shapes, outflaring to slightly outcurving-side bowls and dishes are predominant with ten examples. These were followed in frequency by tripod plates (three), and cylinders (two). The only vessels that did not fall into the serving-vessel category were one rectangular cache vessel, and three miniature jars (and two fragmentary bases that could be miniature jars or broken feet) found together in a single problematical deposit.

The majority of vessels in Imix problematical deposits were decorated serving vessels. Such vessels were common in all contexts and, of course, were the most common as burial offerings. But the problematical deposits did not include sets of three vessels, which were the favored numbers in Imix burials. Consequently, there is no reason to believe that the problematical deposits were from burials.

Only three Imix problematical deposits deserve special mention. Problematical Deposit 54 included a mixture of Ik and Imix vessels. The five

Imix vessels are all of decorated types and serving-vessel shapes. Because the mixture from two complexes was undeniable and because most of the vessels were only fragments, it is unlikely that they represented a single source. Problematical Deposit 76 included two rectangular cache vessels and a Palmar Polychrome outflaring to slightly out-curving-side bowl. Rectangular cache vessels are restricted to deposits that are classified as caches. Decorated serving vessels are also a component of Imix caches and, therefore, it is likely that PD. 76 represented material originally derived from a cache. Finally, PD. 116 from a small structure group consisted of three miniature jars (and two fragmentary bases that could be miniature jars or broken feet); as well as a group of mutilated pottery figurines. Miniature vessels were a characteristic feature of Ik Complex caches, but not usually of Imix Complex caches. It seems likely that the vessels were from a cache, especially if their attribution to the Imix Complex is mistaken and they actually were from the Ik Complex.

X

Eznab Ceramic Complex

Eznab Complex Collections

Introduction

A number of large and well-preserved collections pertaining to the Eznab Complex were recovered at Tikal. Nearly all of these collections are from the same kind of context, refuse deposits that accumulated above the latest construction in and around masonry range structures. Such large refuse accumulations are not found in association with temple structures, although occasional finds suggest that some kinds of ceremonial activity may still have taken place in temples during Eznab times.

The most voluminous Eznab Complex collections are from Gp. 5D-11, the Central Acropolis (Harrison 1970), where there seems to have been a heavy occupation that spanned a considerable length of time. Range structures in the East Plaza, Gp. 5D-3, and the West Plaza, Gp. 5D-10, produced further Eznab collections, as did several such structures in outlying areas of the site (Culbert 1973:68). In contrast to the frequency with which Eznab debris is found in association with masonry structures, few small structure groups at Tikal produced Eznab ceramics in quantities large enough to suggest a major occupation, which may indicate a drastic decline in population at Tikal in Eznab times, a question discussed at greater length elsewhere (Culbert 1973:67–71).

Ceramics from five Eznab locations were analyzed quantitatively. Three of these locations are within the main ceremonial-elite precincts at the heart of the site and are presumed to be squatters who have taken up residence in abandoned structures in the Central Acropolis (Harrison 1970). One is in an intermediate structure, Group 7F-1, and are likely elites living in reduced circumstances (see Haviland TR. 22), and one is in a small structure group, both some distance from the site center. The presumed functional association of all these samples is commoner residential. Although the architecture occupied was of monumental scale, it was no longer being maintained and there was no systematic disposal of the refuse that accumulated inside and outside of buildings, over stairways and piled within courtyards (Harrison 1999:192–198).

Because the only Eznab constructions identified at Tikal are of very small scale and do not contain significant amounts of fill, there is no architectural stratigraphy that can be used to follow changes in Eznab ceramics. Although refuse deposits were deep enough in several locations to separate several levels in the process of excavation, most of these situations involved very rapid accumulation of the deposits, usually redeposited from elsewhere. Consequently, the only indication of ceramic change during the time of the Eznab Ceramic Complex is a seriation of the Eznab samples.

Information on the locations of analyzed Eznab samples is presented in Table 10.1. In addition to these samples, six special deposits classified as burials and twelve classified as problematical deposits contained Eznab ceramics.

TABLE 10.1 (part 1)
Locations of Eznab Samples

Sample #	Op.Sub-Op./Lot	Structure Group and Structure Number	Structure Group Type	Total Sherds-Types	Total Sherds-Shapes	Comments	TR.
Location 1a	79C/14-22	Group 5D-11	Range Structure Group			Post-construction domestic midden in room interior	15[†]
Sample 1a-1		Str. 5D-63		361	—		
Sample 1a-2		Str. 5D-63		327	—		
Sample 1a-3		Str. 5D-63		—	128		
Location 1b	97A/40–41, 43–44, 49–50; 97D/3, 5, 13, 15	Group 5D-11	Range Structure Group			Post-construction domestic midden	15[†]
Sample 1b-1		Str. 5D-54		—	—	Room interior, third story	
Sample 1b-2		Str. 5D-54		—	—	Room interior, third story	
Sample 1b-3		Str. 5D-54		704	—	Room interior, second story	
Sample 1b-4		Str. 5D-54		176	—	Room interior, second story	
Sample 1b-5		Str. 5D-54		136	—	Room interior, second story	
Sample 1b-6		Str. 5D-54		399	—	Room interior, second story	
Sample 1b-7		Str. 5D-54		—	164	Room interior, second story	
Sample 1b-8		Str. 5D-54		—	40	Room interior, second story	
Sample 1b-9		Str. 5D-54		—	74	Terrace in front of second story	
Sample 1b-10		Str. 5D-54		—	87	Room interior, second story	
Location 1c	98L/42; 113C/1	Group 5D-11	Range Structure Group			Post-construction domestic midden	15[†]
Sample 1c-1		Court in front of Str. 5D-44		465	56		
Sample 1c-2		Court in front of Str. 5D-44		—	81		
Location 1d	98A/4–5, 9; 98D/3, 24–27; 98F/2, 4, 6; 98J/1–3; 98K/3–4, 6–7, 9–12, 56; 98M/4–5, 7; 98Q; 98V	Group 5D-11	Range Structure Group			Post-construction domestic midden	15[†]
Sample 1d-1		Str. 5D-46		—	119	Patio on northside	

TABLE 10.1 (part 2)
Locations of Eznab Samples

Sample #	Op.Sub-Op./Lot	Structure Group and Structure Number	Structure Group Type	Total Sherds-Types	Total Sherds-Shapes	Comments	TR.
Sample 1d-2		Str. 5D-46		242	—	Room 1 interior	
Sample 1d-3		Str. 5D-46		—	34	Room 1 interior	
Sample 1d-4		Str. 5D-46		863	134	Exterior, south side	
Sample 1d-5		Str. 5D-46		383	70	Exterior, debris on front steps	
Sample 1d-6		Str. 5D-46		2438	218	Room 4A interior, top stratum	
Sample 1d-7		Str. 5D-46		667	86	Room 4A interior, second stratum	
Sample 1d-8		Str. 5D-46		839	75	Room 4A interior, third stratum	
Sample 1d-9		Str. 5D-46		300	—	Room 4A interior, fifth stratum	
Sample 1d-10		Str. 5D-46		—	150	Room 4A interior, sixth stratum	
Sample 1d-11		Str. 5D-46		213	—	Room 4A interior seventh stratum	
Sample 1d-12		Str. 5D-46		224	—	Room 4A interior, eighth stratum	
Sample 1d-13		Str. 5D-46		325	—	Room 4A interior, ninth stratum	
Sample 1d-14		Str. 5D-46		—	128	Room 4A interior, fourth through ninth strata	
Sample 1d-15		Between 5D-46 and 5D-47		—	70	Rooms between 5D-46 and 5D-57	
Sample 1d-16		Str. 5D-46		297	—	Patio on south side	
Sample 1d-17		Str. 5D-46		239	—	Patio on south side	
Sample 1d-18		Str. 5D-46		—	97	Patio on south side	
Sample 1d-19		Str. 5D-46		464	—	Room 4b interior	
Sample 1d-20		Str. 5D-46		167	—	Room 4b interior	
Sample 1d-21		Str. 5D-46		293	—	Room 4b interior	
Sample 1d-22		Str. 5D-46		—	50	Room 4b interior	

TABLE 10.1 (part 3)
Locations of Eznab Samples

Sample #	Op.Sub-Op./Lot	Structure Group and Structure Number	Structure Group Type	Total Sherds-Types	Total Sherds-Shapes	Comments	TR.
Location 1e		**Group 5D-11**	**Range Structure Group**			Post-construction domestic midden	15[†] Table 10.1. Locations of Eznab Samples
Location 1e-1	107C/5	Str. 5D-47		—	85		
Location 1f		**Group 5D-11**	**Range Structure Group**			Post-construction domestic midden	15[†]
Location 1f-1	100F	Str. 5D-48		—	120	Near small platform in ravine below Str. 5D-48	
Location 1g		**Group 5D-11**	**Range Structure Group**			Post-construction domestic midden	15[†]
Location 1g-1	96H/1–4, 6	Str. 5D-49		—	102	Exterior in front of sturcture	
Location 1h	96D/1, 3, 5–7, 9; 96F/5–6	**Group 5D-11**	**Range Structure Group**			Post-construction domestic midden	15[†]
Sample 1h-1		Str. 5D-51		138	—	Inside east room of structure	
Sample 1h-2		Str. 5D-51		197	—	Inside east room of structure	
Sample 1h-3		Str. 5D-51		525	—	Inside east room of structure	
Sample 1h-4		Str. 5D-51		—	92	Inside east room of structure	
Sample 1h-5		Str. 5D-51		304	363	Exterior courtyard in front of structure	
Sample 1h-6		Str. 5D-51		724	26	Exterior courtyard in front of structure	
Location 1i	44A,C; 45E	**Group 5D-11**	**Range Structure Group**			Post-construction domestic midden	15[†]
Sample 1i-1		Str. 5D-50, -52		—	232	Terrace in front of structures	
Sample 1i-2		Str. 5D-50, -52		—	118	Terrace in front of structures	

TABLE 10.1 (part 4)
Locations of Eznab Samples

Sample #	Op.Sub-Op./Lot	Structure Group and Structure Number	Structure Group Type	Total Sherds-Types	Total Sherds-Shapes	Comments	TR.
Sample 1i-3		Str. 5D-50		218	—	Str. 5D-50, south gallery first story	
Sample 1i-4		Str. 5D-50		—	60	Str. 5D-50, south gallery first story	
Sample 1i-5		Str. 5D-50		—	133	Str. 5D-50, south gallery first story	
Sample 1i-6		Str. 5D-50		360	—	Str. 5D-50, south gallery first story	
Location 1j	108A/2–3	**Group 5D-11**	**Range Structure Group**			**Post-construction domestic midden**	15[†]
Sample 1j-1		Ravine below Str. 5E-41		366	—	Upper level of midden	
Sample 1j-2		Ravine below Str. 5E-41		—	60	Upper level of midden	
Sample 1j-3		Ravine below Str. 5E-41		—	88	Lower level of midden	
Location 1k	106A/1–7	**Group 5D-11**	**Range Structure Group**			**Post-construction domestic midden**	15[†]
Sample 1k-1		Ravine below group		401	—	Upper level of midden	
Sample 1k-2		Ravine below group		352	180	Middle level of midden	
Sample 1k-3		Ravine below group		—	121	Combined midden sample	
Location 1l	105A/5–11	**Group 5D-11**	**Range Structure Group**			**Post-construction domestic midden**	15[†]
Sample 1l-1		Palace Reservoir below Str. 5D-65		132	—	Exterior midden	
Sample 1l-2		Palace Reservoir below Str. 5D-65		198	—	Exterior midden	

TABLE 10.1 (part 5)
Locations of Eznab Samples

Sample #	Op.Sub-Op./Lot	Structure Group and Structure Number	Structure Group Type	Total Sherds-Types	Total Sherds-Shapes	Comments	TR.
Sample 1l-3		Palace Reservoir below Str. 5D-65		—	59	Exterior midden	
Location 2		**Group 5D-3 (East Plaza)**	**Civic-Ceremonial**			**Post-construction domestic midden**	16
Sample 2-1	78T/1–3	Str. 5E-30		209	—	Debris overlying structure	
Sample 2-2	78T/1–3	Str. 5E-30		—	59	Debris overlying structure	
Sample 2-3	78Q/2, 4, 7, 9, 11–12	Str. 5D-40		251	—	Midden	
Sample 2-4	78Q/2, 4, 7, 9, 11–12	Str. 5D-40		279	—	Midden	
Sample 2-5	78Q/2, 4, 7, 9, 11–12	Str. 5D-40		—	95	Midden	
Location 3		**Group 5D-10 (West Plaza)**	**Range Structure Group**				17
Location 3-1	42F/7–8, 12			—	280	Post-construction domestic midden from stairs in front of structure	
Location 4	3D/2–3, 6	**Group 7F-1**	**Intermediate Structure Group**				22
Sample 4-1		Plat. 7F-1 near Str. 7F-29 and 7F-32		—	100	Debris in plaza	
Sample 4-2		Str. 7F-32		190	—	Midden inside and outside of structure	
Sample 4-3		Str. 7F-32		—	148	Midden inside and outside of structure	
Location 5		**Group 2C-1**	**Small Structure Group**				20A
Location 5-1	58G/1–3	Str. 2C-15, -21		—	47	Outside between structures	
	TOTAL SHERDS			15366	4429		

[†] Forthcoming

EZNAB LOCATION 1

Eznab Location 1 includes all of the excavated areas in and near the Central Acropolis that provided ceramics of Eznab date (see TR. 15). Although there are a few fragments of Eznab construction in the Central Acropolis, none of them provided enough ceramics for analysis, so all Eznab samples came from deposits overlying the latest construction. Extensive Eznab middens occurred throughout the Central Acropolis and environs—within rooms, in courtyards, and discarded over the edge of the Acropolis. In several cases, Eznab materials overlay layers of debris from partially collapsed structures, indicating that at least some of the occupation was late enough so that masonry structures had already begun to disintegrate. Although the Central Acropolis had been an elite residential/administrative area of Tikal in earlier times, the disrepair of the buildings and haphazard accumulation of trash, even within rooms, suggests that there were no longer elite activities at Tikal by the time of the Eznab Complex. Hearths and accumulated ash in association with Eznab deposits gave further indication of domestic activities. Because the collections from the Central Acropolis are so numerous and so large, the location has been divided into lettered subdivisions that begin at Str. 5D-63 on the Great Plaza side of the acropolis and move in clockwise fashion around the acropolis.

EZNAB LOCATION 1A

Samples la-1 through la-3: These samples are all from Str. 5D-63, where they were encountered in excavation of the inner room that faces on the Great Plaza. It is uncertain whether the samples represent residence in that room or whether they were thrown down from rooms above after the roof had collapsed. Two samples quantified for type and one combined sample quantified for shape came from location 1a. The samples are alike in that all represent collapse debris and/or midden material.

EZNAB LOCATION 1B

Eznab Samples 1b-1 through 1b–10: This location includes material from all excavations in and around Str. 5D-54. Most of the samples came from debris that had accumulated in several rooms in the second and third stories of the structure. A total of four quantified type samples and four quantified shape samples were from this location.

EZNAB LOCATION 1C

Eznab Samples lc-1 and 1c-2: Only two samples, one quantified for both types and shapes and one quantified only for shapes, were obtained from excavation of the exterior courtyard in front of Str. 5D-44.

EZNAB LOCATION 1D

Eznab Samples 1d-l through 1d-22: The extensive excavations in and around Str. 5D-46 (Location 1d) provided a number of important Eznab Complex samples. The collections came both from deep refuse deposits within rooms of the structure and from middens located in exterior patios and courtyards. In Rm. 4A and 4B, the deep deposits were excavated by natural stratigraphy of banded layers. In both rooms, the material did not accumulate from occupation of the rooms themselves, but was deposited from elsewhere, probably from occupation of the story above after partial collapse of the roof of the lower story had opened holes convenient for refuse disposal. It was hoped that ceramic change within the Eznab Complex might be determined from these carefully excavated deposits, but the ceramics in the nine levels from Rm. 4A (Samples 1d-6 through 1d-14) showed multiple fits between lots that indicate that the material must have been deposited very rapidly, and the three levels from Rm. 4B (Samples ld-19 through 1d-22) show only weak indications of ceramic change, even though they lack the fits between lots of Rm. 4A samples. In all, fifteen type samples and twelve shape samples were obtained from Location 1d.

EZNAB LOCATION 1E

Eznab Samples 1e-1: Only a single sherd sample came from Location 1e, Str. 5D-47. This sample, obtained from a midden outside of the structure was quantified for shapes, but not for types.

EZNAB LOCATION 1F

Eznab Sample 1f-1: Eznab Location 1f consisted of excavation of a small platform located in the ravine S of the Central Acropolis and immediately below Str. 5D-48. It is not known whether the midden material encountered at this location resulted from the use of the platform or was discarded into the ravine from the structure above. Only a single sample, quantified for shapes, was analyzed.

EZNAB LOCATION 1G

Eznab Sample 1g-1: Eznab Location 1g included all of the excavated areas around Str. 5D-49. Only a single sample, quantified for shapes but not for types, was obtained in this location. The sample came from a deposit of refuse located just outside the structure.

EZNAB LOCATION 1H

Eznab Samples 1h-1 through 1h-6: Several large samples of Eznab Complex material were recovered during excavation of Str. 5D-51 (Location 1h). Excavation inside the East room of the structure produced four samples, three quantified for types and one for shapes. A hearth within the room on top of the debris suggested actual residence at some time late in its use. Two additional large samples, quantified for both types and shapes, were recovered from refuse deposits in the courtyard in front of the structure.

EZNAB LOCATION 1I

Samples 1i-1 through 1i-6: Eznab Location 1i included the excavations in and around Str. 5D-50 and 5D-52. Two refuse areas provided the samples. Two samples came from debris on the terrace in front of the structures, while four samples came from within the first-story gallery of Str. 5D-50. Two samples were quantified for types, and four for shapes.

EZNAB LOCATION 1J

Samples 1j-1 through 1j-3: Eznab Location 1j was a midden at the bottom of the ravine below Str. 5E-41. In the ravine near this location was a small platform structure. Two levels were separated in the excavation of the midden. The upper level sample was quantified for types and the lower level of the midden produced two samples that were quantified for shapes.

EZNAB LOCATION 1K

Samples 1k-1 through 1k-3: A midden that had accumulated at the bottom of the ravine below Str. 5D-50 provided the samples in Eznab Location 1k. Two type samples, stratigraphically related to each other, were obtained from the midden together with two stratigraphically unrelated shape samples.

EZNAB LOCATION 1L

Samples 1l-1 through 1l-3: This location is at the bottom of the ravine S of the Central Acropolis and immediately below Str. 5D-65. Two separate type samples and one shape sample were analyzed.

EZNAB LOCATION 2

Eznab Samples 2-1 through 2-5: Eznab Location 2 is in the NW corner of the East Plaza where excavations in the vaulted Str. 5D-40 and the low platform Str. 5E-30 attached to its E end encountered extensive Eznab midden deposits (see TR. 16). The deposits occurred within the rooms and to the front of Str. 5D-40 and overlying Str. 5E-30. They probably are all the result of residence in the vaulted rooms of Str. 5D-40. In all, three type samples and two shape samples were recovered from the location.

EZNAB LOCATION 3

Eznab Sample 3-1: This location included material of Eznab date procured during excavation of Str. 5D-15 on the N edge of the West Plaza (see TR. 17). A single sample quantified for shapes only was obtained from debris lying over and around the central stairway of the structure.

EZNAB LOCATION 4

Eznab Samples 4-1 through 4-3: Eznab Location 4 included Plaza 7F-1 and the structures that surround it (see TR. 22). Eznab material was found in the plaza itself and both inside the rooms and outside of Str. 7F-32. In all, the group produced two Eznab samples quantified for shapes and a single sample quantified for types.

EZNAB LOCATION 5

Eznab Sample 5-1: This location included excavations near Str. 2C-15 and 21 of Gp. 2C-1 (see TR. 20A). A single Eznab shape sample was recovered from refuse between the two structures.

Pastes of the Eznab Complex

Introduction

Considerably more paste types were formally separated in analysis of Eznab Complex ceramics than were separated for either Ik or Imix Complex material. This elaboration of paste types is centered on the ceramic type, Tinaja Red. Unslipped types were still produced from Coarse-carbonate Paste as they had been from the beginning of the Tikal ceramic sequence, and the few Eznab polychromes were made from pastes comparable to those used for polychromes in the Late Classic complexes. Tinaja Red, however, was made from four different pastes in Eznab, as compared to two pastes in Imix and only one in Ik (see Table 10.2).

In spite of this variety of pastes, the majority of Tinaja Red vessels were still made of Tinaja Paste, the paste that characterized the type throughout the Late Classic. It should also be noted that the proliferation of so many pastes is partly an artifact of analysis. The existence of the fine Taman Paste, which is the Tikal manifestation of the general Maya Lowland tendency to utilize fine pastes in the Terminal Classic, made it desirable to sort sherds by paste. Once sorting of sherds by paste was a consistent part of analysis—as it was for the Eznab samples—there was a tendency to split and define as separate units some variants that might have been considered part of the range of variation in samples where paste was not a regular part of the sorting procedure.

Even given these analytical considerations, there is no doubt that pastes showed more variety in Eznab than in earlier complexes. A number of factors were likely involved. The first was probably a stimulus from Fine Orange Ware that spurred a tendency to locally produced fine paste wares at a number of lowland sites, most notably Palenque (Rands 1973). The use of Taman Paste at Tikal must surely have been inspired by knowledge of Fine Orange Ware because Taman Paste was used for Sahcaba Molded-carved, the Petén "imitation" of Fine Orange Pabellon Molded-carved. A second factor that may have been involved in greater paste variety in the Eznab Complex is the larger range of vessel shapes produced from Tinaja Red. In the Ik and Imix Complexes, only large utilitarian bowls and narrow-mouth jars were made from Tinaja Red. In the Eznab Complex varieties of plates, bowls, and dish shapes were added to this repertoire. As smaller "serving" vessels were added to the list of Tinaja Red shapes, it may have been either technologically or aesthetically desirable for potters to change the characteristics of the paste used. Finally, it is possible that the disruption of the social and economic life of Tikal that is undeniably evidenced by Eznab remains may have been associated with the loss of both specialization and standardization in the production of pottery. It should be stressed, however, that Eznab pottery gives no sign of being technologically inferior to pottery of the Imix Complex. Vessels are well shaped and the pottery is hard fired. If anything, Eznab pottery gives the impression of being technologically somewhat better than pottery of the Imix Complex.

Eznab Paste Descriptions

Polychrome types made from the Saxche Paste of the preceding Ik Complex, and Zacatel Paste of the preceding Imix Complex are extremely rare in the Eznab Complex and may be the result of mixed deposits. If polychromes continued to be manufactured in Eznab times, they occur in such low quantities that their presence does not show up in the frequency counts shown in Table 10.2. Ceramics of the Altar Ceramic Group manufactured from Fine Orange Paste are also so infrequent that they do not show up in the paste frequency counts in Table 10.2 except as a trace.

COARSE-CARBONATE PASTE

Identifying characteristics: In all regards identical to the Ix Complex (see Chapter 8).

ZACATEL PASTE

Comments: Although polychrome types were rare in the Eznab Complex, they continued to be made in the standard polychrome paste and, in all regards, identical to the Imix Complex as described in Chapter 9.

SAXCHE PASTE

Comments: A paste that is indistinguishable from Saxche Paste, as described in Chapter 8, occurs on some Eznab polychrome sherds. This seems to be a rejuvenation of a paste that was standard in the Ik Complex but became rare in Imix samples.

TINAJA PASTE

Comments: Eznab Complex examples of Tinaja Paste are as described in the Ik Complex, Chapter 8, except that the Eznab samples average somewhat finer and have less inclusions than the samples from the Ik and Imix Complexes. In addition, yellowish-brown colors occur somewhat more frequently in Eznab, although the typical reddish-yellow colors are still the most common.

TABLE 10.2
Paste Frequencies of the Eznab Complex

Eznab Pastes[1]	Range Structure Group									Civic-Ceremonial	Intermediate Structure Group
	Sample Loc. 1a Gp. 5D-11 Str. 5D-63	Sample Loc. 1b Gp. 5D-11 Str. 5D-54	Sample Loc. 1c Gp. 5D-11 Str. 5D-44	Sample Loc. 1d Gp. 5D-11 Str. 5D-46	Sample Loc. 1h Gp. 5D-11 Str. 5D-51	Sample Loc. 1i Gp. 5D-11 Str. 5D-50,-52	Sample Loc. 1j Gp. 5D-11 Ravine below Str. 5E-41	Sample Loc. 1k Ravine below Gp. 5D-11	Sample Loc. 1l Gp. 5D-11 Palace Reservoir below Str. 5D-65	Sample Loc. 2 Gp. 5D-3 Str. 5E-30, 5D-40	Sample Loc. 4 Gp. 7F-1 Plat. 7F-1 Str. 7F-29, -32
	%	%	%	%	%	%	%	%	%	%	%
Tinaja Paste	64.4	52.9	52.9	54.7	57.7	62.7	51.5	56.5	73.0	56.3	77.8
Toh Paste	3.1	12.6	15.7	19.2	13.0	8.3	22.8	9.1	5.7	18.1	4.8
Taman Paste	2.5	10.1	—	5.0	4.4	5.9	2.0	6.5	9.2	5.1	1.6
Takach Paste	10.9	2.5	4.1	6.0	7.0	11.4	2.0	7.3	—	4.0	—
Tupchaac Paste	19.1	17.1	23.1	10.5	13.5	11.7	18.9	17.2	7.8	12.9	7.9
Course Carbonate Paste	—	4.8	4.1	4.6	4.4	—	3.0	3.4	4.3	3.6	7.9
Total Sherds	320	357	121	1695	385	290	101	232	141	277	63

[1] Zacatel Paste and Saxche Paste occur only rarely in Eznab Complex samples, and may be the result of mixing from Imix Complex vessels. They occur in such low quantities that they do not show up in the frequency counts. Additionally Fine Orange Paste occurs in such small quantities that it does not show up in frequency counts of Eznab Pastes.

TOH PASTE

Identifying characteristics: The fairly heavy temper and alternating bands of color make this paste easy to recognize.

Color: Toh Paste characteristically has alternating bands of color. The paste near the vessel surface is red (2.5YR 5/6, 5/8), while the center of the core is light brownish gray (2.5Y 6/2), brownish yellow (10YR 6/6), yellowish brown (10YR 5/4), or strong brown (7.5YR 5/6). On some sherds, the two colors alternate in several bands or one will be found close to one surface and the other on the opposite side.

Texture: Fine.

Inclusions: Medium amounts of fine to medium particles that include opaque white and amorphous gray particles and sometimes finely divided sparkly particles. Contains carbonate.

Types: Tinaja Red, Toh Brown.

Temporal distribution: Only Eznab Complex.

Comments: Toh Paste is almost invariably used in making curved rim tripod dishes. It is sometimes used for other kinds of "serving" vessels and almost never used for large bowls or jars.

TAMAN PASTE

Identifying characteristics: The very fine paste texture and scarcity of inclusions make the paste easy to identify.

Color: Reddish yellow (7.5YR 6/6, 7/8) is the most common color. Also occurring with some frequency are yellow brown (10YR 5/4), light gray (10YR 7/1, 7/2; 2.5Y 7/0, 7/2), and light brownish gray (2.5Y 6/2).

Texture: Very fine.

Inclusions: The only visible inclusions are rare medium-size white particles that are probably volcanic ash.

Types: The most frequent occurrences of Taman Paste are in Tinaja Red, but it is important that almost all of the examples of Sahcaba Molded-carved are made from Taman Paste.

Temporal distribution: Confined to the Eznab Complex.

Comments: It is likely that Taman Paste represents a local adaptation to the fine paste trend that is characteristic of the Terminal Classic across the Maya lowlands.

TUPCHAAC PASTE

Identifying characteristics: A light brownish color and finely divided inclusions are the identifying features of this paste.

Color: Ranges from reddish yellow (7.5YR 6/6) to yellowish brown (10YR 5/4), light yellow brown (10YR 6/4), and very pale brown (10YR 7/4).

Texture: Fine.

Inclusions: Medium amounts of very finely divided material that includes white particles.

Types: Tinaja Red.

Temporal distribution: Only formalized within the Eznab Complex, but some examples that fall within this range occur throughout the Late Classic.

Comments: The identification of Tupchaac Paste as a separate unit is another artifact that results from the greater attention paid to pastes within the Eznab collections. The paste might be subsumed back within Tinaja Paste except for the fact that it seems to have chronological meaning within the Eznab Complex.

FINE ORANGE PASTE

Identifying characteristics: The extreme fineness, typical orange color, and powdery orange texture of weathered surfaces are very distinctive, although they overlap with the characteristics of Preclassic Mars Orange.

Color: Predominantly light red (2.5YR 6/8), a few reddish yellow (5YR 7/8, 6/8), and red (2.5YR 5/8). A fair number have a tan core (reddish yellow 7.5YR 6/6).

Texture: Very fine.

Inclusions: The only visible inclusions are a few very fine micaceous particles and rare white particles of medium size.

Types: All Fine Orange types.

Temporal distribution: Confined to the Eznab Complex, but seems to occur throughout the span of the complex.

Ceramic Types of the Eznab Complex

Introduction

The Eznab Ceramic Complex includes the 9 ceramic groups and 26 types listed in Table 10.3. There is strong typological continuity between the Imix and Eznab Complexes. Most of the Imix types continue to appear unchanged in Eznab samples except for some changes in polychrome painting. It is beyond question that the producers of Eznab pottery were the descendants of the same population that had produced earlier Late Classic pottery.

Despite this continuity, there are substantial quantitative differences in types that make the Imix and Eznab Complexes easy to distinguish. The most profound of these changes is the drastic decrease in Eznab of the frequency of polychrome types with a corresponding increase in the frequency of Tinaja Red. In this process, a variety of "serving-vessel" shapes that are almost invariably of polychrome types in Imix samples are usually of Tinaja Red in Eznab collections. Another very characteristic feature of the Eznab typology is a substantial increase in frequency of Cambio Unslipped at the expense of Encanto Striated. Although a number of new types are introduced during the Eznab Complex, including those of the Altar and Toh Ceramic Groups, and the types Sahcaba Molded-carved, and Jato Black-on-gray, the new types are not numerically dominant in Eznab collections.

One of the characteristics of Eznab Complex samples is immense variation in type frequencies between lots (see Table 10.4). Consequently, almost every type shows a very wide range of frequency, often

TABLE 10.3
Ceramic Groups and Types of the Eznab Complex

CAMBIO CERAMIC GROUP
Cambio Unslipped: Cambio Variety

ENCANTO CERAMIC GROUP
Encanto Striated: Encanto Variety

TINAJA CERAMIC GROUP
Tinaja Red: Tinaja Variety
Cameron Incised: Cameron Variety
Chinja Impressed: Chinja Variety
Pantano Impressed: Stamped Variety
San Julio Modeled: San Julio Variety
Rosa Punctated: Rosa Variety

ACHOTE CERAMIC GROUP
Achote Black: Achote Variety
Cubeta Incised: Cubeta Variety

MAQUINA CERAMIC GROUP
Maquina Brown: Maquina Variety
Pepet Incised: Pepet Variety

TOH CERAMIC GROUP
Toh Brown: Toh Variety
Tott Incised: Tott Variety

PALMAR CERAMIC GROUP
Palmar Orange Polychrome: Palmar Variety
Chantuori Black-on-orange: Chantuori Variety
Zacatel Cream Polychrome: Zacatel Variety
Zacatel Cream Polychrome: Zacpech Variety
Chinos Black-on-cream: Chinos Variety
Naranjal Red-on-cream: Naranjal Variety
Yuhactal Black-on-red: Yuhactal Variety
Jato Black-on-gray: Jato Variety

TEABO CERAMIC GROUP
Sahcaba Modeled-carved: Sahcaba Variety

ALTAR CERAMIC GROUP
Altar Orange: Altar Variety
Trapiche Incised: Trapiche Variety
Pabellon Molded-carved: Pabellon Variety
Tumba Black-on-orange: Tumba Variety

accompanied by a flat distribution curve without a strong central tendency. The two most common Eznab types are Tinaja Red and Cambio Unslipped. The range of frequencies for Tinaja Red is between 19% and 50%, and, for Cambio Unslipped, it is between 3% and 47%. The next most common type is Encanto Striated, with a range between a trace and 18%. A combined group that includes all polychrome and dichrome sherds has a range between 0 and 10%. Other monochrome ceramics (brown and black) each show ranges between absence and 14%. The Altar Fine Orange Group, Sahcaba Molded-carved, and Toh Brown are all rare types that occur in only a few lots and never reach frequencies of more than one percent.

Eznab Type Descriptions

CAMBIO CERAMIC GROUP

Cambio Unslipped: Cambio Variety

Established: Smith and Gifford (1966)

Group: Cambio

Ware: Uaxactun Unslipped

Ceramic Complex: Eznab (Begins in Ik and continues into Imix and Eznab)

Ceramic Sphere: Tepeu 1–3

Illustrations: Fig. 39.20–24, 39.30–38; 53.1–15; 55.1–9, 55.11–19; 56.34.

Principal identifying attributes: Unslipped surfaces on large wide-mouth jars.

Identifying characteristics and sorting problems: Because the necks and often the bases of Encanto Striated vessels were left unstriated, these sections will be attributed to Cambio Unslipped in sherd sorting. In the Ik and Imix collections, many of the examples counted as Cambio Unslipped are neck and base sections suggesting that few whole vessels were actually Cambio Unslipped. In the Eznab Complex, especially in samples from the late part of the complex, much higher frequencies of unslipped

sherds occur relative to striated sherds, indicating that whole vessels of Cambio Unslipped were much more common than they had been earlier. A number of examples of unslipped double-mouth jars were identified in the collections. In general form, they are similar to unslipped striated Terminal Classic examples from sites in northern Belize (Ball 1983; Chase 1982; Eppich 2000; Kosakowsky and Pring 2001; Walker 1990), however, the Tikal examples are not striated. Similar unslipped double-mouth jars lacking striations have been identified at Blue Creek in northern Belize (Driver and Kosakowsky 2013).

Surface finish and decoration: Surface is very rough. The heavy tempering makes surface smoothing difficult and surfaces show marks where temper particles have been dragged by the careless smoothing that is characteristic of the type.

Shapes: Wide-mouth jars.

Temporal distribution: Occurs throughout the Late Classic, but becomes common in the latter part of the Eznab Complex. Originally Ucum Unslipped was also listed as an Eznab type (TR. 25A) however further analysis has determined that Ucum is only an Ik and Imix type (Tepeu 1–2).

Intersite comparisons: The Cambio Unslipped type is used at Altar de Sacrificios (Adams 1971); Becan (Ball 1977); Calakmul (Dominguez Carrasco 1994); El Mirador (Forsyth 1989); Holmul (Callaghan 2008, 2016e); La Milpa (Sagebiel 2005); Piedras Negras (Muñoz 2006); Seibal (Sabloff 1975); Uaxactun (Smith and Gifford 1966); and Yaxchilan (Lopez Varela 1989). The similar Cayo Unlipped type is used at Barton Ramie (Gifford 1976), Chan (Kosakowsky 2012), and Colha (Valdez 1987). Both Zibal Unslipped and Cambio Unslipped are used at Blue Creek (Kosakowsky and Lohse 2003). An Impressed Variety occurs in the Petexbatun (Foias and Bishop 2013). At Xunantunich the Cambio Group is used for censer forms only (LeCount 1996).

ENCANTO CERAMIC GROUP

Encanto Striated: Encanto Variety

Established: Smith and Gifford (1966)

TABLE 10.4
Ceramic Type Frequencies of the Eznab Complex

Ceramic Group	Sample Loc. 1a Gp. 5D-11 Str. 5D-63	Sample Loc. 1b Gp. 5D-11 Str. 5D-54	Sample Loc. 1c Gp. 5D-11 Str. 5D-44	Sample Loc. 1d Gp. 5D-11 Str. 5D-46	Sample Loc. 1h Gp. 5D-11 Str. 5D-51	Sample Loc. 1i Gp. 5D-11 Str. 5D-50,-52	Sample Loc. 1j Gp. 5D-11 Ravine below Str. 5E-41	Sample Loc. 1k Ravine below Gp. 5D-11	Sample Loc. 1l Gp. 5D-11 Palace Reservoir below Str. 5D-65	Sample Loc. 2 Gp. 5D-3 Str. 5E-30, 5D-40	Sample Loc. 4 Gp. 7F-1 Plat. 7F-1 Str. 7F-29, -32
	%	%	%	%	%	%	%	%	%	%	%
Cambio Group	3.3	35.7	18.9	41.1	47.4	14.4	33.6	26.0	20.0	25.0	27.9
Encanto Group	0.3	11.9	16.8	17.6	8.8	8.7	8.5	8.4	7.0	13.9	2.7
Tinaja Group	46.6	25.6	26.0	21.4	19.5	50.2	27.6	30.8	42.7	37.6	33.3
Achote Group	4.1	2.6	2.0	2.1	2.0	2.1	3.8	1.2	1.5	1.8	1.6
Maquina Group	4.2	1.9	2.0	2.9	1.4	0.9	0.3	2.3	2.4	2.2	1.7
Toh Group	14.5	0.3	0.4	0.2	—	—	—	—	—	0.4	—
Palmar Group	3.6	0.8	10.3	2.5	5.1	5.9	4.1	2.0	2.2	1.6	2.2
Teabo Group	—	—	—	<0.1	—	0.4	—	—	—	0.4	—
Altar Group	0.3	0.6	—	0.3	—	0.3	—	0.1	0.6	—	—
Total Unslipped	3.6	47.6	35.7	58.7	56.2	23.1	42.1	34.4	27.0	38.9	30.6
Total Slipped	73.3	31.8	40.7	29.4	28.0	59.8	35.8	36.4	49.4	44.0	38.8
Unclassified & Rare Types	—	—	0.4	0.5	0.2	0.2	—	—	0.3	—	—
Weathered	23.1	20.6	23.2	11.4	15.6	16.9	22.1	29.2	23.3	17.1	30.6
Total Sherds	688	1397	465	8125	1888	578	366	753	330	739	190

Group: Encanto

Ware: Uaxactun Unslipped

Ceramic Complex: Eznab (Begins in Ik and continues into Imix and Eznab)

Ceramic Sphere: Tepeu 1–3

Illustrations: Fig. 39.20–24, 39.30–38; 52.26–31.

Principal identifying attributes: Unslipped striated surfaces on wide-mouth jars. Crisscross striations occur on bodies of jars and end at the neck.

Identifying characteristics and sorting problems: Striated types are almost identical throughout the Tikal sequence and can only be separated on features of shape.

Paste: Coarse-carbonate Paste.

Firing: Dark cores are common and over one-third of the sherds show fireclouding. Because the fireclouding is more often on the interior than on the exterior, it is probably due to the original firing rather than to smudging from use.

Color: There is a wide range of color, even on a single sherd or vessel. The most common colors range from strong brown (7.5YR 5/6) to pale brown (10YR 7/3; 6/3). There are occasional light gray (10YR 7/2) and some light red brown (5YR 6/4) tones.

Surface finish and decoration: The nature of the paste and coarse inclusions made smoothing difficult. Striations are variable, ranging from fine to heavy. Striations cease abruptly at the necks of vessels, which they approach either vertically or obliquely. Crisscross striations on bodies are common. Bottoms of the rounded bases are often unstriated.

Shapes: Almost entirely wide-mouth jars with tall necks.

Temporal distribution: Begins at the start of the Ik Complex and continues through the Eznab Complex without change.

Intersite Comparisons: The Encanto Striated type is used at Altar de Sacrificios (Adams 1971); Becan (Ball 1977); Calakmul (Dominguez Carrasco 1994); El Mirador (Forsyth 1989); Holmul (Callaghan 2008, 2016e); La Milpa (Sagebiel 2005); Piedras Negras (Muñoz 2006); Seibal (Sabloff 1975); Uaxactun (Smith and Gifford 1966); and Yaxchilan (Lopez Varela 1989). The similar Tu-tu Camp Striated type is used at Barton Ramie (Gifford 1976); Chan (Kosakowsky 2012); Colha (Valdez 1987); and Xunantunich (LeCount 1996). Tu-tu Camp Striated and Encanto Striated are used interchangeably at Blue Creek (Kosakowsky and Lohse 2003).

TINAJA CERAMIC GROUP

Tinaja Red: Tinaja Variety

Established: Smith and Gifford (1966)

Group: Tinaja

Ware: Petén Gloss

Ceramic Complex: Eznab (Begins in Ik and continues into Imix and Eznab)

Ceramic Sphere: Tepeu 1–3

Illustrations: Fig. 50.1, 50.3–5, 50.10, 50.17, 50.19, 50.32, 50.34–36, 50.41–42, 50.44–45, 50.47, 50.52; 51.1–7, 51.12–14, 51.16–22, 51.24–25, 51.28, 51.30–31, 51.33, 51.44–45, 51.48–49, 51.53; 52.3–4, 52.10–11, 52.15–18, 52.23–25; 53.23, 53.32–33, 53.35–36, 53.41–49; 54.2–7, 54.14–29; 55.10, 55.20–25, 55.27–29, 55.33, 55.36, 55.41–43, 55.47, 55.40; 56.6, 56.27; 57.17. See TR. 25A: fig. 145c–d,g; 148g4; 152a3–4,8,c2–3; 153c.

Principal identifying attributes: Light to medium polished monochrome red surfaces on jars and large bowls. Paste is characteristically a pale yellow.

Identifying characteristics and sorting problems: The combination of Tinaja Paste and the shapes produced from it is very characteristic.

Paste: Tinaja Paste. Although Tinaja Paste continued to be the most important paste for Tinaja Red in the Eznab Complex, Eznab collections show a variety of other pastes (see Table 10.2).

Firing: Dark cores and fireclouding are rare.

Slip: Thin to medium slip applied to a surface that has received little attention; the slip wears easily.

Polish: There is a great range of polish. Most examples show low to medium polish, but there are a few highly polished examples.

Color: Most common color is red (10R 4/6, 4/8; 5/6, 5/8; 2.5YR 5/6, 5/8). Occasional weak red (10R 4/4), light red (2.5YR 6/6, 6/8), reddish yellow (5YR 6/6, 6/8), and yellowish red (5YR 5/8) occur.

Shapes: The almost exclusive association of Tinaja Red with narrow mouth jars and large-capacity bowls that characterizes the Ik and Imix Complex came to an end in the Eznab Complex. Although these utilitarian shapes continue to be the most important shapes for Tinaja Red in Eznab collections, better than one-third of Tinaja Red examples are now from tripod plates, slightly incurving to round-side bowls, cylinders, and outflaring and outcurving-side dishes, shapes that in earlier complexes are almost always made from decorated types.

Temporal distribution: Begins at the start of the Ik Complex and continues through the Eznab Complex.

Intersite comparisons: Tinaja Red is used throughout Tepeu (1–3) at Altar de Sacrificios (Adams 1971); Chan Chich (Valdez 1998; Valdez and Houk 2000); Holmul (Callaghan 2008, 2016e); Nakbe (Forsyth 1993); and Rio Azul (Adams 1999; Adams and Jackson-Adams 1991). Tinaja Red: Nanzal Variety is used for the Ik equivalent at El Mirador (Forsyth 1989) and in the Petexbatun (Foias and Bishop 2013). At Uaxactun the Ik equivalent is called Tasital Red (Smith and Gifford 1966). In Belize, type names from Barton Ramie (Gifford 1976) are utilized for the Tepeu 1 monochrome red at Blue Creek (Kosakowsky and Lohse 2003); Chan (Kosakowsky 2102); La Milpa (Sagebiel 2005); and Nohmul (Kosakowsky and Pring 2001). Elsewhere Tinaja Red is used as a type only for the Tepeu 2–3 monochrome red.

Cameron Incised: Cameron Variety

Established: Smith and Gifford (1966)

Group: Tinaja

Ware: Petén Gloss

Ceramic Complex: Eznab (Begins in Ik and continues into Imix and Eznab)

Ceramic Sphere: Tepeu 1–3

Illustrations: Fig. 50.40, 50.50; 51.9–11, 51.15, 51.26–27, 51.32, 51.35, 51.37–38, 51.43, 51.46, 51.56; 52.1–2, 52.5–9, 52.12, 52.14; 53.16–19, 53.31, 53.34, 53.37–40; 54.1, 54.8–13; 55.26, 55.32, 55.34–35, 55.37–38. See TR. 25A: fig. 145*e–f*, 152*a*2,5–6.

Principal identifying attributes: Surface finish and paste similar to Tinaja Red, with the addition of a single incised groove on the exterior of large capacity bowls.

Comments: In all characteristics except incised lines, Cameron Incised is identical to Tinaja Red. As in the Ik and Imix Complexes, the majority of examples continue to be large incurving-side bowls with a single exterior groove. In Eznab, a significant number of tripod plates and cylinders also show simple incised lines. For counting, large bowl and serving-vessel shapes were differentiated, however, this distinction was not maintained in the typology as naming varieties based on vessel shape violates type: variety nomenclature (Gifford 1976). [For example see the differentiation of Tinaja Red from Subin Red at Altar Sacrificios (Adams 1971).]

Intersite comparisons: Similar to Altar de Sacrificios (Adams 1971); Holmul (Callaghan 2008, 2016e); Seibal (Sabloff 1975); and Uaxactun (Smith and Gifford 1966). See intersite comparison discussion for Tinaja Red for more detailed information.

Chinja Impressed: Chinja Variety

Established: Smith and Gifford (1966)

Group: Tinaja

Ware: Petén Gloss

Ceramic Complex: Eznab (Begins in Ik and continues into Imix and Eznab)

Ceramic Sphere: Tepeu 1–3

Illustrations: Fig. 50.6, 50.8–9, 50.12–13, 50.15–16, 50.18, 50.20–22, 50.28, 50.30–31, 50.43, 50.48–49, 50.51; 51.8, 51.23, 51.29, 51.47, 51.50, 51.54–55, 51.57, 51.59–62.

Principal identifying attributes: Surface finish and paste similar to Tinaja Red, with the addition of a single row of finger impressions on the exterior of large capacity bowls.

Surface finish and decoration: Large-capacity bowls have a row of impressions encircling the vessel exterior below the lip. The impressions were made directly on the vessel wall. The impressions were usually made with fingernails, but in a few examples were made with a hollow circular tool (and these latter examples should be reclassified as Rosa Punctated).

Temporal distribution: Chinja Impressed: Chinja Variety occurs in about equal quantities in Ik and Imix collections and is rare in Eznab collections.

Comments: Chinja Impressed: Chinja Variety is identical to Tinaja Red: Tinaja Variety except for the characteristics noted below. Originally called Simple-impressed variety by Culbert (TR. 25A). Some large red bowls in the Eznab collections are still decorated with a band of impressions encircling the exterior. Impressed decoration is considerably less common than in earlier complexes, and the Appliqué Variety is so rare it seems likely that the few examples may be mixed in from earlier complexes. In all other characteristics, Chinja Impressed is identical to Tinaja Red.

Intersite comparisons: Chinja Impressed identified in later time periods at Calakmul (Dominguez Carrasco 1994); El Mirador (Forsyth 1989:86–89); La Milpa (Sagebiel 2005); Nakbe (Forsyth 1993); and in the Nanzal Group at Uaxactun (Smith and Gifford 1966). It is similar to Chaquiste Impressed at Altar de Sacrificios (Adams 1971); Holmul (Callaghan 2008, 2016e); and Seibal (Sabloff 1975). It is similar to Chinja Impressed: Floresas Variety at Holmul (Callaghan 2016e); to Pascua Impressed, Gloria Impressed, and Kaway Impressed at Barton Ramie (Gifford 1976), and to Kaway Impressed at Xunantunich (LeCount 1996). In form it is similar to Subin Red at Altar de Sacrificios (Adams 1971) and San Jose IV and V monochrome red bowls (Thompson 1939).

Pantano Impressed: Stamped Variety

Established: Smith and Gifford (1966)

Group: Tinaja

Ware: Petén Gloss

Ceramic Complex: Eznab

Ceramic Sphere: Tepeu 3

Principal identifying attributes: Monochrome red slip same as Tinaja Red with the addition of stamped decoration at the neck body juncture of jars.

Identifying characteristics and sorting problems: A few examples of jars with stamped decoration occur in the Eznab Complex collections. In all features except those described below, the examples are indistinguishable from Tinaja Red.

Surface finish and decoration: A row of stamped designs occurs around the body of the jar just below the juncture with the neck.

Shapes: All narrow-mouth jars with tall neck, but the necks are straighter than is common in other Tikal monochrome types.

Temporal distribution: Only Eznab Complex.

Comments: Adams (1971) first named this variety for Altar de Sacrificios. Because the variety is very common there and occurs in only a few examples at Tikal, it seems likely that the Tikal examples may be trade pieces.

Intersite comparisons: Altar de Sacrificios (Adams 1971); Caracol (Chase and Chase 2004; El Perú/Waka' (Eppich 2011); Seibal (Sabloff 1975); Uaxactun (Smith and Gifford 1966). It is similar to examples of Remate at Lubaantun (Hammond 1975), the Chiquibul (Kosakowsky et al. 2012), and the southern coast (McKillop 2002).

San Julio Modeled: San Julio Variety

Established: Smith and Gifford (1966)

Group: Tinaja

Ware: Petén Gloss

Ceramic Complex: Eznab

Ceramic Sphere: Tepeu 3

Illustrations: Fig. 52.14; 57.18, 57.23.

Principal identifying attributes: Monochrome red slip the same as Tinaja Red with the addition of modeled decoration.

Identifying characteristics and sorting problems: A few examples of vessels of this type occur in Eznab collections. In most characteristics, the examples are identical to Tinaja Red.

Surface finish and decoration: A face consisting of a crudely modeled nose and eyes occurs on the exterior just below the lip.

Shapes: Small slightly incurving to round-side bowls.

Temporal distribution: Eznab Complex only.

Intersite comparisons: Uaxactun (Smith and Gifford 1966).

Rosa Punctated: Rosa Variety

Established: Smith and Gifford (1966)

Group: Tinaja

Ware: Petén Gloss

Ceramic Complex: Eznab (Begins in Ik and continues into Imix and occasionally Eznab)

Ceramic Sphere: Tepeu 1–2 (occasionally 3)

Illustrations: Fig. 50.11, 50.29, 50.37, 50.46; 51.34, 51.40–41, 51.52. See TR. 25A: fig. 151*d*.

Principal identifying attributes: Surface finish and paste similar to Tinaja Red, with the addition of a single row of punctuated impressions made with a hollow tool on the exterior of large capacity incurving-side bowls.

Identifying characteristics and sorting problems: The occasional examples of large-capacity bowls with a row of impressions made with a hollow circular tool that are noted under the description of Chinja Impressed are technically Rosa Punctated. Rosa Punctated is identical to Tinaja Red except as follows below.

Surface finish and decoration: Rosa Punctated is a highly variable type that includes different kinds of designs on a variety of vessel shapes. The most common examples in the Eznab Complex are tripod dishes. The punctations occur in a line above the break at the vessel base. The punctations are usually small circles, although some diamond-shaped ones also occur. Rosa Punctated also occurs as lines of punctations on jars.

Temporal Distribution: See Chinja Impressed.

Intersite comparisons: For general comparisons see Chinja Impressed. Examples with punctuated fillets are often included in the Chinja Variety at other sites.

ACHOTE CERAMIC GROUP

Achote Black: Achote Variety

Established: Smith and Gifford (1966)

Group: Achote

Ware: Petén Gloss

Ceramic Complex: Eznab

Ceramic Sphere: Tepeu 3

Illustrations: Fig. 52.19–21; 53.20–22, 53.24–25; 56.32. See TR. 25A: fig. 98*a*2,*b*2,*f*; 145*b*; 147*c*; 151*c*2.

Principal identifying attributes: Monochrome black slip on moderately polished surfaces predominately on outflaring-side dishes or round-side bowls.

Identifying characteristics and sorting problems: The type is easily distinguished from all other Eznab Complex types. Typologically, Achote Black does not separate well from Zacec Black of the Imix Complex, but the shapes most common in the two types are different.

Paste: Zacatel Paste.

Firing: Penetration of the black color into the paste indicates that the color was produced by reduction firing; dark cores are rare.

Slip: Thin to medium.

Polish: Quite variable; ranges from low to high.

Color: Color is not well controlled and most sherds show patches in which the black grades off into various shades of brown.

Shapes: The most common shapes in Achote Black are the tripod dish, followed by the slightly incurving to round-side bowls. Some examples of outflaring to slightly outcurving-side dishes and cylinders also occur.

Temporal distribution: Achote Black is considerably more common than the black types of earlier Late Classic complexes. Because the type has a different name from earlier black types, Achote Black at Tikal is confined to the Eznab Complex, but it is only the greater frequency in this complex and the somewhat different assortment of vessel shapes that makes it possible to distinguish Achote Black from Zacec Black in the Ik and Imix Complexes.

Intersite comparisons: Acanmul (Ball and Taschek 2015); Altar de Sacrificios (Adams 1971); Barton Ramie (Gifford 1976); Becan (Ball 1977); Blue Creek (Kosakowsky and Lohse 2003); Calakmul (Dominguez Carrasco 1994); El Mirador (Forsyth 1989); Chan Chich (Valdez and Houk 2000); Colha (Valdez 1987); El Perú/Waka' (Eppich 2011); Holmul (Callaghan 2008, 2016e); La Milpa (Sagebiel 2005); Naachtun (Walker and Reese-Taylor 2012); Nohmul (Kosakowsky and Pring 2001); Rio Azul (Adams 1999; Adams and Jackson-Adams 1991); Seibal (Sabloff 1975) and Uaxactun (Smith and Gifford 1966). Infierno Black is used for the Late Classic at Nakbe (Forsyth 1993).

Cubeta Incised: Cubeta Variety

Established: Smith and Gifford (1966)

Group: Achote

Ware: Petén Gloss

Ceramic Complex: Eznab

Ceramic Sphere: Tepeu 3

Illustrations: Fig. 55.31, 55.39, 55.44, 55.46, 55.48.

Principal identifying attributes: Monochrome black slip on moderately polished surfaces with the addition of simple pre-slip incising on the exterior of vessels.

Identifying characteristics and sorting problems: Cubeta Incised is identical to Achote Black except for the addition of simple horizontal incised lines that encircle the vessels on the exterior. Cubeta Incised is more common at sites in Northern Belize during Tepeu 2/3 than elsewhere in the Maya lowlands.

Intersite comparisons: Chan Chich (Valdez 1998; Valdez and Houk 2000); Colha (Valdez 1987); Seibal (Sabloff 1975); and Uaxactun (Smith and Gifford 1966). Cubeta Incised is used for Spanish Lookout 1 at Barton Ramie (Gifford 1976) and in Tepeu 2 at La Milpa (Sagebiel 2005). Cubeta Incised is used for Tepeu 2/3 at Blue Creek (Kosakowsky and Lohse 2003) and Nohmul (Kosakowsky and Pring 2001).

MAQUINA CERAMIC GROUP

Maquina Brown: Maquina Variety

Established: Smith and Gifford (1966)

Group: Maquina

Ware: Petén Gloss

Ceramic Complex: Eznab (Begins in Ik and continues into Imix and Eznab)

Ceramic Sphere: Tepeu 1–3; most common in Tepeu 3

Illustrations: Fig. 55.30.

Principal identifying attributes: Monochrome brown surfaces that overlap at the extremes with fireclouded Tinaja Red on narrow-mouth jars and large-capacity bowls.

Color: A wide range of colors exists within Maquina Brown without a clustering around any central color. Examples include dark reddish brown (2.5YR 3/4), reddish brown (5YR 4/4, 5/4), brown (7.5YR 5/4), light brown (7.5YR 6/4), grayish brown (10YR 5/2), light brownish gray (10YR 6/2), light yellowish brown (10YR 6/4), and dark yellowish brown (10YR 4/4). These colors range around the edges of the more central reddish shades of Tinaja Red, a fact that increases the probability that many examples called Maquina Brown may be nothing more than misfiring of Tinaja Red.

Shapes: Most examples of Maquina Brown are either narrow-mouth jars or large-capacity incurving-side bowls. These two shapes were separated originally as varieties of the type for counting and in TR. 25A, however, naming varieties on the basis of vessel shape violates the rules of nomenclature in type: variety (Gifford 1976) so both shapes are now included in the Maquina Variety.

Temporal distribution: Maquina Brown sherds occur in all Late Classic complexes. They have a higher frequency of occurrence in the Eznab Complex than in Ik and Imix, but it is possible that this may be an artifact of the better preservation of the Eznab samples.

Intersite Comparisons: Calakmul (Dominguez Carrasco 1994); El Perú/Waka' (Eppich 2011); Holmul (Callaghan 2008, 2016e); Rio Azul (Adams 1999; Adams and Jackson-Adams 1991) and Uaxactun (Smith and Gifford 1966). Some overlap with the Tepeu 2 Tialipa Brown at Barton Ramie (Gifford 1976) and Uaxactun (Smith and Gifford 1966).

Pepet Incised: Pepet Variety

Established: Smith and Gifford (1966)

Group: Maquina

Ware: Petén Gloss

Ceramic Complex: Eznab

Ceramic Sphere: Tepeu 3

Principal identifying attributes: Monochrome brown surfaces that overlap at the extremes with fireclouded Tinaja Red on large capacity incurving-side bowls.

Identifying characteristics and sorting problems: Pepet Incised occurs entirely as large bowls with incurved lip and a restricted orifice that have a single groove around the exterior slightly below the lip. In all other characteristics, Pepet Incised is identical to Maquina Brown.

Intersite comparisons: Uaxactun (Smith and Gifford 1966). An Unspecified Variety is identified in the Tayasal region (Chase 1984). Some overlap with Canoa Incised in Tepeu 2 at Barton Ramie (Gifford 1976); El Perú/Waka' (Eppich 2011); and Uaxactun (Smith and Gifford 1966).

TOH CERAMIC GROUP

Toh Brown: Toh Variety

Established: TR. 25A (Culbert 1993)

Group: Toh

Ware: Petén Gloss

Ceramic Complex: Eznab

Ceramic Sphere: Tepeu 3

Illustrations: Fig. 53.26–30; 56.3.

Principal identifying attributes: Brown surfaces that are heavily pitted and overlap in color with fireclouded Tinaja and Maquina Brown on serving vessels.

Identifying characteristics and sorting problems: The paste, color, and pitting of weathered sherds are the chief diagnostics of the type. The fairly heavy temper and alternating bands of color make the paste easy to recognize, as does the pitting on the surfaces.

Paste: Toh Paste.

Slip: Medium to high polish; pitting of the surface is characteristic of weathered sherds, probably due to the erosion of calcite particles from the paste.

Color: Surface colors mirror those of Maquina Brown and include dark reddish brown (2.5YR 3/4), reddish brown (5YR 4/4, 5/4), brown (7.5YR 5/4), light brown (7.5YR 6/4), grayish brown (10YR 5/2), light brownish gray (10YR 6/2), light yellowish brown (10YR 6/4), and dark yellowish brown (10YR 4/4).

Shapes: Mostly serving vessels among which barrels, cylinders, and tripod dishes occur most commonly.

Temporal distribution: Eznab Complex only.

Intersite comparisons: None specifically noted, due to the pitting on the surfaces, although there may be some overlap with Maquina Brown at other sites in Tepeu 3.

Tott Incised: Tott Variety

Established: TR. 25A (Culbert 1993)

Group: Toh

Ware: Petén Gloss

Ceramic Complex: Eznab

Ceramic Sphere: Tepeu 3

Illustrations: None.

Principal identifying attributes: Brown surfaces that are heavily pitted and overlap in color with fireclouded Tinaja and Maquina Brown on serving vessels. Secondary decoration by means of horizontal incising.

Identifying characteristics and sorting problems: Identical to Toh Brown except for the presence of one or more horizontal lines encircling vessels.

Intersite comparisons: See Toh Brown.

PALMAR CERAMIC GROUP

Palmar Orange Polychrome: Palmar Variety

Established: Smith and Gifford (1966)

Group: Palmar

Ware: Petén Gloss

Ceramic Complex: Eznab (Begins in Imix)

Ceramic Sphere: Tepeu 2–3

Illustrations: Fig. 47.4, 47.14; 48.5–6, 48.9–10, 48.12, 48.15–23; 49.1–3, 49.11; 52.22. See TR. 25A: fig. 97*b*3; 152*c*5.

Principal identifying attributes: Glossy orange slip on a white underslip decorated with red and black designs.

Identifying characteristics and sorting problems: The most easily recognized characteristic is the white background color even though it is overpainted; other colors separate the type from the Saxche Polychrome Group as do many of the shapes involved.

Paste: Zacatel Paste.

Firing: Dark cores and fireclouding are rare.

Slip: As in Zacatel Cream Polychrome a whitish coat was first applied over all surfaces to be decorated. This underslip was then completely covered with the colors noted below.

Polish: Highly polished on well-preserved examples.

Color: The background color is orange (reddish yellow 5YR 7/8, 6/8; light red 2.5YR 6/8; red 2.5YR 5/8). Additional colors are red (red 10R 4/8, 4/6; 7.5R 4/8, 5/8; 5R 5/8; dark red 7.5R 3/8), and black. The black pigment used fires black in an oxidizing atmosphere.

Shapes: Tripod plates, cylinders and slightly incurving to round-side bowls.

Temporal distribution: The great majority of the examples occur in Imix and only a few examples continue to occur in Eznab.

Comments: Many examples of Palmar Orange Polychrome from the Eznab collections are indistinguishable from Imix Complex examples. Quite a few others, however, lack the distinctive underslip that was characteristic of earlier examples and/or show unevenness in the color of orange slip. In addition, the motifs on Eznab examples are less varied than those of Imix examples. In the Eznab Complex, quatrefoils are a very common motif as are various designs involving simple dots. Quite a few complex designs still appear, however, and there is no concentration on a single design as there is in Eznab examples of Zacatel Cream Polychrome.

Intersite comparisons: Altar de Sacrificios (Adams 1971); Barton Ramie (Gifford 1976); Becan (Ball 1977); Blue Creek (Kosakowsky and Lohse 2003); Calakmul (Dominguez Carrasco 1994); Chan (Kosakowsky 2012); Chan Chich (Valdez 1998; Valdez and Houk 2000); Colha (Valdez 1987); El Mirador (Forsyth 1989); Holmul (Callaghan 2008, 2016e); El Peru/Waka' (Eppich 2011); La Milpa (Sagebiel 2005); Naachtun (Walker and Reese-Taylor 2012); Nakbe (Forsyth 1993); Nohmul (Kosakowsky and

Pring 2001); Piedras Negras (Muñoz 2006); Rio Azul (Adams 1999; Adams and Jackson-Adams 1991); Uaxactun (Smith and Gifford 1966); Xunantunich (LeCount 1996). At Seibal, Palmar is lumped with Saxche (Sabloff 1975) and in the Petexbatun it is lumped with Zacatel (Foias and Bishop 2013).

Chantuori Black-on-orange: Chantuori Variety

Established: Smith and Gifford (1966)

Group: Palmar

Ware: Petén Gloss

Ceramic Complex: Eznab (Begins in Imix)

Ceramic Sphere: Tepeu 2–3

Identifying Attributes: Glossy orange slip similar to Palmar Orange Polychrome with the addition of black decoration.

Identifying characteristics and sorting problems: Type is misprinted as "Chantouri" in Culbert (TR. 25A). It is usually impossible to determine which sherds belonged to this type because small sherds with only black and orange may have had additional colors on missing sections. In the absence of whole vessels, sherds are difficult to sort. Chantuori Black-on-orange examples from Eznab collections are identical to Eznab samples of Palmar Orange Polychrome except that they lack red as a part of the decoration.

Intersite comparisons: Uaxactun (Smith and Gifford 1966).

Zacatel Cream Polychrome: Zacatel Variety

Established: Smith and Gifford (1966)

Group: Palmar

Ware: Petén Gloss

Ceramic Complex: Eznab (Begins in Imix)

Ceramic Sphere: Tepeu 2–3

Illustrations: Fig. 47.2, 47.6–9, 47.14–15; 48.1–4, 48.7–8, 48.11, 48.13–14; 49.4–6, 49.8–10, 49.13. See TR. 25A: fig. 97*b*1; 98*d–e*; 151*b*1.

Principal identifying attributes: White to cream glossy slip that matches the underslip on Palmar Orange Polychrome, decorated secondarily with red, black and red-orange designs.

Identifying characteristics and sorting problems: The most easily recognized characteristic is the white slip that underlies all other colors, a characteristic that is not found in the Saxche Polychrome Group; other colors separate the type from the Saxche Group as do many of the shapes involved.

Paste: Zacatel Paste.

Firing: Dark cores and fireclouding are rare.

Slip: A whitish coat was first applied over all surfaces to be decorated. Additional colors were painted over this coat, leaving some areas uncovered to use the whitish layer as part of the design.

Polish: Highly polished on well-preserved examples.

Color: The initial layer is not cream but white (10YR 8/1, 8/2; 2.5Y 8/2), pale brown (10YR 8/3), or pinkish white (5YR 8/2). The most common additional colors are red (red 10R 4/8, 4/6; 7.5R 4/8, 5/8; 5R 5/8; dark red 7.5R 3/8), orange (reddish yellow 5YR 7/8, 6/8; light red 2.5YR 6/8; red 2.5YR 5/8), and black. A weak red (10R 5/4) or pale red (10R 6/4) that is clearly intentional is used in small areas on some examples. The black pigment used fires black in an oxidizing atmosphere.

Shapes: Barrels, cylinders, outflaring to slightly outcurving-side bowls, tripod dishes and plates.

Temporal distribution: The great majority of the examples occur in Imix and a few examples continue to occur in Eznab.

Comments: While Zacatel Cream Polychrome shares the color of the Palmar Orange Polychrome underslip and was therefore grouped together, subsequent researchers have chosen to place the Zacatel type in a separate group. This is more closely aligned with type: variety nomenclature, which is based on surface color and characteristics (Gifford 1976). Some examples of the Zacatel Variety continue to appear in Eznab Complex samples, although the variety is far less common than in the Imix Complex. The only way in which Eznab examples differ from those of Imix is that the number of designs represented is far more restricted. The great majority of Eznab examples are Muan feather designs, usually associated with red bar patterns on another part of the vessel.

Intersite comparisons: Altar de Sacrificios (Adams 1971); Barton Ramie (Gifford 1976); Becan (Ball 1977); Blue Creek (Kosakowsky and Lohse 2003); Colha (Valdez 1987); La Milpa (Sagebiel 2005); Nakbe (Forsyth 1993); Nohmul (Kosakowsky and Pring 2001); the Petexbatun (Foias and Bishop 2013); Rio Azul (Adams 1999; Adams and Jackson-Adams 1991); Uaxactun (Smith and Gifford 1966); Xunantunich (LeCount 1996). At Seibal, it is part of the Saxche/Palmar Group (Sabloff 1975). At El Mirador (Forsyth 1989) and Holmul (Callaghan 2008, 2016e), it is placed in the separate Zacatel Group.

Zacatel Cream Polychrome: Zacpech Variety

Established: Type named by Smith and Gifford (1966); Variety named by Culbert (1993 [TR. 25])

Group: Palmar

Ware: Petén Gloss

Ceramic Complex: Eznab

Ceramic Sphere: Tepeu 3

Principal identifying attributes: Pinkish tone to white/cream glossy slip decorated secondarily with red, black and red-orange designs.

Identifying characteristics and sorting problems: The pinkish tone of the "cream" exteriors is quite distinctive and there are only a few examples that overlap with the range of the Zacatel Variety.

Paste: Mostly Zacatel Paste, but there are a fair number of examples that are indistinguishable from Saxche Polychrome Paste.

Firing: Dark cores are rare. Some firing-related discoloration of the surface occurs on about one-third of the examples.

Slip: An underslip is present on most sherds, but is thinner and less noticeable than on the Zacatel Variety.

Polish: Medium on interior orange surfaces; low on exterior cream surfaces.

Color: The cream is far less white than in the Zacatel Variety. In the Zacpech Variety it ranges from pink (7.5YR 7/4, 8/4) through reddish yellow (7.5YR 7/6) to very pale brown (10YR 7/4, 8/3, 8/4). Some examples that seem to be misfired are yellow brown (10YR 5/4). The interior is usually red (2.5YR 5/8) to reddish yellow (5YR 6/8), sometimes with additional "redder" bands (10R 4/6).

Surface finish and decoration: The interior of the vessels is always simple, usually a solid "orange" with either red or black band at the lip. Bands of black "horseshoes" around the interior lip are also common. By far the most common exterior decoration is the Muan feather design, although other geometric designs also occur on some examples. The design range is certainly much smaller than on Imix Complex examples of the Zacatel Variety.

Shapes: The same as those of the Zacatel Variety.

Temporal distribution: Eznab Complex only.

Intersite comparisons: See Zacatel Cream Polychrome: Zacatel Variety as the pinkish cast to this variety is likely included in the Zacatel Variety at other sites.

Chinos Black-on-cream: Chinos Variety

Established: Smith and Gifford (1966)

Group: Palmar

Ware: Petén Gloss

Ceramic Complex: Eznab (Begins in Imix)

Ceramic Sphere: Tepeu 2–3

Illustrations: See TR. 25A: fig. 97*b*2.

Principal identifying attributes: Glossy white slip decorated with black designs.

Identifying characteristics and sorting problems: It is usually difficult to identify on sherds because small sherds with only black and white may have had additional colors on missing sections. As with Zacatel "Cream" Polychrome, the background color is actually white. The type is identical to Zacatel Cream Polychrome except it lacks any red or red-orange, and is decorated with only black on white or cream.

Surface finish and decoration: The designs seem to cover the same range from simple to complex that is seen in Zacatel Cream Polychrome.

Shapes: In shape as well as decoration the small sample available seems to cover the same range as Zacatel Cream Polychrome.

Intersite comparisons: Becan (Ball 1977) and Uaxactun (Smith and Gifford 1966). At El Mirador (Forsyth 1989), it is placed in the Zacatel Group.

Naranjal Red-on-cream: Naranjal Variety

Established: Smith and Gifford (1966)

Group: Palmar

Ware: Petén Gloss

Ceramic Complex: Eznab (Begins in Imix)

Ceramic Sphere: Tepeu 2–3

Illustrations: Fig. 55.45. See TR. 25A: fig. 152*c*1.

Principal identifying attributes: Glossy white to cream slip decorated secondarily with red designs.

Identifying characteristics and sorting problems: It is usually difficult to identify on sherds because small sherds with only red and cream may have had additional colors on missing sections. A few sherds of Naranjal Red-on-cream appear in the Eznab collections. The sherds are too small to permit significant description. One whole vessel, an outflaring-side bowl with red lip band on the interior and a simple design on the exterior, dates to the Eznab Complex.

Intersite comparisons: Uaxactun (Smith and Gifford 1966).

Yuhactal Black-on-red: Yuhactal Variety

Established: Smith and Gifford (1966)

Group: Palmar

Ware: Petén Gloss

Ceramic Complex: Eznab (Begins in Imix)

Ceramic Sphere: Tepeu 2–3

Principal identifying attributes: Glossy red surface over a white underslip, and secondary decoration with black lines.

Paste: Zacatel Paste.

Slip: The same white underslip that characterizes the Palmar Group was applied first, then overpainted with black and red.

Colors: Colors cover the same range as typical for the Palmar Group.

Surface color and decoration: A red background with broad black horizontal or diagonal bands also occurs as do narrow lines of black on red. No complex designs appear in the small sample. Decoration also consists of a red lip band or bands with the rest of the vessel entirely black.

Shapes: Unknown (sherds too small to identify form).

Intersite comparisons: Barton Ramie (Gifford 1976); Becan (Ball 1977); Mayapan (Smith 1971);

Uaxactun (Smith and Gifford 1966).

Jato Black-on-gray: Jato Variety

Established: Smith and Gifford (1966)

Group: Palmar

Ware: Petén Gloss

Ceramic Complex: Eznab

Ceramic Sphere: Tepeu 3

Principal identifying attributes: Surface colors are reddish gray with the addition of bands of black outlining grooved sections on the exterior of vessels.

Identifying characteristics and sorting problems: Quite distinctive; small sherds merge with misfired or smudged examples of dichromes and polychromes.

Paste: Usually Zacatel Paste.

Slip: Two coats of slip are applied, the first producing the gray color, the second, black. Whether the slips are different or simply the same applied in different thicknesses is impossible to determine.

Polish: Gray sections, very low; black sections, medium to high.

Color: Gray is reddish gray (10R 5/1).

Surface finish and decoration: Simple bands of black on the gray base. Frequently, grooved areas outline the different sections.

Shapes: Cylinders, outflaring to slightly outcurving-side dishes, and slightly incurving to round-side bowls.

Temporal distribution: Eznab Complex only.

Intersite comparisons: At El Perú/Waka' (Eppich 2011) it is placed in the Zacatel Group during the Late Classic (Tepeu 1), and Uaxactun (Smith and Gifford 1966).

TEABO CERAMIC GROUP

Sahcaba Molded-carved: Sahcaba Variety

Established: Smith and Gifford (1966); Originally called Modeled-carved.

Group: Teabo

Ware: Puuc Red

Ceramic Complex: Eznab

Ceramic Sphere: Tepeu 3

Illustrations: TR. 25A: fig. 145*a*.

Principal identifying attributes: Molded-carved decoration with a thin red slip.

Identifying characteristics and sorting problems: The style of decoration is similar to the Fine Orange type Pabellon Molded-carved. Most examples of Sahcaba can be separated from Pabellon on the basis of pastes, although some pieces overlap between the types and pose sorting problems.

Paste: Unspecified.

Firing: Dark cores and fireclouding are rare.

Slip: Thin slip applied to well-polished surface.

Polish: Low.

Color: Red (10R 5/8; 2.5YR 5/8).

Surface finish and decoration: Design panels were produced by molds. The Tikal example is from PD. 133, described in TR. 15 and TR. 33C.

Shapes: Most commonly a pyriform vase with pedestal base; some round-side bowls.

Temporal distribution: Occurs throughout the Eznab Complex.

Intersite comparisons: Teabo Red and the Teabo Ceramic Group identified at Acanmul (Ball and Taschek 2015); Becan (Ball 1977); Caracol (Chase and Chase 2004); Edzna (Forsyth 1979); and Mayapan (Smith 1971).

ALTAR CERAMIC GROUP

Altar Orange: Altar Variety

Established: Adams (1971)

Group: Altar

Ware: Fine Orange

Ceramic Complex: Eznab

Ceramic Sphere: Tepeu 3

Principal identifying attributes: Thin light reddish slip on a fine orange paste without temper.

Identifying characteristics and sorting problems: Most examples can be easily recognized on the basis of the very distinctive color of Fine Orange Paste. Some examples, however, are very close to the range of Tinaja Red pieces made from the fine Taman Paste.

Paste: Fine Orange Paste.

Firing: Dark cores and fireclouding very rare.

Slip: Thin and hard to distinguish from paste.

Polish: Low.

Color: The most common color ranges from light red (2.5YR 6/8) to red (2.5YR 5/6, 5/8), but on many pieces the color ranges to dark brown (10YR 4/3) or black in some areas. Whether the black color is an additional wash as suggested by Sabloff (1975:18a) cannot be determined from Tikal examples.

Shapes: Slightly incurving to round-side bowls, barrels, outflaring to slightly outcurving-side tripod plates, and pyriform vases with pedestal bases occur. It should be noted that the utilitarian forms reported for Altar Orange at Altar de Sacrificios (Adams 1971) are noticeably absent at Tikal.

Temporal distribution: Eznab Complex only but appears to occur throughout the time of the complex.

Intersite comparisons: Altar de Sacrificios (Adams 1971); El Perú/Waka' (Eppich 2011); and Seibal (Sabloff 1975).

Trapiche Incised: Trapiche Variety

Established: Smith and Gifford (1966)

Group: Altar

Ware: Fine Orange

Ceramic Complex: Eznab

Ceramic Sphere: Tepeu 3

Principal identifying attributes: Same as Altar Orange with the addition of simple incised lines on the exterior of vessels.

Identifying characteristics and sorting problems: A few sherds that are otherwise indistinguishable from Altar Orange have simple incised lines encircling the exterior of dishes, plates, or barrels. Usually there is only a single line; occasionally there may be two or three. Trapiche Incised is a definitive Terminal Classic marker at many lowland sites.

Intersite comparisons: Acanmul (Ball and Taschek 2015); Altar de Sacrificios (Adams 1971); Becan (Ball 1977); El Perú/Waka' (Eppich 2011); Holmul (Callaghan 2008, 2016e); and Seibal (Sabloff 1975).

Pabellon Molded (Modeled)-carved: Pabellon Variety

Established: Smith and Gifford (1966). Originally called "modeled-carved," however, the decoration is in fact molded and the type name has been corrected.

Group: Altar

Ware: Fine Orange

Ceramic Complex: Eznab

Ceramic Sphere: Tepeu 3

Illustrations: TR. 25A: fig. 98c1.

Principal identifying attributes: Same as Altar Orange with the addition of molded-carved decoration on the exterior of vessels.

Identifying characteristics and sorting problems: Pabellon Molded-carved is identical to Altar Orange except for the categories discussed below.

Surface finish and decoration: A molded design is applied to the exterior of the vessels.

Shapes: Most examples are from pyriform vases with pedestal vases; some are from slightly incurving to round-side bowls.

Intersite comparisons: Altar de Sacrificios (Adams 1971); Becan (Ball 1977); Calakmul (Dominguez Carrasco 1994); El Perú/Waka' (Eppich 2011); El Mirador (Forsyth 1989); Holmul (Callaghan 2008, 2016e); Rio Azul (Adams 1999; Adams and Jackson-Adams 1991); Seibal (Sabloff 1975); Uaxactun (Smith and Gifford: 1966); and Xunantunich (LeCount 1996). May be related to "San Jose V Carved Orange Ware" (Thompson 1939).

Tumba Black-on-orange: Tumba Variety

Established: Smith and Gifford (1966)

Group: Altar

Ware: Fine Orange

Ceramic Complex: Eznab

Ceramic Sphere: Tepeu 3

Principal identifying attributes: Surface the same as Altar Orange with the addition of monochrome black bands or semicircles on the exterior of vessels.

Identifying characteristics and sorting problems: The fact that many pieces of Altar Orange have a slip that misfires to black in some areas makes it difficult to determine whether small sherds with some black belong in Altar or Tumba. Tumba Black-on-orange is identical to Altar Orange except in the categories that follow:

Slip: A thin black slip with low polish is added over the original orange slip.

Surface finish and decoration: Simple bands or solid semicircles of black are the most common decoration.

Shapes: Although the same shapes reported for Altar Orange occur in Tumba Black-on-orange, slightly incurving to round-side bowls are by far the most common shape for the Tumba type.

Intersite comparisons: Acanmul (Ball and Taschek 2015); Altar de Sacrificios (Adams 1971); Becan (Ball 1977); El Perú/Waka' (Eppich 2011); Seibal (Sabloff 1975). It may be the same as an example from San Jose (Thompson 1939).

Eznab Types: Chronological Change

Although there is clear continuity between the Imix and Eznab Complexes in production techniques and the most important ceramic types, there are also pronounced quantitative differences that make separation of the two complexes unmistakable. One of the most obvious differences is the decline in polychrome (and dichrome) decoration between Imix and Eznab. Although the extreme weathering that made typological counts impossible for many Imix samples weakens quantitative comparison, it can be conservatively estimated that almost all Imix samples included at least 25% polychromes. Among Eznab samples, two-thirds have less than 5% polychromes. There are also important ways in which the polychromes that do occur in the Eznab collections differ from Imix polychromes. First, there is a reduction in the number of decorative motifs represented in Eznab, a reduction most obvious in Zacatel Cream Polychrome but also present to a lesser degree in Palmar Orange Polychrome. Second, the appearance of the Zacpech Variety of Zacatel Cream Polychrome, characterized by a pink to tan background rather than the cream of the Zacatel Variety, seems to represent a deterioration of the firm control of colors present in the Zacatel Variety. Similar deterioration of color control is also noticeable in some examples of Eznab Complex Palmar Orange Polychrome, although in this case the differences are not consistent enough to designate a separate variety. It should be stressed, however, that these changes are by no means universal in Eznab polychromes, as a substantial number of Eznab examples are every bit as good as Imix examples in both color and sophistication of design. It would be very satisfying if it could be demonstrated that the number of polychromes of inferior quality increased through time during the Eznab Complex, but there is no immediately obvious evidence that such was the case.

The decline in frequencies of polychromes in the Eznab Complex is matched by an increase in the frequency of Tinaja Red. The majority of Tinaja Red vessels in Eznab are the same narrow-mouth jars and large bowls characteristic of the type in Imix. In addition, however, a variety of "serving-vessel" shapes in the Eznab collections are Tinaja Red while the counterpart shapes in Imix are almost invariably of decorated types. These shapes include the outflaring to slightly outcurving-side tripod dish or plate, cylinder, and round-side bowls. Such serving vessels of Tinaja Red provide a good type fossil for the Eznab Complex.

Another major change between the Imix and Eznab Complexes is a sharp increase in the type Cambio Unslipped. Finally, the Eznab Complex is marked by the appearance of a number of new types. All of the types of the Altar Fine Orange Group first appear at Tikal in Eznab samples, as does the related Sahcaba Molded-carved. Toh Brown is a distinctive new type of local origin as is Jato Black-on-gray. None of these new types is common, and each of them is missing from at least half the Eznab samples.

An attempt was made to follow typological change within the time period represented by the Eznab Complex by seriating Eznab type samples. An arrangement can be made that suggests an increase in the frequency of Cambio Unslipped from the beginning to the end of the Eznab Complex, accompanied by a decrease in Tinaja Red. Polychrome types are most common in the early segment of the seriation and decrease thereafter, a trend that is very roughly paralleled by Achote Black. The patterns for the seriation are not very convincing, not due to a lack of actual temporal trends within Eznab, but rather to the considerable mixing that has gone on in deposits associated with Eznab occupation at Tikal.

Eznab Types: Social Dimension

The range of archaeological contexts represented by Eznab Complex collections is very limited. In nearly all cases, the samples derive from middens in and around vaulted masonry structures. Such structures obviously served a residential purpose, but it was residence uniformly associated with a lack of construction and maintenance and even with a failure to remove trash from the neighborhood of living areas. One would certainly suspect that there was less class stratification among Eznab populations. There are, of course, substantial differences in type frequencies between Eznab samples. Some of these differences may be of temporal significance; others may be due to random chance or to activity differences that leave no other clues than ceramic frequencies. Unless there are differences in other kinds of artifacts between Eznab lots that suggest activity patterns with which ceramic differences might be associated, the ceramic variations between samples must remain unexplained. The non-vessel offerings in Eznab burials and their recovery contexts do indicate a certain degree of social stratification, but nothing like that in previous Late Classic times (Moholy-Nagy 1994; TR. 27A).

Vessel Shapes of the Eznab Complex

Introduction

Six major shape classes and eleven shapes, listed in Table 10.5 appear in Eznab Complex collections. There is also a miniature vessel shape class and three miniature shapes present in Eznab. A number of distinctive and common shapes appeared for the first time in the Eznab Complex and make it one of the easiest of Tikal complexes to recognize.

Eznab Shape Descriptions

SHAPE CLASS 1: WIDE-MOUTH JARS

Wide-mouth Jar (with Tall Neck)

Illustrations: Fig. 39.20–24, 39.30–38; 52.26–31; 53.1–15; 55.1–9, 55.11–19.

TABLE 10.5
Shape Classes and Shapes of the Eznab Complex

1. **Wide-mouth Jars**

   Wide-mouth Jar (with Tall Neck)

2. **Narrow-mouth Jars**

   Narrow-mouth Jar (with Tall Neck or Bulging Neck)

4. **Large Capacity Bowls**

   Large Incurving-side Bowl

5. **Medium Bowls and Dishes**

   Outflaring to Slightly Outcurving-side Tripod Dish

   Slightly Incurving to Round-side Tripod Bowl

6. **Small Diameter Bowls and Dishes**

   Outflaring to Slightly Outcurving-side Bowl or Dish

   Slightly Incurving to Round-side Bowl

7. **Cylindrical Vessels**

   Barrel

   Pyriform Vase with Pedestal Base

   Cylinder

9. **Large Plates**

   Large Tripod Plate

11. **Miniature Vessels**

    Miniature Jar

    Miniature Bowl or Cylinder

    Miniature Pyriform Vase with Pedestal Base

Comments: The basic characteristics of the shape continue to be the same as those described in the Ik Complex. The varieties of lip represented are quantitatively different in the Eznab Complex.

Lip: All of the lip varieties that occur in the Late Classic complexes continue to appear in Eznab. However, the rounded and rolled lips that are most characteristic of the Ik Complex are no longer common in Eznab, but the flattened and grooved varieties of Imix continue in considerable frequency. Two new lip varieties appear frequently enough in Eznab samples so that they were given names and counted separately. One is the forward-extended lip, in which the upper surface of the lip is either grooved or flattened in a manner that makes the lip broadened on both the interior and exterior surfaces, in contrast to the more common manner in which the lip is broadened only on the exterior. The second new lip variety has a profile that resembles one-half of an arrowhead. As in other complexes, there is great variety in lip treatment so that separation of lip varieties demands many difficult choices.

NARROW-MOUTH JARS

Narrow-mouth Jar (with Tall Neck)

Shape Variant: Tall Neck

Illustrations: Fig. 55.10, 55.21, 55.23–24. See TR. 25A: fig. 145*c*; 147*e*.

Shape Variant: Bulging Neck

Illustrations: Fig. 52.22–23; 54.17–29; 55.20, 55.22. See TR. 25A: fig. 145*g*.

Identifying characteristics and sorting problems: The shape is very easy to identify.

Base and body: No whole examples, but sherds suggest flat base and globular body.

Neck-body juncture: Angular and well marked.

Neck: Restricted at the neck-body juncture and at the point where rim eversion starts. Often rounded outward between these points to give the appearance of bulging.

Rim: Everted, usually quite sharply.

Lip: Usually pointed, sometimes rounded.

Surface: Slipped on vessel exterior and on interior of neck.

Types: Tinaja Red; Maquina Brown.

Lip diameter: The tall neck jar has a median orifice diameter of 16.0 cm. Two size classes are represented in bulging-neck jars. Large: range 18–24 cm; median 20 cm. Small: all examples 14 cm.

Neck height (Tall neck): 5.6 cm. median neck height.

Neck height (Bulging-neck variant): Large: range 5.6–9.4 cm; median 6.9 cm. Small: 4.4–5.8 cm; median 4.6 cm.

Lip diameter/neck height ratio (Tall neck): Median 2.9.

Lip diameter/neck height ratio (Bulging neck variant): Large: range 2.0–4.0; median 3.0. Small: range 2.4–3.2; median 3.0.

Temporal distribution: Eznab Complex.

Comments: The Narrow-mouth jar with tall neck shape continues to appear in the Eznab Complex. It is still the most common narrow-mouth jar in Eznab, but now shares the shape class with the bulging-neck variant that appears for the first time in Eznab. The bulging neck is one of the excellent markers for the Eznab Complex and is common enough so that it is likely to occur in most collections of medium size.

Shape class: 2, narrow-mouth jars.

SHAPE CLASS 4: LARGE CAPACITY BOWLS

Large Incurving-side Bowl

Illustrations: Fig. 50.1–52; 51.1–62; 52.1–9; 53.31–34, 53.37–42; 54.8–13; 55.29, 55.30, 55.32–38. See TR. 25A: fig. 145*e–f*.

Identifying characteristics and sorting problems: Includes examples with incurved rims, and slightly restricted orifices.

Base: Flat.

Orientation of side: Medium to strong restriction of orifice.

Side: Rounded.

Rim: Direct or incurving.

Lip: Rounded, pointed, or slightly beveled. The wall just below the lip is usually somewhat thicker than the wall below.

Surface: About half the examples are unslipped on the interior; the remainder are carelessly slipped. The exterior is slipped, but the section of the wall near the base is often poorly finished and sometimes unslipped.

Types: Mostly Cameron Incised and Tinaja Red as well as Chinja Impressed. Maquina Brown and Pepet Incised occur in very low frequencies.

Diameter: All large bowls of the Eznab Complex show a range of 26 to 46 cm.

Height: The few complete examples show heights of 6.8 to 9.0 cm; this is probably at the low edge of the actual range.

Diameter/height ratio: Two measurable examples: 2.4 to 3.4.

Shape class: 4, large-capacity bowls.

Temporal distribution: Occurs in all Late/Terminal Classic complexes, but is slightly more common in the Eznab Complex.

Comments: Originally separated into three variants in TR. 25A, with restricted orifice, with gradual incurved rim and with sharply incurved rim, however, these are all slightly different rim forms of the same basic vessel shape, a large incurving-side bowl.

SHAPE CLASS 5: MEDIUM DIAMETER BOWLS AND DISHES

Outflaring to Slightly Outcurving-side Tripod Dish

Illustrations: Fig. 52.10–15; 53.20–22. TR. 25A: fig. 97*b*1,*d*3; 98*a*2–3,*c*2,*f*; 122*b*; 145*b*; 147*c*; 152*a*7.

Identifying characteristics and sorting problems: Sherds that do not include feet or ridges might be sorted as outcurving-side dishes. Originally classified as Tripod Dish with Ridge at Base or Composite Silhouette Tripod Bowl or Dish (TR. 25A).

Base: Slightly rounded. Some examples of Achote

Black have a slight ridge just at the point where the wall joins the base.

Orientation of side: Medium outflaring to outcurving.

Rim: Direct or everted.

Lip: Rounded or pointed.

Feet: Rounded, both small and large.

Orientation of side: The upper section of the side is vertical to slightly outflaring or outcurving. This short section joins a widely outflaring lower section at a sharp angle.

Feet: One example has still-attached bulbous feet.

Surface: Slip is present on all surfaces including exterior base.

Types: Predominately Achote Black, but also Tinaja Red, Cameron Incised, and types of the Altar Fine Orange Group are all represented.

Diameter: Range: 20–21 cm; median 20 cm.

Height (without feet): Range: 5.7–7.6 cm; median 6.2 cm.

Diameter/height ratio: Range: 2.6–3.6; median 3.3.

Shape class: 5, medium bowls and dishes.

Temporal distribution: Achote Black examples are confined to the Eznab Complex. Although the total shape is a good Eznab type fossil, sherds without feet attached do not serve to identify it.

Slightly Incurving to Round-side Tripod Bowl

Illustrations: Fig. 52.16–17; 53.35–36, 53.44–48; 55.25–26, 55.47. See TR. 25A: fig. 98*a*1; 152*a*4; 152*c*2.

Identifying characteristics and sorting problems: The short insloping or highly incurving upper section makes the shape easy to identify when the feet are present. Originally separated into two variants: Insloping Tripod Dish and Round-side Tripod Dish in TR. 25A.

Base: Slightly rounded.

Orientation of side: Incurving.

Side: Upper section is slightly incurving, although in one example strongly rounded; lower section rounded.

Rim: Direct.

Lip: Rounded or pointed.

Feet: Rounded or somewhat pointed hollow feet.

Surface: Slipped on all surfaces including exterior base.

Decoration: Painted decoration never occurs. One example shows *molcajete*-like incising on the interior base of a bowl, which may have served as a grater bowl.

Types: Usually Tinaja Red, often with Toh paste; some examples of Toh Brown.

Diameter: Range: 14–22 cm; median 18 cm. Although the median diameter falls within the range of small diameter bowls and dishes, most examples are of medium size.

Height (without feet): Range (3 examples): 5.0–6.4 cm.

Diameter/height ratio: Range (3 examples): 2.8–3.5.

Shape class: 5, medium bowls and dishes.

Temporal distribution: Confined to the Eznab Complex.

Comments: This distinctive shape is one of the excellent shape markers that make the Eznab Complex easy to identify.

SHAPE CLASS 6: SMALL DIAMETER BOWLS AND DISHES

Outflaring to Slightly Outcurving-side Bowl or Dish

Illustrations: Fig. 47.2–3, 47.5, 47.9; 55.41–44. See TR. 25A: fig. 98*d*; 151*b*2,*c*2; 153*b*.

Identifying characteristics and sorting problems: There is considerable variety within this shape, but the best examples with thin, nearly vertical walls and slight outcurve are quite easy to recognize even from sherds. In sherds, some examples are hard to distinguish from cylinders. One example seems more outflaring than outcurving (see TR. 25A: fig. 152*c*1).

Base: Usually flat; sometimes slightly concave.

Orientation of side: Slight to medium outflare.

Side: Usually slightly outcurving; some are medium outcurve. Wall relatively thin.

Rim: Direct.

Lip: Most examples are rounded; some are pointed or rounded bevel.

Types: Achote Black

Diameter: Range 10–44 cm (mostly 10–28 cm); median 18 cm.

Height: Range 4–11 cm; median 7 cm.

Diameter/height ratio: Range 1.0–3.6; median 2.6.

Temporal distribution: Similar shapes occur in all complexes, but in the Late and Terminal Classic the shape is most frequent in the Imix Complex, and less common in Eznab.

Shape class: 6, small-diameter bowls and dishes.

Slightly Incurving to Round-side Bowl or Dish

Illustrations: Fig. 52.14, 52.18–21; 53.24–30, 53.49; 55.27–28, 55.31, 55.48.

Identifying characteristics and sorting problems: Little problem in identification.

Base: The side merges gradually into a small flat area at the base.

Orientation of side: Incurving.

Side: Rounded.

Rim: Usually direct; some examples are everted just below the lip.

Lip: Rounded or pointed.

Surface: Slipped on all surfaces.

Types: A wide variety of types are represented. Tinaja Red is the most common, but other monochrome such as Achote Black, incised types, and all the types of the Altar Fine Orange group also occur frequently. Painted decoration is rare.

Diameter: Range: 12–30 cm; median 20 cm.

Height: Range: 5.0–10.0 cm; median 7.8 cm.

Diameter/height ratio: Range: 1.8–2.8 cm; median 2.6 cm.

Shape class: 6, small-diameter bowls and dishes.

Temporal distribution: The shape occurs in all Tikal complexes. It becomes somewhat more common in the Eznab Complex than in the Late Classic complexes.

SHAPE CLASS 7: CYLINDRICAL VESSELS

Barrel

Identifying characteristics and sorting problems: The relatively thin walls and restricted orifice are the best diagnostics of the shape. There is a nearly continuous overlap with round-side bowls with the two shapes separated on the basis of diameter/height ratio with ratio below 1.5 considered to denote barrel. Among sherds, where the diameter/height ratio cannot be calculated, those with restricted orifice were considered barrels.

Base: About equally divided between flat and slightly concave.

Orientation of side: Slightly restricted orifice.

Side: Rounded, medium curvature.

Rim: Direct.

Lip: Usually pointed; sometimes rounded.

Surface: Interior: usually single color and carelessly finished. Exterior: lip band (usually black) occurs on most examples. The most frequent additional decoration is a band of motifs at mid-point or above on the exterior. Overall exterior decoration also occurs. Glyphs may occur as part of single-band decoration or above additional decoration. In most cases, glyphic inscriptions are meaningful.

Types: Tinaja Red and occasional polychromes. Some examples of Achote Black and Toh Brown.

Diameter: Range 8–20 cm; median 14 cm.

Height: Range 8–14 cm; median 12 cm.

Diameter/height ratio: Range 0.7–1.5; median 1.2.

Temporal distribution: Some barrels occur in the Manik Complex. The shape becomes considerably more frequent in the Ik Complex. Barrels appear in low frequency in Imix and become somewhat more common again in Eznab.

Shape class: 7, cylindrical vessels.

Pyriform Vase with Pedestal Base

Illustrations: Fig. 55.45–46. See TR. 25A: fig. 98*c*1; 145*a*.

Identifying characteristics and sorting problems: The barrel with pedestal is separated from the barrel by the pedestal and by the more exaggerated pear shape of the body. Because these characteristics cannot be noted for sherds, both kinds of barrel were sorted as a single category for sherd samples. There is little overlap with any other vessel shape.

Base: Flat to slightly rounded.

Orientation of side: Slightly restricted orifice.

Side: The vessel is widest just above the base. Above this point, the side is nearly straight and slopes inward to give a characteristic pear shape. On a few examples, the side is recurved so that the upper section is slightly outcurving.

Rim: Direct.

Lip: Rounded or pointed.

Pedestal: Usually 1–3 cm high with bottom either direct or everted. One example has a low annular base.

Surface: Exterior carefully finished; interior less so.

Decoration: Two kinds of decoration occur. One consists of panels of Molded-carved decoration at the exterior mid-point. The other consists of multiple grooved or incised lines just below the lip on the exterior.

Types: Pabellon Molded-carved, Sahcaba Molded-carved, Cameron Incised, Tott Incised, and Tinaja Red are all represented.

Diameter: Range 20–22 cm; median 9 cm.

Height: Range 15.0–20.0 cm; median 17.6 cm.

Diameter/height ratio: Range: 0.4–0.6; median 0.5.

Shape class: 7, cylindrical vessels.

Temporal distribution: Confined to the Eznab Complex.

Cylinder

Illustrations: Fig. 55.39. See TR. 25A: fig. 145*d*.

Identifying characteristics and sorting problems: The straight, vertical side identifies the shape well. There is a minor overlap with the barrel shape. There are both small and large cylinders.

Base: Flat to slightly concave.

Orientation of side: Vertical or nearly so.

Side: Straight to very slightly outcurving.

Rim: Direct.

Lip: Usually rounded; rarely pointed, rounded, bevel or nearly flat.

Diameter: Range 6–28 cm; median 12 cm. The distribution of diameter measurements is weakly bimodal with a smaller and more common cylinder ranging between 6 and 14 cm in diameter and a larger ranging from 16 to 28 cm. Among whole vessels most of the larger cylinders occur in Bu. 116.

Height: Range 8–30 cm; median 18 cm. The large-diameter group ranges from 22 to 30 cm in height, while the smaller group ranges from 8 to 24 cm.

Diameter/height ratio: Range 0.4–1.0; median 0.6. The large and small groups do not differ significantly in diameter/height ratio.

Types: Tinaja Red is the most common though there are occasional polychrome examples, as well as Achote Black and Toh Brown.

Temporal distribution: Most characteristic of the Imix Complex, but quite common in Ik and Eznab.

Shape class: 7, cylindrical vessels.

SHAPE CLASS 9: LARGE PLATES

Large Tripod Plate

Illustrations: Fig. 53.16–19; 54.1–7; 55.40. See TR. 25A: fig. 97*b*3; 98*e*.

Identifying characteristics and sorting problems: If the notched ridge is present, the shape is unmistakable, however, it overlaps with the outflaring or slightly outcurving medium tripod dish. It is differentiated on the basis of its large size.

Comments: The shape continued with little change

in the Eznab Complex, but, like most serving-vessel shapes, the number of polychrome examples declined drastically and was replaced by a predominantly monochrome tradition. The appearance of monochrome examples of the shape is, therefore, a very strong marker for the Eznab Complex. Originally separated into two variants in TR. 25A, one with a beveled lip and the other with a notched Z-angle ridge, however, these variants overlap.

Base: Rounded to nearly flat.

Orientation of side: Medium outflare.

Wall-base juncture: When present, the juncture is marked by a small ridge or sharp z-angle type, which is invariably notched and often serves as a field for incised decoration.

Side: Straight to slight outcurve.

Rim: Direct.

Lip: Although some beveled lips occur, the lips in monochrome types are more often rounded.

Feet: Medium to large hollow feet rounded at the base. The feet are frequently much larger than those in the Imix Complex.

Surface: All surfaces except exterior base slipped and well polished.

Decoration: Most examples have a single incised line just below the lip on the exterior. An incised line just above the flange is common above which is often a line of punctations or impressions. The flange is notched and sometimes impressed.

Types: Mostly Tinaja Red. Some Cameron Incised because there are examples with an incised line on the outside wall below the lip, as well as Rosa Punctated. Also, there are some examples of Achote Black and Cubeta Incised. The polychrome examples are most often Zacatel Cream Polychrome, especially the Zacpech Variety, which is characteristic of the Eznab Complex.

Diameter: Range 25–38 cm; median 32 cm.

Height (without feet): Range 5.0–9.2 cm; median 6.4 cm.

Diameter/height ratio: Range 3.6–6.7; median 4.9.

Shape class: 9, large plates.

Temporal distribution: Eznab Complex. Because the shape is so characteristic, it is an excellent marker for the Eznab Complex.

SHAPE CLASS 11: MINIATURE VESSELS

Miniature Jar

Illustrations: Fig. 56.32, 56.34. See TR. 25A: fig. 148g2–3.

Identifying characteristics and sorting problems: The shape is easy to identify based on size.

Body: Globular.

Neck-body juncture: Outcurving.

Orientation of neck: Vertical.

Neck: Straight.

Rim: Direct.

Lip: Rounded.

Types: Tinaja Red, Achote Black, and Cambio Unslipped.

Lip diameter: Range 2.8–3.2 cm.

Neck height: Range 1.0–2.0 cm.

Total height: Range 4.0–6.0 cm.

Shape class: 11, miniature vessels.

Comments: There is one possible example of a miniature jar, identified solely on the basis of Eznab Toh Paste (see TR. 25A Fig. 148g1). There is one possible Tinaja Red pyriform vase (see TR. 25A: fig. 148g4), also identified on the basis of Toh Paste composition.

Miniature Bowl or Cylinder

Illustrations: Fig. 56.3, 56.6, 56.27.

Identifying characteristics and sorting problems: The shape is easy to identify based on size.

Shapes: Slightly incurving to round-side bowls and cylinders (short).

Types: Tinaja Red, Toh Brown.

Diameter: 2–4 cm.

Height: 4–6 cm.

Diameter/Height ratio: 0.5

Shape class: 11, miniature vessels.

Comments: The cylinders are not true straight-sided cylinders, but have slightly curving sides.

The median values of all Eznab shapes are presented in Table 10.6.

Eznab Shapes: Chronological Change

Dramatic changes in vessel shapes and type/shape combinations occurred between the Imix and Eznab Complexes. As mentioned previously, one of the most obvious is that vessels in the serving-vessel category, which almost invariably had polychrome decoration during Imix, were almost always made from monochrome types (especially Tinaja Red) in Eznab.

In addition, some shapes and a decorative mode on large bowls appeared for the first time in Eznab and are an excellent set of type fossils for identification of the complex. The bulging-neck variant of the narrow-mouth jar with tall neck, and slightly incurving to round-side tripod dish are all very distinctive shapes that can be easily separated from any shapes of the preceding Imix Complex. The decorative mode on large capacity incurving-side bowls that is new in Eznab is the very high position of the groove on some grooved examples, a position that is quite distinct from that of grooves on earlier examples.

As discussed in the earlier section on chronological change in types within the Eznab Complex, it is

TABLE 10.6
Shape Dimensions of the Eznab Complex

Shape Class and Shape	Median Diameter	Median Height	Median Diameter/ Height Ratio
1. Wide-mouth Jar (with Tall Neck)	26.0	8.0	3.2
2. Narrow-mouth Jar (with Tall Neck)	16.0	5.6	2.9
2. Narrow-mouth Jar (with Bulging-neck Small)	14.0	4.6	3.0
2. Narrow-mouth Jar (with Bulging-neck Large)	20.0	6.9	3.0
4. Large Incurving-side Bowl	26.0–46.0	6.8–9.0	2.4–3.4
5. Outflaring to Slightly Outcurving-side Tripod Dish	20.0	6.2	3.3
5. Slightly Incurving to Round-side Tripod Bowl	18.0	5.7	3.2
6. Outflaring to Slightly Outcurving-side Bowl or Dish	18.0	7.0	2.6
6. Slightly Incurving to Round-side Bowl	20.0	7.8	2.6
7. Barrel	14.0	12.0	1.2
7. Pyriform Vase with Pedestal Base	9.0	17.6	0.5
7. Cylinder (small)	12.0	18.0	0.6
7. Cylinder (large)	22.0	26.0	0.6
9. Large Tripod Plate	32.0	6.4	4.9

likely that temporal change within the time covered by the complex is responsible for the considerable variation in shape frequencies in Eznab (see Table 10.7). Nevertheless, no clear trends emerged from the attempted shape seriation of the samples.

Special Deposits of the Eznab Complex

Burials of the Eznab Complex

There are six special deposits classified as burials including vessels that were firmly or tentatively dated to the Eznab Complex (Table 10.8). Three of these burials were from the site center: two in Gp. 5D-2, in Str. 5D-1, Temple I, and Str. 5D-22 on the North Acropolis, and one in Gp. 5D-11, Str. 5D-46, in the Central Acropolis. Three burials were found in Intermediate Structure Groups 5G-1, 6E-2, and 7F-1, Str. 7F-30. Three of the six burials included a single vessel and three had two vessels. Two of the vessels (Bu. 1 and Bu. 6) are Zacatel Cream Polychrome, and both have the characteristic Muan Feather design of the Eznab Complex. One is a tripod plate, the other an outflaring to slightly outcurving-side bowl. One of the polychrome vessels came from Temple 1, the other from Str. 7F-30. Bu. 1 also contained an untyped monochrome red utilitarian bowl. The other vessels, one from Str. 5D-46, the other from Str. 5G-12, were Achote Black tripod vessels, a hallmark of the Eznab Complex. Burial 168 from Str. 6E-143 contained an Achote Black tripod dish and a Tinaja Red tripod dish. Burial 201, in Str. 5D-22, included an Achote Black tripod dish and a Pabellon Molded-carved pyriform vase with pedestal base. In summary, the vessels found in Eznab burials are entirely of the serving-vessel category, as was almost invariably the case in Late Classic burials. Although the same general shapes that characterize Late Classic burials also occur in Eznab, the sets of three vessels that were favored in the Imix Complex did not occur.

TABLE 10.7 (part 1)
Shape Frequencies of the Eznab Complex

Shapes	Range Structure Group								
	Sample Loc. 1a Gp. 5D-11 Str. 5D-63	Sample Loc. 1b Gp. 5D-11 Str. 5D-54	Sample Loc. 1c Gp. 5D-11 Str. 5D-44	Sample Loc. 1d Gp. 5D-11 Str. 5D-46	Sample Loc. 1f Gp. 5D-11 Str. 5D-47	Sample Loc. 1g Gp. 5D-11 Str. 4D-49	Sample Loc. 1h Gp. 5D-11 Str. 5D-51	Sample Loc. 1i Gp. 5D-11 Str. 5D-50,-52	Sample Loc. 1j Gp. 5D-11 Ravine below Str. 5E-41
	%	%	%	%	%	%	%	%	%
All Serving Vessels (Includes Medium and Small diameter bowls and dishes, Cylindrical vessels, and Large plates)	62.5	43.8	61.3	35.5	72.5	36.3	44.6	39.7	41.9
Large Capacity Bowls	14.1	18.9	6.6	15.6	15.0	24.5	16.6	23.3	13.5
Narrow-mouth Jars	20.3	11.2	13.9	10.7	3.3	8.8	4.4	9.6	12.2
Wide-mouth Jars	3.1	26.1	18.2	38.2	9.2	30.4	34.4	27.4	32.4
Total Rims	**128**	**365**	**137**	**1081**	**120**	**102**	**639**	**416**	**148**

TABLE 10.7 (part 2)
Shape Frequencies of the Eznab Complex

Shapes	Range Structure Group		Civic-Ceremonial	Range Structure Group	Intermediate Structure Group	Small Structure Group
	Sample Loc. 1k Ravine below Gp. 5D-11	Sample Loc. 1l Gp. 5D-11 Palace Reservoir below Str. 5D-65	Sample Loc. 2 Gp. 5D-3 Str. 5E-30, 5D-40	Sample Loc. 3 Gp. 5D-10	Sample Loc. 4 Gp. 7F-1 Plat. 7F-1 Str. 7F-29, -32	Sample Loc. 5 Gp. 2C-1 Str. 2C-15, -21
	%	%	%	%	%	%
All Serving Vessels (Includes Medium and Small diameter bowls and dishes, Cylindrical vessels, and Large plates)	28.7	39.0	27.9	18.6	22.6	34.0
Large Capacity Bowls	22.4	13.6	29.2	17.1	32.2	29.7
Narrow-mouth Jars	15.1	16.9	19.5	9.3	10.5	0.0
Wide-mouth Jars	33.8	30.6	23.4	55.0	34.7	34.0
Total Rims	644	59	154	280	248	47

TABLE 10.8
Burials of the Eznab Complex

Burial No.	Op.SubOp./Lot	Str.	Structure Group Type	TR. 25A Illustration	TR.	No. of Vessels
1	3A/12	Gp. 7F-1 Str.7F-30	Intermediate Structure Group	98d	22	2
6	4C/1	Temple I Gp. 5D-2 Str. 5D-1	Civic-Ceremonial	98e	14	1
76	28A/22	Gp. 5G-2 Str. 5G-12	Intermediate Structure Group	98f	21	1
168	73D/24	Gp. 6E-2 Str. 6E-143	Intermediate Structure Group	98a		2
198	98D/35,36	Central Acropolis Gp. 5D-11 Str. 5D-46	Range Structure Group	98b	15	1
201	12T/7	North Acropolis Gp. 5D-2 Str. 5D-22	Civic-Ceremonial	98b	14	2

TABLE 10.9
Problematical Deposits of the Eznab Complex

PD No.	Op.SubOp./Lot	Str.	Structure Group Type	TR. 25A Illustration	TR.	No. of Vessels
6[1]	20E/34	Gp. 4F-1 Str. 4F-4	Small Structure Group	122b	19	1
14[2]	12H/8	North Acropolis Gp. 5D-2 Str. 5D-26	Civic-Ceremonial	122c	14	1
133	98A/5	Central Acropolis Gp. 5D-11 Str. 5D-46	Range Structure Group	145	15[†]	7
134[3]	12T/3	North Acropolis Gp. 5D-2 Str. 5D-22	Civic-Ceremonial	147c	14	1
169[2]	78Q/15	East Plaza Gp. 5D-3 Str. 5D-40	Civic-Ceremonial	148g	16	4
179[1]	12H/54A	North Acropolis Gp. 5D-2 Str. 5D-26	Civic-Ceremonial	151b	14	2
181[1]	120A/5	Gp. 5C-11 Str. 5C-49	Civic-Ceremonial	151c	23C	2
182	120A/2,7,8	Gp. 5C-11 Str. 5C-49	Civic-Ceremonial	151d	23C	1
191	135A	Uolantun SE-486	Minor Center	152a		8
193	135A	Uolantun SE-486	Minor Center	152c		5
201	114I/2	Jimbal Str. 1	Minor Center	153b		1
208[2]	98X/5	Central Acropolis Gp. 5D-11 Str. 5D-46	Range Structure Group	153c	15[†]	1

[1] Imix or Eznab

[2] Possible Eznab

[3] Contains Ik and Eznab ceramics

[†] Forthcoming

Caches of the Eznab Complex

No special deposits classified as caches contained ceramics of the Eznab Complex.

Problematical Deposits of the Eznab Complex

There were twelve special deposits classified as problematical that contained Eznab ceramics (See Table 10.9). Six were from the central area of the site (three from the North Acropolis, two from the Central Acropolis, and one from the East Plaza). Two were from the Mundo Perdido Gp. 5C-11, Str. 5C-49. One was from small structure Gp. 4F-1, Str. 4-F4. Two were from the minor center of Uolantun and one from the minor center of Jimbal.

Six of these problematical deposits contained only a single vessel. PD. 6 contained a weathered tripod plate with beveled lip that is of questionable date; it is either Imix or Eznab. PD. 14 from Str. 5D-26 included a slightly incurving to round-side tripod bowl, probably of Tinaja Red. PD. 182 from Str. 5C-49 included a Rosa Punctated tripod bowl with high sides of unusual shape. A tripod plate of the Palmar Ceramic Group came from PD. 201 from the minor center of Jimbal, and a single tall-neck jar of Tinaja Red was discovered in PD. 208 near Str. 5D-46, in Gp. 5D-11 in the Central Acropolis. A final problematical deposit that contains what may be an Eznab vessel is PD. 134 from the North Acropolis, which is described in the chapter on the Ik Ceramic Complex. PD. 134 contains a series of Ik Complex vessels (see TR. 25A: fig. 147*a,d*), and also includes an outflaring to slightly outcurving-side tripod plate dish of Achote Black that is probably Eznab. It has been suggested that the Ik Complex vessels may have come from Bu. 200, a chamber burial in Str. 5D-22 that was disturbed in Eznab times.

Two problematical deposits contain a pair of Eznab Complex vessels. PD. 179 from Gp. 5D-2, Str. 5D-26, in the North Acropolis included an unusual plate of Zacatel-cream Polychrome with a Muan Feather design. The second is a fragment of a Palmar Orange Polychrome outflaring to slightly outcurving-side bowl or dish. The fact that both vessels are fragmentary raises the question of whether they were actually part of the problematical deposit or stray sherds included therein. The second problematical deposit with two possible Eznab vessels was PD. 181 from Civic-Ceremonial Gp. 5C-11, Str. 5C-49. It included a tripod plate with a quatrefoil design in Palmar Orange Polychrome and an outflaring to slightly outcurving-side bowl of Achote Black. The Eznab Complex assignment of both these problematical deposits is debatable because the types and shapes involved might also be from the preceding Imix Complex. The Muan Feather and quatrefoil designs, however, are more common in Eznab than in Imix.

PD. 169 from Str. 5D-40 in the East Plaza contained four miniature vessels. All were jars of somewhat different shapes. Three were red-slipped and the fourth an unnamed polychrome type. The vessels were associated with other Eznab Complex ceramics and human bones. Miniature vessels are uncommon in the Tikal collections and the slips on all of the PD. 169 examples are outside the usual range of Tikal surface finishes and may be imports.

PD. 193 from the minor center of Uolantun included five vessels: an outflaring to slightly outcurving-side bowl of a Naranjal Red-on-cream, a slightly incurving to round-side tripod bowl and an outflaring to slightly outcurving-side tripod dish (both of Tinaja Red); and basal fragments of two cylinders of the Palmar Ceramic Group. Because all the vessels are fragmentary, one must ask whether or not they were the result of intentional deposition.

Seven vessels were part of PD. 133 from Gp. 5D-11, Str. 5D-46 in the Central Acropolis. They included three vessels of the "serving-ware" category: a Sahcaba Molded-carved pyriform vase with pedestal base; an Achote Black tripod dish, and a Tinaja Red cylinder. There were also four vessels of utility shapes: two narrow-mouth jars of Tinaja Red, one with a bulging-neck jar, and two Cameron Incised large capacity incurving-side bowls.

PD. 191 from the minor center of Uolantun included eight vessels. Six of the vessels were tripod plates (three Cameron Incised, two Tinaja Red and one probably Palmar Ceramic Group). The other two vessels were a base of a cylinder of an unusual gouged-incised type of mottled brown color, and a Tinaja Red slightly incurving to round-side tripod bowl.

In summary, no strong patterns emerge from the study of ceramics in Eznab problematical deposits. Typologically, nearly half the vessels are Tinaja Red and the related Cameron Incised. Polychromes are the next most common ceramics and occur with a frequency considerably greater than in Eznab general sherd deposits. Five of the vessels are outside the usual Tikal ceramic traditions and might be imports. Four of these are the miniature vessels in PD. 169 and the other is the unusual gouged-incised vessel from PD. 191. Among shapes, tripod plates were most common, followed by cylinders and outflaring to slightly outcurving-side bowls and dishes. These were the same vessels that comprised the bulk of burial offerings in the few Eznab burials and those of the preceding Imix Complex. Several narrow-mouth jars, and large-capacity bowls were also included in the sample, but only one problematical deposit mixed such utilitarian vessels with serving vessels (PD. 133). As was true for problematical deposits of other complexes, the interpretation of meaning is by no means clear and it is likely that a number of activities gave rise to them. Ceramically, most of the Eznab problematical deposits have contents that would be appropriate as burial offerings, but are by no means outside the range also represented in general sherd collections.

Appendix I: Catalogue Numbers of Pottery Illustrated in Tikal Report 25A

TR. 25A Figure	Deposit	Catalog Number *duplicated catalog number	Misc. Text	Lot No.
002a01	Bu.158	071F-0105/050		071F/050
002a02	Bu.158	071F-0106/050		071F/050
002a03	Bu.158	071F-0104/050		071F/050
002b01	Bu.122	012P-0347/153		012P/153
002b02	Bu.122	012P-0349/153		012P/153
002c	Bu.123	012P-0343/153		012P/158
002d01	Bu.126	012P-0352/153		012P/159
002d02	Bu.126	012P-0351/159		012P/159
003a	Bu.126	012P-0354/159		012P/159
003b01	Bu.164	012P-0495/170		012P/126,129,170
003b02	Bu.164	012P-0494/170		012P/126,129,170
003b03	Bu.164	012P-0206/129		012P/126,129,170
003b04	Bu.164	012P-0204/126		012P/126,129,170
004a	Bu.085	012P-0091/078		012P/078
004b	Bu.085	012P-0085/078		012P/078
004c	Bu.085	012P-0087/078		012P/078
004d	Bu.085	012P-0088/078		012P/078
005a	Bu.085	012P-0089/078		012P/078
005b	Bu.085	012P-0090/078		012P/078
005c	Bu.085	012P-0080/078		012P/078
005d	Bu.085	012P-0081/078		012P/078
005e	Bu.085	012P-0082/078		012P/078
006a	Bu.085	012P-0083/078		012P/078
006b	Bu.085	012P-0072/078 jar		012P/078
006b	Bu.085	012P-0073/078 top		012P/078
006c	Bu.085	012P-0075/078 jar		012P/078

TR. 25A Figure	Deposit	Catalog Number *duplicated catalog number	Misc. Text	Lot No.
006c	Bu.085	012P-0086/078 top		012P/078
006d	Bu.085	012P-0074/078		012P/078
006e	Bu.085	012P-0076/078		012P/078
006f	Bu.085	012P-0079/078		012P/078
006g	Bu.085	012P-0077/078		012P/078
007a	Bu.085	012P-0096/078		012P/078
007b	Bu.085	012P-0094/078		012P/078
007c	Bu.085	012P-0092/078		012P/078
007d	Bu.085	012P-0095/078		012P/078
007e	Bu.085	012P-0093/078		012P/078
007f	Bu.085	012P-0097/078		012P/078
007g	Bu.085	012P-0078/078		012P/078
008a01	Bu.124	064J-0005/009		064J/009
008a02	Bu.124	064J-0004/009		064J/009
008b01	Bu.128	068I-0007/027		068I/027
008b02	Bu.128	068I-0004/027		068I/027
009a01	Bu.128	068I-0006/027		068I/027
009a02	Bu.128	068I-0002/027		068I/027
009a03	Bu.128	068I-0009/027		068I/027
009a04	Bu.128	068I-0005/027		068I/027
009a05	Bu.128	068I-0008/027		068I/027
009b01	Bu.166	012P-0556/177		012P/177
009b02	Bu.166	012P-0565/177		012P/177
009b03	Bu.166	012P-0548/177		012P/177
009b04	Bu.166	012P-0558/177		012P/177
009b05	Bu.166	012P-0563/177		012P/177
010a	Bu.166	012P-0549/177		012P/177
010b	Bu.166	012P-0564/177		012P/177
010c	Bu.166	012P-0554/177		012P/177
010d	Bu.166	012P-0557/177		012P/177
010e	Bu.166	012P-0555/177		012P/177
010f	Bu.166	012P-0566/177		012P/177
010g	Bu.166	012P-0567/177		012P/177
010h	Bu.166	012P-0562/177		012P/177
011a01	Bu.166	012P-0550/177		012P/177
011a02	Bu.166	012P-0559/177		012P/177
011a03	Bu.166	012P-0561/177		012P/177
011a04	Bu.166	012P-0551/177		012P/177
011a05	Bu.166	012P-0553/177		012P/177
011a06	Bu.166	012P-0560/177		012P/177

TR. 25A Figure	Deposit	Catalog Number *duplicated catalog number	Misc. Text	Lot No.
011a07	Bu.166	012P-0552/177		012P/177
011b	Bu.167	012P-0516/179		012P/179
012a	Bu.167	012P-0510/179		012P/179
012b	Bu.167	012P-0517/179		012P/179
012c	Bu.167	012P-0511/179		012P/179
012d	Bu.167	012P-0509/179		012P/179
012e	Bu.167	012P-0505/179		012P/179
012f	Bu.167	012P-0507/179		012P/179
013a	Bu.167	012P-0508/179		012P/179
013b	Bu.167	012P-0515/179		012P/179
013c	Bu.167	012P-0514/179		012P/179
013d	Bu.167	012P-0506/179		012P/179
013e	Bu.167	012P-0512/179		012P/179
013f	Bu.167	012P-0513/179		012P/179
013g	Bu.167	012P-0518/179		012P/179
014	Bu.010	012C-0508/034		012C/034
015	Bu.010	012C-0489a,b/034		012C/034
016	Bu.010	012C-0546a,b/034		012C/034
017a	Bu.010	012C-0517/034		012C/034
017b	Bu.010	012C-0525/034		012C/034
017c	Bu.010	012C-0548/034		012C/034
017d	Bu.010	012C-0519/034		012C/034
017e	Bu.010	012C-0482,/034		012C/034
017e	Bu.010	012C-0483/034		012C/034
018a	Bu.010	012C-0516/034		012C/034
018b	Bu.010	012C-0481/034		012C/034
019a	Bu.010	012C-0479a,b/034	MT-004	012C/034
019b	Bu.010	012C-0480a,b/034	MT-005	012C/034
019c	Bu.010	012C-0515a,b/034	MT-003	012C/034
020a	Bu.010	012C-0477a,b/034		012C/034
020b	Bu.010	012C-0478a,b/034		012C/034
020c	Bu.010	012C-0514a,b/034		012C/034
020d	Bu.010	012C-0512/034		012C/034
020e	Bu.010	012C-0518a,b/034		012C/034
021a	Bu.010	012C-0488a,b/034		012C/034
021b	Bu.010	012C-0521a,b/034		012C/034
021c	Bu.010	012C-0503a,b/034		012C/034
021d	Bu.010	012C-0531a,b/034		012C/034
021e	Bu.010	012C-0532a,b/034		012C/034
021f	Bu.010	012C-0533ab/034		012C/034

TR. 25A Figure	Deposit	Catalog Number *duplicated catalog number	Misc. Text	Lot No.
021g	Bu.010	012C-0538a,b/034		012C/034
021h	Bu.010	012C-0539a.b/034		012C/034
021i	Bu.010	012C-0540a.b/034		012C/034
021j	Bu.010	012C-0545a,b/034		012C/034
021k	Bu.010	012C-0520/034		012C/034
022ab	Bu.022	012H-0042/018 lid		012H/018
022c	Bu.022	012H-0043/018 bowl		012H/018
023a	Bu.022	012H-0042/018 lid		012H/018
023b	Bu.022	012H-0048/018 lid		012H/018
023b	Bu.022	012H-0049/018 bowl		012H/018
024	Bu.022	012H-0044/018 lid		012H/018
024	Bu.022	012H-0045/018 bowl		012H/018
025a	Bu.022	012H-0050/018 lid		012H/018
025a	Bu.022	012H-0051/018 bowl		012H/018
025b	Bu.022	012H-0039/018 lid		012H/018
025b	Bu.022	012H-0040/018 bowl		012H/018
025c	Bu.022	012H-0055/018		012H/018
025d	Bu.022	012H-0041/018		012H/018
025e	Bu.022	012H-0052e/018		012H/018
025f	Bu.022	012H-0057/018		012H/018
025g	Bu.022	012H-0053/018		012H/018
026a	Bu.022	012H-0046/018 lid		012H/018
026a	Bu.022	012H-0047/018 jar		012H/018
026b	Bu.022	012H-0062/018		012H/018
026c	Bu.022	012H-0060/018 lid	MT-013	012H/018
026c	Bu.022	012H-0061/018 jar	MT-014	012H/018
027a01	Bu.022	012H-0058/018		012H/018
027a01	Bu.022	012H-0059/018		012H/018
027a02	Bu.022	012H-0054/018		012H/018
027a03	Bu.022	012H-0056/018		012H/018
027a04	PD.019	012H-0037/015		012H/015
027a05	PD.019	012H-0038/015		012H/015
027b	Bu.033	020H-0037/009		020H/009
027c01	Bu.035	020H-0045/021		020H/021
027c02	Bu.035	020H-0042/021		020H/021
027c03	Bu.035	020H-0043/021		020H/021
028a01	Bu.035	020H-0044/021		020H/021
028a02	Bu.035	020H-0046/021		020H/021
028a03	Bu.035	020H-0047/021		020H/021
028b01	Bu.047	012O-0186/012		012O/012

TR. 25A Figure	Deposit	Catalog Number *duplicated catalog number	Misc. Text	Lot No.
028b02	Bu.047	012O-0218/012		012O/012
028c	Bu.048	012K-0242/022		012K/022
029a	Bu.048	012K-0238/022		012K/022
029b	Bu.048	012K-0239a/022		012K/022
029c	Bu.048	012K-0239b/022		012K/022
029d	Bu.048	012K-0239c/022		012K/022
029e	Bu.048	012K-0239d/022		012K/022
029f	Bu.048	012K-0239e/022		012K/022
029g	Bu.048	012K-0239f/022		012K/022
029h	Bu.048	012K-0240a/022		012K/022
029i	Bu.048	012K-0240b/022		012K/022
029j	Bu.048	012K-0241/022		012K/022
029k	Bu.048	012K-0232a/022		012K/022
029l	Bu.048	012K-0232b/022		012K/022
029m	Bu.048	012K-0232c/022		012K/022
029n	Bu.048	012K-0232d/022		012K/022
030a	Bu.048	012K-0237/022		012K/022
030b	Bu.048	012K-0236a,b/022		012K/022
031a	Bu.048	012K-0235a,b/022		012K/022
031b	Bu.048	012K-0233a/022		012K/022
031c	Bu.048	012K-0233b/022		012K/022
031d	Bu.048	012K-0233c/022		012K/022
031e	Bu.048	012K-0233d/022		012K/022
031f	Bu.048	012K-0233e/022		012K/022
032a01	Bu.048	012K-0231a,b/022		012K/022
032a02	Bu.048	012K-0243/022		012K/022
032b01	Bu.073	027L-0001/004		027L/004
032b02	Bu.073	027L-0002/004		027L/004
032c	Bu.074	027G-0008/014		027G/014
032d01	Bu.084	030A-0011/005		030A/005
032d02	Bu.084	030A-0012/005		030A/005
032d03	Bu.084	030A-0013/005		030A/005
032e	Bu.094	033A-0027/020		033A/020
033a	Bu.094	033A-0026/020		033A/020
033b01	Bu.095	033A-0033/021		033A/021
033b02	Bu.095	033A-0032/021		033A/021
033b03	Bu.095	033A-0031/021		033A/021
033b04	Bu.095	033A-0034/021		033A/021
033c	Bu.101	033A-0067/031		033A/031
033d01	Bu.107	033A-0083/038		033A/038,48–51

TR. 25A Figure	Deposit	Catalog Number *duplicated catalog number	Misc. Text	Lot No.
033d02	Bu.107	033A-0140/049		033A/038,48–51
033d03	Bu.107	033A-0147/051		033A/038,48–51
034a	Bu.107	033A-0142/051		033A/038,48–51
034b	Bu.107	033A-0148/051		033A/038,48–51
034c	Bu.107	033A-0146/051		033A/038,48–51
034d	Bu.107	033A-0145/051		033A/038,48–51
034e	Bu.107	033A-0132/048		033A/038,48–51
034f	Bu.107	033A-0149/051		033A/038,48–51
035a01	Bu.107	033A-0139/049		033A/038,48–51
035a02	Bu.107	033A-0138/049		033A/038,48–51
035a03	Bu.107	033A-0144/036		033A/036
035a04	Bu.107	033A-0122/048		033A/038,48–51
035a05	Bu.107	033A-0154/048		033A/038,48–51
035b01	Bu.152	068I-0043/020		068I/020
035b02	Bu.152	068I-0044/020		068I/020
035b03	Bu.152	068I-0042/020		068I/020
035b04	Bu.152	068I-0041/020		068I/020
036a01	Bu.160	003B-0089/018		003B/018
036a02	Bu.160	003B-0090/018		003B/018
036a03	Bu.160	003B-0082/018		003B/018
036a04	Bu.160	003B-0088/018		003B/018
036a05	Bu.160	003B-0083/018		003B/018
036a06	Bu.160	003B-0086a,b/018		003B/018
036a07	Bu.160	003B-0087a,b/018		003B/018
036a08	Bu.160	003B-0084/018		003B/018
036a09	Bu.160	003B-0092/018		003B/018
036a10	Bu.160	003B-0091/018		003B/018
036b	Bu.162	003C-0004/007		003C/007
037a01	Bu.169	076B-0010/005		076B/005
037a02	Bu.169	076B-0011/005		076B/005
037b01	Bu.177	087A-0006/006		087A/006
037b02	Bu.177	087A-0007/006		087A/006
037b03	Bu.177	087A-0008/006		087A/006
037b04	Bu.177	087A-0005/006		087A/006
037b05	Bu.177	087A-0009/006		087A/006
037c	Bu.187	112B-0008/006		112B/006
037d	Bu.213	135A-0427/110		135A/110
037e	Bu.217	045G-0017/013		045G/013
038a	Bu.017	020A-1367/047		020A/047
038b	Bu.034	020H-0039/010		020H/010

TR. 25A Figure	Deposit	Catalog Number *duplicated catalog number	Misc. Text	Lot No.
038c01	Bu.115	027A-0065/021		027A/021
038c02	Bu.115	027A-0064/021		027A/021
038c03	Bu.115	027A-0063/021		027A/021
038c04	Bu.115	027A-0062/021		027A/021
038d	Bu.182	098D-0027/009		098D/009
038e01	Bu.206	129D-0001/008		129D/008,9
038e02	Bu.206	129D-0002/008		129D/008,9
038e03	Bu.206	129D-0037/008		129D/008,9
038e04	Bu.206	129D-0003/008		129D/008,9
039a	Bu.023	012K-0086/013	MT-008	012K/011,13,37,39
039b	Bu.023	012K-0085/013	MT-007	012K/011,13,37,39
040a	Bu.023	012K-0084/013	MT-006	012K/011,13,37,39
040b	Bu.023	012K-0091/013		012K/011,13,37,39
040c	Bu.023	012K-0095/013		012K/011,13,37,39
040d	Bu.023	012K-0089/013		012K/011,13,37,39
040e	Bu.023	012K-0090/013		012K/011,13,37,39
040f	Bu.023	012K-0087/013		012K/011,13,37,39
041a01	Bu.023	012K-0094/013		012K/011,13,37,39
041a02	Bu.023	012K-0093/013		012K/011,13,37,39
041a03	Bu.023	012K-0088/013		012K/011,13,37,39
041a04	Bu.023	012K-0092/013		012K/011,13,37,39
041b01	Bu.024	012K-0144/018		012K/018,40,41
041b02	Bu.024	012K-0141/018	MT-002	012K/018,40,41
041b03	Bu.024	012K-0140/018		012K/018,40,41
041b04	Bu.024	012K-0142/018		012K/018,40,41
041b05	Bu.024	012K-0143/018		012K/018,40,41
042a	Bu.024	012K-0139/018	MT-291	012K/018,40,41
042b01	Bu.058	024C-0351/138		024C/138
042b02	Bu.058	024C-0358/138		024C/138
042b03	Bu.058	024C-0349/138		024C/138
042b04	Bu.058	024C-0350/138		024C/138
042c	Bu.072	027A-0046/018		027A/018
043a	Bu.081	030A-0002/002		030A/002
043b	Bu.081	030A-0001/002		030A/002
043c	Bu.081	030A-0003/002		030A/002
043d	Bu.081	030A-0004/002	MT-288	030A/002
044a01	Bu.083	030A-0008/004		030A/004
044a02	Bu.083	030A-0010/004		030A/004
044a03	Bu.083	030A-0009/004		030A/004
044b01	Bu.096	033A-0043/022	MT-097	033A/022

TR. 25A Figure	Deposit	Catalog Number *duplicated catalog number	Misc. Text	Lot No.
044b02	Bu.096	033A-0045/022		033A/022
044b03	Bu.096	033A-0046/022		033A/022
044b04	Bu.096	033A-0044/022		033A/022
044c01	Bu.130	068I-0032/031		068I/031
044c02	Bu.130	068I-0034/031		068I/031
045	Bu.132	003B-0004/004 lid	MT-290	003B/004
045	Bu.132	003B-0005/004 bowl		003B/004
046a01	Bu.132	003B-0003/004		003B/004
046a02	Bu.132	003B-0002/004		003B/004
046b	Bu.134	003B-0021/008		003B/008
046c01	Bu.140	003B-0024/014		003B/014
046c02	Bu.140	003B-0026/014		003B/014
046c03	Bu.140	003B-0025/014		003B/014
046c04	Bu.140	003B-0027/014		003B/014
047a	Bu.150	003B-0065a,b/017	MT-293	003B/017
047b	Bu.150	003B-0068/017		003B/017
047c	Bu.150	003B-0067/017	MT-292	003B/017
047d	Bu.150	003B-0066/017		003B/017
048a	Bu.159	003C-0006/009	MT-098	003C/009
048b	Bu.159	003C-0007/009		003C/009
048c	Bu.159	003C-0008/009	MT-099	003C/009
048d	Bu.159	003C-0009/009		003C/009
049a01	Bu.183	098D-0071/012	MT-148	098D/012
049a02	Bu.183	098D-0070/012		098D/012
049b01	Bu.184	098D-0060/012		098D/017
049b02	Bu.184	098D-0059/012		098D/017
049c	Bu.185	098D-0075/021		098D/021
050a	Bu.195	012U-0039/027		012U/027
050b	Bu.195	012U-0047/027		012U/027
050c	Bu.195	012U-0046/027		012U/027
050d	Bu.195	012U-0041/027		012U/027
050e	Bu.195	012U-0038/027	MT-217	012U/027
050f	Bu.195	012U-0037/027		012U/027
051a	Bu.195	012U-0037/027	MT-216B	012U/027
051b	Bu.195	012U-0037/027	MT-216A	012U/027
052a	Bu.040	020L-0171/040		020L/030
052b01	Bu.054	024C-0308/125		024C/125
052b02	Bu.054	024C-0231/125		024C/125
052b03	Bu.054	024C-0230/125		024C/125
052c	Bu.173	084A-0002/009		084A/009

TR. 25A Figure	Deposit	Catalog Number *duplicated catalog number	Misc. Text	Lot No.
052d	Bu.174	084B-0006/010		084B/010
053a01	Bu.014	020A-1393/093		020A/093
053a02	Bu.014	020A-1394/093		020A/093
053b01	Bu.016	020A-1395/087		020A/097
053b02	Bu.016	020A-1396/087		020A/097
053c	Bu.018	020B-0686/055		020A/055
053d01	Bu.021	020A-0344/059		020A/059
053d02	Bu.021	020A-1391/059		020A/059
053d03	Bu.021	020A-0687/059		020A/059
053e	Bu.026	020B-0037/058		020B/058,59,62
053f	Bu.027	020B-0038/067		020B/067
053g	Bu.028	020B-0105/069		020B/069
053h01	Bu.030	020B-0245/084		020B/084
053h02	Bu.030	020B-0243/084		020B/084
053h03	Bu.030	020B-0244/084		020B/084
053i01	Bu.031	020D-0347/037		020D/037
053i02	Bu.031	020D-0346/037		020D/037
053i03	Bu.031	020D-0345/037		020D/037
054a01	Bu.038	020H-0114/049		020H/049
054a02	Bu.038	020H-0113/049	MT-338	020H/049
054a03	Bu.038	020H-0115/049		020H/049
054b01	Bu.039	020L-0147/029		020L/029
054b02	Bu.039	020L-0149/029		020L/029
054b03	Bu.039	020L-0150/029		020L/029
054c01	Bu.042	020L-0177/033		020L/033
054c02	Bu.042	020L-0176/033		020L/033
054c03	Bu.042	020L-0178/033		020L/033
054d01	Bu.045	024B-0002/001		024B/001
054d02	Bu.045	024B-0003/001		024B/001
054d03	Bu.045	024B-0001/001		024B/001
055a01	Bu.049	024C-0221/069		024C/069
055a02	Bu.049	024C-0219/069		024C/069
055a03	Bu.049	024C-0220/069		024C/069
055b01	Bu.050	024C-0224/070		024C/070
055b02	Bu.050	024C-0223/070		024C/070
055b03	Bu.050	024C-0222/070		024C/070
055c01	Bu.052	024C-0226/104		024C/104
055c02	Bu.052	024C-0228/104		024C/104
055c03	Bu.052	024C-0227/104		024C/104
055d	Bu.053	024C-0229/114		024C/114

TR. 25A Figure	Deposit	Catalog Number *duplicated catalog number	Misc. Text	Lot No.
056a	Bu.056	024C-0347/135		024C/135
056b01	Bu.066	024R-0033/017		024R/017
056b02	Bu.066	024R-0035/017		024R/017
056b03	Bu.066	024R-0034/017		024R/017
056c01	Bu.068	024T-0030/024		024T/024
056c02	Bu.068	024T-0031/024		024T/024
056c03	Bu.068	024T-0032/024		024T/024
056d01	Bu.070	024W-0020/008		024W/008
056d02	Bu.070	024W-0021/008		024W/008
056d03	Bu.070	024W-0022/008		024W/008
056d04	Bu.070	024W-0024/008		024W/008
057a01	Bu.071	027E-0003/007		027E/007
057a02	Bu.071	027E-0002/007		027E/007
057a03	Bu.071	027E-0001/007		027E/007
057a04	Bu.071	027E-0004/007		027E/007
057b01	Bu.075	028B-0030/014		028B/014
057b02	Bu.075	028B-0028/014		028B/014
057b03	Bu.075	028B-0029/014		028B/014
057b04	Bu.075	028B-0027/014		028B/014
057c01	Bu.077	041F-0004/004		041F/001–4
057c02	Bu.077	041F-0005/004	MT-339	041F/001–4
057c03	Bu.077	041F-0006/004		041F/001–4
058a	Bu.077	041F-0001/004		041F/001–4
058b	Bu.077	041F-0002/004	MT-019	041F/001–4
058c	Bu.077	041F-0003/004		041F/001–4
059a01	Bu.078	031A-0004/002		031A/002
059a02	Bu.078	031A-0003/002		031A/002
059a03	Bu.078	031A-0002/002		031A/002
059a04	Bu.078	031A-0001/002		031A/002
059b01	Bu.080	028B-0036/024	MT-289	028B/024
059b02	Bu.080	028B-0035/024		028B/024
060a	Bu.080	028B-0037/024		028B/024
060b	Bu.082	031A-0007/004		031A/004
060c01	Bu.086	030B-0003/007		030B/007
060c02	Bu.086	030B-0004/007		030B/007
060c03	Bu.086	030B-0005/007		030B/007
060c04	Bu.086	030B-0006/007		030B/007
060d01	Bu.087	032A-0002/007		032A/007
060d02	Bu.087	032A-0001/007		032A/007
060d03	Bu.087	032A-0003/007		032A/007

TR. 25A Figure	Deposit	Catalog Number *duplicated catalog number	Misc. Text	Lot No.
060d04	Bu.087	032A-0004/007		032A/007
061a01	Bu.088	033A-0001/009		033A/009
061a02	Bu.088	033A-0003/009		033A/009
061a03	Bu.088	033A-0002/009		033A/009
061b01	Bu.089	033A-0005/012		033A/012
061b02	Bu.089	033A-0007/012		033A/012
061b03	Bu.089	033A-0006/012		033A/012
061c01	Bu.090	033A-0011/013		033A/013
061c02	Bu.090	033A-0012/013		033A/013
061c03	Bu.090	033A-0010/013		033A/013
062a01	Bu.091	033A-0014/016		033A/016
062a02	Bu.091	033A-0016/016		033A/016
062a03	Bu.091	033A-0015/016		033A/016
062b	Bu.092	033A-0018/017		033A/017
062c01	Bu.093	033A-0021/019		033A/019
062c02	Bu.093	033A-0022/019		033A/019
062d01	Bu.097	033A-0050/023		033A/023
062d02	Bu.097	033A-0049/023		033A/023
062d03	Bu.097	033A-0048/023		033A/023
062e	Bu.099	033A-0060/028		033A/028
063a01	Bu.099	033A-0058/028		033A/028
063a02	Bu.099	033A-0059/028		033A/028
063b01	Bu.100	033A-0063/030		033A/030
063b02	Bu.100	033A-0062/030		033A/030
063b03	Bu.100	033A-0061/030		033A/030
063c	Bu.102	033F-0001/017		033F/017
063d	Bu.103	033A-0070/032		033A/032
063e	Bu.104	033F-0011/037		033F/037
063f01	Bu.105	033A-0074/036		033A/036
063f02	Bu.105	033A-0078/036		033A/036
064a01	Bu.105	033A-0072/036		033A/036
064a02	Bu.105	033A-0073/036		033A/036
064b	Bu.113	033F-0130/046		033F/046
064c01	Bu.116	004P-0024/002		004P/002
064c02	Bu.116	004P-0007/002	MT-070	004P/002
064c03	Bu.116	004P-0121/002		004P/002
065a	Bu.116	004P-0003/002	MT-068	004P/002
065b	Bu.116	004P-0001/002		004P/002
066	Bu.116	004P-0028/002		004P/002
067	Bu.116	004P-0118/002		004P/002

TR. 25A Figure	Deposit	Catalog Number *duplicated catalog number	Misc. Text	Lot No.
068A	Bu.116	004P-0008/002	MT-067	004P/002
068a	Bu.116	004P-0008/002	MT-067	004P/002
068b	Bu.116	004P-0002/002	MT-069	004P/002
069	Bu.116	004P-0106/002	MT-057	004P/002
070	Bu.116	004P-0124/002	MT-058	004P/002
071	Bu.116	004P-0107/002	MT-063	004P/002
072a	Bu.116	004P-0109/002	MT-064	004P/002
072b	Bu.116	004P-0122/002	MT-065	004P/002
073	Bu.116	004P-0119/002	MT-059	004P/002
074a	Bu.116	004P-0123/002	MT-060	004P/002
074b	Bu.116	004P-0108/002	MT-061	004P/002
075a	Bu.116	004P-0110/002	MT-062	004P/002
075b	Bu.116	004P-0125/002	MT-066	004P/002
075c	Bu.116	004N-0002/002	MT-071	004N/002
076a01	Bu.118	035C-0003/005		035C/005
076a02	Bu.118	035C-0002/005		035C/005
076b	Bu.133	070A-0002/003		070A/003
076c01	Bu.135	070C-0001/003		070C/003
076c02	Bu.135	070C-0002/003		070C/003
076c03	Bu.135	070C-0003/003		070C/003
076d01	Bu.137	070C-0007/005		070C/005
076d02	Bu.137	070C-0008/005		070C/005
076d03	Bu.137	070C-0006/005		070C/005
077a01	Bu.139	070C-0011/006		070C/006
077a02	Bu.139	070C-0014/006	MT-337	070C/006
077a03	Bu.139	070C-0012/006		070C/006
077a04	Bu.139	070C-0013/006		070C/006
077a05	Bu.139	070C-0010/006		070C/006
077a06	Bu.139	070C-0015/006		070C/006
077b	Bu.141	070D-0001/003		070D/003
077c01	Bu.142	070D-0006/004		070D/004
077c02	Bu.142	070D-0005/004		070D/004
077c03	Bu.142	070D-0004/004		070D/004
078a01	Bu.147	070F-0001/004	MT-294	070F/004
078a02	Bu.147	070F-0002/004		070F/004
078b01	Bu.149	070F-0005/006		070F/006
078b02	Bu.149	070F-0006/006		070F/006
078b03	Bu.149	070F-0007/006		070F/006
078c	Bu.154	070G-0001/003		070G/003
079a01	Bu.154	070G-0002/003		070G/003

TR. 25A Figure	Deposit	Catalog Number *duplicated catalog number	Misc. Text	Lot No.
079a02	Bu.154	070G-0003/003		070G/003
079b01	Bu.155	070G-0006/004		070G/004
079b02	Bu.155	070G-0008/004		070G/004
079b03	Bu.155	070G-0007/004		070G/004
079c01	Bu.156	070G-0010/005		070G/005
079c02	Bu.156	070G-0012/005		070G/005
079c03	Bu.156	070G-0011/005		070G/005
079d	Bu.157	070F-0022/011		070F/011
080a01	Bu.157	070F-0021/011		070F/011
080a02	Bu.157	070F-0020/011		070F/011
080b01	Bu.186	112B-0002/001		112B/001
080b02	Bu.186	112B-0003/001		112B/001
080b03	Bu.186	112B-0001/001		112B/001
080c01	Bu.188	112B-0012/007		112B/007
080c02	Bu.188	112B-0014/007		112B/007
080c03	Bu.188	112B-0013/007		112B/007
080d01	Bu.189	103C-0009/005		103C/005
080d02	Bu.189	103C-0010/005		103C/005
080d03	Bu.189	103C-0011/005		103C/005
081a	Bu.190	003B-0119/019	MT-168	003B/019
081b	Bu.190	003B-0120/019		003B/019
081c	Bu.190	003B-0121/019	MT-166	003B/019
081d	Bu.190	003B-0122/019		003B/019
082a01	Bu.191	003B-0132/021		003B/021
082a02	Bu.191	003B-0133/021		003B/021
082a03	Bu.191	003B-0134/021	MT-169	003B/021
082a04	Bu.191	003B-0136/021		003B/021
082a05	Bu.191	003B-0136/021		003B/021
082b01	Bu.192	003E-0002/027	MT-170	003E/027
082b03	Bu.192	003E-0001/027		003E/027
083a	Bu.192	003E-0003/027		003E/027
083b01	Bu.193	003C-0027/010		003C/010
083b02	Bu.193	003C-0028/010		003C/010
083c	Bu.196	117A-0001/036	MT-176	117A/036
084	Bu.196	117A-0001/036	MT-176	117A/036
085a	Bu.196	117A-0003/036		117A/036
085b	Bu.196	117A-0002/036	MT-177	117A/036
086a	Bu.196	117A-0011/036	MT-334a	117A/036
086b	Bu.196	117A-0006/036	MT-334e	117A/036
087a	Bu.196	117A-0005/036	MT-334c	117A/036

TR. 25A Figure	Deposit	Catalog Number *duplicated catalog number	Misc. Text	Lot No.
087b	Bu.196	117A-0008/036	MT-334b	117A/036
087c	Bu.196	117A-0012/036	MT-334d	117A/036
088a	Bu.196	117A-0010/036	MT-334i	117A/036
088b	Bu.196	117A-0014/016	MT-334g	117A/036
088c	Bu.196	117A-0016/036	MT-334f	117A/036
089a	Bu.196	117A-0013/036	MT-334h	117A/036
089b	Bu.196	117A-0009/036	MT-334k	117A/036
089c	Bu.196	117A-0004/036	MT-334m	117A/036
090a	Bu.196	117A-0007/036	MT-334j	117A/036
090b	Bu.196	117A-0015/036	MT-334l	117A/036
091a	Bu.196	117A-0017/036		117A/036
091b	Bu.196	117A-0018/036		117A/036
091c	Bu.196	117A-0019/036		117A/036
091d	Bu.196	117A-0020/036		117A/036
091e	Bu.196	117A-0021/036		117A/036
091f	Bu.196	117A-0022/036		117A/036
091g	Bu.196	117A-0023/036		117A/036
091h	Bu.196	117A-0024/036		117A/036
091i	Bu.196	117A-0025/036		117A/036
091j	Bu.196	117A-0026/036		117A/036
091k	Bu.196	117A-0027/036		117A/036
091l	Bu.196	117A-0028/036		117A/036
092a	Bu.196	117A-0029/036		117A/036
092b	Bu.196	117A-0030/036		117A/036
092c	Bu.196	117A-0033/036		117A/036
092d	Bu.196	117A-0031/036		117A/036
092e	Bu.196	117A-0032/036		117A/036
092f	Bu.196	117A-0034/036		117A/036
092g	Bu.196	117A-0035/036		117A/036
092h	Bu.196	117A-0039/036	MT-189	117A/036
092i	Bu.196	117A-0040/036		117A/036
093	Bu.196	117A-0036/036	MT-186	117A/036
094a	Bu.196	117A-0037/036	MT-187	117A/036
094b	Bu.196	117A-0038/036	MT-188	117A/036
095a	Bu.196	117A-0041/036		117A/036
095b	Bu.196	117A-0042/036		117A/036
095c	Bu.196	117A-0043/036		117A/036
096a	Bu.196	117A-0044/036		117A/036
096b	Bu.196	117A-0045/036		117A/036
096c	Bu.196	117A-0046/036		117A/036

TR. 25A Figure	Deposit	Catalog Number *duplicated catalog number	Misc. Text	Lot No.
096d	Bu.196	117A-0047/036		117A/036
096e	Bu.196	117A-0048/036		117A/036
097a	Bu.204	128A-0033/011		128A/011,15
097b01	Bu.216	112C-0003/001		112C/001
097b02	Bu.216	112C-0001/001		112C/001
097b03	Bu.216	112C-0002/001		112C/001
097c	Bu.069	024W-0015/020		024T/020
097d01	Bu.212	140A-0003/002		140A/002
097d02	Bu.212	140A-0002/002		140A/002
097d03	Bu.212	140A-0001/002		140A/002
097e	Bu.218	072D-0001/002		072D/002
098a01	Bu.168	073D-0002/024		073D/024
098a02	Bu.168	073D-0001/024		073D/024
098b	Bu.198	098D-0125/035		098D/035
098c01	Bu.201	012T-0015/007		012T/007
098c02	Bu.201	012T-0016/007		012T/007
098d	Bu.001	003A-0014/012		003A/012
098e	Bu.006	004C-0006/001		004C/001
098f	Bu.076	028A-0029/022		028A/022
098g01	Bu.005	004C-0002/001		004C/001
098g02	Bu.005	004C-0001/001		004C/001
099a	Ca.147	012P-0196/136		012P/136
099b	Ca.141	012P-0139/115		012P/115
099c	Ca.168	012P-0599/184		012P/184
099c	Ca.168	012P-0600/184		012P/184
099d01	Ca.024	011D-0089/019		011D/019
099d02	Ca.024	011D-0090/019		011D/019
099e	Ca.205	090C-0001/003		090C/003
099e	Ca.205	090C-0002/003		090C/003
099f	Ca.209	090A-0018a,b/033		090A/033
100a01	Ca.010	012A-0014b/003		012A/003
100a02	Ca.010	012A-0014a/003		012A/003
100b	Ca.013	012B-0239a,b/003		012B/003
100c	Ca.041	012B-0095a,b/014		012B/014
100d	Ca.065	012G-0068a,b/017		012G/017
100e	Ca.079	012J-0028/005		012J/005
100e	Ca.079	012J-0029/005		012J/005
100f	Ca.086	012M-0096a,b/027		012M/027
101a01	Ca.093	012O-0046a,b/008		012O/006,8–11
101a02	Ca.093	012O-0111/010		012O/006,8–11

TR. 25A Figure	Deposit	Catalog Number *duplicated catalog number	Misc. Text	Lot No.
101a02	Ca.093	012O-0113/010		012O/006,8–11
101a03	Ca.093	012O-0177a,b/009		012O/006,8–11
101b01	Ca.102	012O-0194a,b/015		012O/015–17
101b02	Ca.102	012O-0208a,b/016		012O/015–17
101b03	Ca.102	012O-0214a,b/017		012O/015–17
101c01	Ca.120	012J-0130/022		012J/022
101c02	Ca.120	012J/022		012J/022
101d	Ca.140	012R-0157/016		012R/015,16
101d	Ca.140	012R-0158/016		012R/015,16
101e	Ca.140	012R-0154/016		012R/015,16
102a01	Ca.142	012R-0171a,b/018		012R/018
102a02	Ca.142	012R-0170a,b/018		012R/018
102a03	Ca.142	012R-0172a.b/018		012R/018
102a04	Ca.142	012R-0174a,b/018		012R/018
102b	Ca.142	012R-0173a,b/018		012R/018
102c	Ca.188	078M-0028a,b/026		078M/026
102d01	Ca.197	098B-0029a,b/012		098B/012
102d02	Ca.197	098B-0049a,b/012		098B/012
102e	Ca.167	042F-0072a,b/019		042F/019
102f01	Ca.186	012R-0309a,b/028		012R/028
102f02	Ca.186	012R-0330/028		012R/028
103a01	Ca.110	012J-0041a/010		012J/010,13,14
103a02	Ca.110	012J-0041b/010		012J/010,13,14
103a03	Ca.110	012J-0042/010		012J/010,13,14
103a04	Ca.110	012J-0043/010		012J/010,13,14
103a05	Ca.110	012J-0044/013,14		012J/010,13,14
103a06	Ca.110	012J-0045/013,14		012J/010,13,14
103a07	Ca.110	012J-0046/013,14		012J/010,13,14
103a08	Ca.110	012J-0047/013,14		012J/010,13,14
103a09	Ca.110	012J-0049/014		012J/010,13,14
103a10	Ca.110	012J-0050/014		012J/010,13,14
103a11	Ca.110	012J-0051/014		012J/010,13,14
103a12	Ca.110	012J-0052/014		012J/010,13,14
103a13	Ca.110	012J-0053/014		012J/010,13,14
103a14	Ca.110	012J-0054/014		012J/010,13,14
103a15	Ca.110	012J-0055/014		012J/010,13,14
103a16	Ca.110	012J-0056/014		012J/010,13,14
103a17	Ca.110	012J-0057/014		012J/010,13,14
103a18	Ca.110	012J-0058/014		012J/010,13,14
103a19	Ca.110	012J-0059/013,14		012J/010,13,14

TR. 25A Figure	Deposit	Catalog Number *duplicated catalog number	Misc. Text	Lot No.
103a20	Ca.110	012J-0048a,b/014		012J/010,13,14
103b	Ca.132	012R-0021a,b/006		012R/006
104a01	Ca.074	012E-0016a,b/004		012E/004
104a02	Ca.074	012E-0014a,b/004		012E/004
104a03	Ca.074	012E-0015a,b/004		012E/004
104a04	Ca.074	012E-0010a,b/004		012E/004
104a05	Ca.074	012E-0013a,b/004		012E/004
104a06	Ca.074	012E-0026/004		012E/004
104b01	Ca.098	012K-0189a,b/019		012K/019
104b02	Ca.098	012K-0197ab/019		012K/019
104b03	Ca.098	012K-0198ab/019		012K/019
105a	Ca.119	012J-0067ab/020		012J/020
105b	Ca.119	012J-0071ab/020		012J/020
105c	Ca.119	012J-0072ab/020		012J/020
105d	Ca.119	012J-0070ab/020		012J/020
105e	Ca.119	012J-0069ab/020		012J/020
105f	Ca.119	012J-0068ab/020		012J/020
105g	Ca.119	012J-0082ab/020		012J/020
106a01	Ca.119	012J-0073ab/020		012J/020
106a02	Ca.119	012J-0078ab/020		012J/020
106a03	Ca.119	012J-0074ab/020		012J/020
106b01	Ca.119	012J-0075ab/020		012J/020
106b02	Ca.119	012J-0077ab/020		012J/020
106b03	Ca.119	012J-0079ab,/020		012J/020
106b04	Ca.119	012J-0080ab/020		012J/020
106b05	Ca.119	012J-0081ab/020		012J/020
106b06	Ca.119	012J-0076ab/020		012J/020
107a01	Ca.136	012R-0057a,b/012		012R/012
107a02	Ca.136	012R-0054a,b/012		012R/012
107a03	Ca.136	012R-0047a,b/012		012R/012
107a04	Ca.136	012R-0052a,b/012		012R/012
107a05	Ca.136	012R-0051a,b/012		012R/012
107a06	Ca.136	012R-0048a,b/012		012R/012
107a07	Ca.136	012R-0050a,b/012		012R/012
107a08	Ca.136	012R-0046a,b/012		012R/012
107a09	Ca.136	012R-0049a,b/012		012R/012
107a10	Ca.136	012R-0045a,b/012		012R/012
107a11	Ca.136	012R-0053a,b/012		012R/012
107b01	Ca.136	012R-0044b/012		012R/012
107b02	Ca.136	012R-0044a/012		012R/012

TR. 25A Figure	Deposit	Catalog Number *duplicated catalog number	Misc. Text	Lot No.
107b03	Ca.136	012R-0059a/012		012R/012
107b04	Ca.136	012R-0059b/012		012R/012
107b05	Ca.136	012R-0060b/012		012R/012
107b06	Ca.136	012R-0060a/012		012R/012
107b07	Ca.136	012R-0056/012		012R/012
107b08	Ca.136	012R-0058/012		012R/012
107b09	Ca.136	012R-0043/012		012R/012
107b10	Ca.136	012R-0055/012		012R/012
107c	Ca.143	012R-0204a,b/022		012R/022
108a	Ca.043	012C-0234a,b/023		012C/023
108b	Ca.081	012K-0083a,b/012		012K/012
108c	Ca.138	012R-0031a,b/014		012R/014
108d	Ca.198	098B-0044a,b/013	MT-140	098B/013
108e	Ca.228	098X-0001a,b/016		098X/016
108f	Ca.196	098B-0015a,b/010		098B/010
108g	Ca.206	090C-0011a,b/004		090C/004
109a	Ca.053	012B-0208a,b/031		012B/031
109b	Ca.134	012K-0319/029,33,34		012K/029,33,34
109c01	Ca.178	056G-0010/005		056G/005
109c02	Ca.178	056G-0015/005		056G/005
110a01	Ca.131	013F-0001a,b/005		013F/005
110a02	Ca.131	013F-0002a,b/005		013F/005
110b	Ca.161	003B-0044a,b/007		003B/007
110c	Ca.174	012L-0038a,b/008		012L/008
111a	Ca.003	007A-0021/009		007A/009
111b01	Ca.004	007A-0025/010		007A/010
111b02	Ca.004	007A-0024/010		007A/010
111c01	Ca.012	012A-0058b/007		012A/007
111c02	Ca.012	012A-0058a/007		012A/007
111d01	Ca.015	011D-0080/012		011D/011,12,43,52
111d02	Ca.015	011D-0074a/011		011D/011,12,43,52
111d03	Ca.015	011D-0074b/011		011D/011,12,43,52
111d04	Ca.015	011D-0254/043		011D/011,12,43,52
111d05	Ca.015	011D-0253/043		011D/011,12,43,52
111e01	Ca.042	011D-0223/037		011D/037
111e02	Ca.042	011D-0224/037		011D/037
111e03	Ca.042	011D-0225/037		011D/037
111e04	Ca.042	011D-0226/037		011D/037
112a01	Ca.045	011F-0005/006		011F/006
112a02	Ca.045	011F-0006/006		011F/006

TR. 25A Figure	Deposit	Catalog Number *duplicated catalog number	Misc. Text	Lot No.
112a03	Ca.045	011F-0007/006		011F/006
112b01	Ca.050	011D-0236/049		011D/049
112b02	Ca.050	011D-0243a/049		011D/049
112b03	Ca.050	011D-0243b/049		011D/049
112c01	Ca.056	011G-0005/003		011G/003
112c02	Ca.056	011G-0004/003		011G/003
112d	Ca.121	011D-0282/057		011D/057
112e01	Ca.123	008B-0024/010		008B/010
112e02	Ca.123	008B-0028/010		008B/010
112e03	Ca.123	008B-0025/010		008B/010
112e04	Ca.123	008B-0026/010		008B/010
112e05	Ca.123	008B-0027/010		008B/010
113a01	Ca.150	061A-0009/007		061A/007
113a02	Ca.150	061A-0012/007		061A/007
113a03	Ca.150	061A-0011a/007		061A/007
113a04	Ca.150	061A-0010/007		061A/007
113a05	Ca.150	061A-0011b/007		061A/007
113b01	Ca.154	061A-0014/008		061A/008
113b02	Ca.154	061A-0013/008		061A/008
113c	Ca.155	007A-0034/013		007A/013
113d01	Ca.203	005B-0004/002		005B/002
113d02	Ca.203	005B-0005/002		005B/002
114a	Ca.058	012G-0007/004		012G/004
114b01	Ca.080	012G-0116/021		012G/021
114b02	Ca.080	012G-0115/021		012G/021
114c	Ca.108	012M-0095a/028,30		012M/028,30
114d01	Ca.130	012G-0207/041		012G/041
114d02	Ca.130	012G-0208/041		012G/041
114e01	Ca.144	012R-0225a/021		012R/021
114e02	Ca.144	012R-0225b/021		012R/021
114f	Ca.176	056G-0016/003		056G/003
114g	Ca.201	012L-0114/027	MT-085	012L/027
115a	Ca.109	012O-0222/018		012O/018
115b	Ca.085	020B-0010a,b/049		020B/049
115c	Ca.030	No catalog number		nolot
115d	Ca.219	135A-0184/084		135A/084
115d	Ca.219	135A-0194/084		135A/084
115e	Ca.214	135A-0188/054		135A/054
115f	Ca.221	135C-0021/023		135C/023
115g	Ca.222	135A-0186/085		135A/085

TR. 25A Figure	Deposit	Catalog Number *duplicated catalog number	Misc. Text	Lot No.
115h	Ca.232	135A-0749/119		135A/119
115i	Ca.218	135A-0247/082		135A/082
115i	Ca.218	135A-0248/082		135A/082
115j01	Ca.215	129F-0078a,b/007		129F/005,7–12
115j02	Ca.215	129F-0077a,b/007		129F/005,7–12
115j03	Ca.215	129F-0074/0078		129F/005,7–12
115j04	Ca.215	129F-0066/009		129F/005,7–12
116a	PD.001	027B-0062/007		027B/004,7–9
116b	PD.001	027B-0075ab/007		027B/004,7–9
116c	PD.001	027B-0028/007		027B/004,7–9
116d	PD.001	027B-0044/007		027B/004,7–9
116e	PD.001	027B-0036/007		027B/004,7–9
116f	PD.001	027B-0052/007		027B/004,7–9
116g	PD.001	027B-0055/007		027B/004,7–9
116h	PD.001	027B-0041/007		027B/004,7–9
116i	PD.001	027B-0072/009		027B/004,7–9
116j	PD.001	027B-0077/009		027B/004,7–9
116k	PD.001	027B-0073/007		027B/004,7–9
117a	PD.001	027B-0066/007		027B/004,7–9
117b	PD.001	027B-0059/007		027B/004,7–9
117c	PD.001	027B-0039/007		027B/004,7–9
117d	PD.001	027B-0040/007		027B/004,7–9
117e	PD.001	027B-0034/007		027B/004,7–9
117f	PD.001	027B-0033/007		027B/004,7–9
117g	PD.001	027B-0074/007		027B/004,7–9
117h	PD.001	027B-0029/007		027B/004,7–9
117i	PD.001	027B-0063/009		027B/004,7–9
118a	PD.001	027B-0022/007		027B/004,7–9
118b	PD.001	027B-0030/007		027B/004,7–9
118c	PD.001	027B-0037/007		027B/004,7–9
118d	PD.001	027B-0027/007		027B/004,7–9
118e	PD.001	027B-0032/007		027B/004,7–9
118f	PD.001	027B-0026/007		027B/004,7–9
118g	PD.001	027B-0038/007		027B/004,7–9
118h	PD.001	027B-0031/007		027B/004,7–9
118i	PD.001	027B-0067/009		027B/004,7–9
118j	PD.001	027B-0065/009		027B/004,7–9
118k	PD.001	027B-0035/007		027B/004,7–9
118l	PD.001	027B-0023/007		027B/004,7–9
119a	PD.001	027B-0056/007		027B/004,7–9

TR. 25A Figure	Deposit	Catalog Number *duplicated catalog number	Misc. Text	Lot No.
119b	PD.001	027B-0045/007		027B/004,7–9
119c	PD.001	027B-0053/007		027B/004,7–9
119d	PD.001	027B-0064/009		027B/004,7–9
119e	PD.001	027B-0054/007		027B/004,7–9
119f	PD.001	027B-0042/007		027B/004,7–9
119g	PD.001	027B-0058/007		027B/004,7–9
119h	PD.001	027B-0071/009		027B/004,7–9
120a	PD.001	027B-0057/007		027B/004,7–9
120b	PD.001	027B-0049/007		027B/004,7–9
120c	PD.001	027B-0050/007		027B/004,7–9
120d	PD.001	027B-0046/007		027B/004,7–9
120e	PD.001	027B-0048/007		027B/004,7–9
120f	PD.001	027B-0047/007		027B/004,7–9
121a	PD.001	027B-0068/004		027B/004,7–9
121b	PD.001	027B-0069/007		027B/004,7–9
121c	PD.001	027B-0007/004		027B/004,7–9
121d	PD.001	027B-0076/007		027B/004,7–9
121e	PD.001	027B-0051/007		027B/004,7–9
122a	PD.003	027A-0035/006		027A/006
122b	PD.006	020E-0168/034		020E/034
122c	PD.014	012H-0029/008		012H/008
122d	PD.019	012H-0063/015		012H/015
123a	PD.022	012J-0185/017,24		012J/017,23–29
123b	PD.022	012J-0184/017,24		012J/017,23–29
123c	PD.022	012J-0186/017		012J/017,23–29
123d	PD.022	012J/025		012J/017,23–29
123e	PD.022	No catalog number		012J/017,23–29
123f	PD.022	No catalog number		012J/017,23–29
123g	PD.022	012J-0190/017		012J/017,23–29
123h	PD.022	012J-0196/017		012J/017,23–29
124a	PD.022	012J-0193/017,24		012J/017,23–29
124b	PD.022	012J-0192/017		012J/017,23–29
124c	PD.022	No catalog number		012J/017,23–29
124d	PD.022	No catalog number		012J/017,23–29
124e	PD.022	No catalog number		012J/017,23–29
124f	PD.022	012J-0195/017		012J/017,23–29
124g	PD.022	No catalog number		012J/017,23–29
124h	PD.022	012J-0187/017		012J/017,23–29
124i	PD.022	012J-0194/017,25		012J/017,23–29
124j	PD.022	012J-0205/017		012J/017,23–29

TR. 25A Figure	Deposit	Catalog Number *duplicated catalog number	Misc. Text	Lot No.
124k	PD.022	012J-0188/017		012J/017,23–29
124l	PD.022	012J-0199/017		012J/017,23–29
125a	PD.022	012J-0191/017		012J/017,23–29
125b	PD.022	012J-0189/017		012J/017,23–29
125c	PD.022	012J-0198/020		012J/020
125d	PD.022	012J-0204/025		012J/017,23–29
125e	PD.022	No catalog number		012J/017,23–29
125f	PD.022	No catalog number		012J/017,23–29
125g	PD.022	No catalog number		012J/017,23–29
126a	PD.022	012J-0197/017		012J/017,23–29
126b	PD.022	No catalog number		012J/017,23–29
126c	PD.022	No catalog number		012J/017,23–29
126d	PD.022	No catalog number		012J/017,23–29
126e	PD.022	No catalog number		012J/017,23–29
126f	PD.022	No catalog number		012J/017,23–29
126g	PD.022	No catalog number		012J/017,23–29
126h	PD.022	No catalog number		012J/017,23–29
126i	PD.022	No catalog number		012J/017,23–29
126j	PD.022	No catalog number		012J/017,23–29
126k	PD.022	No catalog number		012J/017,23–29
126l	PD.022	No catalog number		012J/017,23–29
126m	PD.022	No catalog number		012J/017,23–29
126n	PD.022	No catalog number		012J/017,23–29
126o	PD.022	No catalog number		012J/017,23–29
126p	PD.022	No catalog number		012J/017,23–29
127a	PD.023	020H-0127/034 top		020H/034
127a	PD.023	020H-0126/034 base		020H/034
127b	PD.024	020H-0030a/034 top		020H/034
127b	PD.024	020H-0030b/034 base		020H/034
127c	PD.025	020H-0027/035 top		020H/035
127c	PD.025	020H-0028/035 base		020H/035
127d	PD.027	012H-0164/028-35		012H/028–35
127e	PD.038	004B-0021/002		004B/002
127f	PD.040	012M-0001/005		012M/005
127g	PD.041,42	013B-0001/001		012L/001,13A/001,13B/001
127h01	PD.044	041G-0021/002		019C,41G
127h02	PD.044	041G-0022ab/002		019C,41G
128a	PD.050	010E-0052/002		010E/002
128b	PD.050	010E-0053/002		010E/002
129a	PD.050	010E-0025/002		010E/002

TR. 25A Figure	Deposit	Catalog Number *duplicated catalog number	Misc. Text	Lot No.
129b	PD.050	010E-0024/002		010E/002
129c	PD.050	010E-0019/002		010E/002
129d	PD.050	010E-0026/002		010E/002
129e	PD.050	010E-0012/002		010E/002
129f	PD.050	010E-0049/002 lid		010E/002
129f	PD.050	010E-0048/002 jar		010E/002
129g	PD.050	010E-0029/002		010E/002
129h	PD.050	010E-0023/002		010E/002
129i	PD.050	010E-0030/002		010E/002
129j	PD.050	010E-0028/002		010E/002
130a	PD.050	010E-0016/002		010E/002
130b	PD.050	010E-0017/002		010E/002
130c	PD.050	010E-0018/002		010E/002
130d	PD.050	010E-0015/002		010E/002
130e	PD.050	010E-0027/002		010E/002
130f	PD.050	010E-0033/002 base		010E/002
130f	PD.050	010E-0042/002 top		010E/002
130g	PD.050	010E-0032/002 base		010E/002
130g	PD.050	010E-0041/002 top		010E/002
130h	PD.050	010E-0047/002 top		010E/002
130i	PD.050	010E-0034/002 base		010E/002
130i	PD.050	010E-0043/002 top		010E/002
130j	PD.050	010E-0031/002 base		010E/002
130j	PD.050	010E-0040/002 top		010E/002
130k	PD.050	010E-0037/002 base		010E/002
130k	PD.050	010E-0046/002 top		010E/002
130l	PD.050	010E-0035/002 base		010E/002
130l	PD.050	010E-0044/002 top		010E/002
130m	PD.050	010E-0039/002		010E/002
130n	PD.050	010E-0036/002		010E/002
130o	PD.050	010E-0038/002		010E/002
131a	PD.054	012C-0114/001		012C/001,6–8,8A,16
131b	PD.054	012C-0112/001		012C/001,6–8,8A,16
131c	PD.054	012C-0113/001		012C/001,6–8,8A,16
131d	PD.054	012C-0117/001		012C/001,6–8,8A,16
131e	PD.054	012C-0115/001		012C/001,6–8,8A,16
131f	PD.054	012C-0120/001		012C/001,6–8,8A,16
131g	PD.054	012C-0169/008		012C/001,6–8,8A,16
132a	PD.064	024C-0225/071		024C/071
132b01	PD.065	24S-0007/003		024S/002,3

TR. 25A Figure	Deposit	Catalog Number *duplicated catalog number	Misc. Text	Lot No.
132b02	PD.065	24S-0005/002		024S/002,3
132b03	PD.065	24S-0002/002		024S/002,3
132b04	PD.065	24S-0006/002		024S/002,3
132b05	PD.065	24S-0001/002		024S/002,3
133a01	PD.067	027G-0044/009		027G/009
133a02	PD.067	027G-0043b/009		027G/009
133a03	PD.067	027G-0043c/009		027G/009
133a04	PD.067	027G-0043a/009		027G/009
133b01	PD.071	028B-0017/006		028B/006
133b02	PD.071	028B-0018/006		028B/006
133c01	PD.076	043C-0018/026		043C/026
133c02	PD.076	043C-0017/026		043C/026
134a	PD.074	043F-0007/017,18*		043F/017,18
134b	PD.074	043F-0086/017,18*		043F/017,18
134c	PD.074	043F-0087/017,18*		043F/017,18
134d	PD.074	043F-0092/017,18*		043F/017,18
134e	PD.074	043F-0025/017,18*		043F/017,18
134f	PD.074	043F-0098/017,18*		043F/017,18
134g	PD.074	043F-0037/017,18*		043F/017,18
134h	PD.074	043F-0089/017,18*		043F/017,18
134i	PD.074	043F-0088/017,18*		043F/017,18
134j	PD.074	043F-0065?/017,18*		043F/017,18
134k	PD.074	043F-0101/017,18*		043F/017,18
134l	PD.074	043F-0100/017,18*		043F/017,18
134m	PD.074	043F-0099/017,18*		043F/017,18
135a	PD.074	043F-0027/017,18*		043F/017,18
135b	PD.074	043F-0113/017,18*		043F/017,18
135c	PD.074	043F-0115/017,18*		043F/017,18
135d	PD.074	043F-0114/017,18*		043F/017,18
135e	PD.074	043F-0073/017,18*		043F/017,18
135f	PD.074	043F-0095/017,18*		043F/017,18
135g	PD.074	043F-0017/017,18*		043F/017,18
135h	PD.074	043F-0094/017,18*		043F/017,18
135i	PD.074	043F-0018/017,18*		043F/017,18
135j	PD.074	043F-0020/017,18*		043F/017,18
135k	PD.074	043F-0022/017,18*		043F/017,18
135l	PD.074	043F-0023/017,18*		043F/017,18
135m	PD.074	043F-0021/017,18*		043F/017,18
135n	PD.074	043F-0024/017,18*		043F/017,18
136a	PD.074	043F-0121/017,18*		043F/017,18

TR. 25A Figure	Deposit	Catalog Number *duplicated catalog number	Misc. Text	Lot No.
136b	PD.074	043F-0122/017,18*		043F/017,18
136c	PD.074	043F-0123/017,18*		043F/017,18
136d	PD.074	043F-0001+3?/017,18*		043F/017,18
136e	PD.074	043F-0102/017,18*		043F/017,18
136f	PD.074	043F-0030/017,18*		043F/017,18
136g	PD.074	043F-0080/017,18*		043F/017,18
136h	PD.074	043F-0032/017,18*		043F/017,18
136i	PD.074	043F-0081/017,18*		043F/017,18
136j	PD.074	043F-0069/017,18*		043F/017,18
136k	PD.074	043F-0124/017,18*		043F/017,18
136l	PD.074	043F-0125/017,18*		043F/017,18
136m	PD.074	043F-0126/017,18*		043F/017,18
136n	PD.074	043F-0049/017,18*		043F/017,18
136o	PD.074	043F-0050/017,18*		043F/017,18
136p	PD.074	043F-0044/017,18*		043F/017,18
137a	PD.074	043F-0068/017,18*		043F/017,18
137b	PD.074	043F-0076/017,18*		043F/017,18
137c	PD.074	043F-0070/017,18*		043F/017,18
137d	PD.074	catalog number lost		043F/017,18
137e	PD.074	043F-0072/017,18*		043F/017,18
137f	PD.074	043F-0082/017,18*		043F/017,18
137g	PD.074	043F-0074/017,18*		043F/017,18
137h	PD.074	043F-0005/017,18*		043F/017,18
137i	PD.074	043F-0103/017,18*		043F/017,18
137j	PD.074	043F-0104/017,18*		043F/017,18
137k	PD.074	043F-0060/017,18*		043F/017,18
137l	PD.074	043F-0059/017,18*		043F/017,18
138a	PD.074	043F-0062/017,18*		043F/017,18
138b	PD.074	043F-0064/017,18*		043F/017,18
138c	PD.074	043F-0015/017,18*		043F/017,18
138d	PD.074	043F-0008/017,18*		043F/017,18
138e	PD.074	043F-0067/017,18*		043F/017,18
138f	PD.074	043F-0010/017,18*		043F/017,18
138g	PD.074	043F-0055/017,18*		043F/017,18
138h	PD.074	043F-0002/017,18*		043F/017,18
138i	PD.074	043F-0061/017,18*		043F/017,18
138j	PD.074	043F-0012/017,18*		043F/017,18
138k	PD.074	043F-0009/017,18*		043F/017,18
138l	PD.074	043F-0119/017,18*		043F/017,18
138m	PD.074	043F-0004/017,18*		043F/017,18

TR. 25A Figure	Deposit	Catalog Number *duplicated catalog number	Misc. Text	Lot No.
138n	PD.074	043F-0013/017,18*		043F/017,18
138o	PD.074	043F-0065?/017,18*		043F/017,18
138p	PD.074	043F-0120/017,18*		043F/017,18
139a	PD.083	012P-0140/118		012P/118
139b01	PD.087	012R-0270/023		012R/017,20,21,23–25
139b02	PD.087	012R-0290/020		012R/017,20,21,23–25
139b03	PD.087	012R-0289/024		012R/017,20,21,23–25
139b04	PD.087	012R-0288/025		012R/017,20,21,23–25
139b05	PD.087	012R-0294/020		012R/017,20,21,23–25
139b06	PD.087	012R-0263a/020		012R/017,20,21,23–25
140a	PD.087	012R-0257/020		012R/017,20,21,23–25
140b	PD.087	012R-0262/020		012R/017,20,21,23–25
140c	PD.087	012R-0264/021		012R/017,20,21,23–25
140d	PD.087	012R-0258/020		012R/017,20,21,23–25
140e	PD.087	012R-0291/020		012R/017,20,21,23–25
140f	PD.087	012R-0293/020		012R/017,20,21,23–25
140g	PD.087	012R-0266/021		012R/017,20,21,23–25
140h	PD.087	012R-0265/021		012R/017,20,21,23–25
140i	PD.087	012R-0259/020		012R/017,20,21,23–25
140j	PD.087	012R-0260/020		012R/017,20,21,23–25
140k	PD.087	012R-0308/020		012R/017,20,21,23–25
140l	PD.087	012R-0261/020		012R/017,20,21,23–25
140m	PD.087	012R-0269/021		012R/017,20,21,23–25
140n	PD.087	012R-0267/021		012R/017,20,21,23–25
140o	PD.087	012R-0282/020		012R/017,20,21,23–25
140p	PD.087	012R-0271/023		012R/017,20,21,23–25
140q	PD.087	012R-0263b/020		012R/017,20,21,23–25
141a	PD.090	064A-0003/006		064A/006
141b01	PD.091	064G-0002/005		064G/005
141b02	PD.091	064G-0001/005		064G/005
141c	PD.093	064J-0002/009		064J/009
141d01	PD.095	065A-0003/003		065A/003
141d02	PD.095	065A-0005/003		065A/003
141d03	PD.095	065A-0006/003		065A/003
142a	PD.097	064A-0004/006		064A/006
142b	PD.098	003B-0035/003,4		003B/003.4
142c01	PD.099	067C-0017a/010		067C/010
142c02	PD.099	067C-0017b/010		067C/010
142c02	PD.099	067C-0017c/010		067C/010
142d01	PD.108	071F-0101/056		071F/056

TR. 25A Figure	Deposit	Catalog Number *duplicated catalog number	Misc. Text	Lot No.
142d02	PD.108	071F-0102/056		071F/056
142d03	PD.108	071F-0100/056		071F/056
142d04	PD.108	071F-0095/056		071F/056
142d05	PD.108	071F-0103/056		071F/056
142d06	PD.108	071F-0094/056		071F/056
143a01	PD.108	071F-0091/056		071F/056
143a02	PD.108	071F-0093/056		071F/056
143a03	PD.108	071F-0097/056		071F/056
143a04	PD.108	071F-0090/056		071F/056
143a05	PD.108	071F-0096/056		071F/056
143a06	PD.108	071F-0092/056		071F/056
143a07	PD.108	071F-0098/056		071F/056
143a08	PD.108	071F-0099/056		071F/056
143b	PD.109	067F-0002/009 lid		067F/009
143b	PD.109	067F-0001/009 bowl		067F/009
143c	PD.111	066P-0034/009		066P/009–11
144a01	PD.114	066X-0075/030		066X/029,30
144a02	PD.114	066X-0074/030		066X/029,30
144b01	PD.116	066X-0036a/020		066X/020
144b02	PD.116	066X-0036b/020		066X/020
144b03	PD.116	066X-0037a/020		066X/020
144b04	PD.116	066X-0036c/020		066X/020
144b05	PD.116	066X-0037b/020		066X/020
144c	PD.122	082A-0005/002		082A/002
144d01	PD.126	076B-0002/008		076B/008
144d02	PD.126	076B-0003/008		076B/008
144d03	PD.126	076B-0005/008		076B/008
144d04	PD.126	076B-0004/008		076B/008
144e	PD.124	076B-0001a,b/013		076B/013
144f01	PD.129	090B-0010/006		090B/006
144f02	PD.129	090B-0011/006		090B/006
145a	PD.133	098A-0008/004		098A/004
145b	PD.133	098A-0027/004		098A/004
145c	PD.133	098A-0026/004		098A/004
145d	PD.133	098A-0030/004		098A/004
145e	PD.133	098A-0028/004		098A/004
145f	PD.133	098A-0029/004		098A/004
145g	PD.133	098A-0031/004		098A/004
146a	PD.134	012T-0014/12,16,18		012T/003,7–9,12,14–18
146b	PD.134	012T-0012/009,12,16		012T/003,7–9,12,14–18

TR. 25A Figure	Deposit	Catalog Number *duplicated catalog number	Misc. Text	Lot No.
146c	PD.134	012T-0017/012,16,18		012T/003,7–9,12,14–18
146d	PD.134	012T-0018/008,9,12,16		012T/003,7–9,12,14–18
146e	PD.134	012T-0082/003,8,9,12,16,20		012T/003,7–9,12,14–18
147a	PD.134	012T-0011/008,9,16,18	MT-102	012T/003,7–9,12,14–18
147b	PD.134	012T-0013/008,9		012T/003,7–9,12,14–18
147c	PD.134	012T-0031/07,12		012T/003,7–9,12,14–18
147d	PD.134	012T-0080/08,9,18		012T/003,7–9,12,14–18
147e	PD.134	012T-0083/009,12,16,18		012T/003,7–9,12,14–18
147f	PD.160,165	012T-0449/078,79,82		012T/078,79,82,86
148a	PD.147	045G-0057/022		045G/022
148b	PD.151	012T-0401/059		012T/059
148c01	PD.152	012T-0402a/060		012T/060
148c02	PD.152	012T-0402b/060		012T/060
148c03	PD.152	012T-0392/060		012T/060
148d01	PD.157	012P-0618/187		012P/187
148d02	PD.157	012P-0619/187		012P/187
148d03	PD.157	012P-0617/187		012P/187
148e	PD.158	098D-0037/016		098D/016
148g01	PD.169	078Q-0018a/014		078Q/014
148g02	PD.169	078Q-0018d/014		078Q/014
148g03	PD.169	078Q-0018b/014		078Q/014
148g04	PD.169	078Q-0018c/014		078Q/014
149a	PD.170	053C-0062a,b/009		053C/009
149b	PD.170	053C-0034a,b/009		053C/009
149c	PD.170	053C-0057a,b/009		053C/009
149d	PD.170	053C-0056a,b/009		053C/009
149e	PD.170	053C-0037a,b/009		053C/009
149f	PD.170	053C-0054a,b/009		053C/009
150a	PD.170	053C-0044a,b/009		053C/009
150b	PD.170	053C-0031a,b/009		053C/009
150c	PD.170	053C-0051a,b/009		053C/009
150d	PD.170	053C-0046a,b/009		053C/009
150e	PD.170	053C-0035a,b/009		053C/009
150f	PD.170	053C-0040a,b/009		053C/009
150g	PD.170	053C-0042a,b/009		053C/009
150h	PD.170	053C-0050a,b/009		053C/009
150i	PD.170	053C-0059/009		053C/009
150j	PD.170	053C-0061/009		053C/009
151a01	PD.170	053C-0058/009		053C/009
151a02	PD.170	053C-0080/009		053C/009

TR. 25A Figure	Deposit	Catalog Number *duplicated catalog number	Misc. Text	Lot No.
151a03	PD.170	053C-0060/009		053C/009
151b01	PD.179	012H-0224/054A		012H/054A
151b02	PD.179	012H-0225/054A		012H/054A
151c01	PD.181	120A-0018/003,4		120A/003–5
151c02	PD.181	120A-0001/003,4		120A/003–5
151d	PD.182	120A-0002/001		120A/001,6–8
151e	PD.184	012U-0141/005		012U/005
152a01	PD.191	135A-0195/001,25,27,67	MT-287	135A/001,18,19,23–27,67–69
152a02	PD.191	135A-0198/027		135A/001,18,19,23–27,67–69
152a03	PD.191	135A-0197/001,18,25,27		135A/001,18,19,23–27,67–69
152a04	PD.191	135A-0241/019		135A/001,18,19,23–27,67–69
152a05	PD.191	135A-0199a/027		135A/001,18,19,23–27,67–69
152a06	PD.191	135A-0199b/927		135A/001,18,19,23–27,67–69
152a07	PD.191	135A-0201/027		135A/001,18,19,23–27,67–69
152a08	PD.191	135A-0204/018,27		135A/001,18,19,23–27,67–69
152b	PD.192	135A-0023/001		135A/001
152c01	PD.193	135A-0655/088		135A/044,88
152c02	PD.193	135A-0252/044,88		135A/044,88
152c03	PD.193	135A-0638/088		135A/044,88
152c04	PD.193	135A-0657/044		135A/044,88
152c05	PD.193	135A-0656/044,88		135A/044,88
153a	PD.199	135C-0029/022		135C/022
153b	PD.201	114I-0004/001		114I/001
153c	PD.208	098X-0009/003		098X/003
153d01	PD.221	140A-0004/001		140A/001
153d02	PD.221	140A-0005/001		140A/001
153e	PD.227	129B-0001/021		129B/021
153f01	PD.231	066H-0050/007,9,12		066H/005–7,9–16
153f02	PD.231	066H-0051/007		066H/005–7,9–16
153f03	PD.231	066H-0053/007,9		066H/005–7,9–16
153f04	PD.231	066H-0019/010		066H/005–7,9–16
154a	PD.231	066H-0017/009		066H/005–7,9–16
154b	PD.231	066H-0020/010		066H/005–7,9–16
154c	PD.231	066H-0049/005-7,10,12		066H/005–7,9–16
154d	PD.231	066H-0021/010		066H/005–7,9–16
154e	PD.231	066H-0048/007,9,12–15		066H/005–7,9–16
155a	PD.233	003D-0024a,b/004		003D/004
155b	PD.235	012K-0057/008		012K/008
155c01	PD.263	072C-0002/005		072C/005
155c02	PD.263	072C-0001/005		072C/005

TR. 25A Figure	Deposit	Catalog Number *duplicated catalog number	Misc. Text	Lot No.
155d	PD.265	012P-0320/137		012P/137
155e	PD.266	012P-0321/144		012P/144
155f	PD.267	012P-0322/145		012P/145
155g	PD.268	012P-0123/060		012P/060

References

Adams, Richard E. W.
    1971   The Ceramics of Altar de Sacrificios. *Papers of the Peabody Museum of Archaeology and Ethnology* 63:1. Cambridge, MA: Harvard University.

    1999   *Rio Azul. An Ancient Maya City*. Norman, OK: University of Oklahoma Press.

Adams, Richard E. W., and Jane Jackson-Adams
    1991   Rio Azul Ceramic Sequence Summary. Unpublished manuscript in possession of author.

Aimers, James J.
    2013   Problems and Prospects in Maya Ceramic Classification, Analysis, and Interpretation. In *Ancient Maya Pottery. Classification, Analysis, and Interpretation*, edited by J. J. Aimers, pp. 229–238. Gainesville: University Pressof Florida.

Awe, Jaime J.
    1992   Dawn in the Land Between the Rivers: Formative Occupation at Cahal Pech, Belize and its Implications for Preclassic Development in the Maya Lowlands. Ph.D. dissertation, University College London.

Bachand, Bruce
    2007   The Preclassic Ceramic Sequence of Punta de Chimino, Petén, Guatemala. *Mayab* 19:5–26.

Ball, Joseph W.
    1977   *The Archaeological Ceramics of Becan, Campeche, Mexico*. Middle American Research Institute Publication Vol. 43. New Orleans: Tulane University.

    1983   Notes on the Distribution of Established Ceramics Types in the Corozal District, Belize. In *Archaeological Excavations in Northern Belize*, edited by Raymond V. Sidrys, pp 203–220. Los Angeles: Institute of Archaeology, University of California Los Angeles.

Ball, Joseph W. and Jennifer T. Taschek
    2015   Ceramic History, Ceramic Change, and Architectural Sequence at Acanmul, Campeche: A Local Chronicle and its Regional Implications. *Ancient Mesoamerica* 26(2):233–273.

Becker, Marshall
    1973   Archaeological Evidence for Archaeological Specialization Among the Classic Period Maya. *American Antiquity* 38:396–406.

Brady, James E., Joseph W. Ball, Ronald L. Bishop, Duncan C. Pring, Norman Hammond, and Rupert A. Housley
    1998   The Lowland Maya Protoclassic: A Reconsideration of Its Nature and Significance. *Ancient Mesoamerica* 9(1):17–38.

Callaghan, Michael G.
    2008   Technologies of Power: Ritual Economy and Ceramic Production in the Terminal Preclassic Period Holmul Region, Guatemala. Ph.D. dissertation, Department of Anthropology, Vanderbilt University, Nashville.

    2016a   Yax Te Complex, Chapter 3. In *The Ceramic Sequence of the Holmul Region, Guatemala*, edited by M. G. Callaghan and N. Neivens de Estrada, pp. 67–91. Anthropological Papers of the University of Arizona, Number 77. Tucson, AZ: The University of Arizona Press.

    2016b   Itzamkanak Complex, Chapter 4. In *The Ceramic Sequence of the Holmul Region, Guatemala*, edited by M. G. Callaghan and N. Neivens de Estrada, pp. 92–110. Anthropological Papers of the University of Arizona, Number 77. Tucson, AZ: The University of Arizona Press.

    2016c   Wayab Subcomplex, Chapter 5. In *The Ceramic Sequence of the Holmul Region, Guatemala*, edited by M. G. Callaghan and N. Neivens de Estrada, pp. 111–121. Anthropological Papers of the University of Arizona, Number 77. Tucson, AZ: The University of Arizona Press.

    2016d   K'ak Complex, Chapter 6. In *The Ceramic Sequence of the Holmul Region, Guatemala*, edited by M. G. Callaghan and N. Neivens de Estrada, pp. 122–159. Anthropological Papers of the University of Arizona, Number 77. Tucson, AZ: The University of Arizona Press.

    2016e   Chak Complex, Chapter 7. In *The Ceramic Sequence of the Holmul Region, Guatemala*, edited by M. G. Callaghan and N. Neivens de Estrada, pp. 160–190. Anthropological Papers of the University of Arizona, Number 77. Tucson, AZ: The University of Arizona Press.

Castellanos, Jeanette E. and Antonia E. Foias
    2017   The Earliest Maya Farmers of Peten: New Evidence from Buenavista-Nuevo San José, Central Peten Lakes Region, Guatemala. *Journal of Anthropology*, vol. 2017, Article ID 8109137, 45 pages; https://doi.org/10.1155/2017/8109137

Chase, Arlen F.
    1984   The Ceramic Complexes of the Tayasal-Paxcaman Zone. *Ceramica de Cultura Maya* 13:27–41.

Chase, Arlen F. and Diane Z. Chase
    2004   Terminal Classic Status-Linked Ceramics and the Maya Collapse: De Facto Refuse at Caracol, Belize. In *The Terminal Classic in the Maya Lowlands: Collapse, Transition, and Transformation*, edited by A. A. Demarest, P. M. Rice, and D. S. Rice, pp. 342–366. Boulder: University Press of Colorado.

Chase, Diane Z.
    1982   Spatial and Temporal Variability in Postclassic Northern Belize. Ph.D. dissertation, University of Pennsylvania. University Microfilms, Ann Arbor.

Cheek, Charles D.
    1970   Tzakol Incised Ceramics from Tikal. M.A. thesis, University of Arizona, Tucson.

Coe, William R.
    1963   Preliminary Research at Tikal, Guatemala. Unpublished report on file at the Penn Museum, Philadelphia.

Coggins, Clemency C.
1975 Painting and Drawing Styles at Tikal: An Historical and Iconographic Reconstruction. Ph.D. dissertation, Department of Anthropology, Harvard University, Cambridge, MA.

Culbert, T. Patrick
1965 *The Ceramic History of the Central Highlands of Chiapas, Mexico*. Papers of the New World Archaeological Foundation, no. 19. Provo, UT: Brigham Young University.

1973 Maya Down Fall at Tikal. In *The Classic Maya Collapse*, edited by T. P. Culbert, pp. 63–92. Albuquerque: University of New Mexico Press

1977 Early Maya Development at Tikal, Guatemala. In *The Origins of Maya Civilization*, edited by R. E. W Adams, pp. 77–101. Albuquerque: University of New Mexico Press.

1993 *The Ceramics of Tikal: Vessels from the Burials, Caches, and Problematical Deposits*. Tikal Report No. 25A. Philadelphia: University of Pennsylvania Museum of Archaeology and Anthropology.

2003 The Ceramics of Tikal. In *Tikal: Dynasties, Foreigners, & Affairs of State*, edited by J. A. Sabloff, pp. 47–82. Santa Fe, NM: School of American Research Press.

Culbert, T. Patrick, Laura J. Kosakowsky, Robert Fry, and William Haviland
1990 The Demography of Tikal. In *Lowland Maya Demography*, edited by T. P. Culbert and D. Rice, pp. 103–122. Santa Fe, NM: School of American Research Press.

Culbert, T. Patrick and Robert Rands
2007 Multiple Classifications: An Alternative Approach to the Investigation of Maya Ceramics. *Latin American Antiquity* 18:181–190.

Demarest, Arthur A., and Robert J. Sharer
1982 The Origins and Evolution of Usulutan Ceramics. *American Antiquity* 47(4):810–822.

Dominguez Carrasco, Maria del R.
1994 *Calakmul, Campeche: Un Analisis de la Ceramica*. Mexico: Universidad Autonoma de Campeche.

Driver, W. David and Laura J. Kosakowsky
2013 Transforming Identities and Shifting Goods: Tracking Sociopolitical Change Through Monumental Architecture and Ceramic Assemblages at Blue Creek, Northwestern Belize. In *Classic Maya Political Ecology, Resource Management, Class Histories, and Political Change in Northwestern Belize*, edited by Jon C. Lohse, pp. 69–98. Los Angeles: Cotsen Institute of Archaeology at UCLA.

Eppich, Keith
2000 Ceramics and Interaction at El Pozito, Belize. M.A. thesis, Department of Anthropology, San Diego State University, San Diego.

2011 Lineage and State at El Perú-Waka': Ceramic and Architectural Perspectives on the Classic Maya Social Dynamic. Ph.D. dissertation, Department of Anthropology, Southern Methodist University, Dallas.

Ferree, Lisa
1972 The Pottery Censers of Tikal, Guatemala. Ph.D. dissertation, Department of Anthropology, Southern Illinois

University, Carbondale, Illinois.

Foias, Antonia E. and Ronald L. Bishop
2013   *Ceramics, Production, and Exchange in the Petexbatun Region: The Economic Parameters of the Classic Maya Collapse.* Nashville: Vanderbilt University Press.

Forsyth, Donald W.
1983   Investigations at Edzna, Campeche, Mexico: Ceramics. *Papers of the New World Archaeological Foundation* 46(2). Brigham Young University, Provo.

1989   The Ceramics of El Mirador, Petén, Guatemala. El Mirador Series, Part 4. *Papers of the New World Archaeological Foundation,* Vol. 63. Provo, UT: Brigham Young University.

1993   The Ceramic Sequence at Nakbe, Guatemala. *Ancient Mesoamerica* 4(1):31–53.

Fry, Robert E.
1979   The Economics of Pottery at Tikal: Models of Exchange for Serving Vessels. *American Antiquity* 44(3):494–512.

1989   Regional Ceramic Distributional Patterning in Northern Belize: The View from Pulltrouser Swamp. In *Prehistoric Maya Economies of Belize, Research in Economic Anthropology*, edited by P. A. McAnany and B. I. Isaac, pp. 91–111. Greenwich , CT: JAI Press.

Gifford, James C.
1976   Prehistoric Pottery Analysis and the Ceramics of Barton Ramie in the Belize Valley. *Memoirs of the Peabody Museum of Archaeology and Ethnology*, Vol. 18. Cambridge, MA: Harvard University Press.

Hammond, Norman
1975   *Lubaantun: A Classic Maya Realm.* Peabody Museum Monographs No. 2. Cambridge, MA: Peabody Museum of Archaeology and Ethnology, Harvard University.

Harrison, Peter D.
1970   The Central Acropolis, Tikal, Guatemala: A Preliminary Study of the Functions of Its Structural Components during the Late Classic Period. Ph.D. dissertation, Department of Anthropology, University of Pennsylvania, Philadelphia.

1999   *The Lords of Tikal.* Thames and Hudson, New York.

Hermes, Bernard
1993   Adiciones tipológicas a los Complejos Eb, Tzec, y Manik de Tikal, Guatemala. *Revista Española de Antropología Americana* 23:9–27.

Iglesias Ponce de León, Maria J.
1988   Análisis de un Deposito Problemático de Tikal, Guatemala. *Journal de la Societe des Americanistes* 74:25–48.

1996   El hombre depone y la arqueología dispone: formas de deposición en la cultura Maya, el caso de Tikal. *Los Investigadores de la Cultura Maya* 4:187–217. Universidad Autónoma de Campeche, Mexico.

Inomata, Takeshi, Daniela Triadan, Kazuo Aoyama, Victor Castillo, and Hitoshi Yonenobu
2013   Early Ceremonial Construction at Ceibal, Guatemala and the Origins of Lowland Maya Civilization. *Science* 340:467–471.

Kidder, Alfred Vincent, Jesse David Jennings, and Edwin M. Shook.
1946   *Excavations at Kaminaljuyu, Guatemala.* Vol. 561. State College, PA: Pennsylvania State University Press.

Kosakowsky, Laura J.
1983   Intra-site Variability of the Formative Ceramics from Cuello, Belize: An Analysis of Form and Function. Ph.D. dissertation, Department of Anthropology, University of Arizona, Tucson.

1987   Preclassic Maya Pottery at Cuello, Belize. *Anthropological Papers of the University of Arizona*, No. 47. Tucson , AZ: University of Arizona Press.

2012   Ceramics and Chronology of the Chan Site. In *Chan: An Ancient Maya Farming Community in Belize*, edited by C. Robin, pp. 42–70. Gainesville: University Press of Florida.

Kosakowsky, Laura J. and Jon C. Lohse
2003   Investigating Multivariate Ceramic Attributes as Clues to Ancient Maya Social, Economic, and Political Organization in Blue Creek, Northwest Belize. Research Report Submitted to the Ahau Foundation. Manuscript on file with the Institute of Archaeology, NICH, Belmopan, Belize.

Kosakowsky, Laura J., Anna C. Novotny, Angela Keller, Nicholas F. Hearth, and Carmen Ting
2012   Contextualizing Ritual: Material Culture from Caches, Burials, and Problematical Deposits from Chan's Community Center. In *Chan: An Ancient Maya Farming Community in Belize*, edited by C. Robin, pp. 289–310. Gainesville: University Press of Florida.

Kosakowsky, Laura J. and Duncan C. Pring
1998 The Ceramics of Cuello, Belize: A New Evaluation. *Ancient Mesoamerica* 9(1):55–66.

2001   The Nohmul Ceramic Sequence: A Summary Analysis. Manuscript on file with the Institute of Archaeology, Belmopan, Belize.

Kosakowsky, Laura J., Kerry L. Sagebiel, and Duncan C. Pring
2018   Long Ago but Not Forgotten: The Early Preclassic Swasey Sphere of Northern Belize. In *Research Reports in Belizean Archaeology: Papers of the 2017 Belize Archaeology Symposium*, edited by J. Morris, M. Badillo, and G. Thompson, Volume 15, pp. 131–140. Belmopan Belize: Institute of Archaeology, NICH.

Kosakowsky, Laura J., Robin Robertson, and Debra S. Walker
2015   The Ceramics from a Terminal Preclassic Chultun Style Burial from the site of Blue Creek, Belize. In *Research Reports in Belizean Archaeology: Papers of the 2014 Belize Archaeology Symposium*, edited by J. Morris, J. Awe, M. Badillo, and G. Thompson, Volume 12, pp. 377–82. Belmopan Belize: Institute of Archaeology, NICH.

Krejci, Estella and T. Patrick Culbert
1995   Preclassic and Classic Burials and Caches in the Maya Lowlands. In *The Emergence of Lowland Maya Civilization: The Transition from Preclassic to Early Classic*, edited by N. Grube, pp. 103116. Acta Mesoamericana. vol. 8. Möckmühl, Germany: Verlag Anton Saurwein.

Laporte, Juan Pedro
1995   Preclasico a Clasico en Tikal: Proceso de Transformacion en Mundo Perdido. In *The Emergence of Lowland Maya Civilization: The Transition from the Preclassic to the Early Classic*, edited by N. Grube, pp. 17–33. Möckmühl, Germany: Verlag Anton Saurwein.

2000   *Ofrenda Cerámica y Cambio Social en Mundo Perdido, Tikal, Guatemala.* Guatemala City: Utz'b. Asociación Tikal.

Laporte, Juan Pedro and Juan Antonio Valdes
1993   *Tikal y Uaxactun en el Preclasico.* Campeche: Universidad Nacional Autonoma de Mexico.

Laporte, Juan Pedro and Vilma Fialko
1987   La Cerámica del Clásico Temprano desde Mundo Perdido, Tikal: Una Reevaluación. In *Maya Ceramics: Papers from the 1985 Maya Ceramics Conference,* edited by P. M. Rice and R. J. Sharer, pp. 123–181. British Archaeological Reports International Series, 345(1). Oxford, UK: British Archaeological Reports.

1990   New Perspectives on Old Problems: Dynastic References for the Early Classic at Tikal. In *Vision and Revision in Maya Studies,* edited by F. Clancy and P. D. Harrison, pp. 33–66. Albuquerque: University of New Mexico Press.

1995   Un Reencuentro con Mundo Perdido, Tikal, Guatemala. *Ancient Mesoamerica* 6(1):41–94.

Laporte, Juan Pedro, Bernard Hermes, Lilian de Zea, and Maria Josefa Iglesias
1992   Nuevos Entierros y Escondites de Tikal: Subfases Manik 3a y 3b. *Ceramica de Cultura Maya* 16:30–101.

LeCount, Lisa
1996   Pottery and Power: Feasting, Gifting, and Displaying Wealth Among the Late and Terminal Classic Maya. Ph.D. dissertation, Department of Anthropology, University of California, Los Angeles.

Lopez Varela, Sandra Lorena
1989   *Análisis y Clasificación de la Cerámica de un Sitio Maya del Clásico: Yaxchilán, México.* British Archaeological Reports International Series, 535. Oxford, UK: British Archaeological Reports.

1996   The K'axob Formative Ceramics: The Search for Regional Interaction Through a Reappraisal of Ceramic Analysis and Classification in Northern Belize. Ph.D. dissertation. London University, London.

Martin, Simon and Nikolai Grube
2000   *Chronicle of the Maya Kings and Queens: Deciphering the Dynasties of the Ancient Maya.* London: Thames & Hudson.

McDow, David A.
1997   An Analysis of the Whole Ceramic Vessels from Kichpanha, Northern Belize. Undergraduate honors thesis, Department of Anthropology, University of Texas, Austin.

McKillop, Heather
2002   *Salt: White Gold of the Ancient Maya.* Gainesville: University Press of Florida.

Moholy-Nagy, Hattula
1994   Tikal Material Culture: Artifacts and Social Structure at a Classic Lowland Maya City. Ph.D. dissertation, Department of Anthropology, University of Michigan, Ann Arbor.

2003b   Beyond the Catalog: The Chronology and Contexts of Tikal Artifacts. In *Tikal: Dynasties, Foreigners, & Affairs of State,* edited by J. A. Sabloff, pp. 83–110. Santa Fe, NM: School of American Research Press.

Moriarty, Matthew D.
2012   History, Politics, and Ceramics: The Ceramic Sequence of Trinidad de Nosotros, El Petén, Guatemala. In *Motul de San José: Politics, History, and Economy in a Classic Maya Polity,* edited by A. E. Foias and K. F. Emery, pp.

194–228. Gainesville: University Press of Florida.

Muñoz, Arturo René
2006 Power, Production and Practice: Technological Change in the Late Classic Ceramics of Piedras Negras, Guatemala. Ph.D. dissertation, Department of Anthropology, University of Arizona, Tucson.

Pring, Duncan C.
1977 The Preclassic Ceramics of Northern Belize. Ph.D. dissertation, University of London, London.

2000 *The Protoclassic in the Maya Lowlands*. British Archaeological Reports International Series, 908. Oxford, UK: British Archaeological Reports.

Rands, Robert L.
1973 The Classic Collapse in the Southern Maya Lowlands: Chronology. In *The Classic Maya Collapse,* edited by T. P. Culbert, pp. 43–62. Albuquerque: A School of American Research Book, University of New Mexico Press.

Rathje, William L.
1967 Tzakol Basal-Flange Polychrome Bowls from Tikal, Guatemala. Undergraduate honors thesis, Department of Anthropology, University of Arizona, Tucson.

Reents-Budet, Dorie and Ronald L. Bishop
2003 More Than Methodology: INAA and Classic Maya Painted Ceramics. In *Patterns and Process: A Festschrift in Honor of Dr. Edward V. Sayre*, edited by L.V. Zelst, pp. 93–106. Smithsonian Center for Materials Research and Education, Washington, DC.

Reents-Budet, Dorie, Ronald L. Bishop, Ellen Bell, T. Patrick Culbert, Hattula Moholy-Nagy, Hector Neff, and Robert Sharer
2003 Tikal y sus tumbas del Clásico Temprano: Nuevos datos químicos de las vasijas de cerámica. In *XVII Simposio de Investigaciones Arqueológicas en Guatemala*, edited by J. P. Laporte, B. Arroyo, H. Escobedo, and H. Mejía, pp. 777–793. Guatemala City: Museo Nacional de Arqueología y Etnología.

Reina, Ruben E and Robert M. Hill
1978 *The Traditional Pottery of Guatemala*. Austin: University of Texas Press.

Rice, Prudence M.
1979a Introduction and the Middle Preclassic Ceramics of Lake Yaxha-Sacnab, Guatemala. *Ceramica de la Cultura Maya* 10:1–36.

1979b Ceramic and Nonceramic Artifacts of Lakes Yaxha-Sacnab, El Petén, Guatemala, Part 1, The Ceramics, Section B, Postclassic Pottery from Topoxte. *Ceramica de Cultura Maya* 11:1–86.

2009 Mound ZZ1, Nixtun-Ch'ich', Petén, Guatemala: Rescue Operations at a Long-lived Structure in the Maya Lowlands. *Journal of Field Archaeology* 34(4):403–422.

2013 Type-Variety: What Works and What Doesn't. In *Ancient Maya Pottery. Classification, Analysis, and Interpretation*, edited by J. J. Aimers, pp. 11–28. Gainesville: University Press of Florida.

Rice, Prudence M. and Timothy W. Pugh
2017 Water, Centering, and the Beginning of Time at Middle Preclassic Nixtun-Ch'ich', Petén, Guatemala. *Journal of Anthropological Archaeology* 48:1–16.

Robertson, Robin A.

2016   Red Wares, Zapatista, Drinking Vessels, Colonists and Exchange at Cerro Maya. In *Perspectives on the Ancient Maya of Chetumal Bay*, edited by D. S. Walker, pp.125–148. Gainesville: University Press of Florida.

Robertson(-Freidel), Robin A.

1980   The Ceramics from Cerros: A Late Preclassic Site in Northern Belize. Ph.D. dissertation, Department of Anthropology, Harvard University, Cambridge, MA. University Microfilms, Ann Arbor.

Sabloff, Jeremy A.

1975   Ceramics. In *Excavations at Seibal, Department of Petén, Guatemala*. Memoirs of the Peabody Museum of Archaeology and Ethnology, Volume 13(2). Cambridge, MA: Harvard University.

Sagebiel, Kerry L.

2005   Shifting Allegiances at La Milpa, Belize: A Typological, Chronological, and Formal Analysis of the Ceramics. Ph.D. dissertation, Department of Anthropology, University of Arizona, Tucson.

Sagebiel, Kerry L. and Helen R. Haines

2015   Never Ending, Still Beginning: A New Examination of the Ceramics of Ka'kabish, Belize. In *Research Reports in Belizean Archaeology, Papers of the 2014 Belize Archaeology Symposium,* Edited by J. Morris, M. Badillo, S. Batty, and G. Thompson, Vol. 12 pp. 358–366. Belmopan, Belize: Institute of Archaeology, NICH.

Schwalbe, Larry A. and T. Patrick Culbert

1987   X-Ray Flourescence Survey of Tikal Ceramics. *Journal of Archaeological Science* 14(6): 635–657.

Shook, Edwin and Alfred V. Kidder

1952   *Mound E-III-3, Kaminaljuyu, Guatemala*. Contributions to American Anthropology and History, no. 53. Carnegie Institution of Washington, Publication 596. Washington, DC: Carnegie Institution of Washington.

Smith, Robert E.

1955   *Ceramic Sequence at Uaxactun, Guatemala*. Middle American Research Institute, Publication 20, I & II. New Orleans: Tulane University.

1971   *The Pottery of Mayapan: Including Studies of Ceramic Material from Uxmal, Kabah, and Chichen Itza*. Papers of the Peabody Museum of Archaeology and Ethnology, Vol. 66:, I & II. Cambridge, MA: Harvard University.

Smith, Robert E. and James C. Gifford

1966   *Maya Ceramic Varieties, Types, and Wares at Uaxactun: Supplement to Ceramic Sequence at Uaxactun, Guatemala*. pp. 125–174. Middle American Research Institute, Publication 28. New Orleans: Tulane University.

Sullivan, Lauren A. and Jaime J. Awe

2013   Establishing the Cunil Ceramic Complex at Cahal Pech, Belize. In *Ancient Maya Pottery: Classification, Analysis, and Interpretation*, edited by James John Aimers, pp. 107–120. Gainesville: University Press of Florida.

Thompson, J. E. S.

1939   *Excavations at San Jose, British Honduras*. Carnegie Institution of Washington Publication 506. Washington, DC: Carnegie Institution of Washington.

Thompson, Raymond H.

1958   Modern Yucatecan Maya Pottery Making. In *Memoirs of the Society for American Archaeology*, No. 15. Salt Lake

City, UT: Society for American Archaeology.

Valdez, Fred
1987 The Prehistoric Ceramics of Colha, Northern Belize. Ph.D. dissertation, Department of Anthropology, Harvard University, Cambridge, MA.

1998 The Chan Chich Ceramic Sequence. In *The 1997 Season of the Chan Chich Archaeological Project*, edited by B. A. Houk, pp. 73–86. Papers of the Chan Chich Archaeological Project No. 3. San Antonio, TX: Center for Maya Studies.

Valdez, Fred Jr., and Brett A. Houk
2000 The Chan Chich Ceramic Complexes. In *The 1998 and 1999 Seasons of the Chan Chich Archaeological Project*, edited by B. A. Houk, pp. 127–140. Papers of the Chan Chich Archaeological Project, No. 4. Mesoamerican Archaeological Research Laboratory. Austin: The University of Texas.

Walker, Debra S.
1990 Cerros Revisited: Ceramic Indicators of Terminal Classic and Postclassic Settlement and Pilgrimage in Northern Belize. Ph.D. dissertation. Department of Anthropology Southern Methodist University, Dallas.

Walker, Debra S. and Kathryn Reese-Taylor
2012 Naachtún, Petén, Guatemala: First Analyses. Report Submitted to the Foundation for the Advancement of Mesoamerican Studies.

Willey, Gordon R., William R. Bullard, John B. Glass, and James C. Gifford
1965 *Prehistoric Maya Settlements in the Belize Valley*. Peabody Museum of Archaeology and Anthropology Papers, Vol.54, Cambridge, MA: Harvard University.

Willey, Gordon R., T. Patrick Culbert, and R. E. W. Adams
1967 Maya Lowland Ceramics: A Report from the 1965 Guatemala City Conference. *American Antiquity* 32(3):289–315.

Tikal Reports (see TR. 12):

TR. 12:
Coe, William R. and William A. Haviland
1982 *Introduction to the Archaeology of Tikal, Guatemala*. Philadelphia: University of Pennsylvania Museum of Archaeology and Anthropology.

TR. 14:
Coe, William R.
1990 *Excavations in the Great Plaza, North Terrace, and North Acropolis of Tikal*. Philadelphia: University of Pennsylvania Museum of Archaeology and Anthropology.

TR. 15:
Loten, H. Stanley, for Peter D. Harrison
n.d. *Excavations in the Central Acropolis of Tikal*.

TR. 16:
Jones, Christopher
1996 *Excavations in the East Plaza of Tikal, Volumes I and II*. Philadelphia: University of Pennsylvania Museum of Archaeology and Anthropology.

TR. 17:
Haviland, William A.
2019 *Excavations in the West Plaza of Tikal*. Philadelphia: University of Pennsylvania Museum of Archaeology and Anthropology.

TR. 18:
Jones, Christopher
n.d. *Excavations in the Twin Pyramid Groups of Tikal*.

TR. 19:
Haviland, William A.
1985 *Excavations in Small Residential Groups of Tikal, Groups 4F-1 and 4F-2*. Philadelphia: University of Pennsylvania Museum of Archaeology and Anthropology.

TR. 20A:
Haviland, William A.
2014 *Excavations in Residential Areas of Tikal: Non-Elite Groups without Shrines. The Excavations*. Philadelphia: University of Pennsylvania Museum of Archaeology and Anthropology.

TR. 20B:
Haviland, William A.
2014 *Excavations in Residential Areas of Tikal: Non-Elite Groups without Shrines. Analysis and Conclusions*. Philadelphia: University of Pennsylvania Museum of Archaeology and Anthropology.

TR. 21:
Becker, Marshall J., with contributions by Christopher Jones
1999 *Excavations in Residential Areas of Tikal—Groups with Shrines*. Philadelphia: University of Pennsylvania Museum of Archaeology and Anthropology.

TR. 22:
Haviland, William A.
2015 *Excavations in Residential Areas of Tikal: Group 7F-1*. Philadelphia: University of Pennsylvania Museum of Archaeology and Anthropology.

TR. 23A:
Loten, H. Stanley
2002 *Miscellaneous Investigations in Central Tikal*. Philadelphia: University of Pennsylvania Museum of Archaeology and Anthropology.

TR. 23C:
Loten, H. Stanley
2018 *Miscellaneous Investigations in Central Tikal: The Plaza of the Seven Temples*. Philadelphia: University of Pennsylvania Museum of Archaeology and Anthropology.

TR. 23D:
Loten, H. Stanley
2018 *Miscellaneous Investigations in Central Tikal: Structures in and around the Lost World Plaza*. Philadelphia: University of Pennsylvania Museum of Archaeology and Anthropology.

TR. 25A:

Culbert, T. Patrick

1993 *The Ceramics of Tikal—Vessels from the Burials, Caches, and Problematical Deposits.* Philadelphia: University of Pennsylvania Museum of Archaeology and Anthropology.

TR. 27A:

Moholy-Nagy, Hattula, with William R. Coe

2008 *The Artifacts of Tikal-Ornamental and Ceremonial Artifacts and Unworked Material.* Tikal Report 27A. Philadelphia: University of Pennsylvania Museum of Archaeology and Anthropology.

TR. 27B:

Moholy-Nagy, Hattula

2003a *The Artifacts of Tikal—Utilitarian Artifacts and Unworked Material.* Philadelphia: University of Pennsylvania Museum of Archaeology and Anthropology.

TR. 33A:

Jones, Christopher, and Linton Satterthwaite, Jr.

1982 *The Monuments and Inscriptions of Tikal—The Carved Monuments.* Philadelphia: University of Pennsylvania Museum of Archaeology and Anthropology.

Illustrations

Figure 1. Color Designations for Tikal Pottery.
Based on Smith 1955: Vol. 2. Additions by L. Ehman and V. Greene. All drawings are presented at 1:4 scale unless otherwise indicated.

FIGURE 1

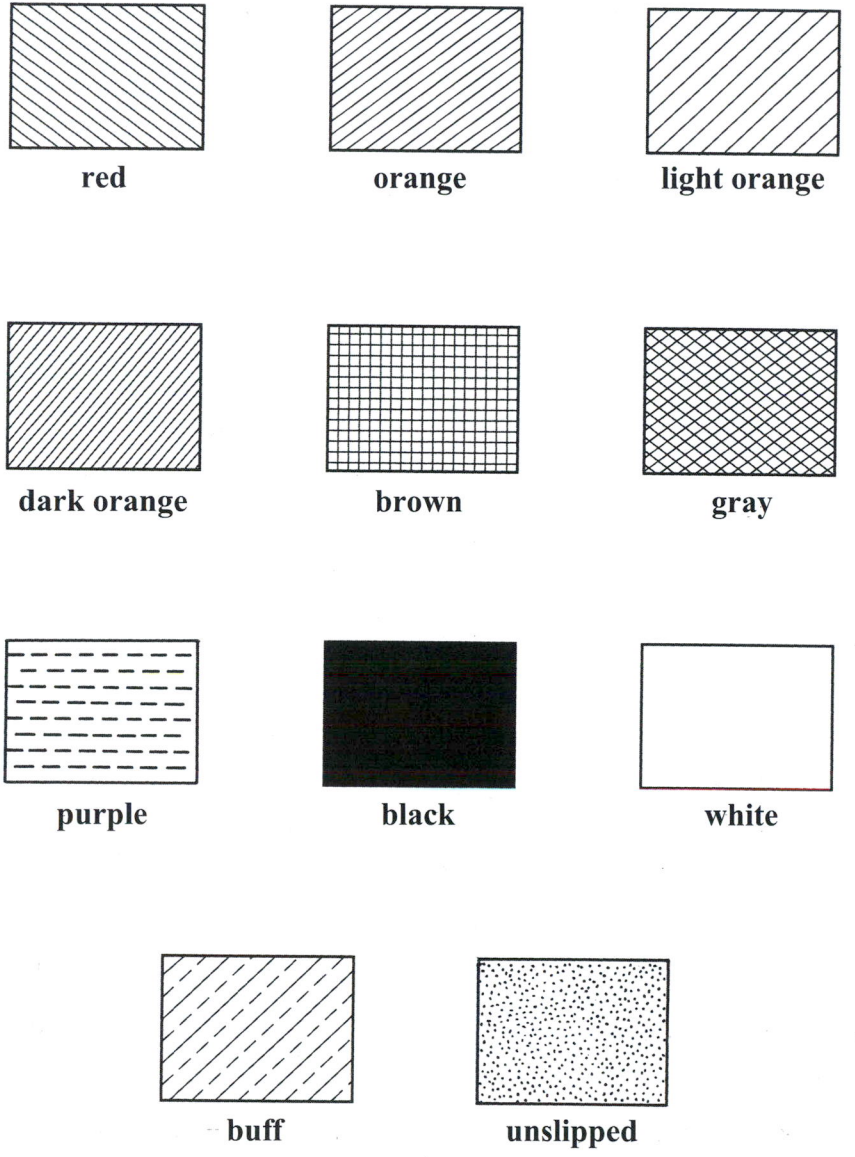

Eb and Tzec
Figure 2

2.1	Guitara Incised: Simple-incised Variety
2.2	Xpokol Incised: Simple-incised Variety (slip not shown)
2.3–4	Calam Buff: Calam Variety
2.5	Amil Chamfered: Amil Variety
2.6–7	Unnamed Monochrome Red: Fine Inclusions Variety
2.8	Unnamed Monochrome Black: Fine Inclusions Variety
2.9	Boolay Brown: Boolay Variety
2.10	Canhel Unslipped: Canhel Variety
2.11	Calam Buff: Calam Variety
2.12	Bechh Incised: Design-incised Variety (slip not shown)
2.13	Unnamed Monochrome Red Incised: Fine Inclusions Variety
2.14–16	Unnamed Monochrome Red: Fine Inclusions Variety
2.17–21	Calam Buff: Calam Variety
2.22	Cabcoh Striated: Cabcoh Variety
2.23	Calam Buff: Calam Buff
2.24–26	Ainil Orange: Ainil Variety
2.27	Amil Chamfered: Amil Variety
2.28	Xpokol Incised: Design-incised Variety (slip not shown)
2.29	Unnamed Monochrome Red: Fine Inclusions Variety
2.30	Unnamed Monochrome Black Incised: Fine Inclusions Variety (slip not shown)
2.31–34	Joventud Red: Ahcax Variety
2.35	Guitara Incised: Simple-incised Variety
2.36–37	Ainil Orange: Ainil Variety
2.38	Amil Chamfered: Amil Variety
2.39	Joventud Red: Ahcax Variety
2.40–41	Guitara Incised: Simple-incised Variety
2.42	Unnamed Monochrome Red Incised: Fine Inclusions Variety
2.43–45	Guitara Incised: Simple-incised Variety
2.46–49	Joventud Red: Ahcax Variety
2.50	Unnamed Monochrome Red Incised: Fine Inclusions Variety (slip not shown)
2.51–54	Joventud Red: Ahcax Variety
2.55	Calam Buff: Unspecified Incised Variety (slip not shown)
2.56	Other Canhel Group: Unslipped Impressed
2.57–60	Cob Red-impressed: Cob Variety
2.61	Unnamed Monochrome Red: Fine Inclusions Variety
2.62	Canhel Unslipped: Canhel Variety
2.63	Cabcoh Striated: Cabcoh Variety

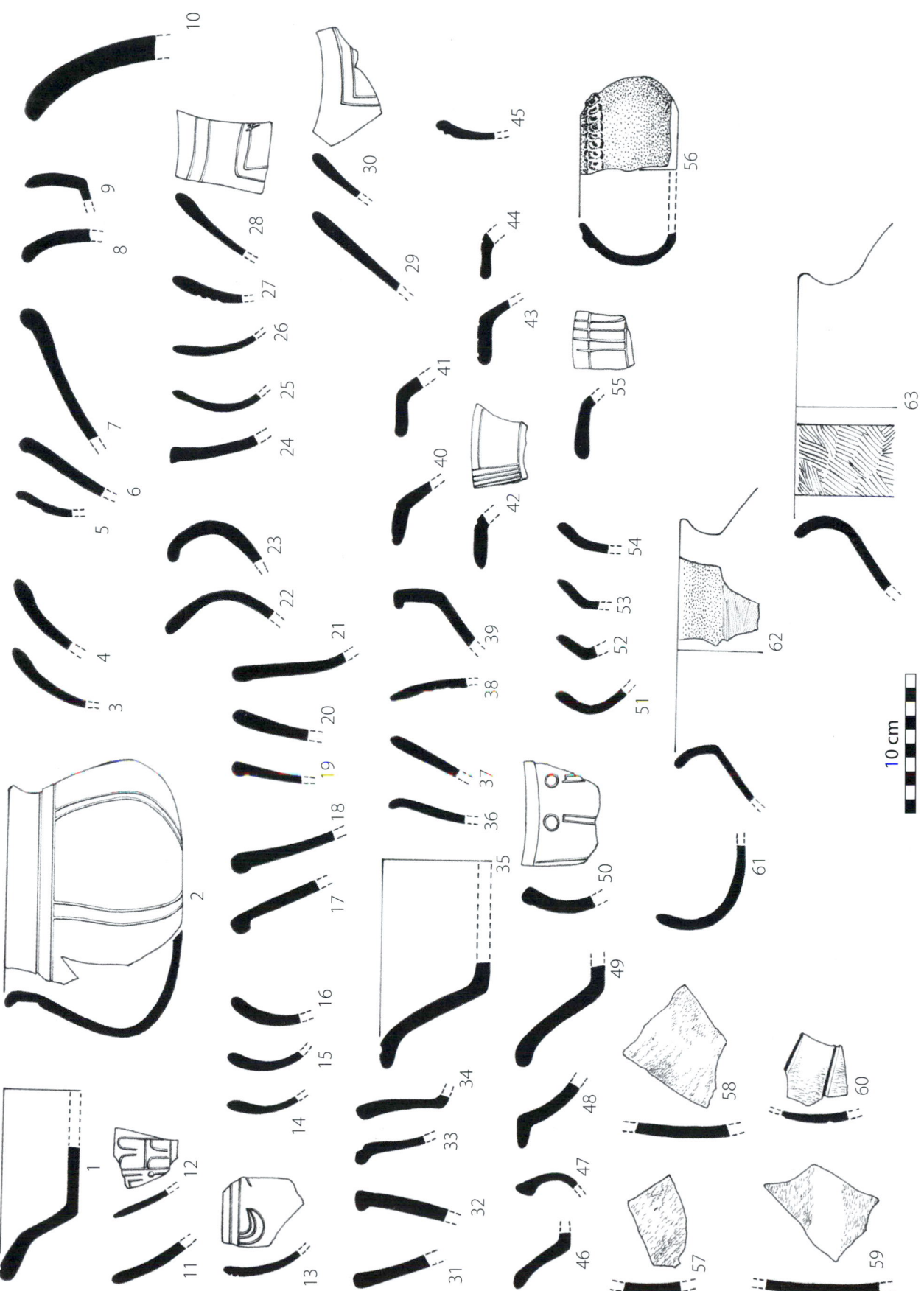

FIGURE 2

Eb and Tzec
Figure 3

FIGURE 3

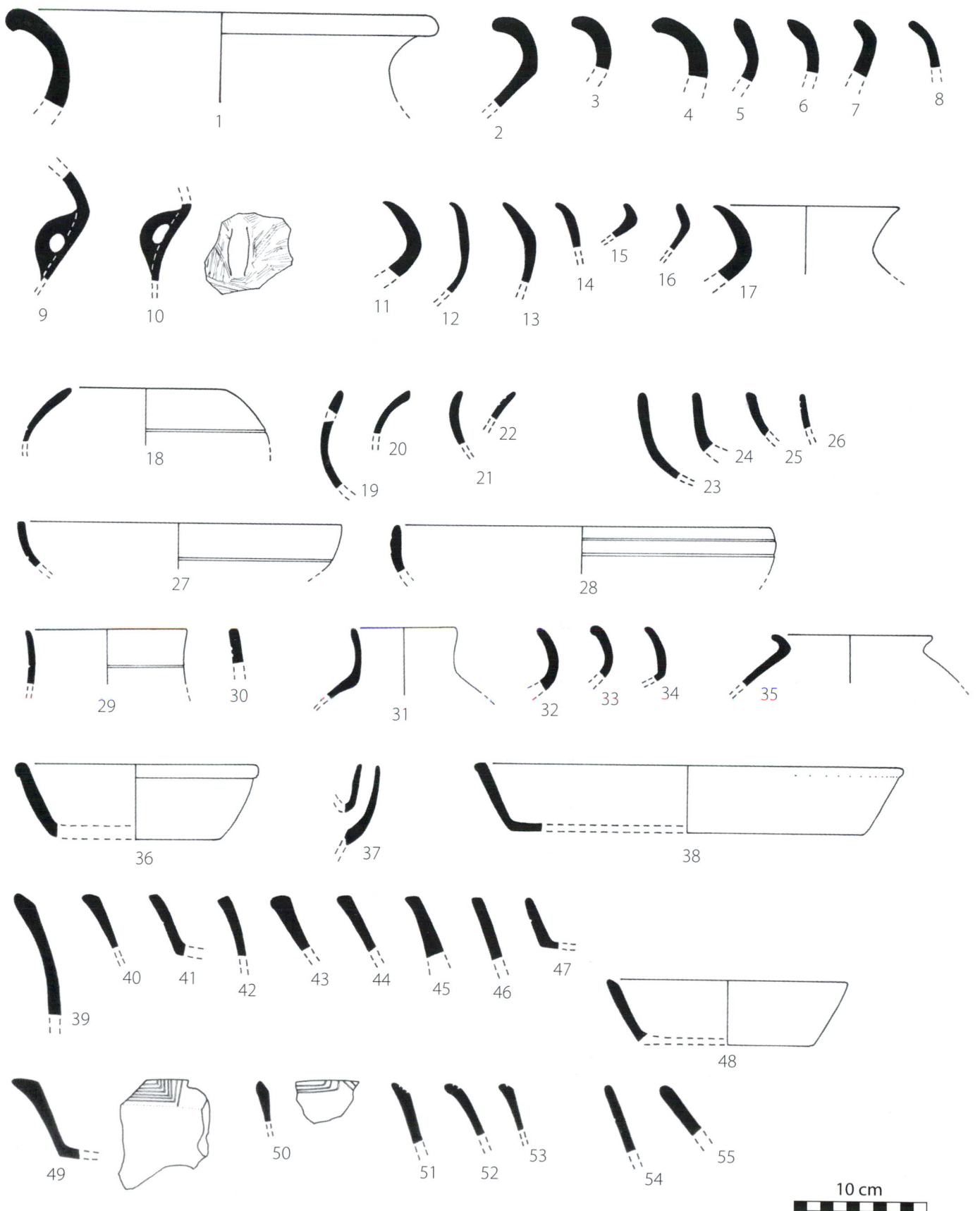

10 cm

Eb and Tzec
Figure 4

4.1	Chunhinta Black: Maach Variety
4.2	Calam Buff: Calam Variety
4.3	Baclam Red-orange: Ahtau Variety
4.4–5	Amil Chamfered: Amil Variety (slip not shown)
4.6–7	Baclam Red-orange: Ahtau Variety
4.8–9	Chunhinta Black: Maach Variety
4.10	Baclam Red-orange: Ahtau Variety
4.11	Boo Composite: Boo Variety
4.12–13	Bechh Incised: Simple-incised Variety
4.14	Guitara Incised: Simple-incised Variety
4.15–18	Pital Cream: Unspecified Variety
4.19	Calam Buff: Calam Variety
4.20–23	Unnamed Monochrome Red: Yellow-paste Variety
4.24	Calam Buff: Calam Variety (slip not shown)
4.25–26	Amil Chamfered: Amil Variety
4.27	Unnamed Monochrome Red Incised: Fine Inclusions Variety (slip not shown)
4.28	Ainil Orange: Ainil Variety
4.29	Baclam Red-orange: Ahtau Variety
4.30	Amil Chamfered: Amil Variety (slip not shown)
4.31–32	Deprecio Incised: Simple-incised Variety (slip not shown)
4.33	Ahmax Chamfered: Ahmax Variety
4.34–36	Deprecio Incised: Simple-incised Variety
4.37	Amil Chamfered: Amil Variety
4.38	Ahmax Chamfered: Ahmax Variety
4.39	Amil Chamfered: Amil Variety
4.40	Boolay Brown: Boolay Variety
4.41	Ainil Orange: Ainil Variety
4.42	Deprecio Incised: Simple-incised Variety (slip not shown)

FIGURE 4

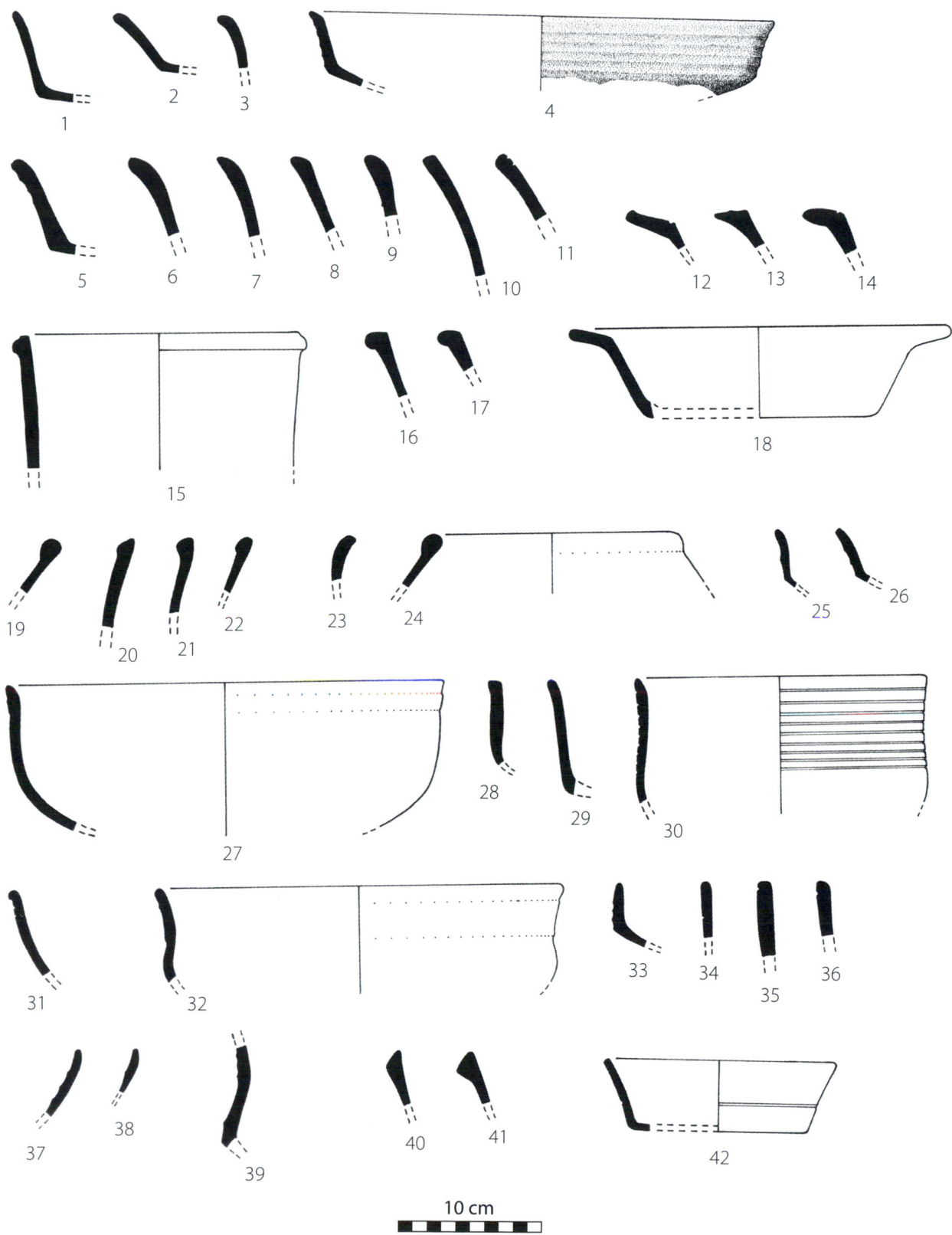

10 cm

Eb and Tzec
Figure 5

5.1 Cabcoh Striated: Cabcoh Variety

5.2–3 Canhel Unslipped: Canhel Unslipped

5.4 Cabcoh Striated: Cabcoh Variety

5.5 Canhel Unslipped

5.6 Cabcoh Striated: Cabcoh Variety

5.7–10 Canhel Unslipped: Canhel Unslipped

5.11 Cob Red-impressed: Cob Variety (slip not shown)

5.12–15 Joventud Red: Ahcax Variety

5.16 Xpokol Incised: Simple-incised Variety (slip not shown)

5.17 Bechh Incised: Simple-incised Variety (slip not shown)

5.18 Guitara Incised: Simple-incised Variety (slip not shown)

5.19–20 Bechh Incised: Simple-incised Variety (slip not shown)

5.21 Xpokol Incised: Simple-incised Variety (slip not shown)

5.22–23 Achiotes Unslipped: Achiotes Variety

5.24 Joventud Red: Ahcax Variety (slip not shown)

5.25 Boolim Red-on-cream: Boolim Variety

5.26 Guitara Incised: Simple-incised Variety (slip not shown)

5.27–30 Joventud Red: Ahcax Variety

5.31 Haleb Composite: Haleb Variety (interior of base also shown)

5.32–33 Haleb Composite: Haleb Variety

5.34 Aac Red-on-buff: Aac Variety

5.35–36 Canhel Unslipped: Canhel Unslipped

5.37 Joventud Red: Ahcax Variety

5.38–39 Boolim Red-on-cream: Boolim Variety

5.40–42 Aac Red-on-buff: Aac Variety

5.43 Boolay Brown: Boolay Variety (punctuated) (slip not shown)

5.44 Boolim Red-on-cream: Boolim Variety

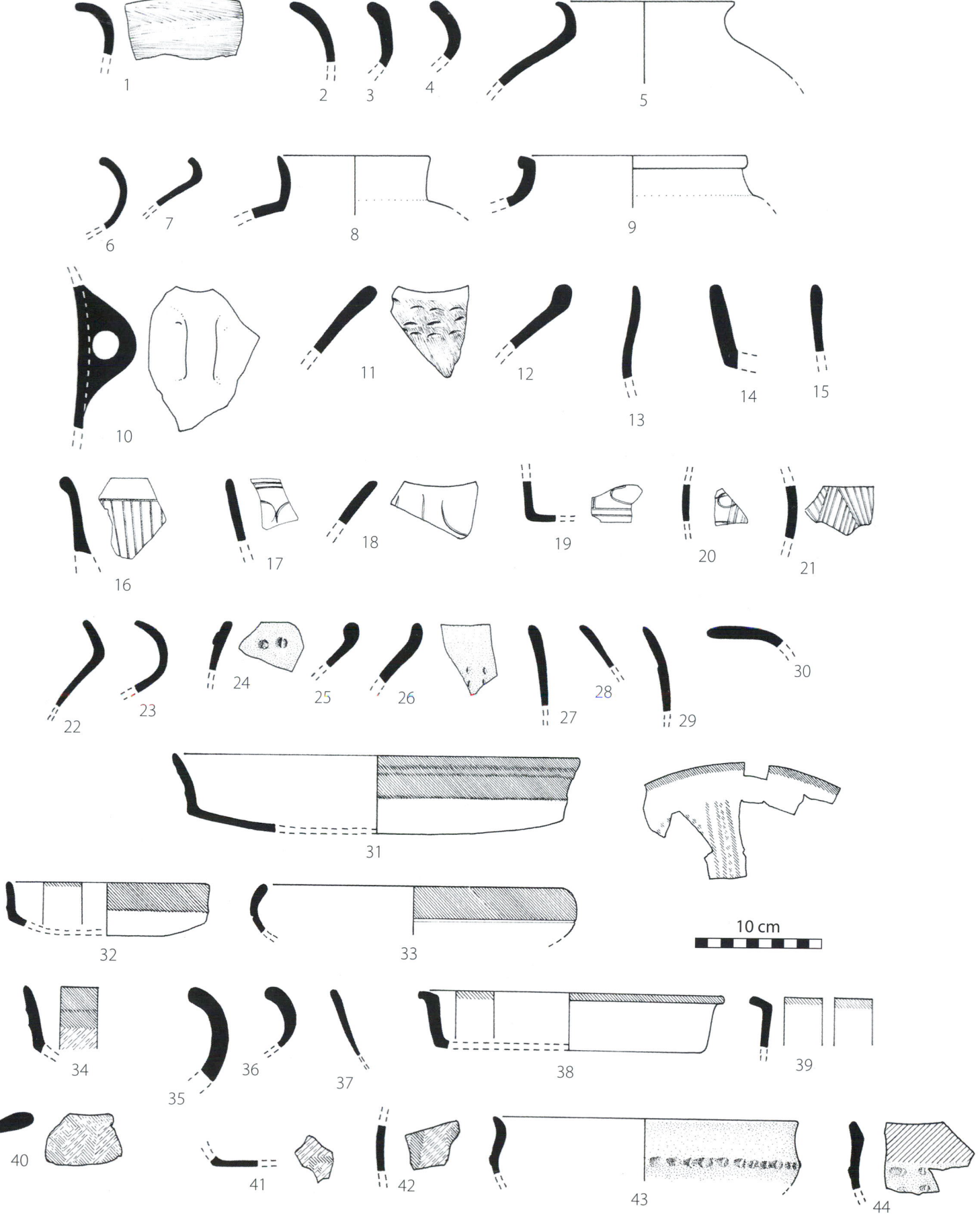

FIGURE 6

Tzec
Figure 6

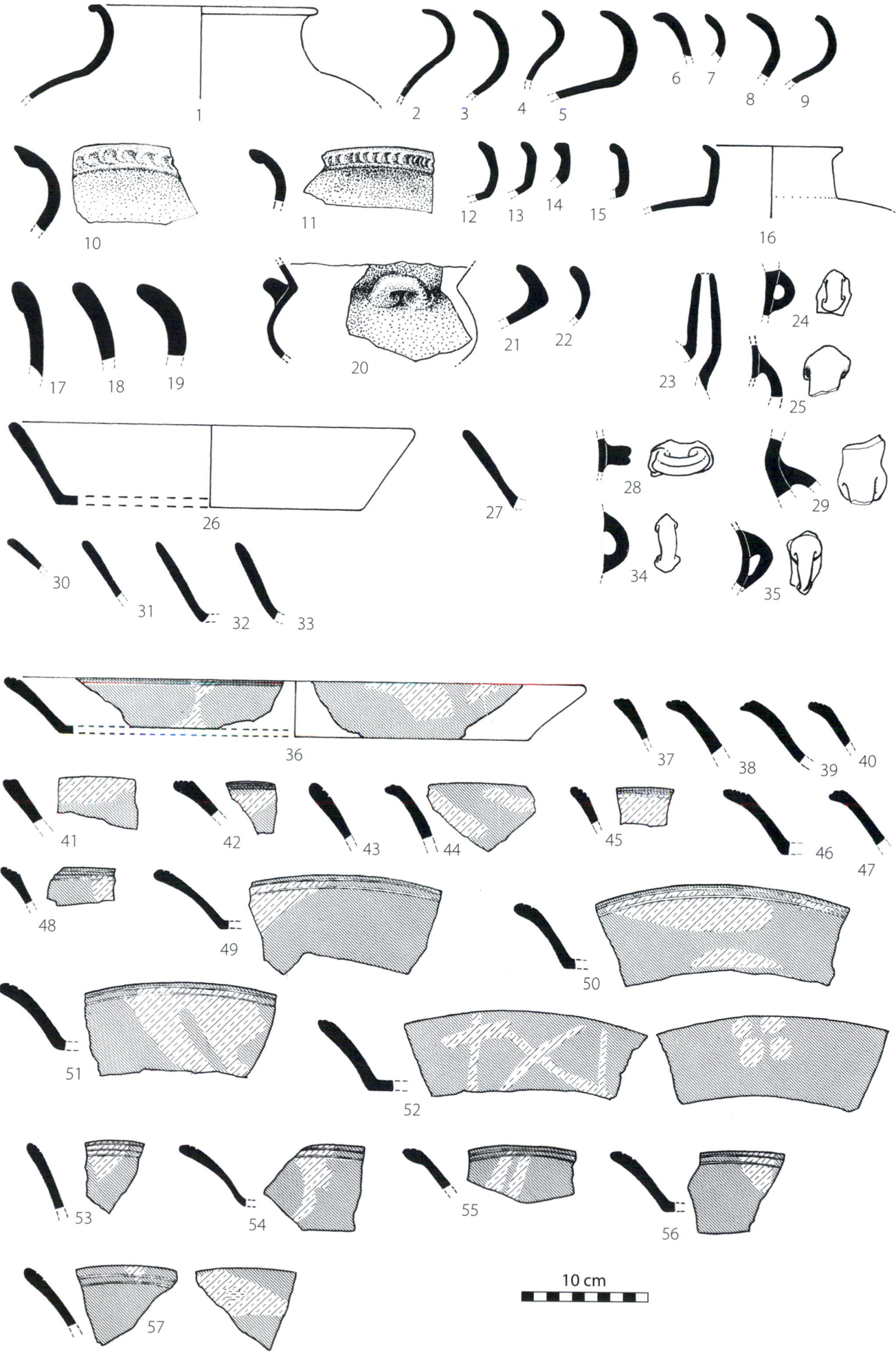

Tzec-Chuen
Figure 7

7.1	Ahmaax Chamfered: Ahmax Variety
7.2–3	Amil Chamfered: Amil Variety
7.4–5	Sierra Red: Sierra Variety
7.6	Polvero Black: Polvero Variety
7.7–8	Pital Cream: Unspecified Variety
7.9–10	Sapote Striated: Sapote Variety
7.11–12	Joventud Red: Ahcax Variety
7.13–15	Baclam Red-orange: Ahtau Variety
7.16–17	Laguna Verde Incised: Simple-incised Variety
7.18	Sierra Red: Sierra Variety
7.19	Amil Chamfered: Amil Variety
7.20	Sierra Red: Sierra Variety (with appliqué) (slip not shown)
7.21	Lagartos Punctated: Lagartos Punctated (slip not shown)
7.22	Joventud Red: Ahcax Variety
7.23	Sierra Red: Sierra Variety
7.24	Joventud Red: Ahcax Variety
7.25	Guitara Incised: Simple-incised Variety
7.26	Pital Cream: Unspecified Variety
7.27	Sierra Red: Sierra Variety
7.28	Deprecio Incised: Simple-incised Variety
7.29	Guitara Incised: Simple-incised Variety
7.30–34	Sierra Red: Sierra Variety
7.35–36	Joventud Red: Ahcax Variety
7.37	Sierra Red: Sierra Variety
7.38–41	Pital Cream: Unspecified Variety
7.42–46	Joventud Red: Ahcax Variety
7.47	Achiotes Unslipped: Achiotes Variety
7.48	Chunhinta Black: Maach Variety (slip not shown)
7.49–50	Amil Chamfered: Amil Variety
7.51	Chunhinta Black: Maach Variety
7.52	Incensario Prong (Chuen Complex)
7.53	Ahchab Red-on-buff: Ahchab Variety
7.54–55	Deprecio Incised: Deprecio Incised
7.56	Sierra Red: Sierra Variety
7.57	Laguna Verde Incised: Simple-incised Variety
7.58	Flor Cream: Flor Variety
7.59	Sierra Red: Sierra Variety
7.60	Polvero Black: Polvero Variety
7.61–64	Sierra Red: Sierra Variety
7.65	Polvero Black: Polvero Variety
7.66–68	Sierra Red: Sierra Variety
7.69	Achiotes Unslipped: Achiotes Variety

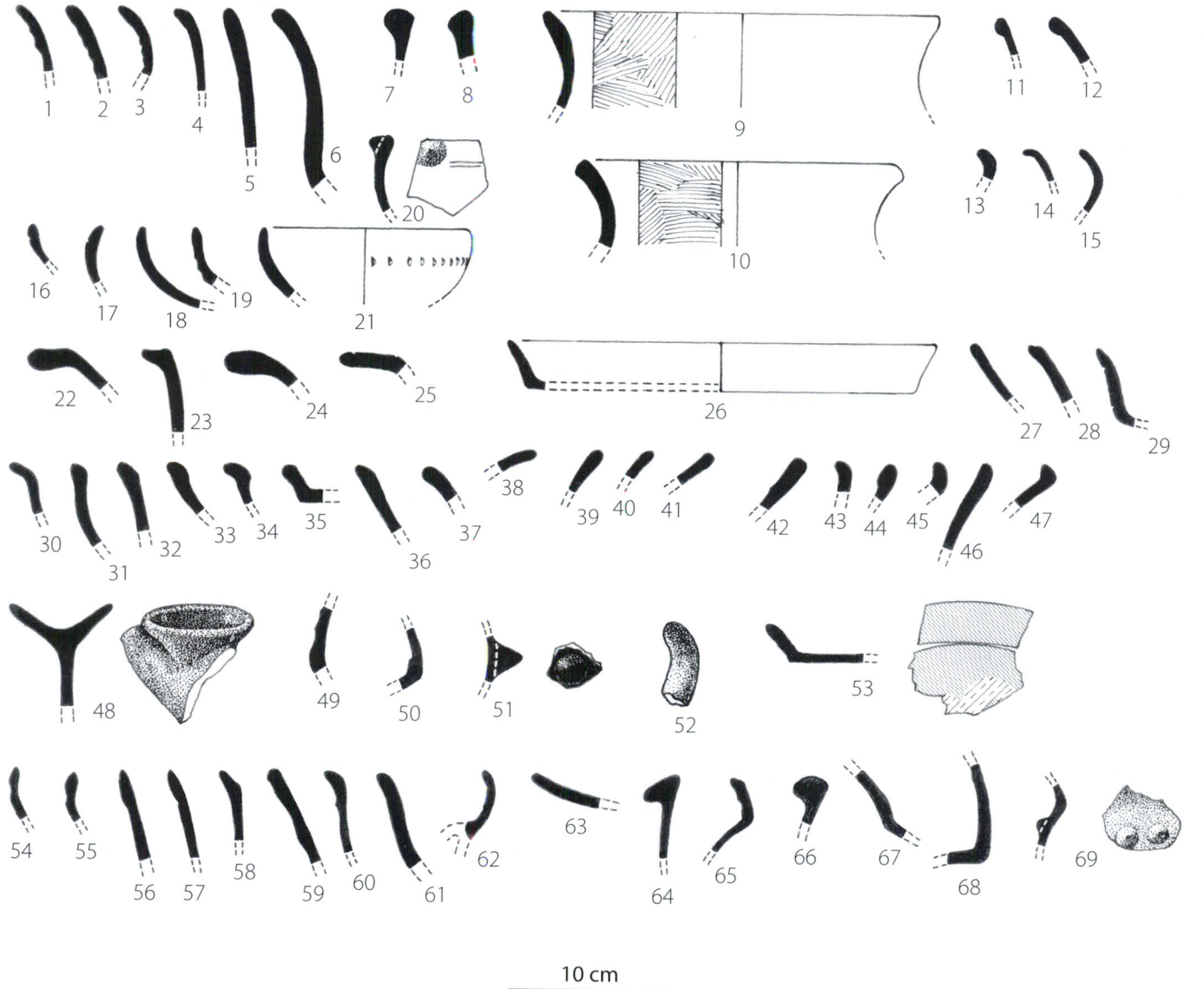

10 cm

FIGURE 7

FIGURE 8

Figure 8
Chuen

8.1	Sierra Red: Sierra Variety (slip not shown)
8.2	Polvero Black: Polvero Variety
8.3–4	Sierra Red: Ahuacan Variety
8.5	Ahchab Red-on-buff: Ahchab Variety
8.6–8	Sierra Red: Ahuacan Variety
8.9	Sierra Red: Sierra Variety (slip not shown)
8.10	Ahchab Red-on-buff: Ahchab Variety
8.11–13	Sierra Red: Ahuacan Variety
8.14	Ahchab Red-on-buff: Ahchab Variety
8.15	Sierra Red: Sierra Variety
8.16–17	Laguna Verde Incised: Simple-incised Variety (slip not shown)
8.18–19	Laguna Verde Incised: Design-incised Variety (slip not shown)
8.20	Polvero Black: Polvero Variety
8.21–25	Laguna Verde Incised: Simple-incised Variety
8.26	Sierra Red (Unnamed modeled) (slip not shown)
8.27–29	Flor Cream: Flor Variety
8.30	Lechugal Incised: Simple Incised Variety
8.31	Laguna Verde Incised: Simple-incised Variety
8.32	Ahcab Red-on-buff: Ahchab Variety
8.33	Lechugal Incised: Design-incised Variety (slip not shown)
8.34	Sierra Red: Sierra Variety
8.35	Ahcab Red-on-buff: Ahchab Variety
8.36	Laguna Verde Incised: Simple-incised Variety
8.37	Polvero Black: Polvero Variety
8.38	Sierra Red: Sierra Variety
8.39–40	Laguna Verde Incised: Simple-incised Variety
8.41	Laguna Verde Incised: Design-incised Variety (slip not shown)
8.42	Polvero Black: Polvero Variety (slip not shown)
8.43	Laguna Verde Incised: Simple-incised Variety (slip not shown)
8.44	Sierra Red: Sierra Variety
8.45–48	Laguna Verde Incised: Simple-incised Variety
8.49	Sierra Red: Sierra Variety

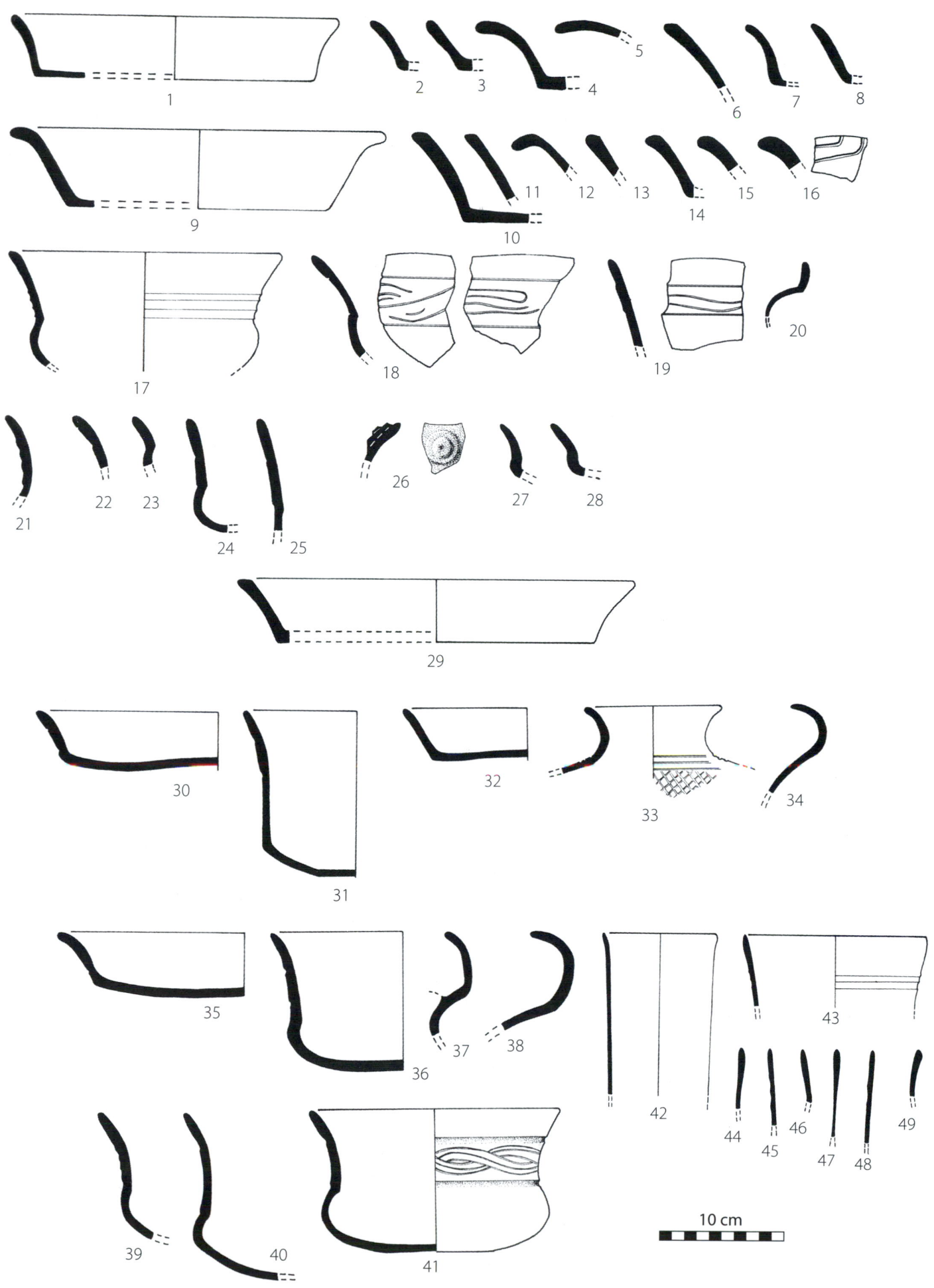

Chuen-Cauac-Cimi
Figure 9

9.1–63   Achiotes Unslipped: Achiotes Variety or Sapote Striated: Sapote Striated (necks are unstriated so difficult to differentiate) (slips not shown)

FIGURE 9

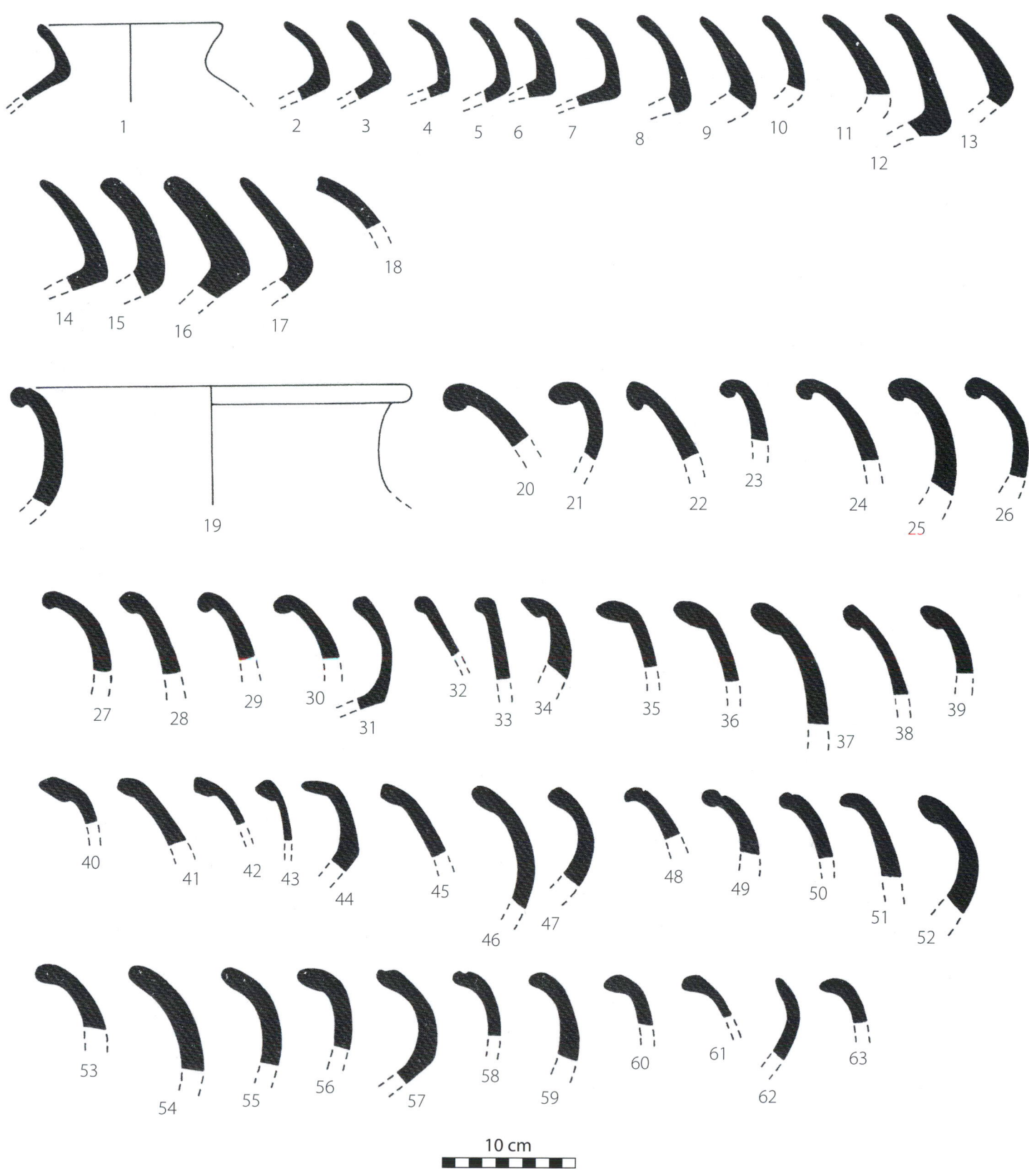

10 cm

FIGURE 10

Chuen-Cauac
Figure 10

10.1–12   Laguna Verde Incised: Simple-incised Variety (slip not shown)

10.13–16   Flor Cream: Flor Variety

10.17–23   Society Hall Red: Society Hall Variety

10.24–27   Sierra Red: Sierra Variety

10.28–31   Laguna Verde Incised: Simple-incised Variety (slip not shown)

10.32–37   Sierra Red: Sierra Variety

10.38   Caramba Red-on-orange: Chic Variety

10.39   Sierra Red: Sierra Variety

10.40   Laguna Verde Incised: Simple-incised Variety

10.41–46   Sierra Red: Sierra Variety (slip not shown)

10.47   Laguna Verde Incised: Simple-incised Variety (slip not shown)

10.48   Flor Cream: Flor Variety

10.49   Sierra Red: Sierra Variety

10.50   Polvero Black: Polvero Variety

10.51   Sierra Red: Sierra Variety

10.52   Mut Red-on-brown: Mut Variety

10.53–62   Sierra Red: Sierra Variety (slip not shown)

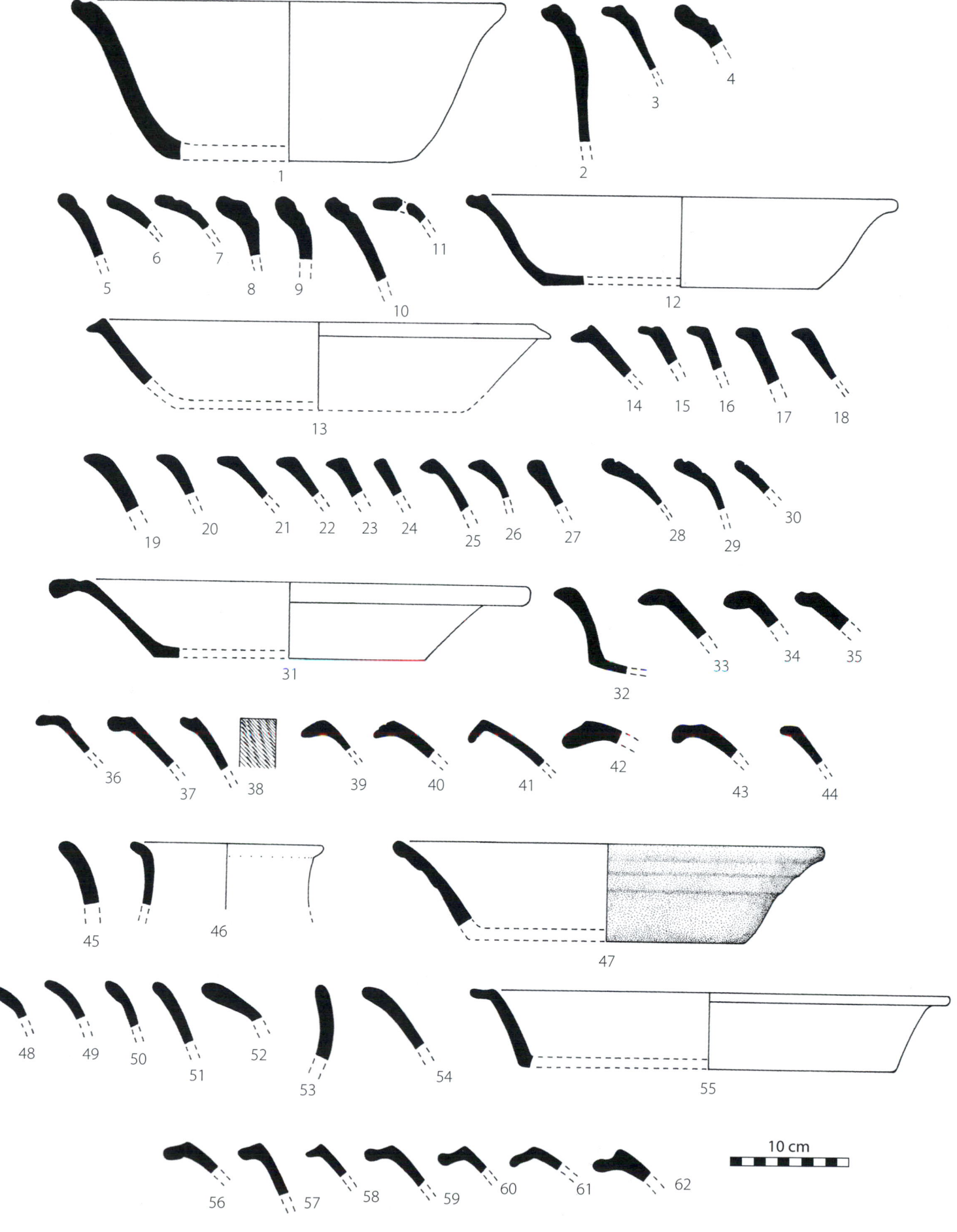

Chuen-Cauac
Figure 11

11.1–18   Sierra Red: Sierra Variety (slip not shown)

11.19–22   Morfin Unslipped: Morfin Variety

11.23   Polvero Black: Polvero Variety

11.24   Flor Cream: Flor Variety

11.25–26   Society Hall Red: Society Hall Variety

11.27   Mut Red-on-brown: Mut Variety

11.28–31   Sierra Red: Sierra Variety (slip not shown)

11.32   Flor Cream: Flor Variety

11.33   Mut Red-on-brown: Mut Variety

11.34   Baclam Red-orange: Baclam Variety

11.35   Sierra Red: Sierra Variety

11.36   Polvero Black: Polvero Variety (slip not shown)

11.37   Flor Cream: Flor Variety

11.38–40   Sierra Red: Sierra Variety

11.41   Flor Cream: Flor Variety

11.42–43   Sierra Red: Sierra Variety (slip not shown)

11.44   Boxcay Brown: Boxcay Variety

11.45   Sierra Red: Sierra Variety

11.46   Boxcay Brown: Boxcay Variety (slip not shown)

11.47   Polvero Black: Polvero Variety (slip not shown)

11.48   Sierra Red: Sierra Variety (slip not shown)

FIGURE 11

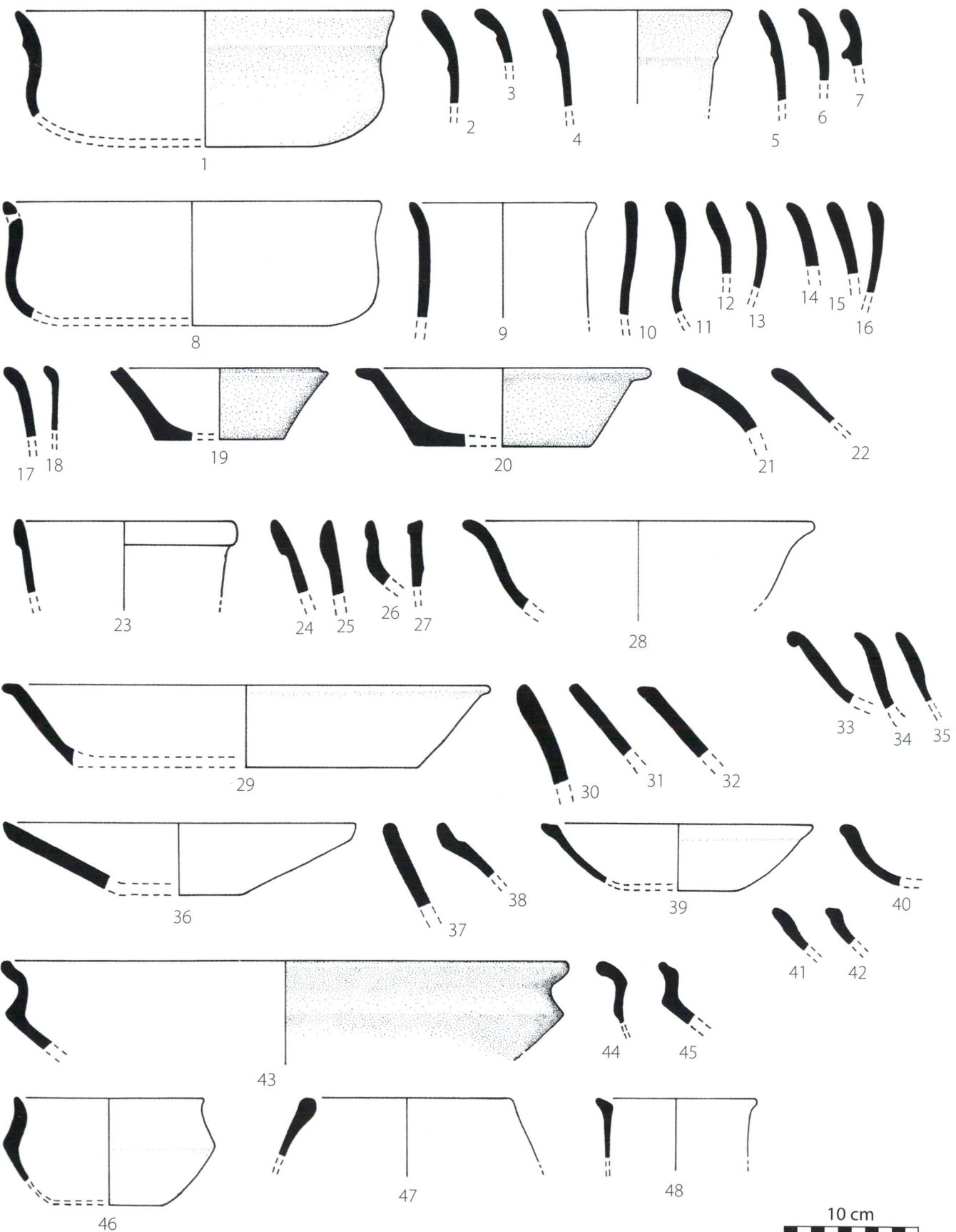

10 cm

Chuen-Cauac
Figure 12

12.1–2   Polvero Black: Polvero Variety (slip not shown)
12.3–5   Sierra Red: Sierra Variety
12.6   Polvero Black: Polvero Variety
12.7   Flor Cream: Flor Cream (slip not shown)
12.8–12   Sierra Red: Sierra Variety
12.13   Polvero Black: Polvero Variety
12.14   Laguna Verde Incised: Simple-incised Variety (slip not shown)
12.15   Metapa Trichrome: Itsul Variety
12.16   Polvero Black: Polvero Variety
12.17–18   Cabro Red: Cabro Variety
12.19–20   Flor Cream: Flor Cream
12.21–22   Sierra Red: Sierra Variety
12.23–27   Flor Cream: Flor Cream
12.28–31   Sierra Red: Sierra Variety
12.32   Flor Cream: Flor Cream
12.33   Sierra Red: Sierra Variety
12.34   Laguna Verde Incised: Design-incised Variety (slip not shown)
12.35–36   Laguna Verde Incised: Simple-incised Variety (slip not shown)
12.37–38   Flor Cream: Flor Cream (slip not shown)
12.39–45   Sierra Red: Sierra Variety
12.46   Accordian Incised: Simple Incised Variety
12.47–53   Sierra Red: Sierra Variety
12.54   Flor Cream: Flor Cream
12.55–58   Sierra Red: Sierra Variety
12.59   Flor Cream: Flor Cream
12.60   Sierra Red: Sierra Variety
12.61–62   Polvero Black: Polvero Variety (slip not shown)
12.63–64   Sierra Red: Sierra Variety
12.65–66   Polvero Black: Polvero Variety
12.67   Sierra Red: Sierra Variety
12.68–73   Sierra Red: Sierra Variety
12.74   Polvero Black: Polvero Variety
12.75–79   Sierra Red: Sierra Variety (slip not shown)

FIGURE 12

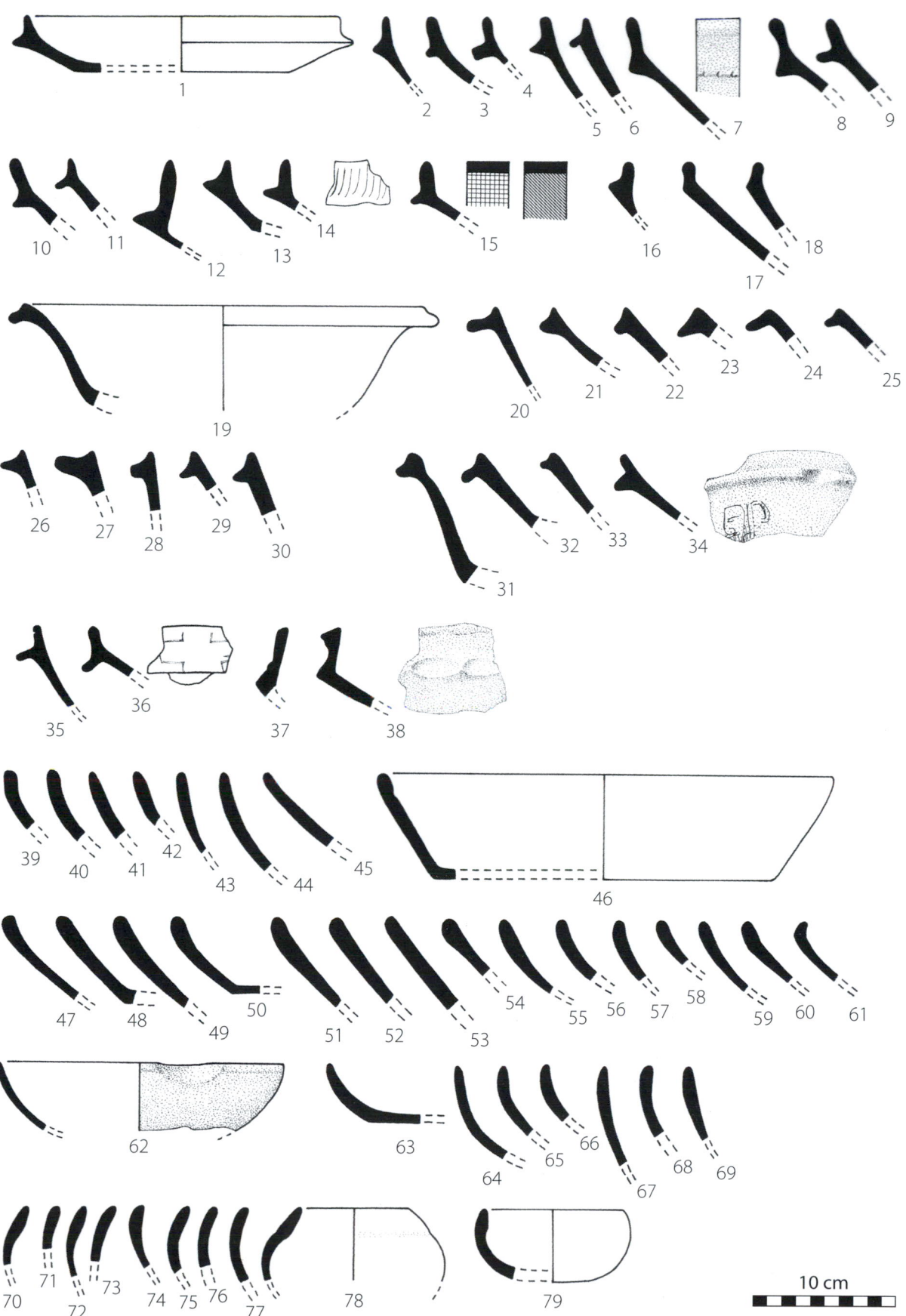

Chuen-Cauac-Cimi
Figure 13

FIGURE 13

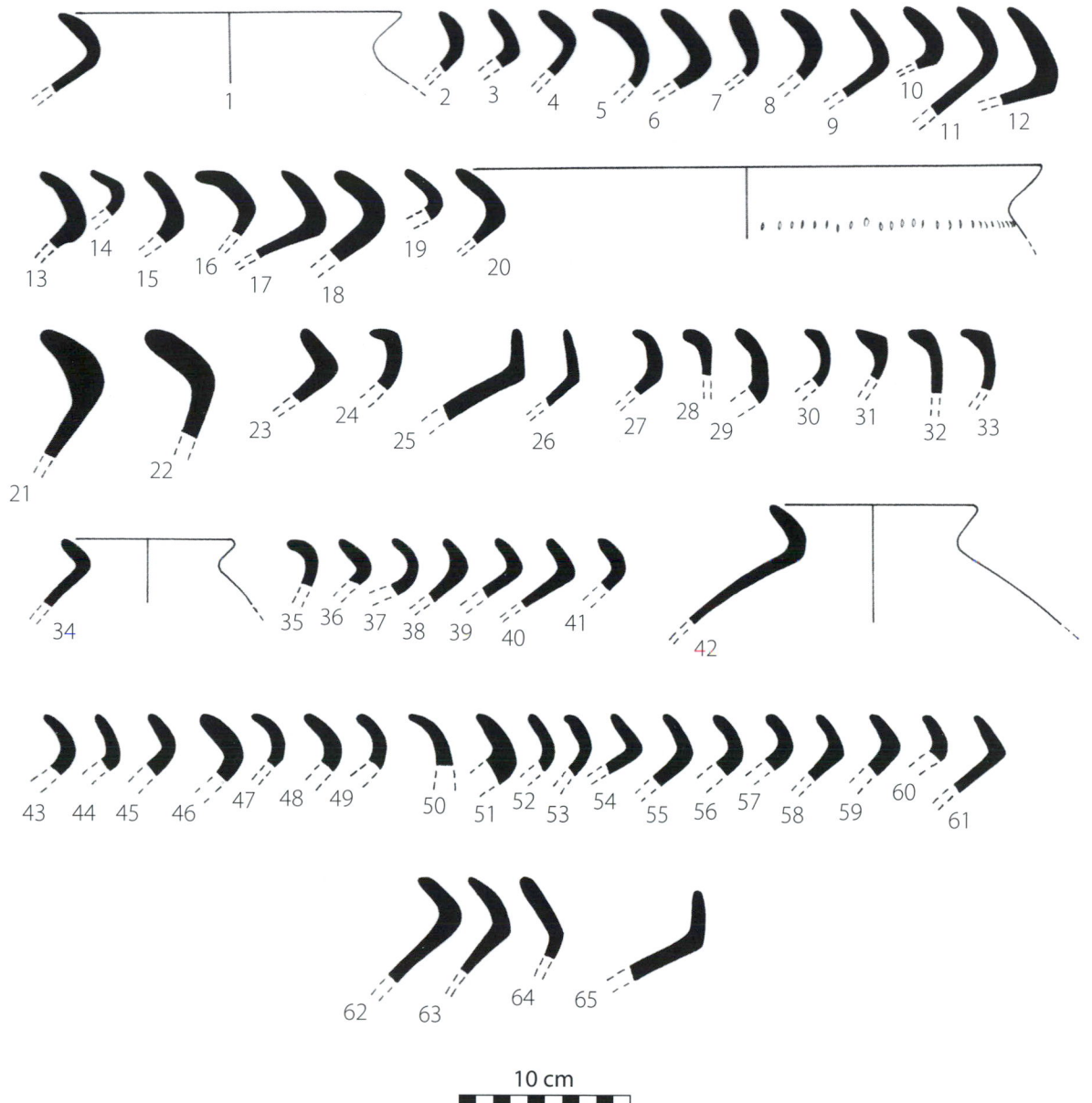

10 cm

Chuen-Cauac-Cimi
Figure 14

14.1	Metapa Trichrome: Itsul Variety (exterior slip not shown)
14.2	Laguna Verde Incised: Usulutan-style Variety (slip not shown)
14.3	Sierra Red: Sierra Variety (slip not shown)
14.4	Cabro Group (possible Tuk Red-on-red Trickle) (slip not shown)
14.5	Cabro Red: Cabro Variety
14.6	Imported Usulutan Resist
14.7	Laguna Verde Incised: Simple-incised Variety
14.8–10	Sierra Red: Sierra Variety
14.11	Caramba Red-on-orange: Chic Variety
14.12	Laguna Verde Incised: Simple-incised Variety
14.13	Sierra Red: Sierra Variety
14.14	Achiotes Unslipped: Achiotes Variety
14.15	Polvero Black: Polvero Variety
14.16–21	Sierra Red: Sierra Variety
14.22	Flor Cream: Flor Variety
14.23–24	Laguna Verde Incised: Design-incised Variety (slip not shown)
14.25–26	Sierra Red: Sierra Variety
14.27	Polvero Black: Polvero Variety
14.28	Sierra Red: Sierra Variety (slip not shown)
14.29–35	Morfin Unslipped: Morfin Variety
14.36	Sierra Red: Sierra Variety
14.37–38	Laguna Verde Incised: Simple-incised Variety
14.39–40	Sierra Red: Sierra Variety
14.41–42	Laguna Verde Incised: Simple-incised Variety
14.43–46	Sierra Red: Sierra Variety
14.47	Flor Cream: Flor Variety
14.48–52	Sierra Red: Sierra Variety

FIGURE 14

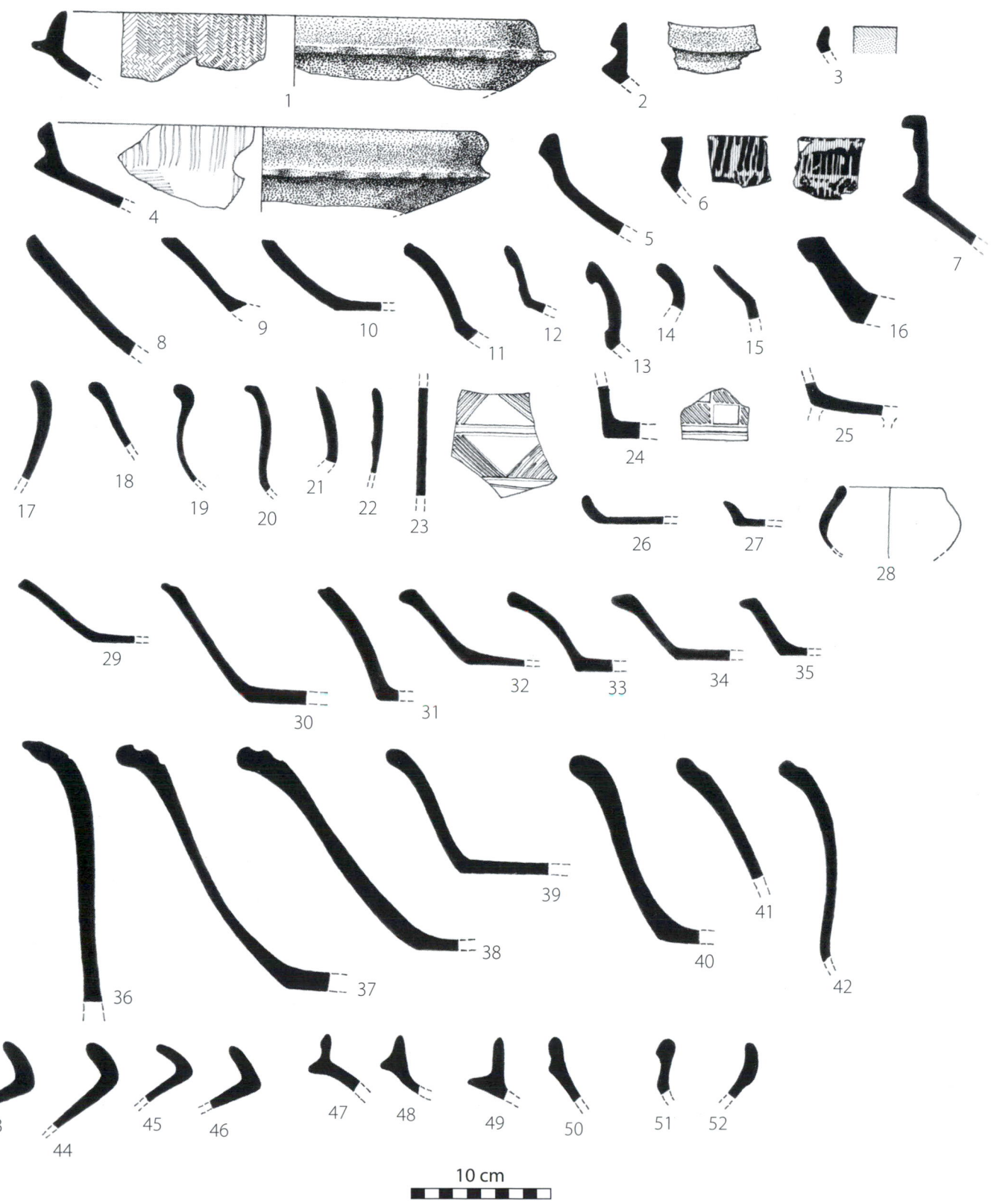

10 cm

FIGURE 15

Chuen-Cauac-Cimi
Figure 15

15.12   Repasto Black-on-red: Repasto Variety

15.3–9   Caramba Red-on-orange: Chic Variety

15.10   Sierra Red: Sierra Variety

15.11   Lechugal Incised: Simple-incised Variety with graffiti (slip not shown)

15.12   Lechugal Incised: Design-incised Variety

15.13   Sapote Striated: Sapote Variety

15.14   Sacluc Black-on-orange: Xux Variety (exterior slip not shown)

15.15–16 Sacluc Black-on-orange: Sis Variety

15.17   Sacluc Black-on-orange: Xux Variety

15.18–24 Sacluc Black-on-orange: Sis Variety

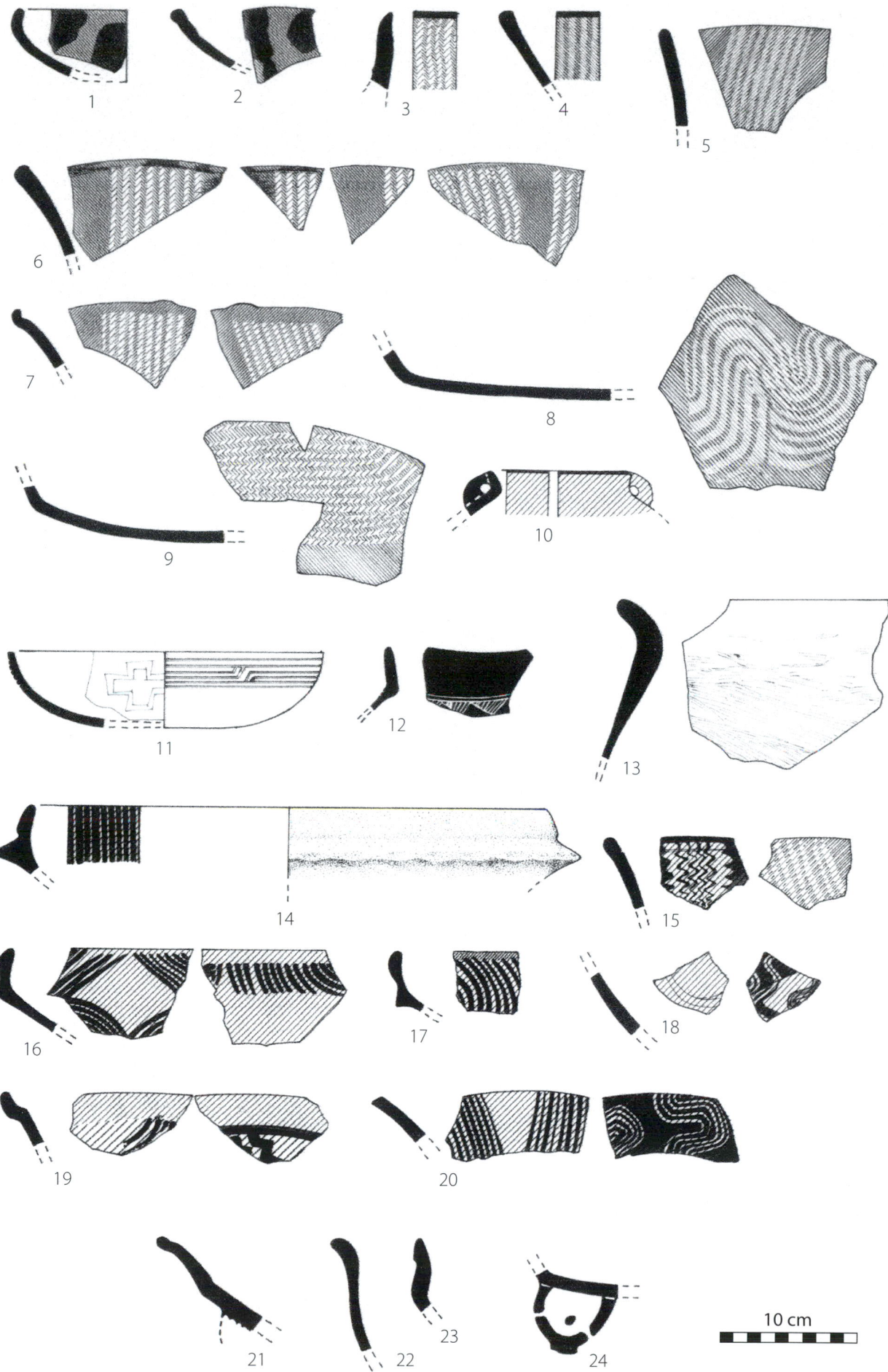

FIGURE 16

Cauac-Cimi
Figure 16

16.1   Cabro Group (Tuk Red-on-red Trickle) (slip not shown)
16.2–4   Metapa Trichrome: Itsul Variety (exterior slip not shown)
16.5   Sierra Group Unnamed Red-and-unslipped (Possibly Puletan Red-and-unslipped)
16.6   Sierra Red: Sierra Variety (slip not shown)
16.7   Correlo Incised-dichrome: Correlo Variety
16.8   Sierra Red: Sierra Variety (slip not shown)
16.9   Xtabcab Incised: Design-incised Variety (slip not shown)
16.10–11   Flor Cream: Flor Variety
16.12   Sierra Red: Sierra Variety (slip not shown)
16.13–14   Metapa Trichrome: Itsul Variety (exterior slip not shown)
16.15   Accordian Incised: Simple-incised Variety
16.16–19   Laguna Verde Incised: Simple-incised Variety (slip not shown)
16.20   Flor Cream: Flor Variety
16.21   Sierra Red: Sierra Variety (slip not shown)
16.22–23   Flor Cream: Flor Variety
16.24   Metapa Trichrome: Itsul Variety
16.25   Laguna Verde Incised: Usulutan-style Variety (exterior slip not shown)
16.26–27   Mut Red-on-brown: Mut Variety
16.28   Sierra Red: Sierra Variety
16.29–30   Metapa Trichrome: Itsul Variety
16.31   Sierra Red: Sierra Variety (slip not shown)

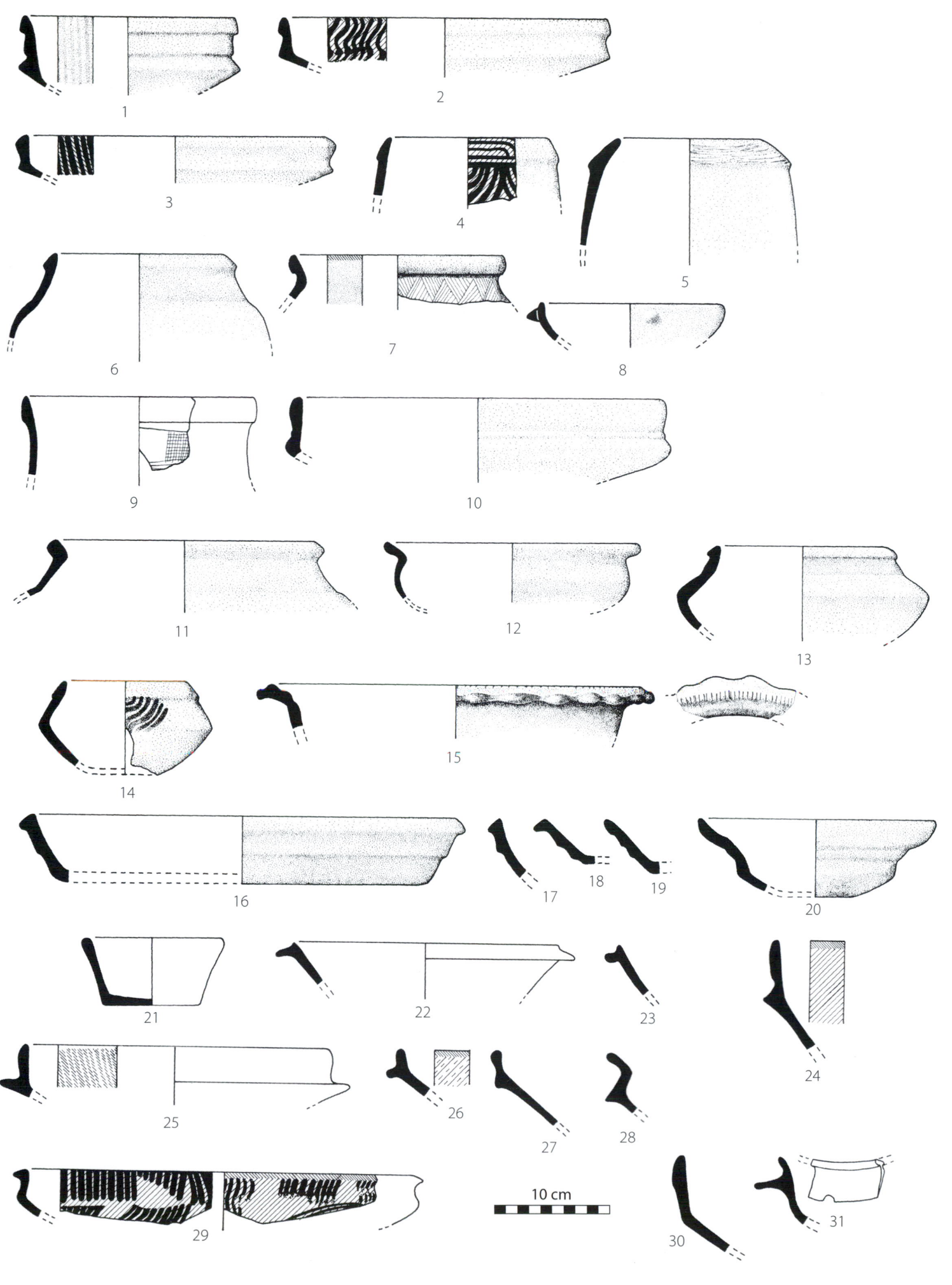

10 cm

Cimi
Figure 17

17.1	Laguna Verde Incised: Design-incised Variety (slip not shown)
17.2	Sacluc Black-on-orange: Xux Variety
17.3	Cayetano Trichrome: Cayetano Variety
17.4	Lechugal Incised: Design-incised Variety
17.5	Caramba Red-on-orange: Chic Variety
17.6–8	Sacluc Black-on-orange: Xux Variety
17.9	Cayetano Trichrome: Cayetano Variety
17.10	Sacluc Black-on-orange: Xux Variety
17.11–12	Metapa Trichrome: Itsul Variety
17.13	Cayetano Trichrome: Xnuk Variety
17.14	Sierra Red: Sierra Variety
17.15	Cayetano Trichrome: Cayetano Variety
17.16–17	Sacluc Black-on-orange: Xux Variety
17.18–21	Sacluc Black-on-orange: Sis Variety
17.22	Mojara Polychrome: Mojara Variety
17.23–25	Caramba Red-on-orange: Chic Variety
17.26–28	Sacluc Black-on-orange: Xux Variety
17.29	Cayetano Trichrome: Cayetano Variety
17.30–31	Caramba Red-on-orange: Chic Variety
17.32	Sacluc Black-on-orange: Sis Variety
17.33	Cayetano Trichrome: Cayetano Variety
17.34	Laguna Verde Incised: Design-incised Variety (slip not shown)
17.35	Cayetano Trichrome: Cayetano Variety

FIGURE 17

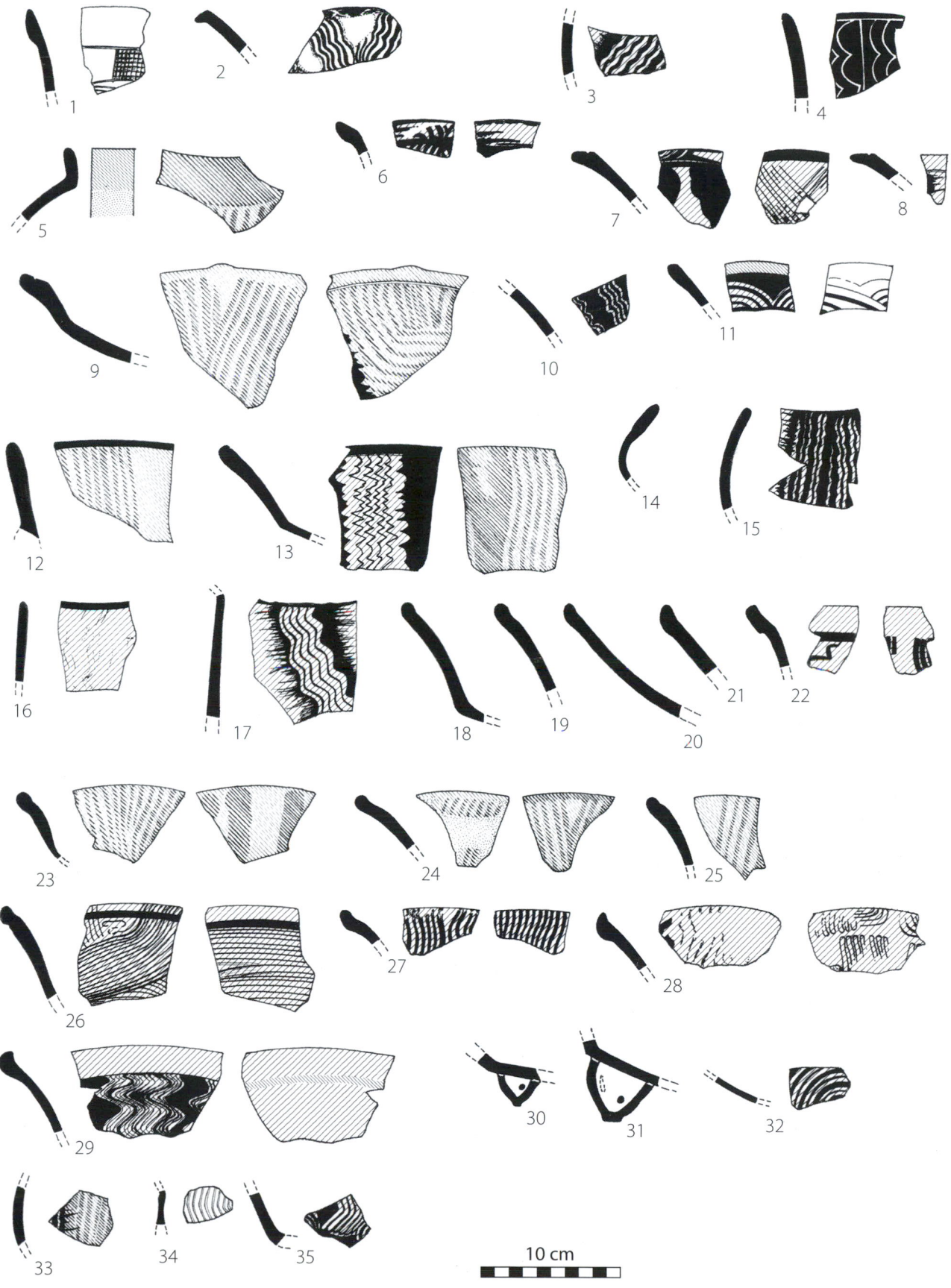

10 cm

Manik
Figure 18

FIGURE 18

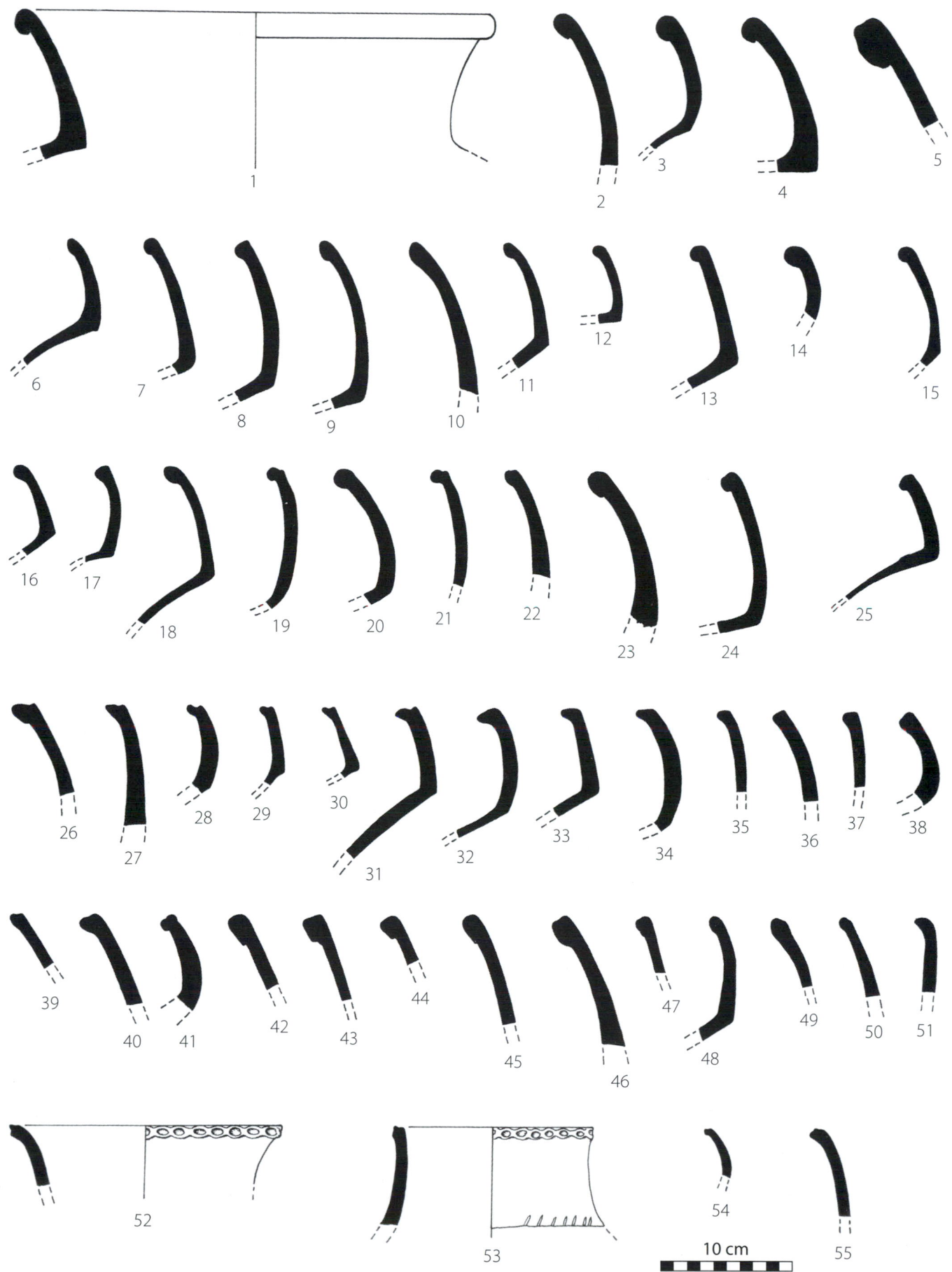

10 cm

Manik
Figure 19

FIGURE 19

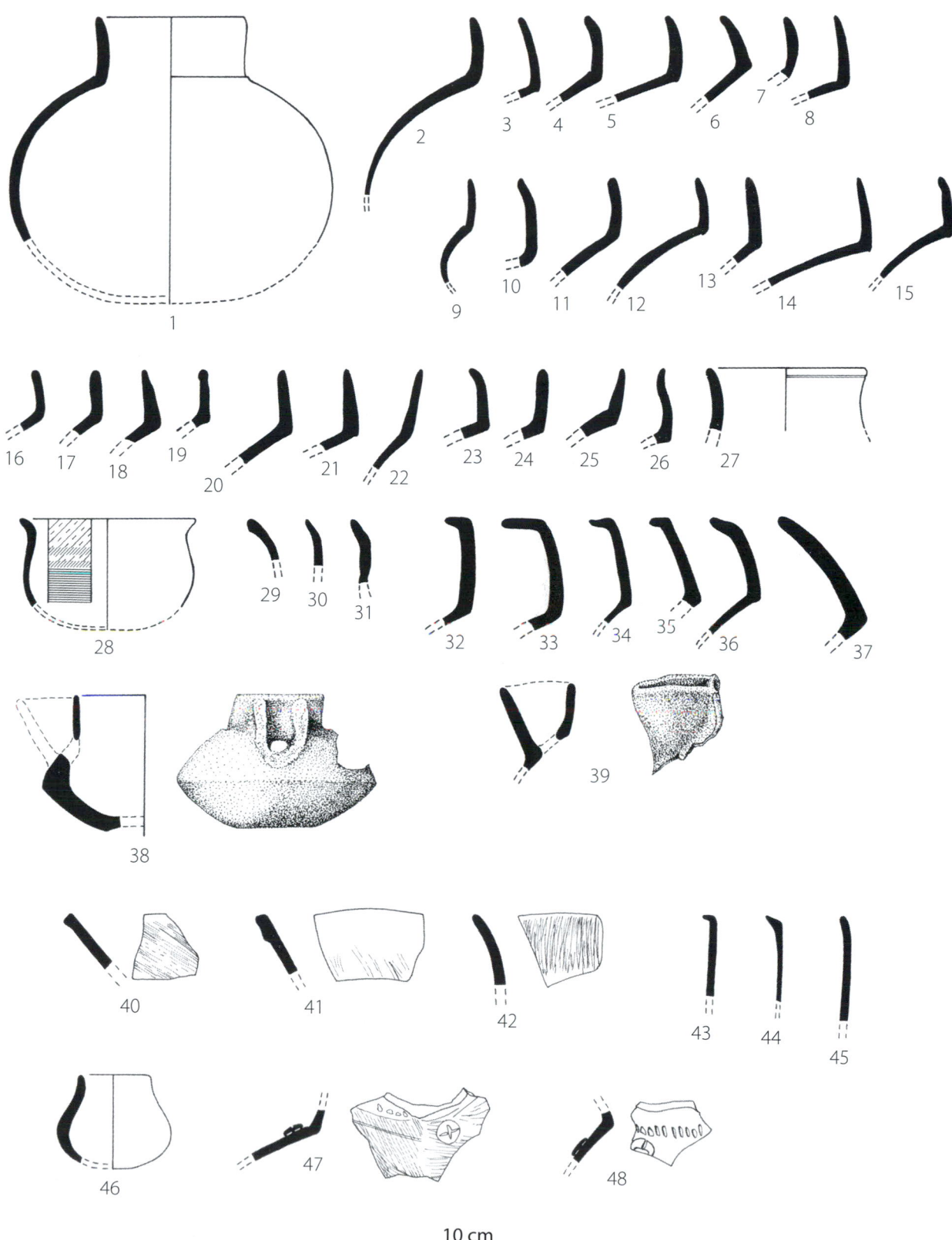

10 cm

Manik
Figure 20

FIGURE 20

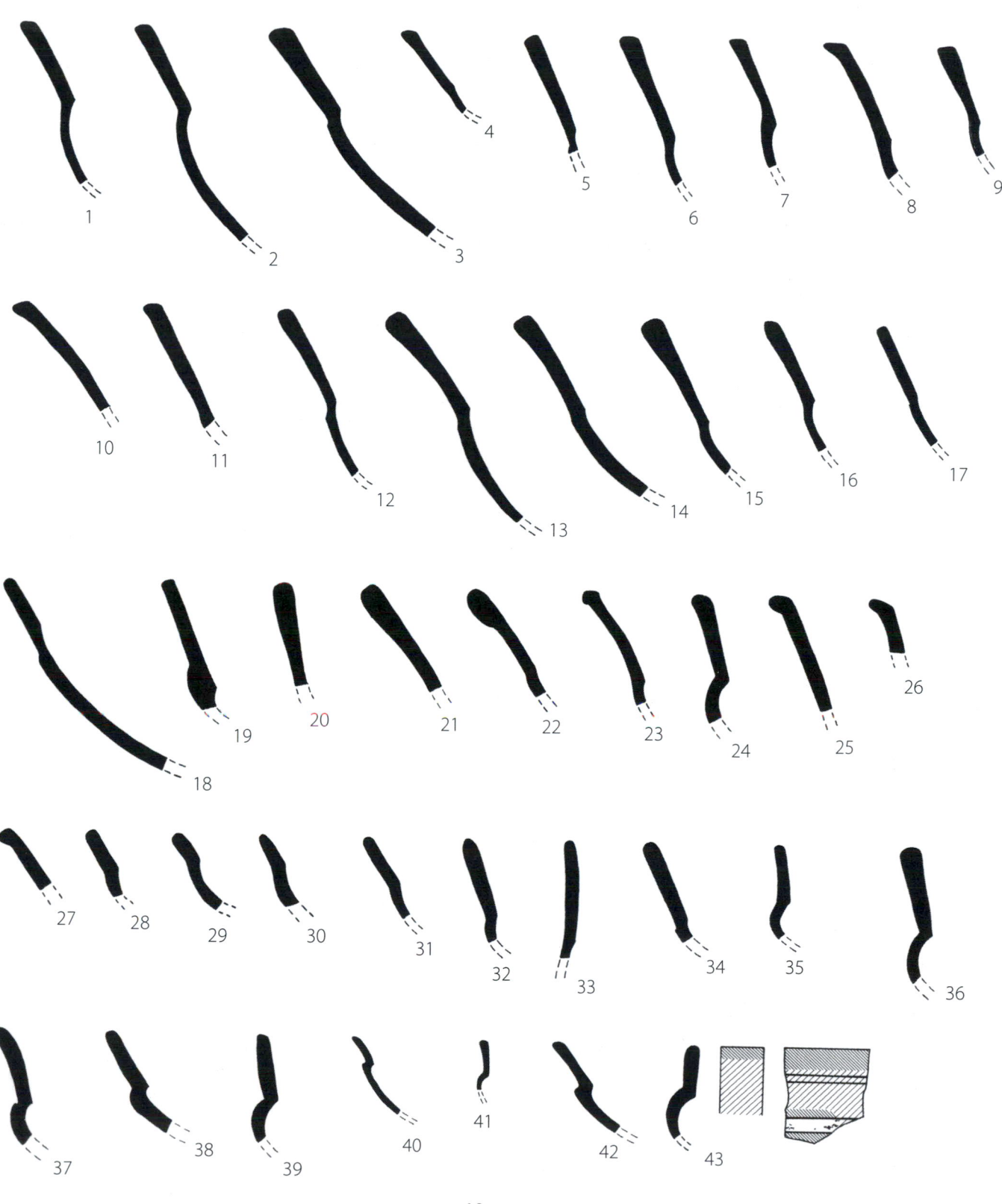

10 cm

Manik
Figure 21

21.1–16   Aguila Orange: Aguila Variety

21.17   Pucte Brown: Pucte Brown

21.18–19   Aguila Orange: Aguila Variety

21.20   Balanza Black: Balanza Black

21.21–22   Aguila Orange: Aguila Variety

21.23–25   Balanza Black: Balanza Black

21.26   Aguila Orange: Aguila Variety

21.27   Balanza Black: Balanza Black

21.28   Pucte Brown: Pucte Brown

21.29–31   Balanza Black: Balanza Black

21.32–46   Aguila Orange: Aguila Variety (slip not shown)

21.47   Aguila Orange: Aguila Variety (with graffiti- slip not shown)

21.48–49   Aguila Orange: Aguila Variety

21.50–51   Aguila Orange: Aguila Variety (slip not shown)

FIGURE 21

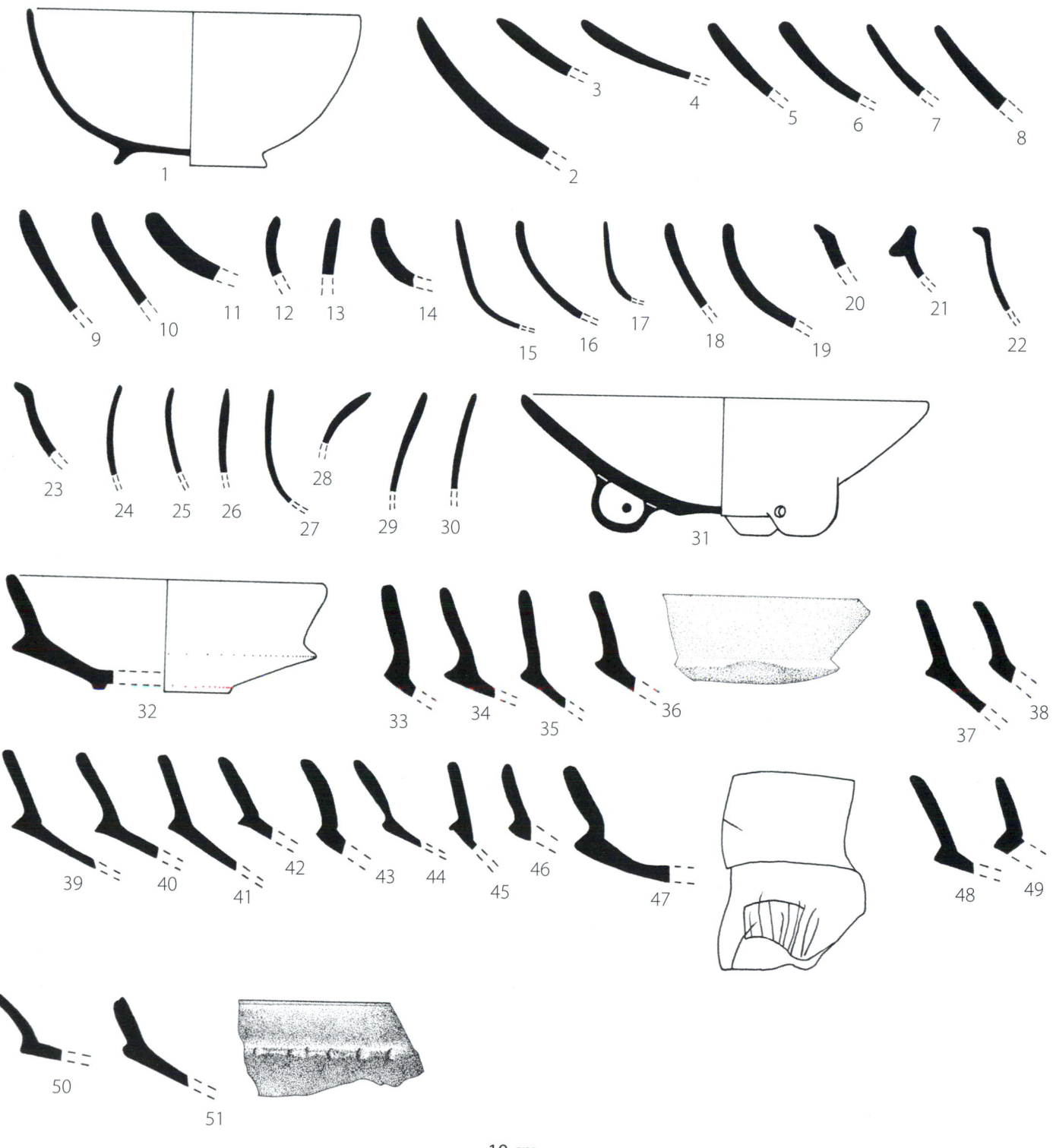

10 cm

Manik
Figure 22

22.1–5 Lucha Incised: Lucha Variety
22.6 Pita Incised: Pita Variety (slip not shown)
22.7–11 Lucha Incised: Lucha Variety
22.12 Pita Incised: Pita Variety (slip not shown)
22.13–23 Lucha Incised: Lucha Variety
22.24 Pita Incised: Pita Variety (slip not shown)
22.25–32 Lucha Incised: Lucha Variety
22.33 Pita Incised: Pita Variety (slip not shown)

FIGURE 22

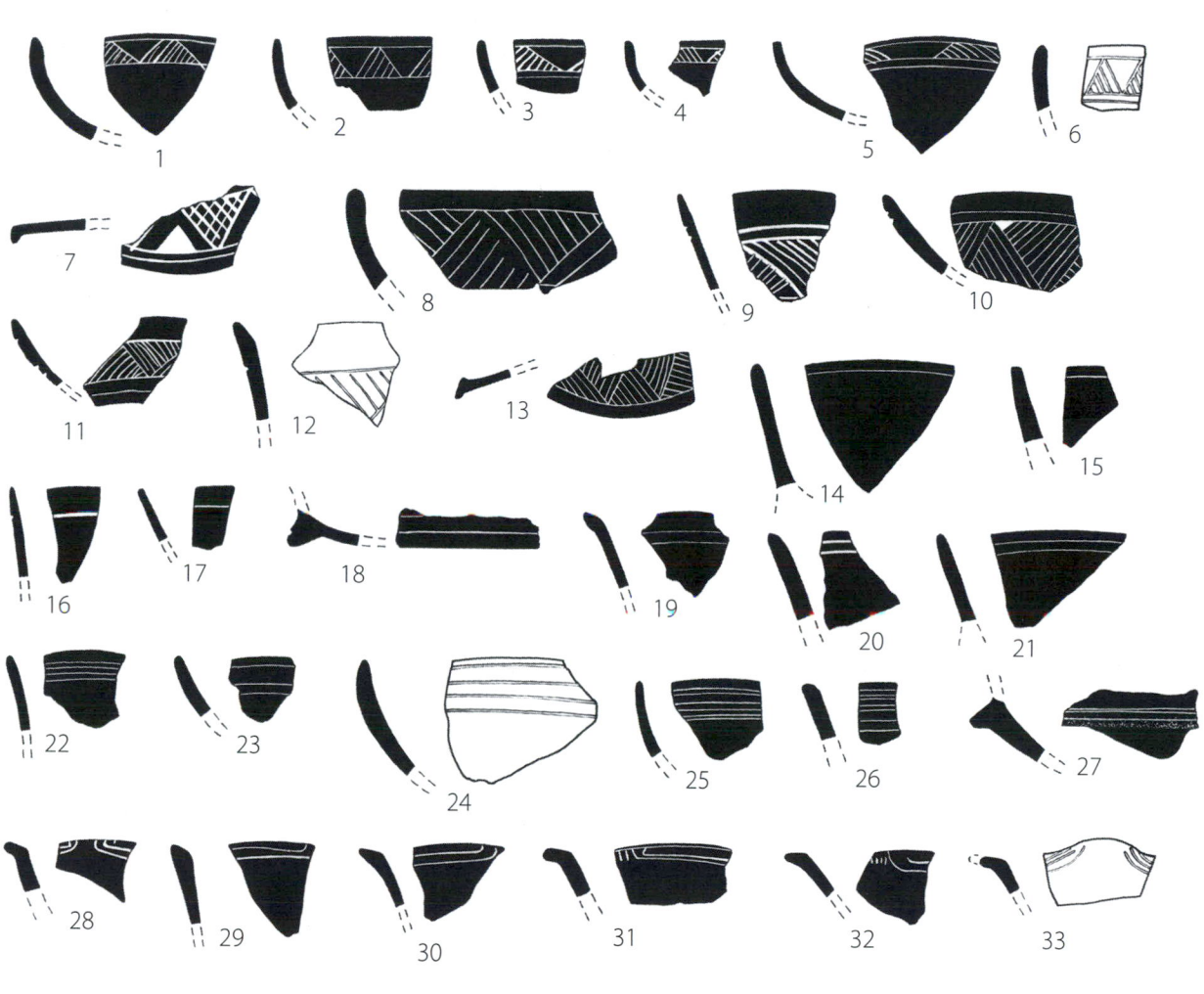

10 cm

Manik
Figure 23

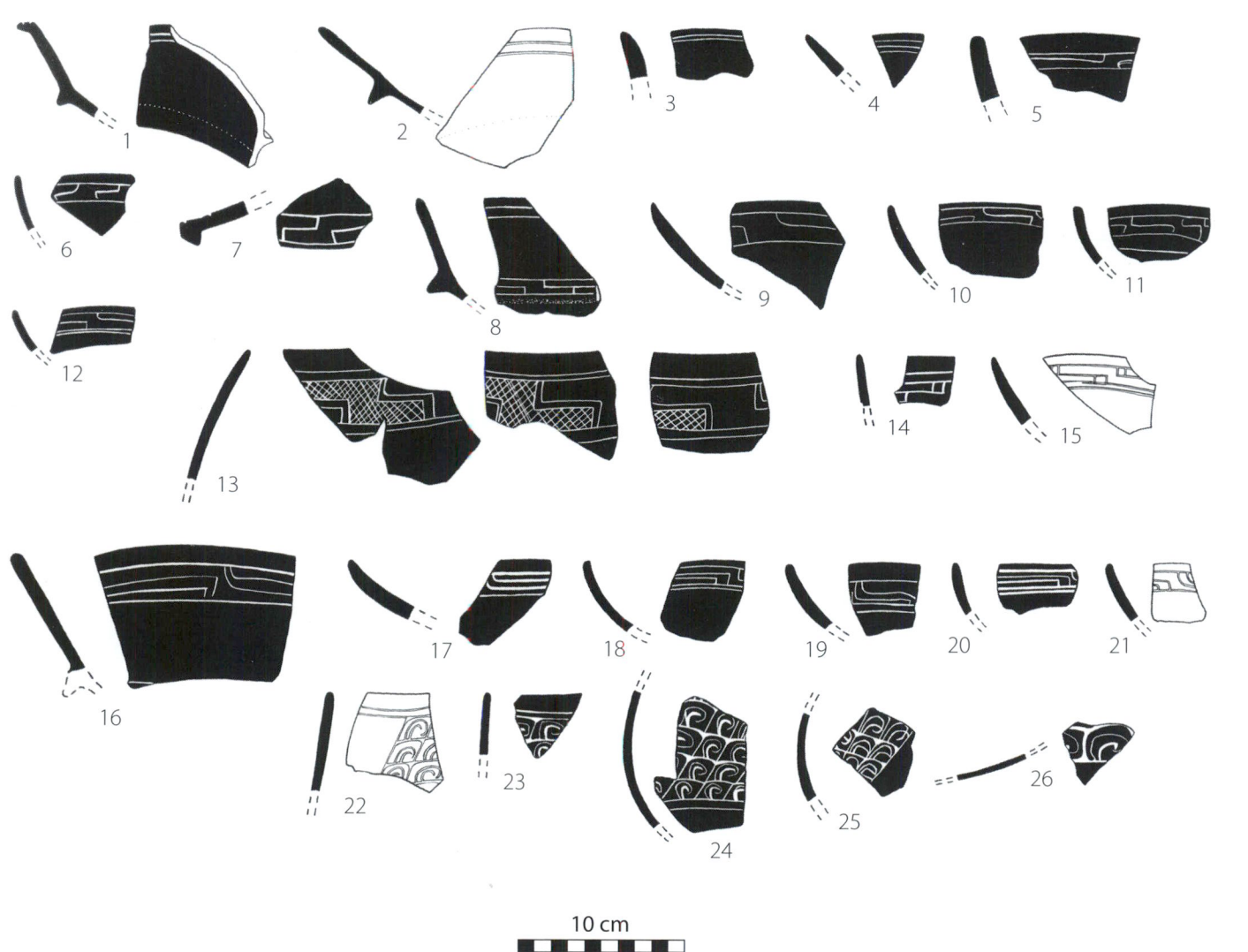

FIGURE 23

10 cm

Manik
Figure 24

FIGURE 24

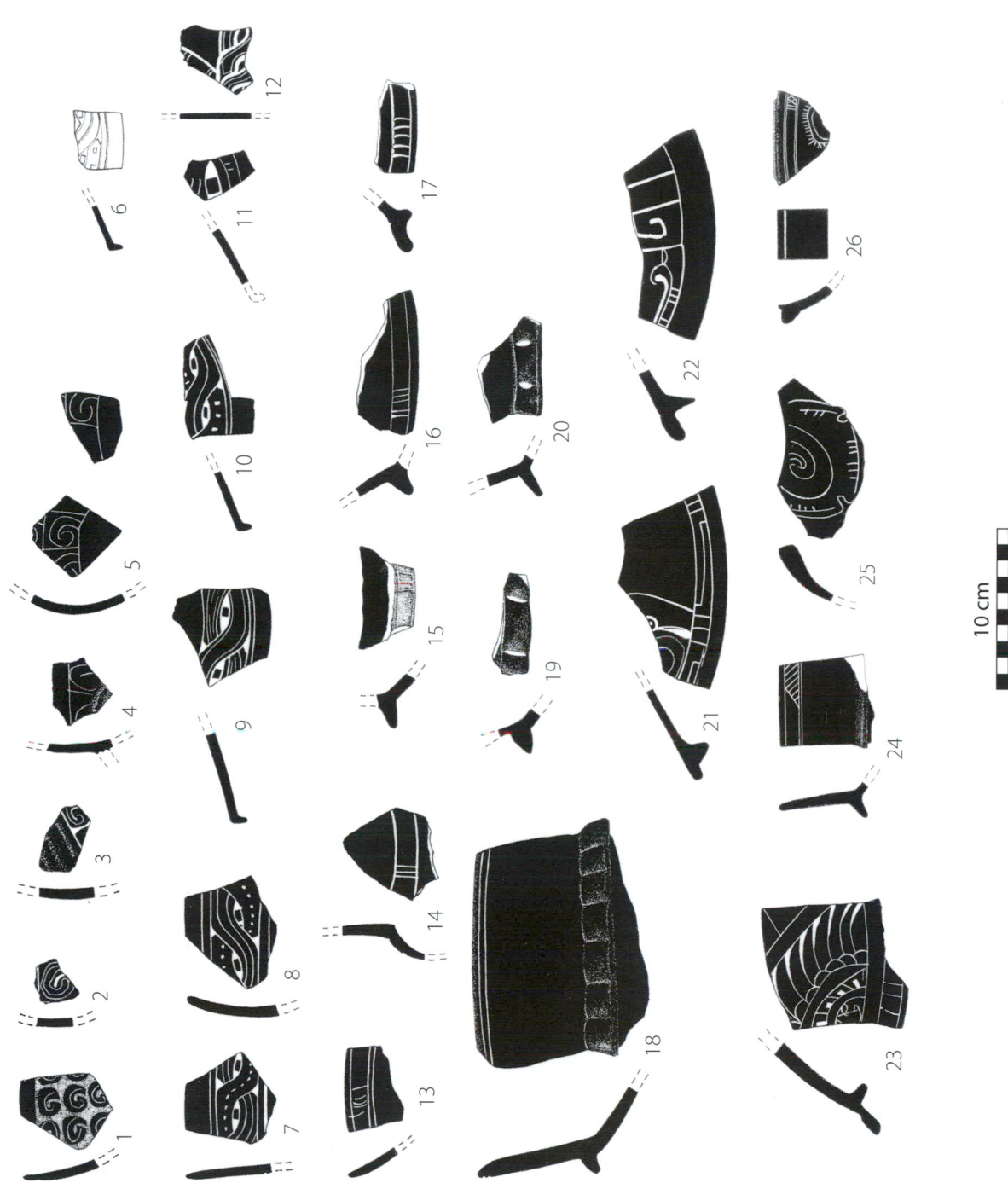

Manik
Figure 25

FIGURE 25

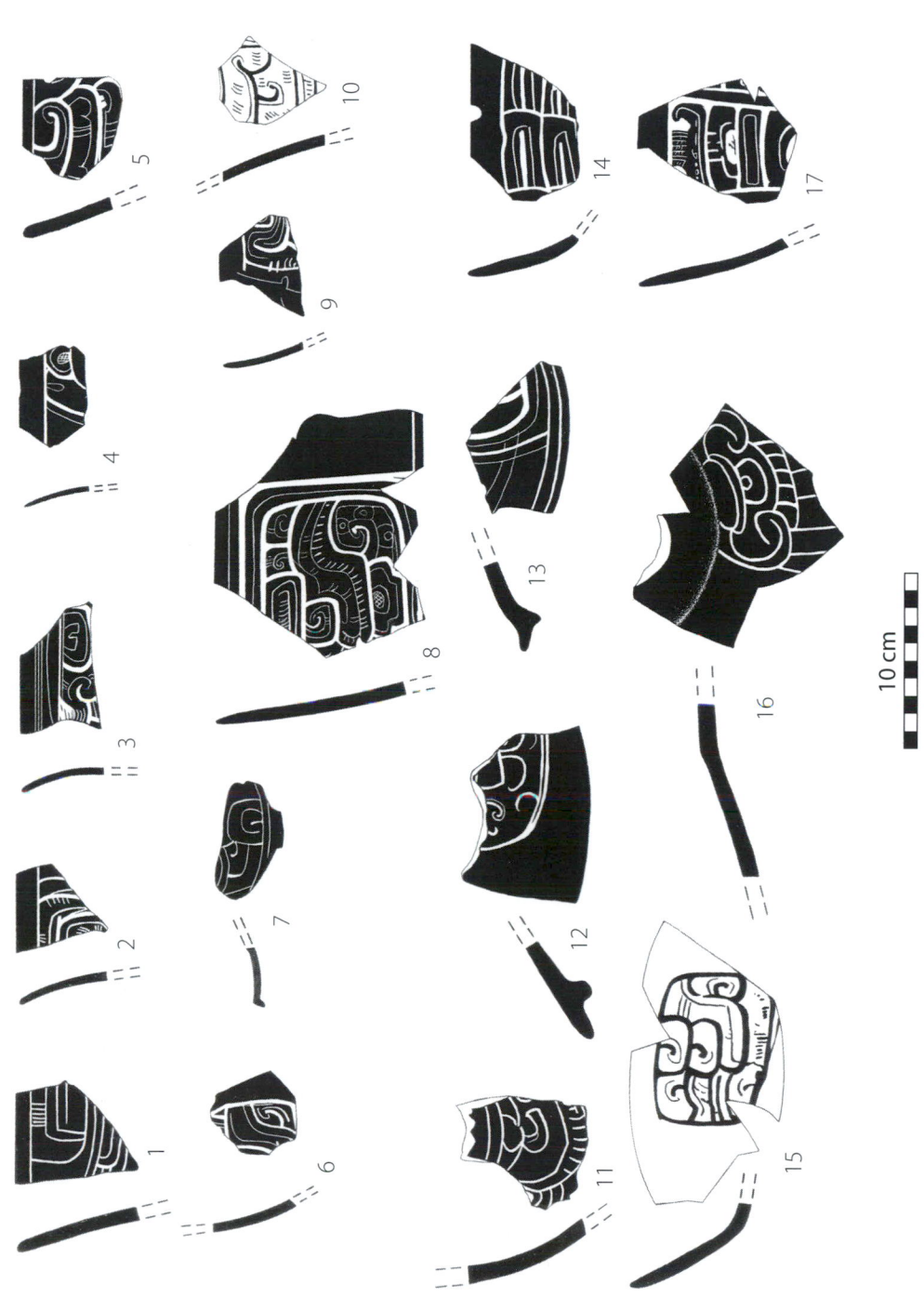

Manik
Figure 26

FIGURE 26

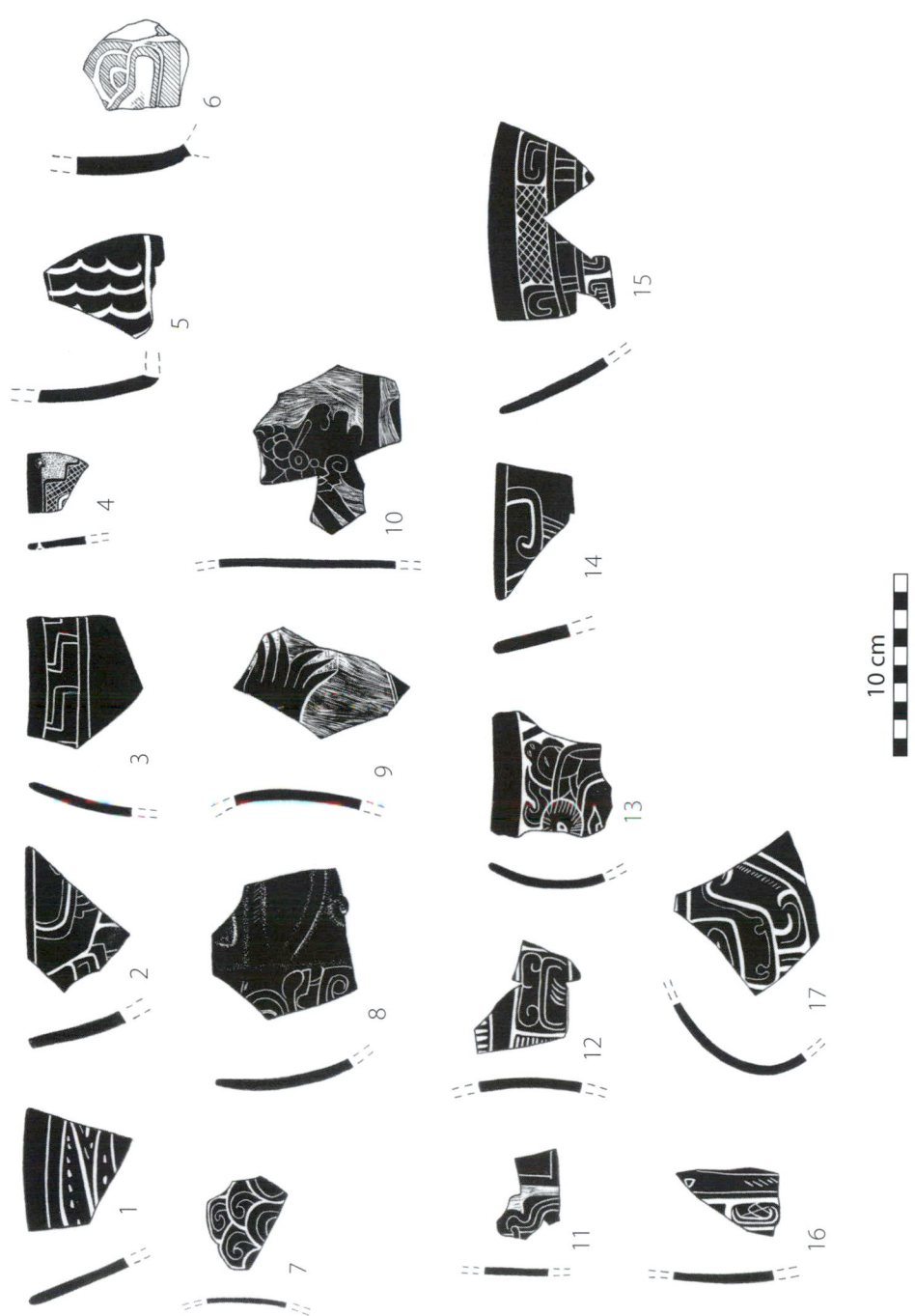

Manik
Figure 27

FIGURE 27

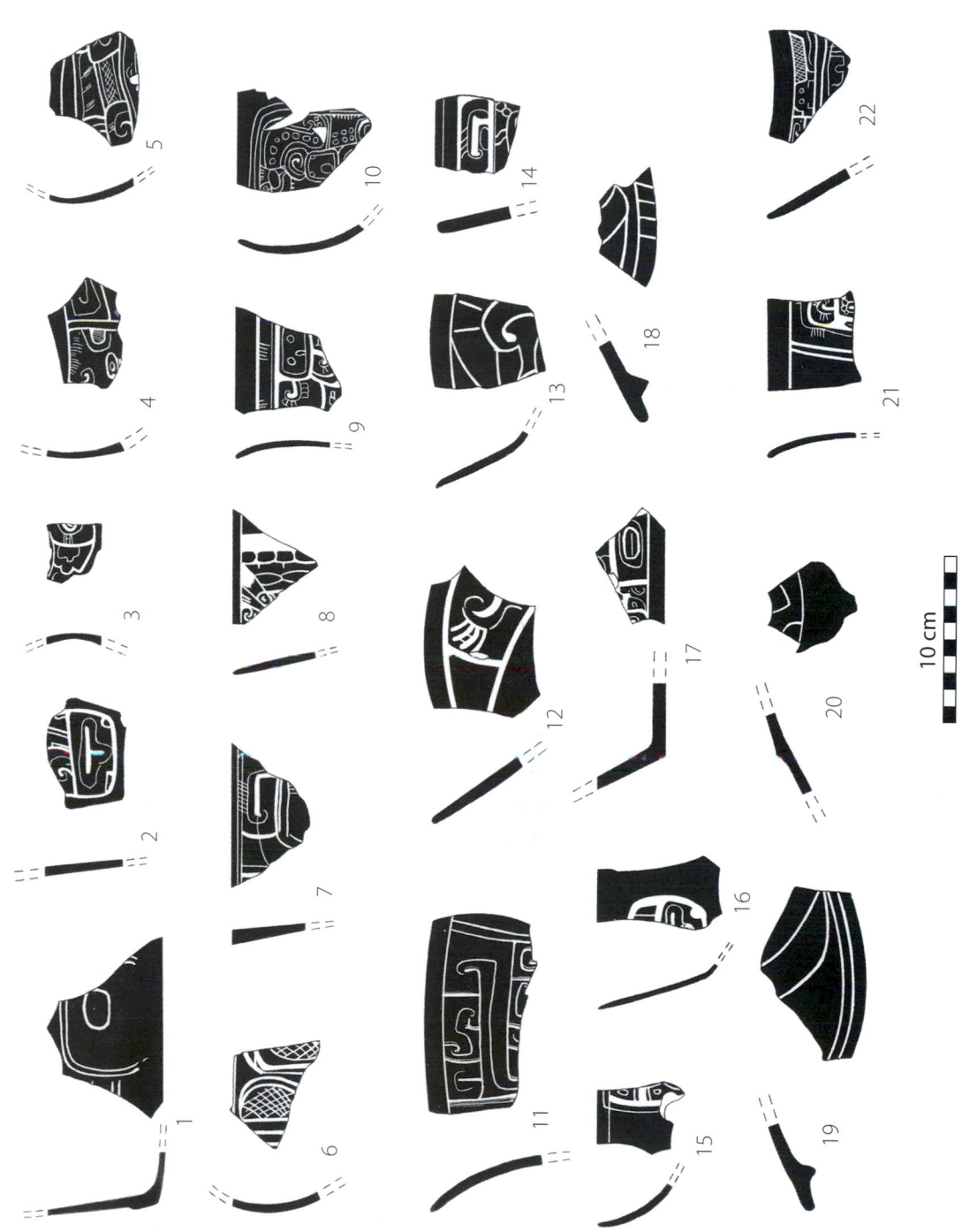

Manik
Figure 28

FIGURE 28

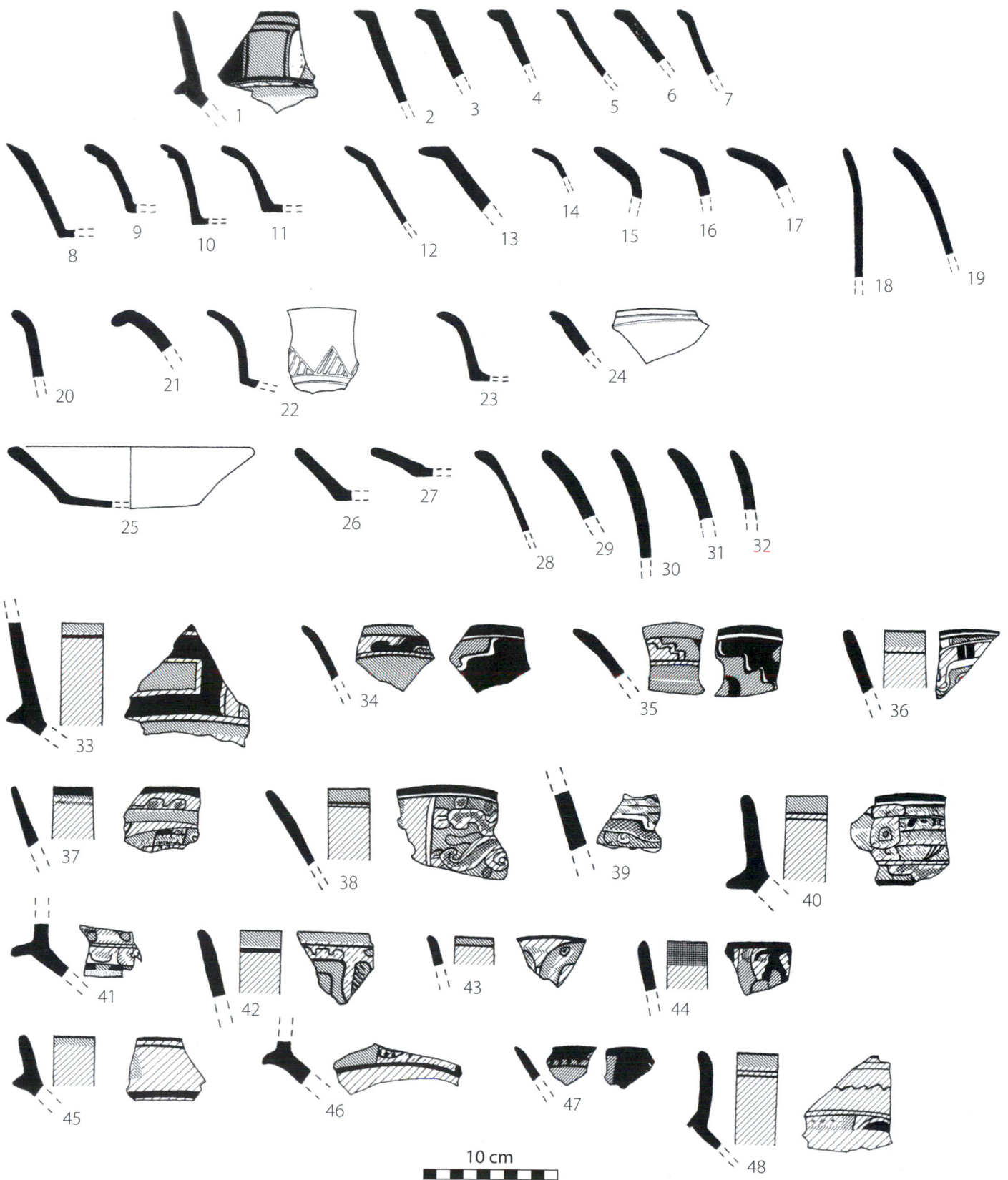

10 cm

Manik
Figure 29

FIGURE 29

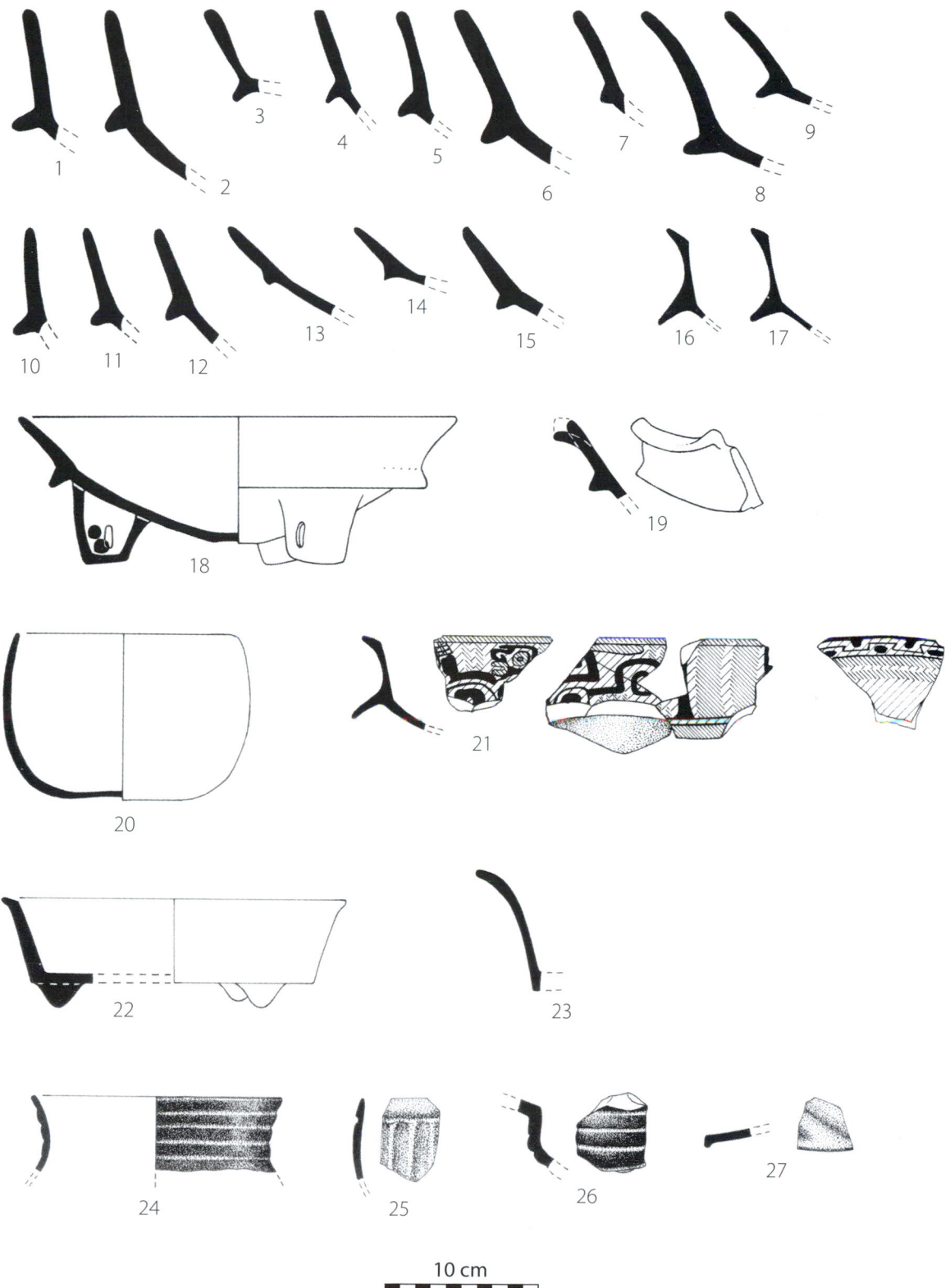

10 cm

Manik
Figure 30

30.1–26   Dos Arroyos Orange Polychrome: Dos Arroyos Polychrome

FIGURE 30

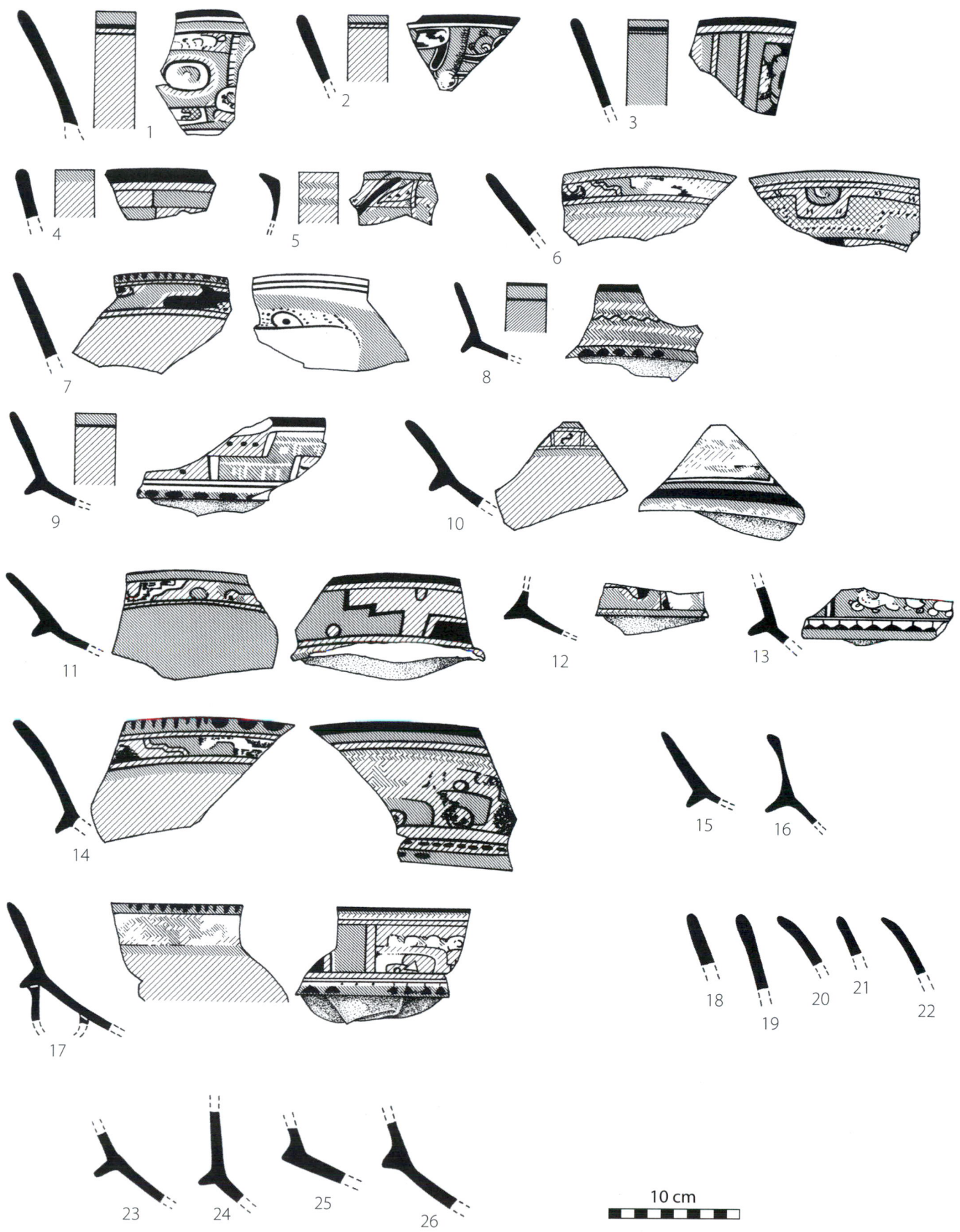

10 cm

Manik
Figure 31

FIGURE 31

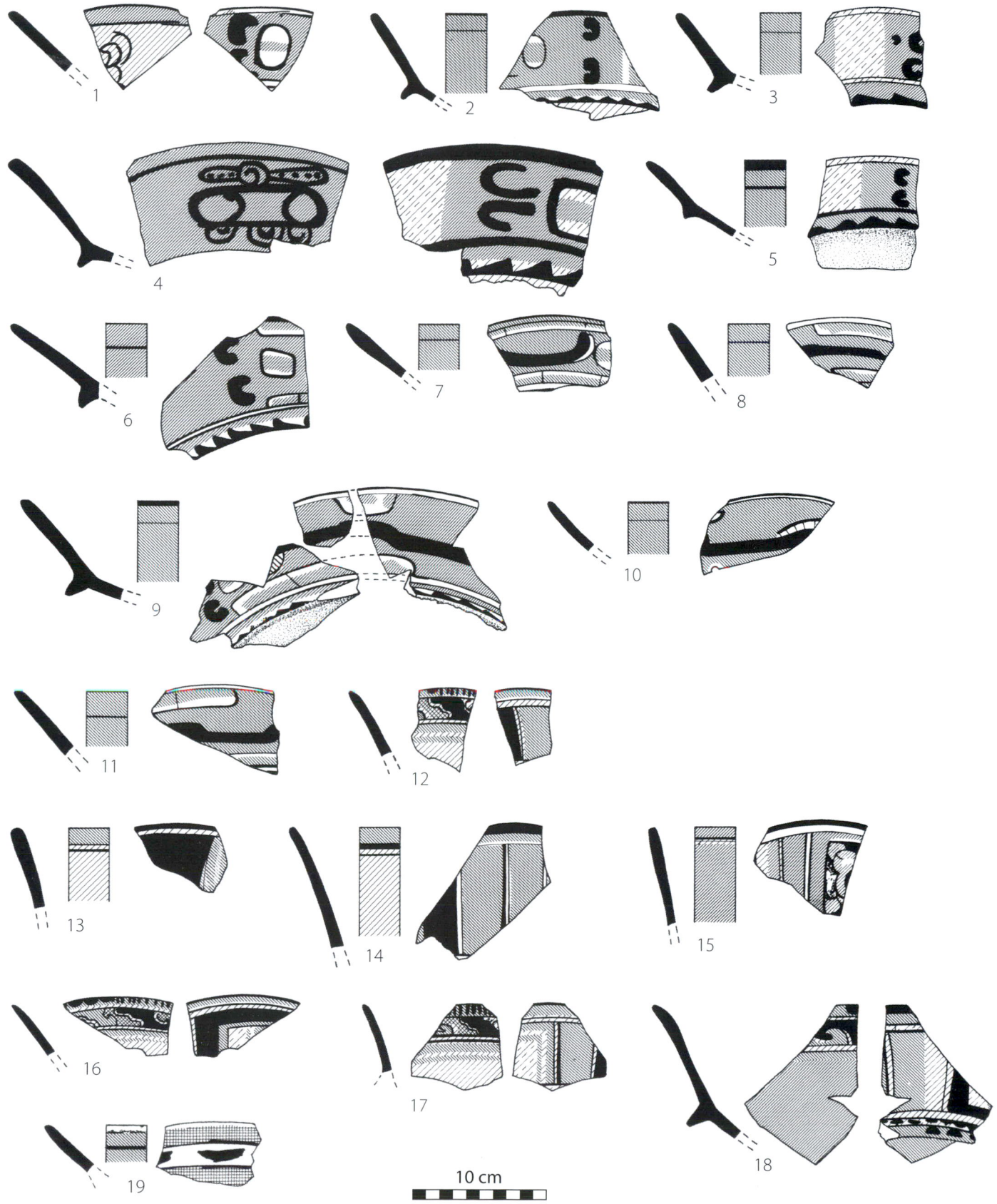

10 cm

Manik
Figure 32

FIGURE 32

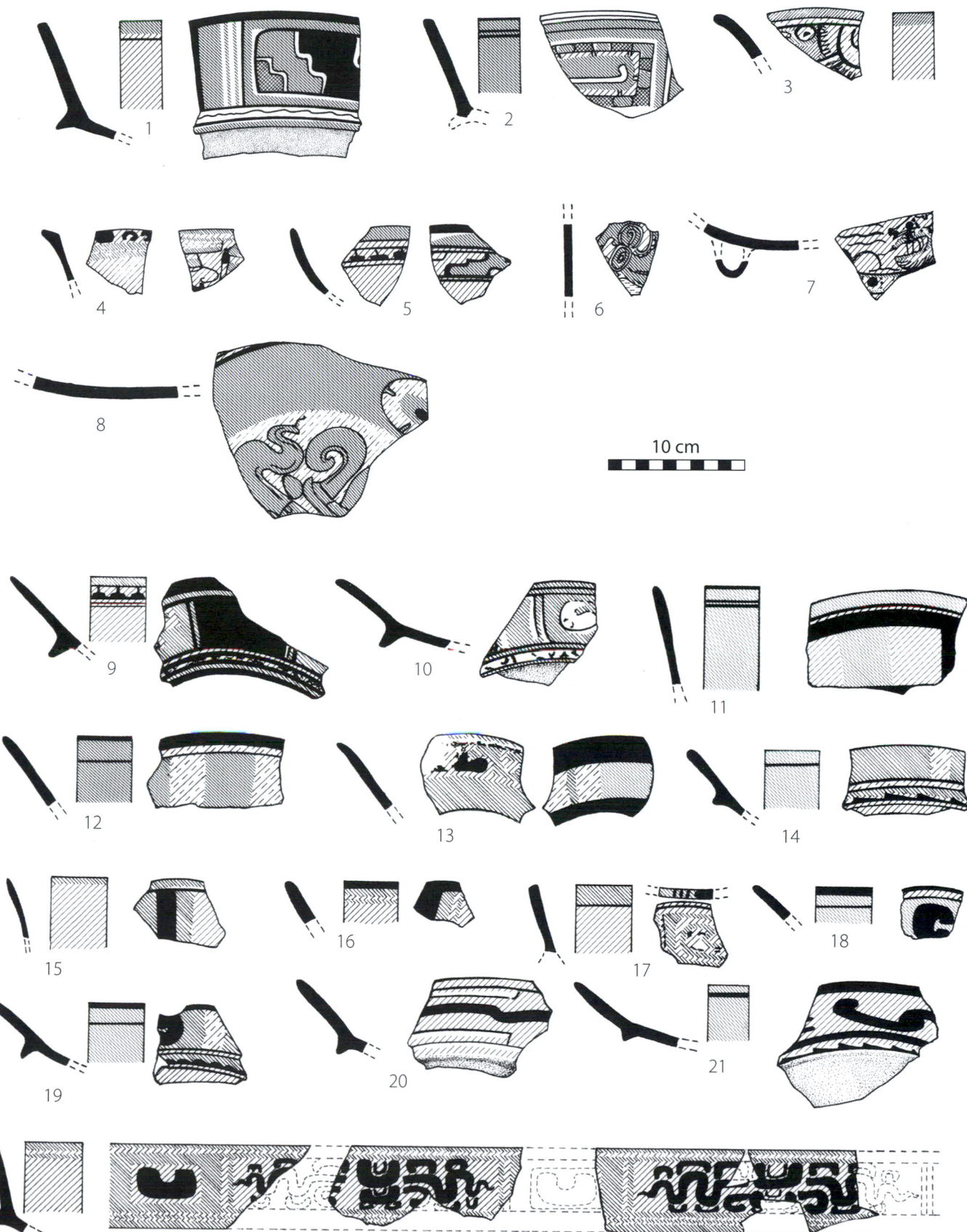

Manik
Figure 33

FIGURE 33

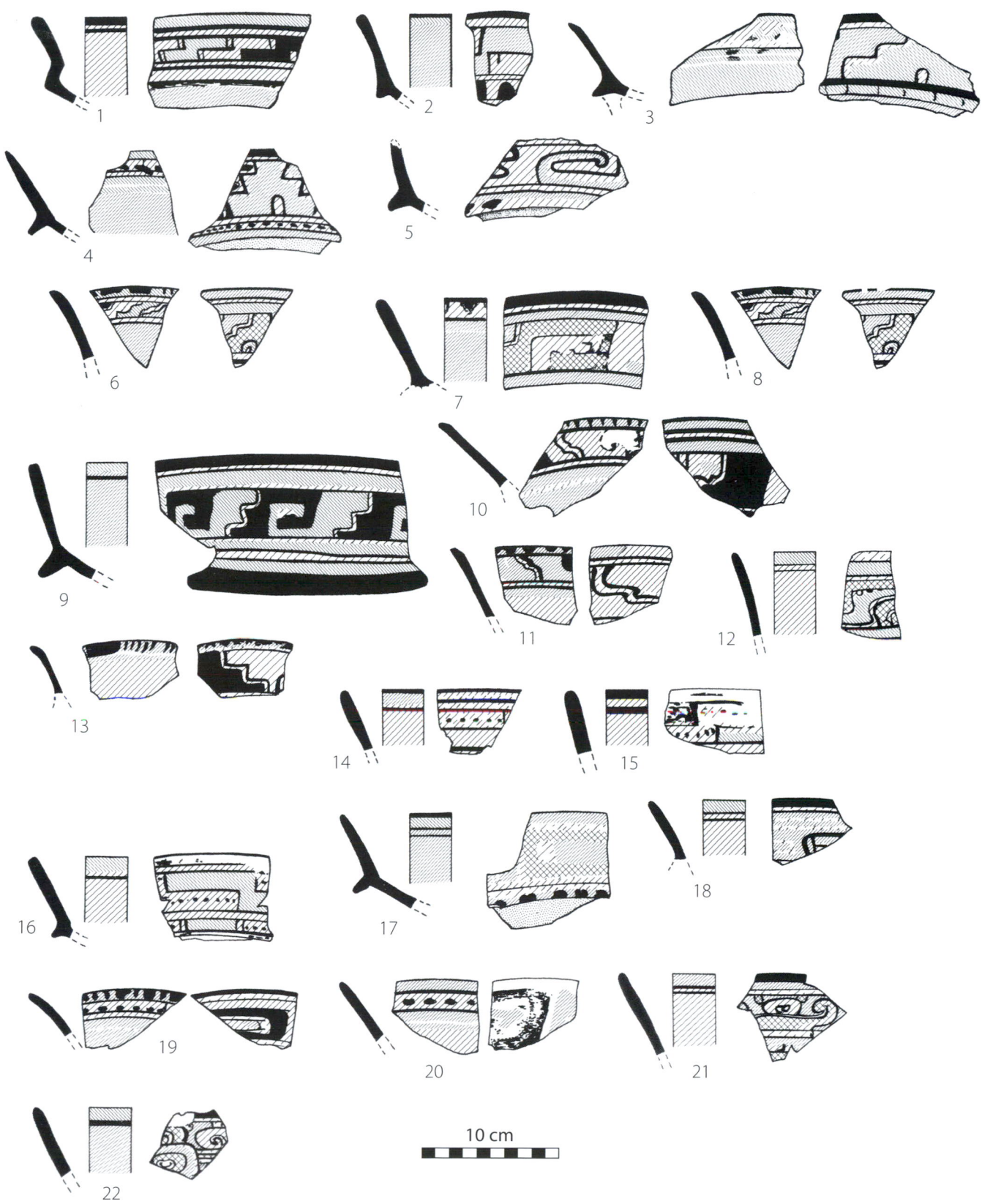

10 cm

Manik
Figure 34

FIGURE 34

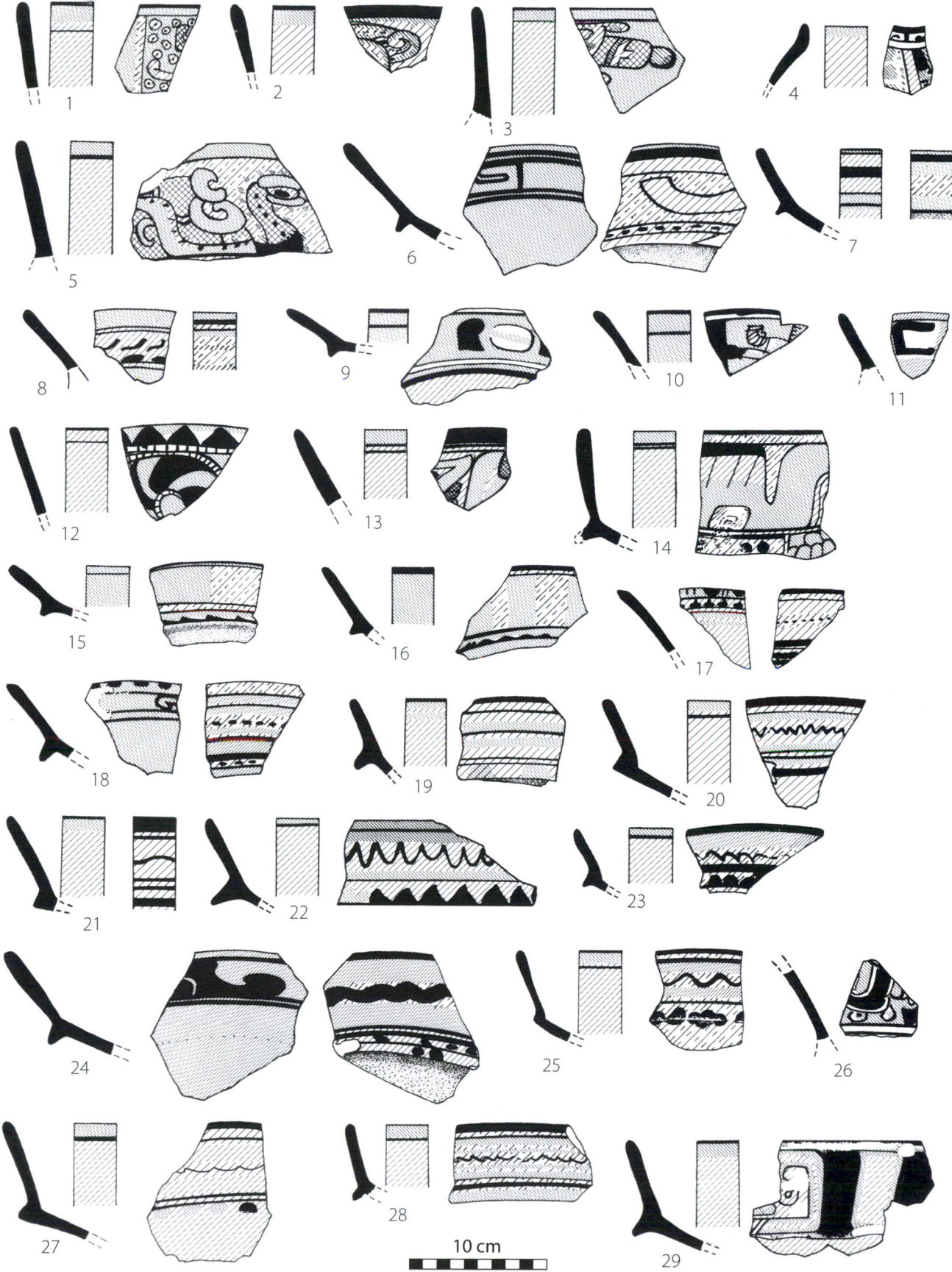

10 cm

Manik
Figure 35

35.1–7	Dos Arroyos Orange Polychrome: Dos Arroyos Variety
35.8	Unnamed Trichrome (Dos Arroyos Group)
35.9	San Blas Red-on-orange: San Blas Variety (interior slip not shown)
35.10–12	Dos Arroyos Orange Polychrome: Dos Arroyos Variety
35.13	San Blas Red-on-orange: San Blas Variety (interior slip not shown)
35.14	Unnamed Trichrome (Dos Arroyos Group)
35.15	Caldero Buff Polychrome: Caldero Variety
35.16–17	Dos Arroyos Orange Polychrome: Dos Arroyos Variety
35.18	San Blas Red-on-orange: San Blas Variety
35.19–21	Dos Arroyos Orange Polychrome: Dos Arroyos Variety
35.22	San Bartolo Red-on-buff: San Bartolo Variety (buff slip not shown)
35.23–26	Dos Arroyos Orange Polychrome: Dos Arroyos Variety
35.27–28	Yaloche Cream Polychrome: Yaloche Variety
35.29	Caldero Buff Polychrome: Caldero Variety
35.30–32	Yaloche Cream Polychrome: Yaloche Variety
35.33–37	Cochol Orange Polychrome: Cochol Variety
35.38	Caldero Buff Polychrome: Caldero Variety
35.39–43	Cochol Orange Polychrome: Cochol Variety

FIGURE 35

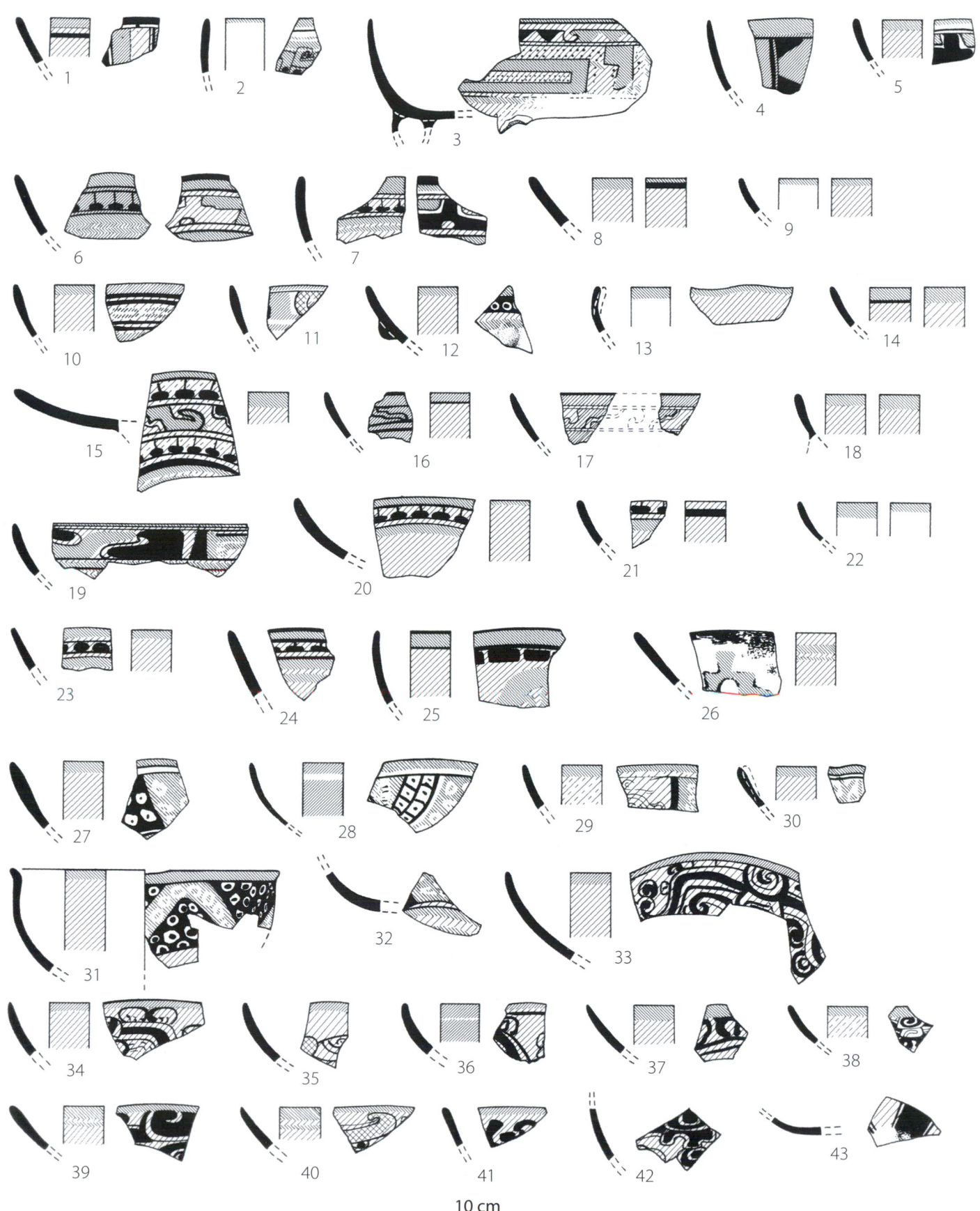

10 cm

FIGURE 36

Manik
Figure 36

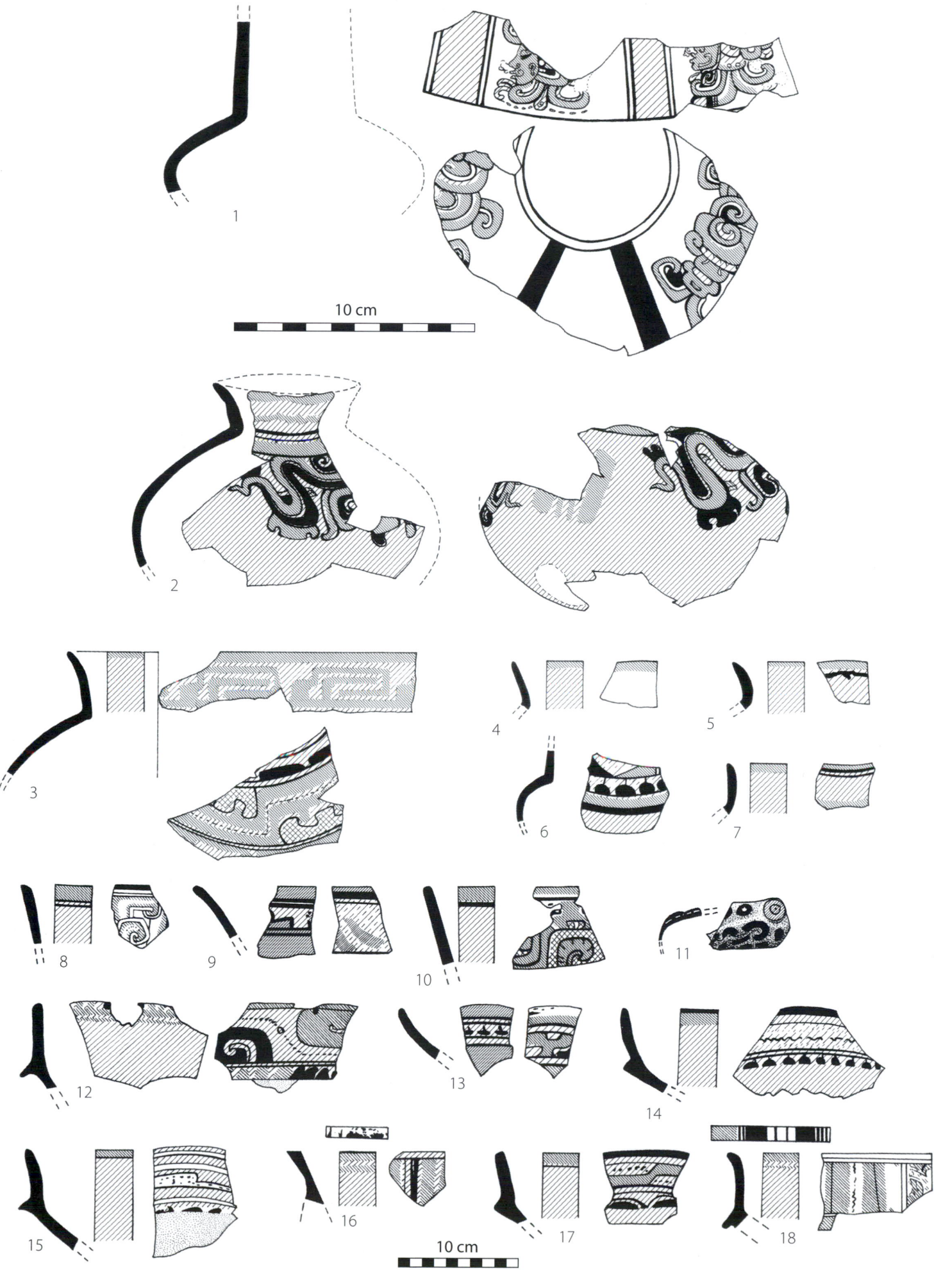

FIGURE 37

Manik
Figure 37

37.1–3	Yaloche Cream Polychrome: Yaloche Variety
37.4	Dos Arroyos Orange Polychrome: Dos Arroyos Variety
37.5	Yaloche Cream Polychrome: Yaloche Variety
37.6–7	Dos Arroyos Orange Polychrome: Dos Arroyos Variety
37.8	Caldero Buff Polychrome: Caldero Variety
37.9	Dos Arroyos Orange Polychrome: Dos Arroyos Variety
37.10–13	Yaloche Cream Polychrome: Yaloche Variety
37.14	Dos Arroyos Orange Polychrome: Dos Arroyos Variety
37.15	Yaloche Cream Polychrome: Yaloche Variety
37.16–17	Dos Arroyos Orange Polychrome: Dos Arroyos Variety
37.18	Yaloche Cream Polychrome: Yaloche Variety
37.19	Caldero Buff Polychrome: Caldero Variety
37.20	Yaloche Cream Polychrome: Yaloche Variety
37.21	Aguila Orange: Aguila Variety
37.22	Dos Arroyos Orange Polychrome: Dos Arroyos Variety
37.23	Aguila Orange: Aguila Variety
37.24	Lucha Incised: Lucha Variety
37.25	Urita Gouged-incised: Urita Variety
37.26	Aguila Orange: Aguila Variety
37.27	San Bartolo Red-on-buff: San Bartolo Variety
37.28–30	Aguila Orange: Aguila Variety
37.31–32	Lucha Incised: Lucha Variety
37.33	Urita Gouged-incised: Urita Variety
37.34	Yaloche Cream Polychrome: Yaloche Variety
37.35–36	Urita Gouged-incised: Urita Variety (slip not shown)
37.37–38	Lucha Incised: Lucha Variety
37.39	Urita Gouged-incised: Urita Variety
37.40	Balanza Black: Balanza Variety
37.41	Urita Gouged-incised: Urita Variety
37.42	Lucha Incised: Lucha Variety
37.43	Urita Gouged-incised: Urita Variety
37.44	Lucha Incised: Lucha Variety
37.45	Urita Gouged-incised: Urita Variety
37.46–47	Balanza Black: Balanza Variety (Appliqué)

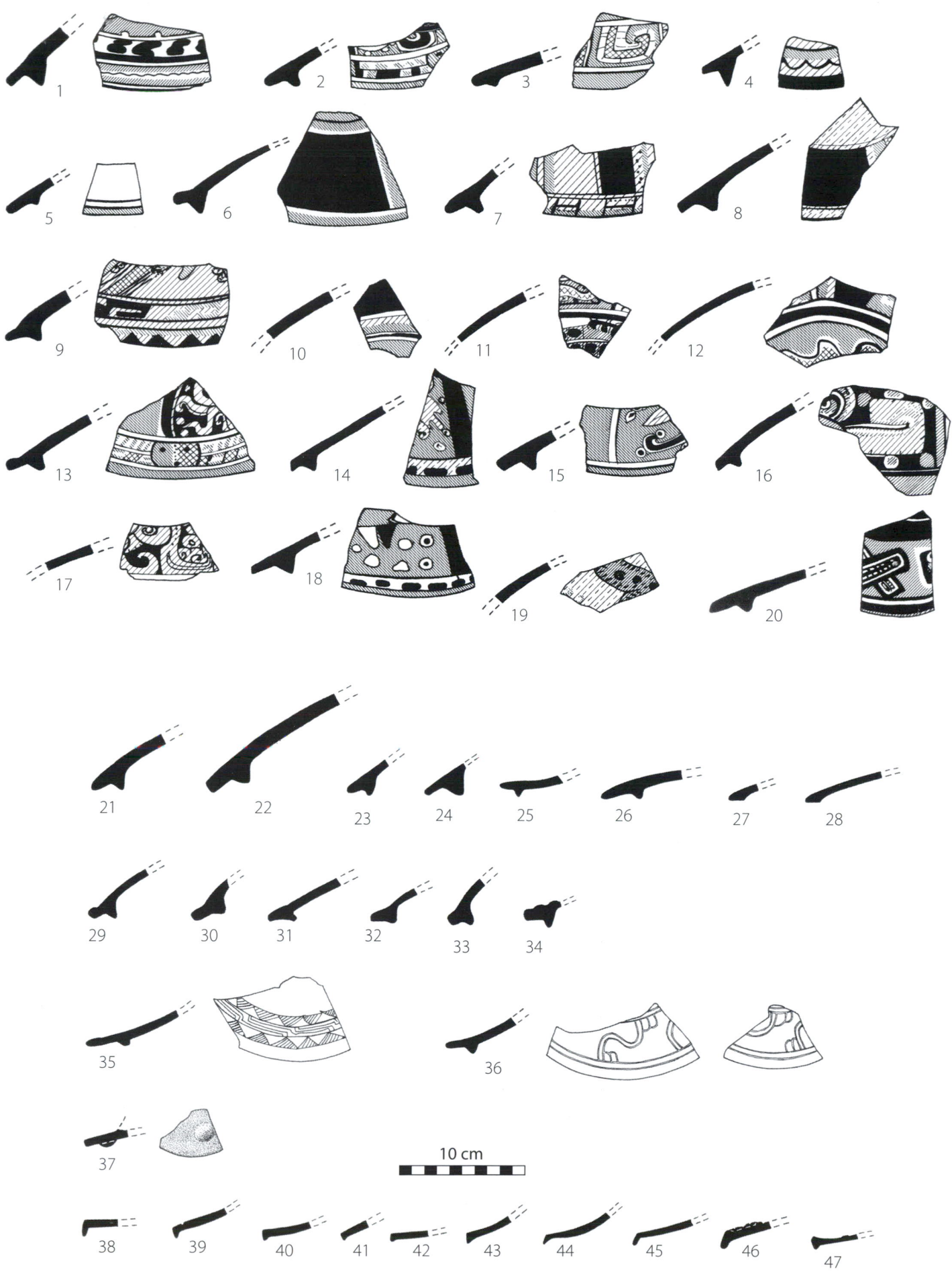

Manik
Figure 38

38.1–4	Aguila Orange: Aguila Variety (Appliqué) (slip not shown)
38.5–8	Balanza Black: Balanza Variety (Appliqué) (slip not shown)
38.9	Aguila Orange: Aguila Variety (Appliqué) (slip not shown)
38.10	Lucha Incised: Lucha Variety
38.11	Balanza Black: Balanza Variety (Appliqué) (slip not shown)
38.12	Urita Gouged-incised: Urita Variety
38.13	Lucha Incised: Lucha Variety
38.14–17	Balanza Black: Balanza Variety (Appliqué) (slip not shown)
38.18	Positas Modeled: Positas Variety (slip not shown)
38.19–20	Pita Incised: Pita Variety (slip not shown)
38.21–25	Balanza Black: Balanza Variety (Appliqué) (slip not shown)
38.26	Lucha Incised: Lucha Variety
38.27	Urita Gouged-incised: Urita Variety
38.28–31	Balanza Black: Balanza Variety (Appliqué) (slip not shown)
38.32	Aguila Orange: Aguila Variety (slip not shown)
38.33	Lucha Incised: Lucha Variety (slip not shown)
38.34	Balanza Black: Balanza Variety (slip not shown)
38.35	San Clemente Gouged-incised: San Clemente Variety (slip not shown)
38.36	Positas Modeled: Positas Variety (slip not shown)
38.37	Pita Incised: Pita Variety (slip not shown)
38.38–47	Balanza Black: Balanza Variety (Appliqué)
38.48	Lucha Incised: Lucha Variety (slip not shown)
38.49	Balanza Black: Balanza Variety (Appliqué) (slip not shown)
38.50–51	Positas Modeled: Positas Variety (slip not shown)
38.53–59	Balanza Black: Balanza Variety (Appliqué)
38.60	San Clemente Gouged-incised: San Clemente Variety (slip not shown)
38.61–70	Balanza Black: Balanza Variety (Appliqué) (slip not shown)
38.71	Positas Modeled: Positas Variety

FIGURE 38

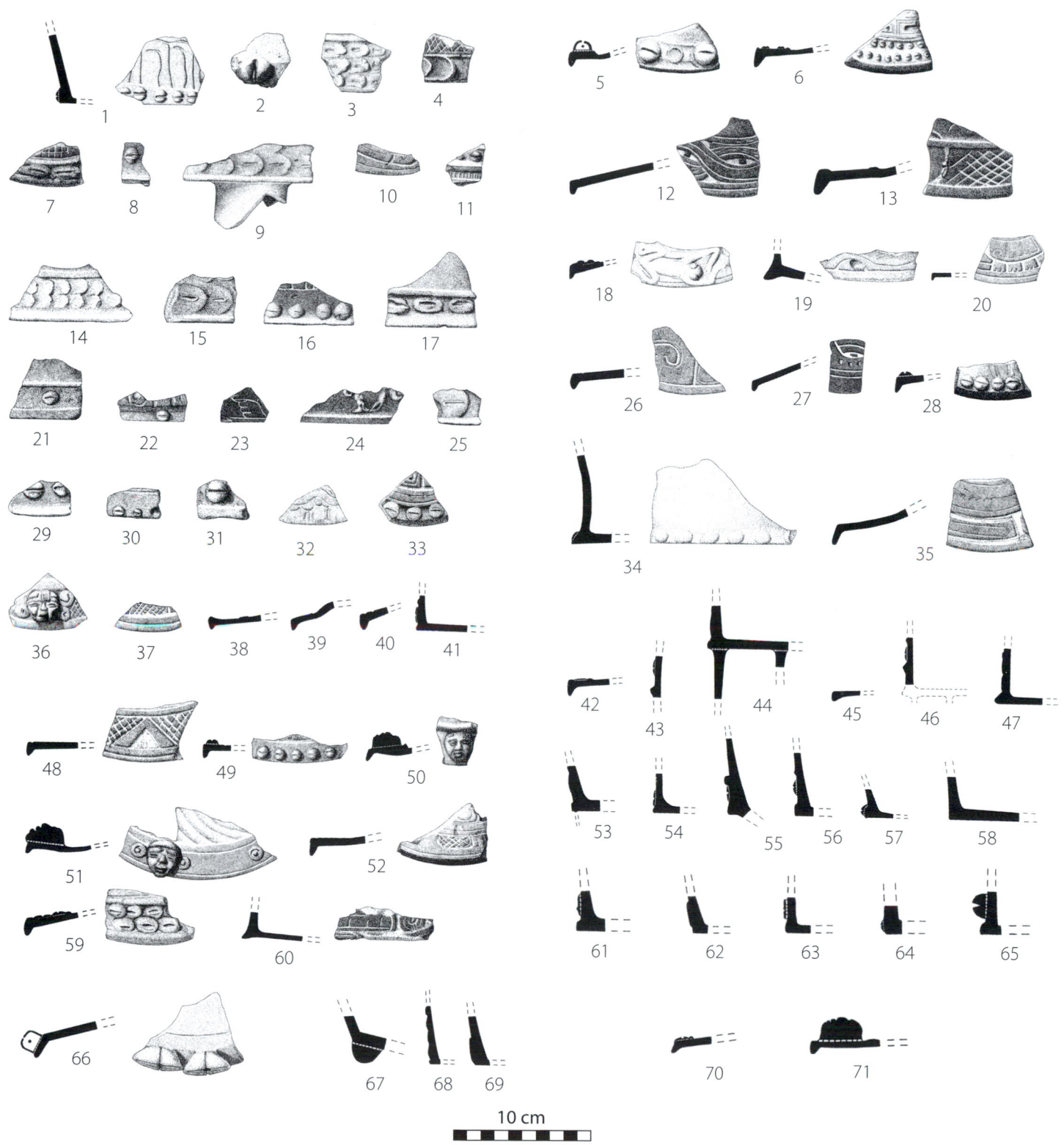

10 cm

Ik-Imix-Eznab
Figure 39

39.1–53   Cambio Unslipped: Cambio Variety or Encanto Striated: Encanto Variety (necks are not striated and rim profiles overlap)

FIGURE 39

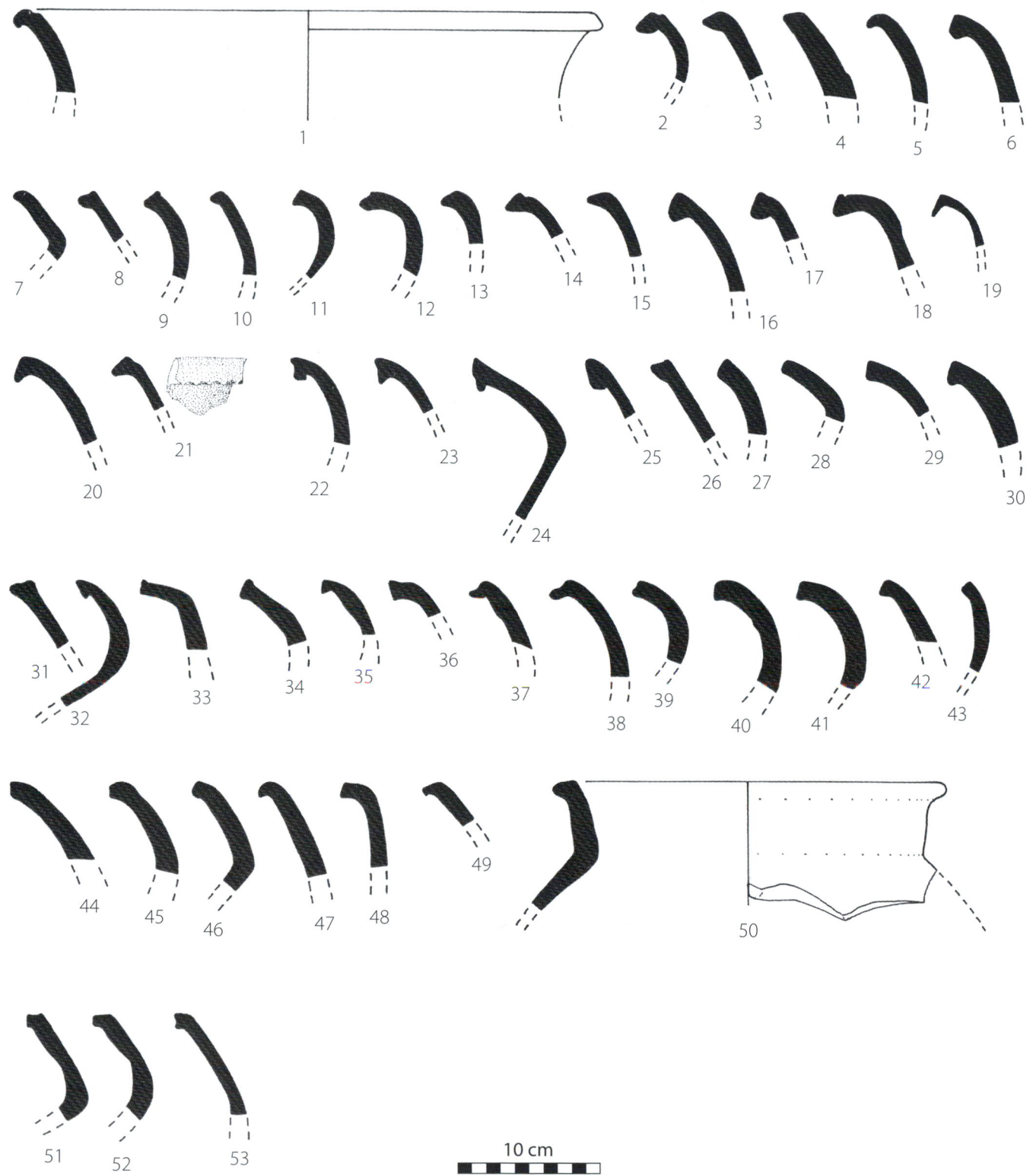

10 cm

FIGURE 40

Ik
Figure 40

40.1–6   Saxche Orange Polychrome: Saxche Variety
40.7   Uacho Black-on-orange: Uacho Variety
40.8–9   Saxche Orange Polychrome: Saxche Variety
40.10   Desquite Red-on-orange: Desquite Variety
40.11–19   Saxche Orange Polychrome: Saxche Variety
40.20   Sibal Buff Polychrome: Sibal Variety
40.21–23   Saxche Orange Polychrome: Saxche Variety

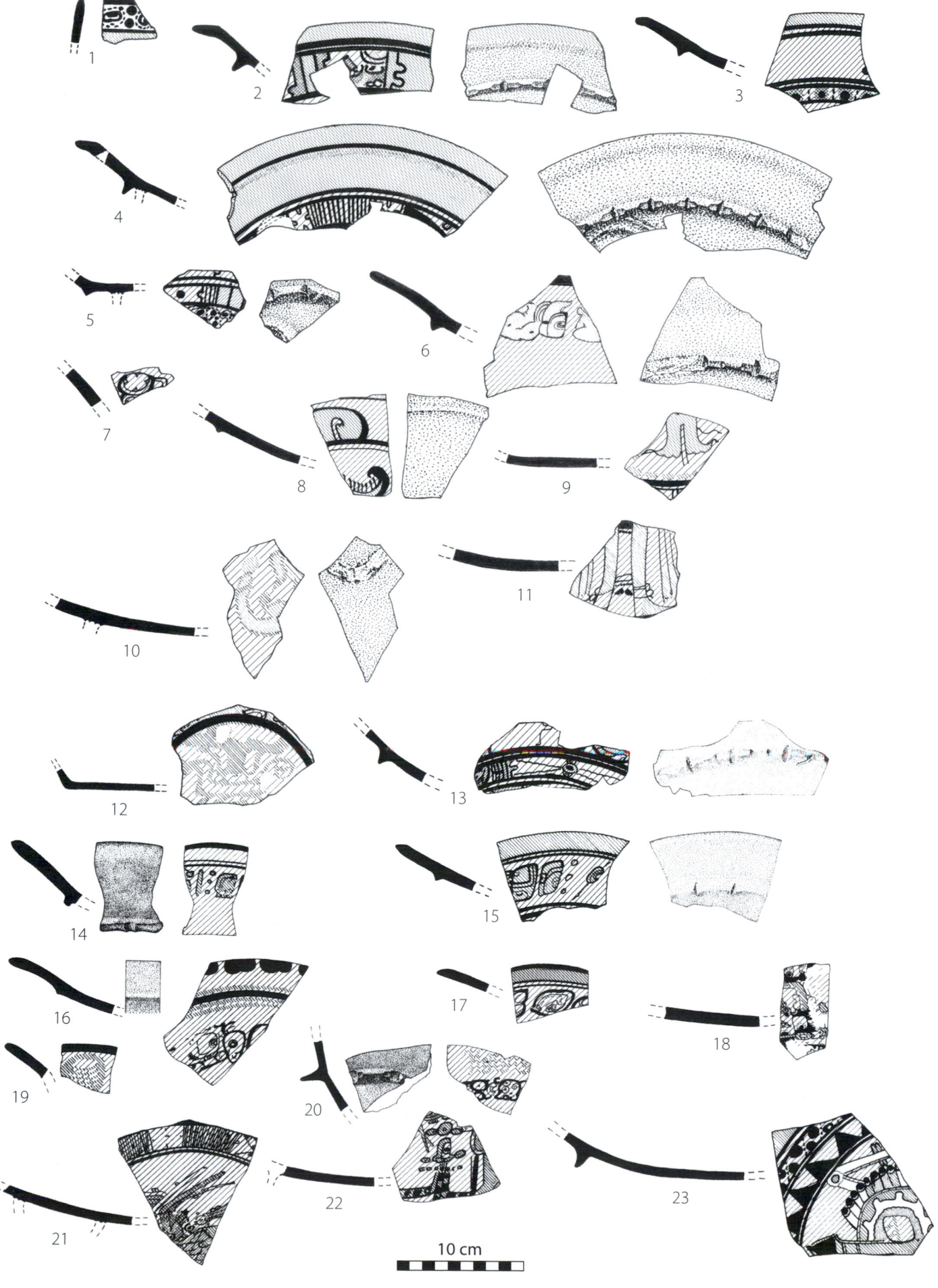

10 cm

FIGURE 41

Ik
Figure 41

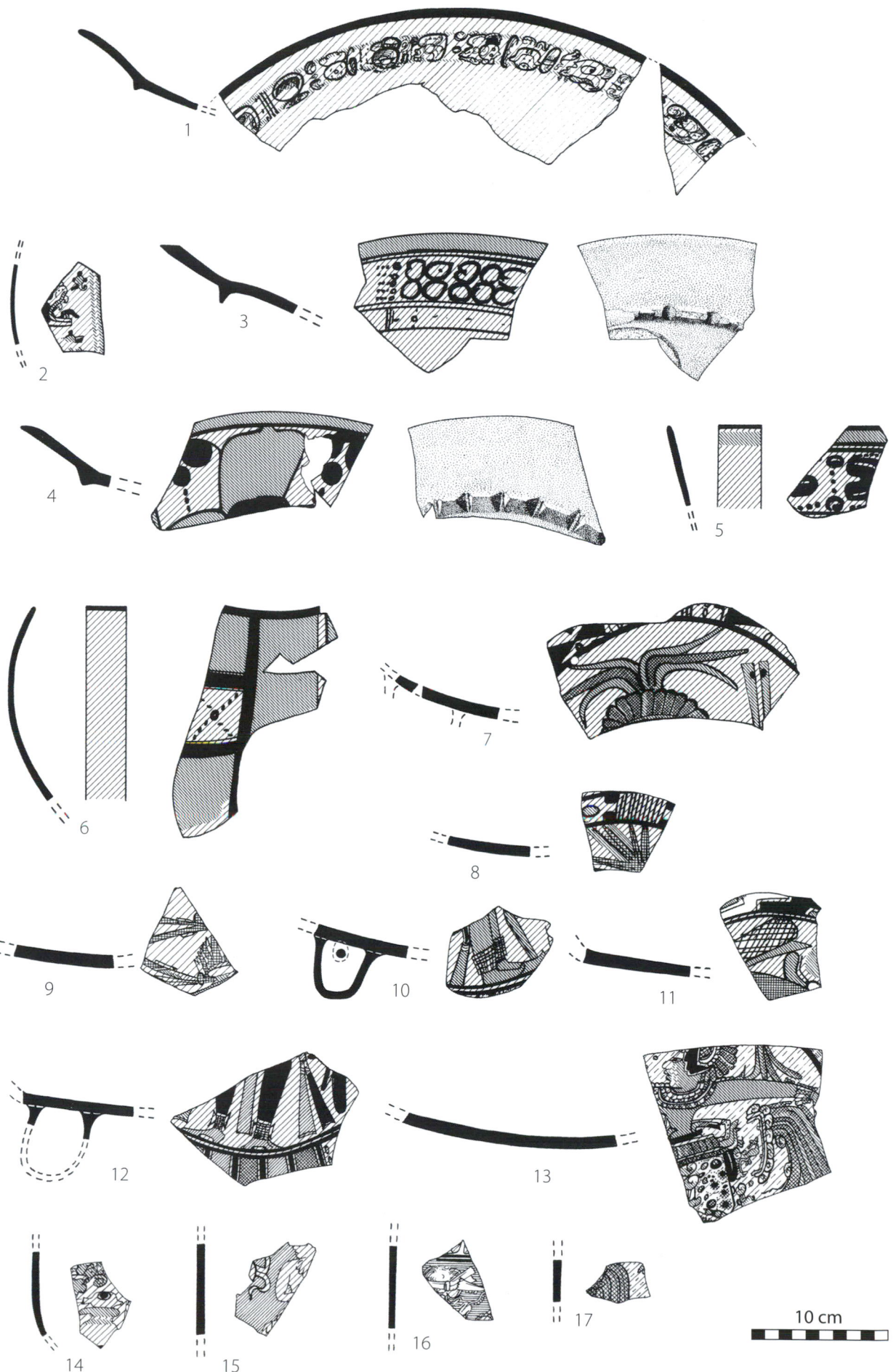

Ik
Figure 42

FIGURE 42

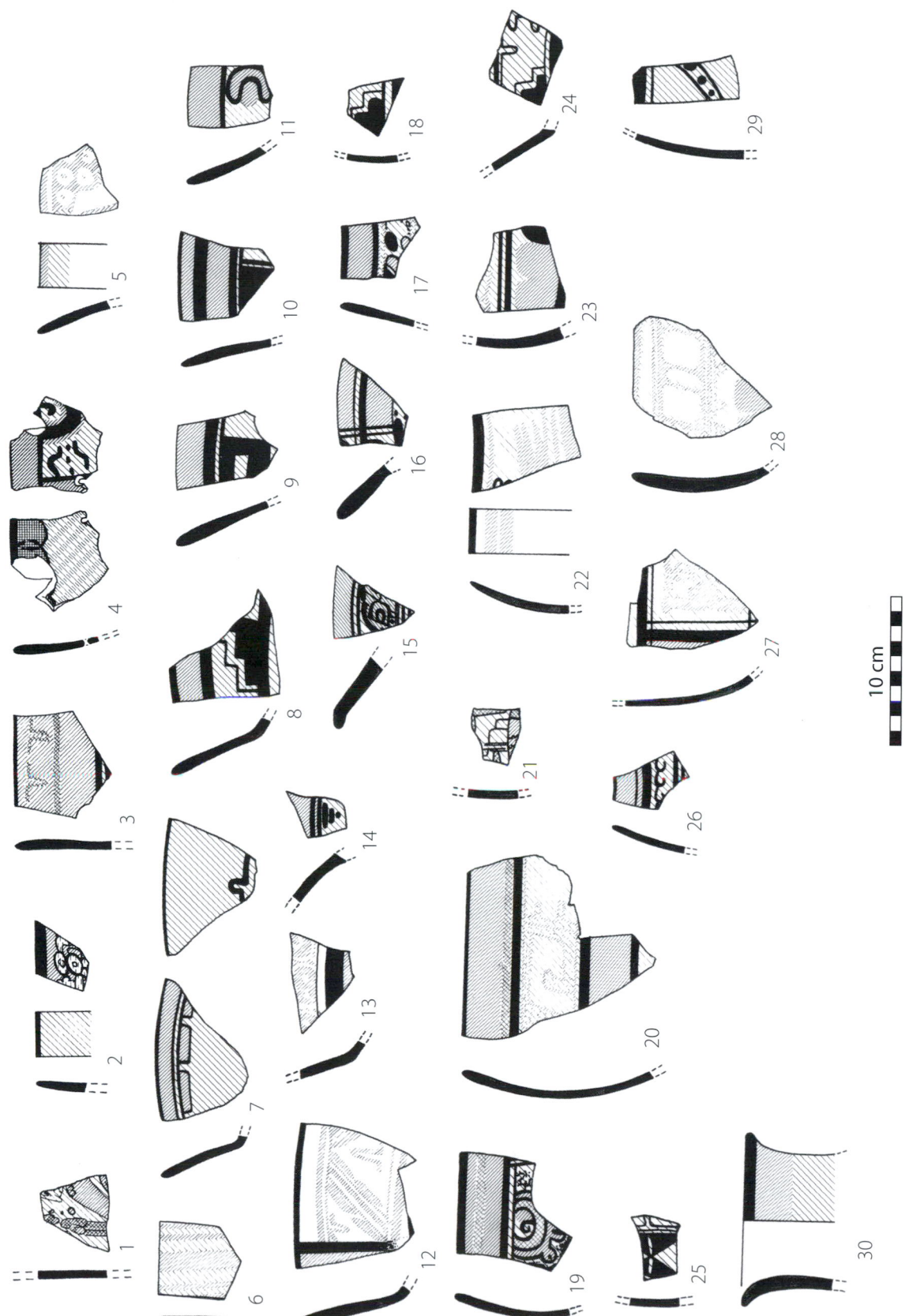

10 cm

Imix
Figure 43

FIGURE 43

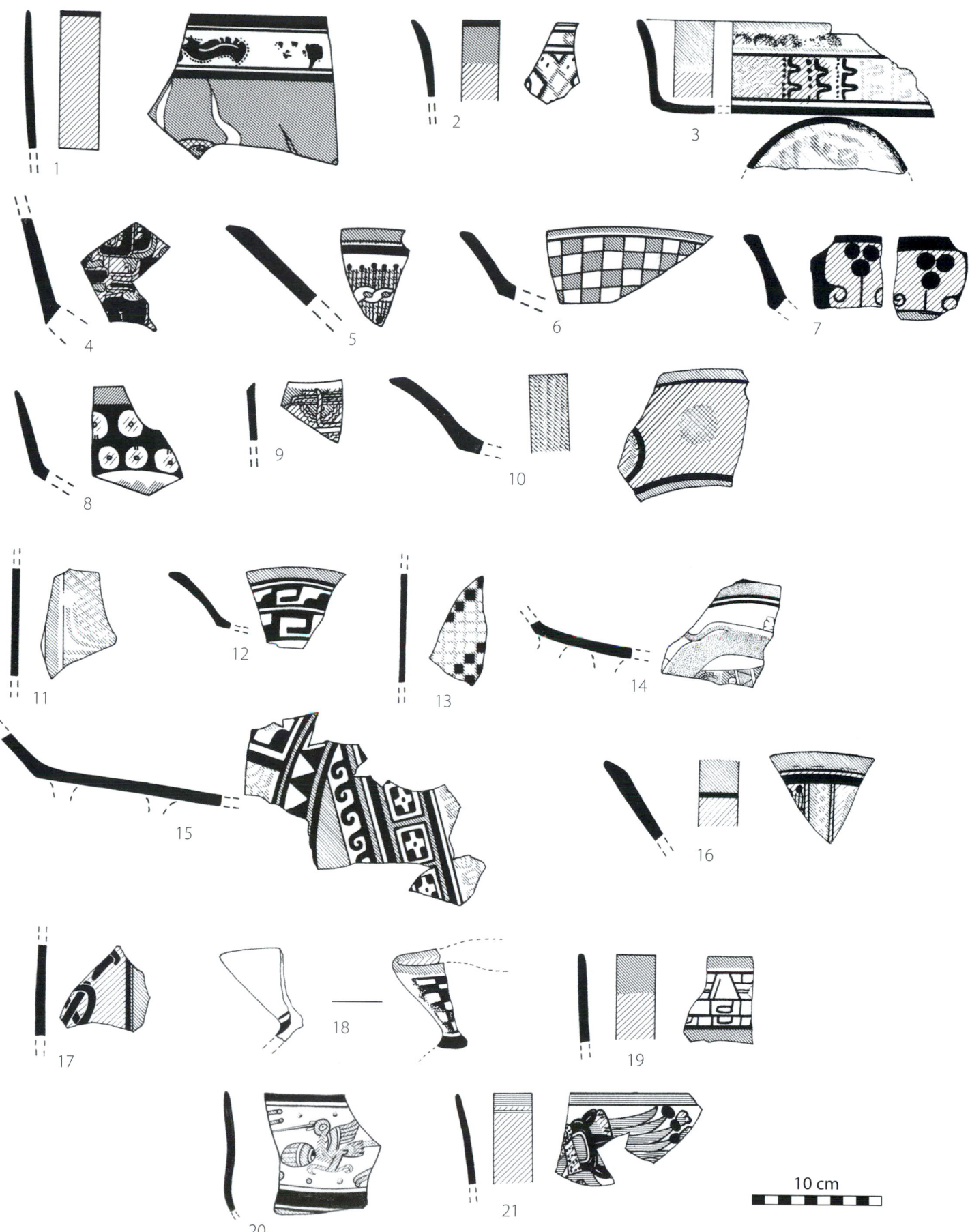

10 cm

Imix
Figure 44

FIGURE 44

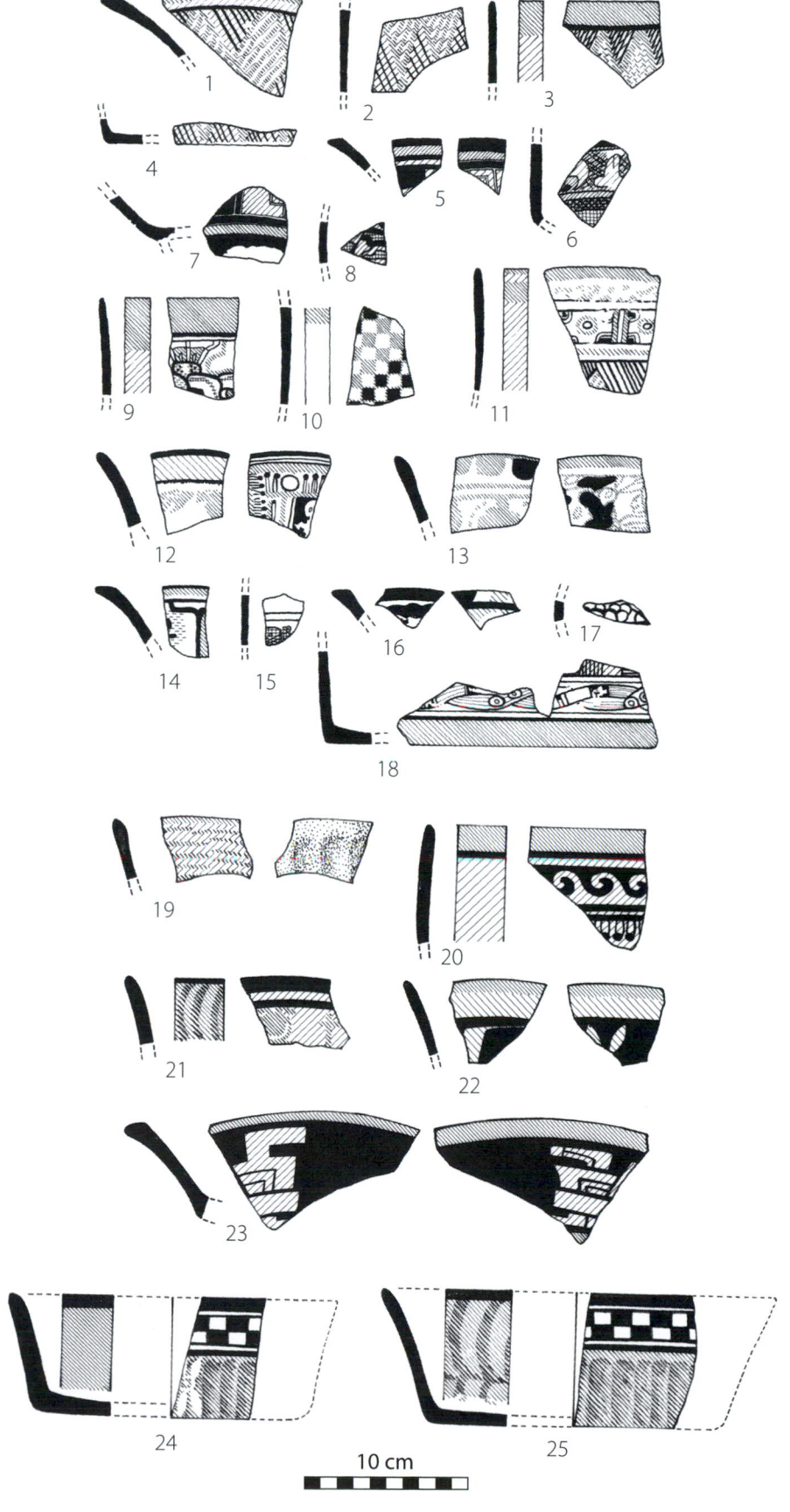

10 cm

Imix
Figure 45

FIGURE 45

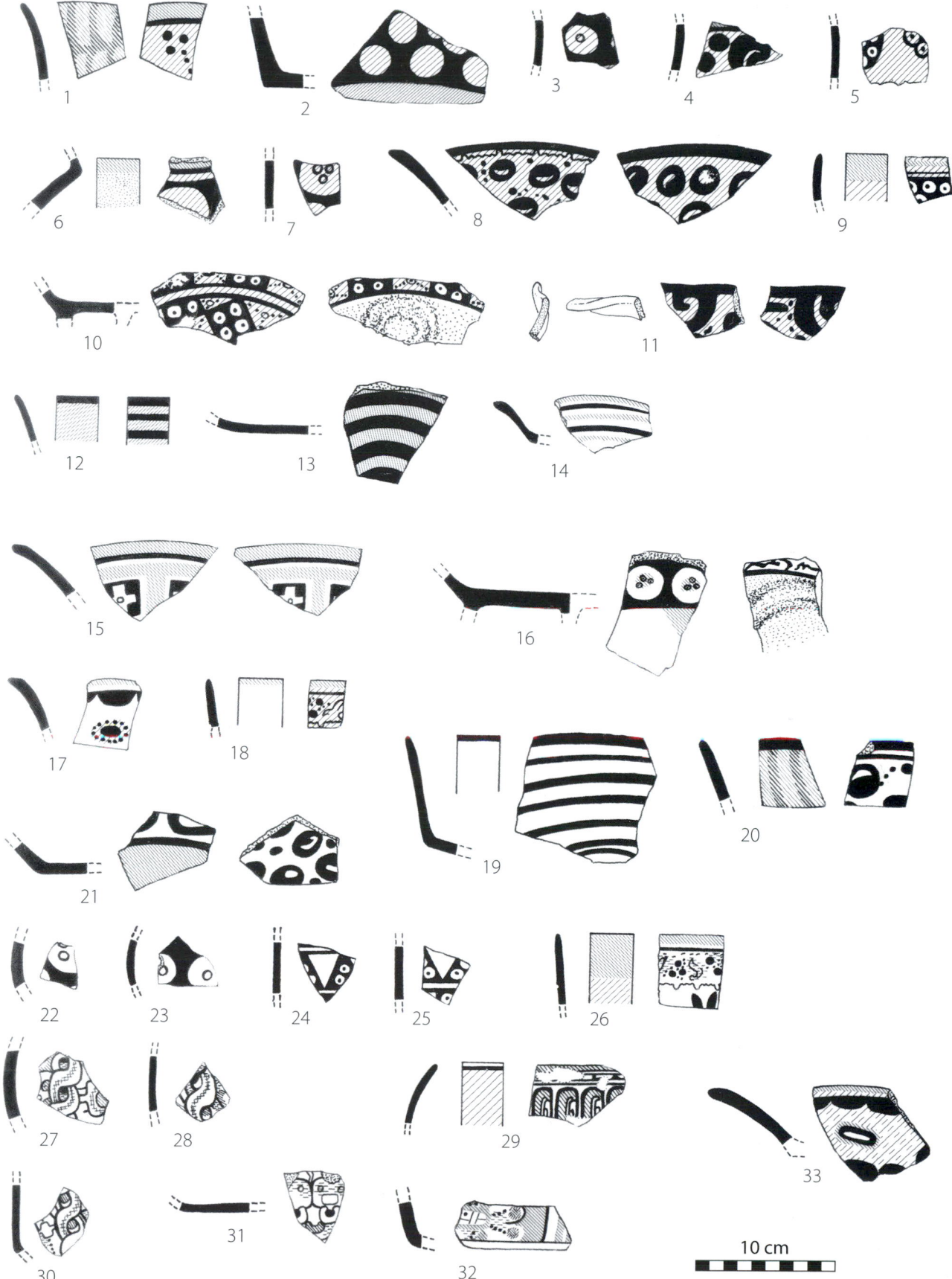

10 cm

Imix
Figure 46

FIGURE 46

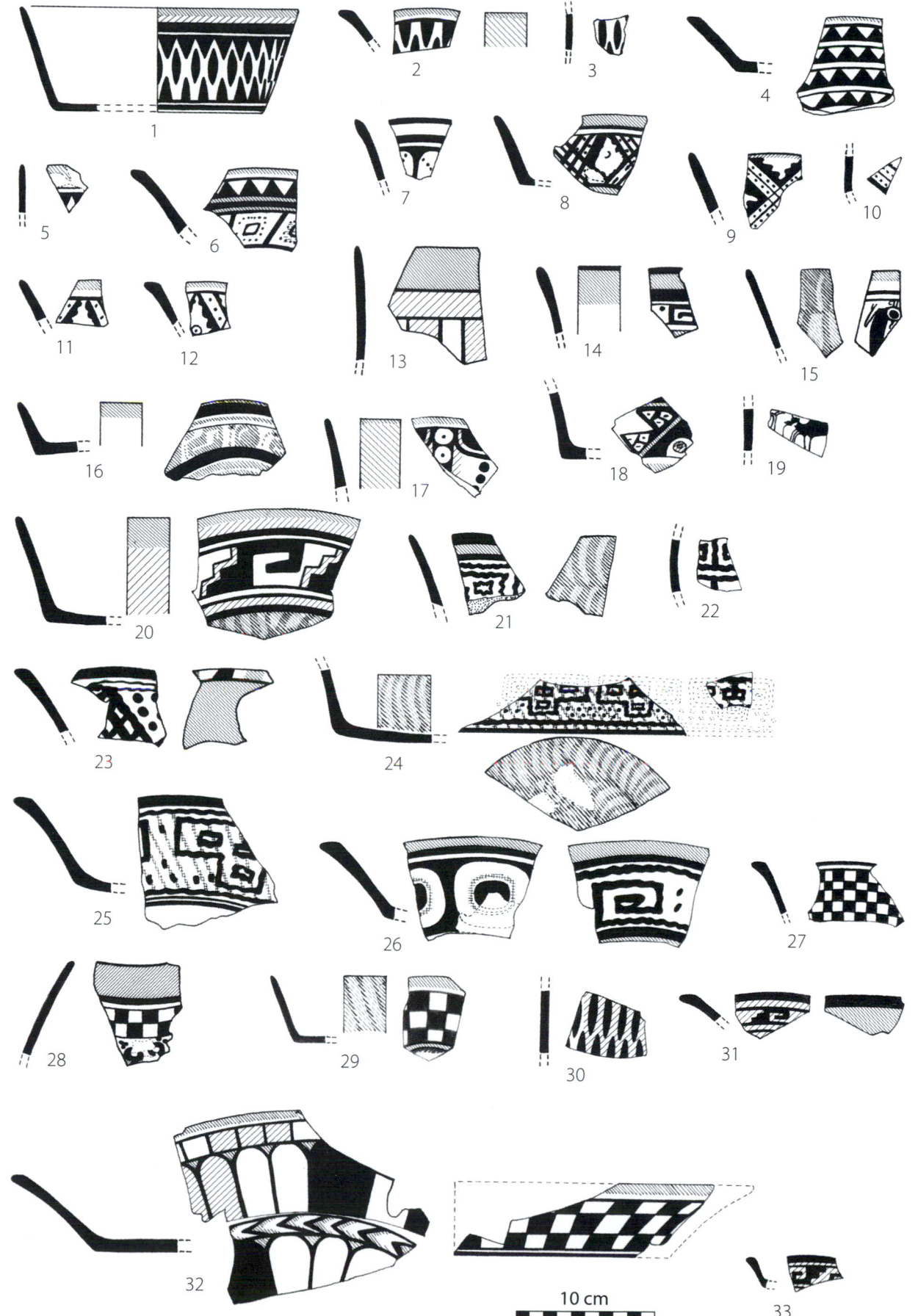

10 cm

Imix-Eznab
Figure 47

FIGURE 47

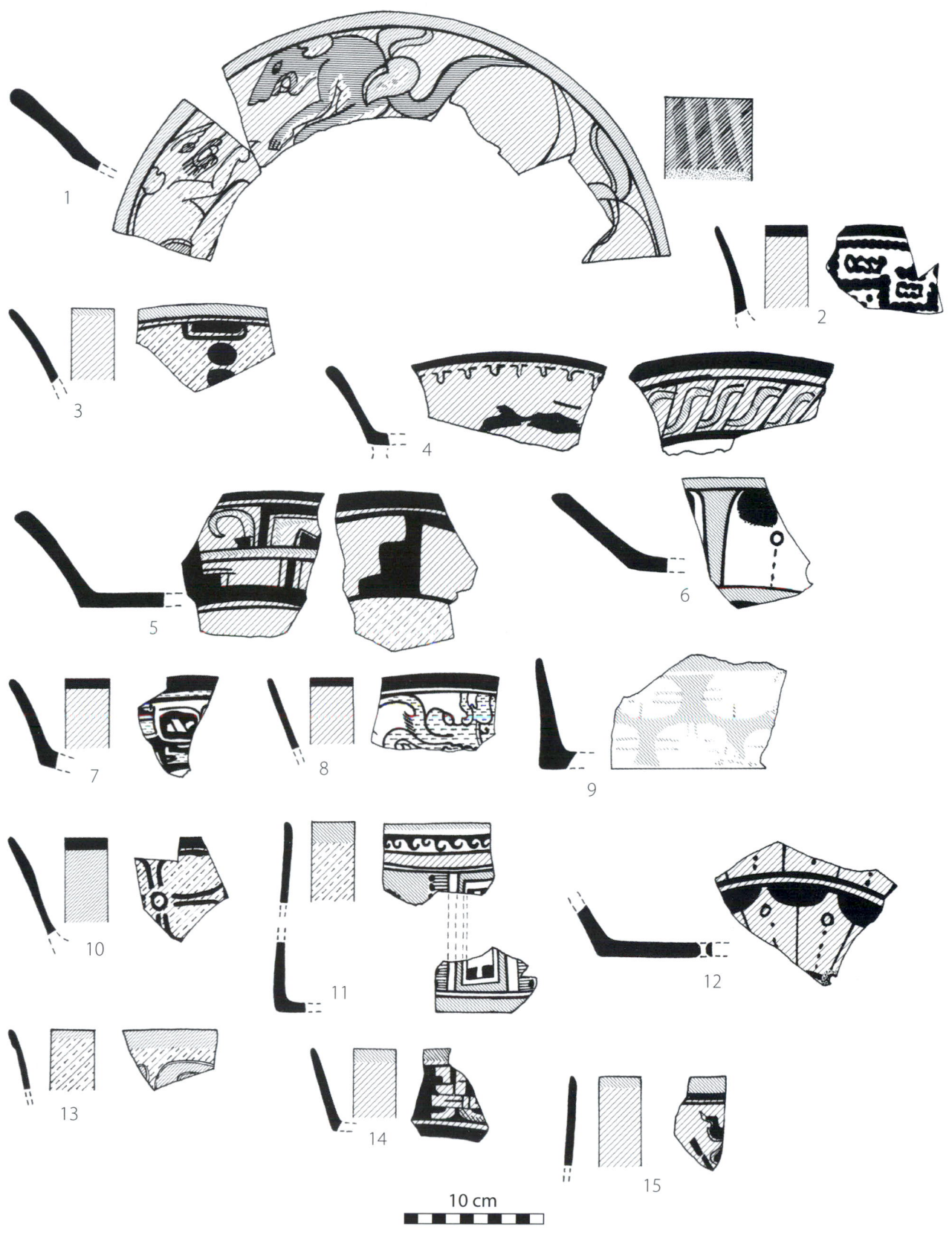

10 cm

Figure 48
Imix-Eznab

48.1–4	Zacatel Cream Polychrome: Zacatel Variety
48.5–6	Palmar Orange Polychrome: Palmar Variety
48.7–8	Zacatel Cream Polychrome: Zacatel Variety
48.9–10	Palmar Orange Polychrome: Palmar Variety
48.11	Zacatel Cream Polychrome: Zacatel Variety
48.12	Palmar Orange Polychrome: Palmar Variety
48.13–14	Zacatel Cream Polychrome: Zacatel Variety
48.15–23	Palmar Orange Polychrome: Palmar Variety

FIGURE 48

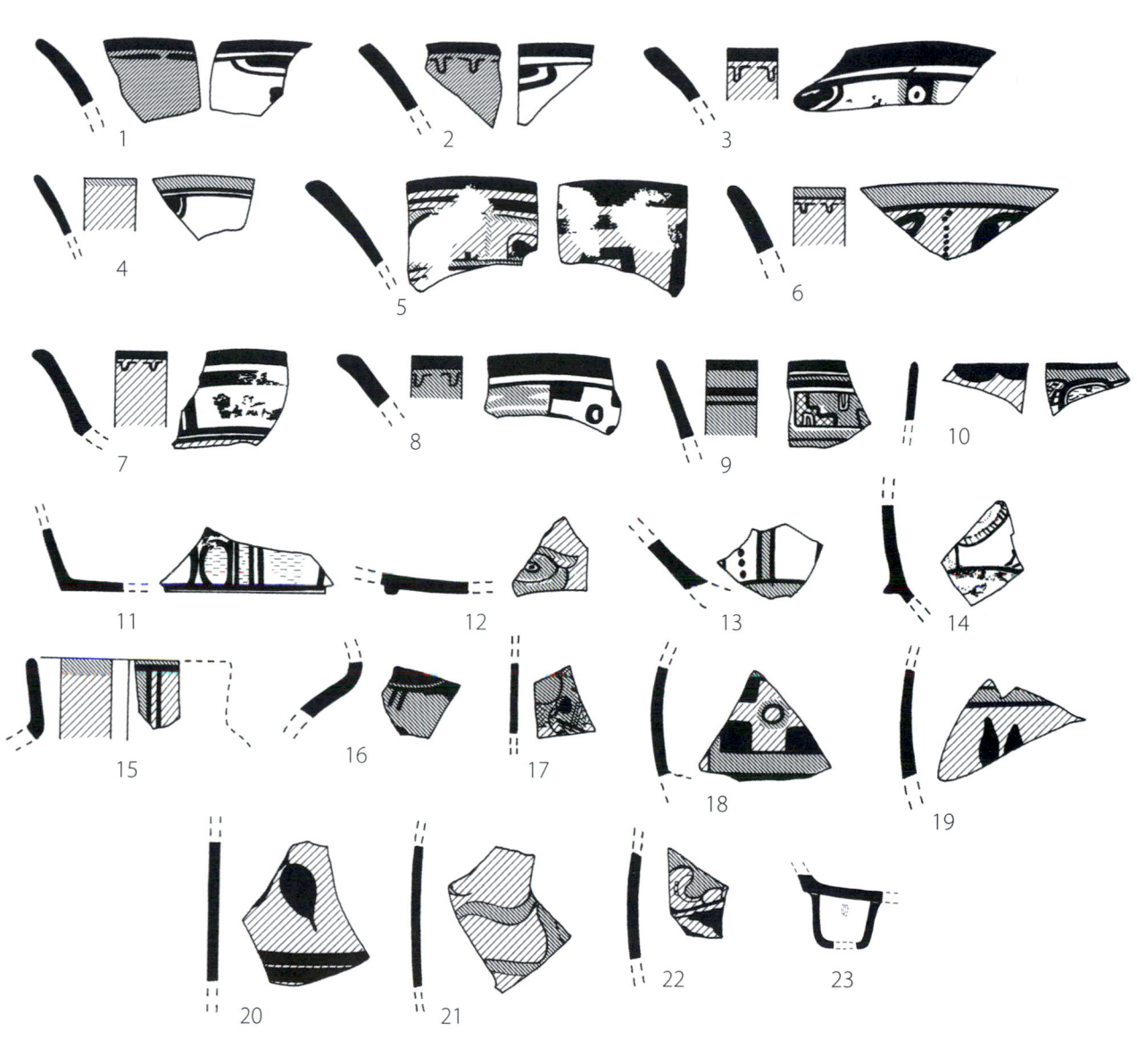

Imix-Eznab
Figure 49

FIGURE 49

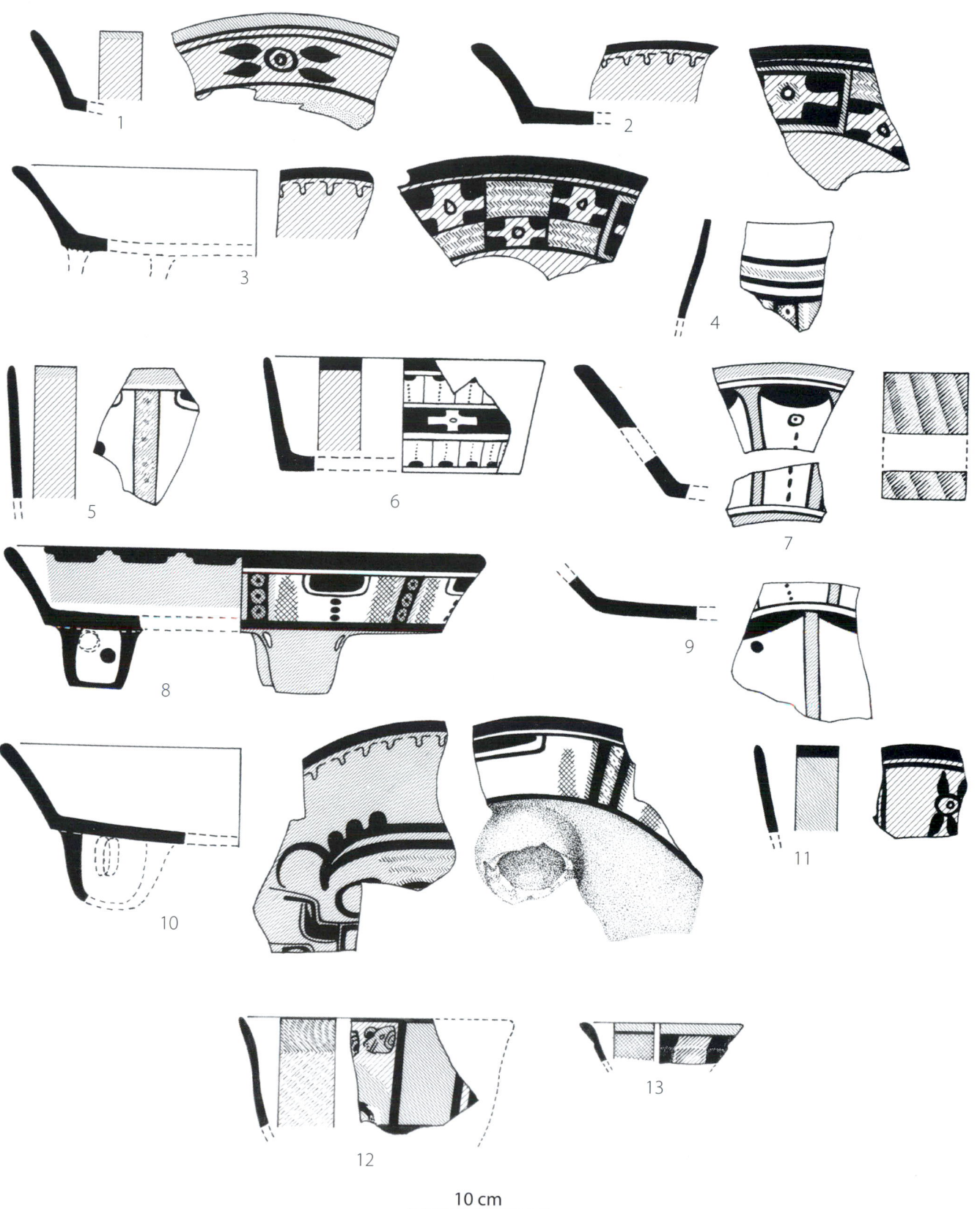

10 cm

Ik-Imix-Eznab
Figure 50

50.1	Tinaja Red: Tinaja Variety
50.2	Chinja Impressed: Appliquéd Variety (slip not shown)
50.3–5	Tinaja Red: Tinaja Variety
50.6	Chinja Impressed: Chinja Variety (slip not shown)
50.7	Chinja Impressed: Appliquéd Variety (slip not shown)
50.8–9	Chinja Impressed: Chinja Variety (slip not shown)
50.10	Tinaja Red: Tinaja Variety
50.11	Rosa Punctated: Rosa Variety (slip not shown)
50.12–13	Chinja Impressed: Chinja Variety (slip not shown)
50.14	Chinja Impressed: Appliquéd Variety (slip not shown)
50.15–16	Chinja Impressed: Chinja Variety (slip not shown)
50.17	Tinaja Red: Tinaja Variety
50.18	Chinja Impressed: Chinja Variety (slip not shown)
50.19	Tinaja Red: Tinaja Variety
50.20–22	Chinja Impressed: Chinja Variety (slip not shown)
50.23–27	Chinja Impressed: Appliquéd Variety (slip not shown)
50.28	Chinja Impressed: Chinja Variety (slip not shown)
50.29	Rosa Punctated: Rosa Variety (slip not shown)
50.30–31	Chinja Impressed: Chinja Variety (slip not shown)
50.32	Tinaja Red: Tinaja Variety
50.33	Chinja Impressed: Appliquéd Variety (slip not shown)
50.34–36	Tinaja Red: Tinaja Variety
50.37	Rosa Punctated: Rosa Variety (slip not shown)
50.38–39	Tinaja Red: Tinaja Variety
50.40	Cameron Incised: Cameron Variety
50.41–42	Tinaja Red: Tinaja Variety
50.43	Chinja Impressed: Chinja Variety (slip not shown)
50.44–45	Tinaja Red: Tinaja Variety
50.46	Rosa Punctated: Rosa Variety (slip not shown)
50.47	Tinaja Red: Tinaja Variety
50.48–49	Chinja Impressed: Chinja Variety (slip not shown)
50.50	Cameron Incised: Cameron Variety
50.51	Chinja Impressed: Chinja Variety (slip not shown)
50.52	Tinaja Red: Tinaja Variety

FIGURE 50

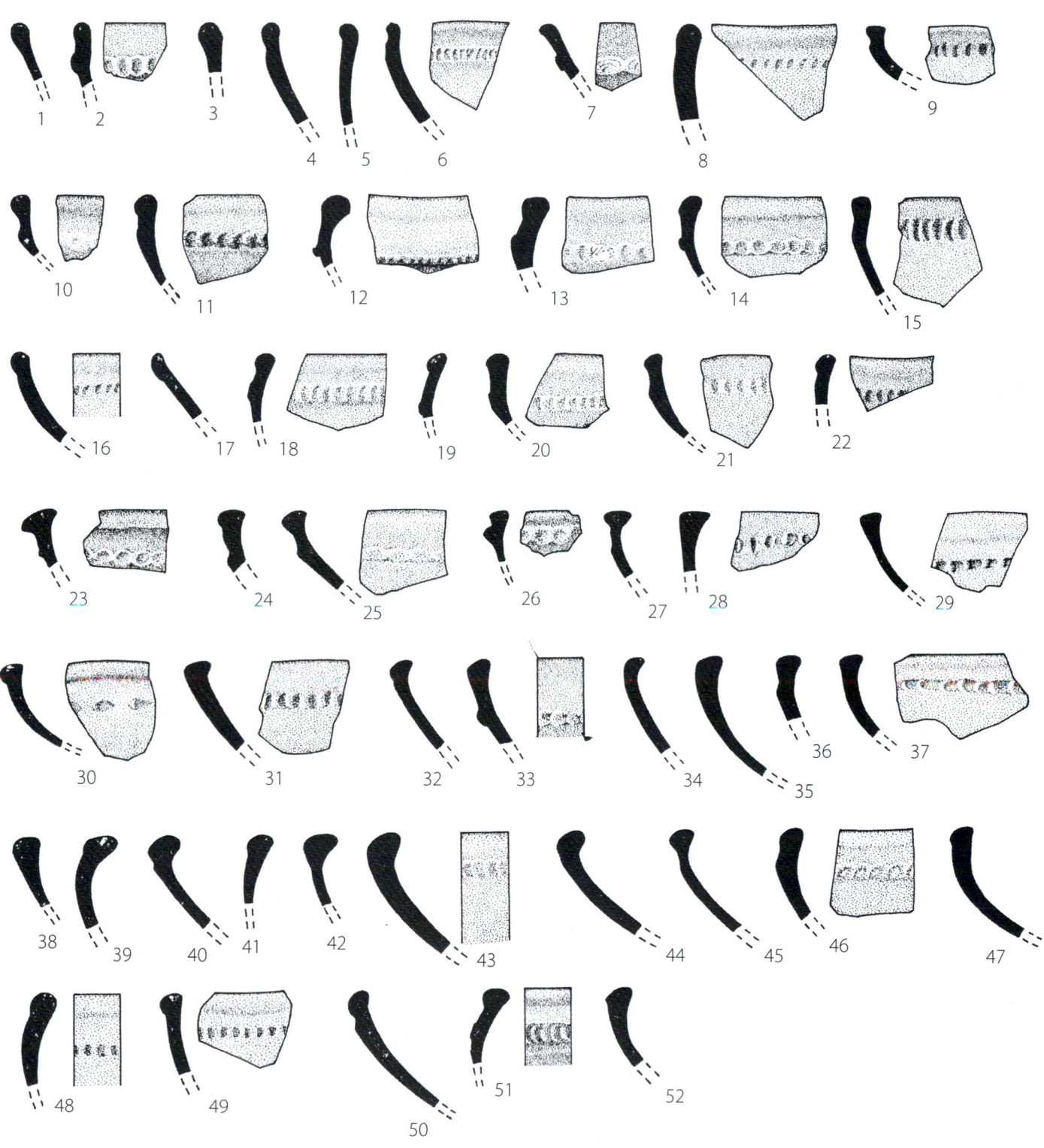

10 cm

Ik-Imix-Eznab
Figure 51

51.1–7   Tinaja Red: Tinaja Variety (slip not shown)
51.8   Chinja Impressed: Chinja Variety (slip not shown)
51.9–11   Cameron Incised: Cameron Variety
51.12–14   Tinaja Red: Tinaja Variety
51.15   Cameron Incised: Cameron Variety
51.16–22   Tinaja Red: Tinaja Variety
51.23   Chinja Impressed: Chinja Variety (slip not shown)
51.24–25   Tinaja Red: Tinaja Variety
51.26–27   Cameron Incised: Cameron Variety
51.28   Tinaja Red: Tinaja Variety
51.29   Chinja Impressed: Chinja Variety (slip not shown)
51.30–31   Tinaja Red: Tinaja Variety
51.32   Cameron Incised: Cameron Variety
51.33   Tinaja Red: Tinaja Variety
51.34   Rosa Punctated: Rosa Variety (slip not shown)
51.35   Cameron Incised: Cameron Variety
51.36   Tinaja Red: Tinaja Variety
51.37–38   Cameron Incised: Cameron Variety
51.39   Chinja Impressed: Appliquéd Variety (slip not shown)
51.40–41   Rosa Punctated: Rosa Variety (slip not shown)
51.42   Chinja Impressed: Appliquéd Variety (slip not shown)
51.43   Cameron Incised: Cameron Variety
51.44–45   Tinaja Red: Tinaja Variety
51.46   Cameron Incised: Cameron Variety
51.47   Chinja Impressed: Chinja Variety (slip not shown)
51.48–49   Tinaja Red: Tinaja Variety
51.50   Chinja Impressed: Chinja Variety (slip not shown)
51.51   Chinja Impressed: Appliquéd Variety (slip not shown)
51.52   Rosa Punctated: Rosa Variety (slip not shown)
51.53   Tinaja Red: Tinaja Variety
51.54–55   Chinja Impressed: Chinja Variety (slip not shown)
51.56   Cameron Incised: Cameron Variety
51.57   Chinja Impressed: Chinja Variety (slip not shown)
51.58   Chinja Impressed: Appliquéd Variety (slip not shown)
51.59–62   Chinja Impressed: Chinja Variety (slip not shown)

FIGURE 51

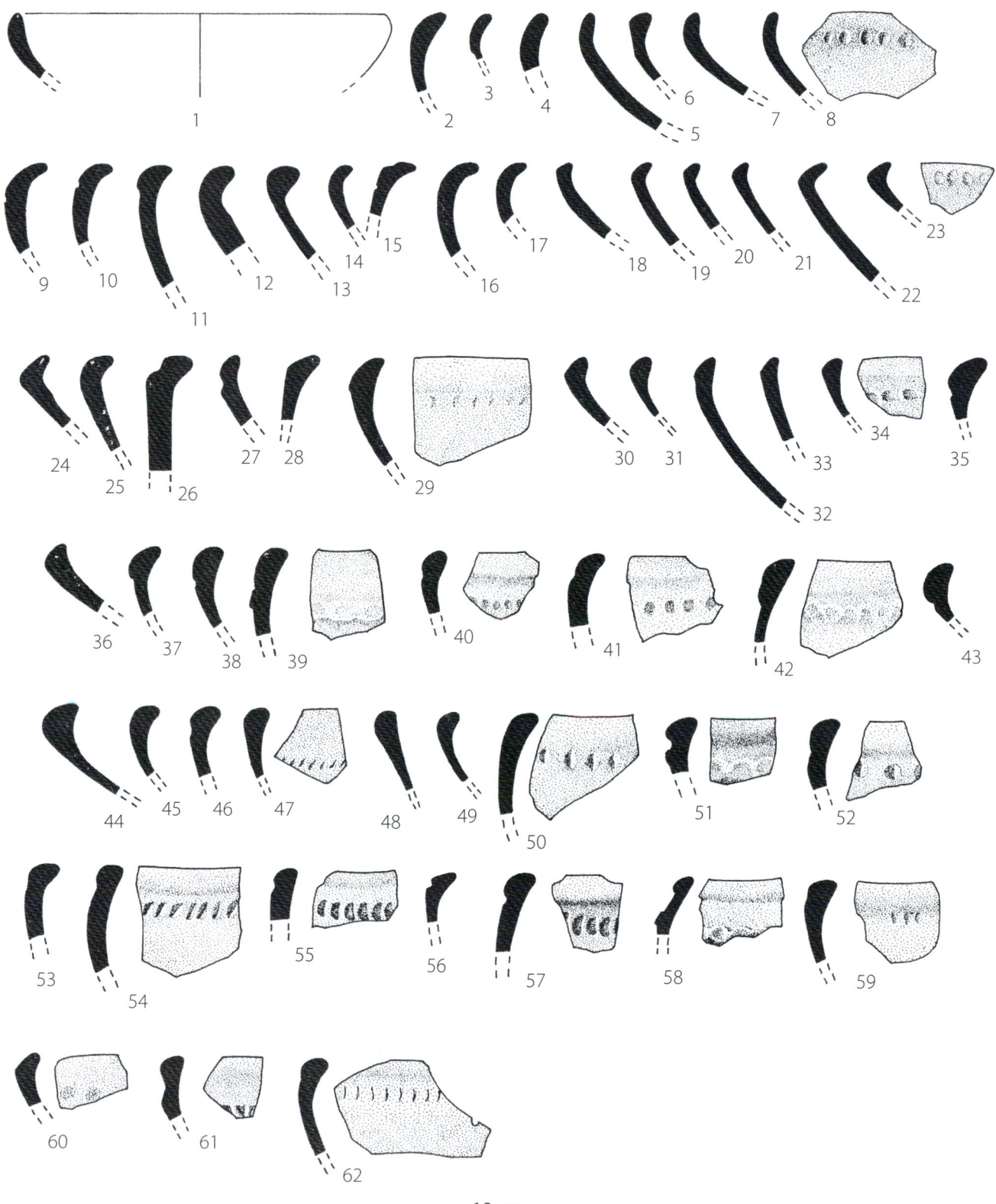

10 cm

Eznab
Figure 52

FIGURE 52

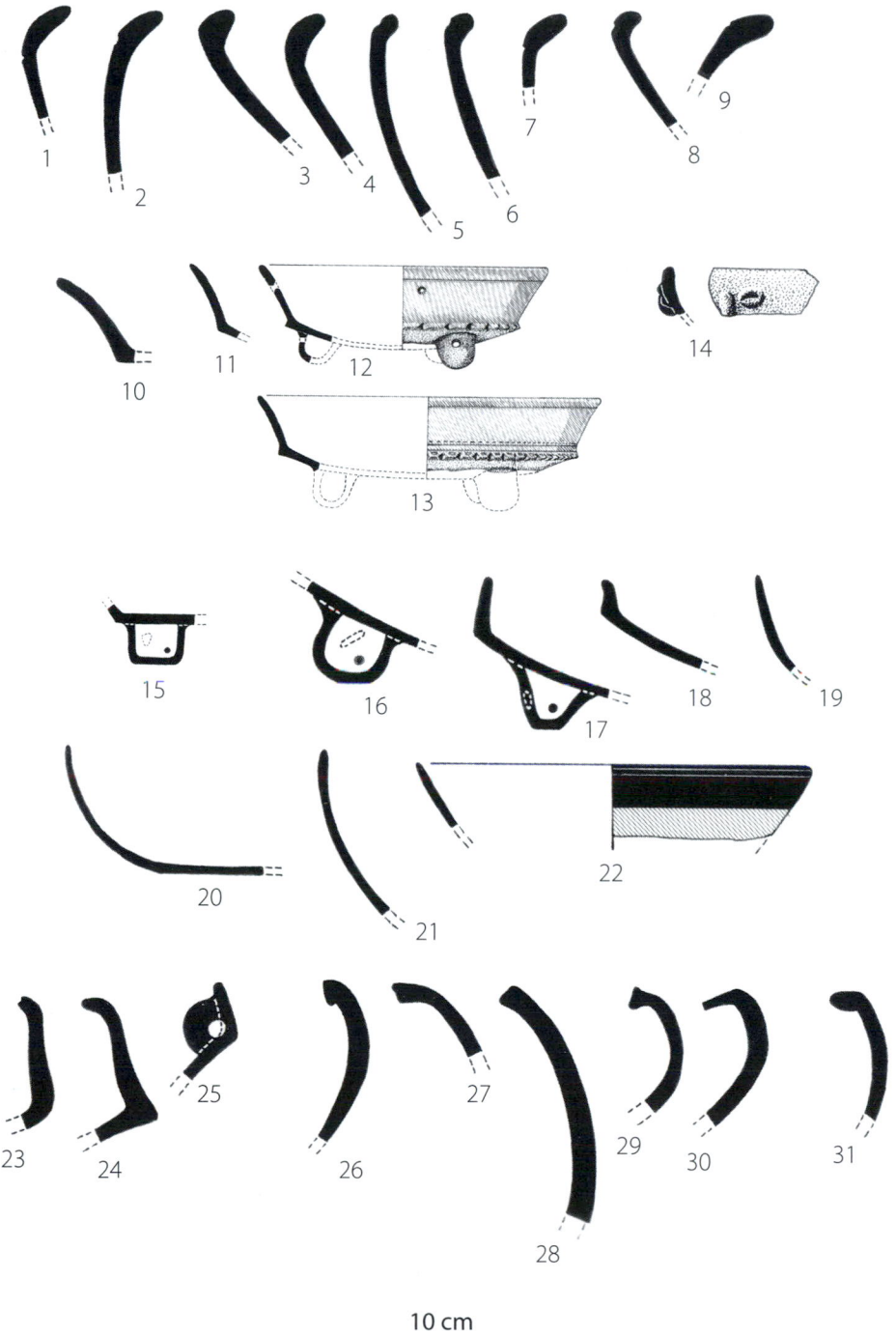

10 cm

Eznab
Figure 53

FIGURE 53

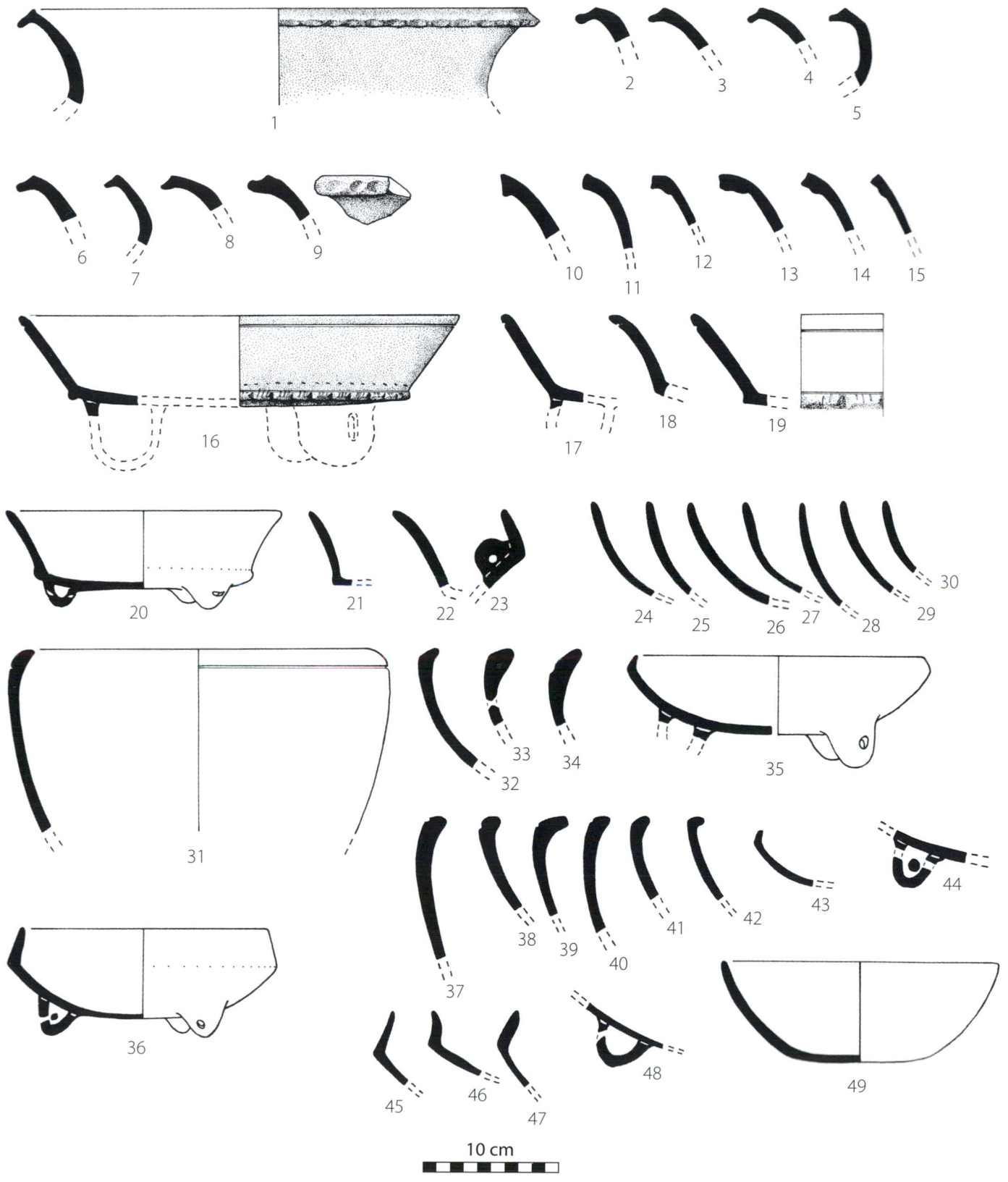

10 cm

Eznab
Figure 54

54.1   Cameron Incised: Cameron Variety (slip not shown)
54.2–7   Tinaja Red: Tinaja Red (slip not shown)
54.8–13   Cameron Incised: Cameron Variety (slip not shown)
54.14–29 Tinaja Red: Tinaja Red (slip not shown)

FIGURE 54

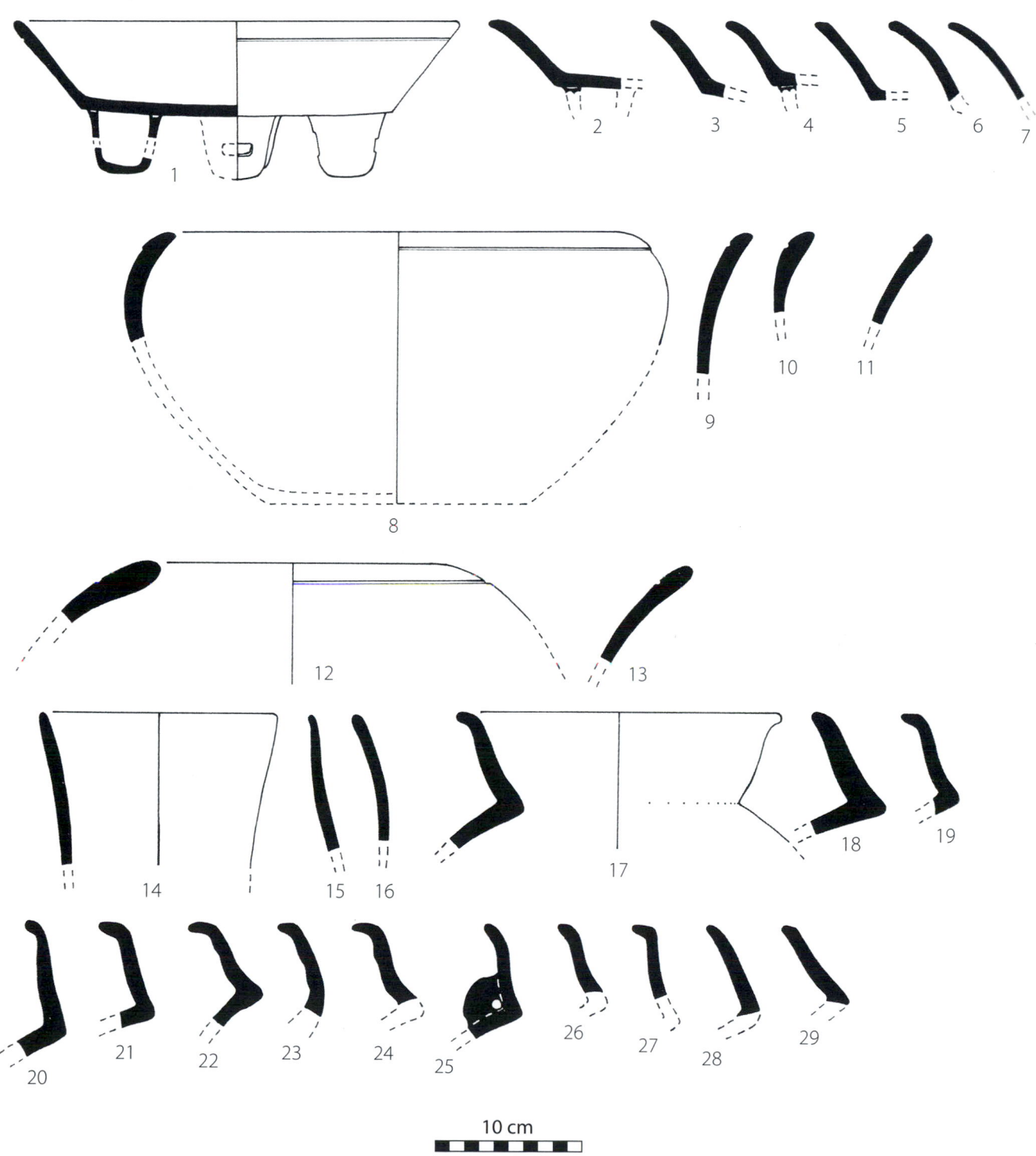

10 cm

Eznab
Figure 55

FIGURE 55

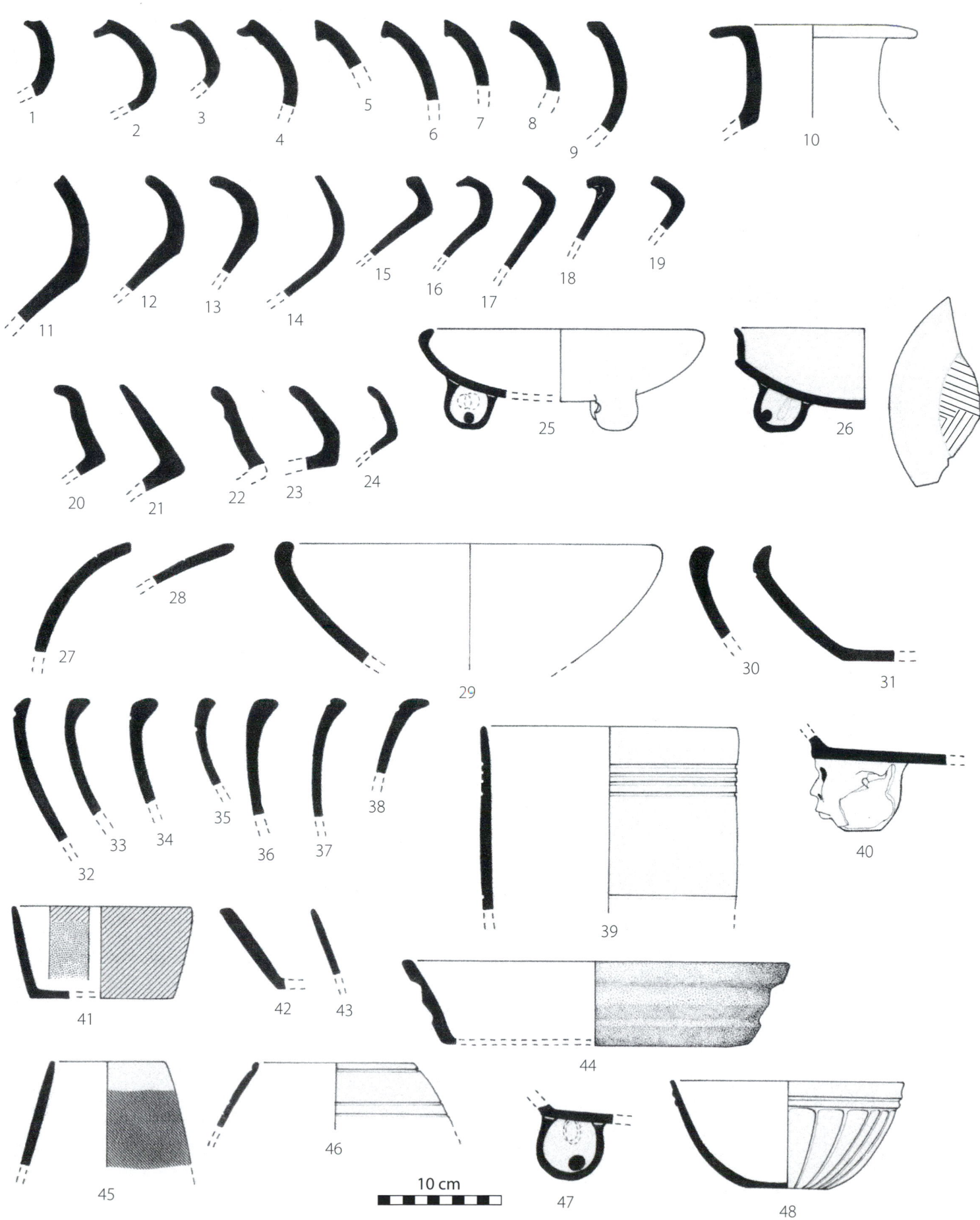

10 cm

Tikal Miniatures
(slip colors not shown)
Figure 56

56.1   **Ik, Imix**: Unknown type (eroded)

56.2   **Cimi**: Polvero Black: Polvero Variety

56.3   **Eznab**: Toh Brown: Toh Variety

56.4   Unknown complex and type

56.5   **Imix**: Unknown type

56.6   **Ik, Imix, Eznab**: Tinaja Red: Tinaja Variety

56.7   Unknown complex and type

56.8   **Imix**: Yuhactal Black-on-red: Yuhactal Variety

56.9   **Manik**: Balanza Black: Balanza Variety

56.10   **Manik**: San Clemente Gouged-incised: San Clemente Variety

56.11   Unidentified monochrome black

56.12   **Late Preclassic, Manik**: Unidentified monochrome black

56.13   **Cauac**: Sierra Red: Sierra Variety

56.14   **Imix PD. 116**: Tinaja Red: Tinaja Variety

56.15   **Manik, Eznab**: Unknown type

56.16   **Late Preclassic, Manik, Imix**: Unknown type

56.17   **Late Preclassic, Manik, Imix**: Unknown type

56.18   **Manik PD. 231**: Unknown type

56.19   **Imix**: Tinaja Red: Tinaja Variety

56.20   Unidentified monochrome red

56.21   Unidentified monochrome red

56.22   **Imix**: Yuhactal Black-on-red: Yuhactal Variety

56.23   **Late Preclassic, Manik, Ik**: Unidentified monochrome red

56.24   Unidentified monochrome orange

56.25   **Manik PD. 275**: Balanza Black: Balanza Variety

56.26   Unidentified monochrome red

56.27   **Ik, Imix, Eznab**: Tinaja Red: Tinaja Variety

56.28   **Cauac**: Sierra Red: Sierra Variety

56.29   **Late Preclassic, Manik, Ik**: Sierra Red: Sierra Variety

56.30   **Ik, Imix**: Tinaja Red: Tinaja Variety

56.31   **Manik, Eznab**: Unidentified Unslipped

56.32   **Eznab**: Achote Black: Achote Variety

56.33   **Manik**: Quintal Unslipped: Quintal Variety

56.34   **Ik, Imix, Eznab**: Cambio Unslipped: Cambio Variety

56.35   **Late Preclassic, Manik**: Unidentified Unslipped

56.36   **Late Preclassic, Manik, Imix**: Unidentified Unslipped

56.37   **Ik, Imix**: Cambio Unslipped: Cambio Variety

56.38   **Imix**: Cambio Unslipped: Cambio Variety

56.39   Unidentified Unslipped

56.40   Unknown Classic: Unidentified Unslipped

56.41   **Manik**: Balanza Black: Balanza Variety

56.42   **Manik**: Balanza Black: Balanza Variety

56.43   **Imix**: Uz Buff: Uz Variety

56.44   **Manik**: Aguila Orange: Aguila Variety

56.45   Unidentified monochrome red

56.46   Unidentified monochrome black

56.47   **Manik**: Balanza Black: Balanza Variety

56.48   Unknown Classic: Unidentified monochrome orange

56.49   **Ik**: Kau Incised: Kau Variety

56.50   Unidentified monochrome orange incised

56.51   **Manik**: Balanza Black: Balanza Variety

56.52   Unknown type

56.53   Unidentified monochrome black

56.54   **Eznab**: Cambio Unslipped: Cambio Variety

FIGURE 56

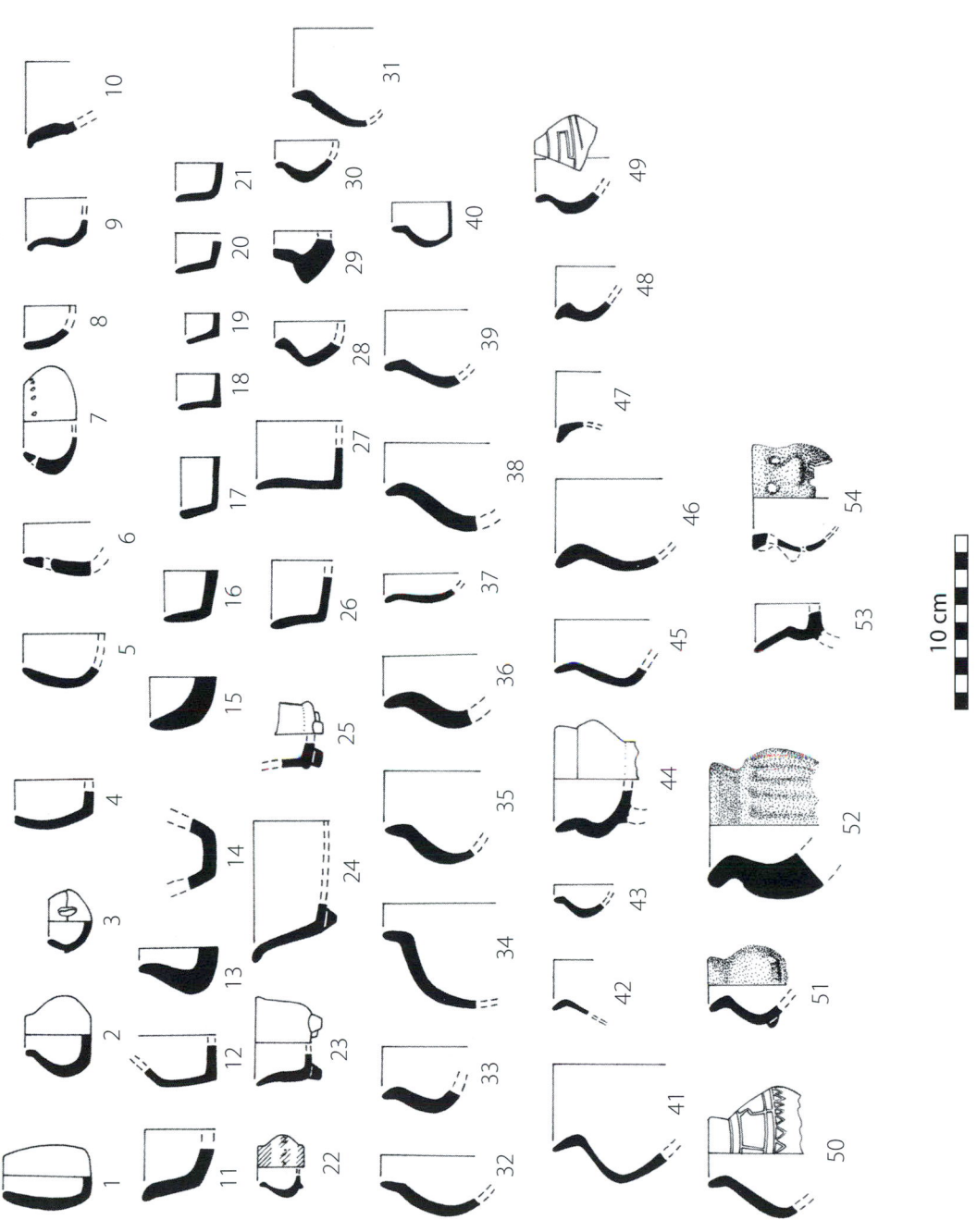

10 cm

Tikal Miscellaneous
(slip colors not shown)
Figure 57

57.1	**Cauac**: Sierra Red: Sierra Variety
57.2	**Chuen, Cauac, Cimi**: Polvero Black: Polvero Variety
57.3	**Cauac**: Polvero Black: Polvero Variety
57.4	**Manik**: Quintal Unslipped: Quintal Variety
57.5	**Manik**: Balanza Black: Balanza Variety
57.6	**Manik 2**: Aquila Orange: Aguila Variety
57.7	**Manik**: Aquila Orange: Aguila Variety
57.8	**Manik**: Balanza Black: Balanza Variety
57.9	**Manik**: Balanza Black: Balanza Variety
57.10	**Manik**: Dos Arroyos Orange Polychrome: Dos Arroyos Variety
57.11	**Manik**: Dos Arroyos Orange Polychrome: Dos Arroyos Variety
57.12	**Manik 3A (PD. 74)**: Aquila Orange: Aguila Variety
57.13	**Manik**: Aquila Orange: Aguila Variety
57.14	**Manik**: Balanza Black: Balanza Variety
57.15	**Manik**: Balanza Black: Balanza Variety
57.16	**Manik 3B**: Balanza Black: Balanza Variety
57.17	**Eznab**: Tinaja Red: Tinaja Variety
57.18	**Eznab**: San Julio Modeled: San Julio Variety
57.19	**Ik**: Zacec Black: Zacec Variety
57.20	**Imix**: Zacec Black: Zacec Variety
57.21	**Imix**: Zacec Black: Zacec Variety
57.22	**Late Imix**: Zacec Black: Zacec Variety
57.23	**Eznab**: San Julio Modeled: San Julio Variety
57.24	**Ik, Imix**: Zacec Black: Zacec Variety

FIGURE 57

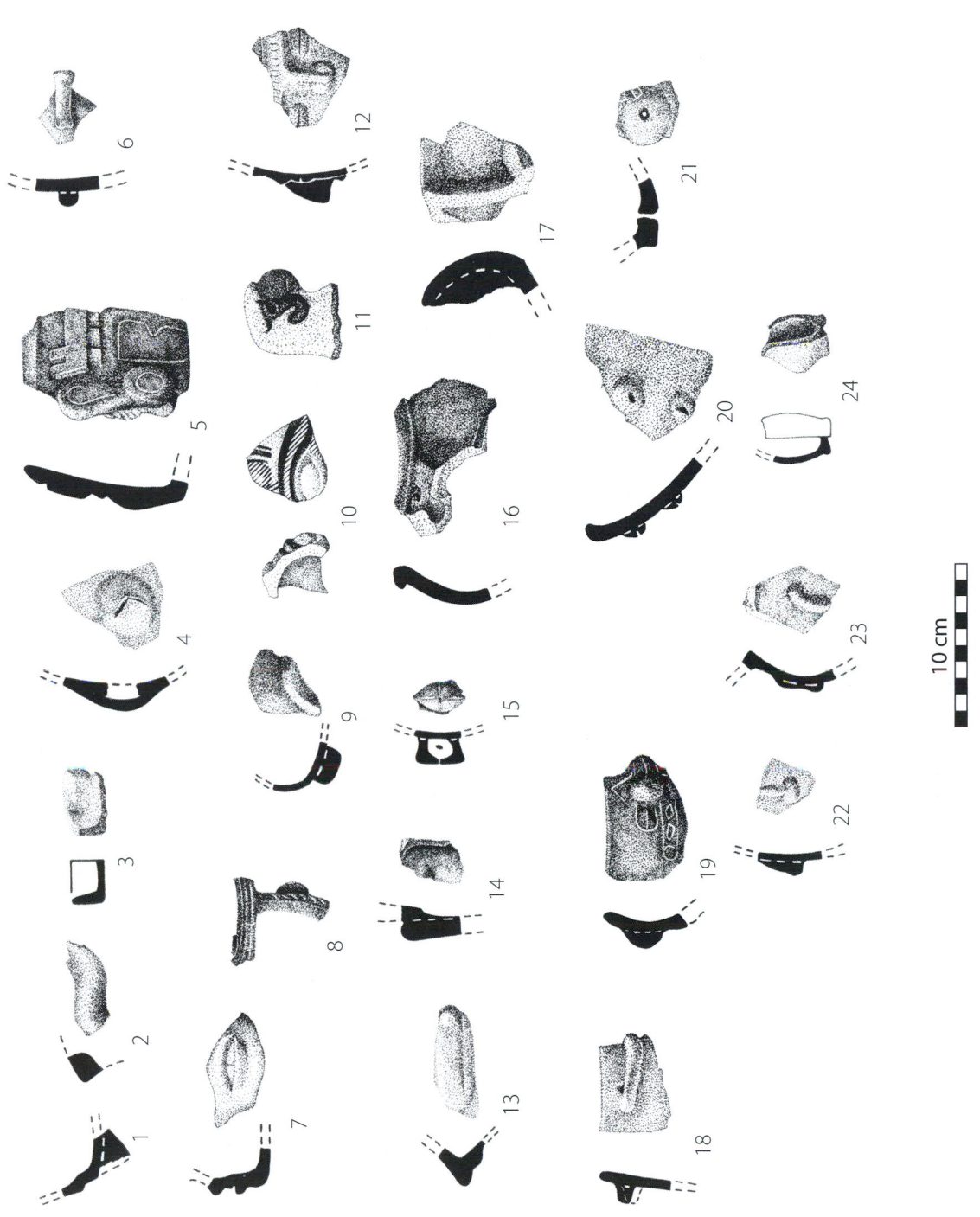

10 cm